Healthcare Delivery in the Information Age

Series Editor
Nilmini Wickramasinghe
Epworth HealthCare
Richmond, VIC
Australia

Deakin University
Burwood, Australia

The healthcare industry is uniquely structured so that the receiver of the services (the patient) often isn't the predominant payer for those services (the insurance company). Healthcare interventions are often complex and typically involve multiple players including providers, payers, patients and regulators. This leads to economic dilemmas such as moral hazard, information asymmetry, and tangential considerations of cost versus quality creating obstacles on the road to delivering efficient and effective health care. Relevant data, pertinent information, and germane knowledge play a vital role in relieving these problems and can be most effectively obtained via prudently structured and well designed healthcare technology. Some of the major challenges facing today's healthcare organizations include demographic (longer life expectancy and an aging population), technology (incorporating advances that keep people healthier), and financial (escalating costs technological innovation) problems. In order to realize technology's full potential it is imperative to understand the healthcare-technology paradigm, develop sustainability models for the effective use of technology in a specific context, then successfully design and implement patient-centric technology solutions. Many of the problems with technology are connected to the platform-centric nature of these systems which cannot support seamless transfer of data and information, leading to inferior health care delivery. This new series focuses on designing effective and efficient technologically enabled healthcare processes to support the delivery of superior health care and provide better access, quality and value. It's main goal will be to identify the barriers and facilitators in moving from idea generation to concept realization and will navigate the key challenges in the field: bringing readers solutions and recommendations while identifying key factors in developing technology-enabled healthcare solutions.

More information about this series at http://www.springer.com/series/8783

Nilmini Wickramasinghe • Jonathan L. Schaffer
Editors

Theories to Inform Superior Health Informatics Research and Practice

Springer

Editors
Nilmini Wickramasinghe
Epworth HealthCare
Richmond, VIC, Australia

Deakin University
Burwood, Australia

Jonathan L. Schaffer
Deakin University
Burwood, Australia

Cleveland Clinic
Cleveland, OH, USA

ISSN 2191-5946 ISSN 2191-5954 (electronic)
Healthcare Delivery in the Information Age
ISBN 978-3-030-10182-4 ISBN 978-3-319-72287-0 (eBook)
https://doi.org/10.1007/978-3-319-72287-0

Softcover re-print of the Hardcover 1st edition 2018

Printed on acid-free paper

This Springer imprint is published by the registered company Springer International Publishing AG part of Springer Nature.
The registered company address is: Gewerbestrasse 11, 6330 Cham, Switzerland

For our families
This series is dedicated to Leo Cussen:
Learned scholar, colleague extraordinare
and good friend

Foreword

The history of progress in most areas of endeavor demonstrates a battle between what we believe to be true and what we really know. The former motivates risky ventures and faith-based investments, while the latter provides sound research data on what actually works best. Of course, both are necessary to advance the human condition, but one without the other leaves us frustrated.

This struggle is no less characteristic of our recent experience in health informatics. For instance, much of recent health policy that has produced major funding and investment in electronic medical records is based on the assumption that more data will produce better care with less cost—without any clear idea about how this is to occur. In a similar way, entrepreneurs have developed new technology and big data solutions to problems that they may not really understand. Both of these fall on the faith-based end of the spectrum.

The clear solution to this problem lies in sound research. To date, the research in health informatics is fragmented and not informed by underlying theory to guide the propositions to be tested. This seminal book is intended to provide this necessary framework.

It starts with articles addressing the basic design and methodologies that underlie good research in this area. This first part uses several specific lenses to define various useful theories. The reader is sure to find useful guidance in determining the best research questions to consider.

The second area expands the frame to include sociotechnical theoretical considerations that may be critical in the interaction between data and users that determine how any given solution might be advanced or blocked. The third part provides examples of actual solutions where the balance between what we want to believe is tested using theoretical principles. For some readers, this last part may be the most important as they struggle with similar problems.

Some may find a complete reading of this volume to be most helpful, while many may see it as a resource to be used with specific problem areas. No matter whether it serves as a textbook or reference source, it will find an honored place in the library of researchers, managers, and policy makers hoping to use informatics as a lever to improve health care for all.

J. B. Silvers
Weatherhead School of Management,
Case Western Reserve University
August 2017

The original version of the book's front matter was revised. The Epilogue section has been moved to the back matter of the book.

Preface

Over the last few decades, the nascent domain of health informatics has expanded and evolved. This evolution provides witness to an expanding volume of research focusing on improving patient care and outcomes through technical assistance platforms including digital health, e-health, big data in health care, healthcare analytics, and implementation of EMRs, to name just a few. Such an exponential increase in research demands sound and solid theories upon which to base these health information technology systems. Industry wide, our research must be appropriately based and appropriately formulated and designed to ultimately improve clinical practices. Through these designs, superior health informatics solutions may indeed be realized and provide for the foundations of the discipline such that patients, clinicians, and future researchers alike can truly benefit.

The editors offer this book to provide, first, a focus on identifying relevant theories from key disciplines and, second, examples of applications of these theories. To date, we have not identified a treatise that has provided this content and transformation in order to facilitate heightened rigor in research within health informatics. The objective of this proposed book is, in one collection, to provide the reader with a set of resources that contains key theories that will enable mature, robust, and quality research programs in health informatics to ensue. This is essential as the discipline matures and establishes itself as a core area within health care and a major contributor to providing greater value in the provision of health care and improved care for patients.

While there has been indeed an exponential growth in the adoption, implementation, and assimilation of numerous technology solutions into various healthcare contexts, the results are still mixed. These solutions have the opportunity to address the key challenges in healthcare delivery today including improving the value in care provision, attacking escalating costs, reversing rising incidence of chronic diseases, correcting workforce shortages, and increasing timely access to care. We contend that to truly address these issues, we need robust and rigorous applied research to be conducted which investigates these critical issues in depth and thereby serves to provide meaningful and sustainable solutions to ameliorate the current state and fully address the key challenges. To do this systematically, effectively, and above all successfully, the healthcare industry requires robust theories that will inform and guide the research endeavors. To accomplish this goal, the research must be based on substantive theories. Given the relatively nascent state of health informatics currently as a discipline as compared to other aspects of health care, robust theories need to be adopted and adapted from other relevant disciplines including information systems, sociology, management, and organizational behavior to provide the basis for development and assessment. This book is a first step toward addressing this very critical void within health informatics today.

The book is structured into three key parts:

Part I focuses on research design and methodologies and consists of the following nine chapters:

Chapter 1 “Design Science Research Opportunities in Health Care” by Hevner and Wickramasinghe

Chapter 2 “Using a Survey Approach to Measure User Satisfaction of Clinical Information Systems: Lessons Learnt” by Schaffer et al.

Chapter 3 “Application of Hermeneutics in Understanding New Emerging Technologies in Health Care: An Example from mHealth Case Study” by Sako et al.

Chapter 4 “IS/IT Governance in Health Care: An Integrative Model” by Haddad et al.

Chapter 5 “Predictive Analytics in Health Care: Methods and Approaches to Identify the Risk of Readmission” by Eigner et al.

Chapter 6 “An Ontology for Capturing Pervasive Mobile Solution Benefits in Diabetes Care: Insights from a Longitudinal Multi-country Study” by Ramaprasad et al.

Chapter 7 “Clustering Questions in Healthcare Social Question Answering Based on Design Science Theory” by Johns and Wickramasinghe

Chapter 8 “Using SWOT to Perform a Comparative Analysis of the German and Australian e-Health Systems” by Eigner et al.

Chapter 9 “The Advantages of Using a Two-Arm Crossover Study Design to Establish Proof of Concept of Technology Interventions: The Case of a Mobile Web-Based Reporting of Glucose Readings in the Management of Gestational Diabetes Mellitus (GDM)” by Wickramasinghe and Goldberg

Part II focuses on sociotechnical considerations and consists of the following nine chapters:

Chapter 10 “Modelling the Business Value of IT in Health Care: Technical and Sociotechnical Perspectives” by Haddad et al.

Chapter 11 “Persuasive Technologies and Behavior Modification Through Technology: Design of a Mobile Application for Behavior Change” by Hamper et al.

Chapter 12 “The Development of a Hospital Secure Messaging and Communication Platform: A Conceptualization” by Muhammad and Wickramasinghe

Chapter 13 “Structuration Theory to Assist in Understanding the Implementation and Adoption of Health Information Systems” by Muhammad and Wickramasinghe

Chapter 14 "Actor-Network Theory to Assist in Understanding the Implementation and Adoption of Health Information Systems" by Muhammad and Wickramasinghe

Chapter 15 "Activity Theory: A Comparison of HCI Theories for the Analysis of Healthcare Technology" by Wiser et al.

Chapter 16 "An Examination of Different e-Health Solutions, Barriers, and Facilitators Using the Fit-Viability Model" by Wickramasinghe et al.

Chapter 17 "Using Foucault to Understand Chronic Disease Management and Self-Monitoring" by Wickramasinghe and Goldberg

Chapter 18 "Healthcare Information Systems (HIS) Assimilation Theory" by Sulaiman and Wickramasinghe

Part III focuses on specific solutions and the principles of knowledge management in the following nine chapters:

Chapter 19 "Knowledge Management to Address Real Healthcare Needs: The Case of Allergy Care in Australia" by Wickramasinghe and Haddad

Chapter 20 "Embracing the Principles of Knowledge Management to Structure a Superior IT Healthcare Paradigm" By Wickramasinghe and Schaffer

Chapter 21 "The Impact of Impaired Executive Functions of ADHD Adults on the Use of IS: Psychologists' Perceptions" by Binhadyan and Wickramasinghe

Chapter 22 "The Development of Intelligent Patient-Centric Systems for Health Care" by Caronongan et al.

Chapter 23 "Applying the Practice Theoretical Perspective to Healthcare Knowledge Management" by Anya et al.

Chapter 24 "Contemporary Development in e-Health" by Troshani and Wickramasinghe

Chapter 25 "A Systematic Framework for EMRs and AHRs" by Gibbings and Wickramasinghe

Chapter 26 "Integrating Hospital Records and Home Monitoring by mHealth Apps" by Marceglia et al.

Chapter 27 "An Investigation on Integrating Eastern and Western Medicine with Informatics" by Han-lin et al.

Clearly, no one volume can provide all relevant and important theories, but we have attempted to provide a sampling of key theories that we believe are essential in assisting the design and development of high-quality research in health informatics as well as successful solutions for practice. We hope you find it enjoyable, informative, and useful as you continue your journey in health informatics and trust it might inspire you to design and develop successful technology solutions for superior healthcare delivery.

Melbourne, Australia Nilmini Wickramasinghe
Cleveland, USA Jonathan L. Schaffer
May 2017

Contents

Part I Research Design and Methodologies

1 **Design Science Research Opportunities in Health Care** 3
Alan R. Hevner and Nilmini Wickramasinghe

2 **Using a Survey Methodology to Measure User Satisfaction with Clinical Information Systems** 19
Jonathan L. Schaffer, Peter Haddad, and Nilmini Wickramasinghe

3 **Application of Hermeneutics in Understanding New Emerging Technologies in Health Care: An Example from mHealth Case Study** 29
Zaid Sako, Sasan Adibi, and Nilmini Wickramasinghe

4 **IS/IT Governance in Health Care: An Integrative Model** 37
Peter Haddad, Steven McConchie, Jonathan L. Schaffer, and Nilmini Wickramasinghe

5 **Predictive Analytics in Health Care: Methods and Approaches to Identify the Risk of Readmission** 55
Isabella Eigner and Andreas Hamper

6 **An Ontology for Capturing Pervasive Mobile Solution Benefits in Diabetes Care: Insights from a Longitudinal Multi-country Study** 75
Arkland Ramaprasad, Steve Goldberg, and Nilmini Wickramasinghe

7 **Clustering Questions in Healthcare Social Question Answering Based on Design Science Theory** 95
Blooma John and Nilmini Wickramasinghe

8 **Using SWOT to Perform a Comparative Analysis of the German and Australian e-Health Systems** ... 109
Isabella Eigner, Andreas Hamper, Nilmini Wickramasinghe, and Freimut Bodendorf

9 **The Advantages of Using a Two-Arm Crossover Study Design to Establish Proof of Concept of Technology Interventions: The Case of a Mobile Web-Based Reporting of Glucose Readings in the Management of Gestational Diabetes Mellitus (GDM)** ... 127
Nilmini Wickramasinghe and Steve Goldberg

Part II Sociotechnical Considerations

10 **Modelling the Business Value of IT in Health Care: Technical and Sociotechnical Perspectives** ... 141
Peter Haddad, Jonathan L. Schaffer, and Nilmini Wickramasinghe

11 **Persuasive Technologies and Behavior Modification Through Technology: Design of a Mobile Application for Behavior Change** ... 163
Andreas Hamper, Isabella Eigner, and Alexander Popp

12 **Integrating Two Sociotechnical Theories to Develop a Suitable Analytic Framework to Assess the Development of a Hospital Secure Messaging and Communication Platform** ... 185
Imran Muhammad and Nilmini Wickramasinghe

13 **Using Structuration Theory to Assist in Understanding the Implementation and Adoption of Health Information Systems** ... 201
Imran Muhammad and Nilmini Wickramasinghe

14 **Actor-Network Theory to Assist in Understanding the Implementation and Adoption of Health Information Systems** ... 219
Imran Muhammad and Nilmini Wickramasinghe

15 **Activity Theory: A Comparison of HCI Theories for the Analysis of Healthcare Technology** ... 235
Fabian Wiser, Carolin Durst, and Nilmini Wickramasinghe

16 **Fit-Viability Model Examination of e-Health Solutions** ... 251
Nilmini Wickramasinghe, Jonathan L. Schaffer, Juergen Seitz, Imran Muhammad, and Doug Vogel

17 **Using Foucault to Understand Self-Monitoring in Chronic Disease Management** ... 271
Nilmini Wickramasinghe and Steve Goldberg

18 **Healthcare Information Systems (HIS) Assimilation Theory** ... 283
Hidayah Sulaiman and Nilmini Wickramasinghe

Part III Specific Solutions and the Principles of Knowledge Management

19 Knowledge Management to Address Real Healthcare Needs: The Case of Allergy Care in Australia 311
Nilmini Wickramasinghe and Peter Haddad

20 Embracing the Principles of Knowledge Management to Structure a Superior IT Healthcare Paradigm 323
Nilmini Wickramasinghe, James Choi, and Jonathan L. Schaffer

21 The Impact of Impaired Executive Functions of ADHD Adults on the Use of IS: Psychologists' Perceptions 337
Bader Binhadyan and Nilmini Wickramasinghe

22 The Development of Intelligent Patient-Centric Systems for Health Care 355
Arturo Caronongan III, Hannah Gorgui-Naguib, and Raouf N. G. Naguib

23 Applying the Practice Theoretical Perspective to Healthcare Knowledge Management 375
Obinna Anya, Hissam Tawfik, and Raouf N. G. Naguib

24 Contemporary Developments in e-Health 391
Indrit Troshani and Nilmini Wickramasinghe

25 A Systematic Framework to Assess EMRs and EHRs 403
Rima Gibbings and Nilmini Wickramasinghe

26 Integrating Hospital Records and Home Monitoring by mHealth Apps 415
Sara Marceglia, Giuseppe Pozzi, and Elena Rossi

27 An Investigation on Integrating Eastern and Western Medicine with Informatics 427
Catherine Han Lin, Angela Wei Hong Yang, David Phillips, and Nilmini Wickramasinghe

Epilogue 443

Index 445

About the Editors

Nilmini Wickramasinghe PhD, MBA, Grad DipMgtSt, BSc, AmusA (violin) AmusA (piano) is the professor-director of Health Informatics Management at Epworth HealthCare and a professor of Health Informatics Management at Deakin University, both in Melbourne, Australia. Professor Wickramasinghe researches and teaches in health informatics with particular focus on developing suitable models, strategies and techniques grounded in various management disciplines to facilitate more effective design, development and implementation of technology solutions to effect superior, patient-centric healthcare delivery. She has collaborated with leading scholars at various premier healthcare organizations throughout Australasia, USA and Europe. She is well published with more than 350 referred scholarly articles, more than 10 books, numerous book chapters, an encyclopaedia and a well-established funded research track record.

Jonathan L. Schaffer MD, MBA FHIMSS FAOA FACS is managing director on the Digital Health team in the Information Technology Division at Cleveland Clinic where he is an arthroplasty surgeon in the Center for Joint Replacement in the Orthopaedic and Rheumatologic Institute. Dr. Schaffer also serves as an Honorary Professor in the Office of the Executive Dean, Faculty of Health at Deakin University. Dr. Schaffer is a graduate of Haverford College, Case Western Reserve University School of Medicine, and the Kellogg Graduate School of Management at Northwestern University. He completed his residency in orthopaedic surgery at the University of Pennsylvania and a fellowship in adult reconstruction at the Brigham and Women's Hospital and Harvard Medical School and a research fellowship at Children's Hospital of Boston and Harvard Medical School.

About the Authors

Sasan Adibi is a lecturer in IT in the Faculty of Engineering at Deakin University. He has had a wide experience with numerous research studies focussing on mobile solutions for health care.

Obinna Anya is a Research Staff Member at IBM Research—Almaden, USA. He holds a PhD in Computer Science and an MSc in Distributed Systems, both from the University of Liverpool, UK. His research interests lie in the areas of user experience research, computer-supported co-operative work, e-health, data analytics and context-aware design.

Bader Binhadyan is a PhD candidate at RMIT University, Australia. He holds a MBIS from Monash University. Bader has worked and studied Business IS in Australia, the Middle East and North America. However, his interests in psychology, human behaviour, and technology have the most influence on his research.

Arturo Caronongan IIIrd obtained his BS and MS degrees in Computer Science from De La Salle University, Philippines, where he is also currently undertaking his PhD studies, focusing on developing gesture recognition concepts for the visually impaired. His publications and research interests involve applying AI concepts in health care, classification, music and game development.

Carolin Durst is associate professor at the Chair of Information Systems II at the Friedrich-Alexander University of Erlangen-Nuremberg. Her research focuses on the development of new methods for the exploration and the design for computer-supported co-operative work (CSCW) systems.

Isabella Eigner holds a master's degree in International Information Systems. Since 2014, she is a member of the research staff and PhD student at the Institute of Information Systems at the University of Erlangen-Nuremberg. Her research focuses on data mining in health care.

Rima Artonian Gibbings has worked as an application developer in healthcare systems and is a current PhD student at the University of Illinois in Chicago. As a health informatics researcher/student, she offers a technical approach that links her background in application development with public health topics, addressing current technical requirements.

Steven Goldberg Mr. Goldberg is president of Inet International Inc., an online data collection agency for market and clinical research. He sits on the Editorial Board of the *International Journal of Networking and Virtual Organisations*. He is a co-author of an international healthcare business model supported by the DiaMond Study. Findings were presented in a poster at the Medicine 2.0 conference at Harvard Medical School, 2012. Mr. Goldberg has a B.A. (Economics and Computer Science) from Western University.

Hannah Gorgui-Naguib obtained her BSc in Regenerative Medicine and Innovation Technology from King's College London, University of London, UK, where she is also currently completing her MBBS. She has conducted clinical and surgical research at King's College, Guy's and St. Thomas' Hospitals, UK, as well as at various hospitals in Texas, USA.

Andreas Hamper holds a master's degree in Information Systems. Since 2011, he is a member of the research staff and PhD student at the Institute of Information Systems at the University of Erlangen-Nuremberg. His research focuses on mobile technologies in health care.

Alan R. Hevner is a Distinguished University Professor in the Information Systems and Decision Sciences Department in the Muma College of Business at the University of South Florida. His areas of research interest include design science research, information systems development, software engineering and healthcare systems. Dr. Hevner received a Ph.D. in Computer Science from Purdue University. He is a Fellow of the American Association for the Advancement of Science (AAAS) and the Association for Information Systems (AIS).

Blooma Johns is a lecturer at RMIT International University, Vietnam. She completed her PhD from Nanyang Technological University (NTU), Singapore. Her research interest is in the area of Text Mining, Question Answering Services and Healthcare Social Media. Her research has been published in journals such as the *Online Information Review*, *IEEE Internet Computing* and *Computers and Education*. Blooma has published in various international conferences. She has international experience in teaching leading information systems and business analytics courses in the Middle East, Singapore, India and Vietnam at both undergraduate and post graduate level.

Catherine Han Lin has worked in the IS/IT profession for over 20 years with many well-known international companies at various positions including System Analyst, BI/BA, ICT Manager, Database Specialist, Research Assistant and IS/IT Lecturer. Her research interest include information systems, information management, health informatics, and IS/IT in complementary and alternative medicine. She is currently working on various health IT research projects at Epworth healthcare and Deakin University Australia.

Sara Marceglia is associate professor of Biomedical Engineering at the University of Trieste, Italy, where she teaches Clinical Engineering and e-Health. She received a PhD in Biomedical Engineering from the Politecnico di Milano, Italy, in 2009. Her research activity focuses on mobile applications for health care and on neuromodulation for chronic diseases.

Imran Muhammad, PhD, MIS, MBus (ERP Systems) is a lecturer at the School of Medicine, Deakin University, Melbourne. He has a broad range of research interests in the areas of management information systems, health information systems, and electronic health records and cross cultural system implementations and adoptions.

Raouf N. G. Naguib is the Director of BIOCORE Research and Consultancy International and a visiting professor in the Faculty of Science, Liverpool Hope University, UK. He was awarded an MSc with Distinction, DIC and PhD from Imperial College of Science, Technology and Medicine, University of London, UK.

David Phillips has a background in biomedical research in the area of inflammatory conditions and processes. He has broad experience and expertise in the support of biomedical and clinical research and its translation in the health context and provides perspectives from laboratory, tertiary education, biotech/commercial and healthcare research environments.

Giuseppe Pozzi has been associate professor of Computer Science at the Politecnico di Milano, Italy, since 2002. His current research interests include process modelling and temporal databases in health care. He co-edited a book on *Process Modeling and Management for Healthcare* (2017).

Elena Rossi received her PhD degree in Biomedical Engineering from the Politecnico di Milano, Italy, in 2016. Her research interests include mobile applications for health care, electronic medical records, standard and recommendations for electronic medical records.

Zaid Sako is currently a Master by Research student in health informatics at Deakin University's Faculty of Health.

J. B. Silvers, PhD is the John R. Mannix Medical Mutual of Ohio Professor of Health Care Finance and professor of banking and finance at Weatherhead School of Management with a joint appointment in the Case Western Reserve University School of Medicine. His research in the areas of financial management and health services has been published in numerous journals including the *Journal of Finance*, *Financial Management*, *Journal of the American Medical Association*, *Medical Care*, *Annals of Family Medicine*, the *Journal of Business Research*, *Journal of Consumer Marketing*, and *New York Times*, *MarketWatch*, *Crain's Cleveland Business* and others. Frequently, Silvers contributes commentary to NPR's Marketplace and other national and local print and broadcast media.

Professionally, Silvers has testified to Congress, several state legislatures, federal and state courts. He has also served on committees at the National Academies and several national and state commissions. Until recently, he was a board member (12 years) and treasurer of the Joint Committee on Accreditation of Healthcare Organizations (TJC/JCAHO) and a board member of SummaCare Insurance Company (14 years). For seven years Silvers was a commissioner on the Prospective Payment Assessment Commission (now MedPAC) advising Congress on Medicare payment. For five years he served on the Board of Mathematical Sciences and their Applications at the National Academy of Science.

From 1997 to 2000, while on leave, he was President and CEO of QualChoice Health Plan and Insurance Company. He currently is vice chair of the board at MetroHealth Medical Center. At Weatherhead, he has served as Department Chair, Senior Associate Dean and Interim Dean.

Hidayah Sulaiman received her PhD in Business Information Systems from RMIT University, Melbourne, Australia, and MSc (Computer Science) and BSc. (Hons) IT from Malaysia. She is currently a senior lecturer at the National Energy University (UNITEN), Malaysia, and her research interests are in healthcare information systems, business analytics and IT governance.

Hissam Tawfik is a professor of Computer Science at Leeds Beckett University with expertise in the areas of biologically inspired computing and health informatics. He holds a PhD in Computer Engineering from the University of Manchester (UK) and has over 120 refereed journal and conference publications.

Indrit Troshani is an associate professor at the University of Adelaide Business School. His research interests include adoption and diffusion of innovations including digital reporting and e-health. His work has been published in several journals including *Information Technology & People*, *Electronic Markets* and *Journal of Computer Information Systems*.

Fabian Wiser is a research associate and Ph.D. student at the Chair of Information Management at Braunschweig University of Technology. His main research activities focus on human-computer interaction, design of sociotechnical systems and innovation management.

Angela Wei Hong Yang has been teaching, researching and practising Chinese medicine for 20 years. Her research focuses on evidence-based medicine and investigation of the quality, safety and effectiveness of Chinese medicine for chronic diseases. She applies an interdisciplinary approach to promote, manage and analyse Chinese medicine knowledge.

Part I
Research Design and Methodologies

Chapter 1
Design Science Research Opportunities in Health Care

Alan R. Hevner and Nilmini Wickramasinghe

1.1 Design Science Research Concepts

Design science research (DSR) seeks to enhance technology and science knowledge bases via the creation of innovative artifacts that solve problems and improve the environments in which they are instantiated. The results of DSR include both the newly designed artifacts (e.g., devices, protocols, systems) and a fuller understanding of why the artifacts provide an enhancement (or even disruption) to the relevant application contexts.

Innovative artifacts are implemented within an application context (e.g., healthcare organizations and environments) for the purpose of improving the effectiveness and efficiency of that context. The utility of the artifact and the characteristics of the targeted application—its work systems, its people, and its development and implementation methodologies—together determine the extent to which that purpose is achieved. Design researchers produce new ideas to improve the ability of human organizations to adapt and succeed in the presence of changing environments. Such new ideas are then communicated as knowledge to the relevant practice communities and scientific disciplines. These prescriptive knowledge bases provide the foundations for current applications and future scientific inquiries (Gregor and Hevner 2013).

Purposeful artifacts are built and evaluated in iterative design cycles to address relevant problems. Design artifacts can be of four types: *constructs*, *models*, *methods*, and *instantiations* (Hevner et al. 2004).

A. R. Hevner (✉)
University of South Florida, Tampa, FL, USA
e-mail: ahevner@usf.edu

N. Wickramasinghe
Deakin University, Kew East, VIC, Australia
e-mail: n.wickramasinghe@deakin.edu.au

N. Wickramasinghe, J. L. Schaffer (eds.), *Theories to Inform Superior Health Informatics Research and Practice*, Healthcare Delivery in the Information Age,
https://doi.org/10.1007/978-3-319-72287-0_1

- *Constructs* provide the vocabulary and symbols used to define and understand problems and solutions, for example, the constructs of "entities" and "relationships" in the field of healthcare data modeling. The correct constructs have a significant impact on the way in which tasks and problems are conceived and represented.
- *Models* are designed representations of the problem and possible solutions, e.g., mathematical models, diagrammatical models, and logic models. Models correspond to the abstract blueprint of an artifact's architecture, which show an artifact's components and how they interact.
- *Methods* are algorithms, practices, and protocols for performing a task. Methods provide the instructions for performing goal-driven activities.
- *Instantiations* are the physical systems that act on the natural world, such as a medical device for monitoring internal pressures in the heart or an information system that stores, retrieves, and analyzes electronic medical record data.

Design science research activities are central to most applied disciplines. Research in design has a long history in many fields including agriculture, architecture, engineering, education, medicine, psychology, and the fine arts (Cross 2001). The field of information technology and systems since its advent in the late 1940s has appropriated many of the ideas, concepts, and methods of design science that have originated in these other disciplines. The healthcare applications of IT solutions as composed of inherently mutable and adaptable hardware, software, and human interfaces provide many unique and challenging design problems that call for new and creative ideas.

1.2 Healthcare Challenges and Design Science Research

Our mission in this chapter is to assess opportunities for design science research (DSR) in the field of health care. The potential for innovation in health care is enormous given the current challenges faced in public health and clinical arenas. However, expectations for major breakthroughs have yet to be achieved. Many IT innovations in health care have been proposed but most have low user acceptance and high failure rates and do not provide clear evidence of higher-quality healthcare impacts. Perhaps poor design is one reason for these issues.

The healthcare field provides unique challenges for design science research.

- Healthcare stakeholders are many and varied. While patients, the receivers of care, are the primary recipient of treatments, other key stakeholders include the providers, the administrators, the payers, and the society. Balancing the needs and wants of these groups is very difficult.
- Measures for assessing the quality of designs are difficult to define and are often controversial. Healthcare designs strive to satisfy a multi-criteria set of objectives drawn from the diverse stakeholder groups. Healthcare quality means different things to different people.

- Healthcare policies are a mix between free-market economies and government regulations resulting in complex governance structures and reimbursement procedures. Special interest groups often have outsized voices in policy considerations. This context shapes all healthcare design choices and decisions.
- Innovative technologies and medical treatments are continually being introduced into healthcare applications. Exploiting the latest ideas in new healthcare designs is subject to arduous scientific studies that provide statistically significant evidence of efficacy (e.g., FDA approvals of devices and drugs). New approaches for design evaluations are required to meet these exacting levels of scientific rigor.
- The ethical design issues of building and evaluating healthcare devices, treatments, policies, organizations, and governance structures are enormous. The design impacts on human well-being and life satisfaction go beyond simple utility and performance considerations.

We cannot hope to address all of these issues in this chapter, but we do offer DSR as a well- defined and effective approach for designing healthcare solutions. DSR provides a rigorous framework in which these challenges can be understood and addressed. We begin with a brief survey of recent DSR projects that provides some insights into the range of healthcare problems that are being studied. Further, two projects are examined in more detail as brief vignettes to demonstrate the potential of DSR in healthcare applications.

1.3 A Survey of Recent DSR Projects in Health Care

We begin an exploration of the design opportunities in health care with a survey of recent research papers that have used DSR methods to design new artifacts in different healthcare application areas. Using Google Scholar, we identified over 50 peer-reviewed healthcare papers that cite Hevner et al. (2004) as the basic DSR reference for the research approach employed. This set of papers has been coded as to the specific healthcare area addressed and the innovative artifact designed and used in the application context. Table 1.1 provides a list of the healthcare areas and a sampling of the design artifacts and research papers in each area. In the remainder of this section, we briefly discuss the design opportunities addressed in each of the ten healthcare areas with several exemplars from the literature briefly described.

1.3.1 Medical Systems

Medical systems design encompasses the development of information systems for particular, bounded care-giving environments. Such environments scale from local practices to hospital systems to state, national, and global healthcare communities.

Table 1.1 Healthcare research areas with recent DSR papers

Healthcare area	Design artifacts	Sample references
1. Medical systems	• Architectures • Ecosystems • Digital health systems	• Baarah et al. (2014) • Dong et al. (2011) • Dünnebeil et al. (2013) • Hai-Hong et al. (2009)
2. Clinical protocols	• Therapy and treatment algorithms • Decision-making procedures • Evaluation methods	• Braun et al. (2014) • Pomares-Quimbaya et al. (2014) • Rapaport et al. (2014) • Zhuang et al. (2013)
3. Medical devices	• Embedded software development • Device security	• Mauro et al. (2011) • Weeding and Dawson (2012)
4. Electronic medical records (EMR)	• Ontologies • Storage schemas • Data quality	• Ben-Zion et al. (2014) • Liu and Zhu (2013) • Gaskin et al. (2011)
5. Healthcare data analytics	• Health informatics systems • Disease trends • Biostatistics • Data warehouses	• O'Connor et al. (2015) • Raptis et al. (2012)
6. Healthcare governance	• Policy formation • Regulatory compliance • Human resource scheduling • Technical and governmental standards	• Fitterer and Rohner (2010) • Krey et al. (2011) • Sadeghi et al. (2012) • Schlieter et al. (2011)
7. Healthcare delivery services	• eHealth provisioning • Homecare health services • Care coordination • Telemedicine • Web services and apps • Mobile services and apps	• Alberts et al. (2014) • Breitschwerdt et al. (2012) • Bui et al. (2013) • de Moraes et al. (2013a, b) • Emrich et al. (2014) • Heldal et al. (2015) • Kao et al. (2014) • Menschner et al. (2011) • Ojo et al. (2015) • Peters et al. (2015) • Walderhaug (2013)
8. Public health and preventive care	• Health care and aging • Vaccinations • Population perspective • Using persuasive social networks	• Holmberg et al. (2011) • Lehto (2012) • Nykänen et al. (2013) • Prinz et al. (2012) • Silva and Correia (2014)
9. Pharmaceutical systems	• Prescription services • Drug interactions	• Lapão et al. (2013)
10. Miscellaneous	• Global health measurements • Alternative medicines and treatments • Green healthcare	• Rissanen (2014) • Sherer (2014) • Vo et al. (2015)

Design components for medical systems would include IT components (HW, SW, communications), human stakeholders (medical providers, patients, administrators), and system procedures (treatment paths, decision models). Several exemplar projects and artifacts in the area are:

- Digital health ecosystems are becoming increasingly important as more healthcare information and treatment options are available as services on digital platforms. Dong et al. (2011) present a design framework for the discovery and classification of the vast amount of information and services present in digital health ecosystems.
- Dünnebeil et al. (2013) address the design of value-added applications on a German healthcare telematics architecture. An electronic referral application is designed and implemented to illustrate the use of the architectural approach.

1.3.2 Clinical Protocols

The design of clinical protocols builds new treatment algorithms and procedures for the care of patients and communities. As new technologies (medical devices), drugs, and therapies become available, the methods of integrating these components into an effective treatment protocol must be designed and tested in appropriate environments. Exemplar projects and artifacts here are:

- A well-known Business Process Model and Notation (BPMN) is used to design clinical pathways by Braun et al. (2014). An example clinical process of wisdom tooth treatment illustrates the new modeling technique.
- Zhuang et al. (2013) design an intelligent decision support system in the context of pathology test ordering by general practitioners. The goal is to support GPs to order pathology tests more effectively and appropriately.

1.3.3 Medical Devices

The design and development of innovative medical devices present many exciting challenges to researchers. A significant challenge is the security of the software applications and the data generated by the device. Some interesting DSR projects include:

- Mauro et al. (2011) study the characteristics of medical devices in order to design a general framework for the integration of medical devices into the IT infrastructure of hospitals. Seamless sharing of information between devices and medical databases is proposed.

- Weeding and Dawson (2012) design a laptop solution for providing healthcare information at the point of care in hospitals. Three design versions of the "laptop on trolley" solution are evaluated in an action research project.

1.3.4 Electronic Medical Records (EMRs)

The electronic medical record (EMR) holds great promise for streamlining the healthcare process across disparate providers and institutions. However, the obstacles in both research and practice for implementing EMRs have been tremendous, and we are far from achieving the promised benefits. New design innovations are needed. Ongoing research on EMRs include:

- Adoption of electronic medical records has been slower than expected. Why? Ben-Zion et al. (2014) propose 26 critical success factors along with design guidance for successful implementation of EMR.
- Liu and Zhu (2013) design an integrated e-service model that supports electronic medical services, EMRs, and application services.

1.3.5 Healthcare Data Analytics

The applications of business intelligence and data analytics to healthcare data are just beginning to realize great promise. New analytics algorithms and systems are being designed to capture, store, organize, and analyze the vast amounts of healthcare data available. Issues of patient privacy are paramount in this research. Some examples of healthcare data analytics research are:

- O'Connor et al. (2015) present the Supporting LIFE (Low-cost Intervention For disEase control) project. An innovative approach is designed for gathering healthcare data of seriously ill children in resource-poor environments.
- The lack of open-source platforms for the sharing of healthcare data has impeded collaboration among healthcare professionals and biostatisticians. Raptis et al. (2012) design such a web-based, open-source platform with a goal to enhance the quality of collaborative healthcare data analytics.

1.3.6 Healthcare Governance

Governance of critical medical and healthcare resources is a hugely important topic for design research. The intersecting roles of governments, nongovernment organizations (NGOs), and businesses (profit and nonprofit) in the establishment of standards, policies, regulations, and societal morals are areas in need of design research. Cutting-edge thinking in healthcare governance is seen in these examples:

- Fitterer and Rohner (2010) present a networkability maturity model to assess a healthcare organization's capacity to support effective collaborations of professionals in a healthcare delivery value chain. The model addresses the interrelationships of strategy, organizational design, and IS design.
- A mashup-based interoperability framework is proposed by Sadeghi et al. (2012) to support more personalized healthcare system.

1.3.7 Healthcare Delivery Services

Much design research in the IT discipline has been devoted to advancing methods of delivery of healthcare services to a wider range of patients and communities. New applications of web-based and mobile technologies can revolutionize the ways in which medicine and treatments are delivered. The effectiveness and efficiencies of these new designs must be evaluated rigorously. We find a large number of research projects in this area to include:

- Ambient assisted living (AAL) holds great promise for many patients desiring home-based treatments. Menschner et al. (2011) introduce a novel approach for designing AAL services.
- Ojo et al. (2015) design and build a mobile phone texting (SMS) system to support the monitoring and delivery of health services to underserved and remote populations.

1.3.8 Public Health and Preventive Care

Issues of public health and the preventive care for the betterment of individuals, communities, and populations are in need of innovative design ideas. Major health problems of obesity, drug/alcohol abuse, and poverty-driven lifestyles will require new grand challenge solutions. Some public health design projects include:

- The use of persuasive technologies is a rapidly expanding field of interest in health care. Lehto (2012) discusses the theory and practice of designing health behavior change interventions.
- Silva and Correia (2014) address issues of aging in the design of online platforms for brain training, stories sharing, and elderly support.

1.3.9 Pharmaceutical Systems

The design of new drugs and drug treatment regimens is not widely found in the IT research literature. However, we envision opportunities for research in the design and delivery of innovative pharmaceutical systems and services using DSR. One example project is:

- The development of Internet-based pharmaceutical services would be an important contribution to more effective chronic disease management. Lapão et al. (2013) study new designs for better integration of pharmaceutical services with electronic health systems.

1.3.10 Miscellaneous

We identified several DSR healthcare projects that do not fit naturally into the above healthcare areas. They include:

- Rissanen (2014) argues that eHealth systems should project minimalism and aesthetic values in design. Examples of "machine beauty" in eHealth systems are presented and shown to better encourage healthier lifestyles.
- We have much to gain from a better understanding of alternative medical practices, such as traditional Chinese medicine (TCM). Vo et al. (2015) study TCM practices and develop an ontology to support integration with modern medical practices.

1.4 Healthcare Case Vignettes

To illustrate more deeply the benefits and assistance that can be gained by incorporating a DSR approach within healthcare contexts, two case vignettes are now briefly discussed. Vignette A focuses on the design of a noninvasive sensor solution for blood glucose detection, while vignette B adopts a DSR approach to assist in the development of a calorie cruncher Facebook application.

1.4.1 Vignette A: Sensors for Monitoring Blood Glucose

Recognizing the growing problem of diabetes globally and the limitations of current blood monitoring techniques, Adibi et al. (2017) have set about to develop a sensor solution to test blood glucose noninvasively, i.e., without finger pricking. This approach is based on terahertz-enabled biosensors. In order to move from idea to realization successfully and expeditiously, they followed a DSR process as described in Table 1.2 Column 3.

Table 1.2 Vignette cases and DSR process mapping

DSR process stages	DSR description	Vignette A: Application for sensors	Vignette B: Application for Calorie Cruncher
Problem identification and motivation	Defining the specific research problem and justifying the value of a solution based on knowledge of the state of the problem	With an increasing diabetes population, and the disadvantages of conventional blood glucose tests, the lack of a reliable and easy-to-use noninvasive technology solution to monitor blood glucose motivates the research	Data collection for the measurement of the influence of Facebook friends on the individual's body weight Design implications for the Health 2.0 Facebook application
Definition of objectives of the solution	The objectives can be qualitative or quantitative, i.e., create or improve an artifact, respectively, based on knowledge of the state of the problem and current solutions, if any, and their efficacy	The objective is to create and refine an artifact, i.e. the sensors	Design of an application (the artifact) that incorporates different features based on different mechanisms that influence health-related behaviors
Design and development	Creating the artifact, including the desired functionality and its architecture based on knowledge of theory that can be used to bear in a solution. This is usually an iterative process	Through several iterations, the exact range for the frequency for the needed terahertz wave beam is to be identified. Once the narrow range for the frequency for the terahertz wave is identified, the CAD/CAM programming will occur	Design of the Calorie Cruncher Facebook application based on 14 qualitative interviews
Demonstration	Demonstrate the use of the artifact to solve the problem	Simulation-based: This will be done in a lab using their simulation setup and mannequins Clinical: Demonstration of the use of a new device to a sample of targeted patient population	Proof of concept of the Calorie Cruncher Facebook application
Evaluation	Iterate back to better design the artifact if needed	Simulation-based: As needed, iterations will take place to fine-tune the needed range for the terahertz wave projections Clinical: Iterative evaluations to ensure that the prototype is truly tailored to meet clinical requirements for the targeted population	Identification of areas to improve the Calorie Cruncher application

(continued)

Table 1.2 (continued)

DSR process stages	DSR description	Vignette A: Application for sensors	Vignette B: Application for Calorie Cruncher
Communication	Publish and let the value of the solution talk about itself	This will include conference publications, journal publications, and other presentation activities	Conference publication to communicate and discuss the results in order to develop this project further

1.4.2 Vignette B: Calorie Cruncher

Globally, clinical obesity is becoming a serious problem. Leveraging previous work on social influences, Wickramasinghe et al. (2014) develop a Facebook application "Calorie Cruncher" to enable friends to share their exercise and diet regimens and thereby invoke social influences to support their healthy eating/healthy lifestyle strategies. In developing this solution, a DSR process was adopted and found to be most helpful in developing a suitable user-friendly solution. Table 1.2 Column 4 highlights key aspects.

These case vignettes serve to illustrate the benefits of adopting a rigorous DSR approach in the context of designing and developing solutions for healthcare contexts. The key benefits achieved in the two examples include high user satisfaction and tailoring of the solution to specifically meet users' needs in a reasonable time frame.

We can see that in both case vignettes, the respective solutions exhibit aspects that are both *innovative* and *purposeful*. Specifically, in vignette A the noninvasive approach using terahertz technology is an extremely *innovative* application of using a specific technology solution; namely, terahertz capabilities, to measure a very key healthcare metric, blood glucose. The measuring of the blood glucose is thus *purposeful* as it is focused on a singular task, that of measuring the level of glucose in the blood. As noted earlier, the purpose of improving the effectiveness and efficiency of the context, in this instance, a noninvasive approach to measure blood glucose, is at the center of its innovativeness. The utility of the artifact and the characteristics of the targeted application—its work systems, its people, and its development and implementation methodologies—together determine the extent to which that purpose is achieved, in this case how accurate is the noninvasive measuring of the blood sugar and does it better meet the needs of the patient and healthcare provider. The new ideas assist to improve and adapt to reach a better end state. However, we also note that the solution exhibits aspects of a purposeful innovation too since it is focused on measuring blood glucose. As can be seen in Table 1.2 above, to ensure the purpose was achieved successfully, it was necessary to traverse iterative cycles of constructs, models, methods, and instantiations.

In vignette B—Calorie Cruncher—a similar juxtaposition is evident. Hence, the use of the Facebook application is both innovative and also purposeful as it focuses specifically to assist the individual to better manage their weight to achieve a healthy lifestyle. These vignettes thus also enable us to see that there exists a synergy between innovative and purposeful elements in all such technology innovations for health care as well as other domains. Often the more innovative the solution, the more challenging it is in a healthcare context to secure the support of the end users, and hence, it becomes more important to carefully traverse the steps in the iterative DSR process cycles.

As is intellectually obvious but often forgotten in practice when developing technology solutions for healthcare contexts, there are often different users in health care all working with the same system. This includes surgeons, physicians, nurses, and allied health professionals as well as patients to name just a few key user groups. Such a heterogeneous group of end users necessitates care in development so that all user needs are identified and addressed as far as practically possible. A case in point concerns a nursing informatics solution designed by the software vendor SmartWard. In this context, Nguyen and Wickramasinghe (2017) used DSR to evaluate the system and identify areas in which the system can be further enhanced in order to better meet/support respective user needs including patients, physicians, nurse unit managers, and nurses. The designed solution enables a clearer picture of how the nursing informatics artifact disrupts many processes traditionally used by nurses using paper based reporting at the bedside. Thus, it is also possible to use DSR as an analytic lens to evaluate existing solutions and from this perspective develop appropriate enhancements and/or strategies to make the adoption and diffusion of the system as well as user adoption more successful. This is further supported to illustrate the power of the DSR approach not only as a tool to assist in designing and development but also to facilitate evaluation and enhancing a given solution in a myriad of healthcare concepts. Given the rapid embracement of technology in healthcare, this becomes an important consideration.

1.5 Discussion

The field of healthcare is ripe with opportunities for the design of innovative and purposeful IT artifacts to improve current situations. Today, technology is a strategic necessity in various aspects of healthcare including acute care contexts, home monitoring, billing, and chronic disease management. However, to date, while we are seeing adoption of technology in healthcare significantly increasing in most instances, most if not all user groups are less than satisfied, and higher value care is not ensuing as expected. We suggest that this might at least in part be due to these systems not being fully fit for purpose with a lack of recognition of multiple user needs including patients, doctors, nurses, and hospital administrators. To address this we proffer that a DSR approach might be the most effective way to address

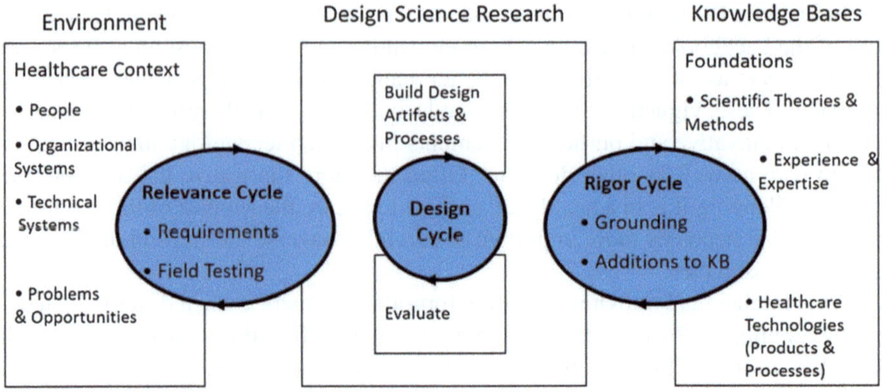

Fig. 1.1 Three-cycle DSR method (Adapted from Hevner 2007)

apparent user dissatisfaction and create solutions that are more suited to all user needs and purposes.

An effective way to view the iterative DSR method is via three intersecting cycles as shown in Fig. 1.1 (Hevner 2007).

- The *Relevance Cycle* bridges the healthcare environment of the improvement project with the DSR activities. The focus in the Relevance Cycle is the purposefulness of the design improvements to be made by the new artifact. What are the practical goals that must be achieved in order to solve the healthcare problem or address the opportunity offered? How can this improvement be measured in the healthcare context? The output from DSR must be returned into the environment for study and evaluation in the application domain.
- The *Rigor Cycle* connects the design science activities with the healthcare knowledge bases of technical and scientific foundations, experience, and expertise that informs the improvement project. Here innovation is the key criterion. The Rigor Cycle provides past knowledge to the research project to ensure its innovation. The design and/or the use of the artifact must provide new knowledge to the organization. This knowledge is validated by clear evidence of the improvements to the healthcare environment.
- The internal *Design Cycle* is the heart of any DSR project. This cycle of design activities iterates rapidly between the construction of the healthcare artifact, its evaluation, and subsequent feedback to refine the design further. This cycle generates design alternatives and evaluates the alternatives against requirements until a satisfactory design is achieved. As discussed above, the requirements are inputted from the Relevance Cycle, and the design and evaluation theories and methods are drawn from the Rigor Cycle. However, the Design Cycle is where the hard work of DSR is done. It is important to understand the dependencies of the Design Cycle on the other two cycles while appreciating its relative independence during the actual execution of the improvement project.

We suggest that faithful adherence to the DSR approach should result in better outcomes in the introduction of new healthcare artifacts that are both purposeful and innovative. We are encouraged to see the increasing use of DSR in healthcare improvement projects as demonstrated by the examples presented in Sects. 3 and 4.

1.6 Conclusions

The goals of this chapter are to survey the state of IT innovation in the field of healthcare and to propose the use of design science research (DSR) as a promising method to enhance the acceptance of future IT innovations. The potential for innovation in healthcare is enormous given the current challenges faced in public health and clinical arenas. However, expectations for major breakthroughs have yet to be achieved. Via a qualitative survey of recent healthcare projects that apply DSR methods, we identify ten areas of ongoing design research. Then, two cases are explored in more detail to demonstrate the use of DSR in challenging healthcare environments. Goals of purposefulness and innovation are identified in the projects. DSR supports the requisite needs of relevance and rigor in healthcare IT projects.

Acknowledgments We gratefully acknowledge the efforts of Avijit Sengupta, Gandhar Pathak, Onkar Malgonde, Vinay Dabhade, Shifa Chaudhary, and Catherine Fernando. This team of University of South Florida graduate students performed a thorough literature review of healthcare papers that used design science research methods.

References

Adibi, S., Nguyen, L., Hamper, A., Bodendorf, F., & Wickramasinghe, N. (2017). A systematic approach to terahertz-based glucose monitoring. *White paper*. Epworth HealthCare.

Alberts, R., Fogwill, T., Botra, A., & Cretty, M. (2014, May). An integrative ICT platform for eHealth. In *IST-Africa conference proceedings, 2014* (pp. 1–8). IEEE.

Baarah, A., Kuziemsky, C. E., Chamney, A., Bindra, J., & Peyton, L. (2014, April). A design strategy for health information systems to address care process management. In *2014 5th international conference on information and communication systems (ICICS)* (pp. 1–6). IEEE.

Ben-Zion, R., Pliskin, N., & Fink, L. (2014). Critical success factors for adoption of electronic health record systems: Literature review and prescriptive analysis. *Information Systems Management, 31*(4), 296–312.

Braun, R., Schlieter, H., Burwitz, M., & Esswein, W. (2014, November). Bpmn4cp: Design and implementation of a bpmn extension for clinical pathways. In *2014 IEEE international conference on bioinformatics and biomedicine (BIBM)* (pp. 9–16). IEEE.

Breitschwerdt, R., Iedema, R. A., Robert, S., Bosse, A., & Thomas, O. (2012). Mobile IT solutions for home health care. In *Advances in health care management: Management issues in health information technology—The international context* (pp. 171–187). Bingley, UK: Emerald Group Publishing Limited.

Bui, D. V., Iacob, M. E., van Sinderen, M., & Zarghami, A. (2013, March). Achieving flexible process interoperability in the homecare domain through aspect-oriented service composition.

In *International IFIP working conference on enterprise interoperability* (pp. 50–64). Berlin: Springer.
Cross, N. (2001). Designerly ways of knowing: Design discipline vs. design science. *Design Issues, 17*(3), 49–55.
de Moraes, J. L. C., de Souza, W. L., Pires, L. F., & do Prado, A. F. (2013a, July). An architecture for health information exchange in pervasive healthcare environment. In *International conference on enterprise information systems* (pp. 385–401). Cham: Springer International Publishing.
de Moraes, J. L. C., de Souza, W. L., Pires, L. F., Cavalini, L. T., & do Prado, A. F. (2013b, June). A novel approach to developing applications in the pervasive healthcare environment through the use of archetypes. In *International conference on computational science and its applications* (pp. 475–490). Berlin: Springer.
Dong, H., Hussain, F. K., & Chang, E. (2011). A framework for discovering and classifying ubiquitous services in digital health ecosystems. *Journal of Computer and System Sciences, 77*(4), 687–704.
Dünnebeil, S., Sunyaev, A., Leimeister, J. M., & Krcmar, H. (2013). Modular architecture of value- added applications for German healthcare telematics. *Business & Information Systems Engineering, 5*(1), 3–16.
Emrich, A., Theobalt, A., Leonhardt, F., Knoch, S., Werth, D., & Loos, P. (2014, January). A pervasive mobile assistance system for health and fitness scenarios. In *2014 47th Hawaii international conference on system sciences* (pp. 2898–2907). IEEE.
Fitterer, R., & Rohner, P. (2010). Towards assessing the networkability of health care providers: A maturity model approach. *Information Systems and E-Business Management, 8*(3), 309–333.
Gaskin, G. L., Longhurst, C. A., Slayton, R., & Das, A. K. (2011). Sociotechnical challenges of developing an interoperable personal health record: lessons learned. *Applied Clinical Informatics, 2*(4), 406–419.
Gregor, S., & Hevner, A. (2013). Positioning and presenting design science research for maximum impact. *MIS Quarterly, 37*(2), 337–355.
Hai-Hong, E., Song, M. N., Song, J. D., Luo, X. X., & Zhang, X. Q. (2009, August). A new service delivery open platform (SDOP) architecture. In *IEEE International Symposium on IT in Medicine & Education, 2009. ITIME'09* (Vol. 1, pp. 404–409). IEEE.
Heldal, I., Lundberg, L., & Hagiwara, M. (2015, October). Technologies supporting longitudinal collaboration along patients' pathway: Planning training for prehospital care. In *International conference on intellectual capital and knowledge management and organisational learning* (pp. 108–116). Kidmore End: Academic Conferences International Limited. Bangkok, Nov 2015.
Hevner, A. (2007). A three cycle view of design science research. *Scandinavian Journal of Information Systems, 19*(2), 87–92.
Hevner, A., March, S., Park, J., & Ram, S. (2004). Design science in information systems research. *MIS Quarterly, 28*(1), 75–105.
Holmberg, N., Steen, O., & Carlsson, S. (2011, May). Service orienting the Swedish vaccination recommendation activity with the business rules centric digital service VacSam. In *International conference on design science research in information systems* (pp. 376–386). Berlin: Springer.
Kao, H. Y., Cheng, Y. T., & Chien, Y. K. (2014, June). Develop and evaluate the mobile-based self- management application for tele-healthcare service. In *International conference on industrial, engineering and other applications of applied intelligent systems* (pp. 460–469). Berlin: Springer International Publishing.
Krey, M., Keller, T., Harriehausen, B., & Knoll, M. (2011). Towards a classification of information technology governance frameworks for the development of a IT GRC healthcare framework. In *Consumer communications and networking conference*. IEEE.
Lapão, L. V., Gregório, J., Cavaco, A., da Silva, M. M., & Lovis, C. (2013). Implementing eHealth services for enhanced pharmaceutical care provision: Opportunities and challenges. In *Advances in information systems and technologies* (pp. 433–443). Berlin: Springer.

Lehto, T. (2012). Designing persuasive health behavior change interventions. In *Critical issues for the development of sustainable e-health solutions* (pp. 163–181). Boston: Springer.

Liu, L., & Zhu, D. (2013). An integrated e-service model for electronic medical records. *Information Systems and e-Business Management, 11*(1), 161–183.

Mauro, C., Leimeister, J. M., & Krcmar, H. (2011). The nature of medical device services. A multiple-case study. In *International conference on biomedical electronics and devices* (BIODEVICES) 2011, Rome, Italy.

Menschner, P., Prinz, A., Koene, P., Köbler, F., Altmann, M., Krcmar, H., & Leimeister, J. M. (2011). Reaching into patients' homes–participatory designed AAL services. *Electronic Markets, 21*(1), 63–76.

Nguyen, L., & Wickramasinghe, N. (2017). An examination of the mediating role for a nursing information system. *Australasian Journal of Information Systems, 21* (in press).

Nykänen, P., Seppälä, A., Ruotsalainen, P., & Blobel, B. (2013, August). Feasibility analysis of the privacy attributes of the personal wellness information model. In *MedInfo* (pp. 219–223).

O'Connor, Y., Hardy, V., Heavin, C., Gallagher, J., & O'Donoghue, J. (2015, May). Supporting LIFE: Mobile health application for classifying, treating and monitoring disease outbreaks of sick children in developing countries. In *International conference on design science research in information systems* (pp. 366–370). Cham: Springer International Publishing.

Ojo, A., Chatterjee, S., Neighbors, H. W., Piatt, G. A., Moulik, S., Neighbors, B. D., et al. (2015, January). OH-BUDDY: Mobile phone texting based intervention for diabetes and oral health management. In *2015 48th Hawaii international conference* on *system sciences (HICSS)* (pp. 803–813). IEEE.

Peters, C., Kromat, T., & Leimeister, J. M. (2015, January). Complex services and according business models--Design and evaluation of an analysis framework in the field of telemedicine. In *2015 48th Hawaii international conference on system sciences (HICSS)* (pp. 1296–1305). IEEE.

Pomares-Quimbaya, A., González, R. A., Bohórquez, W. R., Muñoz, O. M., García, O. M., & Londoño, D. (2014). Improving decision-making for clinical research and health administration. In *Engineering and management of IT-based service systems* (pp. 179–200). Berlin: Springer.

Prinz, A., Menschner, P., & Leimeister, J. M. (2012). Electronic data capture in healthcare—NFC as easy way for self-reported health status information. *Health Policy and Technology, 1*(3), 137–144.

Rapaport, S., Leshno, M., & Fink, L. (2014). A design process for using normative models in shared decision making: A case study in the context of prenatal testing. *Health Expectations, 17*(6), 863–875.

Raptis, D. A., Mettler, T., Tzanas, K., & Graf, R. (2012). A novel open-source web-based platform promoting collaboration of healthcare professionals and biostatisticians: A design science approach. *Informatics for Health and Social Care, 37*(1), 22–36.

Rissanen, M. (2014, April). "Machine beauty"–should it inspire ehealth designers? In *International conference on health information science* (pp. 1–11). Springer International Publishing.

Sadeghi, P., Benyoucef, M., & Kuziemsky, C. E. (2012). A mashup based framework for multi level healthcare interoperability. *Information Systems Frontiers, 14*(1), 57–72.

Schlieter, H., Bögel, S., & Esswein, W. (2011, September). A service oriented method for health care network governance. In *IFIP international working conference on governance and sustainability in information systems-managing the transfer and diffusion of IT* (pp. 249–258). Berlin: Springer.

Sherer, S. A. (2014). Advocating for action design research on IT value creation in healthcare. *Journal of the Association for Information Systems, 15*(12), 860.

Silva, M., & Correia, S. (2014). ActiveBrain: Online social platform for active and healthy ageing. *Procedia Computer Science, 27*, 38–45.

Vo, A., Liu, K., Horan, T. A., & He, Y. (2015, January). Toward global health interoperability: Ontology development of traditional chinese medicine through comparative analyses. In *2015 48th Hawaii international conference on system sciences (HICSS)* (pp. 2843–2852). IEEE.

Walderhaug, S. (2013). Design and evaluation of the ModelHealth toolchain for continuity of care web services. *Automated Software Engineering, 20*(2), 185–235.
Weeding, S., & Dawson, L. (2012). Laptops on trolleys: Lessons from a mobile-wireless hospital ward. *Journal of Medical Systems, 36*(6), 3933–3943.
Wickramasinghe, N., Durst, C., Viol, J., & Theo, S. (2014, December 8–10). Critical issues when designing consumer health 2.0 applications: An investigation of the relationship of online social networks for health-related behaviors. In *Australasian conference on information systems (ACIS)*. Auckland, New Zealand.
Zhuang, Z. Y., Wilkin, C. L., & Ceglowski, A. (2013). A framework for an intelligent decision support system: A case in pathology test ordering. *Decision Support Systems, 55*(2), 476–487.

Chapter 2
Using a Survey Methodology to Measure User Satisfaction with Clinical Information Systems

Jonathan L. Schaffer, Peter Haddad, and Nilmini Wickramasinghe

2.1 Introduction

The healthcare industry is investing heavily in health information systems to enhance patient outcomes, efficiency, and financial performance (Wickramasinghe and Schaffer 2010). Most recently, Gartner has ranked the healthcare industry as the fifth highest spender on information systems/information technology (IS/IT) at ~USD108 billion, with an increase of 2.7% compared to 2013 (Gartner 2015). In Australia, we are now witnessing this trend with significant investments being made by various healthcare organizations for various technology solutions to provide and enable better care delivery (Haddad et al. 2015). IT user satisfaction has been shown in various academic and nonacademic publications as a determinant for successful IS/IT projects (Adam Mahmood et al. 2000; Maldonado and Sierra 2013; Dwivedi et al. 2013; Abelein and Paech 2015). The focus of the vast majority of the current literature are on the factors that affect IT user satisfaction. For example, user involvement in systems development, perceived usefulness, user experience, organizational support, and user attitude toward the IS were reported as key factors influencing user satisfaction in general with IS/IT (Adam Mahmood et al. 2000) and that is in agreement with numerous other studies (Dwivedi et al. 2013; Xiong et al. 2014; Bharati and Chaudhury 2006). While examining IS/IT user satisfaction in healthcare has a lengthy history (Adler 2007; Ammenwerth et al. 2006; Cresswell et al. 2013; Nguyen et al. 2015), measuring user satisfaction with clinical information systems lags behind. This examination of the overall user satisfaction with four

J. L. Schaffer
Cleveland Clinic, Cleveland, OH, USA

P. Haddad · N. Wickramasinghe (✉)
Faculty of Health, Deakin University, Melbourne, VIC, Australia

Health Informatics Management Unit, Epworth HealthCare, Richmond, VIC, Australia

N. Wickramasinghe, J. L. Schaffer (eds.), *Theories to Inform Superior Health Informatics Research and Practice*, Healthcare Delivery in the Information Age,
https://doi.org/10.1007/978-3-319-72287-0_2

clinical information systems qualitatively with the use of descriptive analysis identifies the relationship between the overall satisfaction and five aspects of clinical information systems, namely, key functionalities; efficiency of use; intuitiveness of graphical user interfaces (GUI); communications, collaboration, and information exchange; and interoperability and compatibility issues.

2.2 Methods

An online survey was conducted to collect data on clinical IT user satisfaction at a tertiary, not-for-profit, private healthcare group in Australia. The adopted survey instrument was first tested in another healthcare context to ensure validity of the instrument. As recommended by Miller, three inputs can be used to determine the design of a user satisfaction survey, namely, the objective of the survey, the users' characteristics, and the resources available (Miller 2004). The objective of this survey was to develop a valid measurement of clinical IT user satisfaction. As the participants are predominately clinicians whose schedules are always busy, the design of the survey took this issue into consideration. The survey is relatively short and enables the users to skip sections that are irrelevant. As the selected case is a large healthcare group with multiple sites and locations, an online survey was the preferred option to collect the data. The respondents needed to click a hyperlink to the online survey prior to answering the questions, and a detailed participant information sheet was presented to the respondents about the purpose of this study and how they can take part in it. A total of 107 respondents answered the questionnaire. Due to missing information and incomplete responses, 76 valid questionnaires were used to present the results on clinical IT user satisfaction in the selected context of this study. The response rate was 38.3%. This rate is approximately 3% greater than the average response rate for studies that utilized data collected from organizations through questionnaire/survey methods as was measured by Baruch and Holtom (2008). The questions were focused on four main clinical information systems (Table 2.1) used by various clinicians at the selected healthcare group.

2.3 Results

2.3.1 CIS User Satisfaction

The respondents were first asked on how often they use clinical information systems (CIS) in their daily work with patients. To avoid any confusion, the survey defined a CIS as "any kind of clinical information and communication technology (ICT) system to support patient care (e.g., managing patient information and paperwork,

Table 2.1 The studied CISs in this study and their descriptions

CIS	Description
Computerized physician order entry (CPOE)	This CPOE system is used at the selected healthcare group to facilitate electronic scheduling for oncology patients which was originally a paper-based system at multiple sites and to help with designing its chemotherapy protocols and related processes such as nurse assessment and notes and radiology planning for cancer patients
Scanned Medical Records (SMR) system	SMR is a clinical information system which is seen as a cornerstone of the vision of EMRs. The system is customized and designed to make daily clinical practice easier by enabling higher speed and quality in capturing and distributing health information. The system is web-based and consists of a number of modules such as scanning medical records, e-forms, e-results, and other modules around medical images and medications. The main functions of the system that currently are being used in the selected case are scanning medical records, coding clinical episodes, and tracking paperwork around admissions. The system is used and fully interfaced by seven different pathology and three radiology providers. From a hardware perspective, the system comprises about 30 document scanners and more than 155 computers
Clinical Audit Tool (CAT)	Used as an electronic clinical audit tool. Aims at allowing doctors and other clinical users to create records for each operation or admission that occurs within each specialty. The record will include a structured data set, representing all of the information pertinent to clinical audit within that specialty Recently, CAT for General Surgery and Spinal Surgery went live at the selected case. Both of these projects have extensive clinical content relevant to each specialty. They are also both integrated directly with the group's PAS via HL7. The integration includes patient demographics, diagnosis, theater details, and discharge information
Radiology Results Viewer (RRV)	A web-based application that is embedded within SMR to enable viewing medical images. It supports multimodality readings and has a customized toolset to increase the efficiency of results reading

For ethical considerations, the names of the studied CISs are pseudonym

patients' medication, diagnostic findings, required investigations, etc.)." 51% of the respondents stated they had used CISs several times per day (Fig. 2.1a).

The most used CIS in the examined group of systems was SMR with 97% of the respondents answered with Yes on the question whether they use this system in their daily work. RRV was the second common CIS with 47%, followed by CPOE with 13%, and CAT with only 3% of the population said they had used it in their daily work (Fig. 2.1b).

Answering the question on how the participants were satisfied with the four examined systems, RRV was the most satisfying CIS with 63% of the participants satisfied and 6% very satisfied with it as Table 2.2 summarizes.

In order to identify the reasons behind these levels of satisfactions, the respondents were asked to evaluate sets of statements on their use of the examined systems to perform their tasks. From a system functionality perspective, these statements covered providing decision-making support, preventing medication errors, visualizing data and information to facilitate better work flow, improving health outcomes,

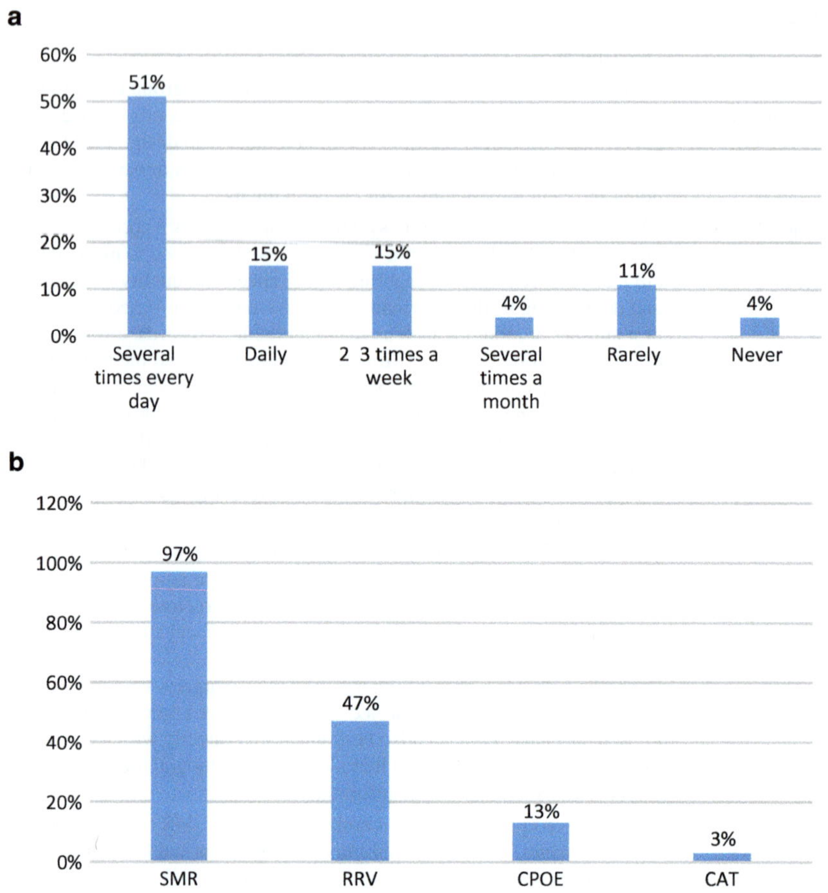

Fig. 2.1 (**a**) How often CISs are used by the respondents. (**b**) The percentage of users who use the examined CISs for their daily work

Table 2.2 The overall satisfaction with the examined CISs in the selected case

CIS	1	2	3	4	5
CPOE	50%	50%			
SMR	22%	22%	23%	33%	
CAT			100%		
RRV		6%	25%	63%	

1: very dissatisfied, 2: satisfied, 3: neutral, 4: satisfied, 5: very satisfied

improving access to important clinical information (lab, radiology, pathology) and documenting these information, improving the quality of information available, and reducing duplicity of effort. As RRV and CPOE were the most and least satisfying CIS, we compared the responses of the statements regarding these two systems. The comparison covered five primary aspects: key functionalities; efficiency of use;

Table 2.3 A comparison between the most and least satisfying CIS in the selected case

Statement	CIS	1	2	3	4	5
This CIS provides support for decision making (reminders and warnings)	CPOE	50%			50%	
	RRV	**20%**	**47%**	**13%**	**20%**	
This CIS helps prevent medication errors	CPOE	50%			50%	
	RRV	**31%**	**44%**	**19%**	**6%**	
This CIS provides a proper summary view (e.g., daily treatment chart) of the patient	CPOE	50%	50%			
	RRV	**38%**	**31%**	**25%**	**6%**	
This CIS helps to improve health outcomes	CPOE		50%	50%		
	RRV		**13%**	**19%**	**50%**	**19%**
This CIS improves access to important clinical information (lab, radiology, pathology)	CPOE	50%	50%			
	RRV			**19%**	**44%**	**38%**
This CIS improves the quality of information available	CPOE	50%	50%			
	RRV		**0%**	**25%**	**56%**	**19%**
This CIS reduces duplicity of effort	CPOE	50%	50%			
	RRV		**6%**	**50%**	**31%**	**13%**
This CIS makes documentation of clinical information easier	CPOE	50%	50%			
	RRV	6 %	13%	19%	50%	12%

intuitiveness of graphical user interfaces (GUI); communication, collaboration, and information exchange; and interoperability and compatibility issues. The summary of this comparison in the area of key functionalities is presented in Table 2.3.

Similar comparisons showed that CPOE has challenges with efficiency of use, intuitiveness, and supporting information exchange, communication, and collaboration in the clinical space. Although the majority of the users thought CPOE was a reliable system, there is an agreement that the system is not easy to communicate with other systems in a way that enables interoperability. On the other hand, RRV seemed to be accepted by the majority of the respondents in terms of its key functionalities (Table 2.3), efficiency of use compared with using paper to facilitate the daily tasks, intuitiveness of GUI, and supporting collaboration in the clinical space. However, RRV seemed to be struggling in terms of supporting access to information in a timely manner.

2.3.2 *Training and Technical Support Satisfaction*

The respondents were surveyed on their satisfaction with IT equipment and systems (hardware and software) in the workplace (Fig. 2.2).

The selected case has an IT hotline in place, the majority of the respondents said they had rarely used this service (79%), and 8% said they had never used it. 29% of the respondents stated that their IT problems were solved immediately over the phone. Similarly, IT-on-call-duty is never used by the respondents. This service relates to IT emergencies and interruptions during the night and on weekends.

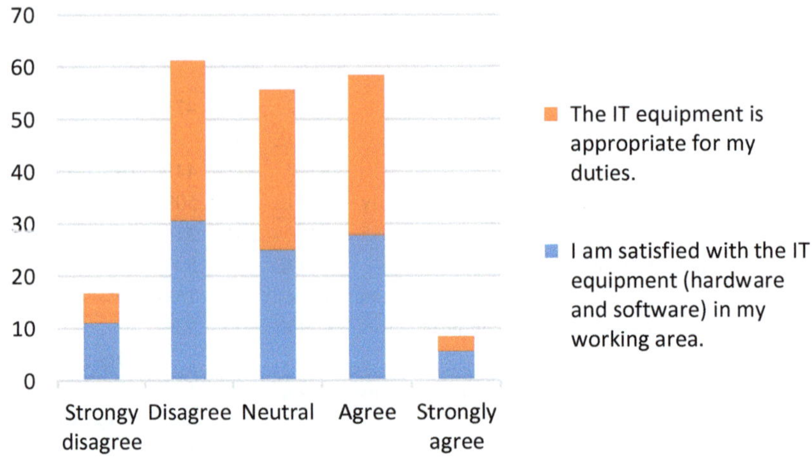

Fig. 2.2 The overall satisfaction with IT equipment at the selected case

Asked about the level on onsite support, 50% of the respondents were neutral, 35% were satisfied, and 10% were very satisfied.

The survey then asked on the amount of trainings which the respondents had attended in the last 12 months. The majority of the respondents stated they had received no training at all, and around 87% of them were dissatisfied with IT training.

2.4 Discussion

This study was performed to qualitatively gain a better understanding of the levels of user satisfaction with four clinical information systems at an Australian healthcare group. Descriptive analysis was also used in this study. The four clinical information systems were of different objectives, the CPOE helps with facilitating electronic drug prescribing, CAT helps create an electronic record for every and each admission to the healthcare group, RRV enables fetching radiology images electronically, and SMR is designed as a system that enables storing all medical records at the selected case in a scanned form. These systems were examined against five primary areas of investigation: key functionalities; efficiency of use; intuitiveness of graphical user interfaces (GUI); communication, collaboration, and information exchange; and interoperability and compatibility issues.

The majority of the participants in this study were satisfied with RRV and dissatisfied about CPOE, and 47% of the participants were satisfied with RRV. RRV is the least expensive system within the examined group of clinical information systems. Yet, it is the most satisfactory system to the majority of its users. The analysis shows that CAT is not widely used at the selected case, and all of its users were neutral about it. This is understandable as the system had been recently implemented at the time of data collection and building conclusions about it might be practically challenging. The most utilized system was SMR with about 97% of the participants using it. The system is seen as a necessary step to EMRs by digitizing all medical records around all admissions that occur at the different sites of the group. Currently, it is used mainly to scan medical records, code clinical episodes, and track paperwork around every admission to all sites of the group.

The system is relatively inexpensive to operate and maintain and is easy to use as described by the majority of the participants. This system, however, suffers from its limited functionality. It is understood that it does not offer the medical records in a way that enables data analytics or business intelligence. This limitation makes this system incapable of coping with today's digital requirements of healthcare delivery. Further, although the system is used group-wide, it only covers inpatient, leaving outpatients out of its scope. The most satisfying system as the results show was RRV, with almost 70% of the participants satisfied and very satisfied with it. A number of characteristics of RRV significantly contributed to this high satisfaction level as the results show. These include supporting information exchange, communications, and collaboration in the clinical space, intuitiveness of user interface, efficiency of use, and the key functionality of the system in terms of improving access to important clinical information as well as providing the clinicians with quality information that support their decisions around respective care episodes. In addition, documenting clinical information is also easily enabled by using RRV as the results show, which contributed to the high level of satisfaction with using this system.

In contrast, CPOE was the least satisfactory system for the participants with 50% of the participants dissatisfied and 50% very dissatisfied with it. CPOE is a sophisticated system that is used primarily by a limited number of clinicians in the area of cancer care for drug prescribing and patient scheduling, which explains the low percentage of use (13%), unlike SMR, for example, which is used by all clinicians in the selected case. The main factors that contributed to lower levels of satisfaction with this system relate to its functionality, ease of use, technical problems, and intuitiveness of the user interface. Indeed 100% of the participants stated that working on paper is more efficient than using the system that is due to technical problems faced by the clinicians with logging in (takes extended times), entering data, and extracting information of the system. As these activities tend to be lengthy procedures and require a broader bandwidth by the clinicians to deal with, 100% of the participants agreed that the use of this system is distracting them from paying attention to their patients. Further, the studied CPOE does not seem to support information exchange, communication, and collaboration within the clinical domain, with 100% of the participants agreeing that this system does not support delivering information about patients to clinicians within or across healthcare providers.

The level of training and technical support on spot have also contributed to the overall satisfaction of CIS users at the selected case. The results show that the majority of participants were satisfied with the IS/IT equipment they have and thought they were appropriate for the type of work assigned to them. However, the level of training both in-house and external was way below the expectations and needs of the users as the results show. Indeed, both CPOE and CAT received lower satisfaction scores due to lacking a proper training that tracks the progress of their utilization of the system and realizing its benefits. The overall satisfaction seems also to be affected by the level of technical support provided on spot. Although all of the participants were happy about the level of help desk provided to them, this support is limited to normal technical issues. With more complex enquiries about sophisticated systems, the technical support seemed to struggle to meet the actual needs of users. Two of the main facilities available for users to use to receive technical support were barely used. These are the IT hotline and IT-on-call-duty services. It is not clear from the results why these are not utilized by the users, which needs a further investigation.

The implications of this study cover both theory and practice. Theoretically, the survey instrument may be used by various types of hospitals and healthcare organizations in general to understand the overall user satisfaction with their clinical information systems. This is particularly timely with the ever-increasing trend to implement electronic medical records (EMRs) in Australia and globally. One of the factors that make this survey valid for different contexts is its coverage to various aspects around the usefulness of clinical information systems in today's healthcare delivery. This includes the systems compatibility with clinicians' tasks in terms of core functionalities, efficiency of use, intuitiveness of user interfaces, accessibility of information, support of collaboration, and interoperability, compatibility, and reliability of the studied systems.

Practically, the results of this study help decision makers and top management at hospitals to better understand the actual needs of clinical information systems' users to better utilize CIS as contemporary assets (Fichman and Melville 2014; Davern and Kauffman 2000). This is crucial with the increased investments in IS/IT in healthcare. Today, healthcare is ranked fourth in investing in IS/IT after retail, banking and securities, and education (Gartner 2015). The study also shows that CIS users are likely to be satisfied if the systems are intuitive and easy to use and enable better access to medical information in a timely manner. This agrees with numerous studies in the literature. See, for example, (Adler 2007; Ammenwerth et al. 2006; Cresswell et al. 2013; Haddad et al. 2014; Nguyen et al. 2015; Wickramasinghe et al. 2014). The results also show that decision makers will need to pay attention to training and technical support channels. The amount and quality of training are key aspects of user satisfaction as the results show. While it is not clear why the vast majority of the participants in this study did not use the IT hotline and IT-on-call-duty services based on the data, further investigation on this matter is likely to clarify this behavior and how to minimize its impact on the overall user satisfaction with clinical information systems.

This study has several limitations. First, the sample size is relatively small and only covers one healthcare organization. Second, the structure of the survey is predominantly qualitative and meant to evaluate the overall user satisfaction with their clinical information systems.

2.5 Conclusion

This study set out to evaluate the overall user satisfaction with clinical information systems at an Australian tertiary, not-for-profit, private healthcare group. Different constructs were considered to evaluate the user satisfaction. The results show that intuitive, easy-to-use, and collaboration enabling systems are more likely to satisfy their users. The level of technical support and training seem to play key roles in determining user satisfaction in the clinical domain. Future research directions include fine-tuning the survey to quantitatively determine user satisfaction based on its constructs in this study, i.e., systems compatibility with clinicians' tasks in terms of core functionalities, efficiency of use, intuitiveness of user interfaces, accessibility of information, support of collaboration, and interoperability, compatibility, and reliability of the studied systems. Also, examining the impact of user satisfaction on the business value of IS/IT in healthcare and moderating role of proper training, coaching, and change management practices on this relationship is planned to be the second phase of this study. A comparison between different healthcare providers is also beneficial and planned to be conducted in the future. Finally, this study highlights the benefits of a survey methodology. The survey used was designed and tested in specific healthcare contexts to establish its validity. A survey methodology can be an appropriate and very meaningful approach to capture key insights from various users, but often further follow-up research is needed to fully understand and unpack key insights gained.

References

Abelein, U., & Paech, B. (2015). Understanding the influence of user participation and involvement on system success–A systematic mapping study. *Empirical Software Engineering, 20*, 28–81.

Adam Mahmood, M. O., Burn, J. M., Gemoets, L. A., & Jacquez, C. (2000). Variables affecting information technology end-user satisfaction: a meta-analysis of the empirical literature. *International Journal of Human-Computer Studies, 52*, 751–771.

Adler, K. G. (2007). How to successfully navigate your EHR implementation. *Family Practice Management, 14*, 33.

Ammenwerth, E., Iller, C., & Mahler, C. (2006). IT-adoption and the interaction of task, technology and individuals: a fit framework and a case study. *BMC Medical Informatics and Decision Making, 6*, 3.

Baruch, Y., & Holtom, B. C. (2008). Survey response rate levels and trends in organizational research. *Human Relations, 61*, 1139–1160.

Bharati, P., & Chaudhury, A. (2006). Product customization on the web: An empirical study of factors impacting choiceboard user satisfaction. *Information Resources Management Journal, 19*(2), 69–81.

Cresswell, K. M., Bates, D. W., & Sheikh, A. (2013). Ten key considerations for the successful implementation and adoption of large-scale health information technology. *Journal of the American Medical Informatics Association, 20*, e9–e13.

Davern, M. J., & Kauffman, R. J. (2000). Discovering potential and realizing value from information technology investments. *Journal of Management Information Systems, 16*, 121–143.

Dwivedi, Y. K., Kapoor, K. K., Williams, M. D., & Williams, J. (2013). RFID systems in libraries: An empirical examination of factors affecting system use and user satisfaction. *International Journal of Information Management, 33*, 367–377.

Fichman, R. G., & Melville, N. P. (2014). How posture-profile misalignment in IT innovation diminishes returns: Conceptual development and empirical demonstration. *Journal of Management Information Systems, 31*, 203–240.

Gartner, I. (2015). *Gartner Says Worldwide IT Spending Across Vertical Industries to Decline 3.5 Percent in 2015*. Stamford, CT: Gartner.

Haddad, P., Gregory, M., & Wickramasinghe, N. (2014). Evaluating business value of IT in healthcare in Australia: The case of an intelligent operational planning support tool solution. In *Bled 2014*. AIS Electronic Library.

Haddad, P., Schaffer, J., & Wickramasinghe, N. (2015). Evaluating business value of IT in healthcare: Three clinical practices from Australia and the US. In *MEDINFO 2015: EHealth-enabled health: Proceedings of the 15th world congress on health and biomedical informatics* (p. 183). Amsterdam: IOS Press.

Maldonado, M., & Sierra, V. (2013). User satisfaction as the foundation of the success following an ERP adoption: an empirical study from Latin America. *International Journal of Enterprise Information Systems (IJEIS), 9*, 77–99.

Miller, L. (2004). User satisfaction surveys. *Australasian Public Libraries and Information Services, 17*, 125.

Nguyen, L., Haddad, P., Mogimi, F., Coleman, K., Redley, B., Botti, M., & Wickramasinghe, N. (2015). Developing an information system for nursing in acute care contexts. In *PACIS 2015 Proceedings, Singapore, 2015*.

Wickramasinghe, N., & Schaffer, J. L. (2010). *Realizing value driven e-health solutions, Improving healthcare series*. Washington, DC: IBM Center for the Business of Government.

Wickramasinghe, N., Kent, B., Moghimi, F., Stien, M., Nguyen, L., Redley, B., Taylor, N., & Botti, M. (2014). Using technology solutions to streamline healthcare processes for nursing: The case of an intelligent operational planning support tool (IOPST) solution. In N. Wickramasinghe, L. Al-Hakim, C. Gonzalez, & J. Tan (Eds.), *Lean thinking for healthcare* (pp. 405–430). New York: Springer.

Xiong, B., Skitmore, M., Xia, B., Masrom, M. A., Ye, K., & Bridge, A. (2014). Examining the influence of participant performance factors on contractor satisfaction: A structural equation model. *International Journal of Project Management, 32*, 482–491.

Chapter 3
Application of Hermeneutics in Understanding New Emerging Technologies in Health Care: An Example from mHealth Case Study

Zaid Sako, Sasan Adibi, and Nilmini Wickramasinghe

3.1 Introduction

Information technology innovation continuum is creating new and innovative solutions for different industries. Particularly, the healthcare industry is witnessing a new era of innovation as new emerging technologies such as Mobile Health (mHealth) and wearable and sensor technologies are being introduced to fight and manage diseases at both global and individual level to deliver better health management platforms. These technologies are delivering innovative solutions through mobile devices that facilitate disease management, tracking of movement and location for fitness and exercise and tracking of different biological signs through smart sensors. These innovative solutions are empowering people and patients to be proactive in managing their health as devices act as a getaway for accessing healthcare services through the exchange of data and information. The exchange of data is through secure data transfer mechanisms between patients and healthcare professionals. The data contains valuable information, and it is the primary driver for the treatment of diseases and empowerment of individuals to self-manage their health (Fig. 3.1).

While new technologies are introduced and solutions have been created, how does one interpret the data captured by such devices to learn more about the underlying IT solution that facilitates the transaction between the different stakeholders of an IT healthcare solution? More specifically, from a research perspective, how does accessing secondary data produced by the devices allow the researchers to understand if the technology is delivering the desired outcome? While from the

Z. Sako · N. Wickramasinghe (✉)
Deakin University, Burwood, Australia

Epworth HealthCare, Richmond, VIC, Australia

S. Adibi
Deakin University, Burwood, Australia

N. Wickramasinghe, J. L. Schaffer (eds.), *Theories to Inform Superior Health Informatics Research and Practice*, Healthcare Delivery in the Information Age,
https://doi.org/10.1007/978-3-319-72287-0_3

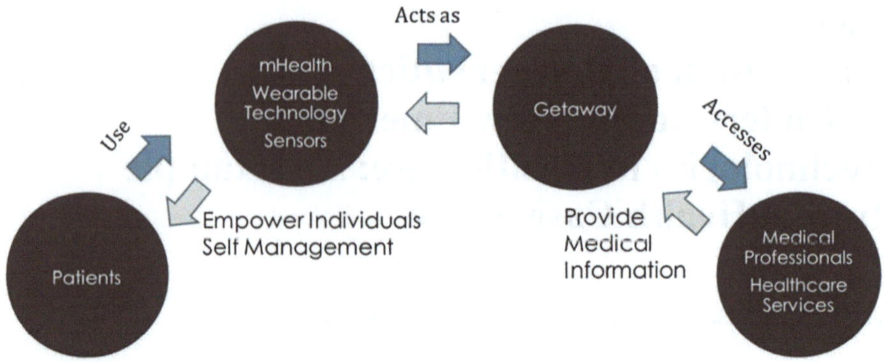

Fig. 3.1 Example of how technologies are becoming a getaway for patients accessing healthcare services

healthcare point of view, how does one evaluate the quality of a solution and whether it is delivering accurate healthcare services?

The technologies are new to the health domain and require a well-established research method to understand how they operate, specifically the IT solution that is delivering healthcare services to people and patients. Although today's modern data analytics platforms are extracting new insights from such technologies to create business values and answer some of the business questions, yet from a scientific perspective, it can be challenging. A way to approach the analysis of secondary data from new, emerging technologies can be accomplished through hermeneutics. Hermeneutics has long been applied in studies where the texts/artefacts are distant from its original authors. The application of hermeneutics in new emerging technologies is to gain a window through interpretation, into the phenomena lived by the patients interacting with healthcare professionals for the management of diseases while using any of the technologies. The essence of interpretation in such case is to understand how the technology is operating, the quality of the primary driver of the technology being data and the integrity of the information based on the data.

With the technologies introduced at the start of the chapter and how they are currently being used in the healthcare domain, this following two sections introduce hermeneutics with background around hermeneutics in the information systems (IS) domain and an example from a current research in progress where hermeneutics is used for analysing secondary data based on an mHealth solution for diabetes.

3.2 Hermeneutics

The term hermeneutics is a modified transliteration of the Greek verb 'hermeneuein', a term that means to express aloud, to explain or interpret and to translate as explained by Schmidt (2014), and it is a technique derived from the interpretive paradigm (Grbich 2013).

It is also known as the process for making a meaning (Esterberg 2002). Hermeneutics was thought to have originated as the study of the interpretation of the Bible (Lee and Dennis 2012) and has been applied in the interpretation of previous work of authors who studied the Bible (Black 2006). Historically, and in ancient Greek, it was believed that Hermes, the mythological messenger god, was equipped with language and understanding that enabled him to interpret the messages from the gods and deliver them to the mortals (Butler 1998). This mythological example illustrates the process for interpreting messages and communicating them with people. The four key terms of language, understanding, interpretation and communication, from the example, are key to hermeneutics. In research, the researcher must be equipped with the language of the subject understudy, understands the messages (data, texts, artefacts) and has a method to interpret the texts to effectively communicate the results from the study to the audiences. Although equipped with language and understanding, the interpretation can become an issue. When interpretation becomes an issue, it is an issue of unintelligibility, and it occurs when a person does not understand an artefact that he or she came across, and it is known as rebelling against successive smooth understanding (Tkácik 2016). In research, unintelligibility can occur when the researcher accesses secondary artefacts that are distant from their original authors and has no access to the language that would enable an understanding of the artefacts.

The objective of using hermeneutics in research is to interpret texts that would allow an understanding of a phenomena and peoples' actions and behaviour and to address questions that fall under the interpretive paradigm. IS research can be classified as interpretive if it is assumed that our knowledge of reality is gained only through social constructions such a language, consciousness, shared meanings, documents, tools and other artefacts (Klein and Myers 1999). Interpreting texts through Hermeneutics is not an easy task and requires in depth understanding of hermeneutics and the interpretation process. The problem with interpretation is that it is a twofold problem. The first is avoiding projecting one's own viewpoint on the text, and the second is the need to successfully communicate to a variety of audiences (Coelho 2001). However, ones' own perceptions and experiences in a subjective, cultural and historical, as referred to as the lifeworld, can be included in the interpretation of texts (Høiseth and Keitsch 2015).

In IS domain, hermeneutics has had a dominant role in the interpretation of information technology(IT)-/IS-related studies, and the results are quite interesting as they provide a fresh view of the IT systems. The widely known paper of Klein and Myers (1999) for set of principles in conducting hermeneutics in IS, Introna (2001) for hermeneutics and meaning making in IS, Boydens and van Hooland (2011) using hermeneutics in quality of empirical databases and Acker (2015) toward a hermeneutics of data are few examples where hermeneutics is key ingredient to the study. They all seek to make meaning of the study and providing guidance in finding a meaning to the study.

Hermeneutics can help render the meaning of a text (object or phenomenon), which has become obscured or 'distanced' in some way, thereby making it no longer immediately obvious (Robert et al. 2011). An obvious everyday example that does not require interpretation is a STOP sign as it is either understood or not (Schmidt 2014).

When is hermeneutics needed? Hermeneutics can provide a rich, detailed interpretation of peoples' experience and texts (Grbich 2013). Traces of data and metadata left in a networked computing infrastructure are becoming computing history where hermeneutics is needed to provide an interpretation of the data (Acker 2015). Interpretive research can help IS researchers understand human thoughts and actions in social and organizational contexts; it has the potential to produce deep insights into information systems phenomena including the managing of information systems and information systems development (Klein and Myers 1999). Hermeneutics was also discussed in the development of information engineering (Fonseca and Martin 2005) due to its powerful ability in interpreting users and the system.

With new emerging technologies, the human action can be understood through the interpretation of data produced by the devices as they are used by people and patients for specific needs, specifically in health care. The data is becoming an extension of people and patients as traces of interaction between patients and medical professionals are captured and exchanged to achieve a desired state of well-being. Yet, while the data has served its purpose, it can contain valuable information that can help in different scenarios. From the technological side of the solution, it sheds light on how the technology functions, how the underlying data quality helps achieve the desired health outcome and what exactly does the data contain that enables this transaction.

With mHealth being a new technology where prototype solutions have been developed and commercially available, studies into the actual quality of data is not looked at thoroughly as the technology is still in its early stages. The following section will elaborate on how hermeneutics is applied to study the emerging technology of mHealth with specific focus on data quality.

3.3 An Example of Hermeneutics in an mHealth Case Study Research

The preceding section has defined hermeneutics and its application in IS studies. This section illustrates with an example, the process of applying hermeneutics in the study of a new emerging technology used for health and disease management. The illustrated example in this chapter is from my current research. The objective of conducting this study is to evaluate data accuracy and information integrity in mHealth solutions, identify how data inaccuracy can occur, test different machine learning algorithms and evaluate the accuracy of the algorithms in detecting inaccurate data. Before diving further into the example, I'd like to begin with Kim's (2013) statement about texts, in which he said:

> Texts do not mean, but we mean with texts.

The selected case study is mHealth for diabetes with the case being patients' data. The selection of the case study was based on the research question, in which it posed as following:

How can Machine Learning be applied in mHealth Solutions to Address Data Accuracy and Information Integrity?

The research question aligns with the study objectives as it is broken down into sections, starting by which type of machine learning, how it can be applied in mHealth and what defines data accuracy and information integrity. The selection of case study was based on the research question, as it is one that conforms to Yin's (2014) criteria for selecting case study, as the form of question is 'How', requires no control of behavioural events and focuses on contemporary events. With using case study, the data is secondary, de-identified data of people with diabetes, and there was no control of behaviour when the data was produced and it presented a contemporary event. The two data sources present both a structured and unstructured cases of data. The first dataset is of patients with diabetes who have glucose measured through both a device and recorded on paper. The second dataset is extracted from hospital admission records where diabetes was either a factor in admission or was recorded during the admission. These two datasets assist in addressing the research question by using the interpretive paradigm as it allows for the reconstruction of understanding of the social world (Denzin and Lincoln 2000). Both datasets allow a rich experience in exploring how different diabetes data is collected and for what purposes, with the patients' experience captured during both scenarios. The hermeneutics method used in this study is adapted from Kim (2013) using the three layers consisting of text, translation and interpretation layer (see Fig. 3.2). The text layer is all the text/data in the study, and it is the first layer of hermeneutics. The text starts with the actual datasets. The datasets are reviewed to form an understanding of what the datasets contain, the format they're in and all the properties of the data including data dictionaries. Once reviewed, the data is then aligned with codes (extracted from thematic analysis) from the literature review that cover data quality (each element of data quality, source of data inaccuracy), information integrity and machine learning. To simulate the process of disease management for patients with diabetes, the data is mapped against the Omaha Client Care Plan that segments the data into Problem Classification Scheme, Intervention Scheme and Problem Rating Scale for Outcomes. The simulation helps in understanding the role of each instance of data in disease management. After the data is examined and mapped against Omaha System, the data is then divided into training and testing data and that is to test different machine learning algorithms. These parts form the text layer as they are mainly text and are yet to bring a meaning that would assist in addressing the research question. The text is translated using thematic analysis. The second layer is the translation layer where thematic analysis is applied to generate themes that can extract meaning from the text. The thematic analysis is adapted from Braun and Clarke (2006). Boyatzis (1998) explains thematic analysis as a process for encoding qualitative information. The text in this study is secondary data, one where there's no access to the patients or the medical professionals and they are open for research. The state of the data does not have a meaning and is therefore stateless data. To understand what the text is, themes look for patterns in information that at minimum describe and organize possible observations while at maximum interpret aspect of

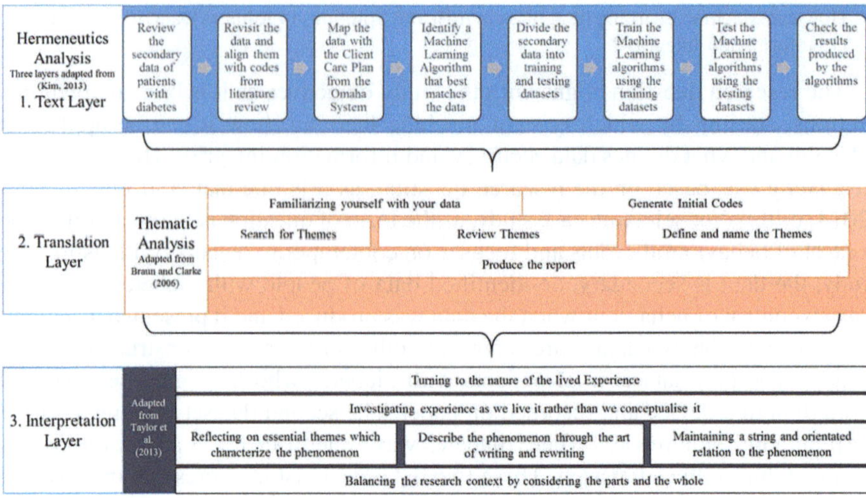

Fig. 3.2 Hermeneutics in studying new emerging technologies

the phenomenon (Boyatzis 1998). The interpretation of the data occurs at the third layer of Kim's (2013) model. The interpretation layer is interpreting the themes to form an understanding about the phenomenon. The interpretation method is adapted from Taylor et al. (2013), and it starts with turning to the nature of the lived experiences, that is, accessing people who would tell about the phenomenon understudy. The lived experience comes from investigating the experience as it has been lived rather than conceptualizing it by accessing data or people who have an experience related to the research question and that is real and has occurred.

Combining the three layers with the thematic analysis and the hermeneutics adapted from Taylor et al. (2013) is to divide the sections with clear and concise objectives that would allow for Hermeneutics technique to be implemented correctly in the right flow. That is by understanding at what stage occurs, the text, the translation and the interpretation of the data.

3.4 Conclusion

Emerging technologies can hold valuable data that require beyond traditional analytics platforms for the analysis of data from a scientific perspective. Hermeneutics has had a role in previous IS studies and has proven to provide a fresh perspective of IS systems. The new technologies are changing the way patients seek advice from medical professionals, disease management and in delivering healthcare services. This change can have many undiscovered, unexplored phenomenon attached to the technologies that are yet to be studied. The role of hermeneutics in this study is to assist in the interpretation of the data through a well-designed process that extracts meaningful information from the themes generated by the data.

References

Acker, A. (2015). Toward a hermeneutics of data. *IEEE Annals of the History of Computing, 37*(3), 70–75. https://doi.org/10.1109/MAHC.2015.68.

Black, C. (2006). *Pico's heptaplus and biblical hermeneutics*. Leiden: Brill.

Boyatzis, R. E. (1998). *Transforming qualitative information: Thematic analysis and code development*. Thousand Oaks, CA: Sage Publications.

Boydens, I., & van Hooland, S. (2011). Hermeneutics applied to the quality of empirical databases. *Journal of Documentation, 67*, 279–289.

Braun, V., & Clarke, V. (2006). Using thematic analysis in psychology. *Qualitative Research in Psychology, 3*, 77–101.

Butler, T. (1998). Towards a hermeneutic method for interpretive research in information systems. *Journal of Information Technology, 13*(4), 285.

Coelho, I. (2001). *Hermeneutics and method: The 'universal viewpoint' in Bernard Lonergan*. Toronto: University of Toronto Press.

Denzin, N. K., & Lincoln, Y. S. (2000). *The handbook of qualitative research* (2nd ed.). Thousand Oaks, CA: Sage Publications.

Esterberg, K. G. (2002). *Qualitative methods in social research* (p. 119). Boston: McGraw-Hill.

Fonseca, F. T., & Martin, J. E. (2005). Toward an alternative notion of information systems ontologies: Information engineering as a hermeneutic enterprise. *Journal of the American Society for Information Science and Technology, 56*(1), 46–57. https://doi.org/10.1002/asi.20099.

Grbich, C. (2013). *Qualitative data analysis: An introduction* (2nd ed.). London; Thousand Oaks, CA: SAGE.

Høiseth, M., & Keitsch, M. M. (2015). Using phenomenological hermeneutics to gain understanding of stakeholders in healthcare contexts. *International Journal of Design, 9*(3), 33–45.

Introna, L. D. (2001). Hermeneutics and Meaning-Making in Information Systems: Oxford University Press.

Kim, Y. S. (2013). *Biblical interpretation: Theory, process, and criteria*. Eugene, OR: Pickwick Publications.

Klein, H. K., & Myers, M. D. (1999). A set of principles for conducting and evaluating interpretive field studies in information systems. *MIS Quarterly, 23*(1), 67–93.

Lee, A. S., & Dennis, A. R. (2012). A hermeneutic interpretation of a controlled laboratory experiment: A case study of decision-making with a group support system. *Information Systems Journal, 22*(1), 3–27. https://doi.org/10.1111/j.1365-2575.2010.00365.x.

Robert, D. G., Wendy, L. C., & Lucas, D. I. (2011). Hermeneutics and meaning making in information systems. In *The Oxford handbook of management information systems: Critical perspectives and new directions*. Oxford: Oxford University Press.

Schmidt, L. K. (2014). *Understanding hermeneutics*. Retrieved from http://deakin.eblib.com.au/patron/FullRecord.aspx?p=3060911

Taylor, B. J., Francis, K., & Hegney, D. (2013). *Qualitative research in the health sciences methodologies, methods and processes*. London: Routledge.

Tkácik, L. (2016). *Introduction to philosophical hermeneutics*. Frankfurt, Germany: Peter Lang GmbH, Internationaler Verlag der Wissenschaften.

Yin, R. K. (2014). *Case study research design and method* (5th ed.). London: SAGE Publications.

Chapter 4
IS/IT Governance in Health Care: An Integrative Model

Peter Haddad, Steven McConchie, Jonathan L. Schaffer, and Nilmini Wickramasinghe

4.1 Introduction

Driven in large by success stories in other industries, digitizing healthcare processes is a relatively common practice today (Haddad and Wickramasinghe 2014; Nguyen et al. 2015), and hence more healthcare providers are moving to IT-enabled solutions. This move requires both up-front and ongoing investments for outcomes that no one can precisely predict (Weill and Ross 2004). This trend provides researchers with the possibility to study the impacts of different information systems/information technology (IS/IT) solutions in various healthcare contexts. Although there is a plethora of such studies, most of these studies have two key limitations. First, there is lack of a comprehensive framework that looks at these systems in their respective contexts. Second, the scope of these studies is mostly limited to the impact of one system on limited measurements regarding outputs. This chapter represents part of a larger research project to comprehensively assess the business value of IT in health care. Business value can only be accurately assessed when the metrics for success are set in advance on project initiation and the metrics are satisfactory and

P. Haddad
Deakin University, Burwood, Australia

S. McConchie
Epworth HealthCare, Richmond, VIC, Australia

J. L. Schaffer
Deakin University, Burwood, Australia

Cleveland Clinic, Cleveland, OH, USA

N. Wickramasinghe (✉)
Epworth HealthCare, Richmond, VIC, Australia

Deakin University, Burwood, Australia

N. Wickramasinghe, J. L. Schaffer (eds.), *Theories to Inform Superior Health Informatics Research and Practice*, Healthcare Delivery in the Information Age,
https://doi.org/10.1007/978-3-319-72287-0_4

acceptable to all stakeholders from administration to clinical services to the corporate oversight structure. Specifically, this model builds an integrative model for IS/IT governance in health care, features both the needs and requirements of various stakeholders in the context of health care, and examines the control measures required to strengthen IS/IT governance practices.

The remainder of this chapter is arranged as follows. First, insights from the literature on the basic definitions and principles of IT governance and how it differs from IT management in contemporary organizations are presented. The need for an integrative model for IT governance in health care is then discussed. Next, a brief summary of the literature on the terms "value" and "business value" is given. The methods and materials used in this research are then presented, followed by the results and their interpretations, as well as implications for both theory and practice.

4.2 Literature Review

The two key areas for this study concern IS/IT governance and the business value of IT and are presented in turn.

4.2.1 IS/IT Governance

Given the increasing need for higher levels of accountability and responsibility in managing IS/IT projects, the term IS/IT governance has emerged (Wim Van and Steven De 2012). A focus on IS/IT governance became important especially as a direct result of the many failures in managing IS/IT projects and generating business value from IT investments (Weill and Ross 2004). This also includes a calculation for the clinical value that is embedded in the business value as these projects should reflect improving the clinical processes and thus increase business value.

The term IT governance has evolved from a need to have a mechanism to manage IT implementation to extend beyond IT contexts and cover the business domain (Weill and Ross 2004). It was defined in the context of the Hawaii International Conference on Systems Sciences (HICSS) as "organizational capacity exercised by the board, executive management and IT management to control the formulation and implementation of IT strategy and in this way ensure the fusion of business and IT" (Van Grembergen and DeHaes 2008). The standardization organization ISO also issued ISO/IEC 38500 in 2008 as a worldwide new standard called "Corporate Governance of IT." Further, Weill and Ross (2004) have defined IT governance as "Specifying the decision rights and accountability framework to encourage desirable behavior in the use of IT" and identified six key assets that enable achieving the strategies of an organization and generating business value – human assets, financial assets, physical assets, intellectual properties (IP) assets, information and IT assets, and relationship assets.

More recently, IS/IT governance practices have been seen as a subset of corporate governance, where IS/IT governance focuses on the relationships required to manage IS/IT assets and resources in a way that achieve the organizational objectives and strategic goals (Korac-Kakabadse and Kakabadse 2001). Given that corporate governance practices focus on board-related issues such as roles, responsibilities compositions, own characteristics, and organizational structures that help achieve corporate strategies, this makes both logical and practical sense (Korac-Kakabadse and Kakabadse 2001).

The scope of IS/IT governance in today's organizations is expanding. Weill and Ross (2005) classify IS/IT governance into five major domains: IT principles, IT architecture, IT infrastructure, business application needs, and prioritization and investment decisions. Each of these decisions is handled, ideally, by different management levels from the top management level down to technical levels. Similarly, Korac-Kakabadse and Kakabadse (2001) scope the coverage of IS/IT governance to cover decisions in three stages—IS/IT projects initiation, IS/IT projects implementation, and realizing the benefits of IS/IT projects (Korac-Kakabadse and Kakabadse 2001).

The leadership in IT governance is controversial (Schyve 2009); IT people argue they know how to manage IT implementations and even reinventing business processes to utilize IT systems and solutions. At the same time, business people and many researchers argue that the leadership of IT governance is the core responsibility of business people, differentiating between effective IT management (the effective delivery of IT services internally) and IT governance, whose aim is to better fit IT implementations into the business strategy (Wim Van and Steven De 2012). Weill (2004) agrees on this, but states the accurate scope of IT governance as

> IT governance is not about making specific IT decisions. That is management. Rather, governance is about systematically determining who makes each type of decision (a decision right), who has input to a decision (an input right) and how these people (or groups) are held accountable for their role.

The literature is rich with studies that attempt to conceptualize IS/IT governance. Alreemy et al. (2016) conducted a literature review to identify the critical success factors (CSF) for IT governance and concluded that these factors can be categorized into ten groups: stakeholders' involvement, management support, financial support, organizational effects (internal), the strategic alignment between IT and business, IT staffing management, IT structure, environment effect (external), managing the implementation, and preparation. Assessing the transparency of IT governance practices and the way firms communicate their IT governance activities have also attracted the interest of both academics and practitioners (see, for example, Chikhale and Mansouri 2015; Joshi et al. 2013). Another notable research direction in the IS literature is integrating IS/IT governance tools and approaches into the traditionally existing organizational processes (see, for example, Heier and Borgman 2012; Peterson 2004). The alignment between IS/IT governance and business strategies has also been studied by numerous studies (see, for example, Boynton et al. 1992; De Haes and Van Grembergen 2009; Haes and Grembergen 2015; Luftman et al. 2012; Orozco et al. 2015; Wu et al. 2015). Although there exists a plethora of studies on IS/IT governance in different industries such as banking (Joshi et al. 2013), technology (Chikhale and Mansouri 2015), manufacturing (Mirbaha 2008), and e-government (Allen et al. 2001), the literature of IT governance in health care lags way behind other industries (Haddad and Wickramasinghe 2014). This may reflect the uniqueness and complexity of health care (Chen et al. 2013), as it has a third key player (the clinicians) beside IT and business players in other industries, and/or that health care has been slower than other industries to embrace IS/IT (Wickramasinghe and Schaffer 2010).

This chapter serves to examine the IS/IT governance structures and approaches in health care, aiming at exploring the best practices of effective IT governance; identifying the main barriers and enablers for such a governance in the three stages of IS/IT projects; initiation, implementation, and potential benefit realization (Korac-Kakabadse and Kakabadse 2001); and then providing a number of recommendations in this regard to enhance the realization of the business value of IS/IT in health care. In order to do so, IS/IT governance practices and structures in a large Australian not-for-profit healthcare organization are closely examined.

4.2.2 Value and Business Value

Healthcare commentary often revolves around universal availability and cost control, i.e., access and cost (Wickramasinghe and Schaffer 2010). Further, value is often defined in terms of the expenditure outcome benefits, divided by the cost expenditure (Porter and Teisberg 2006). The healthcare benefits, from a patient's perspective, include the quality of healthcare outcomes, the safety of the delivery process, and the services associated with the delivery process (Rouse and Cortese 2010; Wickramasinghe and Schaffer 2010).

The term "business value of IT" is commonly used to refer to the organizational performance impacts of IT, i.e., the impact of enterprise architecture (digitizing the operations in a firm) including cost reduction, profitability improvement, productivity enhancement, competitive advantage, inventory reduction, and other measures of performance (Melville et al. 2004).

It is important to emphasize that business value of IT is not a value by itself; rather, it is a model that suggests how value might be generated by implementing different IT solutions (Haddad et al. 2014).

4.3 Research Objective and Research Questions

This study aims to build an integrative model for IS/IT governance in health care. In order to build this model, the impacts of different contextual conditions need to be investigated. Thus, this study attempts to answer the following questions:

1. How can robust IS/IT governance structures help generate the business value of IS/IT in health care?
2. What are the factors that affect IS/IT governance structures for healthcare contexts in the three phases of IS/IT projects—initiation, implementation, and realizing business value?

4.4 Research Design and Methodology

This section presents in turn the research methods, research strategy, and issues around data collection and data analysis.

4.4.1 Research Methodology

This study is predominately qualitative as this approach enables conducting in-depth studies about a broad range of topics with greater latitude in selecting topics of interest (Yin 2014). It also is deemed appropriate to adopt a qualitative approach as it enables examining a relatively new phenomenon, namely, IS/IT governance in health care (Yin 2011). Given the studies on IS/IT governance in health care are scarce, this study is also exploratory in nature, as it is planned to be a "broad-ranging, purposive, systematic, and prearranged undertaking designed to maximize the discovery of generalizations leading to description and understanding of the area of research" (Stebbins 2001).

4.4.2 Research Strategy: Case Study

As noted by Yin (2014), a case study method is appropriate when conducting an exploratory research study especially when the research question is how or why (Yin 2014) as is the case in the current study. The choice of this strategy for this study is justified by the nature of the examined problem, i.e., IS/IT governance in health care, as this strategy is designed for "sticky, practice-based problems where the experiences of the actors are important and the context of action is critical" (Bonoma and Wong 1983). In addition, case study research represents a viable alternative among the other methodological choices to address the complexity of contextual conditions (Posavac 2015; Stufflebeam and Shinkfield 2007; Yin 2013).

The selected case is an Australian not-for-profit tertiary healthcare group that comprises a number of locations and sites in the state of Victoria in the southeast of Australia. The choice of this case is justified by its own characteristics in terms of IS/IT adoption and investments, having multiple business units under the corporate umbrella, and its nature as a not-for-profit hospital, thereby providing an ideal

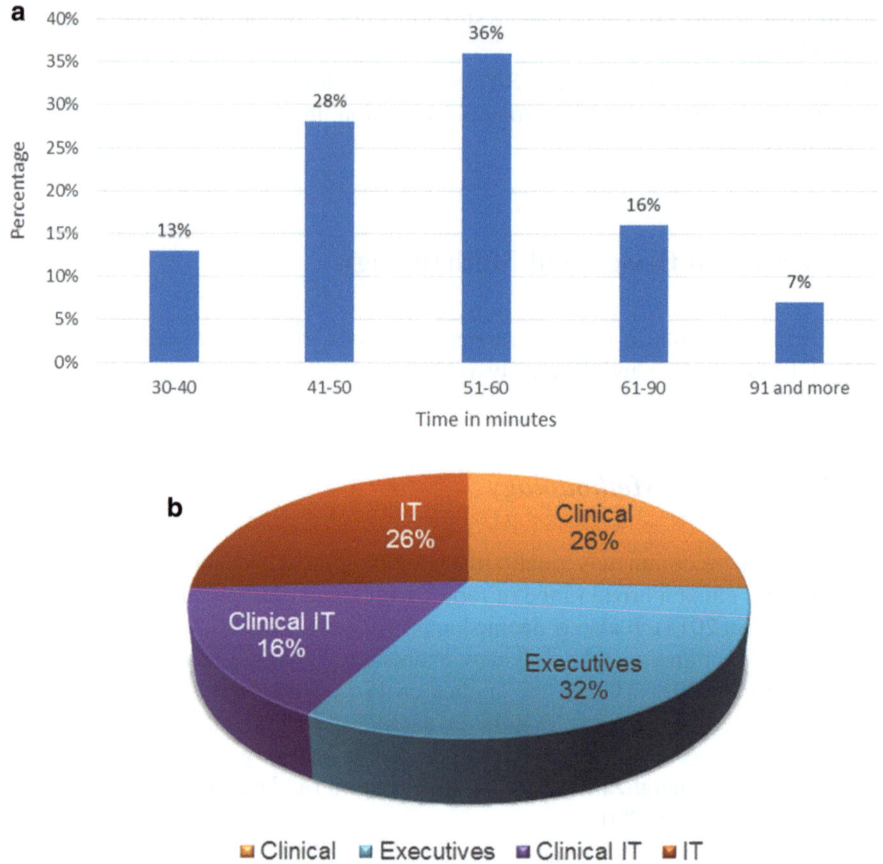

Fig. 4.1 (**a**) The percentage frequency of the duration of conducted interviews. (**b**) The distribution of the interviewees based on their area of expertise/positions

complex environment funding structures, particularly in regard to IS/IT projects, ideally suited for the examination of IS/IT governance issues.

4.4.3 Data Collection and Analysis

To build the IS/IT governance in healthcare model, data were collected by conducting 31 semi-structured interviews in the selected case—Rosetta Healthcare[1] upon the completion of all necessary ethical requirements. The shortest interview was 34 min, and the longest was 102 min. Figure 4.1a depicts the percentage frequency

[1] For ethical reasons, Rosetta Healthcare is used as a pseudonym. The case study is named after Rosetta stone, which was created about 196 BC and discovered in 1799 and led to understanding the ancient Egyptian hieroglyphs.

of the duration of conducted interviews. The interviews enabled gathering insights from four groups of knowledge workers with different levels of influence on IS/IT investments, namely, clinicians, executive and management, and IT personnel (Davenport 2013; Wong et al. 2003), and the group of clinical IT, whose members are clinicians with sound IS/IT knowledge and expertise. The distribution of the interviewees based on area of expertise/positions is shown in Fig. 4.1b.

In addition to the semi-structured interviews, the annual reports for the selected case as well as various archival documents were used to align with recommended practices to enhance the validity of qualitative studies (Johnson 1997). This also helps challenge existing theories and build new theories through data triangulation (Eisenhardt 1989; Eisenhardt 1991), as well as support data and method triangulation, thus enhance the rigor and reliability of the obtained results (Flick 2009).

Iterative thematic analyses were performed on the collected data. These involved the three stages as described by Boyatzis—(1) articulating sampling and other design issues, (2) developing codes and themes accordingly, and (3) testing the validity of the codes and using them to further capture themes (Boyatzis 1998). QSR Nvivo Version 10.2.2 (1380) for Mac was used as a helpful tool to conduct this analysis.

4.5 Findings

The key findings are presented in turn, focusing on the governance structure in place in the selected case, the impact of adopting this structure, and the factors that affect such a structure for IS/IT governance.

4.5.1 The IS/IT Governance Structure in Place

Investing in IS/IT at Rosetta Healthcare goes through a rigorous formal process. Adopting this governance approach started informally in 2009 during a project to change the payroll systems, and over the last few years, it has become more formal, structured, and documented.

This starts with a business initiative, which is handled by a division within the IT department called the project management office (PMO). This initiative undergoes a high-level assessment against the organizational agreed norms. From this point, a project manager will be assigned to the initiative if it is deemed appropriate for the group. The project management approach from this point is Projects in Controlled Environment, version 2 (PRINCE2) (Bentley 2010; Haddad and Wickramasinghe 2014; Hedeman 2006). The resulting document then goes up to the IT Steering Committee, which is the main IT committee at Rosetta Healthcare and whose responsibilities are centered on making the "the right investments in IT," as a senior IT officer describes. Under the central IT steering committee, there exist a number

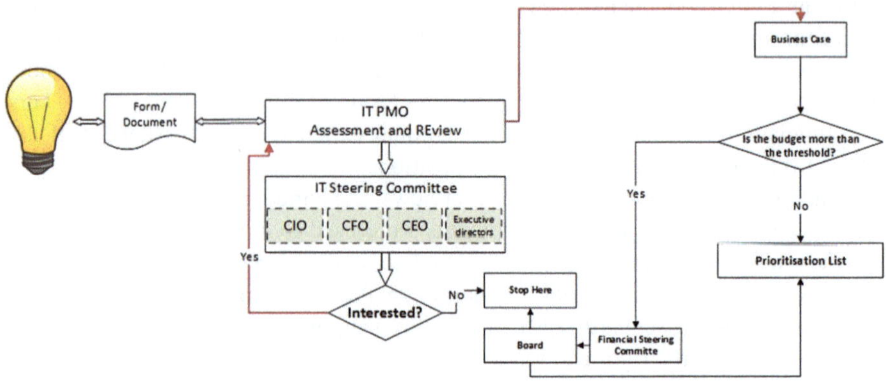

Fig. 4.2 The process of IT governance at the case study, Adapted from Haddad and Wickramasinghe (2014)

of sub-steering committees in different business units (different hospitals) (Haddad and Wickramasinghe 2014). These committees are responsible for managing IT projects based on the approval from the corporate's steering committee. This IT Steering Committee is chaired by the CIO and most of the executive directors and the CEO. It generally discusses whether the group is interested in such a project. This, ideally, depends on its expected benefits and fit with the business strategy and IT architecture of the group. If fit is not apparent, then, more work needs to be done. This starts by deeper discussions between the PMO and the initiator of the project. Upon this, a business case is created. The path from this point depends on the budget required for this project; if it is less than a threshold, then the business case is put in the so-called Prioritization List, on which all planned projects are listed based on their importance to the business. If the required budget is more than this threshold, then the business case is escalated to the Finance Steering Committee and then to the Board, who will decide whether or not this business case will be sent to the Prioritization List (Haddad and Wickramasinghe 2014). Figure 4.2 depicts this process.

If the business case is deemed appropriate and the suggested IT system passes this scrutiny, then a "sponsor" is assigned to the project. A sponsor in the context of the selected case would be a senior employee whose tasks are functionally aligned with the nature of the proposed IT system. Generally, there have been two criteria to appoint a sponsor for an IT project:

1. The nature of the IT project (financial, clinical, administrative, IT, etc.)
2. The experience/expertise required to sponsor each IT project

For example, if the suggested system addresses the financial aspects of the business, then the sponsor would ideally be the Chief Finance Officer (CFO) or the executive director of procurement and facilities depending on the nature of the project. These people would have had enough expertise dealing with similar investments.

The sponsor has a relatively high level of authorization within the dedicated budgets for their assigned projects. If they need additional resources beyond 5% of the allocated budget, they still can ask for it, but they have to go through another cycle of governance to demonstrate the reasons and the commitments to the Board. At the same time, they are fully accountable, and the failure or success of their assigned IS/IT project is their sole responsibility.

4.5.2 The Impact of Adopting This IS/IT Governance Approach

Adopting this IS/IT governance approach has shown an impact on the success of IS/IT projects and generating business value from such IS/IT projects for the hospital. Apart from very few isolated cases, the participants in this research found it difficult to identify a failed IT project since this governance approach was introduced.

All stakeholders at the selected case recognize the importance of a good IT governance for successful IS/IT investments in clinical and business domains:

> Good governance structure has been something we've worked on in the last couple of years, and I feel it absolutely necessary to actually work in this environment. [IT 4]

Besides matching the nature of IT projects with experienced sponsors, the strong governance process gives the business the ability to predict possible failures and prevent it:

> If something was going to fail, you'd see it coming a mile off. Each major project, each month, there is a one-page or a two-page update that goes to the Finance Committee. It says what the status of the project is, what are the key milestones, what are the upcoming activities the next month. There is a track, what we spent today against the budget, what has been committed against the budget. It is really transparent. It's very obvious if something is going to go off track. [EXE 2]

Adopting robust IT governance and project management methodologies that align with the business objectives have another role to play. This is about filtering potential projects and proactively dealing with potential failures for IT projects as one interviewee emphasizes:

> If you've got good IT governance and project management, there's no reason why you should ever have a disaster because you should have certain gates that you go through before you ever hit go on a project. If you don't pass through those gates, then you never hit go. [EXE 6]

Although strong IT governance and project management combined have this important role in this regard, attaining the business value of IT is not a direct result of these practices. Rather, they enable the best opportunity to succeed in delivering IS/IT services as many of the interviewees agreed, especially from the executives and IT groups:

> What we certainly know is without that [governance] structure, it becomes very hard to deliver that initial benefit of actually getting that new system in and transitioned over in a way those benefits or that accommodates the business and the business as usual work. [EXE 3]

The role of the IT department in this practice is more as an advisor and supportive than leading, as the key decision makers at Rosetta Healthcare agreed:

> We don't want IT to say, "Here's your new Internet," and everyone is going, "Well, this is a pile of junk." [EXE 2]

4.5.3 *The Factors That Affect IS/IT Governance in Health Care*

Currently, there seems to exist a number of contextual factors that affect the IS/IT governance structure in place at Rosetta Healthcare, which have reportedly diluted the impact of IS/IT governance during the three stages of IS/IT projects. We examine these in terms of people, process, and technology issues.

4.5.3.1 People Factors

The internal political influences of different stakeholders within healthcare providers seem to limit the efficiency of the current IS/IT governance in place. A number of interviewees noted that internal politics within healthcare organizations is an apparent phenomenon, as noted by this interviewee, who had recently come to the healthcare industry from the defense industry:

> In the medical domain, there are so many political games going on between campuses, divisions within a division; it makes it extremely difficult to talk about IT without politics. [IT 6]

One of the clear aspects of these internal politics relates to the political influence of the visiting medical officers (VMOs). As a not-for-profit private hospital, Rosetta Healthcare does not have many junior doctors employed. Rather, it has a high number of VMOs who are more senior, more experienced, very busy, and tend to have streamlined independent workflows. The Australian Institute of Health and Welfare (2005) defines the VMO as: "A medical practitioner appointed by the hospital board to provide medical services for hospital patients on an honorary, seasonally paid, or fee for service basis" (p. i). In the case of Rosetta Healthcare, VMOs are paid on a fee-for-service basis. Given the VMOs have their own clinics, they run their own IS/IT for managing their patients. As powerful players, the VMOs have impacts on the actual decisions of purchasing IS/IT systems by Rosetta Healthcare. This is due to the fact that they work for/at different healthcare providers and ask for a specific system to be brought based on their experience using this system at a different healthcare provider. In addition, VMOs tend to be reluctant to use the hospital's IS/IT platforms in favor of their own systems. This latter behavior has reportedly limited the business value of IS/IT as it limited the uptake of new IS/IT systems, especially in the clinical space.

The other people aspect is the satisfaction of in-house users (including nurses, allied health, admin and management personnel, etc.). The collected data showed that this group of users lacks the power to have their voice heard and taken into consideration during the purchase process of new IS/IT solutions. It was evident that feedback and inputs from different prospect users of IS/IT were collected, but not taken on board when actually making the decision of investing in IS/IT, which limited their motivation to use these systems and benefit from them. This applies on both business IT and clinical IT. As a result of this behavior, the intention of the internal users to use IS/IT systems when they first know about them dwindles when they realize their inputs were not taken into consideration.

4.5.3.2 Process Factors

From a process perspective, the PMO team at the selected case is assigned a key role during the project start-up and initiation, project delivery, project closure, and analysis and approval. The problem that had been facing this team as the collected data shown is that this team is not dedicated to these projects. Rather, its members are always involved in the day-to-day business, which in many cases caused delays and issues with delivering these projects on time. Similar conditions also apply on the sponsors of these projects, but the pressure on the PMO team is higher as they are specialized in the technical details of starting up and implementing IS/IT projects.

Another aspect of process factors is concerned with the fact that the current IS/IT governance does not consider change management as an integrative part of IS/IT governance processes. This interviewee explains the situation in the selected case: "Some people have been doing some things the same way for 20 years. It's very hard for them to change, but it goes back to making sure that those changes happen in a process. We are trying to say that it's great to put new technology in but you have to change your processes to meet the technology" [IT 3]. Thus, lacking an integrative change management plan in the current IS/IT structure is playing negative roles on the efficiency of IS/IT governance and attaining business value of these IS/IT systems. This is primarily due to the fact that various human resources are not well prepared for the change caused by introducing new technology platforms to their day-to-day processes.

4.5.3.3 Technology Factors

Technology factors that affect the IS/IT governance in place at the selected case included the process of selecting the "right" product, noting the requirements for systems integration, and taking governance issues around the product of IS/IT, namely, data, into consideration.

Selecting the right product is crucial for healthcare organizations as in other industries:

> … Because it is going to affect everyone in the organization in different ways. It's going to affect the doctors in the sense that if it's done properly, it should make it easier for them to get the information. If it's done badly, it's going to obviously undermine them, but it will affect the nursing workflows. It will affect the allied health workflows. It will affect the administrative staff workflows. It will affect HIS [Health Information Systems] workflows. It will affect billing and coding. It will affect business development managers [EXE 4].

From a technological perspective, the healthcare industry seems to be more solution-focused than problem-focused as this interviewee explains:

> Healthcare industry is being solution focused not problem focused: When I look externally, we don't choose a system necessarily based on what solves the problem we have. It was very solution focused, not problem focused so they come in solutions and then look for the problem that it's solving as opposed to what problem I need, what actual things do I need to resolve. [IT 4]

Thus, the principal approach of the current IS/IT governance is to look at different vendors and their systems. Unintentionally adopting this approach has resulted several IS/IT solutions that are not compatible or easy to interface with each other as explained by this interviewee: "You got systems that don't talk to each other; there's already been a lot of investment in one system, and then they don't want to then have to modify" *[IT 3]*.

Each of the newly implemented systems using this approach may have their own dataset that may be used for both clinical and business purposes with almost no data dictionary used universally by all of these datasets. Not only does this limit the benefit of these investments, but it also affects the organization by having to deal with various unstandardized and structurally different dataset, which negatively affects the well-being of the organization itself as the result of this study shown.

4.6 How to Build Robust IS/IT Governance Practices

When asked about the key to creating prudent IS/IT governance practices in health care, the requirements were centered on allocating enough resources, establishing collaborative atmospheres within the healthcare context, ensuring a deeper understanding of the business processes and organizational structure, the existence of adequate upfront planning for IT projects, and carefully assigning leadership to the potential sponsors (Table 4.1).

4.7 Discussion

The results of this exploratory study show that robust IS/IT are increasingly needed to manage the growing IS/IT portfolios in health care as in other industries. The findings also support the work of Korac-Kakabadse et al. that IS/IT governance

Table 4.1 The requirements for a robust IT governance in the healthcare sector, as confirmed by selected quotes from interviewees

Requirements	Selected quotes
Allocating enough resources: IT governance is demanding in terms of human assets, and it needs to be well resourced. This would mean enough personnel equipped with a diverse range of skills and expertise	"We resource it out properly so that we have people not doing it as part of their day jobs. We actually have a dedicated project manager, business analyst, and project team. That has been a real key" [IT 6]
Establishing a collaborative atmosphere within the healthcare context: Successful IT governance needs to be nurtured within a collaborative atmosphere continuously	"We expect that it's going to be a collaborative approach, so it's not someone just running off and doing what they want to do for their site. There needs to be a collaborative approach" [EXE 8]
Deeper understanding of business processes and organizational structures: This understanding is key to all stakeholders, especially to clinicians	"It needs to be at the front end in the sense that they need to basically have a line of sight as to the processes" [IT 7]
Upfront planning for IS/IT projects: IS/IT projects need to be well planned up front. This will lead to a transparent project management and easy to track progress, as well as clarity about expectations	"The fundamental failure up front leads to massive rework, inefficiencies and costs down the back-end and usually leads to immense frustration because it's based on, "I thought I asked for this" and there're no checkpoints along that whole journey" [EXE 4]
Carefully assigning leadership to the potential sponsors (leaders): Although there have been increasing levels of concentration on matching the requirements of specific IS/IT projects and the unique requirements for prospective sponsors, selecting the right sponsor needs to go beyond that, to cover the organizational loyalty. For example, during one IS/IT project, a number of cases of lack of planning and delays happened, even though the same strong IT governance was applied. Asking about the reason, we were advised that the sponsor had not been an employee at the case study	"The role of the sponsor really in my view, it wouldn't have mattered who that person was. It needs to come back to an [Rosetta] executive and someone who's employed and has accountability back to our board for delivering that outcome" [EXE 5]

structures should cover IS/IT projects from initiation through implementation to gaining benefits out these projects (Korac-Kakabadse and Kakabadse 2001).

Successful IS/IT governance structure is a must in order to generate business value from IT investments, but it is not enough on its own. Different factors were found to affect the IS/IT governance.

The chosen IS/IT system and its fit within the business strategy is the main factor in this regard. This is facilitated by a good IT governance structure though.

The results show that the business people should practice the leadership role in IS/IT governance, not IT, whose role should be advising and supporting the front-end role of business. This finding agrees with Weill and Broadbent (1998) who state that decisions around IS/IT investments need to be managed by the top management level rather than the technical level. Nonetheless, IT department still needs to deliver support and practice a mediating role between technology and business, but they should not drive IS/IT governance. This is a priori theme in the literature (see, for example, Van Grembergen and DeHaes 2008; Weill and Ross 2004). Now, we know that this also applies on the healthcare context.

The collected data revealed a number of requirements for a good IT governance structure for health care. Most of these requirements are human and organizational and relate to the maturity of healthcare organizations in dealing with IS/IT assets. From a human perspective, a good IS/IT governance requires to be well equipped with enough dedicated human resources, whose organizational loyalty should be to their organizations and not their own business objectives. That is, they will have to be salaried employees for their hospitals and have accountability back to the board of their hospital (legal employer) to deliver the expected outcomes. From the organizational point of view, hospitals need to encourage collaborative atmospheres between three different groups of knowledge workers, clinicians, business, and IT personnel, and also they need to nurture upfront planning and reengineering of the organizational processes. Thus, IS/IT governance can play a role as an enabler for organizational development and should benefit from it in return.

The results from this study also showed that the current IS/IT structure needs to principally change to focus on the problems faced by the selected case rather than the available IS/IT solutions in the market. Most importantly, IS/IT governance practices need to take systems integration as a must requirement for new IS/IT projects. Further, IS/IT governance structures need to stretch to cover not only IS/IT solutions but also their product, i.e., clinical and nonclinical data. In this regard, the current IS/IT governance structure covers both the initiation and implementation phases of IS/IT projects and neglects the third stage around attaining the business value of IS/IT due to poor quality of produced data through these systems.

In addition, the political influence of different stakeholders needs to be neutralized in order to enhance the alignment with the organizational interest and business objectives. In-house users need also to have their voice actively heard and taken into consideration to enhance the contribution of IS/IT governance to the success of IS/IT projects. Table 4.2 summarizes the factors affect the existing IS/IT governance structure at the selected case for this study and which phases of IS/IT projects are affected by each of these factors.

The results also indicate that when considering IS/IT governance in health care, it is prudent to take a sociotechnical perspective and hence consider various contemporary issues around people, process, and technology.

Based on the results of this study, it is possible to conceptualize IS/IT governance practices in health care from initiation to attaining the business value of these investments as Fig. 4.3 depicts. It is understood that the level to which the business value of existing IS/IT projects is realized affects the initiation of new IS/IT products based on the results of this study.

Based on the discussion above, this study has answered the two research questions by showing the impact of adopting IS/IT structures on attaining the business

Table 4.2 Factors affect IS/IT governance in the selected case

Factor		Initiation	Implementation	Attaining business value
People	VMOs	✓		✓
	In-house users	✓		✓
Process	Leadership	✓	✓	✓
	Project management	✓	✓	✓
	Change management	✓	✓	✓
	aligning to business objectives	✓		✓
Technology	Selecting appropriate IS product	✓	✓	✓
	Taking systems integration into consideration	✓	✓	✓
	Data governance	✓	✓	✓

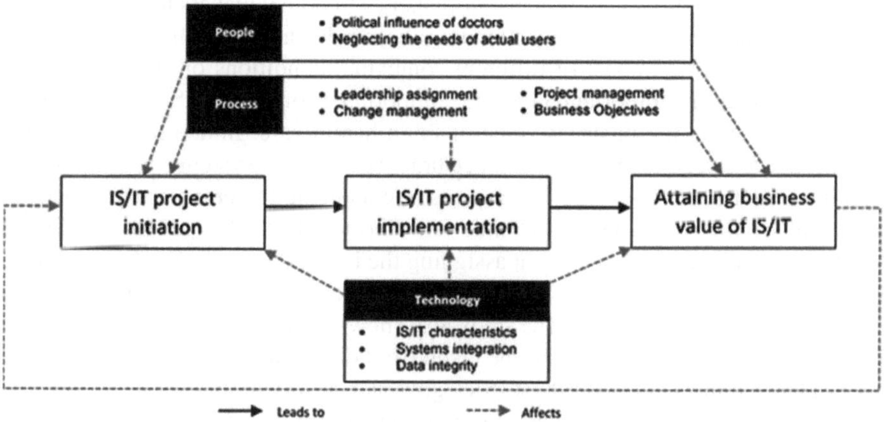

Fig. 4.3 IS/IT governance in healthcare model

value of IS/IT in health care and identifying three primary streams of factors that affect IS/IT governance structures in the healthcare contexts, namely, people, processes, and technology.

This study has two limitations. First the data were collected from a single case study. Even though the selected case comprises a number of hospitals, they all follow the same governance structures. Thus, conducting deeper examinations for different IS/IT governance structures adopted by other healthcare providers may help compare the results and further assess the validity of the integrative model developed in this study. In addition, the interviewees were not comfortable to share information on the cost and bottom line of their organization. Most of the findings on impacts of IS/IT governance on the business value of IS/IT are limited to intangible benefits. Monetized benefits were not easy to be captured in this study. Future directions for this research will benefit from its current limitations. Extending this research to quantitatively investigate this model in multiple case studies is one of the directions for future research. In addition, comparing public and private healthcare settings and their adopted IS/IT governance structure is an option for future research.

The implications of this study extend beyond the theory to cover practices in the area of IS/IT governance in health care. This model helps conceptualize different IS/IT governance structures in health care. The theoretical implications of this chapter is building an integrative model for IS/IT governance in health care. This model is integrative as it has both control and stakeholders functionalities as recommended by Korac-Kakabadse and Kakabadse (2001), who stated that the former is about featuring the necessary control of various stakeholders, while the latter is about meeting their needs and requirements. The model of this research addresses both of these arms by featuring the requirements and the needs of different stakeholders in the context of health care, as well as the control measures required to strengthen IS/IT governance structures and maximize their impacts on IS/IT projects during the start-up, implementation, and post-implementation phases.

Practically, this model helps decision-makers and policy makers to enhance their IS/IT governance by further understanding the needs and requirements of various stakeholders and the impact of different contextual conditions on these practices. This is particularly important given the importance of robust IS/IT governance structures to attain the business value of IT in health care. In addition, this study extends the coverage of IS/IT governance practices to cover systems integration and data integrity issues. These are key aspects of enhancing the organizational performance of healthcare providers (Conrad and Shortell 1996; He and Da Xu 2014; Hiatt et al. 2015). It also shows that assigning the leadership to the top management level is one of the best practices to maximize the success rates for S/IT projects and their perceived business value. The study also shows what roles can be played by the IT department and which inputs to be taken from different stakeholders (clinicians, users, IT personnel) to build robust IS/IT governance structures.

Our future research will focus on applying the proposed framework in other healthcare contexts.

4.8 Conclusion

Based on the discussion above, the need for a systematic, integrative conceptual model for IS/IT governance in health care was established. To address this need, a suitably robust model was developed based on data collected from a large not-for-profit tertiary private hospital in Victoria, Australia.

In closing, to ensure sound IS/IT governance strategies, we have provided a suitable integrative model to assist these practices by both identifying the needs and requirements for different stakeholders and the control measures required to strengthen IS/IT governance practices and maximize their impact on the success of IS/IT projects.

References

Allen, B. A., Juillet, L., Paquet, G., & Roy, J. (2001). E-Governance & government on-line in Canada: Partnerships, people & prospects. *Government Information Quarterly, 18*(2), 93–104.

Alreemy, Z., Chang, V., Walters, R., & Wills, G. (2016). Critical success factors (CSFs) for information technology governance (ITG). *International Journal of Information Management, 36*(6, Part A), 907–916.

Australian Institute of Health and Welfare. (2005). Visiting medical officer.

Bentley, C. (2010). *Prince2: A practical handbook*. New York: Routledge.

Bonoma, T. V., & Wong, K. B. (1983). *A case study in case research*. Boston: Division of Research, Graduate School of Business Administration, Harvard University.

Boyatzis, R. E. (1998). *Transforming qualitative information: Thematic analysis and code development*. Thousand Oaks: Sage.

Boynton, A. C., Jacobs, G. C., & Zmud, R. W. (1992). Whose responsibility is IT management? *MIT Sloan Management Review, 33*(4), 32.

Chen, D. Q., Preston, D. S., & Xia, W. (2013). Enhancing hospital supply chain performance: A relational view and empirical test. *Journal of Operations Management, 31*(6), 391–408.

Chikhale, M. M., & Mansouri, M. (2015). An agile and collaborative framework for effective governance to enhance management in large-scale enterprise business systems: The case of Apple Inc. *Global Journal of Flexible Systems Management, 16*(3), 283–293.

Conrad, D. A., & Shortell, S. M. (1996). Integrated health systems: Promise and performance. *Frontiers of Health Services Management, 13*(1), 3.

Davenport, T. H. (2013). *Thinking for a living: How to get better performances and results from knowledge workers*. Boston: Harvard Business Press.

De Haes, S., & Van Grembergen, W. (2009). An exploratory study into IT governance implementations and its impact on business/IT alignment. *Information Systems Management, 26*(2), 123–137.

Eisenhardt, K. M. (1989). Building theories from case study research. *Academy of Management Review, 14*(4), 532–550.

Eisenhardt, K. M. (1991). Better stories and better constructs: The case for rigor and comparative logic. *The Academy of Management Review, 16*(3), 620–627.

Flick, U. (2009). *An introduction to qualitative research*. London: Sage.

Haddad, P., & Wickramasinghe, N. (2014). The role of IT governance in generating business value from IT investments in healthcare: Lessons from an Australian experience. In *Bled 2015*. Bled, Slovenia.

Haddad, P., Gregory, M., & Wickramasinghe, N. (2014). Business value of IT in healthcare. In L. A.-H. C. G. N. Wickramasinghe & T. Joseph (Eds.), *Lean thinking for healthcare. Healthcare delivery in the information age*. New York: Springer.

Haes, S. D., & Grembergen, W. V. (2015). *Enterprise governance of information technology achieving alignment and value*. Cham: Springer.

He, W., & Da Xu, L. (2014). Integration of distributed enterprise applications: A survey. *IEEE Transactions on Industrial Informatics, 10*(1), 35–42.

Hedeman, B. (2006). *Project management based on PRINCE2TM-PRINCE2 edition 2005*. Zaltbommel: Van Haren Publishing.

Heier, H., & Borgman, H. P. (2012). Improving the organizational integration of IT governance tools: An explorative study. In *Business strategy and applications in enterprise IT governance* (pp. 202–217). Hershey, PA: IGI Global.

Hiatt, R. A., Tai, C. G., Blayney, D. W., Deapen, D., Hogarth, M., Kizer, K. W., Lipscomb, J., Malin, J., Phillips, S. K., & Santa, J. (2015). Leveraging state cancer registries to measure and improve the quality of cancer care: A potential strategy for California and beyond. *Journal of the National Cancer Institute, 107*(5), djv047.

Johnson, R. B. (1997). Examining the validity structure of qualitative research. *Education, 118*(2), 282.

Joshi, A., Bollen, L., & Hassink, H. (2013). An empirical assessment of IT governance transparency: Evidence from commercial banking. *Information Systems Management, 30*(2), 116–136.
Korac-Kakabadse, N., & Kakabadse, A. (2001). IS/IT governance: Need for an integrated model. *Corporate Governance: The International Journal of Business in Society, 1*(4), 9–11.
Luftman, J. N., Ben-Zvi, T., Dwivedi, R., & Rigoni, E. H. (2012). IT Governance: An alignment maturity perspective. In *Business strategy and applications in enterprise IT governance* (pp. 87–101). Hershey, PA: IGI Global.
Melville, N., Kraemer, K., & Gurbaxani, V. (2004). Review: Information technology and organizational performance: An integrative model of it business value. *MIS Quarterly, 28*(2), 283–322.
Mirbaha, M. (2008). *IT governance in financial services and manufacturing*. Citeseer.
Nguyen, L., Bakewell, L., Wickramasinghe, N., Haddad, P., Muhammad, I., Moghimi, H., et al. (2015). Transition from paper to electronic nursing documentation in residential aged care: An actor network theory analysis. *electronic Journal of Health Informatics, 9*(1), 4.
Orozco, J., Tarhini, A., & Tarhini, T. (2015). A framework of IS/business alignment management practices to improve the design of IT Governance architectures. *International Journal of Business and Management, 10*(4), 1.
Peterson, R. R. (2004). Integration strategies and tactics for information technology governance. In *Strategies for information technology governance* (Vol. 2, pp. 37–80). Hershey, PA: Idea Group Publishing.
Porter, M. E., & Teisberg, E. O. (2006). *Redefining health care: Creating value-based competition on results*. Boston: Harvard Business School Press.
Posavac, E. (2015). *Program evaluation: Methods and case studies*. New York: Routledge.
Rouse, W. B., & Cortese, D. A. (2010). *Engineering the system of healthcare delivery*. Amsterdam: IOS Press.
Schyve, P. M. (2009). *Leadership in healthcare organizations: A guide to joint commission leadership standards, a governance institute white paper*. Governance Institute.
Stebbins, R. A. (2001). *Exploratory research in the social sciences*. Thousand Oaks: Sage.
Stufflebeam, D. L., & Shinkfield, A. J. (2007). *Evaluation theory, models, and applications* (1st ed.). San Francisco: Wiley.
Van Grembergen, W., & DeHaes, S. (2008). *Implementing information technology governance: Models, practices, and cases*. Hershey, PA: IGI Publishing.
Weill, P. (2004). Don't just lead, govern: How top-performing firms govern IT. *MIS Quarterly Executive, 3*(1), 1–17.
Weill, P., & Broadbent, M. (1998). *Leveraging the new infrastructure: How market leaders capitalize on information technology*. Boston: Harvard Business School Press.
Weill, P., & Ross, J. W. (2004). *IT governance: How top performers manage IT decision rights for superior results*. Boston: Harvard Business Press.
Weill, P., & Ross, J. (2005). A matrixed approach to designing IT governance. *MIT Sloan Management Review, 46*(2), 26–34.
Wickramasinghe, N., & Schaffer, J. (2010). *Realising value driven e-health solutions*. Washington, DC: IBM Center for the Business of Government.
Wim Van, G., & Steven De, H. (2012). A research journey into enterprise governance of IT, business/IT alignment and value creation. In *Business strategy and applications in enterprise IT governance* (pp. 1–13). Hershey, PA: IGI Global.
Wong, D. H., Gallegos, Y., Weinger, M. B., Clack, S., Slagle, J., & Anderson, C. T. (2003). Changes in intensive care unit nurse task activity after installation of a third-generation intensive care unit information system. *Critical Care Medicine, 31*(10), 2488–2494.
Wu, S. P.-J., Straub, D. W., & Liang, T.-P. (2015). How information technology governance mechanisms and strategic alignment influence organizational performance: Insights from a matched survey of business and IT managers. *Mis Quarterly, 39*(2), 497–518.
Yin, R. K. (2011). *Applications of case study research*. Los Angeles: Sage.
Yin, R. K. (2013). Validity and generalization in future case study evaluations. *Evaluation, 19*(3), 321–332.
Yin, R. K. (2014). *Case study research: Design and methods* (5th ed.). London: SAGE.

Chapter 5
Predictive Analytics in Health Care: Methods and Approaches to Identify the Risk of Readmission

Isabella Eigner and Andreas Hamper

5.1 Introduction

Hospital readmissions have become a critical measure of the quality and cost in health care (Shams et al. 2015, p. 19). According to a report by Medicare (Medicare 2007, pp. 103ff.), readmissions can indicate issues and weaknesses in coordinated care. A key finding of the report is that 13.3% of readmissions that occur 30 days after discharge are classified as potentially preventable in the USA. This results in expenses of 12 billion US dollars. A similar result is also found in a study by the US Veterans Administration, which investigates the cost of readmissions within 30 days in 119 acute hospitals, stating that 2140 US dollars can be saved on average for a preventable, 30-day readmission (Carey and Stefos 2016, p. 241). According to a study by Golmohammadi and Radnia (2016, 151f.), one of ten hospital stays in the USA is potentially avoidable. Germany presents a similar situation, where approximately 2 million hospital stays are considered to be avoidable (Bohsem 2015).

A preventive measure against these trends is the introduction of predictive analyses that can support medical decision-makers in various tasks. On the one hand, the identification of high-risk patients and prognosis of readmissions can be specified, and on the other hand, the effects of various risk factors on the likelihood of readmissions can be determined.

Studies show that current risk prediction models often fail to achieve an acceptable level of accuracy. Comparability of these studies is often complex due to the use of different prediction methods and evaluation techniques. Furthermore, there is no

I. Eigner (✉) · A. Hamper
Institute of Information Systems, University Erlangen-Nuremberg, Nuremberg, Germany
e-mail: isabella.eigner@fau.de; andreas.hamper@fau.de

N. Wickramasinghe, J. L. Schaffer (eds.), *Theories to Inform Superior Health Informatics Research and Practice*, Healthcare Delivery in the Information Age,
https://doi.org/10.1007/978-3-319-72287-0_5

clear definition of readmissions as studies often differ in the investigated time of readmissions (e.g. within 30 days) or use various distinctions ranging from scheduled and unscheduled readmissions (Shams et al. 2015, p. 19f.), clinically related and unrelated, or preventable and non-preventable readmissions. The aim of this study therefore is to analyse current risk prediction models in health care based on their investigated area, applied methods and the prediction accuracy. This chapter is structured as follows: first, an overview and definition of predictive analytics is given as well as a general approach for building a predictive model. Subsequently, application areas of predictive risk models are presented. Finally, identified risk prediction models in health care are analysed and presented in detail.

5.2 Background

5.2.1 Predictive Analytics

To determine the right suggestion to the relevant stakeholders, predictive analytics methods are used to extract patterns from historical data to create empirical predictions as well as methods for assessing the quality of those predictions in practice (Shmueli and Koppius 2010). Predictive analytics are part of data mining, which aims at deriving models that can, e.g. use patient-specific information to predict a specific outcome. As opposed to descriptive models that aim to identify human-interpretable patterns and associations in existing data based on predefined attributes, predictive analytics tries to foresee outcomes or classifications for new input data using a special response variable, thus the classification (Bellazzi and Zupan 2008).

Shmueli and Koppius (2010, pp. 22ff.) present a general approach for conducting predictive analyses. They postulate that in general, predictive analyses consist of two components: first, the empirical predictive model, such as statistical methods or data mining algorithms, and, second, methods that evaluate the predictive power of a model. The latter refer to the ability of a predictive model to accurately represent new observations. The explanatory power, in turn, is related to the strength of the association induced by the statistical model (Shmueli and Koppius 2010, p. 5ff.). Figure 5.1 illustrates the general process steps, which are carried for the creation of an empirical model.

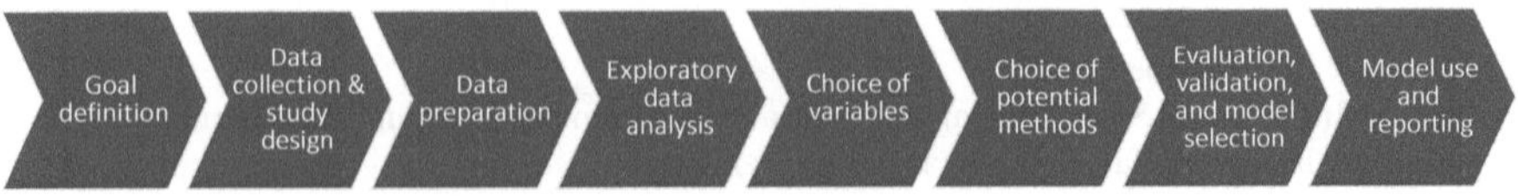

Fig. 5.1 Steps of building an empirical model (Shmueli and Koppius 2011, p. 563)

5.2.2 Application Areas

Besides health care, the use of data mining and predictive analytics to gain knowledge of future trends and behaviours has become popular in various economic sectors. The most prominent areas are presented in the following:

5.2.2.1 Sales and Marketing

The use of large customer databases can enable companies to understand and segment their customers as well as predict future buying and behaviour patterns. Based on the analysis of this data, customers can be individually addressed, and thus marketing measures can be taken more efficiently. As a result, the consumer receives more appropriate offers, and the cross-selling opportunities can be identified more easily. Predictive analyses can also be used to adjust business models, as well as pricing strategies (Hair 2007, p. 307). Hit ratios or customer retention rates can also be increased by analysing purchase patterns of potential customers. Hit ratios determine how often a marketing function generates a sale for each contact with a potential customer. The retention rate defines the number of persistent customers depending on the total number of customers (Nyce 2007, p. 5f.). In addition, the increasing use of web and social media (podcasting, blogs, etc.) encourages customers to retrieve product information online before making a purchase. When using these kinds of media, consumers produce data that can be used to generate demographic profiles of the customers. As a result, the optimum time and place for the placement of an advertisement can be determined (Hair 2007, p. 309f.).

5.2.2.2 Insurance

In insurance companies, predictive analyses are especially useful to detect suspicious or unexpected claims or fraud (Mishra and Silakari 2012, p. 4435). Furthermore, analyses can support the rating and prioritization of individual claims. Another application is the evaluation of insurance risks. By comparing common and more unusual insurance cases, unqualified claims can be filtered out prematurely (Nyce 2007, p. 4ff.).

5.2.2.3 Finance

According to Orem (2015), there are four essential applications of predictive analysis in finance:

- Better forecasting of online revenue
- Reduction of unscheduled expenses
- Improving supply chain efficiency
- The optimization of labour costs

First, the evaluation of customer data can help to identify customer paths that most likely lead to a purchase and hence direct consumers to a profitable page when they reach the retailer's website through an external advertisement. The reduction of unscheduled expenditure can be achieved by identifying areas of underperformance, e.g. by identifying patients at risk of readmission that might lead to financial penalties. In the field of supply chain efficiency, predictive analyses can provide real-time forecasts of demands to optimize inventory or shipping.

5.2.2.4 Law Enforcement

Predictive analyses are also used within the area of law enforcement. Predictive policing uses data from different sources, analyses them and uses the results for the prevention of future crimes. The main aim of the analysis is the identification of patterns in criminal behaviour or locations. Thus, policemen can be appointed in the right place at the right time, thus reducing personnel costs (Pearsall 2010, p. 16ff.; Wang et al. 2013, p. 515f.).

5.2.2.5 Health Care

Predictive analytics in health care, or healthcare analytics, has been a growing research area for the past few years (Koh and Tan 2005; Raghupathi and Raghupathi 2014), often used for fraud detection (Aral et al. 2012; Christy 1997) and risk prediction (Son et al. 2010) or supporting financial and administrative actions, e.g. by reducing patient length of stay (Kudyba and Gregorio 2010). One application of healthcare analytics is clinical decision support, which aims at providing insights to clinical providers by "disseminating timely, actionable information" (Strome 2015) at the right place and time. Therefore, relevant stakeholders can be supported with "relevant, intelligently filtered information at appropriate times, to enhance health and health care" (Osheroff et al. 2007). Predictive analytics can be used to support clinical decision-making for prognosis, diagnosis or treatment planning (Bellazzi and Zupan 2008). Different methods for predictive modelling have been adapted for analytical healthcare purposes and decision support systems, such as the Bayesian classifier (Chan and Lan 2001), Bayesian networks, k-nearest neighbour (Liang and Gong 2015), decision trees (Chae et al. 2003; Delen et al. 2005), artificial neural networks (Delen et al. 2009), support vector machines (Son et al. 2010) or regression models (Chechulin et al. 2014; Phillips-Wren et al. 2008).

After the preceding general view on the fields of application of predictive analyses, an overview of predictive models specifically in risk prediction and their use in the healthcare sector is explained in more detail in the following abstract.

5.3 Risk Prediction Models in Health Care

5.3.1 Overview

The result of this study is primarily based on the systematic analyses of predictive risk models of Kansagara et al. (2011), Ross (2008), van Walraven et al. (2011) and Desai et al. (2009). These analyses examine a total of 216 studies and thus provide a representative insight into the objectives of predictive risk models in health care. In addition to analysing four systematic reviews, 17 additional studies that have been published in the recent past are taken into consideration. The results of these studies show that a retrospective study design is predominantly used (Kansagara et al. 2011, p. 1688), while some studies follow a prospective study design. Retrospective studies thereby use data that was originally documented for other purposes. In the field of health care, this mainly includes medical records (Hess 2004, p. 1171ff.). The main advantage is that data already exists in the form of patient records and does not have to be collected. In contrast, prospective studies collect the data for the purpose of the study allowing to exactly define and gather the required data points. A disadvantage, however, lies in the required waiting time, in which events (e.g. readmissions of a patient group) first have to be documented, before they can be analysed (Song and Chung 2010, pp. 2234ff.).

5.3.1.1 Sample Size

The sample size varies greatly between the identified studies. For example, Huang et al. (2014, p. 1180) use only 520 treated patients with lung inflammation for the development of a readmission prediction model. Futoma et al. (2015, p. 230) use approx. 3,300,000 hospital episodes for the comparison of various predictive risk models. The analysis of 26 predictive risk models according to Kansagara et al. (2011, p. 1690) also indicates a large variance of the sample size, varying between 173 and 2,700,000 patients in the identified studies.

5.3.1.2 Split Ratio

The split ratio of the analysed data into a derivation cohort (DC) and validation cohort (VC) also varies strongly between the different predictive risk models. For example, Howell et al. (2009, p. 1ff.) use an algorithm to predict readmissions within 12 months, using multivariate logistic regression, with 13207 (~75%) patients for the DC and 4492 (~25%) for the VC (Kansagara et al. 2011, p. 1691). Krumholz et al. (2009, p. 407ff.) use a more balanced relationship between DC (226545) and VC (226706) (Kansagara et al. 2011, p. 1691).

5.3.1.3 Object of Investigation

The object of investigation between the analysed studies also varies. For example, Hilbert et al. (2014) focus on the development of a model for patients with acute myocardial infarction, cardiac failure and lung inflammation or pneumonia. Au et al. (2012) also focus on patients with heart failure, and Philbin and Disalvo (1999) limit their study to patients diagnosed with cardiac insufficiency. In addition to patients with heart failure, Howell et al. (2009) also consider patients with chronic obstructive pulmonary disease, diabetes and dementia (Howell et al. 2009). Shulan et al. (2013), on the other hand, take into account all admitted patients. The analysis of the studies shows that most risk prediction models are based on all types of diagnoses. The study by Ross (2008, p. 1379) also obtains similar results, with most studies from the USA taking into account all the diagnoses for readmissions. This is followed by studies investigating patients with cardiac diseases.

5.3.1.4 Readmission Period

The readmission period between the initial admission to the hospital and the readmissions also varies between studies. The analysis of the studies shows that readmissions are primarily investigated within a period of 30 days. Other intervals are 2-month, 6-month and yearly readmissions. In a systematic study analysing prediction models for patients with acute heart muscle infarction, Desai et al. (2009, p. 501f.), on the other hand, find that most models are based on readmissions rate within 1 year.

5.3.1.5 Independent Variables

An overview of the most frequently used variables in predictive risk models based on the studies by Kansagara, Ross and Desdai is shown in Table 5.1. It is important to note that especially socio- demographic variables such as age, gender, insurance status and income are frequently used. In addition, specific variables concerning the patients' disease or comorbidities are used. These include, among others, the severity of the illnesses as well as information on the mental health condition. Predictive risk models, which focus on specific diagnoses, such as, for example, myocardial infarction, also document serum values.

5.3.1.6 Issues

Regression analyses are most frequently used for the evaluation of these data, which are selected with regard to their practical and statistical relevance with regard to the available data. However, the prognosis of future results is often linked to various problems, some of which are described below. A fundamental problem in the

Table 5.1 Common independent variables in risk prediction models

Variable	Kansagara et al. (2011)	Ross (2008)	Desai et al. (2009)
Socio-demographic variables			
Age	X	X	X
Sex	X	X	X
Race/ethnicity	X	X	X
Insurance status	X	X	X
Education	X	X	X
Marital status	X	X	
Living status		X	X
Income	X	X	X
Availability of caregiver	X		
Access to care or limited access	X		
Discharge location	X		
Comorbid variables			
Specific medical diagnoses or comorbidity index	X	X (Heart failure)	X (Myocardial infarction)
Mental illness/depression	X		X
Diabetes mellitus		X	X
Hypertension		X	X
Renal disease		X	X
Myocardial infarction		X	X
Coronary artery disease		X	X
Heart failure		X	X
COPD		X	X
Stroke		X	X
Arterial fibrillation		X	
Previous PTCA		X	
Precious CABG surgery		X	
Tobacco/substance abuse	X		X
Hypercholesterolemia			X
Prior revascularization			X
Severity of disease			
	Severity index	Left ventricular ejection fraction	Location of myocardial infarction
			Coronary angiographic findings
		New York Heart Association Class	Length of stay
			Revascularization
			Physical exam results
Serum markers			
Troponin		X	X
Haematocrit or haemoglobin		X	X

(continued)

Table 5.1 (continued)

Variable	Kansagara et al. (2011)	Ross (2008)	Desai et al. (2009)
Blood urea nitrogen/creatinine		X	X
Natriuretic peptide		X	X
Sodium		X	

derivation of knowledge is that the present record may contain peculiarities. These are then included in the predictive algorithm, as well as in the prognosis. This can lead to incorrect conclusions drawn from the data. A basic problem is under- or overfitting. With underfitting, important forecast variables are not identified in the derived data set. This can have different causes. On the one hand, random variation can lead to the fact that the values of important forecast variables do not differ significantly, within different forecast groups of the available data collection. On the other hand, important prediction factors cannot be taken into account due to limitations in the derivation of the data set. With overfitting, on the other hand, the prediction model is too much focused on the derivation data and cannot generalize well enough to be applied to new data. Essentially, the compatibility of the models for further applications has to be validated. Altman & Royston (2000, p. 454ff.) define a clinically validated model as such, that is, has to reach a satisfactory performance under defined statistical criteria. They see a need for validation of prognosis models to ensure that the predictors are appropriate for the purpose, and thus various problems can be identified and corrected. These issues include deficits in the application of standard modelling methods, the design of the prognostic studies and the transferability of the models.

5.3.2 *Methods*

The following table provides an overview of the methods used within predictive risk models in health care. Each method is presented shortly and subsequently evaluated (Table 5.2).

5.3.2.1 Regression Analysis

In health care, the regression analysis is one of the most important statistical methods for evaluating medical data. Through this method, relationships between individual factors such as, for example, hypertension and the age of the patient can be identified. In essence, the regression analysis allows to examine three aspects and, on the one hand, the relationship between the independent and dependent variables, which are described using a regression analysis. On the other hand, the dependent variable can be estimated by the observed independent variables. The third aspect is the

Table 5.2 Applied methods in risk prediction studies

	Amarasingham et al.	Au et al.	Billings et al.	Bottle et al.	Futoma et al.	Halfon et al.	Hasan et al.	Hilbert et al.	Howell et al.	Huang et al.	Lee	Morrissey et al.	Philbin et al.	Shams et al.	Shulan et al.	Sushmita et al.	Yamokoski et al.
Regression analysis	X		X	X	X	X	X		X	X	X	X	X	X	X	X	X
Decision trees								X			X					X	
Random forest		X			X									X		X	
Support vector machine					X											X	
Neural networks											X						

identification of relevant risk factors as well as the generation of individual predictions (Schneider et al. 2010, p. 776). There are different kinds of regression analyses, the fields of application which are as follows (Backhaus et al. 2016, p. 67):

- Causal analysis: here, we examine how a certain variable is influenced by the regression analysis.
- Impact analysis: the degree of change of a dependent variable can be investigated when an independent variable is modified.
- Time series analyses: in this application area, the change of a variable is analysed in the time sequence.

In essence, simple and multiple regression, as well as linear and non-linear regression, can be differentiated (von der Lippe 1993, pp. 259ff.). A regression method often used in the medical field is the so- called *logistic regression (LR).* There are two types of logistic regression: the binary logistic regression and the multinomial logistic regression. The former is used for dependent variables with two possible characteristics. For example, a patient is readmitted or not readmitted. The latter is for a dependent variable which can take more than two characteristics. The main difference between the logistic and the linear regression is that the logistic regression only estimates the occurrence probability of the selected characteristic of the dependent variable and not the magnitude of this variable itself (Albers 2007, p. 199). As an alternative to logistic regression models, the "*penalized*" *regression analyses (PRA)* apply. These are mainly used in the analysis of high-dimensional data. Among the most popular PRA methodologies are LASSO, adaptive LASSO and the elastic net (Brown 2016). Finally, the Poisson's regression is used to model count data as a dependent variable and continuous or categorical independent variables (Schneider et al. 2010, p. 777).

5.3.2.2 Support Vector Machines (SVMs)

A support vector machine represents data objects as vectors in a d-dimensional data space to enable a separation of these objects by means of binary classification rules. For this purpose, the training data is separated from each other, depending on the number of dimensions, by a line, plane or hyperplane according to learned classification rules (Harrach 2014, p. 150; Müller and Lenz 2013, p.). SVMs are used to describe the extent to which new examples can be classified from a learning set. Each learning set has n examples and is composed of a feature vector and a classification. The classification Y can be 1 (positive) or −1 (negative). The feature vector summarizes all feature values of the example and must contain real numbers. The aim of SVM is to select the hyperplane with the maximum distance between the positive and negative data points (Görz 2014, S. 427ff.). In addition, the initial feature space can be represented in a higher-dimensional space, which may allow an easier identification of separating boundaries between the data sets. For the conversion of a function of data objects into a higher- dimensional space, so-called kernel functions are used (Müller and Lenz 2013, p. 107). Thus, SVM can also have complex non-linear classification rules (Görz 2014, p. 432). SVMs are mainly used when a large number of features have to be interpreted, e.g. in text classification (Kaiser 2009, S. 93f.). An advantage of SVMs is that if the kernels are correctly specified, a high classification quality can be obtained. Another advantage is that, after completing the classifier's training, new data objects can be quickly categorized onto the right side of the separating hyperplane. A shortcoming in the use of SVM is that a large number of irrelevant attributes lead to overfitting. Another drawback with SVM is that the kernel function and its parameters must be estimated for each data set. This requires a large training data set so that the classification quality and the cross-validation can still be reliably determined (Harrach 2014, p. 151; Müller and Lenz 2013, pp. 106f.).

5.3.2.3 Decision Trees (DT)

Complex, unbalanced and missing values of health data result in a non-linear relationship between health outcomes and their underlying determinants. Thus, methods that can deal with non-linear relationships, such as decision trees, are often applied in health care. A distinction is made between two different types of trees: classification trees and regression trees. The former can be used for the prediction of categories, whereas the latter can be used, for example, to identify relationships of related health data. Both are used for the investigation of dependent variables, whereby classification trees use a limited number of disordered values. Regression trees, on the other hand, use ordered, discrete values. In general, both methods are considered machine-based learning methods, which can generate prediction models from data (Loh 2011, p. 14; Speybroeck 2012, p. 243). When using decision trees for classifying new examples, a set of already classified examples has to be prepared first. This data set is divided into a training data set and a test data set. The training data set is used to develop the decision tree and the test data set to test the accuracy of the obtained model. First, all attributes (input data) that define a specific case are described. Next, all attributes, which are relevant for the decision of a given problem (output data), are selected. For each input variable, specific value classes are defined according to the following rules: if an attribute can only accept one of a few discrete values, then each value has its own class. If an attribute can hold various numerical values, characteristic intervals are defined. In this case, each interval can again represent a different class. Each of these attributes can then represent an internal node in the generated decision tree. The leaves of the decision tree characterize decisions by means of value classes. The derived rules that have been developed based on solved cases can then be transferred to new examples. In principle, a decision tree is generated by means of a "divide and conquer" algorithm from the objects of the training data set. If all objects belong to the same decision class, the resulting tree consists of a single node with a correct decision. Otherwise, the objects must be split according to the category of the selected attributes. For each branch, an induction process is repeated within the remaining objects until no further branches and divisions are possible (Podgorelec et al. 2002, S. 446f).

5.3.2.4 Random Forests (RF)

The approach of random forests uses so-called bootstrap samples to build several decision trees (Singh and Xie 2008, S. 2). Each of these trees differs by a unique, random sampling of subsets of predictors (Prasad et al. 2006, p. 184) and results in an individual prediction. There are two methods for generating multiple classifications and the following aggregations of results, called "bagging" and "boosting". In bagging, each tree is created using a bootstrap sample, which is replaced in the training data. This mechanism allows a simple reduction of prognosis errors for unstable predictors. The average prediction of all generated trees thus allows a reduction in the variance, which can be achieved by minimizing the correlation between average quantities. This can also be achieved by the random selection of many predictors (Segal 2004, p. 3). In boosting, extra weights are added to successive trees for incorrect predictors in previous predictions. A weighted aggregation is then used for the prediction (Liaw and Wiener 2002, p. 18). Random forests are particularly suitable for medical diagnoses, since there are a large number of input variables with only a small amount of information for each variable. Therefore, individual decision trees can only provide predictions with little precision, whereas a combination of multiple trees can significantly improve the predictability (Breiman 2001, p. 6). Furthermore, the predicted output is mainly dependent on the user-specified parameters, with a large number of predictors randomly selected for each node. In addition, by using random forests, precise predictions can be made for the accuracy of the results if certain input variables are changed randomly. As a result, the relative weightings of the variables can also be filtered out (Prasad et al. 2006, p. 185).

5.3.2.5 Artificial Neural Networks (ANN)

Artificial neural networks consist of parallel distributed processors, which in turn consist of single processing units, the so-called neurons (Haykin 1999, p. 24). The processing of an ANN is performed analogously to that of a brain. Here, the communication happens by transmitting electrical impulses via neural networks consisting of axons, synapses and dendrites. Since ANNs are based on the principle of information processing of a biological nervous system, some analogies exist between the two (Krogh 2008, p. 195). One the one hand, external information form the basis for the information processing for ANN. On the other hand, information processing is based on a large number of single connected elements, which are referred to as neurons in both ANN and biological nervous systems. Another important analogy is that knowledge is generated by learning processes and information processing is carried out in parallel (Backhaus et al. 2015, p. 298). According to Haykin (1999, p. 24), there is another commonality in the weights between neurons, also known as synaptic weights, which are responsible for storing the learned knowledge. Neural networks can be divided into supervised and unsupervised networks based on the underlying learning rules (Backhaus et al. 2015, p. 300). In the case of unsupervised learning, the main goal is the discovery of clusters with similar characteristics within the data. Supervised learning, on the other hand, focuses on building a model with predefined classes based on already classified training data (Guerra et al. 2011, p. 74f). ANNs can be further categorized in "feedforward" and "feedback" networks. In feedforward networks, the state of any neuron in the network is determined only by the input-output patterns and is thus classified as static. Feedback networks, on the other hand, are characterized by at least one existing feedback loop; thus they are also referred to as dynamic networks.

5.3.3 Evaluation of Methods

A statistical method for evaluating the performance of a model is C-statistics or the area under the curve (AUC) below the receiver operating characteristic (ROC) curve (Uno et al. 2011, p. 1105f.). C-statistics can be calculated for each method that generates predictive values. These include, among others, logistic regression and machine-based learning classifications. C-statistics can take values between 0.5 and 1, with 0.5 indicating an insufficient classification and 1 a perfect classification (Westreich et al. 2011, p. 2). Kansagara et al. (2011, p. 1689) further specify the interpretation of these statistics. Thus, models with C-statistics of less than or equal to 0.7 have inadequate discriminative ability. Values up to 0.8 have an acceptable performance, and models with C-statistics greater than 0.8 show good discriminative performance. An analysis of current studies with regard to the C-statistics shows that a large part of the developed models show only a poor discriminative ability (cf. Table 5.3).

While the setups vary greatly between different studies as shown in paragraph 3, some studies exist that compare specific methods within the same study configuration (population/subject, etc.) A study comparing the performance of SVM, DT, RF and LR by Sushmita et al. (2016, p. 453ff.), for example, evaluates the prediction of readmissions for patients within 30 days, as well as their resulting costs. The data is based on a large hospital group in the USA, comprising 221,000 admissions that are analysed according to demographic information (e.g. age, ethnicity), clinical information (e.g. primary diagnosis), insurance information, administrative data and payment information. The LACE index (length of stay, acuity of admission, Charlson comorbidity index, number of ED visits) is used to compare the performance of individual methods. LACE is an acknowledged method to assess the statistical risk of preventable readmissions. Table 5.4 gives an overview of the results of the study.

According to Sushmita et al. (2016, p. 458ff.), three essential findings are obtained from the study. First, three out of five methods achieved a sensitivity of over 80%, while their specificity and accuracy were similar to that of the compared LACE algorithm. The sensitivity and precision results of the DT and SVM were both relatively high and also comparable to the LACE algorithm. Nevertheless, the specificity of both algorithms, which indicates the correct identification of low risks,

Table 5.3 C-statistics of identified studies

Author	Method	C-statistics
Amarasingham et al.	LR	0.72
Au et al.	RF	0.57–0.61
Billings et al.	LR	0.69
Bottle et al.	LR	0.72
Futoma et al.	LR, PLR, RF, SVM	LR = 0.648
		RF = 0.684
		PLR = 0.683
		SVM = 0.671
Halfon et al.	PR	0.72
Hasan et al.	LR	0.61
Hilbert et al.	DT	PN: 0.65
		AMI: 0.612
		HF: 0.583
Howell et al.	LR	0.65
Huang et al.	SVM	nA
Lee	LR, DT, ANN	nA
Morrissey et al.	LR	0.7
Philbin et al.	LR	0.6
Shams et al.	Hybrid approach: LR + RF	0.8
Shulan et al.	LR	0.8
Sushmita et al.	SVM, LR, DT, RF	nA
Yamokoski et al.	LR	0.6

Table 5.4 Results of the performance comparison of different methods (Sushmita et al. 2016)

Algorithm	Sensitivity (%)	Specificity (%)	Accuracy (%)
LACE	76.42	38.95	31.63
SVM	98.1	1.84	26.98
DT	94.07	9.04	27.65
RF	84.76	25.60	29.63
LR	92.47	13.24	28.26

is quite low. Second, the sensitivity and specificity varies only slightly between the methods. Third, the maximum value for all methods lies between 50% and 60% when aiming at a perfect balance of all measurements (sensitivity, specificity, accuracy).

Another study by Futoma et al. (2015, pp. 230ff.) also investigates various predictive risk models for readmissions. A record of the New Zealand Ministry of Health is used, comprising information on approximately 3.3 million hospital admissions between 2006 and 2012. Independent variables included race, sex, age, length of stay, type of institution (private/public) and if the patient was transmitted

Table 5.5 Results of performance comparison (Lee 2012)

	LR	DT	ANN
Standard error			
Training data	0.385	0.373	0.384
Validation data	0.385	0.369	0.383
Misclassification rate			
Training data	0.214	0.180	0.214
Validation data	0.217	0.177	0.211

from another hospital. In addition, previous hospital visits within the last year were considered. In this study, the predictive performance of LR, MR, PLR, RF and SVM is compared using C-statistics. RF (AUC value 0.684) and PLR (AUC value 0.683) presented the best performance. In addition, a pre-coupled neural network was tested resulting in significantly better AUC values compared to the PRA.

Lee (2012, p. 259ff.) compares the performance of predictive risk models using LR, DT and ANN, based on readmissions to a university hospital in Seoul from January to December 2009. They included demographic data (age, gender, etc.), treatment and clinical data (department, treating physician, number of comorbidities, etc.) and healthcare utilization data (type of insurance, length of stay, etc.). Table 5.5 shows the results of the standard error and rate of misclassification across all methods.

Here, DT resulted in the highest predictive performance with regard to the misclassification rate and the AUC value (Lee 2012, p. 262).

5.4 Discussion

Literature shows that a large number of diverse, predictive risk models with different objectives and approaches already exist that are, however, difficult to compare and often result in an inadequate predictive performance. One way to assess their meaningfulness is to provide C-statistics. Kansagara et al. (2011, p. 1694ff.) state that the forecast of readmissions using predictive models is considered a complex and difficult process, which is also reflected in the poor C-statistics of the predictive risk models under study. Van Walraven et al. (2011, p. 397) propose another problem in identifying whether a readmission should be classified as avoidable or unavoidable. While there is a lot of potential in these methods to reduce healthcare costs and improve the overall quality of care by supporting more evidence-based decision-making and delivery of healthcare services, the performance of these models and overall understanding of readmissions still need to be improved in future studies.

References

Albers, S. (2007). *Methodik der empirischen forschung*. Wiesbaden: Springer Fachmedien.

Altman, D. G., & Royston, P. (2000). What do we mean by validating a prognostic model? *Statistics in Medicine, 19*(4), 453–473.

Aral, K. D., Güvenir, H. A., Sabuncuoğlu, I., & Akar, A. R. (2012). A prescription fraud detection model. *Computer Methods and Programs in Biomedicine, 106*(1), 37–46.

Au, A. G., McAlister, F. A., Bakal, J. A., Ezekowitz, J., Kaul, P., & van Walraven, C. (2012). Predicting the risk of unplanned readmission or death within 30 days of discharge after a heart failure hospitalization. *American Heart Journal, 164*(3), 365–372. https://doi.org/10.1016/j.ahj.2012.06.010.

Backhaus, K., Erichson, B., & Weiber, R. (2015). *Fortgeschrittene multivariate analysemethoden*. Berlin: Springer. https://doi.org/10.1007/978-3-662-46087-0.

Backhaus, K., Erichson, B., Plinke, W., & Weiber, R. (2016). *Multivariate analysemethoden*. Berlin: Springer. https://doi.org/10.1007/978-3-662-46076-4.

Bellazzi, R., & Zupan, B. (2008). Predictive data mining in clinical medicine: Current issues and guidelines. *International Journal of Medical Informatics, 77*(2), 81–97.

Bohsem, G. (2015). *Millionen überflüssige Klinikaufenthalte,* Sueddeutsche Zeitung.

Breiman, L. (2001). *Machine Learning, 45*(1), 5–32. https://doi.org/10.1023/A:1010933404324.

Brown, A. (SAS Institut, Hrsg.). (2016). *Top five reasons for using penalized regression for modeling your high-dimensional data.* Zugriff am December 13, 2016, Verfügbar unter https://communities.sas.com/t5/SAS-Communities-Library/Tip-Top-five-reasons-for-using-penalized-regression-for-modeling/ta-p/223734

Carey, K., & Stefos, T. (2016). The cost of hospital readmissions: Evidence from the VA. *Health Care Management Science, 19*(3), 241–248. https://doi.org/10.1007/s10729-014-9316-9.

Chae, Y. M., Kim, H. S., Tark, K. C., Park, H. J., & Ho, S. H. (2003). Analysis of healthcare quality indicator using data mining and decision support system. *Expert Systems with Applications, 24*(2), 167–172.

Chan, C. L., & Lan, C. H. (2001). A data mining technique combining fuzzy sets theory and Bayesian classifier – An application of auditing the health insurance fee. In *Proceedings of the International Conference on Artificial Intelligence*.

Chechulin, Y., Nazerian, A., Rais, S., & Malikov, K. (2014). Predicting patients with high risk of becoming high-cost healthcare users in Ontario (Canada). *Healthcare Policy, 9*(3), 68–79.

Christy, T. (1997). Analytical tools help health firms fight fraud. *Insurance & Technology, 22*(3), 22–26.

Delen, D., Walker, G., & Kadam, A. (2005). Predicting breast cancer survivability: A comparison of three data mining methods. *Artificial Intelligence in Medicine, 34*(2), 113–127.

Delen, D., Fuller, C., McCann, C., & Ray, D. (2009). Analysis of healthcare coverage: A data mining approach. *Expert Systems with Applications, 36*(2), 995–1003.

Desai, M. M., Stauffer, B. D., Feringa, H. H. H., & Schreiner, G. C. (2009). Statistical models and patient predictors of readmission for acute myocardial infarction: a systematic review. *Circulation. Cardiovascular Quality and Outcomes, 2*(5), 500–507. https://doi.org/10.1161/CIRCOUTCOMES.108.832949.

Futoma, J., Morris, J., & Lucas, J. (2015). A comparison of models for predicting early hospital readmissions. *Journal of Biomedical Informatics, 56*, 229–238. https://doi.org/10.1016/j.jbi.2015.05.016.

Golmohammadi, D., & Radnia, N. (2016). Prediction modeling and pattern recognition for patient readmission. *International Journal of Production Economics, 171*, 151–161. https://doi.org/10.1016/j.ijpe.2015.09.027.

Görz, G. (2014). *Handbuch der künstlichen Intelligenz* (5th, revised. and updated edition). München: Oldenbourg.

Guerra, L., McGarry, L. M., Robles, V., Bielza, C., Larranaga, P., & Yuste, R. (2011). Comparison between supervised and unsupervised classifications of neuronal cell types: A case study. *Developmental Neurobiology, 71*(1), 71–82. https://doi.org/10.1002/dneu.20809.

Hair, J. F. (2007). Knowledge creation in marketing. The role of predictive analytics. *European Business Review, 19*(4), 303–315. https://doi.org/10.1108/09555340710760134.

Harrach, S. (2014). *Neugierige strukturvorschläge im maschinellen lernen. Eine technikphilosophische verortung* (Edition panta rei). Bielefeld: transcript.

Haykin, S. (1999). *Neural networks. A comprehensive foundation* (2nd ed.). Delhi: Pearson Education.

Hess, D. R. (2004). Retrospective studies and chart reviews. *Respiratory Care, 49*(10), 1171–1174.

Hilbert, J. P., Zasadil, S., Keyser, D. J., & Peele, P. B. (2014). Using decision trees to manage hospital readmission risk for acute myocardial infarction, heart failure, and pneumonia. *Applied Health Economics and Health Policy, 12*(6), 573–585. https://doi.org/10.1007/s40258-014-0124-7.

Howell, S., Coory, M., Martin, J., & Duckett, S. (2009). Using routine inpatient data to identify patients at risk of hospital readmission. *BMC Health Services Research, 9*, 96. https://doi.org/10.1186/1472-6963-9-96.

Huang, J. S., Chen, Y. F., & Hsu, J. C. (2014, January). Design of a clinical decision support model for predicting pneumonia readmission. In W.-Y. Chen (Ed.), *International symposium on computer, consumer and control (IS3C), 2014. 10–12 June 2014, Taichung, Taiwan; proceedings* (S. 1179–1182). Piscataway, NJ: IEEE.

Kaiser, C. (2009). Opinion mining im web 2.0—Konzept und fallbeispiel. *HMD Praxis der Wirtschaftsinformatik, 46*(4), 90–99. https://doi.org/10.1007/BF03340384.

Kansagara, D., Englander, H., Salanitro, A., Kagen, D., Theobald, C., Freeman, M., et al. (2011). Risk prediction models for hospital readmission: a systematic review. *JAMA, 306*(15), 1688–1698. https://doi.org/10.1001/jama.2011.1515.

Koh, H. C., & Tan, G. (2005). Data mining applications in healthcare. *Journal of Healthcare Information Management, 19*, 64–72.

Krogh, A. (2008). What are artificial neural networks? *Nature Biotechnology, 26*(2), 195–197. https://doi.org/10.1038/nbt1386.

Krumholz, H. M., Merrill, A. R., Schone, E. M., Schreiner, G. C., Chen, J., Bradley, E. H., et al. (2009). Patterns of hospital performance in acute myocardial infarction and heart failure 30-day mortality and readmission. *Circulation. Cardiovascular Quality and Outcomes, 2*(5), 407–413. https://doi.org/10.1161/CIRCOUTCOMES.109.883256.

Kudyba, S., & Gregorio, T. (2010). Identifying factors that impact patient length of stay metrics for healthcare providers with advanced analytics. *Health Informatics Journal, 16*(4), 235–245.

Lee, E. W. (2012). Selecting the best prediction model for readmission. *Journal of Preventive Medicine and Public Health = Yebang Uihakhoe Chi, 45*(4), 259–266. https://doi.org/10.3961/jpmph.2012.45.4.259.

Liang, C., & Gong, Y. (2015). Enhancing patient safety event reporting by K-nearest neighbor classifier. *Studies in Health Technology and Informatics, 218*, 93–99.

Liaw, A., & Wiener, M. (2002). Classification and regression by randomForest. *R News, 2*(3), 18–22. Verfügbar unter http://CRAN.R-project.org/doc/Rnews/

Loh, W.-Y. (2011). Classification and regression trees. *Wiley Interdisciplinary Reviews: Data Mining and Knowledge Discovery, 1*(1), 14–23. https://doi.org/10.1002/widm.8.

Medicare (Medicare Payment Advisory Comission, Hrsg.). (2007). *Report to the congress. Promoting greater efficiency in medicare.* Zugriff am November 28, 2016, Verfügbar unter http://medpac.gov/docs/default-source/reports/Jun07_EntireReport.pdf?sfvrsn=0

Mishra, N., & Silakari, S. (2012). Predictive analytics: A survey, trends, applications, oppurtunities & challenges. *International Journal of Computer Science and Information Technologies, 3*, 4434–4438.

Müller, R. M., & Lenz, H.-J. (2013). *Business intelligence*. Berlin: Springer. https://doi.org/10.1007/978-3-642-35560-8.

Nyce, C. (American Institute for Chartered Property Casualty Underwriters/Insurance Institute of America, Hrsg.). (2007). *Predictive analytics. White Paper.* Zugriff am November 13, 2016, Verfügbar unter http://www.hedgechatter.com/wp-content/uploads/2014/09/predictivemodelingwhitepaper.pdf

Orem, T. (IBM, Hrsg.). (2015). *4 ways predictive analytics in finance can help companies see the future.* Zugriff am December 02, 2016, Verfügbar unter http://www.ibmbigdatahub.com/blog/4-ways-predictive-analytics-finance-can-help-companies-see-future

Osheroff, J. A., Teich, J. M., Middleton, B., Steen, E. B., Wright, A., & Detmer, D. E. (2007). A roadmap for national action on clinical decision support. *Journal of the American Medical Informatics Association: JAMIA, 14*(2), 141–145.

Pearsall, B. (2010). Predictive policing: The future of law enforcement. *National Institute of Justice Journal, 266*, 16–19.

Philbin, E. F., & DiSalvo, T. G. (1999). Prediction of hospital readmission for heart failure: Development of a simple risk score based on administrative data. *Journal of the American College of Cardiology, 33*(6), 1560–1566.

Phillips-Wren, G., Sharkey, P., & Dy, S. M. (2008). Mining lung cancer patient data to assess healthcare resource utilization. *Expert Systems with Applications, 35*(4), 1611–1619.

Podgorelec, V., Kokol, P., Stiglic, B., & Rozman, I. (2002). *Journal of Medical Systems, 26*(5), 445–463. https://doi.org/10.1023/A:1016409317640.

Prasad, A. M., Iverson, L. R., & Liaw, A. (2006). Newer classification and regression tree techniques. Bagging and random forests for ecological prediction. *Ecosystems, 9*(2), 181–199. https://doi.org/10.1007/s10021-005-0054-1.

Raghupathi, W., & Raghupathi, V. (2014). Big data analytics in healthcare: promise and potential. *Health Information Science and Systems, 2*(1), 3.

Ross, J. S. (2008). Statistical models and patient predictors of readmission for heart failure: A systematic review. *Archives of Internal Medicine, 168*(13), 1371. https://doi.org/10.1001/archinte.168.13.1371.

Schneider, A., Hommel, G., & Blettner, M. (2010). Linear regression analysis: Part 14 of a series on evaluation of scientific publications. *Deutsches Arzteblatt International, 107*(44), 776–782. https://doi.org/10.3238/arztebl.2010.0776.

Segal, M. R. (2004). *Machine learning benchmarks and random forest regression*. Verfügbar unter http://escholarship.org/uc/item/35x3v9t4.pdf

Shams, I., Ajorlou, S., & Yang, K. (2015). A predictive analytics approach to reducing 30-day avoidable readmissions among patients with heart failure, acute myocardial infarction, pneumonia, or COPD. *Health Care Management Science, 18*(1), 19–34. https://doi.org/10.1007/s10729-014-9278-y.

Shmueli, G., & Koppius, O. (2011). Predictive analytics in information systems research. *SSRN Electronic Journal.* https://doi.org/10.2139/ssrn.1606674

Shulan, M., Gao, K., & Moore, C. D. (2013). Predicting 30-day all-cause hospital readmissions. *Health Care Management Science, 16*(2), 167–175. https://doi.org/10.1007/s10729-013-9220-8.

Singh, K., & Xie, M. (2008). *Bootstrap: A statistical method.* Unpublished manuscript, Rutgers University, USA. Retrieved from http://www.stat.rutgers.edu/home/mxie/RCPapers/bootstrap.pdf

Son, Y.-J., Kim, H.-G., Kim, E.-H., Choi, S., & Lee, S.-K. (2010). Application of support vector machine for prediction of medication adherence in heart failure patients. *Healthcare Informatics Research, 16*(4), 253–259.

Song, J. W., & Chung, K. C. (2010). Observational studies: Cohort and case-control studies. *Plastic and Reconstructive Surgery, 126*(6), 2234–2242. https://doi.org/10.1097/PRS.0b013e3181f44abc.

Speybroeck, N. (2012). Classification and regression trees. *International Journal of Public Health, 57*(1), 243–246. https://doi.org/10.1007/s00038-011-0315-z.

Strome, T. L. (2015). *Healthcare analytics: From data to knowledge to healthcare improvement.* Hoboken: Wiley.

Sushmita, S., Khulbe, G., Hasan, A., Newman, S., Ravindra, P., Roy, S. B., et al. (2016). *Predicting 30-day risk and cost of "all-cause" hospital readmissions*. Verfügbar unter http://www.aaai.org/ocs/index.php/WS/AAAIW16/paper/view/12669

Uno, H., Cai, T., Pencina, M. J., D'Agostino, R. B., & Wei, L. J. (2011). On the C-statistics for evaluating overall adequacy of risk prediction procedures with censored survival data. *Statistics in Medicine,* 30(10), 1105–1117.

Van Walraven, C., Bennett, C., Jennings, A., Austin, P. C., & Forster, A. J. (2011). Proportion of hospital readmissions deemed avoidable: A systematic review. *CMAJ: Canadian Medical Association Journal = journal de l'Association medicale canadienne, 183*(7), E391–E402. https://doi.org/10.1503/cmaj.101860.

von der Lippe, P. (1993). *Deskriptive statistik* (UTB für Wissenschaft Uni-Taschenbücher Wirtschaftswissenschaften, Bd. 1632). Stuttgart: Fischer.

Wang, T., Rudin, C., Wagner, D., & Sevieri, R. (2013, January). Learning to detect patterns of crime. In *Joint European conference on machine learning and knowledge discovery in databases* (S. 515–530).

Westreich, D., Cole, S. R., Funk, M. J., Brookhart, M. A., & Sturmer, T. (2011). The role of the c-statistic in variable selection for propensity score models. *Pharmacoepidemiology and Drug Safety, 20*(3), 317–320. https://doi.org/10.1002/pds.2074.

Isabella Eigner studied International Information Systems at the University of Erlangen-Nuremberg. Since 2014, she is a member of the research staff and PhD student at the Institute of Information Systems. In her research she is focusing on predictive analytics in health care.

Andreas Hamper studied Information Systems at the University of Erlangen- Nuremberg. Since 2011, he is a member of the research staff and PhD student at the Institute of Information Systems. In his research he is focusing on mobile technologies and health care.

Chapter 6
An Ontology for Capturing Pervasive Mobile Solution Benefits in Diabetes Care: Insights from a Longitudinal Multi-country Study

Arkland Ramaprasad, Steve Goldberg, and Nilmini Wickramasinghe

6.1 Background

Globally, two key and unconnected trends are evident: (1) the prevalence of diabetes is increasing exponentially (Help4Diabetes 2012), and (2) the adoption of pervasive mobile solutions is increasing rapidly (Degusta 2012). Globally, diabetes mellitus [diabetes] is one of the leading chronic diseases (Geisler and Wickramasinghe 2005). The total number of diabetes patients worldwide is estimated to rise to 366 million in 2030 from 171 million in 2000 (Wild et al. 2004). Contemporaneously, conservatively, over 6.4 billion mobile internet subscriptions are predicted by 2019, and by 2030 everyone is predicted to be using mobile banking.

In Australia alone, an estimated 275 individuals develop diabetes daily (Diabetes Australia 2016) making Australia a significant contributor to this projected global trend. Further, an estimated 700,000 Australians, representing approximately 3.6% of the population, were diagnosed with diabetes in 2004–2005. Further, between 1989–1990 and 2004–2005, the proportion of Australians diagnosed with this disease more than doubled from 1.3% to 3.3% (Diabetes Australia 2016). Additionally, between 2000–2001 and 2004–2005, Australian diabetes hospitalization rate increased by 35% from 1932 to 2608 per 100,000 people (AIHW 2008). Hence, most agree that diabetes is one of the fastest growing chronic diseases in Australia (AIHW 2008; Catanzariti et al. 2007; Chittleborough et al. 2007).

A. Ramaprasad (✉)
UIC, Chicago, IL, USA

S. Goldberg
Inet International Inc., Thornhill, ON, Canada

N. Wickramasinghe (✉)
Deakin University, Burwood, Australia

Epworth HealthCare, Richmond, VIC, Australia

N. Wickramasinghe, J. L. Schaffer (eds.), *Theories to Inform Superior Health Informatics Research and Practice*, Healthcare Delivery in the Information Age,
https://doi.org/10.1007/978-3-319-72287-0_6

In addition to the unpleasantness of this disease to its sufferers, it must also be kept in mind that diabetes and its complications incur significant costs for careers, governments, and the entire health system (Geisler and Wickramasinghe 2005; Colagiuri et al. 2002). In the United States, in 2010–2011, costs associated with diabetes were US$174 billion ($116 billion direct medical costs and at least $58 billion indirect costs) (Help4Diabetes 2012), while in 2004–2005 direct healthcare expenditure on diabetes in Australia was AU$907 million, which constituted approximately 2% of the allocable recurrent health expenditure in that year (AIHW 2008; Catanzariti et al. 2007; Chittleborough et al. 2007; Colagiuri et al. 2002; Wickramasinghe et al. 2013). Further costs include societal costs that represent productivity losses for both patients and their careers (Colagiuri et al. 2002).

In Germany and China, diabetes is also a significant healthcare issues and represents a national concern for these two countries whose combined spending (with the United States) contributed 60% of the total global health expenditure on diabetes as of 2015 (International Diabetes Federation 2015). Given that China is the most populous country, it currently is home to the largest number of adults living with diabetes. According to International Diabetes Federation (2015), both countries had 10.6% diabetes national prevalence as of 2015, while China had a higher diabetes age-adjusted comparative prevalence (10.6–10.9%) compared to 8.7% in Germany.

Further, the prevalence of gestational diabetes mellitus (GDM) increased in both Germany and China during the last 15 years. While more cases have been diagnosed with GDM in China as compared to Germany (adjusted for population differences), the two countries have similar trends in the prevalence of GDM, with slightly higher rate in Germany than in China. Specifically, the adjusted prevalence of gestational diabetes mellitus increased by 2.8 times during 1999–2008, from 2.4% to 6.8% ($P < 0.0001$ for linear trend) (Zhang et al. 2011); the highest rate was in the age group 30–34 (11.3%), and the lowest was among women aged 25 and under (1.2%). A similar trend can be seen in Germany, over a period of 11 years (2002–2013); the documented prevalence of GDM increased 2.9 times (compared to 208 times in China) from 1.5% to 4.4% (Kleinwechter et al. 2011; AQUA 2013).

In the United States, 29.1 million people or 9.3% of the population have diabetes; 21.0 million people have been diagnosed with diabetes, with estimated 8.1 million people with undiagnosed diabetes (Centers for Disease Control and Prevention 2014). Further, The prevalence of gestational diabetes mellitus (GDM) in the United States may be as high as 9.2%, with 1–14% of pregnant women in the United States could develop GDM annually (DeSisto et al. 2014). According to Centers for Disease Control and Prevention (Centers for Disease Control and Prevention 2014), the total medical costs and lost work and wages for people with diagnosed diabetes is USD 245 billion.

Recognizing the growing problem of diabetes as well as noting that simultaneously there has been an exponential rise in the penetration, use, and uptake of mobile phone solutions and applications, it seems logical to investigate the possibility of developing a pervasive mobile solution to support and facilitate better care of individuals with diabetes. As diabetes is a global health concern, this longitudinal study examines the use of the proffered pervasive solution in several countries, namely, Australia, Canada, China, German, Sri Lanka, and the USA. In Australia, Germany, and the USA, the focus of the patient cohort is on GDM (gestational diabetes), while in Canada, China, and Sri Lanka the focus is on type 2 diabetes. To understand the use of the proffered pervasive solution then, it is first necessary to understand the key aspects of chronic disease management and diabetes self-care as well as the case of GDM as the following describes. Then we present the insights to date from the longitudinal multi-country study. However, in conducting the multiple studies and examining the insights collected to date, an important void became apparent to us, the need for a universal framework to examine the benefits of pervasive mobile solutions for various populations of patients with diabetes. We address this void by developing an ontology for diabetes care which is presented in the discussion section of the paper.

6.1.1 Diabetes Care and the Importance of Self-Management

Currently, there is no cure for diabetes. Recommended treatment protocols require effective and ongoing lifestyle management, together with particular attention and monitoring by healthcare professionals and patients (Britt et al. 2009). In order to be effective, it is essential that patients are both informed and be active participants in their treatment regimen (AIHW 2008, 2007). Thereby, continuous self-management is an essential part of prudent diabetes care (ICIC 2008; Colagiuri et al. 1998; Poulton 1999; Rasmussen et al. 2001; Wellard et al. 2008).

Nevertheless, self-management is time-consuming and requires significant self-discipline (Russell et al. 2005). Current support strategies include regular assessment, goal setting, action planning, problem-solving, and follow-up (ICIC 2008). However, since effective self-management often requires ongoing patient interaction with their healthcare professionals (Knuiman et al. 1996), difficulties often arise when diabetes sufferers encounter problems ranging from making appointments to needing to travel to many locations (Wellard et al. 2008; Van Eyk and Baum 2002; Zgibor and Songer 2001). There may be temporal gaps in appointment, geographical gaps due to travel distances, and informational gaps due inadequate communication.

Solutions for supporting self-management to date (Chau and Turner 2007; Rudi and Celler 2006) have not always been effective, as they have been complex and awkward for patients to embrace easily (Reach et al. 2005). It has been noted that computer-assisted telemedicine can help diabetes sufferers improve both their self-management (Balas et al. 2004) and their relationship with healthcare professionals (Bodenheimer et al. 2002; Downer et al. 2006), and thus the use of a pervasive mobile solution would appear to have merit.

6.1.2 Gestational Diabetes

The global problem of diabetes is well documented, and public health agencies globally are trying to develop appropriate awareness, education, and treatment programs to address this silent crisis (Help4Diabetes 2012; Geisler and Wickramasinghe 2005). These discussions, however, tend to focus only on type 1 and type 2 diabetes; less attention is given to gestational diabetes mellitus (GDM) (Geisler and Wickramasinghe 2005). GDM is also an important consideration when examining the chronic disease of diabetes, and thus we endeavor to include it in many of our trials.

Gestational diabetes mellitus (GDM) is a form of diabetes which presents in pregnancy, and is usually detected by routine screening in asymptomatic women (Wickramasinghe et al. 2013). Typically, incidence is 4.6% of pregnancies, i.e., greater than 12,400 women per year, in Australia (Templeton and Pieris-Caldwell 2008). Some women, especially those in whom the diagnosis of GDM was made early in pregnancy, may have pre-existing undiagnosed diabetes. In Australia and New Zealand, universal screening for GDM is recommended by the Australasian Diabetes in Pregnancy Society (ADIPS) (Hoffman et al. 1998); however, the uptake of the recommendation is rather variable (Rumbold and Crowther 2001). Most commonly the diagnosis of gestational diabetes is made following routine screening at 24–28 weeks gestation, with smaller numbers of women diagnosed earlier or later in pregnancy. Maternal complications of GDM include polyhydramnios and premature labor, preeclampsia, and perineal trauma (Hoffman et al. 1998). Perinatal complications include macrosomia, shoulder dystocia, bone fractures, and nerve palsy (Crowther et al. 2005a). It recurs in subsequent pregnancy in 30–80% of women, the incidence varying with ethnicity, being lower in Caucasian women (Kim et al. 2007).

Treatment of women with GDM aims to control maternal, and therefore fetal, hyperglycemia and the associated tendency to fetal hyperinsulinemia. They are at the root of the fetal complications (Metzger et al. 2008). Critical to the treatment of women with GDM is careful and systematic monitoring of maternal glycemia and appropriate adjustment of lifestyle, dietary, and pharmacological therapy (Crowther et al. 2005a; Metzger et al. 2008; Crowther et al. 2005b).

6.1.3 The Development of a Pervasive Mobile Solution

In order to develop the solution, it was first necessary to understand the key elements of chronic disease management as set out by Rachlis (2006). Integral to this model is the interaction between an informed patient and a proactive care team. Both of these are possible only with solutions that can facilitate better management and monitoring (Goldberg 2002a, 2002b, 2002c, 2002d, 2002e; Wickramasinghe and Goldberg 2003, 2004).

To develop such a solution, a user-centered design (UCD) approach was adopted. UCD can be considered in general terms as a type of user interface design (Vredenburg et al. 2002). In addition, it is a process where attention is given to the needs, wants, and desires of end users of a product or solution and is characterized by a multistage problem-solving process including planning and feasibility, requirements, design, implementation, test and measure, post release, and analysis (Vredenburg et al. 2002). In the case of the design and development of a pervasive mobile solution, this included a 30-day e-business acceleration project in collaboration with many key players in hospitals, such as clinicians, medical units, administration, and IT departments. At the completion of this e-business acceleration project, a scope document to develop a proof-of-concept specific to the unique needs of a particular environment was delivered.

The web-based model (Fig. 6.1) provided the necessary components to enable the delivery framework to be positioned in the best possible manner. It can facilitate enacting the key components of the chronic disease model successfully. In addition, the web-based model is designed to be flexible and dynamic. It can be adapted to suit the complex nature of healthcare environments by iteratively, systematically, and rigorously incorporating lessons learnt from data into healthcare processes to ensure superior healthcare delivery. This method not only maximizes the value of past data and learning but also makes processes amendable as complex needs and requirements evolve.

What makes this model unique and most beneficial is its focus on enabling and supporting all areas necessary for the actualization of ICT (information communication technology) initiatives in health care. By design, the model identifies the inputs necessary to bring an innovative chronic disease management solution to market (Rumbold and Crowther 2001; Crowther et al. 2005a; Kim et al. 2007; Metzger et al. 2008; Crowther et al. 2005b; Rachlis 2006; Goldberg 2002a). These solutions are developed and implemented through a physician-led mobile e-health project. This project is the heart of the model that bridges the needs and requirements of many different players into a final (output) deliverable, a "wireless healthcare program."

Succinctly, the final technology solution works as follows. The individual takes their blood glucose readings. These are then either directly transferred to the mobile device or manually entered and then sent to the designated member of the clinical care team who on reading the information can send a message back to the patient.

6.2 Methods

Given the preceding, we set out to investigate the possibility of applying the pervasive mobile solution in several countries. Specifically, we wanted to investigate the benefits of a pervasive technology to facilitate and enable superior self-care for patients suffering with diabetes. As highlighted in Table 6.1, in some of the countries, we only focused on GDM (gestational diabetes mellitus), while in other

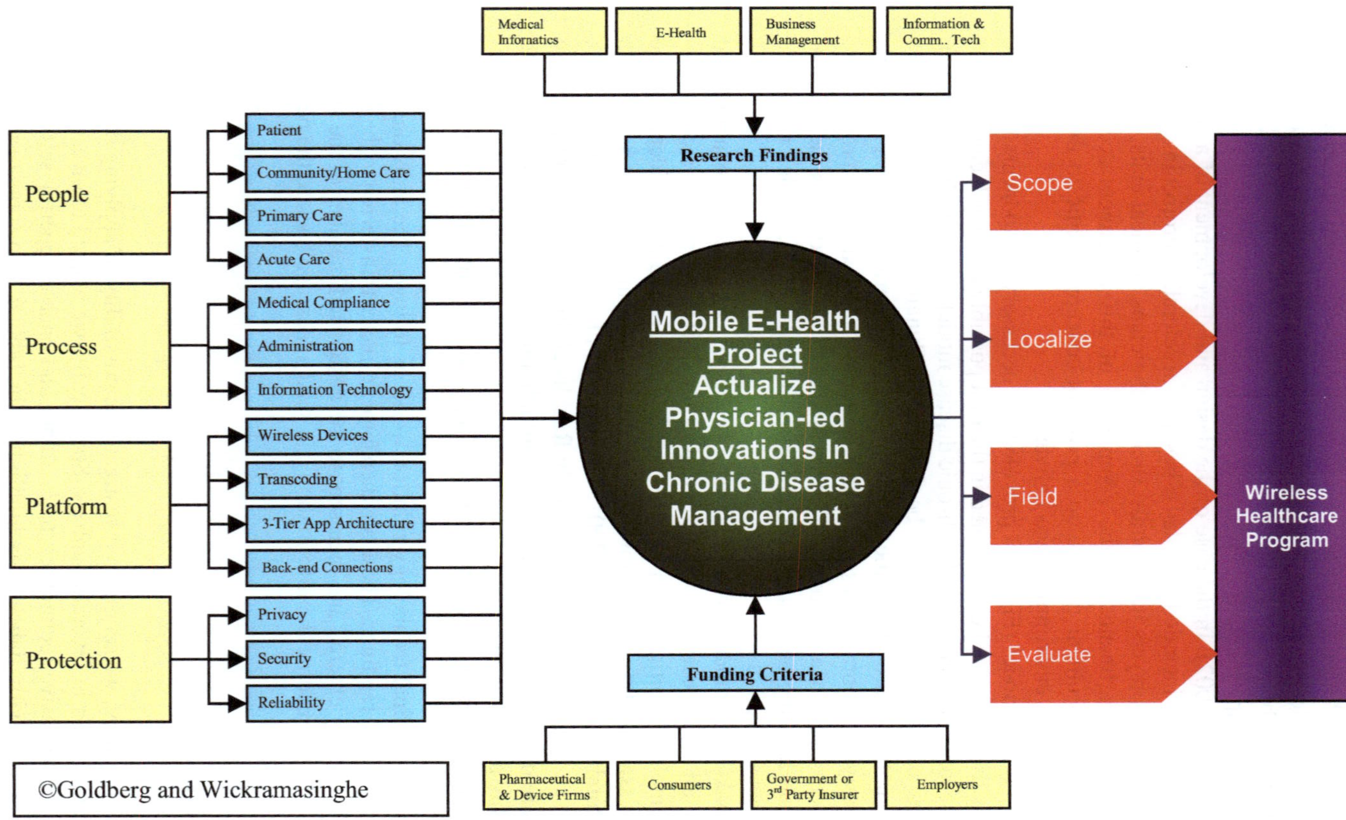

Fig. 6.1 Depiction of the underlying conceptual model and delivery framework. As can be seen the emphasis is on four key inputs of people, processes, platform and technology. The project is always clinician led. Moreover, it also captures the dynamic nature of health care by continually enabling latest research findings to be incorporated. The sustainability of the solution is ensured through the multiple sources of funding. These all support the four key aspects of the delivery framework; namely, scope, localize, field and evaluate

Table 6.1 Summary of results

Country	Stage	Comments
Australia—GDM	Completed	All patient and clinical users preferred the technology solution, and usability, fidelity, and usability were established
Canada—type 2	Completed	Pre and post levels of HbA1c were recorded to monitor glycemic control. The study showed that all patients using the technology solution recorded their blood sugar daily indicating a higher level of self-management which in turn led to better glycemic control
China—type 2	Recruiting	Currently the recruiting process is proving to be difficult since culturally Chinese do not like to take blood sugar four times a day as required, and some patients have been trying to sell the test strips
Germany—GDM	Tailoring the solution	Several bespoke requirements have been requested by the hospital, and these are being considered and integrated into the mobile solution
Sri Lanka—type 2	Recruiting	We are in the process of finalizing the recruitment stage
United States—GDM	Recruiting	We are in the process of finalizing the recruitment stage

countries we focused on type 2 diabetes. In any single trial in a particular context/country, we did not mix type 2 and GDM patients. Thus each trial was either made up of a GDM patient cohort or a type 2 diabetes cohort.

Research Design The DiaMonD (Diabetes monitoring device) study used the established techniques adapted by Wickramasinghe and Goldberg (Goldberg 2002a, 2002b, 2002c, 2002d, 2002e; Wickramasinghe and Goldberg 2003, 2004, 2007) to date, i.e., the AMR (adaptive mapping to realization) methodology. In addition, a crossover style unblended RCT (randomized control trial) was utilized which means that the control group at a predetermined time converts to using the technology solution, while the intervention group at this same point in time then reverts to the traditional solution. This strategy is deemed appropriate in studies of this nature so that it is possible for patients to compare with/without technology scenarios.[1] We note that for GDM trials crossover was set at 4 weeks while for the type 2 trials crossover was set at 3 months.

Established qualitative and quantitative techniques have been employed to analyze the collected data. Specifically, from the qualitative data, thematic analysis was performed in accordance with standard approaches described by Boyatzis (1998) and Kvale (2009), while simple regression techniques and exploratory data mining techniques will form the major focus for the quantitative part.

[1] www.implementationscience.com/content/4/1/69.

6.2.1 Data Collection Strategy

The data collection strategy included collecting data at the start, at the cross over point, and at the end of each respective patient's participation in the trial via an interview and the administration of open-ended questionnaires. In addition, clinician data would be captured at the start and conclusion of the project via interview and the administration of open-ended questionnaires.

6.3 Results

The results to date of this research in progress are summarized in Table 6.1.

As can be seen from Table 6.1, the study is at various stages of progression across the different data sites in each country with the trial completed in Australia (focusing on GDM) and Canada (focusing on type 2). In addition to the relative stages of the actual trial, the study has also established an appropriate delivery framework and web-based conceptual model that were tailored to each context, namely, Australia, Canada, China, Germany, Sri Lanka, and the United States. This was an essential first step in order to successfully apply the pervasive mobile solution. From this, it was possible to then program the solution to the required local processes and requirements. Once the solution was approved by the clinicians and ethics clearance received, it was then used in the technology arm of the trial.

6.3.1 Key Insights

From the Australian case results, we are able to note that whether patients started with standard care and then migrated to the technology arm or vice versa, all patients interviewed have preferred the technology solution over the standard care approach. The standard care approach in the Australian context essentially consisted of keeping logs of blood sugar readings and food intake and when required insulin usage. One patient noted (and all patients to date have expressed similar sentiments):

> …as a busy working person I have no time to note things down but with the mobile solution I can record things as I go so easily. I cannot believe this solution has not been used yet…. (patient 3)

Patients also commented about the benefit of the solution in a geographic sense, since they did not have to drive for regularly checkups but could through the technology solution transfer key data and be advised when they must come in for a checkup.

All members of the healthcare team (obstetricians, diabetic educator, and endocrinologists) were supportive of the technology solution. They claimed it enabled them to provide a higher quality of care in a timely fashion to their patients. When the findings were discussed with hospital administration, they were supportive of the solution to improve quality of care for patients but were also focused on if there were more labor requirements for members of the clinical team especially if scale increased to manage the backend and provide timely replies and feedback.

From the Canadian study, patients reported that the technology solution facilitated them to record their blood sugar regularly which in turn led to higher levels of self-management with the result of higher compliance. This was considered to be of value to the patients and also the clinicians.

In all the trials to date, the focus has been on monitoring and self-management; however, when we look at the literature around diabetes care, one is also aware of other important aspects such as coaching and education (Wolever et al. 2013; Mullins et al. 2012).

6.4 Discussion

Even though this longitudinal multi-country study is in progress, to date we have not had any patient prefer the standard care over the technology solution. However, a more pressing void than the access to a pervasive technology solution per se has been uncovered, while we have been conducting the respective trials and working with the clinicians and hospital administrators in order to move forward with our respective trials. Specifically, we realized that a void in the literature is the presence of a universal framework of diabetes care to facilitate maximization of the benefits of a pervasive technology solution in the context of supporting the delivery of superior care in diabetes exists. We believe this is particularly important today given the global problem of diabetes and the variety of technology solutions that are now being developed to support various aspects of diabetes care. For example, studies on diabetes management such as (3,4,13,50,51) discuss only a subset of all stakeholders, many do not discuss GDM even though this is a recognized type of diabetes, and some do not discuss the geographic angle or traveling. Thus, to address this void, we constructed the following ontology (Fig. 6.2) and discuss key aspects of it below.

6.4.1 Ontology of Diabetes Care

Figure 6.2 presents the ontology for diabetes care that was derived by combining our literature review with results to date from the current longitudinal multi-country study. To understand the ontology, it is first necessary to realize that it is difficult to effectively present the full complexity of diabetes care using linear natural (English) narrative as the narrative would not only be too voluminous but also increase the risk of simplification and the bias of selection in its description. On the other hand, a structured natural English representation using an ontology can be parsimonious

Ontology of Diabetes Care

Stakeholder		Medium		Semiotics: Phase		Semiotics: Process		Continuity		Function		Diabetes		Value	
Providers	['/'s]	Paper	[-based]	Data	[+]	Generation	[for]	Temporally	[continuous]	Detection	[of/for]	GDM	[diabetes to manage]	Quality	[of care]
Hospitals		Person		Information		Application		Geographically		Treatment		Pre-		Outcomes	
Clinics		AI/Robot		Knowledge				Informationally		Monitoring		Type 1		Compliance	
Retail		Technology						Private		Education		Type 1.5		Glycemic Control	
Physicians		Web						Confidential		Coaching		Type 2		Safety	
Endocrinologists		Smart/Mobile						Secure						Satisfaction	
GP/PCP		Phone						Integral						Cost	
OBGYN		Wearable												Monetary	
HCPs (non-physicians)		SMS												Insurance	
CDEs		E-mail												Fees/Co-payments	
Dietitians		Fax												Travel	
DNEs		Phone												Non-monetary	
Diabetes Rehab.														Time	
Pharmacists														Services	
Physician Assistants															
Nurses															
Social Workers															
Payers															
Private															
Government															
Regulators															
Pharmaceuticals															
Recipients															
Patients															
Families															
Caretakers															
Communities															
Populations															

GP/PCP - General Practitioner/Primary Care Physician
OBGYN - Obstetrics and Gynecology
HCP - Health care Professionals
CDE - Certified Diabetes Educator
DNE -Diabetes Nurse Educator
GDM - Gestational Diabetes Mellitus

Illustrative Components:

Providers-Hospitals' paper-based data generation for temporally continuous detection of GDM diabetes to manage quality-outcomes-compliance of care.

Recipients-families' technology-web-based knowledge application for informationally-private continuous monitoring of Type 1.5 diabetes to manage cost-monetary of care.

Payers-Private's person-based information generation for geographically continuous education for Type 2 diabetes to manage cost-non-monetary-time of care.

Fig. 6.2 The proposed ontology

and effective in capturing the complexity of diabetes care and making it visible and comprehensible. The ontology then serves as a combinatorial, visual, natural English representation (Churchman 1967; Ramaprasad and Syn 2014; Ramaprasad and Syn 2015; Cimino 2006). (It can be in other languages too.)

Thus in developing the presented ontology, we deconstruct diabetes care into seven dimensions, one of them with two subdimensions. These dimensions emerged from our pilot studies as well as the literature reviewed to date. Specifically, these include (a) stakeholders in the care, (b) medium of care, (c) semiotics of care, (d) continuity of care, (e) function of care, (f) diabetes type, and (g) value of care. The semiotics of care has two subdimensions—semiotic phase and semiotic process. The underlying argument is that the stakeholders use the media-based semiotics to assure the continuity of the various functions of diabetes care to manage the value of care. This argument can be expressed as:

Value = f (Stakeholder, Medium, Semiotics (Phase, Process), Continuity, Function, Diabetes)

The stakeholders in diabetes care are many—both a cause and a consequence of the complexity of diabetes care. They are enumerated as a two-level taxonomy under the Stakeholder dimension (column) in Fig. 6.3. (Notes: We will capitalize the words that refer to the dimensions and elements in the ontology, except in narrative descriptions of full or partial components. The dimensions and elements of

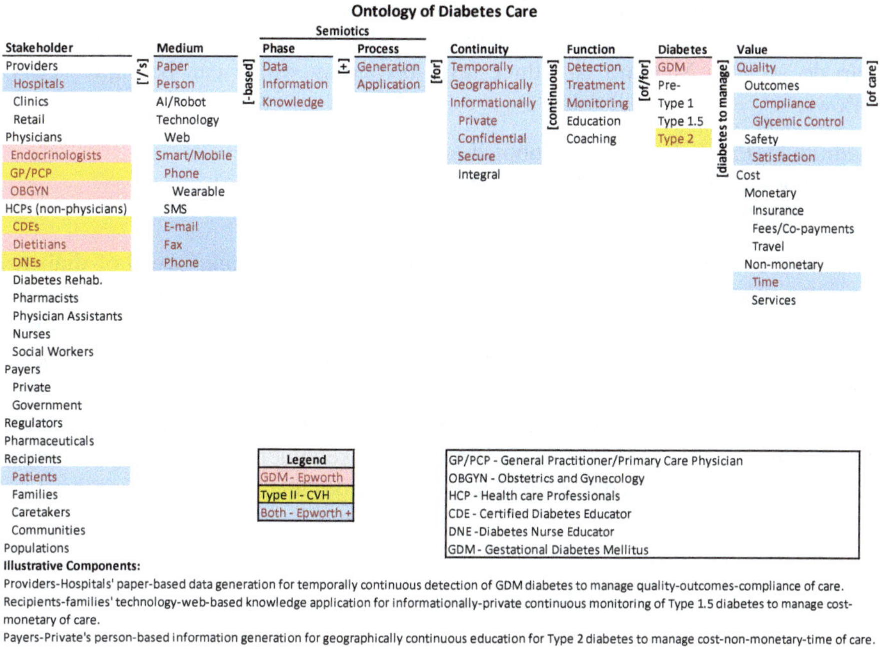

Fig. 6.3 Mapping of case study data to ontology

the ontology are defined in greater detail in the glossary in the Appendix.) The stakeholder can be expressed as:

Stakeholder ⊂ (Providers, Physicians, Healthcare Professionals, Payers, Regulators, Pharmaceuticals, Recipients)
Providers ⊂ (Hospitals, Clinics, Retail)
Physicians ⊂ (Endocrinologists, General Practitioners/Primary Care Physicians, Obstetricians/Gynecologists)
Healthcare Professionals (non-physicians) ⊂ (Certified Diabetes Educators, Dietitians, Diabetes Nurse Educators, Diabetes Rehabilitation Specialists, Pharmacists, Physician Assistants, Nurses, Social Workers)
Payers ⊂ (Private, Government)
Recipients ⊂ (Patients, Families, Caretakers, Communities, Populations)

Part of the complexity of diabetes care is, in addition to the individual interventions of the stakeholders, one has to include the many interactions among them. The Stakeholder dimension helps identify the stakeholders in a specific context; a Stakeholder x Stakeholder table can help map the interactions among them systematically.

The media employed in diabetes care are shown in the Medium dimension of the ontology. It includes both the traditional and emerging media. The emergence of new media, their capabilities, and the interaction of the new and traditional media in innovative ways can help transform diabetes care. To unleash their power to transform, it is necessary to understand the stakeholders' use of the media and its effects on semiotics (discussed next) systemically and systematically. The ontology can help do so. The Medium is a three-level taxonomy which can be expressed as follows:

Medium ⊂ (Paper, Person, AI/Robot, Technology)
Technology ⊂ (Web, Smart/Mobile, SMS, E-mail, Fax, Phone)
Smart/Mobile ⊂ (Phone, Wearable)

Semiotics is the core engine of the logical and translational work of diabetes care. The logical work is performed through the iterations of Data-Information-Knowledge in the Phase subdimension of the ontology. The translation work is performed through the iterations of Generation-Application labeled the Process subdimension. Thus, Semiotics consists of the six combinations of Data-Generation, Information-Generation, Knowledge-Generation, Data-Application, Information-Application, and Knowledge-Application. The stakeholders, individually and interactively, may use the media, individually and in combination, to perform these six semiotic functions. Thus:

Semiotics = (Phase, Process)
Phase ⊂ (Data, Information, Knowledge)
Process ⊂ (Generation, Application)

Continuity is a critical dimension of diabetes care. Diminution of continuity can diminish the value of care significantly. The emergence of new media has made it easier, efficient, and effective for the stakeholders to maintain the continuity of care through collaboration and coordination. While continuity is commonly perceived a temporal continuity, geographical and informational continuity are equally important in assuring the value of diabetes care. A recipient should be able to obtain timely care, irrespective of location, based on the same information. It is also necessary for information continuity that it be private, confidential, secure, and correct. Thus:

Continuity ⊂ (Temporally, Geographically, Informationally)
Informationally ⊂ (Private, Confidential, Secure, Integral)

There are five basic functions of diabetes care—detection, treatment, monitoring, education, and coaching. They are in roughly ordinal—each following the other—and iterative. From education one may move back to treatment and then monitoring, etc. Different stakeholders using a portfolio of media may be involved in performing these functions. The semiotics of these functions too is connected but separate. The semiotics of treatment is related to but different from that for education, for example. Yet, it is necessary to maintain the temporal, geographical, and informational continuity in performing these functions. Thus:

Function ⊂ (Detection, Treatment, Monitoring, Education, Coaching)

There are different types of diabetes each of which requires a different type of care. The five types considered are gestational diabetes mellitus, prediabetes, type 1 diabetes, type 1.5 diabetes, and type 2 diabetes. The functions, continuity, semiotics, media, and stakeholders may be different for each. Thus:

Diabetes ⊂ (GDM, Pre-, Type 1, Type 1.5, Type 2)

The values sought from diabetes care are the improvement in the quality and cost of care. The Value can be expressed as a three-level taxonomy. Quality may be in terms of its outcomes, safety, and satisfaction with it. The outcomes can be further in terms of compliance with care and glycemic control. The cost may be monetary or nonmonetary. Monetary costs may be insurance costs, fees/co-payments, and travel costs. The nonmonetary costs may be of time and for services. The value profile may vary by the type of diabetes, function of care, continuity of care, semiotics of care, media used for care, and the stakeholders. Further, the Quality elements may affect cost and vice versa. One can map the interaction among the value elements using a Value × Value table. Thus:

Value ⊂ (Quality, Cost)
Quality ⊂ (Outcomes, Safety, Satisfaction)
Outcomes ⊂ (Compliance, Glycemic Control)
Cost ⊂ (Monetary, Nonmonetary)
Monetary ⊂ (Insurance, Fees/Co-payments, Travel)
Nonmonetary ⊂ (Time, Services)

6.4.2 Interactions Among Dimensions of Diabetes Care

There are seven dimension of diabetes care in the ontology. We have discussed each dimension in the context of the others in the above. One may also systematically analyze the interaction between each of the 21 pairs of dimensions to obtain the following insights:

Stakeholder × Medium—Use of media by stakeholders in diabetes care
Stakeholder × Semiotics—Semiotics of diabetes care by different stakeholders
Stakeholder × Continuity—Role of stakeholders in different aspects of continuity of diabetes care
Stakeholder × Function—Role of stakeholders in different functions of diabetes care
Stakeholder × Diabetes—Role of stakeholders in different types of diabetes care
Stakeholder × Value—Role of stakeholders in delivering different types of value in diabetes care
Medium × Semiotics—Semiotics of media in diabetes care
Medium × Continuity—Role of media in different aspects of continuity of diabetes care
Medium × Function—Role of media in different functions of diabetes care
Medium × Diabetes—Role of media in different types of diabetes care

Medium × Value—Role of media in delivering different types of value in diabetes care
Semiotics × Continuity—Semiotics of different aspects of continuity of diabetes care
Semiotics × Function—Semiotics of different functions of diabetes care
Semiotics × Diabetes—Semiotics of different types of diabetes care
Semiotics × Value—Semiotics of delivering different types of value in diabetes care
Continuity × Function—Continuity of different functions of diabetes care
Continuity × Diabetes—Continuity of different types of diabetes care
Continuity × Value—Value of continuity in diabetes care
Function × Diabetes—Role of functions in different types of diabetes care
Function × Value—Value of functions in diabetes care
Diabetes × Value—Value of care of different types of diabetes

6.4.3 Components of Diabetes Care

The arrangement of the dimensions of the ontology left to right with adjacent punctuations/words/phrases makes it convenient to concatenate all the logical components of diabetes care in natural English. Each component consists of an element from each dimension together with the adjacent punctuation/words/phrases. Three illustrative components are shown at the bottom of Fig. 6.1 and reproduced below.

1. Providers-hospitals' paper-based data generation for temporally continuous detection of GDM diabetes to manage quality-outcomes-compliance of care.
2. Recipients-families' technology-web-based knowledge application for informationally private continuous monitoring of type 1.5 diabetes to manage cost-monetary of care.
3. Payers-private's person-based information generation for geographically continuous education for type 2 diabetes to manage cost-nonmonetary-time of care.

There are 23 × 10 × 3 × 2 × 6 × 5 × 5 × 9 = 1,863,000 potential components of diabetes care encapsulated in the ontology. It would be laborious and voluminous to enumerate all of them. The ontology provides a convenient and concise "big picture" of the diabetes care in a limited space. It helps visualize its combinatorial complexity. A component may be instantiated in many different aspects of the diabetes care. Consider the first illustrative component above. An instance of it can be a hospital's paper-based system to collect GDM compliance data. An instance of the second can be a patient's family's online search and study to minimize the monetary cost of type 1.5 diabetes care. Last, an instance of the third can be a regional education program instituted by an insurer to save time spent on type 2 diabetes care.

Some components of diabetes care may be instantiated frequently, some infrequently, and some not at all in a system. The frequently instantiated components will constitute the dominant themes, the infrequently instantiated ones the less-dominant themes, and the un-instantiated one the non-dominant themes or potential gaps in diabetes care. The frequency of instantiation of a component may not necessarily indicate its importance, centrality, criticality, or other priority. A dominant theme may simply be a product of convenience or a "herd effect"; a less-dominant theme may be a product of inexperience or oversight; and a gap may in fact have been overlooked or infeasible.

In summary, the ontology can be used to study the anatomy of diabetes care systemically and systematically. It can be used to study both the research on and the practice of diabetes care. Mapping the growing research corpus on the topic will highlight its areas of emphasis, lack of emphasis, and oversights. Mapping its practice will highlight the priority of different elements and components in practice. The insights from such mappings can be used to develop a roadmap for future research and practice.

Returning briefly to our pilot studies, the presented ontology or universal framework of diabetes care supports both the GDM trial conducted in Australia and the type 2 study conducted in Canada. The relevant paths are highlighted in Fig. 6.3, respectively. This serves to illustrate the benefits of the proposed ontology. Our future work will focus on validating the ontology. What Fig. 6.3 clearly highlights is that the studies only serve to capture part of the picture of all elements that impact diabetes care (the shaded parts respectively red and yellow). Indeed we can see that the studies do have overlap, i.e., indicated by the blue shaded cells; however, this figure also has many unshaded cells which are the parts not captured by the studies but captured by our ontology. Diabetes is a global phenomenon, and many multiplicity of factors need to be considered in order to provide the full benefits of the pervasive mobile solution. If these factors are not recognized and modeled, it is likely they will not be addressed. The proffered ontology thus serves to capture all these factors.

6.5 Conclusion

The DiaMonD study is a longitudinal multi-country study that supports a pervasive mobile technology solution, which, while not exorbitantly expensive, has the potential to facilitate the superior monitoring and management of diabetes suffers. The proposed solution enables patient empowerment by way of enhancing self-management. This is not only a noted desirable objective because it allows patients to become more like partners with their clinicians in the management of their own health care (Opie 1998; Radin 2006; Lacroix 1998) but also to date yet to be achieved in an optimal or satisfactory fashion (Colagiuri et al. 1998). Further, by enhancing the traditional clinical-patient interactions (Mirza et al. 2008; Gururajan and Murugesan 2005), the solution should provide better data management and effective and efficient clinical care focus.

Our results to date have served to provide directional data to support the benefits of using a pervasive technology solution to facilities superior care delivery. More importantly, however, our results underscored the need for an organizing framework to facilitate the maximizing of benefits to patients suffering from diabetes. We have addressed this by presenting an ontology for diabetes care which has been developed by combining our results to date with our findings from analyzing the extant literature. Three illustrative components of diabetes care were derived from the ontology. Our method of constructing an ontology is explained by Ramaprasad and Syn (2014) and Ramaprasad and Syn (2015). It was iterative among the authors of the paper (a physician, a healthcare executive, and two information systems professors—all involved in diabetes care and/or healthcare research). The challenge was to construct an ontology which is logical, parsimonious, and complete. It had to be logical in the deconstruction of the domain, parsimonious yet complete in the representation of the domain. It had to be a closed description of the diabetes care domain. We should note that the ontology presented is one of many possible ontologies of the mHealth domain.

Current debate on healthcare delivery in the United States and globally is focusing on delivering value and being patient centered. The proffered pervasive mobile solution promises to deliver on both these, and our directional data to date support this position. However, if we are to understand the complex context of diabetes, we need an organizing framework so that we can systematically evaluate value and patient-centered aspects. To address this we present the ontology of diabetes care. A complex domain like diabetes care can be studied from many points of view, each with its own ontology. It is a "wicked" (Churchman 1967) problem with many potential formulations. Our future research will serve to unpack these perspectives in detail. We contend this is essential if we are to understand the true influences, barriers, and facilitators to effecting superior diabetes care. In so doing we will also be able to address critical issues regarding value-based health care, quality outcomes, patient centeredness, and access, all critical considerations in today's healthcare delivery landscape. Indeed diabetes is a pressing issue in global health care, and it is necessary to understand the full and far-reaching aspects of this domain, so we can design and develop solutions to address this problem. The presented ontology promises to assist in this pursuit. We close by noting the benefits for using ontology to assist mapping problem domains in healthcare contexts.

Acknowledgments Funding for this study was received from a Schoeller Senior Fellowship and Epworth Research Institute seed funding grant.

References

AIHW. (2007). *National indicators for monitoring diabetes: Report of the Diabetes Indicators Review Subcommittee of the National Diabetes Data Working Group, Diabetes series 2007*. Canberra, ACT: The Australian Institute of Health and Welfare.

AIHW. (2008). *Australian facts 2008*. Canberra: Australian Institute of Health and Welfare.

AQUA. (2013). *Bundesauswertung zum Erfassungsjahr*. National evaluation report. http://www.sqg.de/sqg/upload/CONTENT/Qualitaetsberichte/2013/AQUA-Qualitaetsreport-2013.pdf.

Balas, E. A., et al. (2004). Computerized knowledge management in diabetes care. *Medical Care, 42*, 610–621.
Bodenheimer, T., et al. (2002). Patient self-management of chronic disease in primary care. *JAMA, 288*(19), 2469–2475.
Boyatzis, R. E. (1998). *Transforming qualitative information: Thematic analysis and code development*. Thousand Oaks, CA: Sage.
Britt, H., et al. (2009). *General practice activity in Australia 2008-09*. Australian Institute of Health and Welfare, and University of Sydney.
Catanzariti, L., Faulks, K., & Waters, A.-M. (2007). *National diabetes register: A statistical profile 1999-2005*. Australian Institute of Health and Welfare.
Centers for Disease Control and Prevention. (2014). *National diabetes statistics report: Estimates of diabetes and its burden in the United States, 2014*. Atlanta, GA: US Department of Health and Human Services.
Chau, S., & Turner, P. (2007). Utilisation of mobile handheld devices for care management at an Australian aged care facility. *Electronic Commerce Research and Applications, 5*(4), 305–312.
Chittleborough, C. R., et al. (2007). The increasing prevalence of diabetes in South Australia: The relationship with population ageing and obesity. *Public Health, 121*(2), 92–99.
Churchman, C. W. (1967). Wicked problems. *Management Science, 14*(4), B-141–B-142.
Cimino, J. J. (2006). In defense of the Desiderata. *Journal of Biomedical Informatics, 39*(3), 299–306.
Colagiuri, S., Colagiuri, R., & Ward, J. (1998). *National diabetes strategy and implementation plan* (pp. 1–281). Canberra, ACT: Diabetes Australia.
Colagiuri, S., et al. (2002). DiabCost Australia-assessing the burden of type 2 diabetes in Australia. In *Diabetologia*. New York: Springer.
Crowther, C. A., et al. (2005a). Effect of treatment of gestational diabetes mellitus on pregnancy outcomes. *New England Journal of Medicine, 352*(24), 2477–2486.
Crowther, C., et al. (2005b). Australian carbohydrate intolerance study in pregnant women (ACHOIS) trial group effect of treatment of gestational diabetes mellitus on pregnancy outcomes. *The New England Journal of Medicine, 352*(24), 2477–2486.
Degusta, M. (2012, October). *Smartphones spreading faster than any other technology*. Available from http://www.technologyreview.com/news/427787/are-smart-phones-spreading-faster-than-any/
DeSisto, C. L., Kim, S. Y., & Sharma, A. J. (2014). Prevalence estimates of gestational diabetes mellitus in the United States, pregnancy risk assessment monitoring system (PRAMS), 2007-2010. *Preventing Chronic Disease, 11*, E104.
Diabetes Australia. (2016). *Diabetes in Australia*. April 11, 2016. Available from https://www.diabetesaustralia.com.au/diabetes-in-australia
Downer, S. R., et al. (2006). SMS text messaging improves outpatient attendance. *Australian Health Review, 30*(3), 389–396.
Geisler, E., & Wickramasinghe, N. (2005). The role and use of wireless technology in the management and monitoring of chronic diseases. DC. http://www.businessofgovernment.org/report/role-and-use-wireless-technology-management-and-monitoring-chronic-diseases.
Goldberg, S. (2002a). HTA quality assurance component summary. Internal INET documentation.
Goldberg, S. (2002b). *Building the evidence for a standardized mobile internet (wireless) environment in Ontario, Canada*. January Update, Internal INET Documentation.
Goldberg, S. (2002c). *HTA presentation rendering component summary*. Internal INET documentation.
Goldberg, S. (2002d). *HTA presentational selection and aggregation component summary*. Internal documentation.
Goldberg, S. (2002e). *Wireless POC device component summary*. Internal INET documentation.
Gururajan, R., & Murugesan, S. (2005). Wireless solutions developed for the Australian healthcare: A review. In *International Conference on Mobile Business, 2005. ICMB 2005*. IEEE.
Help4Diabetes. (2012 [cited 2012 September 2012]). *Diabetes: Aa-worldwideepidemic*. Available from http://www.hope4diabetes.info/general-information/diabetes-a-worldwide-epidemic.html

Hoffman, L., et al. (1998). Gestational diabetes mellitus-management guidelines—The Australasian Diabetes in Pregnancy Society. *Medical Journal of Australia, 169*(2), 93–97.
ICIC. (2008). Improving chronic illness care: The chronic care model. http://www.ic-ic.org/2008/SpecialSession.htm.
International Diabetes Federation. (2015). *IDF diabetes* (7th ed.). Brussels: International Diabetes Federation.
Kim, C., Berger, D. K., & Chamany, S. (2007). Recurrence of gestational diabetes mellitus a systematic review. *Diabetes Care, 30*(5), 1314–1319.
Kleinwechter, H., et al. (2011). Gestationsdiabetes mellitus (GDM). Evidenzbasierte Leitlinie zu Diagnostik, Therapie u. Nachsorge der Deutschen Diabetes-Gesellschaft (DDG) und der Deutschen Gesellschaft für Gynäkologie und Geburtshilfe (DGGG) (www.deutsche-diabetes-gesellschaft.de).
Knuiman, M. W., Welborn, T. A., & Bartholomew, H. C. (1996). Self-reported health and use of health services: a comparison of diabetic and nondiabetic persons from a national sample. *Australian and New Zealand Journal of Public Health, 20*(3), 241–247.
Kvale, S., & Brinkmann, S. (2009). *Interviews: Learning the craft of qualitative research interviewing*. Los Angeles: Sage.
Lacroix, A. (1998). International concerted action on collaboration in telemedicine: G8 sub-project 4. *Studies in Health Technology and Informatics, 64*, 12–19.
Metzger, B. E., et al. (2008). Hyperglycemia and adverse pregnancy outcomes. *The New England Journal of Medicine, 358*(19), 1991–2002.
Mirza, F., Norris, T., & Stockdale, R. (2008). Mobile technologies and the holistic management of chronic diseases. *Health Informatics Journal, 14*(4), 309–321.
Mullins, C., Abdulhalim, A. M., & Lavallee, D. C. (2012). Continuous patient engagement in comparative effectiveness research. *JAMA, 307*(15), 1587–1588.
Opie, A. (1998). "Nobody's asked me for my view": Users' empowerment by multidisciplinary health teams. *Qualitative Health Research, 8*(2), 188–206.
Poulton, B. C. (1999). User involvement in identifying health needs and shaping and evaluating services: is it being realised? *Journal of Advanced Nursing, 30*(6), 1289–1296.
Rachlis, M. (2006). *Key to sustainable healthcare system*. Retrieved June, 2006. Vol. 21. p. 2008.
Radin, P. (2006). "To me, it's my life": Medical communication, trust, and activism in cyberspace. *Social Science & Medicine, 62*(3), 591–601.
Ramaprasad, A., & Syn, T. (2014). Design thinking and evaluation using an ontology. In M. Helfert, B. Donnellan, & J. Kenneally (Eds.), *Design science: Perspectives from Europe* (pp. 63–74). Cham: Springer International Publishing.
Ramaprasad, A., & Syn, T. (2015). Ontological meta-analysis and synthesis. *Communications of the Association for Information Systems, 37*, 138–153.
Rasmussen, B., Wellard, S., & Nankervis, A. (2001). Consumer issues in navigating health care services for type I diabetes. *Journal of Clinical Nursing, 10*(5), 628–634.
Reach, G., et al. (2005). Adjusting insulin doses: From knowledge to decision. *Patient Education and Counseling, 56*(1), 98–103.
Rudi, R., & Celler, B. G. (2006). Design and implementation of expert-telemedicine system for diabetes management at home. In International Conference on Biomedical and Pharmaceutical Engineering, 2006. ICBPE 2006. IEEE.
Rumbold, A. R., & Crowther, C. A. (2001). Guideline use for gestational diabetes mellitus and current screening, diagnostic and management practices in Australian hospitals. *Australian and New Zealand Journal of Obstetrics and Gynaecology, 41*(1), 86–90.
Russell, L. B., Suh, D.-C., & Safford, M. (2005). Time requirements for diabetes self-management: Too much for many. *The Journal of Family Practice, 54*(1), 52–56.
Templeton, M., & Pieris-Caldwell, I. (2008). *Gestational diabetes mellitus in Australia, 2005-06*. Canberra, ACT: Australian Institute of Health and Welfare.
Van Eyk, H., & Baum, F. (2002). Learning about interagency collaboration: Trialling collaborative projects between hospitals and community health services. *Health & Social Care in the Community, 10*(4), 262–269.

Vredenburg, K., et al. (2002). A survey of user-centered design practice. In *Proceedings of the SIGCHI Conference on Human factors in Computing Systems*. ACM.

Wellard, S. J., Rennie, S., & King, R. (2008). Perceptions of people with type 2 diabetes about self-management and the efficacy of community based services. *Contemporary Nurse, 29*(2), 218–226.

Wickramasinghe, N., & Goldberg, S. (2003). The wireless panacea for healthcare. In *Proceedings of 36th Hawaii International Conference on System Sciences, Hawaii.*

Wickramasinghe, N., & Goldberg, S. (2004). How M= EC^2 in healthcare. *International Journal of Mobile Communications, 2*(2), 140–156.

Wickramasinghe, N., & Goldberg, S. (2007). Adaptive mapping to realisation methodology to facilitate mobile initiatives in healthcare. *International Journal of Mobile Communications, 5*(3), 300–318.

Wickramasinghe, N., et al. (2013). A transaction cost assessment of a pervasive technology solution for gestational diabetes. In *Healthcare information technology innovation and sustainability: Frontiers and adoption: Frontiers and adoption* (p. 109). Hershey, PA: IGI Global.

Wild, S., et al. (2004). Global prevalence of diabetes estimates for the year 2000 and projections for 2030. *Diabetes Care, 27*(5), 1047–1053.

Wolever, R. Q., et al. (2013). A systematic review of the literature on health and wellness coaching: Defining a key behavioral intervention in healthcare. *Global Advances in Health and Medicine, 2*(4), 38–57.

Zgibor, J. C., & Songer, T. J. (2001). External barriers to diabetes care: Addressing personal and health systems issues. *Diabetes Spectrum, 14*(1), 23.

Zhang, F., et al. (2011). Increasing prevalence of gestational diabetes mellitus in Chinese women from 1999 to 2008. *Diabetic Medicine, 28*(6), 652–657.

Chapter 7
Clustering Questions in Healthcare Social Question Answering Based on Design Science Theory

Blooma John and Nilmini Wickramasinghe

7.1 Introduction

In healthcare social media, users connect with patients and professionals without time and space boundaries to seek and share healthcare-related information (Denecke and Stewart 2011). A classic example of a Medicine 2.0 application is a healthcare Social Question Answering (SQA) service. Healthcare SQA services are redefining healthcare delivery and supporting patient empowerment. Healthcare SQA services allow users to seek information, communicate with others on similar problems, share health guidance, and compare treatment and medication strategies (Blooma and Wickramasinghe 2014). Examples of healthcare SQA services are *MedHelp*, *BabyHub*, and *Drugs.com*. The growing activities in online healthcare communities, asking questions and sharing answers, play an important role in users' health information inquiries (Zhang and Zhao 2013). Individual behaviors, in particular health-related behaviors such as physical activity, diet, sleep, smoking, and alcohol consumption, as well as adherence to medical treatments and help-seeking behavior (Hyyppä 2010), appear to be significant in SQA services.

On the other hand, there is a need to aid in assisting and mining the content shared to make the process of retrieving quality content, relevant to users, easier. For millions of users who ask questions in a healthcare SQA service like *Drugs.com*, the answers for the past questions submitted comprise a valuable knowledge repository. As the quality and the source of the questions and answers vary widely,

B. John (✉)
University of Canberra, Bruce, ACT, Australia
e-mail: blooma.john@canberra.edu.au

N. Wickramasinghe
Deakin University, Melbourne, VIC, Australia

Epworth HealthCare, Richmond, VIC, Australia

N. Wickramasinghe, J. L. Schaffer (eds.), *Theories to Inform Superior Health Informatics Research and Practice*, Healthcare Delivery in the Information Age,
https://doi.org/10.1007/978-3-319-72287-0_7

there is a need to further study the relationship between the users and the content they post, particularly with respect to health-related questions and answers. Earlier studies (Agichtein et al. 2008; Bian et al. 2009) classified high quality content from various SQA services. However, there were very few studies that focused on SQA services in the healthcare social media. Hence, the research question addressed in this paper is:

- How can we cluster similar questions shared on SQA services in healthcare social media based on the quality of the content shared by users?

We used quadri-link cluster analysis based on various features related to questions, answers, and users to cluster similar content and a similarity measure to classify content. Based on an earlier work (Blooma et al. 2016), the similarity measure was developed based on the user profile and the relationship network between the users and the types of information disclosed. We extended the features used by earlier studies (Bian et al. 2009; Agichtein et al. 2008) and used the similarity measure to cluster similar content based on a design science approach (Hevner et al. 2004).

This paper proceeds as follows. In the literature review, we review studies related to health informatics, design science, and cluster analysis. We then present the methodology and quadri-link cluster analysis to cluster similar questions. We describe our data collection and analysis procedures. We present the results of our pilot study and explain the precision based on a preliminary content analysis. We finally conclude with the contributions of this paper and propose future work.

7.2 Literature Review

Health informatics is a relentless pursuit of helping people to improve health by using information technology (Friedman 2012). Health informatics is an integration of elements from broadly defined information science and health science. On the other hand, studies in health informatics tend to miss either the health problem or the information technology problem. For example, De Vries et al. (2013) reviewed 55 heart failure risk computational models and showed clear evidence that only a few had been implemented in clinical practice. In general, previous studies highlighted that innovations fail to achieve sustainability because the health technology disregards the relationship between the technology and the people involved.

Today, social media has empowered users to post content that is publicly available, and the dangers and threats of inaccurate diagnoses are formidable (George et al. 2013). Hence, as we propose a novel method to cluster similar content shared by users of SQA services in healthcare social media, we based our similarity measures on the quality and the relationship of the content and users. For the design of this proposed cluster analysis, we used design science guidelines as reviewed in the following section.

Design science is an important and legitimate research paradigm in information systems (Gregor and Hevner 2013). Design science research involves constructing a wide range of sociotechnical artifacts, such as new software, processes, algorithms, or systems intended to improve or solve an identified problem (Myers and Venable 2014). Hevner et al. (2004) presented seven guidelines for understanding, executing, and evaluating design science research. The seven guidelines are design as an artifact, problem relevance, design evaluation, research contributions, research rigor, design as a search process, and communication of research. Design science guidelines originated from information systems design theory originally proposed by Walls et al. (1992a; b) as "a prescriptive theory which integrates normative and descriptive theories into design paths intended to produce more effective information systems." Eventually, Peffers et al. (2007) expanded design theory into a design science research methodology by incorporating the principles, practices, and procedures required to carry out research by applying design science theory. They suggested that design science theory as a methodology needs to be consistent with prior literature, provide a nominal process model for doing design science research, and provide a mental model for presenting and evaluating design science research (Peffers et al. 2007). While we used cluster analysis, the nature of design science theory provides a foundation for more systematically specifying its design. Based on Arnott and Pervan (2012) and Xu et al. (2007), we used design science theory guidelines to propose a model to cluster similar questions in SQA services.

Cluster analysis groups together similar objects into meaningful clusters based on the similarities among the objects (Balijepally et al. 2011). Information systems research uses cluster analysis as an analytical tool for classifying configurations of various entities that comprise the information technology artifact. Because of the nature of the questions posed in SQA services, keywords alone do not provide a reliable basis for clustering user-generated questions effectively, particularly in SQA services for health care (Bian et al. 2009; Agichtein et al. 2008). To overcome the disadvantages of keyword-based clustering, extant research focuses on additional criteria. Blooma et al. (2016) used the content and user relationship to identify similar questions. Leung et al. (2008) introduced the notion of concept-based graphs. Bian et al. (2009) used a mutually coupled bipartite network to identify high quality content and users. However, there is a lack of studies that applied cluster analysis in health care to identify similar questions and reuse the existing answers for new questions.

Thus, in this paper, we propose a novel cluster analysis based on a design science approach by considering the relationship between the questions, answers, askers, and answers to cluster similar questions as detailed in the next section.

7.3 Methodology

In this section we identify a set of features related to questions, answers, and users to classify similar questions in healthcare social media. The features are based on Bian et al. (2009), Agichtein et al. (2008), Chan et al. (2010), and Angeletou et al. (2011).

Table 7.1 Features for questions

Feature	Description	References
Question	Words in the question subject and question detail	Bian et al. (2009), Agichtein et al. (2008)
Subject length	Number of words in the question subject	
Detail length	Number of words in the question detail	
Posting time	Date and time when the question was posted	
Question votes	Number of positive votes	
Number of answers	Number of answers received	
Punctuation density	Number of punctuation marks divided by the total number of characters	
Question's category	Tags/topics assigned to questions by the asker	
Number of words per sentence	Average number of words per sentence in the current question	
Capitalization errors	Number of sentences not starting with capitalized letters	
The Flesch–Kincaid (F–K) reading grade level	The FK reading score indicates the level of difficulty in reading	

The four distinct sets of entities are questions, answers, users, and concepts. In this model we combine both answerer and asker into one entity—user. This is mainly because the actual role of the user is not determined a priori in this extended model when compared to Blooma et al. (2016); instead, the computed values of features regarding the social role will resolve their final role as an asker or an answerer. The second major inclusion in this model is that we considered concepts as a new entity that contains rich information. However, we simplified the concept extraction as the extraction of unique nonstop words as meaningful words. Although we used unique nonstop words in this study, we can further extend the concepts using a medical thesaurus to be very specific in healthcare medical terms.

In particular, the features used to represent questions are given in Table 7.1 and are mainly used to focus on intrinsic content quality metrics. The features are text related as the questions and answers we analyzed are primarily textual in nature. In addition to the content itself, there is a wide array of noncontent information available, from links between items to explicit and implicit features of the content, such as posting time, questions, votes, punctuation, typos, and semantic complexity measures.

With respect to an answer, in addition to the intrinsic content quality metrics as well as noncontent information, we also used the relationship features of questions and users. Word overlap and the ratio between the lengths of the question and the answer are features that are based on the relationship between the question and its answer. Features such as positive votes and negative votes are based on the

Table 7.2 Features for answers

Feature	Description	References
Overlap	Words shared between the question and answer	Bian et al. (2009), Agichtein et al. (2008)
Number of comments	Number of comments added by other participants	
Total positive votes	Total number of positive votes for the answer	
Total negative votes	Total number of negative votes for the answer	
Answer length	Number of words in the answer	
Unique words	Number of unique words in the answer	
QA ratio	Ratio between the question length and the answer length	
Number of words per sentence	Average number of words per sentence in the current question	
Capitalization errors	Number of sentences not starting with capitalized letters	
The Flesch–Kincaid (F–K) reading grade level	The FK reading score indicates the level of difficulty in reading	

relationship between the answer and users. The list of features used for answers is listed in Table 7.2.

The user features were mainly adopted from Angeletou et al. (2011) and Chan et al. (2010). The features in-degree, out-degree, hub score, authority score, and initialization are used to reflect the structural network properties of a user within the community and the user's popularity in the community. These features, along with their relationship with the questioning and answering in which they participate, helped us enhance the quality of the cluster analysis, based on the relationship between the content and the users. It is highly important to put emphasis on the authority of the users' in a healthcare-related community to improve the quality of the outcome. The features used with respect to the users are detailed in Table 7.3.

Thus, to plot the relationship between the content and users, we separated the content and users into four distinct sets of entities and six distinct types of links as given in Fig. 7.1.

After we framed the quadri-link model, we calculated similar measures for questions, answers, and users. We introduced the similarity measure to compute the similarity score between two sets of questions, answers, or users by considering two components: link count to the same concepts and value of other features. We used the Jaccard similarity index (for a discrete set) and its extended general form for nonnegative real values as suggested by Charikar (2002). The equations for all three entities (answers, questions, and users) are similar, and they consist of four parts: the Jaccard index of the bag of words, the general Jaccard index of features, and the Jaccard indices of graph links to the two other clusters. The equations to calculate similarity between answers (sim(*ai*, *aj*), questions sim(*qi*, *qj*), and users sim(*ui*, *uj*) are given below.

Table 7.3 Features for users

Feature	Description	References
Questions asked	Number of questions asked across all Q and A groups	Chan et al. (2010), Angeletou et al. (2011)
Total answers	Number of posted answers across all Q and A groups	
Votes	Total votes the user received	
In-degree	Number of other users answered by this user	
Out-degree	Number of other users that answered this user	
Hub score	Hub score for the user computed by the HITS algorithm	
Authority score	Authority score for the user computed by the HITS algorithm	
Average votes per answer	Average votes per answer divided by the total number of answers	
Initialization	Number of questions asked by this user divided by all questions asked	
% in-degree	The in-degree of this user divided by unique in-degrees	

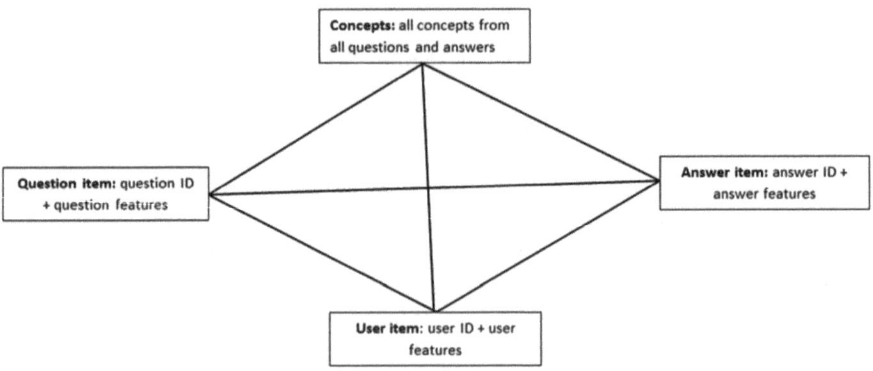

Fig. 7.1 Quadri-link model

$$\begin{aligned}\mathrm{Sim}\left(a_i,a_j\right) &= \frac{\text{Common concepts}}{\text{Total distinct concepts of both } a_i \text{ and } a_j} \\ &+ \text{If their questions are the same or in the same cluster 0 else 1} \\ &\text{If their users are the same or in same cluster 0 else 1} \\ &+ \text{Jaccard similarity of features in the framework}\end{aligned} \tag{7.1}$$

$$\begin{aligned}\mathrm{Sim}\left(q_i,q_j\right) &= \frac{\text{Common concepts}}{\text{Total distinct concepts of both } q_i \text{ and } q_j} \\ &+ \text{If their answers are the same or in the same cluster 0 else 1} \\ &\text{If their users are the same or in same cluster 0 else 1} \\ &+ \text{Jaccard similarity of features in the framework}\end{aligned} \tag{7.2}$$

$$\begin{aligned}\mathrm{Sim}\left(u_i,u_j\right) &= \frac{\text{Common concepts}}{\text{Total distinct concepts of both } u_i \text{ and } u_j} \\ &+ \text{If their questions are the same or in the same cluster 0 else 1} \\ &+ \text{If their answers are the same or in same cluster 0 else 1} \\ &+ \text{Jaccard similarity of features in the framework}\end{aligned} \tag{7.3}$$

We used the above similarity measures to cluster similar answers, questions, and users iteratively. We used complete linkage similarity to find the most similar clusters (Defays 1977). We clustered all three entities (question, answer, and user) as we proceeded with the iteration. However, we needed to choose the order of clustering. The user needs information from the question and answer clusters rather than the individual questions or answers. Their user score will be computed last in the iteration. Similarly, questions need information from answers (two questions do not share the same individual answer); thus their score will be computed second. Consequently, the score of answers will be computed first since they only need the information of the individual entities from the other three sets. Therefore, the suggested order of clustering is answer, question, and user, and the proposed clustering algorithm is called quadri-link cluster analysis.

We also propose two ways to terminate the algorithm:

1. Run the algorithm until completion (everything is in one cluster), plot a dendrogram, and then select the number of clusters based on the plot.
2. Terminate upon reaching a certain condition (there is no similarity score above a certain threshold).

As we proceed, we first compute the feature value as shown in Tables 7.1, 7.2, and 7.3. Once we compute all the features, we feed the computed similarity scores to perform quadri- link cluster analysis. The steps used to calculate the quadri-link cluster analysis are listed below.

The steps of quadri-link cluster analysis:

1. Obtain the maximum similarity score of all answer clusters according to the similarity function above.
2. Merge the answer clusters with the highest similarity score.
3. Obtain the maximum similarity score of all question clusters according to the similarity function above.
4. Merge the question clusters with the highest similarity score.

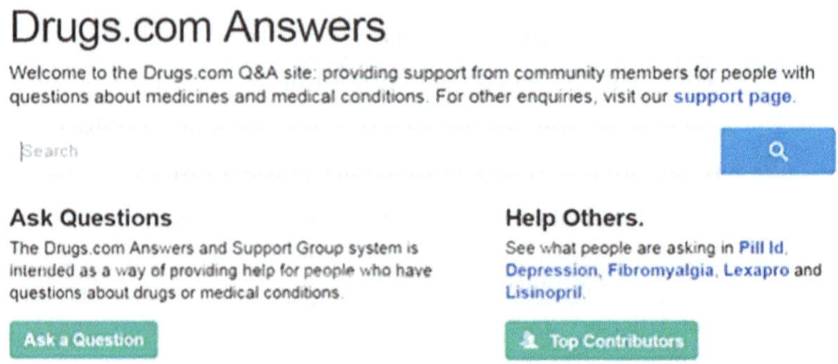

Fig. 7.2 Drugs.com question and answer site

5. Obtain the maximum similarity score of all user clusters according to the similarity function above.
6. Merge the user clusters with the highest similarity score.
7. Repeat step 1–7, unless the similarity score falls below the threshold.

While merging, if several clusters shared the same maximum score, they were merged in the same iteration. For example, if clusters A–B had 3.5, B–C had 3.5, and D–E had 3.5, then after merging we will have two new clusters A–B–C and D–E. For the general Jaccard index of features, we used a complete linkage criterion; thus during merging we used the minimum similarity score as the representative score of the new merged cluster. The similarity score between the new merged cluster A–B and cluster C was the minimum of {A–C, B–C}. For the graph link, the merge was an OR function of all sets of links. For example, when merging user clusters A–B, user A had links to question clusters C and D and answer cluster E, and user B had links to question cluster C and answer cluster F. The new user cluster A–B will have links to question clusters C and D and answer clusters E and F.

We conducted a pilot study by collecting publicly available data from the Drugs.com question and answer site[1] and tested the quadri-link cluster analysis to identify similar questions. A sample screenshot from Drugs.com is shown in Fig. 7.2. We collected 200 resolved questions related to obesity so that we could focus on the obesity domain in health care for testing and analysis. Along with the questions, we collected the answers for the resolved questions and the user details involved. We also collected the number of votes obtained for the answers.

Thus, to summarize, the main features that we collected for questions are question ID, user ID, title, description, topic, date, and total number of answers. For maintaining anonymity and privacy, identifications for questions, answers, and users were created as we collected the respective data. Similarly, the main features that we collected for answers are listed as answer ID, user ID, question ID, date, votes, text, and total comments. The main features that we collected for users are user ID, total questions asked by the user, total answers answered by the user, and

[1] https://www.drugs.com/answers/.

points earned by the user. Based on the collected data, the features listed in Tables 7.1, 7.2, and 7.3, respectively, for questions, answers, and users were calculated before we tested the proposed quadri-link cluster analysis. The results and findings from a pilot testing of the proposed quadri-link cluster analysis are discussed in the following section.

7.4 Results

We analyzed the content of the clustered questions by looking back at the answers and the users involved in the question to judge the similarity of the questions rather than the wording of the question itself. We found that the majority of the questions users asked contained a detailed description of a personal problem that required an answer. We also found that 79% of the questions had detailed descriptions with an average word count of 56.

The question with the longest description had 788 words, and it is a detailed explanation about diet, exercise, and metformin with a little personal history and story such as this "….So let me tell you my story and maybe you can share any ideas that you might have regarding what it is I suffer from,…." The question also had detailed answers, with the longest answer having 505 words. The answers, in turn, had comments that held the conversation lively. Yet another interesting fact was that the question was asked in 2012 and it continued getting replies, with the last answer posted in 2015. The first answer to the question was answered on the same day it was asked. Examples of the sample question and answer are given in Figs. 7.3 and 7.4. User details are the points they earned in participation and their questions and answers as illustrated in Fig. 7.5.

We then evaluated the results of the proposed quadri-link cluster analysis using three different combinations of datasets. We compared the results by using quadripartite cluster analysis (Blooma et al. 2016).

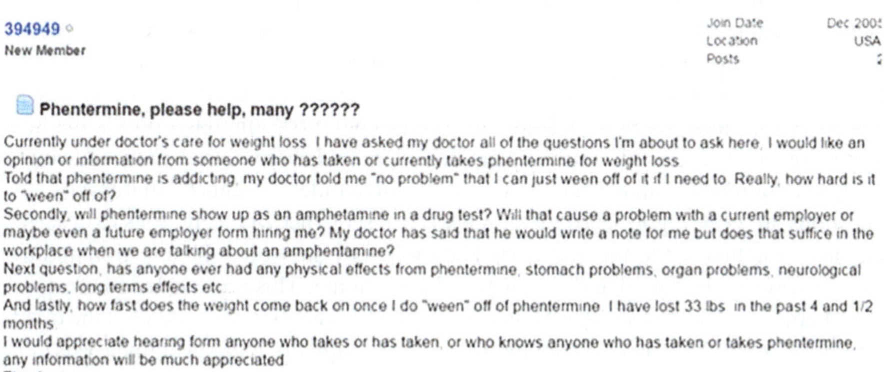
394949
New Member

Join Date Dec 200:
Location USA
Posts :

Phentermine, please help, many ??????

Currently under doctor's care for weight loss I have asked my doctor all of the questions I'm about to ask here, I would like an opinion or information from someone who has taken or currently takes phentermine for weight loss
Told that phentermine is addicting, my doctor told me "no problem" that I can just ween off of it if I need to. Really, how hard is it to "ween" off of?
Secondly, will phentermine show up as an amphetamine in a drug test? Will that cause a problem with a current employer or maybe even a future employer form hiring me? My doctor has said that he would write a note for me but does that suffice in the workplace when we are talking about an amphentamine?
Next question, has anyone ever had any physical effects from phentermine, stomach problems, organ problems, neurological problems, long terms effects etc…
And lastly, how fast does the weight come back on once I do "ween" off of phentermine. I have lost 33 lbs in the past 4 and 1/2 months
I would appreciate hearing form anyone who takes or has taken, or who knows anyone who has taken or takes phentermine, any information will be much appreciated
Thank you,

Fig. 7.3 A sample question

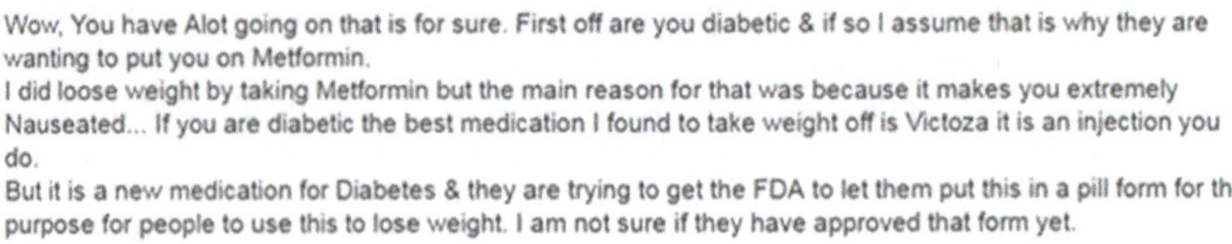
Wow, You have Alot going on that is for sure. First off are you diabetic & if so I assume that is why they are wanting to put you on Metformin.
I did loose weight by taking Metformin but the main reason for that was because it makes you extremely Nauseated... If you are diabetic the best medication I found to take weight off is Victoza it is an injection you do.
But it is a new medication for Diabetes & they are trying to get the FDA to let them put this in a pill form for the purpose for people to use this to lose weight. I am not sure if they have approved that form yet.

Fig. 7.4 A sample answer

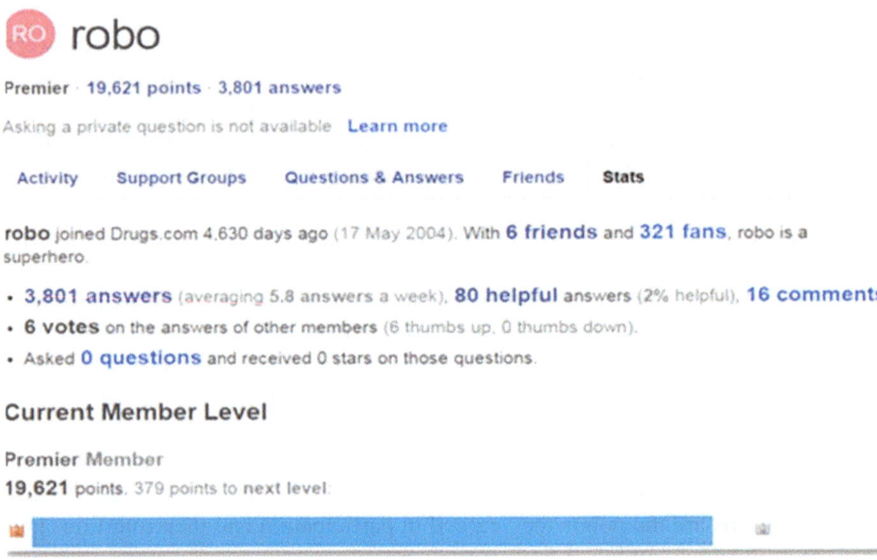

Fig. 7.5 A sample user profile

In quadripartite cluster analysis, the most similar questions that evolved were "Do Chlordiazepoxide/clidinium pills cause weight gain?" and "Can periactin increase your appetite?". In this case, the user and the response were the same and that lead to the clustering, which is a result of the algorithm used. However, as suggested by the study, there is an immense need to put more emphasis on the medical terms. Yet another set of similar questions identified were "Drug induced weight gain; any solutions?" and "Can you take this with antidepressants?". In this case, the questions are very vague. The question leads to a sequence of discussions to describe the medicine that led to the question. The same user answered the question and the answer was to ask more details regarding the medicine. This process led to the questions being clustered as similar. Hence, based on the analysis, we extended the quadripartite cluster analysis to gauge the features as in quadri-link cluster analysis.

In the quadri-link cluster analysis, the first pair of questions that were clustered are "Does trazodone cause constipation or weight gain?" and "Does buspar cause weight gain or constipation?". In this case, they were found to be similar. On analysis, it was interesting to note that both of the questions were asked by the same user on the same day. The questions had a different cohort of users answering the question; however, the answers were not the same but did agree that the drugs caused weight gain or constipation. This is clear evidence of the precision of quadri-link cluster analysis. Another example of similar questions is "Kindly inform me about the recommended medicine that causes weight to lose?" and "Just to get rid of obesity, which drug is beneficial?". On analysis, it is not only the questions that were similar but also the same user asked both questions. The answers for the questions were differently worded but had the same meaning. Hence, this is yet more clear evidence of the precision of quadri-link cluster analysis. Another example of similar questions asked and answered by different users that were clustered is "Feedback on prozac? Can anybody give me feedback on Prozac, especially, energy level, weight loss ..." and "Prozac—like it? Can someone give me some information about Prozac?"

On the other hand, quadri-link cluster analysis did not distinguish between different medical terms when the questions were phrased the same except for the medical terms. For example, "Does cyclobenzaprine cause weight gain?" and "Does polyethylene glycol 3350 cause weight gain?" were clustered, and "Does cymbalta (60 mg) cause weight gain?" and "Does this effexor cause weight gain?" were found similar. "Does Lupron injections cause weight gain in women?" and "Does Trileptal or the Generic cause weight gain?" are yet another combination of questions that were found similar. Although quadri-link cluster analysis was found to be more precise than quadripartite cluster analysis, there is a need to emphasize the use of a medical thesaurus to identify similar medical terms to avoid clustering questions that have all of their features similar except for the medical terms (Zhang and Zhao 2013; Blooma and Wickramasinghe 2016).

7.5 Discussion

The application of design science theory as a cluster analysis technique is a novel step toward identifying similar questions. We present the findings of this study based on the five activities as detailed by Peffers et al. (2007).

Activity 1—Problem identification and motivation: The specific research problem is identifying similar questions in healthcare SQA services. Health information needs and the omnipresence of social media have made users seek and answer queries in various arenas like SQA services. Hence, the motivation for this study was significant as the quality and the source of the questions and answers varied widely. Moreover, little is known about how to identify similar questions to reuse the content collected in healthcare SQA services.

Activity 2—Define the objective of a solution: We focused on developing quadri-link cluster analysis based on the relationship between content and the users involved to solve the complexity of searching through user-generated content in healthcare social media. Most importantly, we produced a viable artifact in the form of quadri-link cluster analysis. Thus, applying design science theory, we aided in assisting and mining the content shared to make the process of retrieving quality content relevant to users easier.

Activity 3—Design and Development: The designed artifact in this study is an instantiation of quadri-link cluster analysis. As we designed the artifact, we defined the list of features used with respect to questions, answers, and users. We then framed the quadri-link model comprised of questions, answers, users, and concepts to calculate the similarity measure. We finally developed the similarity measure and the algorithm to cluster similar questions.

Activity 4—Evaluation: We evaluated the artifact based on a pilot study as detailed in the results section. The evaluation resulted in clear evidence of improved precision of quadri-link cluster analysis. Although the findings from this study are a pilot attempt, there is a need to extend the analysis to various variations of similarity measures and datasets collected from other SQA services, like MedHelp, to evaluate the precision of quadri-link cluster analysis. This study can be extended to apply and evaluate other types of content in social media to cluster similar content, like tweets in Twitter and postings and comments in Facebook.

Activity 5—Communication: We published the algorithm and its applicability on healthcare social media. We also emphasize the fact that the nature and use of design science theory and quadri-link cluster analysis will be compared and contrasted in future studies.

7.6 Conclusion

Healthcare SQA services enable patient empowerment and the better transfer of pertinent information and germane knowledge with the potential end result being superior healthcare delivery. Furthermore, regarding the nature of chronic diseases where prevention is a key factor, a healthcare SQA service plays a major role in supporting healthier lifestyle practices. The pervasive nature of healthcare SQA services means that this is a benefit that most, if not all, people can enjoy. In many ways a healthcare SQA service has the potential to revolutionize current healthcare delivery practices and/or roles. In addition, it has a key role to play regarding public health and enabling education and change of lifestyle for all. Hence, this research sheds light on how various factors that influence specific types of health outcomes contribute to both theory and practice.

In particular, the proposed quadri-link cluster analysis contributes to the healthcare informatics domain by introducing content-, user-, and concept-based clustering applicable to sort the issues faced in content-based similarity. Based on a design science approach, the quadri-link model, similarity measures, and the cluster analysis algorithm showed that similarity was improved with respect to not only the words in the questions but also the context, which in turn improved the precision. Although the results in this paper were tested using 200 questions and the top results analyzed, there is a need to test quadri-link cluster analysis for various combinations of data as part of future work. As highlighted in the earlier section, there is also a need to integrate a medical thesaurus so that we can further extend the concepts to be very specific for medical terms.

References

Agichtein, E., Castillo, C., Donato, D., Gionis, A., & Mishne, G. (2008). Finding high- quality content in social media. In *Proceedings of the 2008 International Conference on Web Search and Data Mining* (pp. 183–194).

Angeletou, S., Rowe, M., & Alani, H. (2011). Modelling and analysis of user behaviour in online communities. In *The Semantic Web-ISWC 2011* (pp. 35–50). Berlin: Springer.

Arnott, D., & Pervan, G. (2012). Design science in decision support systems research: An assessment using the Hevner, March, Park, and Ram Guidelines. *Journal of the Association for Information Systems, 13*(11), 923.

Balijepally, V., Mangalaraj, G., & Iyengar, K. (2011). Are we wielding this hammer correctly? A reflective review of the application of cluster analysis in information systems research. *Journal of the Association for Information Systems, 12*(5), 375.

Bian, J., Liu, Y., Zhou, D., Agichtein, E., & Zha, H. (2009). Learning to recognize reliable users and content in social media with coupled mutual reinforcement. In *Proceedings of the 18th International Conference on World Wide Web* (pp. 51–60).

Blooma, M. J., & Wickramasinghe, N. (2014, December). Research issues in healthcare social question answering services. In *Australian Conference on Information Systems 2014*, Auckland, New Zealand.

Blooma, M. J., & Wickramasinghe, N. (2016). Prevalence of social question answering in healthcare social media. In *Contemporary consumer health informatics*. Cham: Springer.

Blooma, M. J., Chua, A. Y. K., Goh, D. H., & Wickramasinghe, N. (2016, October). Graph-based cluster analysis to identify similar questions: A design science approach. *Journal of the Association for Information Systems, 17*, 590.

Chan, J., Hayes, C., & Daly, E. M. (2010). Decomposing discussion forums and boards using user roles. *ICWSM, 10*, 215–218.

Charikar, M. S. (2002). Similarity estimation techniques from rounding algorithms. In *STOC 02, Montreal, Quebec, Canada.*

De Vries, J. J. G., Geleijnse, G., Tesanovic, A., & Van de Ven, A. R. T. (2013, September). Heart failure risk models and their readiness for clinical practice. In *2013 IEEE international conference on healthcare informatics (ICHI)* (pp. 239–247). IEEE.

Defays, D. (1977). An efficient algorithm for a complete link method. *The Computer Journal, 20*(4), 364–366.

Denecke, K., & Stewart, A. (2011). Learning from medical social media data: Current state and future challenges. In *Social media tools and platforms in learning environments* (pp. 353–372). Berlin: Springer.

George, D. R., Rovniak, L. S., & Kraschnewski, J. L. (2013). Dangers and opportunities for social media in medicine. *Clinical Obstetrics and Gynecology, 56*(3), 453. https://doi.org/10.1097/GRF.0b013e318297dc38.

Gregor, S., & Hevner, A. R. (2013). Positioning and presenting design science research for maximum impact. *MIS Quarterly, 37*(2), 337–355.

Friedman, C. P. (2012). What informatics is and isn't. *Journal of the American Medical Informatics Association, 20*(2), 224–226.

Hevner, A. R., March, S. T., Park, J., & Ram, S. (2004). Design science in information systems research. *MIS Quarterly, 28*(1), 3.

Hyyppä, M. T. (2010). *Healthy ties: Social capital, population health and survival*. New York: Springer.

Leung, K. W. T., Ng, W., & Lee, D. L. (2008). Personalized concept-based clustering of search engine queries. *IEEE Transactions on Knowledge and Data Engineering, 20*(11), 1505–1518.

Myers, M. D., & Venable, J. R. (2014). A set of ethical principles for design science research in information systems. *Information & Management, 51*(6), 801–809.

Peffers, K., Tuunanen, T., Rothenberger, M. A., & Chatterjee, S. (2007). A design science research methodology for information systems research. *Journal of Management Information Systems, 24*(3), 45–77.

Walls, J. G., Widmeyer, G. R., & El Sawy, O. A. (1992a). Building an information system design theory for vigilant EIS. *Information Systems Research, 3*(1), 36–59.

Walls, J., Widmeyer, G., & El Sawy, O. (1992b). Building an information system design theory for vigilant EIS. *Information Systems Research, 3*(1), 36–59. Retrieved from http://www.jstor.org/stable/23010780

Xu, J., Wang, G. A., Li, J., & Chau, M. (2007). Complex problem solving: identity matching based on social contextual information. *Journal of the Association for Information Systems, 8*(10), 524.

Zhang, J., & Zhao, Y. (2013). A user term visualization analysis based on a social question and answer log. *Information Processing and Management, 49*(5), 1019–1048.

Chapter 8
Using SWOT to Perform a Comparative Analysis of the German and Australian e-Health Systems

Isabella Eigner, Andreas Hamper, Nilmini Wickramasinghe, and Freimut Bodendorf

8.1 Introduction

The use of technology to increase efficiency and transparency in organizations has been widely accepted worldwide and transformed operations in many sectors, e.g. commerce, finance or education. In health care, the need for technological support is becoming even more prominent. Developed countries are suffering from increasing cost pressure and rising consumer expectations. The lack of trained professionals leads to an expanding need for more efficient communication and collaboration between healthcare professionals. Even though many countries already adopted information and communication technologies to support individual healthcare processes, a comprehensive solution and infrastructure for integrated healthcare processes has yet to be developed. The requirements for the success and a positive effect of e-health strategies are threefold. Firstly, the acceptance and access of both providers and consumers, i.e. healthcare professionals and patients, highly influences the actual increase in efficiency and speed of adoption. Secondly, governmental support and legal requirements have to be established to determine how and which processes in the healthcare ecosystem can be improved or have to be adapted. The required technology and nationwide standards are lastly essential to facilitate the introduction of networked applications. The forecast for the development of the global digital health market shown in Fig. 8.1 projects a continuous rise for e-health applications worldwide, e.g. telehealth and electronic health records (Little 2016).

I. Eigner (✉) · A. Hamper · F. Bodendorf
Institute of Information Systems, University Erlangen-Nuremberg, Nuremberg, Germany
e-mail: isabella.eigner@fau.de

N. Wickramasinghe
Deakin University, Kew East, VIC, Australia

N. Wickramasinghe, J. L. Schaffer (eds.), *Theories to Inform Superior Health Informatics Research and Practice*, Healthcare Delivery in the Information Age,
https://doi.org/10.1007/978-3-319-72287-0_8

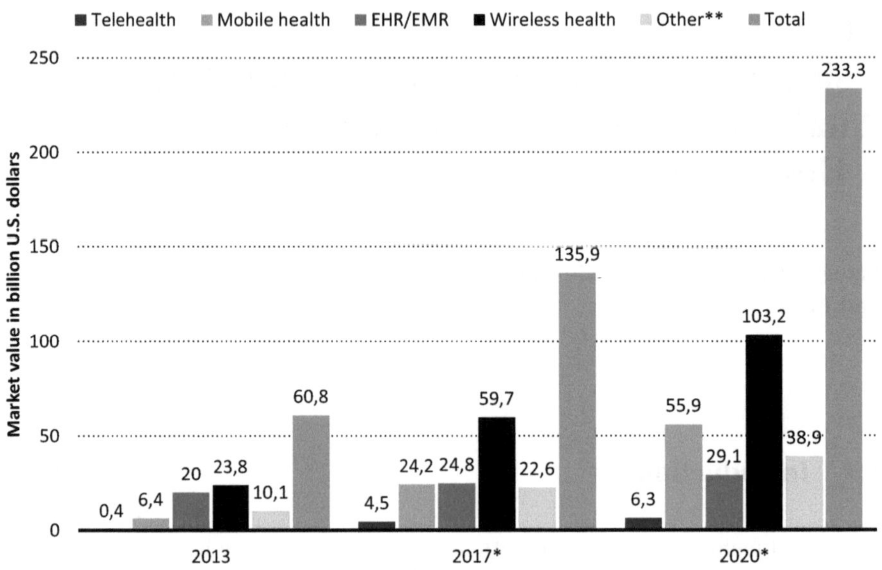

Fig. 8.1 Global digital health market from 2013 to 2020, by segment (in billion US dollars) (Little 2016)

To support this steady growth and enable scalability throughout various e-health application areas, national strategies for setting an e-health vision and its implementation have been introduced by a majority of nations. Although healthcare systems in developed countries are confronted with similar issues, e.g. an aging population and increasing cost pressure, approaches of national e-health solutions vary in their execution.

This chapter aims at identifying strategies for the successful adoption of national e-health projects, by comparing the Australian and German e-health systems. While both countries' healthcare systems bear similar traits in the "offline" setting considering insurance and financial administration, the execution and goals of their nationally initiated e-health solutions show vast differences.

8.2 Background

8.2.1 Healthcare Systems in Germany and Australia

Both Australia and Germany follow a universal two-tiered system, offering private and statutory health insurance. While public and private insurance can be taken complementary in Australia, Germany only allows one type of primary insurance and limits the transfer to the private system with a minimum required level of income. With health expenditures of 11.3% of the country's GDP, Germany spends slightly more on health care compared to Australia's 9.4% (OECD 2015). Both countries are also among the top rates in life expectancy and quality of care. Besides demographic similarities, hospital administration and billing follow similar approaches due to corresponding patient classification systems based on diagnosis-related groups.

"Diagnosis-related groups" (DRG) are admitted patient classification systems which provide a clinically meaningful way of relating a hospital's casemix to its required resources. Patients with similar clinical conditions requiring similar hospital resources are categorized in groups and priced accordingly (Fetter et al. 1980). Initially originating in the USA in 1980, the development of the Australian National DRG (AN-DRG) system began in 1988 and was released in July 1992. It is based on the US-developed "All Patient Diagnosis-Related Groups" (AP-DRG). The system has been renamed to Australian Refined DRG (AR-DRG) after introducing the ICD-10-AM diagnosis and procedure codes (Lüngen and Lauterbach 2002). The current AR-DRG version 6.0 is mainly based on the seventh edition of ICD-10-AM, classifying patients based on major diagnostic categories (MDC), procedures, medical conditions and other factors that differentiate processes of care (AIHW 2016).

In 2003, Germany adapted the Australian DRG (diagnosis-related groups) system to bill patients according to diagnosis-related case rates. The goal behind this adaption was to reduce variation in pricing and provide more efficiency and transparency of hospital services. As the AR-DRG system was not commercially bound, but managed by the Australian government, the choice of adopting it to the German healthcare system was mainly supported by the lack of licencing costs and international acceptance (Lüngen and Lauterbach 2002). Since then, hospital costs for health services have been reduced by 0.6% a year in Germany until 2012 with clear indication for this to be a result of the DRG implementation (Haeussler et al. 2014). However, even with this increase in efficiency, hospitals have suffered a funding gap of over 11 billion euro since 2004 due to continuously reduced compensation by health insurances (Neumann 2014). Since the implementation in 2003, the DRG system has undergone major revisions and changes from the first adaption of the Australian DRG system. The basis for the German DRG system relies on the ICD-10-GM, the international classification of diseases and health problems, and the OPS, the classification for operations and procedures (InEK GmbH 2016).

8.2.2 *e-Health*

The rapid development of information and communications technologies in the past years has led to an increased usage of the Internet and electronical devices to search, access and monitor health information, communicate with peers or health professionals and manage personal health records. This phenomenon termed e-health has been broadly defined as the transfer of health resources and support of healthcare processes by electronic means. It comprises three main areas, i.e. the "delivery of *health information*, for health professionals and health consumers, through the

Internet and telecommunications", "using the power of IT and e-commerce to improve *public health services*" as well as "the use of e-commerce and e-business practices in *health systems management*" (WHO 2016). According to the 5 "Cs" model by Eng (2001), the functions and capabilities of e-health encompass *content*, *community*, *commerce*, *connectivity* and *care*. Alongside these fields of e-health, Eysenbach (2001) proposes ten characterizations for e-health and its goals. The overall purpose of e-health is the improvement of efficiency and enhancing quality of care by using evidence-based methods and approaches. To improve community and connectivity, Eysenbach (2001) emphasizes the empowerment of consumers and patients and the encouragement of better relationships between patient and health professionals. By educating physicians through online services and by enabling information exchange and communication in a standardized way, the scope of health care can be extended beyond its conventional boundaries. Ethical concerns arising through new methods of patient-physician interaction have to be considered as well as the assertion to make access and usage of e-health equitable to all populations.

Dietzel (2001) identifies three core problems in today's healthcare delivery that can be supported by e-health:

- *Patient information:* The medical biography of patients is not complete, and its documentation is still unfit for efficient communication between stakeholders.
- *Integrated treatment chain:* Treatment often occurs as an addition of individual diagnosis and treatment episodes that result in unnecessary duplicate actions.
- *Isolated solutions:* e-health applications and IT solutions are isolated and follow individual goals. A holistic scope and introduction of standards is required to support e-health on a broader scale.

Key to a successful use of e-health technologies is the controlled access of information for relevant stakeholders. Although the concept of electronic medical records to store and share patient and treatment information has already been implemented in some countries, including Australia and Germany, acceptance is not at a peak yet. Castillo et al. (2010) identify six main issues for the adoption of electronic medical records comprising user attitude towards information systems, workflow impact, interoperability, technical support, communication among users and expert support. This research shows that especially user acceptance and the technical infrastructure are vital to ensure successful e-health operations. The framework for assessing e-health preparedness proposed by Wickramasinghe et al. (2005) determines four main areas that influence a country's e-health potential, i.e. Information and Communication Technology Architecture and Infrastructure, Standardization, Policies, Protocols and Procedures, User Access and Accessibility Policies and Infrastructure and Governmental Regulations and Roles. Based on these prior findings, influencing aspects for a national e-health strategy can be viewed according to macro-environmental aspects, i.e. political, economic, social, technological, legal and environmental factors (Kotler and Armstrong 2010).

8.3 Comparison of e-Health Systems

To enable successful e-health development, the various motivations and perspectives of key stakeholders have to be considered. According to Eng (2001), major stakeholders can be categorized into consumers, application developers, clinicians, policymakers, healthcare organizations, public health professionals, employers and purchasers. The interactions and decisions of these individual groups have a high impact on acceptance and enablement of e-health initiatives. Furthermore, Boonstra and Broekhuis (2010) identify eight critical factors for the adoption of electronic medical records including financial, technical, time, psychological, social, legal, organizational and change process. Hage et al. (2013) argue that e-health only leads to sustainable adoption when the implementation carefully considers and aligns the e-health content, the pre-existing structures in the context and the interventions in the implementation process. Successful e-health implementation therefore relies on the infrastructural prerequisites and technical standards, governmental and policy support as well as user acceptance and accessibility. Based on these influencing areas, the following sections analyses the implementation, key challenges and opportunities of e-health systems in Germany and Australia and develop suggestions with regard to their present experiences.

Figure 8.2 summarizes the scope of e-health and its influencing macro-economic factors that are considered in our analysis.

8.3.1 e-Health in Germany

The German healthcare system is suffering from demographic change, increasing costs and lack of skilled professionals. Telemedicine can help counter these problems (Krüger-Brand 2011) by improving treatment efficiency and quality, increasing access speed to relevant information and enabling networking between all stakeholders of the care value chain. e-Health can support current issues regarding coordination, integration and networks between stakeholders and enhance decision-making and planning throughout the entire value care chain.

8.3.1.1 Governmental and Policy Support

Until 2004, Germany offered a basic health insurance card (KVK) providing minimum information about a patient's personal and insurance information as a credential for patients to claim health services. Due to limitations in storage and applications of this insurance card, the modernization act by the statuary health insurance in January 2004 proposed the extension of the insurance card to the electronic health card (EHC), which was finally implemented in early 2006. The goal behind the EHC was to provide health service providers access to patient information through

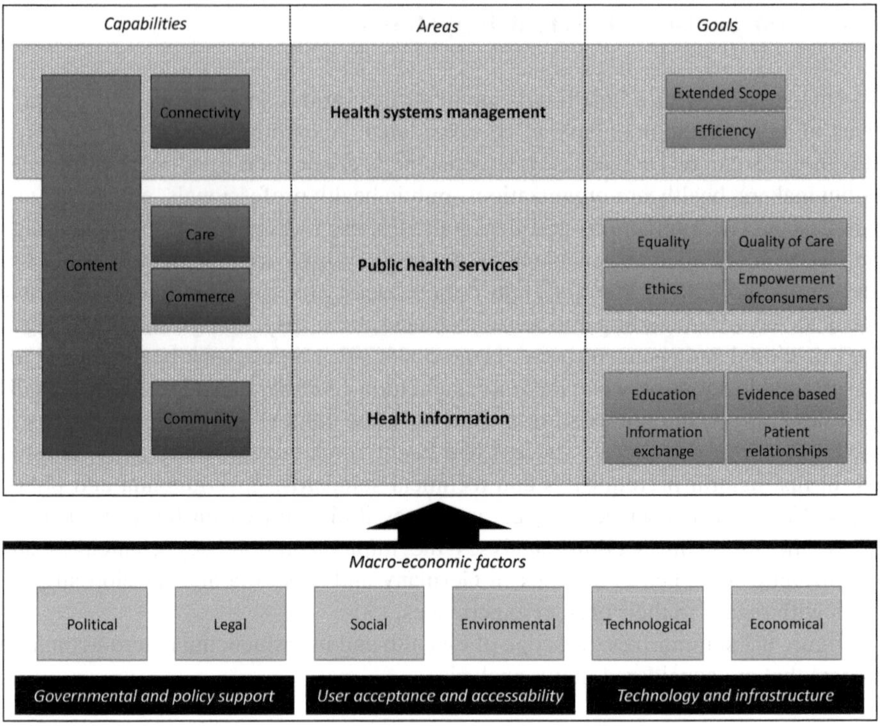

Fig. 8.2 Scope of e-health

IT to increase treatment quality and control health service processes and quality for medical treatments (GKV Spitzenverband 2015a).

Since January 1, 2015, the "electronic health card (EHC)" is the mandatory credential in Germany to claim services covered by the health insurance. Table 8.1 summarizes the required and optional information on the EHC with their respective legal codes.

Data security is provided by following a two-key principle. Both an electronic healthcare ID by the professional and the personal healthcare card and PIN code of the patient are required to access their medical data. Although not yet implemented, the EHC is designed to include electronic patient records, medical reports, care records and medication records in the future.

Besides internal regulations and investments, Germany can additionally benefit from EU initiatives and funding schemes. The topic of health, demographic change and wellbeing addressed in the Horizon2020 programme provides extensive funding possibilities for e-health applications and development. The Digital Agenda for Europe focuses an entire pillar of their Europe 2020 strategy on ICT-enabled benefits for the EU society, including actions to enable secure online access to medical health data and a widespread telemedicine deployment (Action 75); define a minimum common set of patient data (Action 76); foster EU-wide standards,

Table 8.1 Required and optional information on the EHC

Information	Required/ optional	Legal code
Name of the issuing health insurance	Required	SGB §291a (2), SGB §291 (2)
First and last name of the insurant		
Date of birth		
Sex		
Address		
Insurance number		
Insurance status		
Out-of-pocket payment		
Date of insurance commencement		
Date of expiration time (for fixed-term insurance)		
Medical prescriptions in electronic and machine-usable form	Optional	SGB §291a (2)
Credential for health treatment in an EU or EEA member state and Switzerland		
Medical data	Optional	SGB §291a (3)
Medical reports		
Electronic patient record		
Additional data provided by the insurant		
Information and consent form on organ and tissue donation		
Information to verify drug therapy security		

interoperability testing and certification of e-health (Action 77); and reinforce the Ambient Assisted Living (AAL) Joint Programme (Action 78) (European Commission 2015).

8.3.1.2 Technology and Infrastructure

Germany is a leading country in technology development considering financial and human resources devoted to R&D as well as patents granted per capita (Florida et al. 2011). In health care, Germany currently ranks high considering quality of care, access to health care services, efficiency and equity as well as expenditure per capita. Especially access to health care shows above-average results in international comparisons. Space for improvement is still found in the area of coordinated care, which constitutes a major issue to be solved by e-health (Davis et al. 2014).

Besides access to advanced technology, a main requirement for a successful national e-health strategy is the underlying infrastructure to integrate applications and provide and access data in a structured and protected environment. For a strategical conception and implementation of the EHC and telematics infrastructure, the company for EHC telematics applications *gematik* was founded in Germany in 2005 (gematik 2016). The company's core responsibility lies in managing the development, implementation and maintenance of a countrywide telematics infrastructure. Although first rollout was projected for mid-2015, security issues and the highly technical requirements for connecting hospitals, apothecaries, medical practices and care facilities throughout Germany are still delaying deployment. In December 2015, the German parliament passed a new legislation for secure digital communication and applications in health care, legally replacing the preceding health insurance card with the EHC. This legislation lays down a timeframe for a nationwide integration of hospitals and practices into the developed infrastructure until 2018 (Bundestag 2015).

8.3.1.3 User Access and Accessibility

From a professional standpoint, the e-health acceptance rate in Germany shows a below-average increase on an EU level of 31% since 2007. While the country's professional-to-patient initiatives in telehealth, e.g. remote monitoring and consultation, show good results in international comparisons, the professional-to-professional dimension including online education and joint consultation is still lagging behind. The combination of a mandatory insurance proof and an optional extension for further information lowers the barriers of adopting a new system for users. Since over 97% of the insured population is now provided with an EHC (GKV Spitzenverband 2015b), the extension of additional services, e.g. electronic health records, can be added more easily to the already distributed systems. Issues with user participation for the basic system can therefore be eliminated; however, the use of additional services could still be obstructed by user acceptance.

8.3.1.4 Key Challenges

Although the EHC was already implemented in 2006, an integrated, accessible and data security-compliant infrastructure for telemedical services has yet to be developed. Through many regional projects, individual solutions have been brought up that already exploit parts of what e-health can offer, but further reinforce redundancies in development. Investments in healthcare structures and concepts are still scarce, leading to a pool of isolated applications within a diverse, fragmented market. Another issue obstructing e-health development stems from the lagged development of IT standards in the healthcare sector and missing secure networks. Lack of investments, scarce awareness and indolence of decision-makers also hinder a fast development of national e-health initiatives. Questions of liability and security also cause for delay.

8.3.2 e-Health in Australia

The Australian healthcare system is argued to be among the best providers of outstanding quality of care. In comparison to Germany, the unrestricted access to healthcare services is not as prominent, but the coordination of care shows overall better results (Davis et al. 2014). This stems from the early attempts on utilizing e-health to increase transparency and efficiency in care, starting with the introduction of the e-health technology programme in 1991. Since then, the Australian e-health strategy has been continuously refined and analysed to adapt to emerging issues in health care.

8.3.2.1 Governmental and Policy Support

In 2004–2005 the National E-Health Transition Authority (NEHTA) was established to develop the e-health agenda with the development of e-health standards, clinical terminologies and patient and provider identifiers. In 2008, the new Labour government asked consultants from Deloitte to help develop a new direction. They found that lack of financial support was one of the main problems. Three months after the submission of Deloitte's report, the government introduced its national e-health strategy. This adoption strategy of e-health in Australia was implemented incrementally following three main principles (Australian Health Ministers' Council 2008):

- To leverage currently existing resources in the Australian e-health landscape
- To manage underlying variation in capacity across health sector and states and territories
- To allow scope for change during the implementation process

In 2009 the National Health and Hospitals Reform Commission released a report advocating the introduction of personal electronic health records. In 2010–2012 the Personally Controlled E-Health Records (PCEHR) platform was founded and launched in July 2012. The objective behind this system was the establishment and operation of a voluntary national system for the provision of access to health information. The main goal of the PCEHR system was to improve availability and quality of health information and reduce fragmentation, minimize the occurrence of adverse medical events and duplication of treatment and support coordination of health care provided to consumers by different healthcare providers.

Australia has passed a legislative framework that includes governance arrangements, a privacy and security framework and a registration regime or the My Health Record system (Australian Government 2012). However, in contrast to Germany, Australia still lacks appropriate governance and regulatory mechanisms to manage, monitor and control the system.

Table 8.2 Australian e-health infrastructure (Bunker 2011)

Personally controlled electronic health record	Clinical information	Individual information	Shared information	Others
e-Health services	Shared health profile	Event summaries	Self-managed care	Complex care management
e-Health solutions	e-Diagnostics	e-Discharge	e-Referral	e-Medications
National infrastructure components	Clinical terminology information	Secure messaging	Identifiers	Authentication

8.3.2.2 Technology and Infrastructure

Although Australia doesn't rank as high in international comparisons considering technology and R&D in general (Florida et al. 2011), the use of healthcare technologies has been developed. Similar to Germany's gematik, Australia's NEHTA is leading a national approach to develop a national e-health infrastructure and IT standards to enable connected health. So far, a national terminology for medicines (AMT), a clinical terminology (SNOMED) and a Secure Message Delivery (SMD) system were implemented as a first step for setting national standards. The goal is to build these foundations within the My Health Record platform as the national e-health infrastructure. Table 8.2 summarizes the main components of the PCEHR system, intended services and solutions and the underlying infrastructure.

8.3.2.3 User Access and Accessibility

Up until today, only 11% of the Australian population are yet registered on the platform and just slightly over 8000 healthcare provider organizations, mainly general practices (Australian Department of Health 2015). Without legal enforcement to adapt the platform for, e.g. billing or insurance claims, usage rates have not yet reached the lower limit for a comprehensive adoption of e-health services. Due to the lack of meaningful use of the PCEHR system, the platform will be changed to an opt-out solution and renamed to My Health Record in 2016. A resulting wider uptake of the system is projected to increase the value for healthcare professionals and consequently their willingness to use the system. Registration barriers for healthy persons or disadvantaged patients thus should be eliminated (Australian Department of Health 2013).

8.3.2.4 Key Challenges

The aging population, increasing incidence of chronic disease, rising customer demand for more costly, complex and technologically advanced procedures and the simultaneous lack of skilled health sector workers are causing a major rise in cost and complexity for the Australian healthcare system. Pre-existing e-health solutions to counter these issues are implemented as discrete islands of information with significant barriers to effective sharing of information between healthcare participants. Without proper national coordination, extensive service duplication, avoidable expenditures and solutions that cannot be scaled or integrated can drastically decrease the potential of e-health. In addition, Australia still lacks the required legal and infrastructural foundations to enable a nationwide implementation of their e-health platform.

8.4 SWOT Analysis

8.4.1 Comparison of the Systems

Table 8.3 summarizes the advantages and handicaps of the German e-health system in a SWOT analysis. The resulting strategies give suggestions on further developments e-health can endorse to enhance quality of health care in Germany.

8.4.2 Strategies Derived from the SWOT Analysis

Germany and Australia pursue different approaches with their national e-health strategy. Whereas Australia initially invested in an open, voluntary platform solution, Germany instructed a long-term statutory basis for an integrated infrastructure for extensive e-health services based on a mandatory insurance card. Changing the My Health Record platform to an opt-out model can reduce the barriers for user registration; meaningful use of the proposed service, however, will require additional effort by the Australian government. The German example shows that the utilization of national technology resources and know-how can be used to systematically invest and plan for comprehensive e-health applications. Applications can therefore be developed on a common ground, facilitating the reuse of key insights and results. The downside in the implementation of a nationwide e-health project is reflected in protracted legal changes and limited reaction to changing requirements. On the other hand, although development of individual applications may increase implementation flexibility and speed and allow for modular adjustments, the subsequent integration of fragmented solutions can result in major adaption requirements, insufficient scalability and unnecessary duplicates.

Tables 8.4 and 8.5 summarize the derived insights from the SWOT analysis, indicating strategies for Germany and Australia to utilize the countries' capabilities for exploiting the proposed opportunities and handle emerging threats.

Table 8.3 SWOT analysis of German and Australian e-health system

Germany	Australia
Strengths	
S1: Advanced technological foundation and development	*S1*: General guidelines based on the commonwealth privacy act 1988 and the Australian privacy principles (APP)
S2: Legal requirements for e-health explicitly defined in fifth social security code	*S2*: Flexible infrastructural solutions
S3: Regulations for data safety and security	*S3*: First attempts at national standards
S4: High mobile penetration and broadband coverage	*S4*: Secure messaging system
S5: Governmental support	*S5*: High quality of care
S6: Funding opportunities on international level (EU)	*S6*: Adaptability of e-health strategy
S7: Integrated solution of mandatory EHC and optional e-health applications in one system	*S7*: Nationwide platform for interaction and information exchange
	S8: Lower usage barriers through change to an opt-out model
Weaknesses	
W1: Lack of IT standards in health care	*W1*: No legal binding to use or adapt e-health
W2: Isolated solutions	*W2*: Isolated solutions
W3: High bureaucracy through governmental involvement	*W3*: Fragmented system
W4: Common infrastructure still not available	*W4*: Missing nationwide governmental cooperation
W5: Lack of experience with patient involvement	*W5*: Dispersed data storage
Opportunities	
The mandatory cross-linkage between healthcare providers can enable an *uninterrupted communication network*	Flexibility in strategical decision enables *fast adjustments*
Lower adoption barriers through combination of mandatory and voluntary services	*Lower adoption barriers* through change to an opt-out model
Better *information exchange*	Better *information exchange*
Increase in *efficiency* and *transparency* of healthcare delivery	Increase in *efficiency* and *transparency* of healthcare delivery
Citizen's mobility requires *increased data sharing*	Citizen's mobility requires increased *data sharing*
Increased *computer literacy* and *ICT skills*	Increased *computer literacy* and *ICT skills*
Reuse of knowledge and applications	*Reuse* of knowledge and applications
Reduced *unnecessary* and *duplicate treatments*	Reduced *unnecessary* and *duplicate treatments*
Increased *scalability* of e-health solutions	Increased *scalability* of e-health solutions
Threats	
Delayed roll-out of holistic infrastructure	Low *adoption rates* by healthcare professionals
Protracted *legal changes*	Weighing between *effort* and *benefits* for individual providers

(continued)

Table 8.3 (continued)

Germany	Australia
High *bureaucracy implications* for nationwide decisions	Difficulties *integrating* fragmented e-health market
User acceptance of e-health innovations	*User acceptance* of e-health innovations
Lack of *skilled professionals*	Lack of *skilled professionals*
Incomplete documentation	*Incomplete documentation*
Data privacy, confidentiality, liability and *data protection*	*Data privacy, confidentiality, liability* and *data protection*

8.5 Discussion and Conclusion

In this chapter, we analysed the potentials and challenges of national e-health strategies in Australia and Germany. Based on macro-environmental factors, i.e. governmental support and policies, technology and infrastructure and user acceptance and accessibility, key capabilities and handicaps were identified for each country. Based on these results, we derived strategies on how to exploit the positive effects and opportunities of e-health and how to handle challenges that might arise concurrently. Our results suggest similar findings for developed countries, especially with regard to major challenges in health care that are planned to be addressed by e- health solutions. Both countries attempt to increase efficiency and transparency in health care, increase communication and collaboration between healthcare participants and provide overall better quality of care. The meaningful use of health information, development of national standards and regulations and application integration are also focused in the individual e-health strategies. Two approaches to reach these goals have been identified: The German strategy combines partly statutory and voluntary information sharing within an integrated system, whereas the Australian platform-based solution relies on an entirely optional system. Both countries can profit from different insights already gathered from other national e-health approaches. With Germany as a leading player in technology advancements and an already well-established legal foundation for e-health regulations on the one hand and Australia's flexible adaptions and early experiences within e-health in contrast, both countries can provide different knowledge aspects for successful e-health implementation and a high level of quality of care to other countries. At the moment, however, major changes are also taking place in both countries. In Germany, a new e-health law has laid down an obligation to link healthcare providers in the national telematics infrastructure currently under development. First results and the impact of this regulation will be seen in the following years. The change of an opt-in to an opt-out model for the Australian e-health platform My Health Record will also entail major alterations in the country's e-health strategy and development that should be addressed in future studies. Finally, we note in closing that a SWOT analysis can be a suitable tool to assist in conducting a systematic analysis of various factors both strengths and weaknesses from which it is then also possible to develop appropriate strategies to assist with developing sustainable solutions for specific healthcare contexts.

Table 8.4 Opportunities for Germany and Australia

Opportunity	Germany	Australia
O1: Integrated healthcare data + applications	*S1/S2*: Use the mandatory linkage of all healthcare providers to combine health information from all linked partners as well as patients in an integrated system to gain holistic insights over bigger patient cohorts *W4/S1/S5/S6*: Support and contribute to infrastructural development with funding projects	*W1/W2/S2*: Two-sided approach to integrate currently isolated solutions and adapt infrastructure accordingly
O2: Cross-linking of healthcare providers	*S2/S5*: The cross-linkage of healthcare providers is already determined by law and currently tested in field studies. Collaboration should be further supported and monitored by the government	*W1/S1*: Provide more binding regulations to join the nationwide network *S4*: Create awareness for e-health advantages in field studies
O3: Increasing user acceptance + IT literacy	*S4*: With high mobile penetration and broadband coverage of German citizens and healthcare providers, mobile applications and IT solutions to link healthcare consumers should be implemented	*S7/S8*: Engage consumers in participating in voluntary e-health services by providing comprehensible personal insights
O4: Better information exchange	*S3/S4/S7*: Provide easy and secure methods to share and exchange data	*S3/S4*: Provide easy and secure methods to share and exchange data
O5: Increase efficiency and transparency of healthcare delivery	*S2/S5*: Continuous monitoring of healthcare expenditure and health quality indicators to monitor performance and impact of e-health solutions	*W4/S5/S6*: Continuous monitoring of healthcare expenditure and health quality indicators to monitor performance and impact of e-health solutions
	W5/S7: Engage consumers in participating in voluntary e-health services by providing comprehensible personal insights	*S8:* Engage consumers in participating in voluntary e-health services by providing comprehensible personal insights
O6: Increased communication and collaboration	*S1/W5:* Implement secure messaging service to enable communication and coordination between patients and healthcare providers	*S4:* Secure messaging system already in place.
O7: Reuse of knowledge and applications	*W1*: Develop open IT standards based on insights from pre-existing solutions *S1:* Initiate national open source platform for e-health development to share experiences	*S1/S7:* Extend national platform for to share experiences in e-health service development

(continued)

Table 8.4 (continued)

Opportunity	Germany	Australia
O8: Reduce unnecessary and duplicate treatments	*S7:* Create structured overviews/ templates for patients including treatments, medications and personal data as a single source of truth *W2:* Integrate existing isolated solutions into national infrastructure	*W2/S2:* Two-sided approach to integrate currently isolated solutions and adapt infrastructure accordingly *S7:* Aggregate collected data on my health record platform to provide a structured history for each patient

Table 8.5 Threats for Germany and Australia

Threat	Germany	Australia
T1: Incomplete documentation	*S3/S4/S7*: Provide easy and secure methods to share and exchange data *S7*: Create structured overviews/ templates for patients including treatments, medications and personal data as a single source of truth	*W1/S1*: Provide more binding regulations to participate in the nationwide network *S3/S4/S7*: Provide easy and secure methods to share and exchange data *S7*: Aggregate collected data on my health record platform to provide a structured history for each patient
T2: Legal changes	*W3/S2*: Systematically monitor issues in e-health development to enable fast reactions for necessary changes	*W4/S1*: Introduce legal regulations for e-health on a national level
T3: Bureaucracy implications	*W3*: Encourage close cooperation between government and healthcare providers for shorter discussion paths	*W4*: Increase national governmental cooperation
T4: User acceptance	*S4*: With high mobile penetration and broadband coverage of German citizens and healthcare providers, mobile applications and IT solutions to link healthcare consumers should be implemented	*S7/S8*: Engage consumers in participating in voluntary e-health services by providing comprehensible personal insights
T5: Data privacy, confidentiality, liability and data protection lack of skilled	*S1/S3/S5*: Ensure secure and stable networks and regulate data access according to different stakeholders; data authority lies with the consumer *S5*: Offer training and raise transparency for e-health services	*W5*: Appoint a single institution to store, manage and secure healthcare data in a structured and reliable way *S5*: Offer training and raise professionals transparency for e-health services

References

AIHW. (2016). *Australian refined diagnosis-related groups (AR-DRG) data cubes: AR-DRG cubes for 1997–98 to 2013–14*. Retrieved February 03, 2016, from http://www.aihw.gov.au/hospitals-data/ar-drg-data-cubes/

Australian Department of Health. (2013). *Review of the personally controlled electronic health record.* from http://www.health.gov.au/internet/main/publishing.nsf/content/17BF043A41D470A9CA257E13000C9322/$File/FINAL-Review-of-PCEHR-December-2013.pdf

Australian Department of Health. (2015). *My health record statistics.* from https://myhealthrecord.gov.au/internet/ehealth/publishing.nsf/Content/pcehr-statistics

Australian Government, Federal Register of Legislation. (2012). *Personally Controlled Electronic Health Records Act 2012*.

Australian Health Ministers' Council. (2008). *National E-Health Strategy.*

Boonstra, A., & Broekhuis, M. (2010). Barriers to the acceptance of electronic medical records by physicians from systematic review to taxonomy and interventions. *BMC Health Services Research, 10*, 231.

Bunker, D. (2011). E-health and NEHTA: Integrating heterogeneous data sources: A technology or policy challenge.

Castillo, V. H., Martínez-García, A. I., & Pulido, J. R. G. (2010). A knowledge-based taxonomy of critical factors for adopting electronic health record systems by physicians: A systematic literature review. *BMC Medical Informatics and Decision Making, 10*, 60.

Davis, K., Stremikis, K., Squires, D., & Schoen, C. (2014). *Mirror, mirror on the wall: How the performance of the U.S. health care system compares internationally*. New York: The Commonwealth Fund.

Deutscher Bundestag. (2015). *Gesetz für sichere digitale Kommunikation und Anwendungen im Gesundheitswesen sowie zur Änderung weiterer Gesetze*.

Dietzel, G. (2001). E-Health und Gesundheitstelematik: Herausforderungen und Chancen. *Deutsches Ärzteblatt, 98*(4), 158–160.

Eng, T. R. (2001). *The eHealth landscape: A terrain map of emerging information and communication technologies in health and heath care*. Princeton, NJ: Robert Wood Johnson Foundation.

European Commission. (2015). *Digital agenda for Europe: A Europe 2020 initiative,* from https://ec.europa.eu/digital-agenda/en/our-goals

Eysenbach, G. (2001). What is e-health? *Journal of Medical Internet Research, 3*(2), E20.

Fetter, R. B., Shin, Y., Freeman, J. L., Averill, R. F., & Thompson, J. D. (1980). Case mix definition by diagnosis-related groups. *Medical Care, 18*(2), i-53.

Florida, R., Mellander, C., Stolarick, K., Silk, K., Matheson, Z., & Hopgood, M. (2011). *Creativity and prosperity: The global creativity index,* from http://martinprosperity.org/media/GCI%20Report%20Sep%202011.pdf

gematik. (2016). *gematik Unternehmensorganisation.* Retrieved February 06, 2016, from https://www.gematik.de/cms/de/gematik/unternehmensorganisation/historie_1/historie_1.jsp

GKV Spitzenverband. (2015a). *Elektronische Gesundheitskarte (eGK),* from https://www.gkv-spitzenverband.de/krankenversicherung/telematik_und_datenaustausch/egk/egk.jsp

GKV Spitzenverband. (2015b). *Das Wichtigste über Das Wichtigste über die elektronische Gesundheitskarte.*

Haeussler, B., Zich, K., & Bless, H.-H. (2014). Does the implementation of a new payment system for hospital services induce changes in the quality of health care? Experiences from Germany. *BMC Health Services Research, 14*(Suppl 2), O18.

Hage, E., Roo, J. P., van Offenbeek, M. A., & Boonstra, A. (2013). Implementation factors and their effect on e-health service adoption in rural communities: A systematic literature review. *BMC Health Services Research, 13*, 19.

InEK GmbH. (2016). *G-DRG-System 2016,* from http://www.g-drg.de/cms/

Kotler, P., & Armstrong, G. (2010). *Principles of marketing* (13th ed.). Upper Saddle River, NJ: Pearson Education.

Krüger-Brand, H. (2011), TeleHealth 2011 – digitale Medizin: Telemedizin und Gesundheits-Apps, Deutsches Ärzteblatt International

Little, A. D. (2016). *Global digital health market from 2013 to 2020, by segment (in billion U.S. dollars)*, from http://www.statista.com/statistics/387867/value-of-worldwide-digital-health-market-forecast-by-segment/

Lüngen, M., & Lauterbach, K. (2002). Ergebnisorientierte Vergütung bei DRG. In *Qualitätssicherung bei pauschalierender Vergütung stationärer Krankenhausleistungen. Gesundheitsmanagement*. Berlin, Germany: Springer.

Neumann, K. (2014). *Blick für das Ganze*, from http://www.iges.com/kunden/gesundheit/forschungsergebnisse/2014/gesundheitswirtsch aft/index_ger.html#ZMS_HIGHLIGHT=raw&raw=drg

OECD. (2015). *OECD Health Statistics 2015*, from http://www.oecd.org/els/health-systems/health-data.htm

WHO. (2016). *eHealth: Glossary of globalization, trade and health terms*, from http://www.who.int/trade/glossary/story021/en/

Wickramasinghe, N. S., Fadlalla, A. M. A., Geisler, E., & Schaffer, J. L. (2005). A framework for assessing e-health preparedness. *International Journal of Electronic Healthcare, 1*(3), 316–334.

Chapter 9
The Advantages of Using a Two-Arm Crossover Study Design to Establish Proof of Concept of Technology Interventions: The Case of a Mobile Web-Based Reporting of Glucose Readings in the Management of Gestational Diabetes Mellitus (GDM)

Nilmini Wickramasinghe and Steve Goldberg

9.1 Introduction

The need for improvement in the delivery of health care is paramount. Today, much of the literature pertaining to health care continually discusses the many severe challenges such as exponentially increasing costs, pressures to provide appropriate quality and access as well as incorporate best practice and recent new findings at the point of care (Wickramasinghe and Schaffer 2010; Geisler and Wickramasinghe 2009; Wickramasinghe et al. 2012). Government agencies and the private sector are alarmed with rising costs and the decline in quality, access and availability of care. In addition, we are now witnessing the increased role of chronic diseases as a major contributor to cause of death and morbidity, replacing communicable diseases which only serves to further stress the resources of an already strained healthcare delivery system.

Without a question then, there is a clear need for short- and long-term solutions to this current crisis in the delivery of care. Such a search for a solution has led to the growing focus on technology, especially telemedicine and remote care, as a useful alternative to the prevailing models of inpatient care. The utilisation of information communication technologies (ICT) seems particularly attractive given its allure in the support and enablement of a cost-effective model of care for patients with chronic diseases. Moreover, mobile phone penetration has been exponentially increasing over the last decade with most individuals now having at least one mobile

N. Wickramasinghe (✉)
Deakin University, Burwood, VIC, Australia

S. Goldberg
Inet International Inc., Thornhill, ON, Canada
e-mail: sgoldberg@inet-international.com

N. Wickramasinghe, J. L. Schaffer (eds.), *Theories to Inform Superior Health Informatics Research and Practice*, Healthcare Delivery in the Information Age,
https://doi.org/10.1007/978-3-319-72287-0_9

device. (Business insider Australia 2013) However, the implementation of new ICT infrastructures needs to consider the users and the management of the information that can be captured and shared by such systems.

This chapter sets out to describe a two-arm crossover research design that was adopted to assess the usability and fidelity issues and establish proof of concept of a unique technology solution that focusses on a specific issue to address this current dilemma, the use of smart phones to effect better information access and sharing between patients and clinicians and, thus, improved control of a chronic illness.

9.2 Prevalence of Diabetes

Today, chronic diseases have replaced infectious diseases as the top global causes of deaths and morbidity (Zimmet 2000; Zuvekas and Cohen 2007). Noncommunicable diseases—such as cardiovascular disorders and strokes, respiratory illnesses such as asthma, arthritis and diabetes—now account for more deaths, and for a disproportionate burden on healthcare budgets of governments, than infectious diseases such as tuberculosis, HIV/AIDS and malaria. This trend is magnified by the demographic realities of this century. The aging of the population and the increased longevity of major segments of the population are key contributors to the emerging picture of a crisis in the delivery of health services. More patients afflicted by chronic diseases will continue to be a burden on an already drained healthcare delivery system (Windrum 2008; Wickramasinghe and Geisler 2008). Diabetes, the leading chronic disease, has been described by the WHO as the silent epidemic (WHO 2012; Wild et al. 2004).

Chen et al. (2012) indicate that over the last three decades, the number of people with diabetes mellitus worldwide has more than doubled. Their comment is based on data collected up to 2011 and reinforces the concern of other research that identified the continued global prevalence of diabetes mellitus. The 2012 update of the International Diabetes Federation Atlas (IDF 2012) indicates that 8.3% of the global adult population live with diabetes, and of these, 50% are undiagnosed, usually type 2 (non-insulin-dependent) diabetics. The Federation predicts that by 2030 the prevalence of diabetes will have risen to 9.9% of the global adult population (IDF 2012).

Uncontrolled diabetes can lead to other very unpleasant complications, and thus there is a broader medical impact of diabetes which includes co-morbidities and higher risks of contracting other diseases (WHO 2012). One of the measures of diabetic control and management is the haemoglobin A1c (or HbA1c) blood test, which is used to indicate the average blood sugar control over a period of time, generally 3-month intervals (WHO 2013). Stratton (2000) indicated that a 1% decrease in the results of the A1c test can lead to substantial decreases in the risk of associated conditions. The results of Stratton's (2000) study suggest that this could be a 43% decrease in the risk of peripheral vascular disease, 37% decrease in microvascular disease and 14% decrease on myocardial infarction (heart attack). This reinforces the importance of controlling diabetes as tighter control leads to less complications and therefore to less impact on the medical infrastructure.

Where tighter control is explicitly required is in the management of gestational diabetes mellitus (GDM) (Hoffman et al. 1998). Diabetes Australia estimates that between 3% and 8% of pregnant women will develop GDM (Diabetes Australia 2012). Unmanaged GDM has many problematic concerns including the impact of the mother passing high levels of glucose to the baby, which may then lead to several complications at birth and beyond for both mother and baby. Tight control and management of GDM is therefore necessary, and a team of medical practitioners, diabetic nurses and dieticians are needed to assist the mother to manage her blood sugar during the pregnancy. Getahun et al. (2008) note that there is an increased prevalence of GDM in women ages between 25 and 34 years.

9.3 The Management of Diabetes

Diabetes is a chronic disease and therefore by definition there is no cure for diabetes. This makes the adoption of various management strategies paramount in the successful care of diabetic patients (Britt et al. 2007; AIHW 2007; AIHW 2008).

The management of diabetes is typically based on a mixture of self-management protocols linked with the support of a dedicated medical care team (Victorian Government 2007). An essential element of self-management relies on regular testing of blood glucose, using a glucometer or blood glucose monitor. These monitors provide a point in time reading of blood sugar, which then inform the diabetic of the need for insulin (if type 1) or activity/exercise (if type 2). The preferred range of readings for type 1/2 diabetic is between 4 and 8 mmol/L (Hoffman et al. 1998).

Gestational diabetes mellitus (GDM) requires tight control of blood sugar levels, with a preferred range of readings between 4 and 6 mmol/L (Hoffman et al. 1998; Siri and Thomas 1999; Diabetes Australia 2012). The management of GDM is conducted over a shorter period of time (that of the pregnancy), and thus a tighter management of sugar levels is required. The need for such control draws into question the information that a diabetic may need when self- managing their condition.

In 2008, Hedtke posed the question as to whether "wireless technology enable new diabetes management tools?" (Hedtke 2008). The question was raised in relation to the ways that mobile phone technology could assist in the recording and management of blood glucose monitor. More specifically, can mobile communication and data sharing be integrated with the process of glucose reading? Hedtke (2008) suggested that mobile technology and glucose monitoring technology could be integrated in 3 ways. The first is "user integration", where the technology is not physically integrated, but rather the information is by having the user rekey data from glucose monitor into a mobile phone application. The second is "cable/ Bluetooth integration", where the glucose monitor and phone are connected through a direct (physical) cable or through a close vicinity network (Bluetooth or infrared communication). And the third approach is "physical integration", where the glucose monitor is built into or attached to the mobile phone.

This paper extends the notion of integration, by reporting on the development of a pilot solution to support GDM which has been adapted from a technology solution developed in North America. The study has demonstrated proof of concept but also has uncovered other important aspects. Blood glucose monitors and even smartphone apps tend to act as recording devices. Any information is transferred to medical practitioners as a 'batch' data transfer, usually at the time of medical visit. This study, however, proposes that diabetes control may be more easily managed if there is integration of the captured mobile data with the e-health systems employed by key medical staff in real time.

Specifically, this exploratory study is examining usability and fidelity issues focusing on:

Can the mobile phone "integrate" glucose monitoring as real-time data for the effective management of GDM?

How do patients and clinicians find the use of such a mobile solution for GDM management?

The focus is on GDM as this short-term form of diabetes may benefit from immediate feedback that an integrated information and communication process can provide. Moreover, the patient population in GDM is highly motivated and generally technology savvy and desirous to have better strategies to effectively and efficiently monitor their blood sugar levels.

9.4 The Information and Support Model

A comprehensive review of the literature around the development of technology solutions to assist in diabetes care was performed by Le Rouge and Wickramasinghe (2013). They found that an integral key success criterion is the incorporation of a user-centred design approach (ibid). It is precisely this, a subscription to a user-centred paradigm, that has guided the development of the mobile web-based solution developed by INTEL Intl. Inc. (2013). This mobile solution is web-based and has been developed over several years (Goldberg 2002a, b, c, d, e; Wickramasinghe and Goldberg 2004, 2007; Wickramasinghe et al. 2010).

The development of this mobile solution and information sharing model aims to assist in the information management processes needed for the self-care and self-management of diabetes. Often a system-based development focusses on the technology and how it can be adopted and integrated. This project, however, explores the potential of mobile development from the perspective of the patient and the clinical team, thus the user-centred nature of the project. However, the project team is also drawing on principles of information need and information management that stem from the understanding of library science. Thus, the project will examine whether increased access to information and feedback can assist in patient self-care.

Chronic illnesses, such as GDM, rely on the ability of the patient to self- monitor their daily condition. Blood glucose readings form the basis for this process. However, such self-monitoring also needs to draw on the "knowledge base" of the clinical professionals. This is usually done during clinical visits, where the blood readings over a period of time are accessed and discussed. If aspects of the "knowledge base" can be accessible on a daily basis, then there is a potential that this information can alter the patient behaviour earlier and lead to and maintain tighter control of the diabetic condition. The blood monitoring processes provide patients with information about their glucose readings at any given time. However, the information solution proposed in this study adds to this a layer of knowledge access that is not readily available for individual readings. That is, the "real-time" nature of the information sharing between the patient and the clinical team means that feedback can be accessed on readings that are out of the norm.

Winter et al. (2001) suggests that "Information management in hospitals is the sum of all management activities in a hospital that transpose the potential contribution of information processing to fulfill the strategic hospital goals into hospital's success". The existing information management of patient glucose readings would be based on the record of HbA1c results of tests ordered by the clinical team. The daily glucose readings of the patient will be reviewed at clinical appointments, but they may not be recorded and stored, unless the data is batch uploaded from the monitor and then stored against the patient record. However, such information management processes would generally not be conducted, and rather the daily readings may be reviewed only during the patient/clinician discussion. The model, being tested in this research, captures and stores the daily glucose readings and makes this accessible to the clinical team. These readings can be displayed graphically and the patterns of daily reading can be easily monitored. This information can then complement other patient tests, such as the HbA1c data. Thus, the project has the potential to offer an information management process that improves access to the daily glucose readings of a patient. This information can then assist in identification of trends in daily care that can support the information decisions associated with HbA1c data. However, as Winter et al. (2001) suggests, this then needs to form part of the overall information management practice and systems employed by a hospital. This study can also examine how the clinical team use, monitor and exploit the additional information processes that the project's mobile solution can provide.

Figures 9.1 and 9.2 depict the respective web-based model and how the solution actually works. In particular Fig. 9.1 highlights the key inputs (people process, protection and platform) all essential considerations for a solution of this type that impacts a clinical environment of care. In addition, the dynamic nature of health care is captured by ensuring ongoing updating and integration of new research findings as well as the sustainability of the solution is achieved through the broad based of financing options. Lastly, the model supports the necessary delivery framework and the interaction of the patient and clinician with the clinician being the lead on all projects and the patient being the empowered consumer of the data and information.

From Fig. 9.2 we see how the solution works: (1) the patient must take their blood sugar reading, then enter it into the mobile solution and submit it. Once the

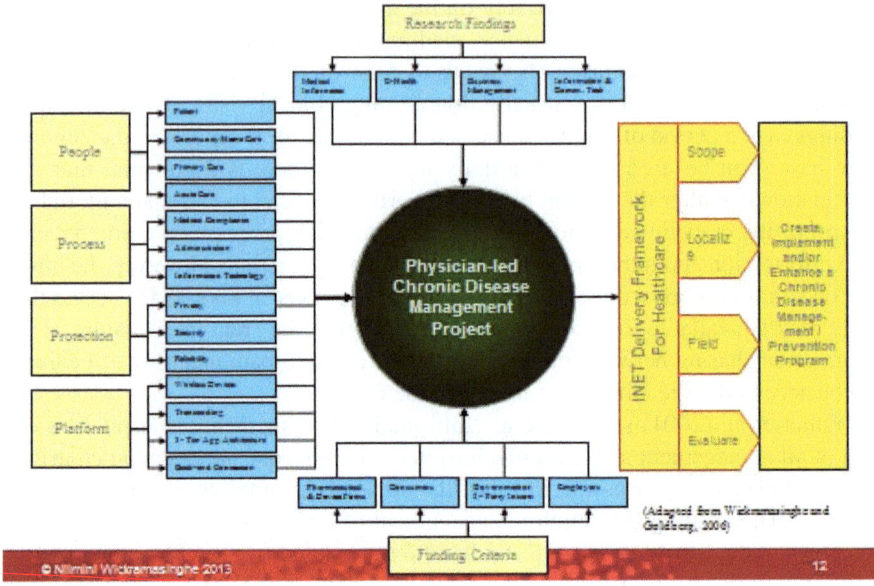

Fig. 9.1 Web-based model

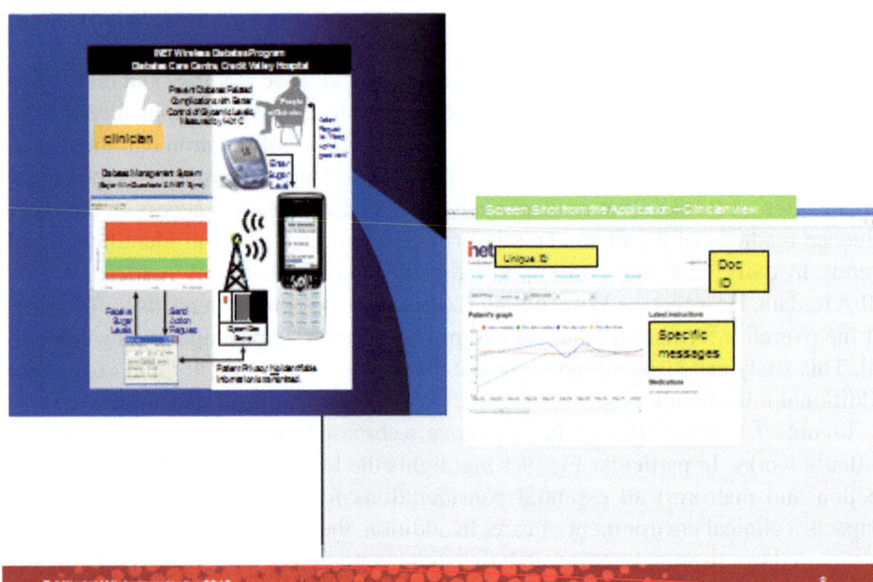

Fig. 9.2 Solution in a nutshell

solution is received by the designated clinician, it is processed and reviewed by the clinician in conjunction with all other relevant medical data before a recommendation is then sent back to the patient. To the right of Fig. 9.2, it is possible to see a typical screenshot showing the four readings normally taken for GDM patients, i.e. before breakfast, 2 h after breakfast, 2 h after lunch and 2 h after dinner. Patients can also write messages about their food and exercise consumption to the right, and the clinician can review all these aspects on receipt.

The process means that there is a continued information sharing between the patient and clinician. While not unique in the management of glucose readings, the graphic representations assist clinicians in identifying trends associated with the glucose management. The ability to add further information to the digital record (e.g. food intake or increased exercise) can assist the clinician in interpreting what may be impacting on these trends or changes in the glucose readings. What is different to current glucose recording processes is the ability for the clinician to then send feedback to the patient if there are concerns with the readings. Usually such feedback is provided during a patient's physical visit with the clinical team; however, this mobile-based solution provides the opportunity for ongoing or "real-time" feedback if required. As suggested above, this assists in the communication dialogue between the patient and clinical team and has the potential to, therefore, change the information exchange and knowledge sharing between the two parties. In a review of literature associated with GDM, Devsam et al. 2013 p.70) suggests that "Women reported feeling 'shocked', 'upset', 'panicked', 'scared', 'numbed', 'depressed', 'fearful', 'terrified', 'disappointed', 'surprised', 'horribly sad', 'anxious' and 'worried' when first diagnosed with GDM". Devsam et al. 2013 p.70) then indicates that when information about the condition was presented, "Women expressed they felt unprepared and unable to assimilate this knowledge because everything was new and uncertain to them". While this initial shock may still be evident for the participants in this study, the mobile data collection and information management processes, proposed in this pilot, may assist in alleviating the information uncertainty that Devsam et al. (2013) has identified.

Carolan (2013) indicates that "In terms of support from health professionals, the women's experiences differed quite substantially, and information and support were rated from excellent to poor. When the woman felt she had sufficient information at her disposal to self- manage her condition, then she generally was satisfied". The near real-time information exchange that is made possible by this pilot study may assist in reinforcing women's need for adequate information access during the management of their GDM. An outcome of the study may be perceived improved support for the participants as they will engage in a potential two-way dialogue through the mobile model being tested.

9.5 Methodology

A quasi-experimental approach was adopted (Campbell and Stanely 1963) employing a two-period crossover clinical trial strategy (Hills and Armitage 1979; Rigby 2003; Senn 2002) over a 10-week duration. Specifically, 2 groups were used. The first group experienced "standard care" protocols and treatments, and the second group was introduced to the "technology solution". Patients were offered the opportunity to participate in the trial once a diagnosis of gestational diabetes had been made, based on a glucose tolerance test administered between 26 and 28 weeks in pregnancy. Enrolment in the study was done by the endocrinologist under the supervision of the consultant obstetricians and was totally optional. At the time of enrolment, all pertinent information regarding the study was shared with patients including the crossover strategy employed. Following enrolment in the study, patients were randomly allocated to either the "technology solution" or "standard care" arms of the study. All patients were then educated in the technique of blood glucose monitoring (BSLs) by a diabetic educator, as per standard clinical practice. They were also then educated in the use of "technology-based" or "traditional" recording techniques for BSLs. Decisions regarding the need for insulin or other medical therapy were always made at the discretion of the clinician and based on current treatment guidelines and standard care. At the time of enrolment into the study, patients were asked to complete a short questionnaire, exploring demographic details, their familiarity with technology in general and their understanding of gestational diabetes. Five weeks into the study, crossover occurred; thus patients initially in the "standard care" arm now entered the "technology solution" arm and vice versa. Once again the diabetic educator provided the necessary education regarding the use of "technology-based" or "traditional" recording techniques for BSLs. Also at this time a short questionnaire was administered to patients regarding their experiences during the first 5 weeks. At the completion of the study, patients again completed a questionnaire, this time also evaluating their experiences with the respective techniques. In addition, data was collected on patient outcomes, including the use of insulin, frequency of "out of target range" BSLs, compliance with monitoring (number of readings actually completed) and baby birth weight and delivery outcomes. At the completion of the study, the clinicians involved (diabetic educator, endocrinologist, obstetricians) also completed a questionnaire evaluating their experiences, in particular their opinions of the technology, relative to standard techniques. All participants participated in a debriefing session at the conclusion of the study.

Established qualitative techniques have been employed to analyse the collected data (Kvale 1996; Boyatzis 1998; Yin 1994). Specifically, from the qualitative data, thematic analysis was performed in accordance with standard approaches described by Kvale (1996) and Boyatzis (1998).

9.5.1 Anticipated Benefits and Potential Outcomes

The study aims to determine if this approach to diabetic information management can assist in maintaining a tighter control of GDM. It hopes that the mobile solution may provide a more enticing way to maintain information associated with glucose reading logs. While glucose monitors have a memory of readings, there are still some who maintain a written journal as an approach to information capturing for their glucose readings. The mobile phone (as a personal information device) may add an enticement for a more frequent recording of glucose readings. The feeding back of this information to the clinical team may also provide reassurance to the patient that their management is being monitored and that the information that they collate is being accessed regularly.

9.6 Initial Results

It is noted that the sample size (7 participants) in this pilot is small; thus while not statistically significant, we have established proof of concept and demonstrated the benefit of a real-time smart phone solution to facilitate the self-management and monitoring of GDM patients. Most notably all patients preferred the technology solution to the standard care, and those patients who start with the technology solution found the change to the standard care disappointing. "Can't I just stay with the smart phone" [Patient 1] was what one patient said, and this sentiment was repeated by all the others who had the technology solution for the first 5 weeks. In addition the clinical care team (obstetricians, diabetic educator and endocrinologist) preferred the technology solution over the standard care approach. The questionnaires and debrief sessions also generated many useful and innovative suggestions for additional features such as an interactive food diary. In keeping with a user-centred design approach, these suggestions will now be incorporated into the technology solution for the next larger-scale trial.

9.7 Discussion and Conclusion

This paper serves to report on a research in progress that focused on the application of a smart technology solution to assist in the enablement of self-management and patient empowerment for sufferers of GDM. The technology solution itself has been designed and developed following a user-centred design approach, and this pilot trial represented the first of its type in an Australian healthcare context. The directional data obtained to date has served to establish proof of concept and that patients and clinicians alike for similar and different reasons prefer the solution to standard care approaches. Clearly, future studies will serve to provide statistically significant results to support this and confirm hypotheses that this study will generate.

The study also serves to uncover some important implications from an information management perspective. In particular, it would appear that presenting patients with pertinent information in an easy to understand form (i.e. a graph of blood sugar results) anytime anywhere has the result of facilitating better and appropriate behaviour modification towards control of blood sugar. We know that pregnant women represent a group in the population that is highly motivated to follow suggested beneficial behaviour modifications for the benefit of their unborn child, but our study shows that the way the information is presented as well as the time and regularity appears to be effective in facilitating the rapid adoption of appropriate and prudent behaviour modification for their own and baby's better health and wellbeing.

In conclusion, we believe that solutions of this type that try to incorporate leading edge technology possibilities to support better patient care represent a key imperative for the future of healthcare delivery especially in regard to superior chronic disease management in today's challenging healthcare environment.

References

AIHW. (2007). National indicators for monitoring diabetes. In *Report of the diabetes indicators review subcommittee of the national diabetes data working group: AIHW cat. No. CVD 38*. Canberra, ACT: AIHW.

AIHW. (2008). *Diabetes: Australian facts 2008*. Canberra, ACT: Australian Institute of Health and Welfare.

Boyatzis, R. E. (1998). *Transforming qualitative information: Thematic analysis and code development*. Thousand Oaks, CA: Sage.

Britt, H., Miller, G. C., Charles, J., Pan, Y., Valenti, L., Henderson, J., et al. (2007). *General practice activity in Australia 2005–06, Cat. No. GEP 16*. Canberra, ACT: AIHW.

Business Insider Australia. (2013). "*Chart: Global mobile phone penetration nears 100 percent*. Retrieved July 30, 2013, from http://www.businessinsider.com.au/mobile-penetration-nears-100-percent-2013-7

Campbell, D., & Stanely, J. (1963). *Experimental and quasi-experimental designs for research*. Boston: Houghton Mifflin Company.

Carolan, M. (2013). Women's experience of gestational diabetes self management: A qualitative study. *Midwifery, 29*, 637–645.

Devsam, B. U., Bogossian, E., & Peacock, A. S. (2013). An interpretative review of women's experiences of gestational diabetes mellitus, proposing a framework to enhance midwifery assessment. *Women and Birth, 26*, 69–76.

Diabetes Australia. (2012). *Gestational diabetes*, Canberra, ACT: Diabetes Australia. Retrieved April 29, 2013, from http://www.diabetesaustralia.com.au/living-with-diabetes/gestational-diabetes/

Geisler, E., & Wickramasinghe, N. (2009). *The role and use of wireless technology in the management and monitoring of chronic diseases*. Washington, DC: IBM Center for The Business of Government.

Getahun, D., Nath, C., Ananth, C. V., et al. (2008). Gestational diabetes in the United States: Temporal trends 1989 through 2004. *American Journal Obstetrics Gynecology, 198*, 525.e1–525.e5.

Goldberg, S. (2002a). *Building the evidence for a standardized mobile internet (wireless) environment in Ontario, Canada. January Update. Internal INET documentation*. North York, ON: INET.
Goldberg, S. (2002b). *HTA presentational selection and aggregation component summary. Internal INET documentation*. North York, ON: INET.
Goldberg, S. (2002c). *Wireless POC device component summary. Internal INET documentation*. North York, ON: INET.
Goldberg, S. (2002d). *HTA presentation rendering component summary. Internal INET documentation*. North York, ON: INET.
Goldberg, S. (2002e). *HTA quality assurance component summary. Internal INET documentation*. North York, ON: INET.
Hedtke, P. (2008). Can wireless technology enable new diabetes management tools? *Journal of Diabetes Science and Technology, 2*(1), 127–130.
Hills, M., & Armitage, P. (1979). The two-period cross-over clinical trial. *British Journal of Clinical Pharmacology, 58*(7), 7–20.
Hoffman, L., Nolan, C., Wilson, J. D., Oats, J., & Simmons, D. (1998). Gestational diabetes mellitus-management guidelines. *Medical Journal of Australia, 169*, 93–97.
IDF Diabetes Atlas. (2012). *5th edition–2012 update, International Diabetes Federation*. Retrieved July 05, 2013, from http://www.idf.org/diabetesatlas/5e/the-global-burden
Inet International Inc. (2013). Retrieved July 30, 2013, from www.inet-international.com
Kvale, S. (1996). *InterViews: An introduction to qualitative research interviewing*. London: Sage.
Le Rouge, C., & Wickramasinghe, N. (2013). A review of user-centered design for diabetes-related consumer health informatics technologies. *Journal of Diabetes Science and Technology, 7*(4), 1039–1056.
Chen, L., Magliano, D. J., & Zimmet, P. Z. (2012). The worldwide epidemiology of type 2 diabetes mellitus–present and future perspectives. *Nature Reviews Endocrinology, 8*(4), 228–236.
Rigby, A. (2003). Cross-over trials in clinical research. *Journal of the Royal Statistical Society, 52*(3), 417–418.
Senn, S. (2002). *Cross-over trials in clinical research* (2nd ed.). New York: Wiley.
Siri, L., & Thomas, A. (1999). Gestational diabetes mellitus. *New England Journal of Medicine, 341*, 1749–1756.
Stratton, I. M., et al. (2000). Association of glycaemia with macrovascular and microvascular complications of type 2 diabetes '(UKPDS 35): Prospective observational study'. *BMJ, 321*, 405–412.
Victorian Government. (2007). *Diabetes prevention and management: A strategic framework for Victoria 1007–2010*. Melbourne, VIC: Victorian Government, Department of Human Services.
Wickramasinghe, N., & Goldberg, S. (2004). How M=EC^2 in healthcare. *International Journal of Mobile Communications, 2*(2), 140–156.
Wickramasinghe, N., & Goldberg, S. (2007). Adaptive mapping to realisation methodology (AMR) to facilitate mobile initiatives in healthcare. *International Journal of Mobile Communications, 5*(3), 300–318.
Wickramasinghe, N., Troshani, I., & Goldberg, S. (2010). An investigation into the use of pervasive wireless technologies to support diabetes healthcare. In A. Coronato & G. De Pietro (Eds.), *Pervasive and smart technologies for healthcare: Ubiquitous methodologies and tools* (Vol. 114–129). New York: IGI Global.
Wickramasinghe, N., & Schaffer, J. (2010). *Realizing value driven patient centric healthcare through technology*. Washington, DC: IBM Center for The Business of Government.
Wickramasinghe, N, Bali, R., Troshani, I., & Goldberg, S.. (2012). Pervasive knowledge management for healthcare. New York: Springer.
Wickramasinghe, N., & Geisler, E. (Eds.). (2008). *Encyclopedia of healthcare information systems*. Hershey, PA: IGI Global.
Wild, S., Roglic, G., Green, A., Sicree, R., & King, H. (2004). Global prevalence of diabetes: Estimates for the year 2000 and projections for 2030. *Diabetes Care, 27*(10), 1047–1053.

Windrum, P. (2008). *Innovation in public sector services entrepreneurship, creativity and management*. New York: Edward Elgar.

Winter, A. F., et al. (2001). Strategic information management plans: The basis for systematic information management in hospitals. *International Journal of Medical Informatics, 64*(2–3), 99–109.

WorldHealthOrganisation.(2012)."*WorldHealthStatistics2012report*.RetrievedJuly31,2013,from http://www.euro.who.int/en/what-we-do/health-topics/noncommunicable-diseases/sections/news/2012/5/world-health-statistics-2012-report-increase-of-hypertension-and-diabetes

World Health Organisation. (2013). "*Use of glycated haemoglobin (HbA1c) in the diagnosis of diabetes mellitus*. Retrieved July 31, 2013, from http://www.who.int/diabetes/publications/diagnosis_diabetes2011/en/index.html

Yin, R. (1994). *Case study research*. Thousand Oaks, CA: Sage.

Zimmet, P. (2000). 21st century review: Globalization, coca-colonization, and the chronic disease epidemic: Can the doomsday scenario be averted? *Journal of Internal Medicine, 247*(3), 301–310.

Zuvekas, S., & Cohen, J. (2007). Prescription drugs and the changing concentration of healthcare expenditures. *Health Affairs, 26*(1), 249–257.

Part II
Sociotechnical Considerations

Chapter 10
Modelling the Business Value of IT in Health Care: Technical and Sociotechnical Perspectives

Peter Haddad, Jonathan L. Schaffer, and Nilmini Wickramasinghe

10.1 Introduction

Driven in large by success stories in other industries, digitizing healthcare processes is a relatively common practice today (Haddad and Wickramasinghe 2014; Nguyen et al. 2015), and more healthcare providers are now moving to IT-enabled solutions. These moves require both upfront and ongoing investments for optimizing outcomes that defy precise prediction (Weill and Ross 2004). This trend provides researchers with the possibility to study the impacts of different information systems/information technology (IS/IT) solutions in various healthcare contexts. Although there is a plethora of such studies, most of these studies have two key limitations: first, the lack of a comprehensive framework that looks at these systems in their respective contexts; and, second, the scope of these studies is mostly limited to the impact of one system on limited measurements regarding outputs. This chapter represents part of a larger research project to comprehensively assess the business value of IS/IT in health care.

The remainder of this chapter is arranged with a literature review on the use of information systems in health care followed by a discussion of the concepts of 'value' and 'business value of IT' in health care. Based on this discussion, the business

P. Haddad
Deakin University, Burwood, VIC, Australia

J. L. Schaffer
Deakin University, Burwood, VIC, Australia

Cleveland Clinic, Cleveland, OH, USA

N. Wickramasinghe (✉)
Epworth HealthCare, Richmond, VIC, Australia

Deakin University, Burwood, VIC, Australia

N. Wickramasinghe, J. L. Schaffer (eds.), *Theories to Inform Superior Health Informatics Research and Practice*, Healthcare Delivery in the Information Age,
https://doi.org/10.1007/978-3-319-72287-0_10

value of IT in healthcare model is introduced, by, first, introducing its theoretical underpinnings and then compiling its various components based on a literature review focusing on the subject of using information technology in health care.

10.2 Literature Review

This section discusses the use of information systems for health care and the 'concepts of value' and 'business value of IT' in this context.

10.2.1 Information Systems for Health Care

The healthcare industry is investing heavily in IS/IT to enhance different outputs, such as patient outcomes (Brenner et al. 2015; Freedman et al. 2014; Kellermann and Jones 2013; Nurek et al. 2015; Piette et al. 2015; Roshanov et al. 2013), safety (Elliott et al. 2013; Kaushal et al. 2003; Nanji et al. 2014; Nuckols et al. 2014; Shekelle et al. 2011; Tang 2003), efficiency (DesRoches et al. 2013; Georgiou et al. 2011; Kellermann and Jones 2013; Lippi et al. 2015; Waterson 2014; Wickramasinghe et al. 2016), and financial performance (Appari et al. 2012; Frisse et al. 2012; Kern et al. 2012; Low et al. 2013; McCoy et al. 2012; Unertl et al. 2012).

This increased use of IS/IT in health care can also be seen from the figures for IS/IT investments (OECD 2013), with more healthcare providers moving towards digitizing their processes and different levels of care delivery (Haddad et al. 2015). Most recently, Gartner (2015) has ranked the healthcare industry as the fifth largest spender on IS/IT with about USD108 billion, behind banking, communications, education, and government and with growth of 2.7% compared to 2013 (Table 10.1).

Table 10.1 IT spending by industry in 2014–2015 (Gartner 2015)

Industry	2014 spending	2014 growth (%)	2015 spending	2015 growth (%)
Banking and securities	498,377	2.1	486,278	−2.4
Communications: media services	444,639	1.5	428,675	−3.6
Education	66,524	1.0	64,182	−2.5
Government	447,114	−1.2	424,660	−5.0
Health care	107,934	2.7	104,982	−2.7
Insurance	187,958	1.8	182,572	−2.8
Manufacturing and natural resources	498,995	1.0	476,546	−4.5
Retail	179,538	2.5	176,916	−1.5
Transportation	133,785	1.6	129,696	−3.1
Utilities	149,379	1.3	143,479	−3.9
Wholesale trade	87,707	0.69	82,011	−3.2
Total market	2,798,950	1.2	2,699,998	−3.5

In this list, health care was ahead of other industries which had previously invested heavily in IS/IT such as manufacturing and natural resources, retail, and transport. Even with the worldwide decline in IT spending in 2015 across divergent vertical industries due to the rising US dollar and the relative slowdown in emerging markets (particularly Russia, Brazil, and China), the healthcare industry was ranked fourth in investing in IT in 2015 after retail, banking and securities, and education (Gartner 2015) as demonstrated in Table 10.1.

The data in Table 10.1 supports other forecasts that rank the healthcare industry first in the list of fastest growing industries in adopting IS/IT over the 2015–2019 forecast period with a 5-year compound annual growth rate (CAGR) of 5.5% ((IDC) 2016). According to the same source, spending on software will be the fastest growing market with a 6.7% CAGR, led by the healthcare and financial services investments. In addition, the healthcare industry will also represent, with telecommunication industry, the strongest opportunities for the IS/IT hardware market (IDC 2016).

Today, investing in IS/IT within healthcare contexts covers a broad range of applications and systems to facilitate the healthcare delivery at different levels, from detection to recovery (Rouse 2009). Table 10.2 describes the main healthcare IS/IT applications that have been widely used in a quest to enhance healthcare outcomes. In addition to this array of clinical information systems, healthcare providers use another array of systems that facilitate the business part of healthcare organisations. This is not any different from other industries (Anderson et al. 2006).

Investing in IS/IT for health care is not limited to healthcare organisations on a meso level. Today, governments around the world are deploying initiatives on a macro level to leverage the possibilities of IS/IT nationally. These initiatives have different names in different countries but are all centred on providing so-called e-health. While this term has been used widely to describe digitized healthcare delivery on a national level, the literature has different definitions of this term (Oh et al. 2005). However, all of these definitions are centred on leveraging IS/IT to provide care. For example, Eysenbach (2001, p. 4) defines e-health as

> an emerging field in the intersection of medical informatics, public health, and business, referring to health services and information delivered or enhanced through the Internet and related technologies. In a broader sense, the term characterizes not only a technical development, but also a state-of-mind, a way of thinking, an attitude, and a commitment for networked, global thinking, to improve health care locally, regionally, and worldwide by using information and communication technology.

Different countries have different structures of their e-health initiatives (Troshani and Wickramasinghe 2016), such as the National Program for IT in the UK (Greenhalgh and Keen 2013; Waterson 2014), the Electronic Health Card (eHC) in Germany (Muhammad et al. 2013b; Wirtz et al. 2012), and Australia's My Health Record (Andrews et al. 2014; Muhammad and Wickramasinghe 2014).

These increasing investments in health IS/IT have created numerous studies to evaluate the impact of these investments on the different levels of healthcare delivery (Chaudhry et al. 2006; Das et al. 2011). The following section focuses on a holistic literature review regarding the business value of IT in general and then delineating this concept to cover the healthcare domain.

Table 10.2 The most popular clinical IS/IT in today's clinical practices. Adapted from (HIMSS 2013; HIMSS Analytics 2009)

IS system	Definition/description
Clinical data repository (CDR)	A centralised database that allows organisations to collect, store, access, and report on clinical, administrative, and financial information collected from various applications within or across the healthcare organisation that provides healthcare organisations with an open environment for accessing/viewing, managing, and reporting enterprise information
Clinical decision support systems (CDSS)	An application that uses pre-established rules and guidelines that can be created and edited by the healthcare organisation and integrates clinical data from several sources to generate alerts and treatment suggestions Example: All patients who have potassium below 2.5 mg% should not have a cardiac glycoside. The physician would enter into the system the prescription for a cardiac glycoside, and the system would pop up an alert to the fact that the patient should not be given this medicine due to the low level of potassium in their blood
Computerised practitioner order entry (CPOE)	An order entry application specifically designed to assist clinical practitioners in creating and managing medical orders for inpatient acute care services or medications. This application has a particular electronic signature, workflow, and rules engine functions that reduce or eliminate medical errors associated with practitioner ordering processes. It is a computer application that accepts the provider's orders for diagnostic and treatment services electronically instead of the clinician recording them on an orders sheet or prescription pad
Laboratory information systems (LIS)	An application to streamline the process management of the laboratory for essential services such as haematology and chemistry. This application may provide general functional support for microbiology reporting, but does not generally support blood bank functions. It provides an automatic interface to laboratory analytical instruments to transfer verified results to nurse stations, chart carts, and remote physician offices. The module allows the user to receive orders from any designated location, process the order, and report results and maintain technical, statistical, and account information. It eliminates tedious paperwork, calculations, and written documentation while allowing for easy retrieval of data and statistics
Nursing documentation (ND)	This software documents nursing notes that describe the care or service. Health records may be paper documents or electronic documents, such as electronic medical records, faxes, emails, audio or videotapes, and images. Through documentation, nurses communicate their observations, decisions, actions, and outcomes of these actions for clients. Documentation software tracks what occurred and when it occurred
Order entry (OE)	A legacy HIS application that allows for entry of orders from multiple sites including nursing stations, selected ancillary departments, and other service areas allows viewing of single and composite results for each patient order. The function creates billing records as a by-product of the order entry function

(continued)

Table 10.2 (continued)

IS system	Definition/description
Pharmacy management system (PMS)	An application that provides complete support for the pharmacy department from an operational, clinical, and management perspective, helping to optimise patient safety, streamline workflow, and reduce operational costs. It also allows the pharmacist to enter and fill physician orders and, as a by-product, performs all of the related functions of patient charging, general ledger updating, resupply scheduling, and inventory reduction/statistics maintenance. During order entry, the module automatically checks for drug-drug and food-drug interactions and monitors for allergy contraindications. Maintenance of an on-line patient medication profile allows easy access by the pharmacist and may be viewed by nursing stations, ancillary departments, and physicians
Physician documentation (PD)	The use of structured template documentation by physicians to capture any of their patient findings that are part of the electronic medical record (e.g. history and physicals, diagnostic findings, discharge notes, etc.). The structured template documentation captures discreet data that is used for interaction with the clinical decision support system relative to evidence-based medicine guidelines and/or protocols
Radiology information system (RIS)	An automated RIS system manages the operations and services of the radiology department. This functionality includes scheduling, patient and image tracking, and the rapid retrieval of diagnostic reports. The RIS can be integrated with the hospital information system and a picture archiving and communication system (PACS) to provide an efficient environment for users to collect, process, and manage data

10.2.2 The Business Value of IT in Health Care

The health informatics literature is relatively new (Dalrymple 2011). In the past decade, the healthcare industry has started to invest heavily in various health IS/IT programs to enhance the quality of care and control the escalating costs. These two aspects have been among the major criteria to be addressed by health informatics researchers (Jones et al. 2014). Today, there exists a plethora of studies that investigate the impact of IS/IT on specific aspects of healthcare delivery such as patient outcomes (e.g. Goldzweig et al. 2013; Tucker et al. 2014), patient safety (e.g. Farley et al. 2013; Middleton et al. 2013), quality of care (e.g. Kellermann and Jones 2013), the efficiency of healthcare delivery operations (e.g. Goldzweig et al. 2013; Lee 2013), and the cost of these operations (e.g. Balabanova et al. 2013). The majority of the reviewed studies, however, share two types of limitations: (1) they tend to study specific systems and their impacts on a particular output. Therefore, their results are not easily generalisable, and (2) most of these studies lack the adoption of sociotechnical aspects to cover the different levels of healthcare delivery, making their findings questionable, especially when issues around patient outcomes and safety are of concern (Haddad et al. 2014a).

Furthermore, a considerable portion of the current studies on the impact of IS/IT in health care tended to be vague in terms of specifying the examined IS/IT (Haddad et al. 2015), which also raises questions about the usefulness of these studies and their findings. For example, Frimpong et al. (2013) examined the relationship between 'health information technology capacity' and quality of care in 776 federally qualified health centres (FQHCs) in the USA. The study found a positive association between health information technology capacity and quality of care in terms of receipt of discharge summaries, the use of a patient notification system for preventive and follow-up care, and timely appointment for specialty care. The problem with these findings is the lack of analysis to show which IS/IT in the studied centres helped enhance and those that did not enhance the quality of care.

Similarly, Lee et al. (2013) studied the relationship between 'health information systems' and cost in 577 US hospitals. Using structural equation modelling, they found that 'health information systems' were negatively but not statistically significantly associated with the hospitals' total expenses. The major flaw this study shares with many other studies is being generic, and the examined IS/IT systems were not specified (Chaudhry et al. 2006; Lee et al. 2013).

This lack of IS/IT system specificity is a flaw that has represented a gap in the current health IS/IT literature and which has encouraged some researchers to conduct studies that address this limitation by adopting classifications of health IS/IT according to varied criteria. For example, Menon et al. (2000) analysed the impact of IT in a healthcare setting using a longitudinal sample of hospital data from 1976 to 1994 in the USA by classifying hospitals' IS/IT into three components: IT capital, medical capital, and medical information technology capital. IT capital included data processing and communication capital (mainly for administrative purposes) (Menon et al. 2000). Medical information technology capital included equipment used for diagnosis and therapeutic purposes, i.e. to collect data from patients or report information to medical personnel (e.g. X-ray machines, magnetic resonance imaging, etc.). Medical capital consisted of equipment used solely for therapeutic purposes (e.g. improvements in acute care wards or lasers). Labour was also classified into two components: medical and IT labour (Menon et al. 2000). The results obtained from this study showed that both IT and medical IT capital exhibited a positive influence on output. In addition, results indicated that IT labour and medical labour exhibited a positive influence on output as well as a positive impact on mean marginal revenue (Menon et al. 2000).

Similar to prior research that aggregates across various types of capital, this study is subject to problems that occur when the productivity impacts of different information technologies are averaged (Williams et al. 2011). Furthermore, hospitals today are way faster in adopting new IS/IT compared to the time this study was conducted (Maklan et al. 2015).

In another study, Das et al. (2010) developed a framework that disaggregates investments in IT in the healthcare industry into four categories: investments in patient management IT (PMIT), transactional support IT (TSIT), communications IT (CIT), and administrative IT (AIT). This study investigated two problems related to the effect of IT investments on productivity in a healthcare setting (as a branch of the tree of service industry)—the lag (i.e. when the effect is observed, which can be immediate, i.e. near term or late) and the durability (i.e. duration of the effect, which can be short or long term). The authors of this paper concluded that investing in IT in a healthcare setting was associated with improvements in several performance measures, with their model also revealing the types of healthcare IT investments that have an immediate effect and those that have a later effect (Das et al. 2010).

Although this study claims IS/IT investments were classified into four 'distinct' categories, their findings have two limitations. Firstly, it ignored the need for a socio-technical perspective (Muhammad et al. 2013a) when examining the role of health IS/IT in enhancing the organisational performance in favour of economic value, lag, and duration. Secondly, the four categories of health IS/IT cover non-clinical IS/IT, leaving the complexity of examining the role of clinical IS/IT neglected (Haddad et al. 2014a).

Furthermore, the majority of the current literature examines different IS/IT apart from their business objectives, which raises questions about their findings and how valid they are to be used in various contexts (Kumar et al. 2008; Weill and Woerner 2013). This gap was the reason for adopting the IT Portfolio of Weill and Broadbent (1998) as one of the theoretical bases for this research.

In addition, the current literature shows contradictory results from different studies on the impact of IS/IT on different outputs such as quality of care, patient safety, patient outcomes, cost, and efficiency (Chaudhry et al. 2006; Jones et al. 2014). Not only do these results call for a deeper examination of the business value of IS/IT in health care, but they also mirror the need for developing a comprehensive framework that takes the contextual conditions into consideration when investigating the impact of IS/IT on the organisational performance of healthcare providers.

10.2.3 Value in Health Care

Given the difficulties faced by different healthcare systems around the world, many initiatives have been established to support the move to adopting value-based care delivery systems (Kaplan and Witkowski 2014; Kawamoto et al. 2015; Rotar et al. 2016). Particularly, creating rational approaches to lessen healthcare cost growth and enhancing the centredness of healthcare procedures around patients has been shown as an essential step to building such value-based healthcare systems (CMS 2013; OECD 2010). In addition, one of the predominant perceptions with value-based health care is identifying and encouraging care delivery patterns that are not only of higher quality but also more cost-efficient (CMS 2013). The current state of care delivery, though, tends to be on the other side in many cases, i.e. delivering care of poorer quality at higher costs (Wilson et al. 2016).

Porter (2010) and Porter et al. (2013) expound that lacking a precise definition of 'value' in health care and adopting it is the central dilemma that has been challenging the efforts to enhance healthcare outcomes. Instead of adopting such a definition to guide different initiatives to reform healthcare systems, these initiatives have used other aspects such as economic measures like profitability and cost containment (Blumenthal and Jena 2013; VanLare and Conway 2012), safety (Chatterjee et al. 2012), patient experience (Hibbard et al. 2012), and quality (OECD 2010). The problem with adopting different goals in health care is that they cannot be used as a reliable indicator of value in health care because of flawed reimbursement and lack of competition based on actual results (Porter 2010, p. 2480).

It is important to emphasise that the business value of IT is not a value by itself; rather, it is a model that suggests the value that might be generated by implementing specific IS/IT solutions (Haddad et al. 2014a, p. 78).

10.3 The Business Value of IT in Healthcare Model

This section presents the business value of IT in healthcare model as developed in this research. Firstly, the theoretical underpinnings are presented followed by the model itself.

10.3.1 Theoretical Underpinnings

This section presents the theoretical foundations used in this study, namely, the IT Portfolio (Weill and Broadbent 1998) and the Enterprise of Health Delivery (Rouse and Cortese 2010).

10.3.1.1 IT Portfolio

Weill and Broadbent (1998) argue that IT in the service industry is the production technology, i.e. the equivalent of the machine tools and production lines of manufacturing. They define IT in this setting as:

> A firm's total investments in computing and communications technology. This includes hardware, software, telecommunications, the myriad of devices for collecting and representing data, all electronically stored data, and the people dedicated to providing these services (human resources). That includes information technology investments implemented by internal groups (insourced), and those outsources by other providers. The sum of these investments is viewed as the information technology portfolio, which must be managed like a financial portfolio, balancing risks and returns to meet management goals strategies for customer and shareholders. (p. 6)

Principally, firms invest in IT to achieve four fundamentally different management objectives: transactional, infrastructure, informational, and strategic. These management objectives then lead to informational, transactional, infrastructural, and strategic

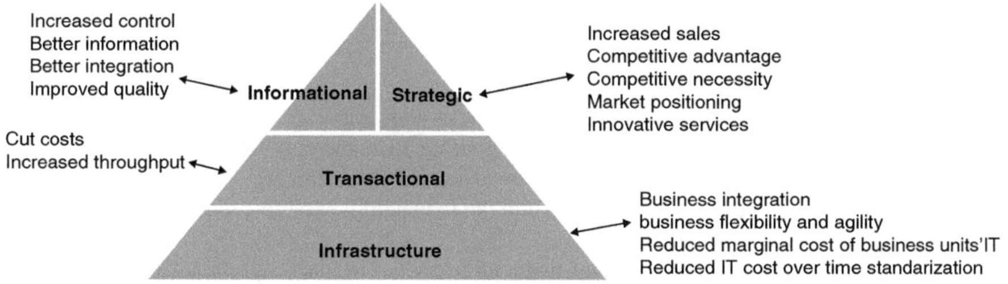

Fig. 10.1 The IT Portfolio model, adapted from (Weill and Broadbent 1998)

systems, which make up the information technology investment portfolio (Weill and Broadbent 1998). Figure 10.1 depicts these different management objectives and their relationships as they form the information technology portfolio.

The four categories of IT investments have unique characteristics and are used differently in different contexts and industries (Weill and Broadbent 1998). Table 10.3 briefly describes the objectives of these four categories of IT investments.

The underpinning theory states that the use of information technology in a firm is governed by a set of rules and policies, which is called 'information technology architecture' (Weill and Broadbent 1998). One of the main roles of this architecture is to draw the path to the way business will be done in both the near and far futures. This architecture is not expected to give rules of decision-making; rather, it provides the technical guidelines for the decision-making process (Weill and Broadbent 1998). This architecture, which needs to be dynamic and subject to regular reviews, is necessary for a firm-wide infrastructure to:

- Achieve compatibility among various systems
- Specify the policies and mechanics for delivering the information technology strategy
- Describe the technological model of the organisation
- Cut through multivendor chaos and move towards vendor independence (Weill and Broadbent 1998, p. 15)

According to this model, the ultimate objective of information technology is to provide business value in two related ways: to successfully implement current strategies and to use the technology to enable new strategies (Weill and Broadbent 1998). The alignment between information technology portfolio and strategy is tough, as they fundamentally have different characteristics. There is enough evidence of better payoff of the information technology investments if well aligned with business strategies (Weill and Broadbent 1998). This alignment, however, is hard to achieve and maintain, due to the constantly changed business circumstances (Weill and Broadbent 1998). Nevertheless, each unique strategic context leads to different strategic objectives and different types of information technology portfolios. Thus, a firm's information technology capabilities are a top management responsibility (Weill and Broadbent 1998). As the size of investments in IT and the strategic role it may play make investing in IT a very challenging business decision,

Table 10.3 The objectives of the IT Portfolio model, adapted from (Weill and Broadbent 1998, pp. 26–28)

Objectives	Description
Infrastructure	• The foundation of information technology capacity which is delivered as reliable services shared throughout the firm and coordinated centrally, usually by the information technology group (IT Department) • Include both the technical and the managerial expertise required to provide reliable services • Having the required infrastructure services in place significantly increases the speed with which new applications can be implemented to meet new strategies, thus increasing the firm's strategic agility and flexibility
Transactional	• Process and automate the basic, repetitive transactions of the firm. These include systems that support order processing, inventory control, bank cash withdrawal, statement production, account receivable, accounts payable, and other transactional processing • Transactional systems aim to cut costs by substituting capital for labour or to handle higher volumes of transactions with greater speed and less unit cost. These systems build on and depend on a reliable infrastructure capacity
Informational	• Provide information for managing and controlling the firm • Systems in this category typically support management control, decision-making, communication, and accounting. These systems can summarize and report this firm's product and process performance across a wide range of areas • Two examples of these systems come from Ford Australia (Electronic Corporate Memory) and from the consulting firm Bain & Company which developed Bain Resources Access for Value Addition (BRAVA)
Strategic	• The objective of strategic technology investments is quite different from those of the other parts of the portfolio • Strategic investments are made to gain competitive advantage or to position the firm in the marketplace, most often by increasing market share or sales • Firms with successful strategic information technology initiatives have usually found a new use of information technology for an industry at a particular point in time • Two good examples of theses strategic initiatives are inventing automatic teller machines (ATMs) and designing a system that provides immediate 24-hour, 7-day-a-week loan approvals in car dealerships using expert systems technology. Both of these innovative systems have changed their industries forever

these are far too important to be left to the technical people or, worse, to outsource these resources to third parties or sub-contractors with their own business objectives (Weill and Broadbent 1998).

The use of this classification to be one of the theoretical underpinnings of this study is justified by the need to avoid one of the biggest flaws in the current health information systems literature (Haddad et al. 2014a, b). That is, approaching different IS/IT from a heterogeneous perspective, i.e. generalising the findings from evaluating specific information systems to all other information systems that have different business objectives (Berg 1999; Eysenbach et al. 2002; Haddad et al. 2015).

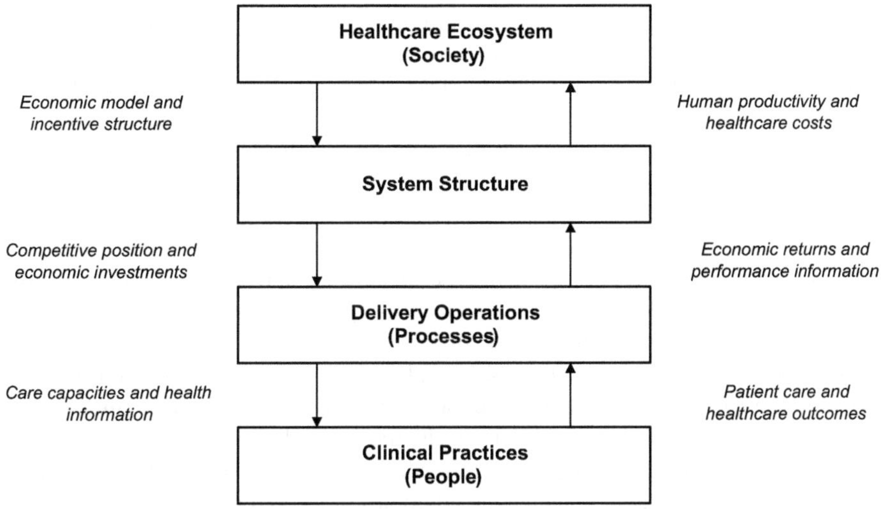

Fig. 10.2 The enterprise of healthcare delivery, adapted from (Rouse and Cortese 2010)

10.3.1.2 The Enterprise of Healthcare Delivery

The second theoretical basis of this study is the Enterprise of Healthcare Delivery by Rouse and Cortese (2010). In their book *Engineering the System of Healthcare Delivery*, Rouse and Cortese propose an architecture of the enterprise of healthcare delivery as shown in Fig. 2.6. According to this architecture, the healthcare delivery consists of four main layers:

- *The Healthcare Ecosystem*: Covers the society of the healthcare organisations from a macro perspective
- *The System Structure*: Meant to cover the healthcare organisations on a meso level
- *The Delivery Operations*: Covers different stages of healthcare delivery from detection to recovery on a micro level
- *The Clinical Practices*: Covers different clinical practices within healthcare organisations that target people from a functional perspective

These four layers are interrelated in a way that the efficiencies can be gained at the lowest level and are limited by the nature of the next level (Fig. 10.2). For example, functionally organised practices are much less efficient than delivery organised around processes. Similarly, the efficiencies that can be gained in operations are limited by the level above (system structure). Functional operations are driven by organisations structured around specialties, e.g. anaesthesiology and radiology. Furthermore, efficiencies in system structures are limited by the healthcare ecosystem in which healthcare organisations operate (Rouse and Cortese 2010).

According to this model, the interaction between different sequential levels is bidirectional. For example, prudent clinical practices positively affect the delivery operations from patient care and healthcare outcome perspectives, and good delivery operations serve to provide higher care capabilities and better health information to clinical practices (Rouse and Cortese 2010). At the same time, these good delivery operations help create economic returns and usable performance information, while well-structured healthcare organisations help delivery operations take competitive positions and benefit from firms' investments' portfolios (Rouse and Cortese 2010).

The use of this framework to support this study is justified by the potential of this model to cover the sociotechnical aspects of healthcare delivery. Looking at healthcare delivery from this perspective is an increasingly used and needed approach to evaluating health information systems, in particular with the increasing recognition of the importance of the interaction between human, social, and organisational contexts and the role it plays to determine the success or failure of health information systems (Aarts et al. 2010). In other words, the interrelation between technology and its social environment is crucial to evaluating the role of health information technology that can play to enhance the outcomes of the healthcare delivery in general, either on a macro level such as national e-health initiatives (Muhammad et al. 2013a, b; Waterson 2014) or on a meso and/or micro level (Singh et al. 2013; Westbrook et al. 2007).

10.3.2 Developing the Conceptual Framework

The model builds on two prior structures: the first is the theory of IT Portfolio by Weill and Broadbent (1998), who classified IT investments into infrastructural, transactional, strategic, and informational. This classification is based on their business objectives. The second is the model of the Enterprise of Healthcare Delivery by Rouse and Cortese (2010), which covers the sociotechnical aspects of the healthcare delivery. This includes the healthcare ecosystem (society), system structure (organisation), delivery operations (processes), and clinical practices (people) (Rouse and Cortese 2010). In addition, the conceptual mode of this study is based on a rigorous literature review to cover different aspects of healthcare delivery (Fichman and Melville 2014; Kohli and Grover 2008; Maklan et al. 2015; Melville et al. 2004; Melville and McQuaid 2012; Ramirez et al. 2010). The following subsections serve to explain the elements of the conceptual model.

10.3.2.1 Healthcare Ecosystem (Society)

Healthcare intervention is complex and typically involves a multiplicity of factors that might be conceptualised as a web of healthcare players (Wickramasinghe and Schaffer 2010). These players together form the health ecosystem (Fig. 10.3). By analogy with natural life ecosystem, Serbanati, Ricci, Mercurio, and Vasilateanu (2011, p. 628) defined a health ecosystem as '*the network of a multitude of agents:*

Fig. 10.3 Healthcare ecosystem, adapted from (Wickramasinghe and Schaffer 2010)

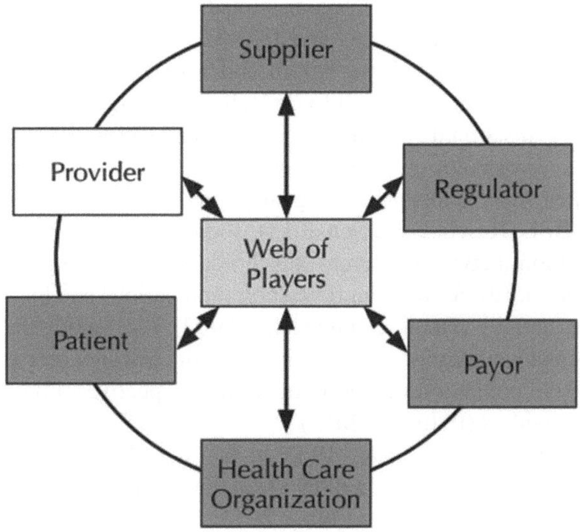

care providers (physicians, nurses, pharmacists, and other health professionals), health suppliers, together with their organisations and information systems, care consumers, plus the socio-economic environment and including the health institutional and regulatory frameworks'.

Digitizing the concept of ecosystem enables the dynamic networking of the organisations, which, in turn, drives the dynamic cooperation of the players on the territory and the connection of the resources in a system, resulting in a community that shares business, knowledge, and infrastructures (Nachira 2002). It is a self-organising digital infrastructure aimed at creating a digital environment for networked organisations that support the cooperation, the knowledge sharing, and the development of open and adaptive technologies and evolutionary business models (Serbanati et al. 2011). In order to achieve the cooperation and knowledge sharing among the components of the health ecosystem, relevant data, pertinent information, and knowledge can be obtained only via the prudent structure and design of technology (von Lubitz and Wickramasinghe 2006; Wickramasinghe 2007; Wickramasinghe et al. 2006).

10.3.2.2 System Structure (Organisation)

The evolution of technology during the last few decades has caused tremendous changes in the organisational structures of healthcare organisations (Dahlgren and Cokus 2007). Traditional hierarchical constructs no longer exist, at least in practice (Eybers et al. 2013). The use of IS/IT to reshape organisational structures began with the use of voice communications (telephone) and then started to evolve using high-speed data lines and facsimiles, which in turn opened the door to the use of computers and related technologies like e-mail, Internet, intranet, extranet, etc. in the different levels of organisational processes. The amount of information generated by these technologies and the ease of information sharing (in theory) between different stakeholders within and across organisations, coupled with other social changes since the World War II, have had significant influences on the conventional organisational structures (Dahlgren and Cokus 2007).

The evolution of information technology to information systems is still playing key roles in reshaping organisational processes or business process improvement (BPI) (Raschke and Sen 2013). Today, BPI projects aim at achieving better collaborations between different stakeholders, higher integration between the various levels of operations, and improved communications and knowledge sharing internally and externally (Dahlgren and Cokus 2007). Facilitating these projects is one of the principal justifications of more investments and spending on IS/IT nowadays, especially from collaboration and integration perspectives, both within and among healthcare providers (Laliberte 2012).

The trend of using IS/IT to facilitate BPI initiatives has created an interest in measuring the impact of IS/IT on the organisational structures in different industries (Bank 2015; Pope and Mays 2013). The lack of clear frameworks and measurement for their impacts on the organisational structures, and acutely in health care, has caused the majority of these projects to fail (Business Process Improvements 2011), which necessitates the design of a framework that is capable of measuring the mutual impacts of IS/IT and organisational structures (Raschke and Sen 2013).

10.3.2.3 Delivery Operations (Processes)

A typical care cycle consists of four interrelated processes: detection, diagnosis, treatment, and recovery (Rouse 2009). Each stage utilises both labour and technological resources (Fig. 10.4). In order to reduce healthcare delivery costs, IS/IT has been shown as a 'labour eliminator' in all of these four stages. For example, web-based scheduling and account management can enable patients to substitute their labour for that of providers, as has been experienced in the airline, banking, and retail industries. Adopting information technology in this area could result in better care, greater patient satisfaction, and lower cost (Rouse 2009).

The above suggested the use of information technology instead of labour is limited to transactional IT, whose primary concern is to perform repetitive duties online instead of communicating with human resources (labour). This trend can be found in different industries, such as banking and manufacturing, and is not limited to the healthcare contexts (Weill and Broadbent 1998). However, the use of IS/IT to handle more complex processes within the care cycle may be prone to risk (Jones et al. 2014). Given the use of IS/IT in the operationalisation of the actual care delivery has potential impacts and risks at the time. Thus, a comprehensive framework to assess the impact of different IS/IT on the different stages of care delivery is crucial.

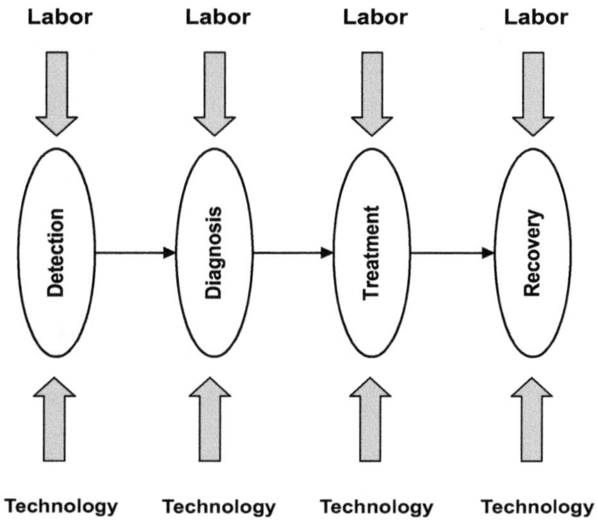

Fig. 10.4 Four stages of care cycle, adapted from (Rouse 2009)

10.3.2.4 Clinical Practices (People)

Nowadays, electronic medical records (EMRs) and electronic medical administration records (eMAR) are the most popular emerging clinical IS/IT in the healthcare industry. HIMSS (2013, p. ii) defines an EMR as a '*longitudinal electronic record of patient health information generated by one or more encounters in any care delivery setting. Included in this information are patient demographics, progress notes, problems, and medications, vital signs, past medical history, immunizations, laboratory data and radiology reports*'.

EMRs and eMAR have been in use for more than 20 years (Ilie et al. 2007; Park et al. 2014), and they are gradually replacing the paper-based medical and administration records. Today, EMRs as enterprise systems are not only integrating most of the departments within a healthcare provider but also creating an integrative environment between different healthcare providers. In doing so, EMRs use a compilation of clinical practices, such as clinical data repositories (CDR), clinical decision support systems (CDSS), laboratory information systems (LIS), nursing documentation (ND) systems, order entry (OE), pharmacy management systems (PMS), physician documentation (PD), and radiology information systems (RIS). A summary of these systems and their definitions and functions were presented in Sect. 10.2 (Information Systems for Health Care).

In combining the two models (IT Portfolio and the Enterprises of Healthcare Delivery) with the literature review conducted to cover the different aspects of healthcare delivery, the conceptual model of this study is shown in Fig. 10.5.

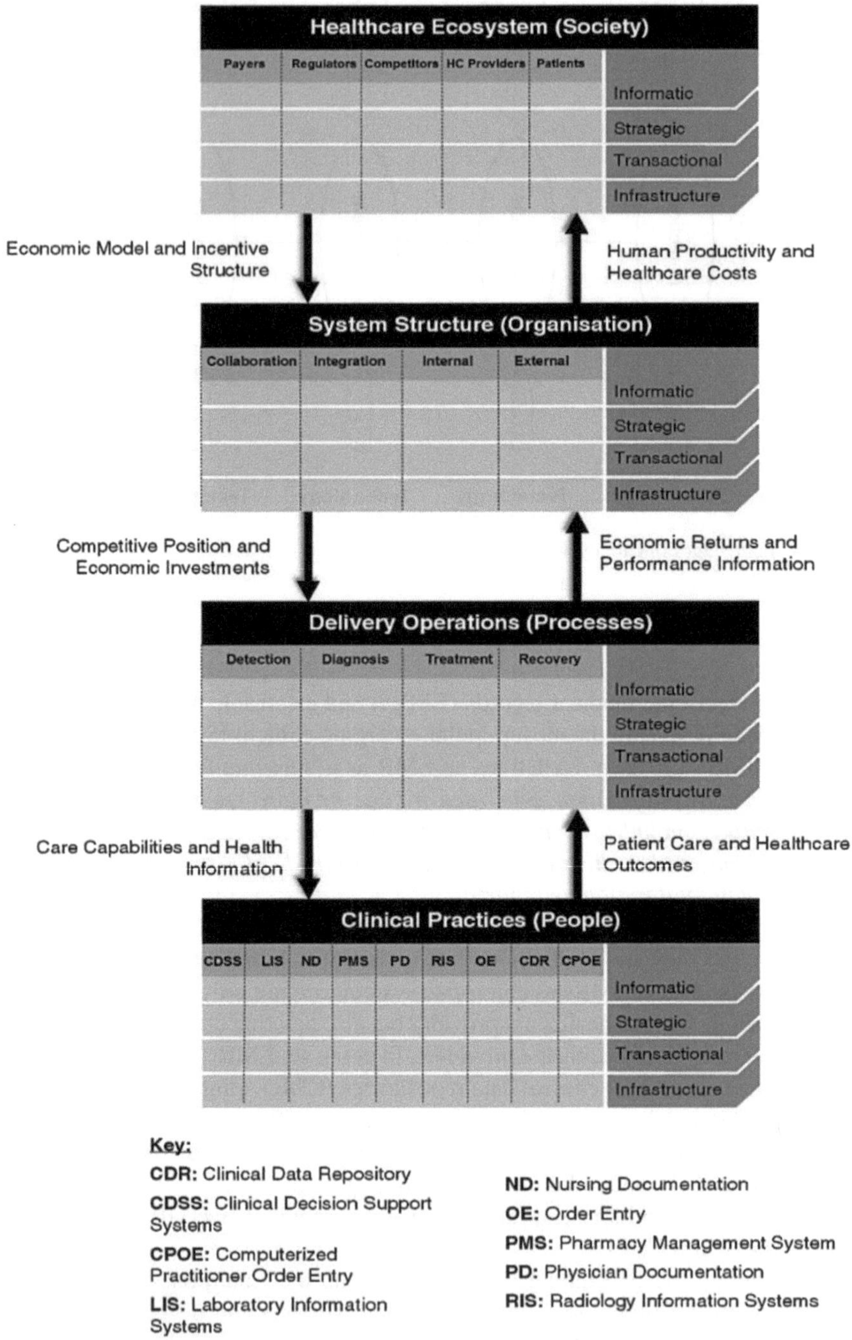

Fig. 10.5 The conceptual mode of the research: the BVIT in healthcare model

10.4 Summary

This chapter has discussed different issues pertaining to the business value of IT in health care. It started with giving an overview of the challenges facing healthcare delivery systems globally, the increasing costs and pressures to improve patients' outcomes and quality of care. These problems have encouraged policy- and decision-makers to adopt IS/IT, which was also discussed in this chapter. Following this increased use of IS/IT in health care, the impacts of these costly investments have started to be questioned. This was covered in the third section of this chapter. In order to help answer some of the questions on the business value of IS/IT in health care, this study develops a conceptual model that takes into consideration two points: the first is the need of a prudent classification of IS/IT based on their business/management objectives, and the second is the need for sociotechnical lenses to examine the healthcare domain. These two points clearly represent a current void in the health IS literature. The two models that serve to provide these platforms were discussed in this chapter. Then, the different levels and elements of the conceptual model of this study were presented in details.

The literature review has shown a clear evidence that a comprehensive conceptual model to evaluate the business value of IT in health care is crucial, in particular with the notable trend to invest heavily in health IS/IT with little to show for it in the output.

References

(IDC), I. D. C. (2016). Worldwide semiannual IT spending guide: Vertical and company size [Press release].

Aarts, J., Callen, J., Coiera, E., & Westbrook, J. (2010). Information technology in health care: Socio-technical approaches (Vol. 79, pp. 389–390).

Anderson, G. F., Frogner, B. K., Johns, R. A., & Reinhardt, U. E. (2006). Health care spending and use of information technology in OECD countries. *Health Affairs, 25*(3), 819–831.

Andrews, L., Gajanayake, R., & Sahama, T. (2014). The Australian general public's perceptions of having a personally controlled electronic health record (PCEHR). *International Journal of Medical Informatics, 83*(12), 889–900.

Appari, A., Carian, E. K., Johnson, M. E., & Anthony, D. L. (2012). Focus on health information technology, electronic health records and their financial impact: Medication administration quality and health information technology: A national study of US hospitals. *Journal of the American Medical Informatics Association: JAMIA, 19*(3), 360.

Balabanova, D., Mills, A., Conteh, L., Akkazieva, B., Banteyerga, H., Dash, U., et al. (2013). Good health at low cost 25 years on: Lessons for the future of health systems strengthening. *The Lancet, 381*(9883), 2118–2133.

Bank, T. W. (2015). World Health Organization Global Health Expenditure database. Retrieved 17/05/2015, from The World Bank http://data.worldbank.org/indicator/SH.XPD.TOTL.ZS

Berg, M. (1999). Patient care information systems and health care work: A sociotechnical approach. *International Journal of Medical Informatics, 55*(2), 87–101. https://doi.org/10.1016/S1386-5056(99)00011-8

Blumenthal, D., & Jena, A. B. (2013). Hospital value-based purchasing. *Journal of Hospital Medicine, 8*(5), 271–277.

Brenner, S. K., Kaushal, R., Grinspan, Z., Joyce, C., Kim, I., Allard, R. J., et al. (2015). Effects of health information technology on patient outcomes: A systematic review. *Journal of the American Medical Informatics Association: JAMIA, 23*(5), 1016–1036.

Business Process Improvements. (2011). Business Process Improvement (BPI) projects – the top ten reasons why they often end in failure [Press release]. Retrieved from https://www.newswire.com/business-process-improvement-bpi/103958

Chatterjee, P., Joynt, K. E., Orav, E. J., & Jha, A. K. (2012). Patient experience in safety-net hospitals: Implications for improving care and value-based purchasing. *Archives of Internal Medicine, 172*(16), 1204–1210.

Chaudhry, B., Wang, J., Wu, S., Maglione, M., Mojica, W., Roth, E., et al. (2006). Systematic review: Impact of health information technology on quality, efficiency, and costs of medical care. *Annals of Internal Medicine, 144*(10), 742–752. https://doi.org/10.7326/0003-4819-144-10-200605160-00125

CMS. (2013). Roadmap for implementing value driven healthcare in the traditional Medicare fee-for-service program: Centers for Medicare & Medicaid Services.

Dahlgren, J. W., & Cokus, M. S. (2007). Real options and flexibility in organizational design (pp. 1–7).

Dalrymple, P. W. (2011). Data, information, knowledge: The emerging field of health informatics (Feature). *Bulletin of the American Society for Information Science and Technology, 37*(5), 41.

Das, S., Yaylacicegi, U., & Menon, N. M. (2010). The effect of information technology investments in healthcare: A longitudinal study of its lag, duration, and economic value. *IEEE Transactions on Engineering Management, 58*(1), 124–140. https://doi.org/10.1109/TEM.2010.2048906

Das, S., Yaylacicegi, U., & Menon, N. M. (2011). The effect of information technology investments in healthcare: A longitudinal study of its lag, duration, and economic value. *IEEE Transactions on Engineering Management, 58*(1), 124–140. https://doi.org/10.1109/TEM.2010.2048906

DesRoches, C. M., Charles, D., Furukawa, M. F., Joshi, M. S., Kralovec, P., Mostashari, F., et al. (2013). Adoption of electronic health records grows rapidly, but fewer than half of US hospitals had at least a basic system in 2012. *Health Affairs*, https://doi.org/10.1377/hlthaff.2013.0308

Elliott, R. A., Putman, K., Franklin, M., Verhaeghe, N., Annemans, L., Eden, M., et al. (2013). *Economic evaluation of a pharmacist-led IT-based intervention with simple feedback in reducing rates of clinically important errors in medicines management in general practices (PINCER)*. Birmingham: Department of Health Patient Safety Research Portfolio, University of Birmingham.

Eybers, S., Kroeze, J. H., & Strydom, I. (2013). Towards a classification framework of business intelligence value research. *Italian Chapter of AIS (itAIS 2013)*.

Eysenbach, G. (2001). What is e-health? *Journal of Medical Internet Research, 3*(2), e20. https://doi.org/10.2196/jmir.3.2.e20

Eysenbach, G., Powell, J., Kuss, O., & Sa, E. (2002). Empirical studies assessing the quality of health information for consumers on the world wide web: A systematic review. *JAMA, 287*(20), 2691–2700. https://doi.org/10.1001/jama.287.20.2691

Farley, H. L., Baumlin, K. M., Hamedani, A. G., Cheung, D. S., Edwards, M. R., Fuller, D. C., et al. (2013). Quality and safety implications of emergency department information systems. *Annals of Emergency Medicine, 62*(4), 399–407.

Fichman, R. G., & Melville, N. P. (2014). How posture-profile misalignment in IT innovation diminishes returns: Conceptual development and empirical demonstration. *Journal of Management Information Systems*, 31(1), 203–240. https://doi.org/10.2753/MIS0742-1222310109

Freedman, S., Lin, H., & Prince, J. (2014). Information technology and patient health: An expanded analysis of outcomes, populations, and mechanisms. *Social Science Research Network SSRN Scholarly Paper ID, 2445431*.

Frimpong, J. A., Jackson, B. E., Stewart, L. M., Singh, K. P., Rivers, P. A., & Bae, S. (2013). Health information technology capacity at federally qualified health centers: A mechanism for improving quality of care. *BMC Health Services Research, 13*(1), 1.

Frisse, M. E., Johnson, K. B., Nian, H., Davison, C. L., Gadd, C. S., Unertl, K. M., et al. (2012). The financial impact of health information exchange on emergency department care. *Journal of the American Medical Informatics Association, 19*(3), 328–333.

Gartner, I. (2015). Gartner says worldwide IT Spending across vertical industries to decline 3.5 percent in 2015 [Press release].

Georgiou, A., Lang, S., Rosenfeld, D., & Westbrook, J. (2011). The use of computerized provider order entry to improve the effectiveness and efficiency of coagulation testing. *Archives of Pathology & Laboratory Medicine, 135*(4), 495–498.

Goldzweig, C. L., Orshansky, G., Paige, N. M., Towfigh, A. A., Haggstrom, D. A., Miake-Lye, I., et al. (2013). Electronic patient portals: Evidence on health outcomes, satisfaction, efficiency, and attitudes: A systematic review. *Annals of Internal Medicine, 159*(10), 677–687.

Greenhalgh, T., & Keen, J. (2013). England's national programme for IT. *British Medical Journal, 346*, f4130.

Haddad, P., Gregory, M., & Wickramasinghe, N. (2014a). Business value of IT in healthcare. In L. Al-Hakim, C. Gonzalez, N. Wickramasinghe, & T. Joseph (Eds.), *Lean thinking for healthcare*. New York: Springer.

Haddad, P., Gregory, M., & Wickramasinghe, N. (2014b). Evaluating business value of IT in healthcare in australia: The case of an intelligent operational planning support tool solution. Paper presented at the Bled 2014.

Haddad, P., Schaffer, J., & Wickramasinghe, N. (2015). *Evaluating business value of IT in healthcare: Three clinical practices from Australia and the US*. Paper presented at the MEDINFO 2015: EHealth-enabled Health: Proceedings of the 15th World Congress on Health and Biomedical Informatics.

Haddad, P., & Wickramasinghe, N. (2014). *The role of IT governance in generating business value from IT investments in healthcare: Lessons from an Australian experience*. Paper presented at the Bled 2015, Bled, Slovenia.

Hibbard, J. H., Greene, J., Sofaer, S., Firminger, K., & Hirsh, J. (2012). An experiment shows that a well-designed report on costs and quality can help consumers choose high-value health care. *Health Affairs, 31*(3), 560–568.

HIMSS. (Ed.). (2013). HIMSS.

HIMSS Analytics. (2009). HIMSS analytic database definitions. Retrieved 10 June 2012, from HIMSS http://www.himssanalytics.org/hcproider/emradoption.asp

Ilie, V., Courtney, J. F., & Van Slyke, C. (2007). Paper versus electronic: Challenges associated with physicians' usage of electronic medical records.

Jones, S. S., Rudin, R. S., Perry, T., & Shekelle, P. G. (2014). Health information technology: An updated systematic review with a focus on meaningful use. *Annals of Internal Medicine, 160*(1), 48–54. https://doi.org/10.7326/M13-1531

Kaplan, R. S., & Witkowski, M. L. (2014). Better accounting transforms health care delivery. *Accounting Horizons, 28*(2), 365–383.

Kaushal, R., Shojania, K. G., & Bates, D. W. (2003). Effects of computerized physician order entry and clinical decision support systems on medication safety: A systematic review. *Archives of Internal Medicine, 163*(12), 1409–1416.

Kawamoto, K., Martin, C. J., Williams, K., Tu, M.-C., Park, C. G., Hunter, C., et al. (2015). Value driven outcomes (VDO): A pragmatic, modular, and extensible software framework for understanding and improving health care costs and outcomes. *Journal of the American Medical Informatics Association, 22*(1), 223–235.

Kellermann, A. L., & Jones, S. S. (2013). What it will take to achieve the as-yet-unfulfilled promises of health information technology. *Health Affairs, 32*(1), 63–68.

Kern, L. M., Wilcox, A., Shapiro, J., Dhopeshwarkar, R. V., & Kaushal, R. (2012). Which components of health information technology will drive financial value? *The American Journal of Managed Care, 18*(8), 438–445.

Kohli, R., & Grover, V. (2008). Business value of IT: An essay on expanding research directions to keep up with the times. *Journal of the Association for Information Systems, 9*(1), 23–28, 30–34, 36–39.

Kumar, R., Ajjan, H., & Niu, Y. (2008). Information technology portfolio management: Literature review, framework, and research issues. *Information Resources Management Journal, 21*(3), 64.

Laliberte, B. (2012). The most important consideration for justifying IT purchases in 2012 [Press release].

Lee, K., Wan, T. T., & Kwon, H. (2013). The relationship between healthcare information system and cost in hospital. *Personal and Ubiquitous Computing, 17*(7), 1395–1400.

Lee, T.-F. (2013). An efficient chaotic maps-based authentication and key agreement scheme using smartcards for telecare medicine information systems. *Journal of Medical Systems, 37*(6), 1–9.

Lippi, G., Brambilla, M., Bonelli, P., Aloe, R., Balestrino, A., Nardelli, A., et al. (2015). Effectiveness of a computerized alert system based on re-testing intervals for limiting the inappropriateness of laboratory test requests. *Clinical Biochemistry, 48*(16), 1174–1176.

Low, A., Phillips, A., Ancker, J., Patel, A., Kern, L., & Kaushal, R. (2013). Financial effects of health information technology: A systematic review. *The American Journal of Managed Care, 19(10 Spec No)*, SP369–SP376.

Maklan, S., Peppard, J., & Klaus, P. (2015). Show me the money. *European Journal of Marketing, 49*(3/4), 561.

McCoy, A. B., Waitman, L. R., Lewis, J. B., Wright, J. A., Choma, D. P., Miller, R. A., & Peterson, J. F. (2012). Focus on health information technology, electronic health records and their financial impact: A framework for evaluating the appropriateness of clinical decision support alerts and responses. *Journal of the American Medical Informatics Association: JAMIA, 19*(3), 346.

Melville, N., Kraemer, K., & Gurbaxani, V. (2004). Review: Information technology and organizational performance: An integrative model of IT business value. *MIS Quarterly, 28*(2), 283–322.

Melville, N., & McQuaid, M. (2012). Generating shareable statistical databases for business value: Multiple imputation with multimodal perturbation. *Information Systems Research, 23*(2), 559–574, 596.

Menon, N. M., Lee, B., & Eldenburg, L. (2000). Productivity of information systems in the healthcare industry. *Information Systems Research, 11*(1), 83–92.

Middleton, B., Bloomrosen, M., Dente, M. A., Hashmat, B., Koppel, R., Overhage, J. M., et al. (2013). Enhancing patient safety and quality of care by improving the usability of electronic health record systems: Recommendations from AMIA. *Journal of the American Medical Informatics Association, 20*(e1), e2–e8.

Muhammad, I., Teoh, S., & Wickramasinghe, N. (2013a). The need for a socio-technical analysis in E-health: The case of the PCEHR. *International Journal of E-Health and Medical Communications (IJEHMC), 4*(2), 65–79.

Muhammad, I., & Wickramasinghe, N. (2014). How an actor network theory (ANT) analysis can help us to understand the personally controlled electronic health record (PCEHR) in Australia. In *Technological Advancements and the Impact of Actor-Network Theory*, 15.

Muhammad, I., Zwicker, M., & Wickramasinghe, N. (2013b). *Using ANT to understand key issues for successful e-Health solutions*. Paper presented at the 46th Hawaii International Conference on System Sciences (HICSS).

Nachira, F. (2002). Toward a network ofdigital business ecosystems fosteringthe local development. Retrieved 15/12/2015, 2014, from http://www.digital-ecosystems.org/doc/discussionpaper.pdf

Nanji, K. C., Slight, S. P., Seger, D. L., Cho, I., Fiskio, J. M., Redden, L. M., et al. (2014). Overrides of medication-related clinical decision support alerts in outpatients. *Journal of the American Medical Informatics Association, 21*(3), 487–491.

Nguyen, L., Bakewell, L., Wickramasinghe, N., Haddad, P., Muhammad, I., Moghimi, H., et al. (2015). Transition from paper to electronic nursing documentation in residential aged care: An actor network theory analysis. *Electronic Journal of Health Informatics, 9*(1), 4.

Nuckols, T. K., Smith-Spangler, C., Morton, S. C., Asch, S. M., Patel, V. M., Anderson, L. J., et al. (2014). The effectiveness of computerized order entry at reducing preventable adverse drug events and medication errors in hospital settings: A systematic review and meta-analysis. *Systematic Reviews, 3*(1), 1.

Nurek, M., Kostopoulou, O., Delaney, B. C., & Esmail, A. (2015). Reducing diagnostic errors in primary care. A systematic meta-review of computerized diagnostic decision support systems by the LINNEAUS collaboration on patient safety in primary care. *European Journal of General Practice, 21*(sup1), 8–13.

OECD. (2010). *Improving value in health care*: OECD Publishing.

OECD. (2013). *Strengthening health information infrastructure for health care quality governance*: OECD Publishing.

Oh, H., Rizo, C., Enkin, M., & Jadad, A. (2005). What is eHealth (3): A systematic review of published definitions. *Journal of Medical Internet Research, 7*(1), e1. https://doi.org/10.2196/jmir.7.1.e1

Park, S. L., Parwani, A. V., & Pantanowitz, L. (2014). *Electronic medical records practical informatics for cytopathology* (pp. 121–127). New York: Springer.

Piette, J. D., Striplin, D., Marinec, N., Chen, J., Gregory, L. A., Sumerlin, D. L., et al. (2015). Improving post-hospitalization transition outcomes through accessible health information technology and caregiver support: Protocol for a randomized controlled trial. *Journal of Clinical Trials, 5*(5), 240.

Pope, C., & Mays, N. (2013). *Qualitative research in health care*. Hoboken: John Wiley & Sons.

Porter, M. (2010). What is value in health care? *The New England Journal of Medicine, 363*(26), 2477–2481. https://doi.org/10.1056/NEJMp1011024

Porter, M. E., Pabo, E. A., & Lee, T. H. (2013). Redesigning primary care: A strategic vision to improve value by organizing around patients' needs. *Health Affairs, 32*(3), 516–525.

Ramirez, R., Melville, N., & Lawler, E. (2010). Information technology infrastructure, organizational process redesign, and business value: An empirical analysis. *Decision Support Systems, 49*(4), 417–429. https://doi.org/10.1016/j.dss.2010.05.003

Raschke, R. L., & Sen, S. (2013). A value-based approach to the ex-ante evaluation of IT enabled business process improvement projects. *Information & Management, 50*(7), 446–456. https://doi.org/10.1016/j.im.2013.07.007

Roshanov, P. S., Fernandes, N., Wilczynski, J. M., Hemens, B. J., You, J. J., Handler, S. M., et al. (2013). Features of effective computerised clinical decision support systems: Meta-regression of 162 randomised trials. *BMJ, 346*, f657.

Rotar, A. M., van den Berg, M. J., Kringos, D. S., & Klazinga, N. S. (2016). Reporting and use of the OECD health care quality indicators at national and regional level in 15 countries. *International Journal for Quality in Health Care, 28*(3), 398–404.

Rouse, W. (2009). Engineering perspectives on healthcare delivery: Can we afford technological innovation in healthcare? *Systems Research and Behavioral Science, 26*(5), 573–582. https://doi.org/10.1002/sres.991

Rouse, W. B., & Cortese, D. A. (2010). *Engineering the system of healthcare delivery*. Amsterdam: IOS Press.

Serbanati, L. D., Ricci, F. L., Mercurio, G., & Vasilateanu, A. (2011). Steps towards a digital health ecosystem. *Journal of Biomedical Informatics, 44*(4), 621–636. https://doi.org/10.1016/j.jbi.2011.02.011

Shekelle, P. G., Pronovost, P. J., Wachter, R. M., Taylor, S. L., Dy, S. M., Foy, R., et al. (2011). Advancing the science of patient safety. *Annals of Internal Medicine, 154*(10), 693–696.

Singh, H., Spitzmueller, C., Petersen, N. J., Sawhney, M. K., Smith, M. W., Murphy, D. R., et al. (2013). Primary care practitioners' views on test result management in EHR-enabled health systems: A national survey. *Journal of the American Medical Informatics Association, 20*(4), 727–735.

Tang, P. (2003). *Key capabilities of an electronic health record system*. Washington, DC: Institute of Medicine of the National Academies.

Troshani, I., & Wickramasinghe, N. (2016). An organizing vision perspective for developing and adopting e-health solutions. In *Contemporary consumer health informatics* (pp. 271–281). Cham: Springer.

Tucker, C. A., Cieza, A., Riley, A. W., Stucki, G., Lai, J. S., Ustun, T. B., et al. (2014). Concept analysis of the patient reported outcomes measurement information system (PROMIS®) and the international classification of functioning, disability and health (ICF). *Quality of Life Research, 23*(6), 1677–1686.

Unertl, K. M., Johnson, K. B., & Lorenzi, N. M. (2012). Focus on health information technology, electronic health records and their financial impact: Health information exchange technology on the front lines of healthcare: Workflow factors and patterns of use. *Journal of the American Medical Informatics Association: JAMIA, 19*(3), 392.

VanLare, J. M., & Conway, P. H. (2012). Value-based purchasing – National programs to move from volume to value. *New England Journal of Medicine, 367*(4), 292–295.

von Lubitz, D., & Wickramasinghe, N. (2006). Networkcentric health care: Outline of entry portal concept. *International Journal of Electronic Business Management (IJEBM), 1*, 16–28.

Waterson, P. (2014). Health information technology and sociotechnical systems: A progress report on recent developments within the UK National Health Service (NHS). *Applied Ergonomics, 45*(2), 150–161.

Weill, P., & Broadbent, M. (1998). *Leveraging the new infrastructure: How market leaders capitalize on information technology*. Boston: Harvard Business School Press.

Weill, P., & Ross, J. W. (2004). *IT governance: How top performers manage IT decision rights for superior results*. Boston: Harvard Business Press.

Weill, P., & Woerner, S. L. (2013). Optimising your digital business model. *MIT Sloan Management Review, 54*(3), 71.

Westbrook, J., Braithwaite, J., Georgiou, A., Ampt, A., Creswick, N., Coiera, E., & Iedema, R. (2007). Multimethod evaluation of information and communication technologies in health in the context of wicked problems and sociotechnical theory. *Journal of the American Medical Informatics Association, 14*(6), 746–755.

Wickramasinghe, N. (2007). Fostering knowledge assets in health care with the KMI model. *International Journal of Management and Enterprise Development (IJMED), 4*(1), 52–65.

Wickramasinghe, N., Geisler, E., & Schaffer, J. (2006). Realising the value proposition for healthcare by incorporating KM strategies and data mining techniques with the use of information and communication technologies.(knowledge management systems) (Author abstract). *International Journal of Healthcare Technology and Management, 7*(5), 303.

Wickramasinghe, N., Haddad, P., & Vaughan, S. (2016). Using actor network theory and agency theory to identify critical factors in the adoption and implementation of a chemotherapy ordering system: A case study from the Australian Private Health-Care Sector. In *Contemporary consumer health informatics* (pp. 443–460). Cham: Springer.

Wickramasinghe, N., & Schaffer, J. L. (2010). *Realizing value driven e-health solutions. Improving healthcare series*. Washington, DC: IBM Center for the Business of Government.

Williams, M. D., Rana, N. P., Dwivedi, Y. K., & Lal, B. (2011). *Is UTAUT really used or just cited for the sake of it? A systematic review of citations of UTAUT's originating article*. Paper presented at the ECIS.

Wilson, H., Gole, J., Mishra, B., & Mishra, J. (2016). Value based healthcare. *Advances in Management, 9*(1), 1.

Wirtz, B. W., Mory, L., & Ullrich, S. (2012). eHealth in the public sector: An empirical analysis of the acceptance of Germany's electronic health card. *Public Administration, 90*(3), 642–663.

Chapter 11
Persuasive Technologies and Behavior Modification Through Technology: Design of a Mobile Application for Behavior Change

Andreas Hamper, Isabella Eigner, and Alexander Popp

11.1 Introduction

As of 2017, smartphone usage is still rapidly increasing, even in developed countries. Almost two-thirds of the entire US population is expected to own a smartphone at the end of the year, in comparison to 2012, where the penetration rate was below 40% (Statista: Smartphone Market 2016). Even though, only 2.97% of all available apps at the Apple App Store are in the Health & Fitness category (Statista: App Store Categories 2016), about 60% have downloaded at least one of them (Krebs and Duncan 2015). The reasons for using these kinds of apps are the adoption of a healthier lifestyle or tracking numbers, like weight or calories (Dennison et al. 2013).

However, there are two problems with the usage of health and fitness applications. On the one hand, there is a significant proportion of users (45.7%) who discontinue using the downloaded apps (Krebs and Duncan 2015). Making people reopen the app for a long period of time is not only desirable for the developer but also the only way to support a long-term behavior change, like a healthier lifestyle (Dennison et al. 2013).

On the other hand, only about 30% of users reported that their health improved considerably (Krebs and Duncan 2015). Although there are currently over 75,200 apps in the Health & Fitness category at the App Store (Apple: Health and Fitness Apps 2016), most of them have the same features as well as the same functionality. Additionally, this majority is developed only for people that are already physically active and does not support a long-term behavior change (Hofer 2016).

The two problems can be summarized to a low usage of downloaded health and fitness apps as well as limited effects for the majority of users, which lead to the

A. Hamper (✉) · I. Eigner · A. Popp
University Erlangen-Nuremberg, Institute of Information Systems, Nuremberg, Germany
e-mail: andreas.hamper@fau.de; isabella.eigner@fau.de

N. Wickramasinghe, J. L. Schaffer (eds.), *Theories to Inform Superior Health Informatics Research and Practice*, Healthcare Delivery in the Information Age, https://doi.org/10.1007/978-3-319-72287-0_11

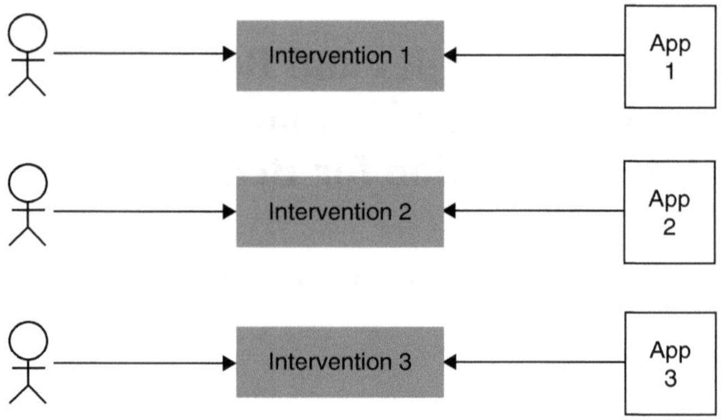

Fig. 11.1 Matching users with applications

following research question: How can behavioral interventions, in form of fitness apps, be tailored to specific users to increase their usage as well as effects?

The goal is to develop a process to identify apps for individual users at a specific point of time to support a long-term behavior change.

In order to achieve this, there has to be a methodology in place to describe and discover characteristics of users that are connected to influencing factors of behavior change. Furthermore, multiple applications have to be analyzed regarding the same influencing factors. This analysis can be built on the already existing examination of 29 different fitness apps regarding their characteristics of the transtheoretical model (TTM) and Fogg's Behavior Model (FBM) (Hofer 2016).

By translating these common factors to interventions for behavior change, they provide a method to match users with applications. The image below outlines this principle (Fig. 11.1).

Finally, a prototype will be built to demonstrate this process. It will analyze the user and match him with a suitable health and fitness service. Previous studies, though, discovered a lack of applications for certain characteristics (Hofer 2016), so the missing functionality will also be implemented to complete this demonstration.

11.2 Influencing User Behavior for Health and Fitness

Behavioral interventions appear to be more effective if they are individually tailored to the target (Bock et al. 2001), as well as perceived more positively and with a greater impact (Spittaels et al. 2007). However, tailoring behavioral interventions for each target individually leads to an exponentially increasing effort. There are numerous factors altering and affecting the behavior which make it challenging to limit or control their correlations. As a consequence, the exponential effort can be confined by clustering all possible targets into target groups. These represent a distinct set of properties and characteristics to which interventions, to a certain

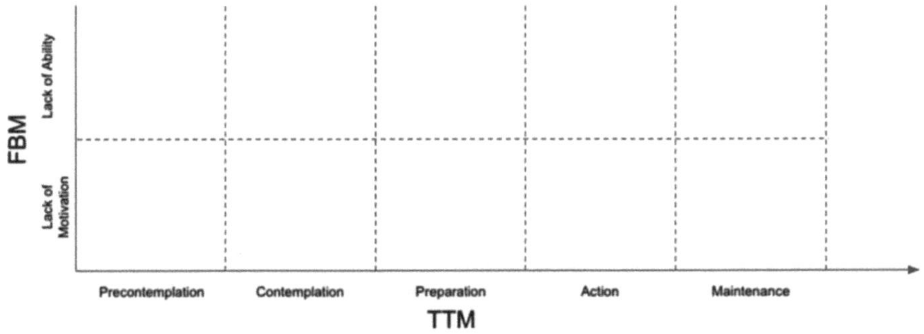

Fig. 11.2 Sociodemographic target groups

degree, can be tailored to. It might be necessary for some use cases to have extremely individual behavioral interventions, which can be achieved by increasing the number of target groups up to the number of original targets. For the results of this work, it is sufficient to have ten different groups.

There are many studies developing or elaborating new models for target groups. Most of them differ on the applications or purposes they are intended for. However, Rütten et al. (2007) take one model into account, the transtheoretical model (TTM), which focuses on behavior change. It describes a process with five different stages (precontemplation, contemplation, preparation, action, and maintenance), which individuals must go through to change and maintain a certain behavior (Glanz et al. 2008). The TTM has been used in multiple studies and can be used to develop and apply behavioral interventions (Fig. 11.2).

Nevertheless, these five stages are not enough to tailor precise interventions since there is no distinction between different types of people within one stage. TTM and FBM can be seen as a two-dimensional matrix. The FBM lists different personal factors, which influence human behavior. It helps to understand how and why people move from one stage of the TTM to the next (Fogg 2009). To simplify the resulting target groups, participants will be differentiated only by their combined core motivators and simplicity factors. These two factors will be referenced as "lack of motivation" and "lack of ability".

The combination of the TTM and FBM results into a matrix with ten different values (Fig. 11.3). Each of these values represents one sociodemographic target group. In this work, the term "sociodemographic target group" is defined by a target group that can be identified by exactly one TTM stage and a set of components from the FBM.

In order to decide how to classify participants into sociodemographic target groups, psychological questionnaires can be used:

The first one identifies the TTM stage by asking questions about the past, present, and future of the intended behavior. It is based on the staging algorithm, described by the Psychologisches Institut Freiburg (2001), which exploits the fact that the stages are linked in a timely manner (Prochaska et al. 1992).The second one simply

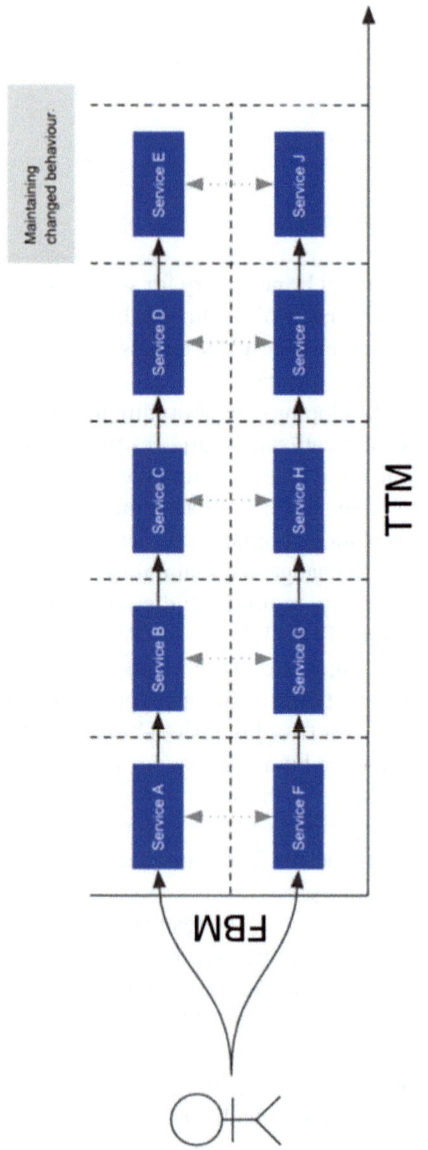

Fig. 11.3 Services for target groups

asks for the presence and significance of elements of motivation and elements of simplicity from Fogg's Behavior Model (Fogg 2009).

As a result, ten sociodemographic target groups, associated with processes of change from the TTM and behavior influencing factors from the FBM, can be differentiated. Furthermore, with the two questionnaires, there is a reliable and repeatable method to categorize people into these target groups.

Since the goal of this work is to change a behavior and preferably also maintain it, people have to get to the last stage of the TTM. This is where the desired behavior is already achieved and "people are working to prevent relapse" (Prochaska and Velicer 1997, p. 39). To get there, according to the TTM, the processes of change can be utilized to help targets proceed to the next stages. According to Prochaska and Velicer (1997, p. 39), "processes of change provide important guides for intervention programs." As explained above, tailored interventions are more effective; thus a tailored intervention to a specific target group helps them to move to the next stage and ultimately change and maintain a certain behavior.

Derived from the processes of change, this work will use services to create and apply interventions. As a result, one or more services that incorporate a process of change can be applied to progress to another stage.

Furthermore, these services should not only be tailored to the TTM stage but also to the influencing factors of the FBM to fully match with the target groups. The classification of services into target groups has been demonstrated by Hamper et al. (2016) with a Delphi study. By analyzing applications regarding their usefulness for each TTM stage and appealing to each Fogg factor, they can "be placed inside a two-dimensional matrix" (Hamper et al., 2016, p. 3353), which in turn represents all sociodemographic target groups.

One important difference between the two dimensions of the target groups is that the categorization into the TTM is temporally based (Prochaska and Velicer 1997), in contrast to the FBM. The influencing factors of the FBM do not necessarily have to be static, but they can be (Fogg 2009). The image below demonstrates the progress of a user through the different stages with the help of different services. For each target group, there is one individually tailored service.

However, it is quite complex to differentiate and work with so many services, especially if the vertical axis may be broken down further into more fine-grained FBM factors. To achieve an additional layer of standardization and abstraction, the term "service archetype" will be used for services that are in one TTM stage. It is based on the definition by the openEHR Foundation (2007) which states that archetypes are "expressions of a domain content model," "are all expressed in the same formalism," and are "defined for a wider reuse." In this work, a service archetype is an abstract structure, consisting of at least one service, which has an objective and several manifestations that explain how to achieve that objective.

11.2.1 Technical Requirements for Tailored Interventions

To translate the tailored interventions from the section before into actual software, it is necessary to develop concrete requirements to "reap the benefits of reduced integration and test costs, higher software reliability and maintainability, and more user-responsive[ness]" (Boehm 1984, p. 75) and, of course, simply to understand what it has to do and how (Wiegers and Beatty 2013). This section will first describe the theoretical background of requirements and then combine it with the service archetypes. The final result will be detailed requirements that can be used to actually implement this concept.

Software requirements describe a necessity for something, often combined with a prioritization and time specification. Nevertheless, there are many different levels and types of requirements for multiple purposes like project management or quality assurance. In order to keep it as clear and simple as possible, the focus will be on two very specific types that are used to describe systems: functional and nonfunctional requirements (Wiegers and Beatty 2013). Since the differentiation is of great importance for an exact tailoring, this section will introduce and describe both types.

Functional requirements describe "the necessary task, action or activity that must be accomplished" (Lightsey 2001, p. 36). It is not about in what way or manner this can be achieved but only about what it "must be able to do." The Institute of Electrical and Electronics Engineers (1984, p. 20) tries to summarize functional requirements into specifying the "inputs, processing, and outputs" of the software so that it can behave like a "finite state machine." It basically means that the system behaves solely, but also repeatable and predictable, based on its input and past behavior (Institute of Electrical and Electronics Engineers 1984). To summarize, functional requirements specify a concrete task, its necessary information, and possible results.

Nonfunctional requirements, on the other hand, are not related to the functionality of the software (Chung and do Prado Leite 2009). Although there are many different definitions and there is "still no consensus in the requirements engineering community what non-functional requirements are" (Glinz 2007, p. 21), the most common interpretation is that they are "attribute[s] of or constraint[s] on a system" (Glinz 2007, p. 25). They describe nonfunctional characteristics and general attributes of the software, like "efficiency, human engineering or understandability" (Chung and do Prado Leite 2009, p. 365).

A visualization by Glinz (2007) demonstrates the different classifications of requirements (Fig. 11.4). It indicates that functional as well as nonfunctional requirements are part of the system requirements. The important conclusion of this visualization is that it is necessary to define both types, functional and also nonfunctional, to properly design and develop a whole system.

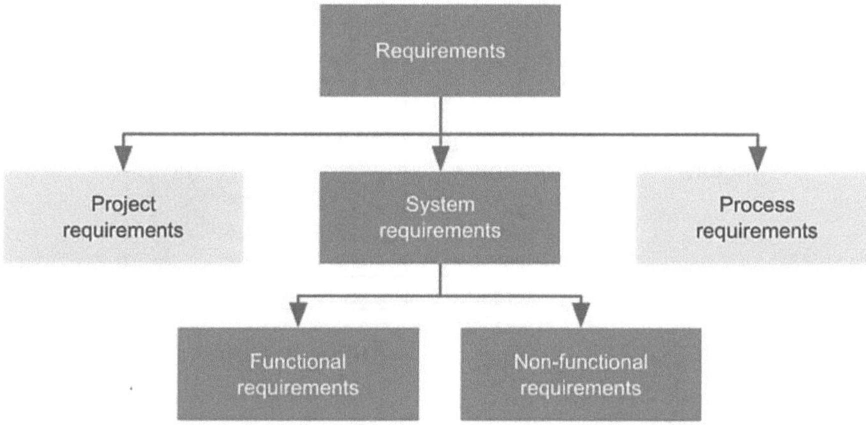

Fig. 11.4 Classification of requirements

11.2.2 Defining Requirements for Services

Concrete functional, as well as nonfunctional requirements, can now be derived from the service archetypes. Five different archetypes with multiple manifestations are necessary to change and maintain a certain behavior.

Due to the fact that each service archetype has an exact "objective," it can be matched with the definition of functional requirements, which can be described as a "concrete task" with a result. Furthermore, the manifestations of service archetypes "explain how to achieve that objective," have multiple constraints, and are individually tailored to the FBM. Considering the definition of nonfunctional requirements by Glinz (2007, p. 25), which states that they are "attribute[s] of or [a] constraint[s] on a system," it can be matched with the different manifestations.

As a consequence, the objective of a service archetype is determined by the TTM stage and represents functional requirements. The manifestations, in turn, are determined by the FBM factors and influence nonfunctional requirements. Figure 11.5 documents these correlations.

Consecutively, the requirement derivations for one service archetype can be applied to Fig. 11.6. This results into five service archetypes with distinct functional but a common set of two different nonfunctional requirements.

The next step is to define concrete requirements for each archetype, which can be used in the following sections to implement it into a prototype.

Functional requirements are already established by Prochaska et al. (1992) by means of the processes of change within the TTM. These are defined as "activities people use to get through stages" and "provide guides for intervention programs" (Glanz et al. 2008, p. 101), hence they directly relate to the definition of functional requirements. Moreover, there are "systematic relationships between people's stages and the processes" (Glanz et al. 2008, p. 105). Considering this and the fact

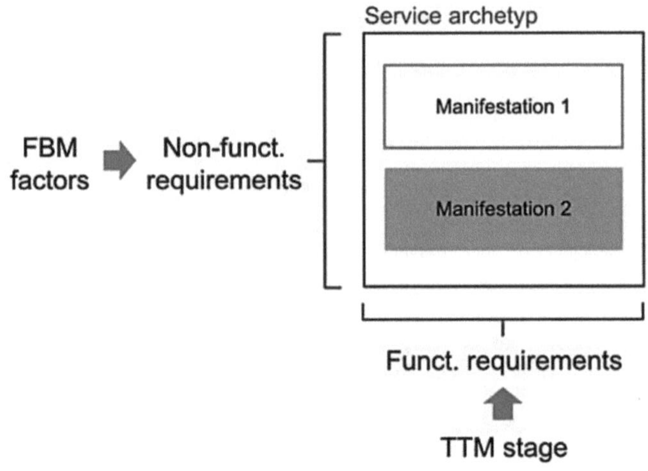

Fig. 11.5 Requirement derivation for a service archetype

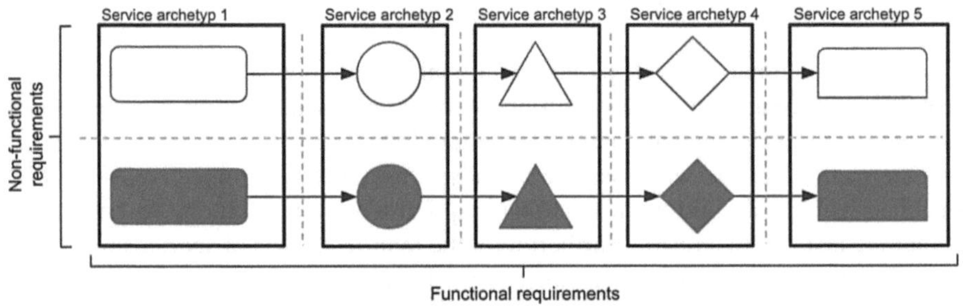

Fig. 11.6 Requirements for service archetypes

that each service archetype is placed at exactly one stage, the processes of change can be mapped to the five different archetypes.

- *Service archetype 1 (risk and fitness)*

- Raising consciousness for a particular behavior and its "causes, consequences, and cures" (Glanz et al. 2008, p. 101).
- *Service archetype 2 (coaching and advice)*
- Combining "increased emotional experiences" with an "anticipated relief" as soon as the desired behavior has taken place (Glanz et al. 2008, p. 101).
- *Service archetype 3 (progress monitoring)*
- Illustrating, cognitively as well as affectively, effects and consequences of the desired behavior to one's self-image (Glanz et al. 2008).
- *Service archetype 4 (rewards)*
- Reconfirming and supporting the "belief that one can change and the commitment and recommitment to act on that belief" (Glanz et al. 2008, p. 101).
- *Service archetype 5 (social and competition)*

- Adding signals to carry out the desired behavior as well as removing or avoiding signals for unwanted behaviors (Glanz et al. 2008).

In contrary to the section above, nonfunctional requirements have to be developed manually, because they are not directly related to the FBM factors.

Since there are many different nonfunctional requirements, the first step is to detect which ones can actually influence FBM factors. Distinct keywords, so-called indicator terms, in a text can be used to identify nonfunctional requirements. By applying the top 15 indicator terms of this study to the description of the FBM factors by Fogg (2009), the relevant requirements can be extracted.

Especially two requirements, "look and feel" and "usability," have an actual influence on multiple FBM factors. Another finding is that some of the factors cannot be influenced at all by nonfunctional requirements.

The next step is to specify the influence of "look and feel" as well as "usability" on both types of manifestations of service archetypes. They can be described as "lack of motivation" and "lack of ability," which in turn means that either elements of motivation or elements of ability have to be supported. This can be achieved by comparing characteristics of existing software with both types of FBM elements and the corresponding nonfunctional requirements. A list of 29 different health-related services, assembled by Wendt and Hofer (Hofer 2016), served as a base for this examination. Subsequently, a set of features can be described for both manifestations, lack of ability and lack of motivation, based on the, previously discovered, influencing requirements.

11.3 Prototypical Implementation of Tailored Interventions for Mobile Devices

Based on the requirements of the previous section, technical guidelines for the implementation as a mobile application will be described in the following section. The structure of the software, as well as the interactions with the user, is also laid out and explained. Furthermore, several rules and guidelines for organizing and building up the code base are mentioned along with the underlying reasons. The result does not only provide basic knowledge for other developers to further improve this prototype but also as a demonstration of how the previously described theoretical model can actually be implemented.

As already described, the platform has two tasks: firstly, it has to analyze the user and, secondly, it has to recommend suitable services. These recommendations have the form of simple links or redirections to existing services from other developers. This leads to two external parties. The use case diagram below (Fig. 11.7) demonstrates the connections and relations between the platform and the external actors.

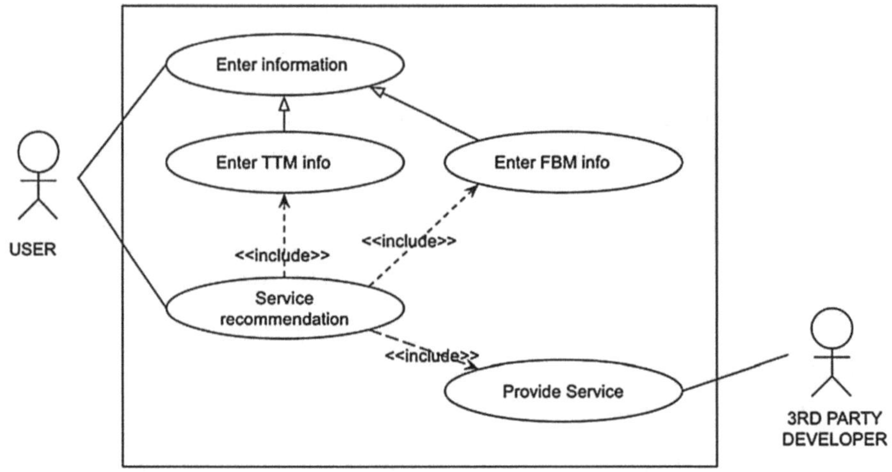

Fig. 11.7 Use case diagram for the platform

The first external actor is the developer who provides the necessary services. There may be multiple developers, but they can be regarded as one entity, especially when the Google Play Store is taken into account.

The second external actor is the user, who has two different interactions. On the one hand, he can enter some information about himself, which consists of data about his influencing FBM factors and current TTM stage. And on the other hand, he has access to service recommendations. These are based on the personal information about himself as well as the available third-party services.

We create a so-called feed. Since the classification into one TTM stage is not completely reliable, there won't be just one service recommendation. Instead, one service for each stage will be presented and arranged according to its relevance. As a result, there are five sorted "ServiceCards," one for each TTM stage (Prochaska and Velicer 1997), which act as links to services and have additional information, like the name of the service or the relevance. These are displayed within the feed and represent the service archetypes from Sect. 11.3.2. This structure fits perfectly to the role as a prototype. It does not focus on the user experience but on the demonstration of this concept. Future enhancements should tackle this issue and move the focus from a prototype to a release version. The image below (Fig. 11.8) visualizes this concept.

There are five ServiceCards, sorted by their relevance according to the TTM stage, the user is currently in, with multiple links. As stated in the requirements, there might be the case that there is only one link with an adapting service. This scenario is demonstrated for "ServiceCard 3" at Fig. 11.8. Another scenario, as displayed for "ServiceCard 5," is two links: one for lack of motivation and one for lack of ability.

Nevertheless, it is possible that the user simply does not like the recommended service. For this scenario, there will be another adaption. Some ServiceCards do not

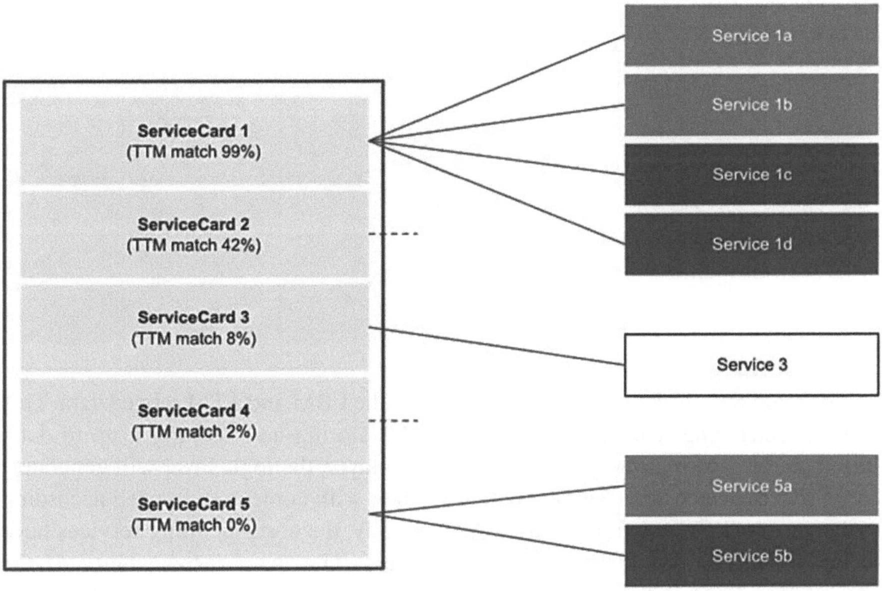

Fig. 11.8 Feed with five ServiceCards

just have one alternative but a list of equally matching services, the user can choose from ("ServiceCard 1").

11.3.1 Software Design Pattern and Abstraction

To "reduce system complexity" and build "reusable software," the goal is to use appropriate design patterns to structure the code. However, in this prototype, they have been used on two different tiers but for the same above- described purposes.

On a very abstract level they ensure "high reusability and interoperability" (Cortez and Vazhenin 2013, p. 132) of the code itself. Correspondingly, they have nothing to do with the concrete requirements but only with general code quality. Examples for this are the "abstract factory" or the "chain of responsibility."

On a more detailed level, these patterns are not designed on a class level but on a software component level, which means they are modeled out of entire fully functional components. The platform itself is built out of three software components: the data layer, logic layer, and presentation layer. It is important not to confuse this division into three with the model-view-controller pattern, which can rather be classified into the previously described, abstract type of patterns (Cortez and Vazhenin 2013). Instead, each of these three components can consist of multiple other patterns; they are only named after their main responsibility (Fig. 11.9).

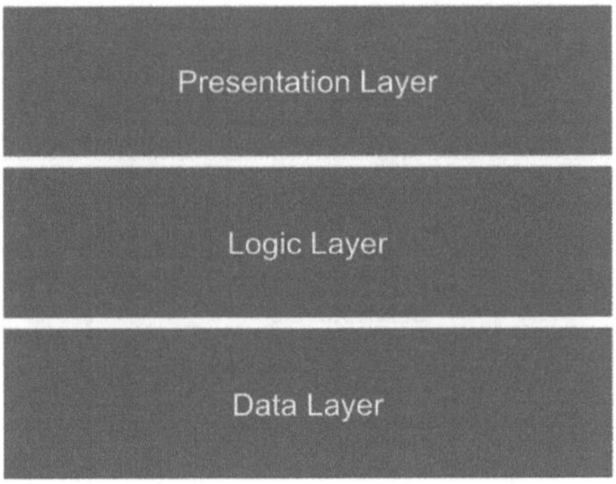

Fig. 11.9 Overview of the platform system architecture

The main task of the data layer is to provide the FBM and TTM related data. This includes retrieving it from the user as well as storing and keeping it up to date. Based on the information, provided by the data layer, the logic layer will generate a list of five ServiceCards. These have to be filled with content and sorted according to the current TTM stage of the user. Additionally, the corresponding services have to be filtered by the influencing FBM factors. The main responsibility of the presentation layer is to render these ServiceCards properly on the user interface. Furthermore, it has to provide the necessary information and ensure a smooth redirecting of the user to the external services.

The following three sections will give a more detailed insight into how these components are structured as well as their concrete tasks, interfaces, and relations.

Previous sections already indicated that the system of linking to other services has one flaw. Necessary applications with matching FBM factors for the right TTM stage might not exist. According to Hofer (2016), this problem is especially serious for the first two stages, since there are almost no applications tailored for the precontemplation and contemplation stage. In contrast, there are a huge number of services for the later stages. As a consequence, this section will outline the structure, design, and implementation of a service, tailored for the first stage of the TTM. Additionally, this service will adapt automatically to match to the influencing FBM factors of the user. To illustrate the software design, the following section describes the design of services for the precontemplation stages in technical detail based on software design patterns.

11.3.2 Implementation

People are usually in the precontemplation stage "because they are uninformed or underinformed about the consequences of their behavior" (Prochaska and Velicer 1997, p. 39). They can be moved to the next stage by raising consciousness and awareness of the consequences and effects of their lifestyle. They need to understand that there is a problem that has to be solved, which can be done with education as

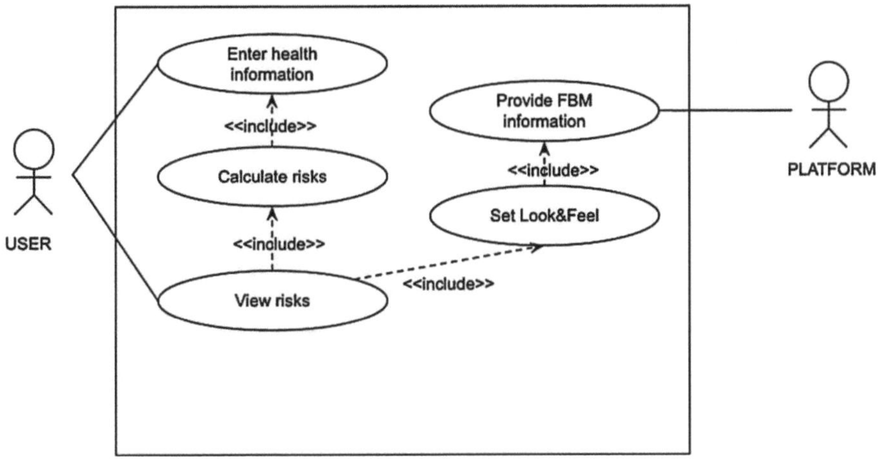

Fig. 11.10 Use case diagram for the service

well as confrontation (Prochaska and Velicer 1997). The main goal of the prototype is to increase the physical activity of the user, so this service should focus on educating and confronting about problems that can actually be tackled by that.

As a result, the implemented service has two tasks. Firstly, it has to calculate some risk factors, based on the health and physical condition of the user. Secondly, it has to adapt its nonfunctional factors dynamically according to the FBM, which relies on data provided by the platform. The use case diagram below (Fig. 11.10) visualizes these tasks with its corresponding external actors.

On the one hand, there is the user, who can enter information about his physical condition. This data is necessary to calculate the risk to suffer from selected problems and diseases. On the other hand, there is the platform that can provide information about the FBM profile of the user. This separation highlights the concept of service archetypes. The whole service is one archetype with exactly specified functional requirements: calculating risks according to fixed algorithms. These risks, however, are presented differently to the user, depending on the influencing FBM factors, which translate to different nonfunctional requirements.

11.3.2.1 Data Layer

The algorithms and questionnaires to calculate health risks rely on multiple types of data. As already mentioned, some need the user to enter a simple number or a free text, while others are developed in a multiple-choice style. Additionally, some information are not known to the user or are constantly changing which leads to accessing external sources to obtain it. However, not all users are using external services, for example, for tracking their daily steps, so this service has to handle this case as well. In a nutshell, obtaining the data has to be abstract, to support multiple

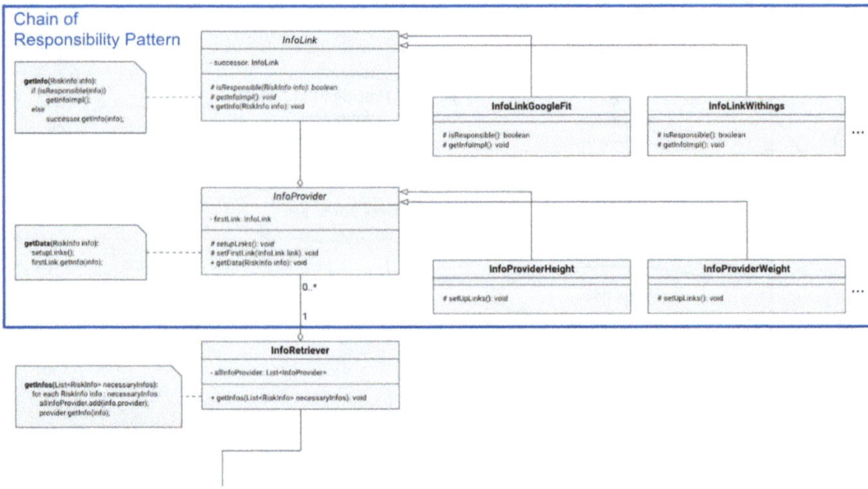

Fig. 11.11 Class diagram of InfoProvider with InfoLinks

data types, reusable for multiple algorithms that need the same information, and flexible in case of unreliable sources.

To achieve these three requirements, the concept of "InfoProviders" has been developed. One InfoProvider is responsible for obtaining exactly one specified information and has a reusable interface. It is decoupled from data sources which makes it abstract and can be used for multiple risk algorithms that need the same information. Each InfoProvider, in turn, consists of at least one "InfoLink." Their main task is to actually retrieve information from a source. In contrary to the InfoProviders, InfoLinks have a fixed data source but can return multiple types of information. To further increase reusability, they can be reused for various InfoProviders. Furthermore, each InfoLink has the possibility to signal that it cannot retrieve the desired information at the moment, which makes it possible to connect them in series and create a fallback system. Due to their abstract interface, InfoLinks can be used in any order and combination for every InfoProvider.

As a result, this concept has a high degree of abstraction, because of the fixed InfoProvider interfaces, and reusability, because of the possibility to reuse on the one hand the same InfoProvider for multiple algorithms and on the other hand the same InfoLink for multiple InfoProviders. Moreover, the arbitrary order and combination of InfoLinks lead to more flexibility.

The concrete implementation is done with the "chain-of-responsibility" design pattern which is highlighted in the class diagram below (Fig. 11.11). This design pattern should be used, whenever there are "more than one object [that] may handle a request" (Vlissides et al. 1995, p. 253), like retrieving a certain information, and results in reduced coupling between a sender and receivers as well as added flexibility.

There are two abstract classes, *InfoProvider* and *InfoLink*, which have concrete inheritances for certain information and data sources. The *InfoRetriever* acts as a unified interface for the logic layer to conveniently access the data. The most important detail is the "GetData(...)" method. Whenever it is called, the concrete implementation of an InfoProvider first has to set up its InfoLinks (*setupLinks()*). This basically creates all necessary InfoLink objects and orders them correctly. After that, the first InfoLink will be called for the desired information. The concrete InfoLink implementation, in turn, implements two methods that are structured and called by their abstract superclass, as demonstrated in "GetInfo(...)." The first method checks whether it can provide this exact data from the data source, and the second one actually returns it. Additionally, it has a reference to the next InfoLink, so it can redirect the request if it cannot provide the data.

11.3.2.2 Logic Layer

The main responsibility of the logic layer is to calculate health risks. However, it is quite difficult, especially for a non-expert user, to correctly understand and interpret the results. Without any background knowledge or comparisons, it is hard to know whether a value, for example, the risk to suffer from a stroke, is good or bad. As a consequence, there won't be just the calculation of the result but also a percentage-based valuation. This classifies the absolute values into a scale from 0 to 100%, whereby "100%" means that it is the best and correspondingly "0%" the worst possible outcome. Another adaption will be the possibility to swap out algorithms. There are numerous ways to calculate these health risks. Some are more suitable for certain demographics (Li et al. 2014) and some proof to be correct only after a long period of time (Assmann et al. 2002). Furthermore, science will progress so there might always be the case to change an algorithm. To tackle this problem, the six health risks will be fixed, but their way of calculation can be changed dynamically. Just like the data layer, the logic layer is also based on the principles of well-known design patterns. The main part is structured according to the template pattern which "lets subclasses redefine certain steps of an algorithm without changing the [...] structure" (Vlissides et al. 1995, p. 360). This is useful, since there are always the same three parts in the same order but with different implementations: retrieving necessary data, calculating the health risk, and evaluating the result.

The class diagram above (Fig. 11.12) outlines the structure of the logic layer. To have access to information about the user, each "RiskAlgorithm" has a reference to the InfoRetriever, which was already described in the data layer. The method "calculate(...)" of the abstract class RiskAlgorithm is the core of the template pattern. It structures the flow of the calculation by combining functions of subclasses with the InfoRetriever. However, there is one addition to the classical pattern. There is not only one level of subclasses below the RiskAlgorithm but two. The first level represents the six different health risks and the second one the actual implementations of the different algorithms. In combination, the lowest level, e.g., "RiskAlgorithmCardioPROCAM," incorporates the calculation of health risks. Its

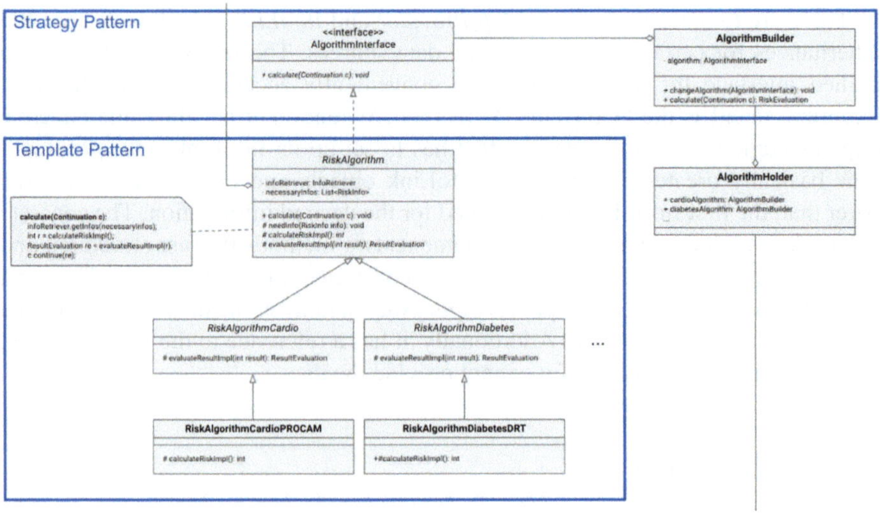

Fig. 11.12 Class diagram of the logic layer

superclass in turn, e.g., "RiskAlgorithmCardio," can evaluate this calculation. The final superclass "RiskAlgorithm" actually calls these functions and redirects their results.

To be able to swap out algorithms, preferably during run time, the strategy pattern is put on top of the template. Its use case is to "define a family of algorithms, encapsulate each one, and make them interchangeable" (Vlissides et al. 1995, p. 349) so that they are independent from the code that uses them. As illustrated above, there is an "AlgorithmInterface" on top of the RiskAlgorithm to have fixed interfaces, which can be used by the compositor. In this scenario, the "AlgorithmBuilder" is the compositor, whose responsibility is to have a reference to one AlgorithmInterface and calls its "calculate" function or swap out the entire reference whenever the algorithm needs to be changed. Whenever an object wants to trigger the calculation of an algorithm, it needs to call the corresponding function of the AlgorithmBuilder. This abstraction decouples the RiskAlgorithm from the triggering object.

11.3.2.3 Presentation Layer

The next step is to display the calculated and evaluated health risks properly, according to the influencing FBM factors of the user. To achieve this, the view has to be able to adapt or change to different requirements that are presented in Table 11.1: look and feel and usability. Since not only the user interface has to change (look and feel) but also its behavior (usability), the concept of fragments fits perfectly. They are Android-specific elements whereby "each fragment defines its own layout and its own behavior" (Android: Fragments 2016). This also highlights

Table 11.1 Features for service archetype manifestations

	Features for	
	Lack of ability	Lack of motivation
Usability	• Simple and efficient usage • Style of usage according to OS guidelines • Easy to understand • No frills	• Informational • Clear and distinct status information
Look and feel	• Simply structured • Identical/similar representations • Succinctly	• Extreme colors • Clear connection between progress and UI • Emotional pictures and text

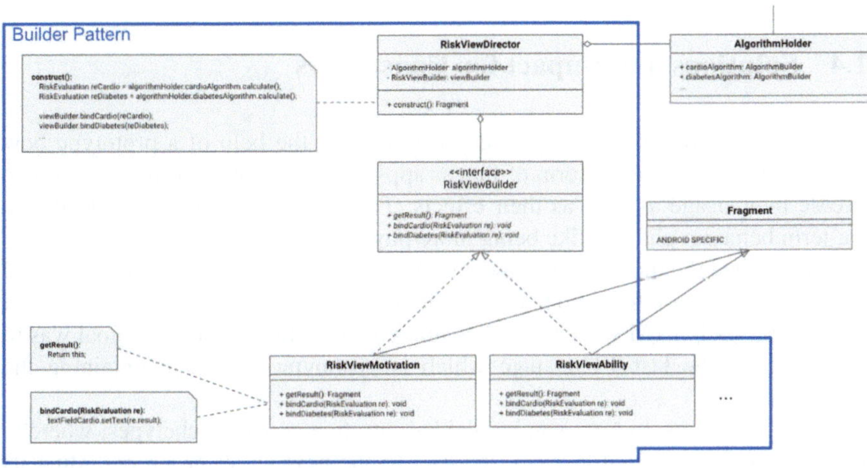

Fig. 11.13 Class diagram of the presentation layer

why the system architecture of the service cannot be compared with the model-view-controller pattern. The presentation layer consists not only of a plain view, which would only affect the look and feel, but also some logic, or controller code, to influence the behavior and thereby the usability differently.

This leads to two fragments with different user interfaces and actions, depending on the FBM factors. One for "lack of motivation" and one for "lack of ability." Nonetheless, they receive exactly the same data from the logic layer. This can be realized with the builder pattern which allows to "separate the construction of a complex object from its representation so that the same construction process can create different representations" (Vlissides et al. 1995, p. 110). In this case, the representation is a fragment with only two different manifestations. The second section indicated that the split of the FBM into two groups might be broken down even further in the future. This architecture combined with the builder pattern supports this change since it would be easy to simply add more representations (Fig. 11.13).

The central point of the presentation layer is the “RiskViewDirector.” It contains the “AlgorithmHolder” which encapsulates the six AlgorithmBuilder, presented in the previous section. Additionally, it will be instantiated with a “RiskViewBuilder,” depending on the FBM factors that can be retrieved from the shared preferences. The initial instantiation might look like the following.

Summed up, the presentation layer combines fragments with evaluated health risks, depending on FBM factors. The health risks, in turn, are calculated and evaluated at the logic layer and are combined and accessible through one AlgorithmHolder. To be able to calculate these risks, the logic layer needs access to information that can be provided by the data layer through the InfoRetriever. These fixed interfaces enable fast and easy changes for future developments.

11.4 Solutions and Impact for Consumers

The objective of this work was to demonstrate with the help of a prototype how behavioral interventions, in form of fitness apps, can be tailored to specific users to increase their usage as well as their effects. These interventions aim to lead to a long-term behavior change, like being more physically active.

We described the theoretical framework behind tailored interventions. We stated that users can be classified into ten different target groups, based on a questionnaire that analyzes their TTM stage as well as influencing FBM factors. The goal was to move users to the last TTM stage which is synonymous with maintaining the changed behavior.

The target groups, in turn, can be divided into five service archetypes, whereby each of these has the goal to move the user to the next target group regarding its TTM stage. The archetypes differ only in the way they try to achieve this goal, the processes of change. Additionally, each service archetype has two manifestations that indicate different ways to influence the user. These two variants are derived from a set of influencing FBM factors.

The prototype is modeled strongly on this theoretical framework. It first navigates the user through a tutorial with a questionnaire to determine the most suitable target group. Afterward, a list of ServiceCards is displayed. Each one represents exactly one service archetype. Based on the target group of the user, these ServiceCards can be sorted, so that the most relevant service archetype is at the first and the least relevant at the last position.

By just linking from a ServiceCard to an already existing app, which incorporates the matching process of change, they do not have to be developed all over again. However, there is a lack of suitable applications for the first service archetype or the first TTM stage. For this reason, a service, the risk test, has been implemented to fill this gap. To address the two manifestations, there is not just one link to a fixed service; instead, the user will be redirected to another application depending on the target group he is currently in whenever the service is not capable of adapting what was demonstrated at the risk and fitness test.

Fig. 11.14 Matching users with applications

To develop a process to decide to which services can be linked from which archetypes and which manifestations, the two components of the target groups, the TTM and FBM, are translated to functional and nonfunctional requirements. This leads to a set of different tailored requirements for each target group which allows to either match existing applications with them or to exactly tailor new services.

The image above (Fig. 11.14) demonstrates the combination of the theoretical framework and the actual implementation. There is still the classification into ten target groups, whereby the shape indicates the service archetype and the color the manifestation. By means of a questionnaire, users can be put into one target group. In this example, user A is in the white rounded rectangle, user B in the white triangle, and user C in the black diamond.

As a result, each one of these users will get recommendations for different services. User A starts at the beginning with the motivational version of the self-implemented service. As he progresses through the TTM stages, he will finally get the same recommendation as user B currently has. User C has a different set of influencing FBM factors, so he will be redirected to different applications. The sequences below (Fig. 11.15) highlight that users will have different, individually tailored recommendations to services that incorporate the exact process of change with the matching influencing FBM factors to move them to the next TTM stage, which ultimately leads to a behavior change. The task of the last service is to keep the user at this stage and maintain the changed behavior.

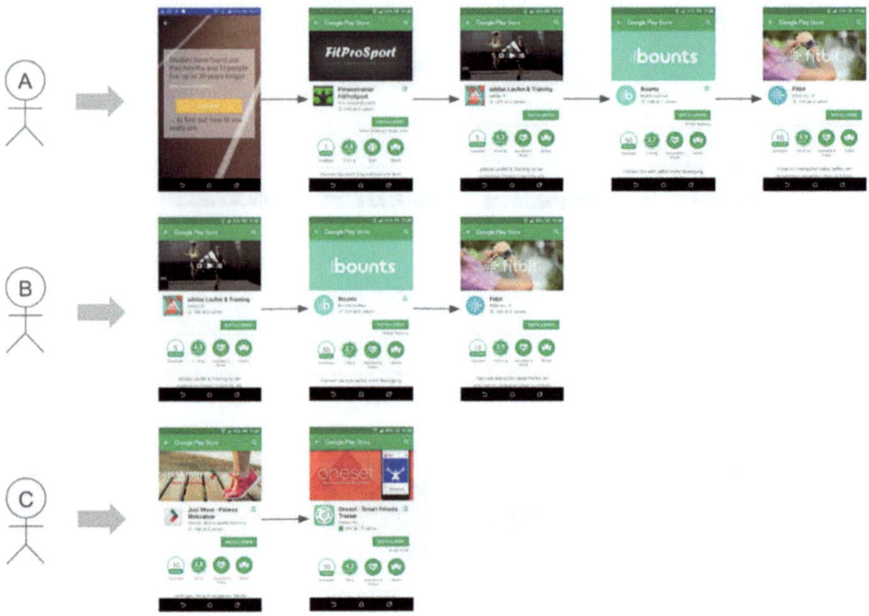

Fig. 11.15 Tailored recommendations of different services

Two problems of current health and fitness applications are addressed. They very often have only a limited effect, and many users stop using them after a while. Both issues prevent the change and maintaining of a healthier lifestyle. The prototype, resulting from this work, tackled these problems by incorporating a theoretical framework to increase usage as well as effects of fitness apps. However, the purpose of the implementation was to move from a theoretical to a practical perspective and demonstrate this framework in form of an Android application. It is not yet intended for normal users because there are some features that serve well for demonstrating the theory but not for a practical usage.

As already described, the feed, the list of five ServiceCards, should be simplified. Early test users, who were not familiar with the TTM concept, were confused by the amount of content. Only the first ServiceCard is important, so the last four can be hidden. Since this basically makes the list layout ineffective, a complete change of the main screen can be useful. A similar problem occurred at selecting a concrete service. At the moment, the user can choose between several applications, which appeared to be too confusing.

According to Krebs and Duncan (2015), a big proportion of users discontinue using an app because it takes too much time to enter data. This is likely to be the case for the questionnaire at the beginning. Solutions might be to reduce the number of questions or delay them until they are absolutely necessary. The FBM classification, for example, is only needed when the actual service has to be selected and not for rendering the list of ServiceCard at the beginning.

Eventually, it might be interesting to implement these recommended changes and compare the long- term success of this application with several others that are currently available. By increasing the number of target groups, which allows more precise recommendations, or adjusting the match with services, there are multiple changes that can be made to perform extensive A/B tests.

In conclusion, users can be analyzed and receive individually tailored recommendations to different services. These services have various functionalities and are each one step to changing and maintaining the desired behavior to be more physically active.

References

Android: Fragments. (2016). Retrieved December 19, 2016, from https://developer.android.com/guide/components/fragments.html

Apple: Health & Fitness Apps. (2016). Retrieved December 19, 2016, from https://itunes.apple.com/us/genre/ios-health-fitness/id6013

Assmann, G., Cullen, P., & Schulte, H. (2002). Simple scoring scheme for calculating the risk of acute coronary events based on the 10-year follow-up of the prospective cardiovascular Münster (PROCAM) study. *Circulation, 105*(3), 310–315.

Bock, B. C., Marcus, B. H., Pinto, B. M., & Forsyth, L. (2001). Maintenance of physical activity following an individualized motivationally tailored intervention. *Annals of Behavioral Medicine, 23*(2), 79–87.

Boehm, B. W. (1984). Verifying and validating software requirements and design specifications. *IEEE Software, 1*(1), 75–88.

Chung, L., & do Prado Leite, J. C. (2009). On non-functional requirements in software engineering. In *Conceptual modeling: Foundations and applications* (pp. 363–379). Berlin Heidelberg: Springer.

Cortez, R., & Vazhenin, A. (2013). Developing re-usable components based on the Virtual-MVC design pattern. In *International Workshop on Databases in Networked Information Systems* (pp. 132–149). Springer Berlin Heidelberg.

Dennison, L., Morrison, L., Conway, G., & Yardley, L. (2013). Opportunities and challenges for smartphone applications in supporting health behavior change: Qualitative study. *Journal of Medical Internet Research, 15*(4), e86.

Fogg, B. J. (2009). A behavior model for persuasive design. In *Proceedings of the 4th International Conference on Persuasive Technology* (p. 40). ACM.

Glanz, K., Rimer, B. K., & Viswanath, K. (Eds.). (2008). *Health behavior and health education: Theory, research, and practice*. San Francisco: John Wiley & Sons.

Glinz, M. (2007). On non-functional requirements. In *15th IEEE International Requirements Engineering Conference (RE 2007)* (pp. 21–26). IEEE.

Hofer, S. (2016). *Consumer Healthcare Wearables – A teardown of health and fitness solutions to understand their impact on behavior change.* Master's Thesis, Friedrich Alexander Universität Erlangen-Nürnberg.

Institute of Electrical and Electronics Engineers. (1984). *IEEE guide to software requirements specifications.* IEEE.

Krebs, P., & Duncan, D. T. (2015). Health App use among US mobile phone owners: A national survey. *JMIR mHealth uHealth, 3*(4), e101.

Li, K., Hüsing, A., & Kaaks, R. (2014). Lifestyle risk factors and residual life expectancy at age 40: A German cohort study. *BMC Medicine, 12*(1), 59.

Lightsey, B. (2001). *Systems engineering fundamentals*. Ft. Belvoir: Defense Acquisition University.
openEHR Foundation. (2007). In T. Beale & S. Heard (Eds.), *Archetype definitions and principles. 1.0*.
Prochaska, J. O., DiClemente, C. C., & Norcross, J. C. (1992). In search of how people change: applications to addictive behaviors. *American Psychologist, 47*(9), 1102.
Prochaska, J. O., & Velicer, W. F. (1997). The transtheoretical model of health behavior change. *American Journal of Health Promotion, 12*(1), 38–48.
Psychologisches Institut Freiburg. (2001). Erfassung der "Stages of Change" im Transtheoretischen Modell Prochaska's – eine Bestandsaufnahme. *Forschungsberichte des Psychologischen Instituts der Albert-Ludwigs-Universität Freiburg i. Br.*
Rütten, A., Abu-Omar, K., Adlwarth, W., & Meierjürgen, R. (2007). Sedentary lifestyles. Classification of different target groups for the promotion of health-enhancing physical activities. *Gesundheitswesen (Bundesverband der Arzte des Offentlichen Gesundheitsdienstes (Germany)), 69*(7), 393–400.
Spittaels, H., Bourdeaudhuij, I. D., Brug, J., & Vandelanotte, C. (2007). Effectiveness of an online computer-tailored physical activity intervention in a real-life setting. *Health Education Research, 22*(3), 385–396.
Statista: App Store Categories. (2016). Retrieved December 19, 2016, from https://www.statista.com/statistics/270291/popular-categories-in-the-app-store/
Statista: Smartphone Market. (2016). Retrieved December 19, 2016, from https://www.statista.com/topics/2711/us-smartphone-market/
Vlissides, J., Helm, R., Johnson, R., & Gamma, E. (1995). Design patterns: Elements of reusable object-oriented software. *Reading: Addison-Wesley, 49*(120), 11.
Wiegers, K., & Beatty, J. (2013). *Software requirements*. London: Pearson Education.

Andreas Hamper studied Information Systems at the University of Erlangen-Nuremberg. Since 2011, he is a member of the research staff and PhD student at the Institute of Information Systems. In his research he is focusing on mobile technologies and health care.

Isabella Eigner studied International Information Systems at the University of Erlangen-Nuremberg. Since 2014, she is a member of the research staff and PhD student at the Institute of Information Systems. In her research she is focusing on data mining in health care.

Alexander Popp studied Information Systems at the University of Erlangen-Nuremberg. In 2016, he did his master's work on mobile technology for preventive health care at the Institute of Information Systems.

Chapter 12
Integrating Two Sociotechnical Theories to Develop a Suitable Analytic Framework to Assess the Development of a Hospital Secure Messaging and Communication Platform

Imran Muhammad and Nilmini Wickramasinghe

12.1 Introduction

Pagers and phone conversations have been the stalwarts of hospital communication with good reason; they are simple, reliable and relatively inexpensive. However, with the increasing complexity of patient care and the need for greater speed and revolutionary progress of health technology, hospital communication systems appear to be increasingly inefficient, non-secure and inadequate (Coiera 2006; Grisot and Vassilakopoulou 2011).

In a broader context, implementing health information systems has been viewed as a potential solution to addressing issues faced in healthcare service provision, such as process inefficiencies, high healthcare costs, poor access to high-quality and safe health care and low patient satisfaction (e.g. see Edwards et al. 2008; Lau 2007). Consequently, there is an impetus towards the use of technology in many areas of healthcare administration and care processes. However, the complexities associated with the coordination, communication and delivery of health care at the point of care present challenges for the design and implementation of hospital secure messaging and communication system. According to surveys conducted by the American College of Physicians and American EHR Partners (2013), user satisfaction and usability ratings for health information systems (HISs) decreased between March 2010 and December 2012. During this period, overall user satisfaction decreased by 12%, and users who were "very dissatisfied" increased by 10%. Overriding of the system, duplication of documentation and a reversion to familiar systems such as paper recording have been reported as workaround strategies used to continue delivery of safe and reliable clinical communication and care in the face

I. Muhammad · N. Wickramasinghe (✉)
Deakin University, Burwood, VIC, Australia

Epworth HealthCare, Richmond, VIC, Australia

N. Wickramasinghe, J. L. Schaffer (eds.), *Theories to Inform Superior Health Informatics Research and Practice*, Healthcare Delivery in the Information Age,
https://doi.org/10.1007/978-3-319-72287-0_12

of technological solutions that do not meet clinicians' needs (Dowding et al. 2009; Lau et al. 2010; Viitanen et al. 2011).

In the information systems literature, development and sequential implementation of a technology solution have been commonly agreed to be a process of social change involving active and interwoven relationships between the social and technical systems (Alexander and Silvis 2014; Cho et al. 2008; Hanseth et al. 2004; Iyamu and Sekgweleo 2013; Tatnall and Gilding 2005). Particularly in health care, end users and the socio-organisational context have been argued to play a crucial role to the success of technology implementation (Meijden et al. 2003; Stevenson et al. 2010; Vimarlund and Timpka 2002). Among different sociotechnical approaches, actor-network theory (ANT) (Latour 2005; Law and Hassard 1999) and activity theory (AT) (Leontiev 2009) have been adopted to develop a rich understanding into the complexity of the heterogeneous network of multiple social and technical actors and the process of social change associated with technology introduction. Thus, this study draws from these two theories to develop a conceptual framework for the theoretical underpinning of the research study and to answer the key research question: "How can a sociotechnical perspective-based integrated theoretical framework help us understand the complexities and challenges regarding communication inefficiencies within health care, and, furthermore, how can this framework aid in the development, implementation and adoption of ICT (information communication technology)-based hospital communication solutions?"

12.2 Study Background

A recent report by the Ponemon Institute examined the financial burden resulting from communication inefficiencies in health care (Ponemon Institute 2014). An average US hospital is estimated to lose USD1.75 million annually due to poorly implemented communication among health staff. Some of the key findings included (Ponemon Institute 2014):

- The average healthcare provider wastes 45 min every day by using substandard communication systems such as pagers.
- During admission of a patient, a significant portion of time is wasted due to inefficient communication, costing USD 728,000 per year per hospital.
- Secure text messaging has the potential to reclaim 20 min per patient in the patient transfer alone.
- The use of two-way secure text messaging has the potential to improve productivity, saving an estimated USD 918,000.00 per hospital annually.

It is unsurprising then that methods other than pagers and phone calls are often utilised—be it residents communicating with other residents, nurses seeking consultant feedback or patients seeking advice from their clinicians (Wu et al. 2013). These methods include smartphone text and image messaging, email, VOIP, video calls, etc. While efficient, these methods are insecure, and with the introduction of new health privacy laws, there has been increased scrutiny on the way staff involved in patient care share information about their mutual patients (Wu et al. 2013).

Mobile health platforms (mHealth) offer a promising solution to some of the more important problems facing the current healthcare messaging systems (Harvey and Harvey 2014). Mobile technologies have become the platform of choice with more than 6 billion mobile subscribers worldwide (Smith 2012). Integral to mobile health is the use of mobile and wireless devices to improve health outcomes, healthcare services and health research (Varshney 2014). The topic of mobile health (mHealth) seeks to capture the dynamics of using mobile devices for various aspects of healthcare delivery such as access to government resources, social networking and interactions between organisations, institutions, individuals and all relevant interested parties (Vogel et al. 2013).

Mobile health has many applications. It can be used to facilitate data collection and to encourage healthcare consumers to adopt healthy lifestyles or to self-manage chronic conditions. It can also be used to improve healthcare service delivery processes by targeting healthcare providers or communication between these providers and their patients. So, for example, mobile technologies can be used to provide clinical management support in settings where there are no specialist clinicians, and they can be used to send patients' test results and timely reminders of appointments (Free et al. 2013).

In 2013, Free at al. conducted a systematic review to investigate the effectiveness of mobile health technologies to improve healthcare service delivery. 334 studies and 42 mHealth trials, published between January 1990 and September 2010, were included in the review. The study found that some mHealth interventions designed to improve healthcare service delivery processes are modestly effective, but it also highlighted the need for more trials of these interventions (Free et al. 2013). In terms of mHealth interventions targeting communication between healthcare providers and communication with patients, the study concluded that SMS appointment reminders have modest benefits. Researchers suggested that such solutions be implemented more broadly to improve all aspects of healthcare communication (Free et al. 2013). However, such a broad application is often challenging, due to concerns regarding the security of smartphone technologies when dealing with personal health information.

Thus, this study attempts to answer the research question: "How can a sociotechnical perspective-based integrated theoretical framework help us understand the complexities and challenges regarding communication inefficiencies within health care, and, furthermore, how can this framework aid in the development, implementation and adoption of ICT (information communication technology)-based hospital communication solutions?"

To answer this question, this study has developed an integrated theoretical framework for the evaluation of the hospital communication ICT secure messaging solution at a private hospital in Melbourne, by applying two strong theories, actor-network theory (ANT) and activity theory (AT), to make a robust body of knowledge for the proposed solution.

12.3 Methodology

Based on the criteria given by Yin (2010), the choice of methodology for this research study is a qualitative single-case study. This study is about health information systems implementation and adoption and subsequently, its use. To understand the phenomenon, it is important to understand the processes, interactions between human and non-human actors and their perceptions and expectations, which can be best served by a qualitative approach as it can serve better in providing the insights necessary to understand the participant's role in the event and their perceptions of the experience (Yin 2010).

The part one of this study is theoretical underpinning of the study. To answer the research question and development of the theoretical framework, several archival records and documents relating to the health information and communication technology implementation and adoption in healthcare service delivery settings were critically analysed. These documents were of great value in developing an understanding of the need for a hospital communication tool and factors important for the implementation and adoption of hospital communication tool. This analysis assisted in developing the theoretical research framework and in planning the primary data collection strategies for the larger study. A priori themes were developed through a pilot survey, and then literature was analysed using thematic analysis and hermeneutic analysis, and then we performed a gap analysis. The analysis led us towards the sociotechnical perspective of this study. A comprehensive review of two sociotechnical theories, namely, ANT and AT, was conducted that leads to the development of a conceptual framework for the study that serves to build the theoretical foundations of the study. Phase two of this multimethod study will then serve to test this model and build the artefact.

12.4 Theoretical Foundations of the Study

Healthcare systems are complex systems especially when they integrate information technology. The challenge of this study is further complicated by the interaction of different human and non-human actors that mainly leads to failed technology-based healthcare interventions and implementations. As a result, failure rates are unsurprisingly high and costly and have far-reaching impacts (Cresswell et al. 2011). Thus, it becomes necessary and important to evaluate these interventions with theoretically informed techniques to enable a deeper understanding which in turn can facilitate a successful development, implementation and adoption of health information technology such as hospital communication application (Cresswell et al. 2011).

We believe that a sociotechnical systems perspective can provide the foundations for a better understanding of these systems so that there is a better evaluation and provision of specific solutions to address gaps in their current development, implementation and adoption. Furthermore, it can also enhance our understanding by providing a mechanism to study the relationships between technology organisation, people, social and financial factors that influence the success of hospital communication application development as well as implementation and adoption. We believe that a viable healthcare system can only be improved if these considerations are jointly optimised.

Our goal here is to investigate this in the specific context of a hospital communication application, in a private hospital in Melbourne, Australia. The initial analysis and the conceptual framework presented for the application development in hospitals to date show that the processes underlying the development, implementation and adoption of hospital communication application are inherently sociotechnical in nature. A sociotechnical approach of study therefore will allow more flexibility in system design and adoption.

We have argued here that this approach will be of benefit to both practitioners for better design and implementation and researchers for better evaluation. The researchers, however, acknowledge that sociotechnical theory as Berg et al. (2003) rightly indicate does have its shortcomings and suggest that to overcome these one should combine such an analysis with other theories, namely, actor-network theory and activity theory which provided the impetus to proceed as follows.

12.4.1 Actor-Network Theory (ANT)

Actor-network theory (ANT) is a sociological theory developed by French sociologists Bruno Latour and Michel Callon and British sociologist John Law (Latour 2005; Law 1999). Its fundamental premise is that technologies and people are linked in an often complex network. ANT tries to bridge the gap between a sociotechnical divide by denying the existence of purely social or technical relations. In doing so, it takes a very radical stance and goes as far as challenging many of the conventional epistemological ideas and rejecting any distinction between subject or object, nature or culture and technology and society.

ANT assumes that each entity (such as technologies, organisations and humans) is an actor. Therefore, the actors have the potential to transform and mediate social relationships (Cresswell et al. 2011). ANT further emphasises that entities regardless of their nature, whether human, technologies, activities or process, are not fixed. Thus, they do not have any significance on their own, but rather their significance depends on the nature of their relations with other entities in the network and their role which may change as their relations change (Law 2004). This means that neither actors nor their relations are static and permanent; they change over time and across social and political contexts (Singleton and Michael 1993).

Actors are essentially considered heterogeneous in nature, representing negotiations at different levels (e.g. political, social, technical and/or economic levels). Further, the degrees of commitment, skills, constraints and prejudice among actors also can vary. Often, these represent a mixture of one or two of social, technical or personal levels (Latour 2005). At the technical level, the role of technology may be involved to facilitate users by giving them accurate and up-to-date information when it is needed. For example, in health care, the accuracy (effectiveness and efficiency) of the technology would be best determined or disputed by the users (nurses, clinicians, pharmacists and patients). To better understand relationships and how they create meaning and describe the role of different actors (e.g. the patient, GPs, nurses, different diagnostic tests, different medical technologies, different communication channels, standards, protocols and decision-makers and policymakers), ANT suggests we should think in terms of networks of relations or actor-networks (Williams-Jones and Graham 2003).

In the context of hospital messaging, a new technology actor is to be introduced to an existing sociotechnical network to replace an existing actor (communication tool/pager) who has a long-term established role in the network. This change is both complex and risky especially in an acute care hospital environment. This has been acknowledged in health care, which is a strongly people-centred sector where technology is dealt with more as an intruder, disrupts the healthcare professionals' way of doing things and can be considered as a competitor to this people-centred model (Berler et al. 2005). Among many problems attributing to this complexity, acceptability and usability are well-known reasons (Darbyshire 2004; Stevenson et al. 2010).

Therefore, impacts of a specific system on the health service providers and their reactions are difficult to predict and need to be examined carefully. ANT can help to understand how the resistance to sociotechnical change can be met by reorganising the relations in actor-networks and translating their interests into common goals. Counterclaims and disagreements that arise from different actors in a network can harm the stability of the network. The concerns regarding aggravated costs, healthcare quality, safety and efficiency of communication channels and most importantly acceptance of a new system shape the problemisation stage. The Hospital Secure Messaging and Communication Platform is the primary actor as well as the obligatory passage point between other actors. Competing roles between the incoming primary actor (Hospital Secure Messaging and Communication Platform) and the outgoing actor (old hospital messaging and communication tools) require that links between the latter (old hospital messaging and communication tools) and other actors (e.g. nurses, medical staff, allied health professionals and patients) are weakened. In addition, the ties (interests) between the incoming actor (Hospital Secure Messaging and Communication Platform) and the other actors need strengthening, through interessement, to be successful. If this process succeeds, then it can facilitate the enrolment stage in which actors accept and align their positions in new networks where the actor old hospital messaging and communication-based tools leaves the network and the Hospital Secure Messaging and Communication Platform enters the network. Mobilisation happens when the new networks become active and stable with the new actor.

The foundation of networks is built upon the rules of interactions between actors. Therefore, continuous translation of interests at different levels is a primary source of social order. It is, therefore, also important to understand the role of controlling elements and their influences and contribution (Law, 2004).

12.4.1.1 Critique and Limitations of ANT

Although ANT has been applied to the implementation and adoption of many IT-based healthcare innovation studies (Berg et al. 2003; Cresswell et al. 2010, 2011; Hall et al. 2010), it is important to note that ANT has also been criticised for its limitations (Cresswell et al. 2010, 2011; Greenhalgh and Stones 2010 Walsham 1997). Some of the key limitations of ANT identified in the literature include a lack of ability to consider the broader social structures (Walsham 1997) and a lack of ability to consider the macro-environmental factors (McLean and Hassard 2004). However, the advocates of ANT have argued that the macro level structures of the system or society are made up of the same artefacts and activities so they can be analysed in the same way as micro level structures and activities. Further the advocates of ANT have argued that ANT is flexible enough to allow different levels of analysis. As (Latour 2005) argues, the difference between network and actor are two faces of same phenomenon. Combining activity theory with ANT can help in overcoming this problem as it can link multiple levels of analysis. Further, it is argued that this can help to understand the transformation from individual activities to organisation level settings (Walsham 1997).

Another criticism of ANT is concerned with its inability to explain the formation of relationships between actors and different changes of events in networks because individual events and activities take place because of change in circumstances (Cresswell et al. 2011; Greenhalgh and Stones 2010; Kaghan and Bowker 2001). This criticism can also be dealt with by combining activity theory as it can explain the role of mediating factors and transformation. ANT's assumption of symmetry between the social and technological actors has also been criticised (Mutch 2002). There is an argument that all actors are not the same as some can have more influence than others and human feelings and emotions can play a strong role in different circumstances (Mutch 2002; Walsham 1997).

Yet another criticism of ANT relates to its methodological standing. It has been argued that ANT is a method of describing rather than explaining; however, Latour (2005) counters this criticism by explaining that ANT does not try to explain the actor's reasons for joining the network but searches for procedural activities that happen during negotiations between different actors. Thus ANT never intends to explain the behaviour, but ANT is a way to understand why and how the actors behave (Law and Hassard 1999), a subtle but significant distinction.

To overcome these limitations, many researchers have suggested that ANT can be combined with other theoretical lenses such as activity theory (AT) (Kaptelinin and Nardi 2006; Engeström 2001; Miettinen 1999), which is what is proffered in this chapter.

12.4.2 Activity Theory (AT)

Activity theory, or cultural-historical theory of activity (Vygotsky 1978), was first developed in the 1920s and 1930s by Lev Vygotsky, a Russian psychologist, together with his colleagues. The fundamental building block of the theory is a human activity involving a subject, i.e. a human agent, and an object, i.e. an objective or goal of activity. This subject-object relationship is mediated by a tool(s), i.e. an instrument(s) that can be physical tools, signs and/or cultural means. Activity theory with its core triangle of subject-object-tool aims to study the human doer and his/her complex and mediated activity in context.

Activity theory was extended by Leontiev (2009) to describe a three-layer model of human activity consisting of activity, actions and operations. Along with these, there is another hierarchy of motivation consisting of motive, goals and conditions. An activity is associated with motive at the top level and can be characterised as high level, significant and holistic. Activity can be achieved through a set of actions and each consisting of operations. An action can be associated with an intention (to achieve a specific goal) and operations. An operation is to be performed routine to complete the action under certain conditions.

Activity theory was further extended by Engeström (1987) and Engeström (1999) to include the collective characteristic of the human activity system. The extended model includes additional collective elements of rules, community and division of labour. Rules and division of labour can be explicit or implicit. Rules refer to conventions, regulations and social relations within a community, and division of labour refers to the organisation of a community to enable the transformation. Therefore, rules mediate the relationship between subject and community, while division of labour mediates the relationship between object and community. The mediating roles of tools, rules and division of labours are historically formed and evolve over time. Further, Engeström's (1987) structure of activity also emphasises the transformation of an object to an outcome.

As shown in Fig. 12.1, the structure of an individual human activity includes a subject, e.g. an individual worker or member of the workplace community; tools,

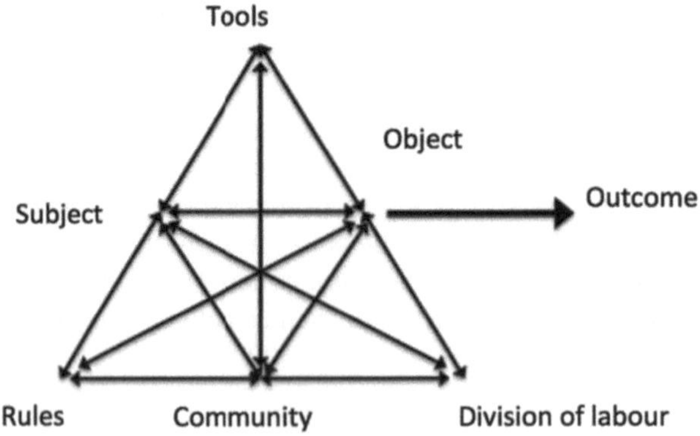

Fig. 12.1 Structure of human activity in activity theory

e.g. conceptual models, tools and/or equipment he/she uses to work; the rules that govern their work; and the purpose to which the subject directs their activity. This structure of individual human activity can be further extended to denote the interaction between multiple human activities where the activities share common goals, rules and division of labours.

Engeström (1987) described human activity as goal-oriented and culture-mediated tool. Furthermore, he added the dynamic, historical dimension to the human activity through the concepts of externalisation and internalisation. Externalisation can be described as the process of change driven by tensions and conflicts motivating for changes and improvements; as a result, new tools are created and introduced. Internalisation can be described the process of reproduction of culture through training of members of the community to adopt changes and fit in the new culture. These two processes are referred to as the dynamic cycle of learning and enable both the historical continuity and adaptation of the culture of the human activity system.

12.4.2.1 Use of Activity Theory in Information Systems

Activity theory has been first argued for use in the information systems (IS) discipline by Nardi (1996) and Kuutti (1995). Both these authors emphasise the notion of technology mediation in activity theory. Technology can be seen as tools or "mediators of human thought and behaviour" (Nardi 1996). Thus, to design an effective mediating technology solution, we should understand users' thoughts and behaviours in the context of use. In the context of IS development, software development can be seen as an activity in which the developer (subject) creates a software application (object) using various tools including analysis and design methods, computers and programming tools (Kuutti 1995; Fjeld et al. 2002). In the context of IS use, an information system can be seen as a mediating tool used by a human agent to pursue an object, according to the workplace rules, coordinated with other members of the community (Hashim and Jones 2007). It has been postulated that in this context, activity theory can be useful to study how people collectively undertake their activities towards an outcome using IS as a mediating tool in a specific workplace environment.

Activity theory has been explored and argued to be a useful theoretical lens to study in information systems (Crawford and Hasan 2006; Häkkinen and Korpela 2007; Hasan and Banna 2010; Sadeghi et al. 2014). A framework has been proposed to describe each research study as a human activity using this theory (Crawford and Hasan 2006). In this framework, the researcher is the individual undertaking research activity using a research tool to achieve a research objective. Activity theory has been found to be useful to explore and elicit users' requirements for an information system as a mediating tool to achieve their professional goals in the healthcare context (Häkkinen and Korpela 2007; Sadeghi et al. 2014). Activity theory was found to be an effective framework to unpack communication activities when assessing hospital communication application in private hospitals in

Melbourne. In the context of IS design, activity theory was found to be a powerful unit of analysis to gain deep understandings of the complexity and dynamics of human activities in health care (Hasan and Banna 2010).

12.5 Conceptual Framework

The initial conceptual framework for the current study identifies the human and non-human factors for a successful hospital communication device development, implementation and adoption as can be seen in Fig. 12.2. At this stage, we have combined the two presented sociotechnical theories to form the conceptualization of the framework. Documents and archival records of healthcare service provider organisations, government agencies and private organisations involved in healthcare service delivery and hospital communication mobile application development and implementation were also analysed in developing this framework. Important activities involved in hospital communication were identified coupled with key considerations and enabling and inhabiting factors for the successful implementation and adoption of communication solutions. All these financial, organizational

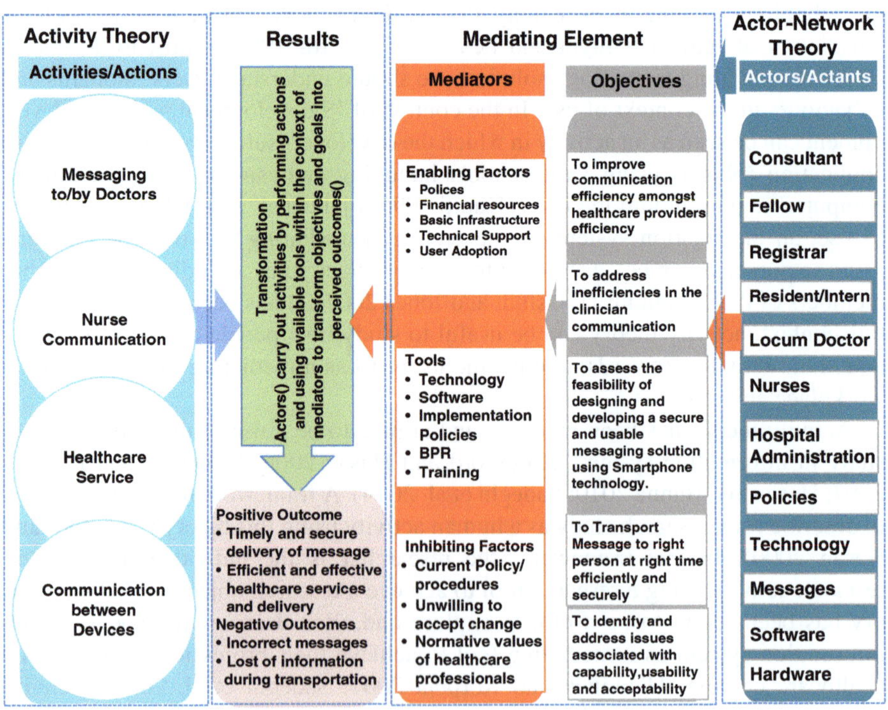

Fig. 12.2 Conceptual framework

and social/people and technological factors were analysed at the micro, meso and macro level, respectively. This has facilitated the development of the proposed conceptual framework.

The proposed model identifies a network of different actors interconnected to each other. It further illustrates that a central issue with the evaluation of IT-based health care is influenced by the complexity of the evaluation objects and includes both social and technical considerations (Ammenwerth et al. 2003). For instance, the nature of the integration of healthcare information systems with the culture and business processes of healthcare organisations puts more emphasis on the evaluation methods and goes beyond the technology aspects of hardware and software. Furthermore, external and internal environmental factors as well as an understanding of the diverse nature of system effects in the healthcare settings are required (Ammenwerth et al. 2003). This emphasis is on creating a better fit between human, contextual and technological factors for the successful implementation and adoption of health information systems (Dansky et al. 2006; Kukafka et al. 2003; Yusof et al. 2008).

To study this complex network of interactions of humans with technology in organisations and certain individual levels, a sociotechnical system (STS) perspective is indeed prudent (Cresswell et al. 2011).

The researchers note that in the conceptual model (Fig. 12.2), it is possible to view these factors at different levels. In particular, micro level issues (i.e. issues related to the individual user level, such as technology acceptance and communication failures), meso level issues (i.e. issues related to the organisational level such as organisation-wise communication policy) and macro level issues (i.e. issues related to the governance such as national health standards) are dealing with policy regarding funding and privacy aspects. However, it is important to remember that the actual factors concerned to the activities in hospital information and communication delivery and distribution are relevant at all levels (micro, meso and macro levels) and together form a heterogeneous network as per actor-network theory (Latour 2005), and thus it is important at least initially to view them at the same level much like the way actants are all treated equally in ANT (Latour 2005).

Therefore, to study this complex network of interactions of humans with technology as the hospital communication platform project necessitates, the holistic approach is a necessity. Holistic means that analysis should be done as a whole including all the interdependent parts of the system and avoid any separate or individual analysis (Latour 2005). This approach serves to capture all issues relating to financial such as funding, organisational such as policy and procedures and social, people and technological factors such as technology acceptance and use during the design, implementation and adoption phases of the hospital communication application.

Our initial investigation into hospital communication solutions and their adoptions has served to indicate a great need to start focusing on social and organisational issues and shift away from the current technocentric obsession of how the technical system can be made to work right. The literature clearly outlines that the failure is not just because of a poor understanding of technological issues but also, and more importantly, about a lack of understanding and interest in organisational, cultural and social issues (Sharma et al. 1999). Ignoring the existing organisational workflows and social interactions in redesigning the organisational processes may hinder the implementation and adoption process, which could have adverse effects on healthcare service outcomes (Muhammad et al. 2012). Therefore, the information system alone might not be the decisive factor, but the social factors are likely to have much more importance in the decision-making process. A sociotechnical design provides a well-thought-out approach to acknowledge the complexities of the healthcare environment and explain the interaction between a social system, hospital activities and a technology (Altman 1997; Atkinson et al. 2001; Coiera 2011). Hence the researchers believe it is only through the adoption of a sociotechnical approach that it will be possible to not only fully capture the complexities and richness of healthcare operations but also be able to analyse them effectively and appropriately and thereby assess critical issues for successful development and implementation to ensue.

12.6 Conclusion and Recommendations

The need for IT-based interventions in the healthcare service delivery to improve information and communication flow is well recognised all around the globe. Different e-health solutions are being implemented with mixed success to address this challenge (Protti and Smit 2006; Basch 2005; DesRoches et al. 2008; Greenhalgh and Stones 2010). It is, therefore, important to evaluate these technologies with theoretically informed approaches to enjoy more successful outcomes.

We believe it is important to develop a deeper understanding of the sociotechnical complexities to the development, adoption, implementation and diffusion of various hospital communication solutions. Specifically, we suggest that a sociotechnical approach can inform and facilitate such evaluations, and we illustrate this by presenting a conceptual framework for the development and implementation of hospital communication system in a private hospital based in Melbourne, Australia. To achieve the required level of robustness, we combined ANT with AT. We are confident that this approach can be beneficial to both practitioners and researchers.

This paper has served to outline the key concepts of ANT and AT that are relevant in the context of the hospital communication system adoption and implementation and discussed the appropriateness of a theoretical lens for the evaluation of hospital communication system in very complex environment of healthcare service delivery. We have also noted that ANT has been criticised by several scholars based on its appropriateness as an ontology and/or epistemology (Latour 2005). Therefore, we recommend that to reduce the negative impact of these limitations, the use of activity theory along with actor-network theory be incorporated. A theoretically conceptualised framework in Fig. 12.2 offers a practical approach to viewing a complex sociotechnical phenomenon such as the development, implementation and adaption and deployment of ICT-based communication tools in hospital environment and its integration into healthcare services and delivery. Practically, this sociotechnical framework offers analytical tools that can assist managers, policymakers and other actors to make sense of the underlying factors surrounding the implementation of technology policies in the societal settings at different levels local in hospital and at macro level including government levels. Further, it will serve to establish proof of concept by theoretical conceptualization of hospital messaging system and usability and feasibility of the proffered solution.

References

Alexander, P. M., & Silvis, E. (2014). Towards extending actor-network theory with a graphical syntax for information systems research. *Information Research*, 19(2), paper 617.

Altman, R. B. (1997). Informatics in the care of patients: Ten notable challenges. *The Western Journal of Medicine, 166*(2), 118–122.

Ammenwerth, E., Gräber, S., Herrmann, G., Bürkle, T., & König, J. (2003). Evaluation of health information systems-problems and challenges. *International Journal of Medical Informatics, 71*(2–3), 125–135.

Atkinson, C., Eldabi, T., Paul, R., & Pouloudi, A. (2001). Investigating integrated socio-technical approaches to health informatics (pp. 10–pp SRC – GoogleScholar).

Basch, P. (2005). Electronic health records and the national health information network: Affordable, adoptable, and ready for prime time? *Annals of Internal Medicine, 143*(3), 227–228.

Berg, M., Aarts, J., & van der Lei, J. (2003). ICT in health care: Sociotechnical approaches. *Methods of Information in Medicine, 42*(4), 297–301.

Berler, A., Pavlopulous, S., & Koutsouris, D. (2005). Using key performance indicators and knoweldge management tools. *IEEE Trans Inf Tech Biomed, 9*(2), 184–192.

Cho, S., Mathiassen, L., & Nilsson, A. (2008). Contextual dynamics during health information systems implementation: An event-based actor-network approach. *European Journal of Information Systems, 17*(6), 614–630.

Coiera, E. (2006). Communication systems in healthcare. *Clinical Biochemist Reviews, 27*(2), 89–98.

Coiera, E. (2011). Do we need a national electronic summary care record? *The Medical Journal of Australia, 194*(2), 90–92.

Crawford, K., & Hasan, H. (2006). Demonstrations of the activity theory framework for research in information systems. *Australasian Journal of Information Systems, 13*, 49–68.

Cresswell, K., Worth, A., & Sheikh, A. (2011). Implementing and adopting electronic health record systems: How actor-network theory can support evaluation. *Clinical Governance: An International Journal, 16*(4), 320–336. https://doi.org/10.1108/14777271111175369

Cresswell, K. M., Worth, A., & Sheikh, A. (2010). Actor-network theory and its role in understanding the implementation of information technology developments in healthcare. *BMC Medical Informatics and Decision Making, 10*, 67. https://doi.org/10.1186/1472-6947-10-67

Dansky, K. H., Thompson, D., & Sanner, T. (2006). A framework for evaluating eHealth research. *Evaluation and Program Planning, 29*(4), 397–404. https://doi.org/10.1016/j.evalprogplan.2006.08.009

Darbyshire, P. (2004). Rage against the machine? *Journal of Clinical Nursing, 13*, 17–25.

DesRoches, C. M., Campbell, E. G., Rao, S. R., Donelan, K., Ferris, T. G., Jha, A., et al. (2008). Electronic health records in ambulatory care – A national survey of physicians. *New England Journal of Medicine, 359*(1), 50–60. https://doi.org/10.1056/NEJMsa0802005

Dowding, D., Mitchell, N., Randell, R., Foster, R., Lattimer, V., & Thompson, C. (2009). Nurses' use of computerised clinical decision support systems: A case site analysis. *Journal of Clinical Nursing, 18*(8), 1159–1167.

Edwards, P. J., Moloney, K. P., Jacko, J. A., & Sainfort, F. (2008). Evaluating usability of a commercial electronic health record: A case study. *International Journal of Human-Computer Studies, 66*(10), 718–728.

Engeström, Y. (1987). *Learning by expanding: An activity-theoretical approach to developmental research*. Orienta-Konsultit: Helsinki.

Engeström, Y. (1999). Outline of three generations of activity theory. Available at: http://www.bath.ac.uk/research/liw/resources/Models%20and%20principles%20of%20Activity%20Theory.pdf

Engeström, Y. (2001). Expansive learning at work: Toward an activity theoretical reconceptualization. *Journal of Education and Work, 14*(1), 133–156.

Fjeld, M., Lauche, K., Bichsel, M., et al. (2002). Physical and virtual tools: Activity theory applied to the design of groupware, a special issue of computer supported cooperative work (CSCW): Activity theory and the practice of design. In B. A. Nardi & D. F. Redmiles (Eds.), *Computer supported cooperative work* (Vol. 11, pp. 153–180).

Free, C., Phillips, G., Watson, L., Galli, L., Felix, L., Edwards, P., & Haines, A. (2013). The effectiveness of mobile-health technologies to improve health care service delivery processes: A systematic review and meta-analysis. *PLoS Medicine, 10*(1), e1001363.

Greenhalgh, T., & Stones, R. (2010). Theorising big IT programmes in healthcare: Strong structuration theory meets actor-network theory. *Social Science & Medicine* (1982), *70*(9), 1285–1294. https://doi.org/10.1016/j.socscimed.2009.12.034

Grisot, M., & Vassilakopoulou, P. (2011). Challenges in institutionalising electronic platforms for patient? Healthcare provider communication. *International Journal of Electronic Healthcare, 6*(2–4), 138–152.

Häkkinen, H., & Korpela, M. (2007). A participatory assessment of IS integration needs in maternity clinics using activity theory. *International Journal of Medical Informatics, 76*, 843–849.

Hall, L. M., Ferguson-Paré, M., Peter, E., White, D., Besner, J., Chisholm, A., & Mildon, B. (2010). Going blank: Factors contributing to interruptions to nurses' work and related outcomes. *Journal of Nursing Management, 18*(8), 1040–1047.

Hanseth, O., Aanestad, M., & Berg, M. (2004). Guest editors' introduction: Actor-network theory and information systems. What's so special? *Information Technology & People, 17*(2), 116–123.

Harvey, M. J., & Harvey, M. G. (2014). Privacy and security issues for mobile health platforms. *Journal of the Association for Information Science and Technology, 65*(7), 1305–1318.

Hasan, H., & Banna, S. (2010). The unit of analysis in IS theory: The case for activity. In *The Fifth Biennial ANU Workshop on Information Systems Foundations*. Canberra, Australia: ANU, pp. 1–18.

Hashim, N., & Jones, M. L. (2007). Activity theory: A framework for qualitative analysis. In *4th International Qualitative Research Convention (QRC)*, Malaysia.

Iyamu, T., & Sekgweleo, T. (2013). Information systems and actor-network theory analysis. *International Journal of Actor-Network Theory and Technological Innovation (IJANTTI), 5*(3), 1–11. https://doi.org/10.4018/jantti.2013070101

Kaghan, W., & Bowker, G. (2001). Out of machine age?: Complexity, sociotechnical systems and actor network theory. *Journal of Engineering and Technology Management, 18*(1), 253–269.

Kaptelinin, V., & Nardi, B. A. (2006). *Acting with technology: Activity theory and interaction design*. Cambridge: MIT Press. https://books.google.com.au/books?hl=en&lr=&id=qYj6AQAAQBAJ&oi=fnd&pg=PP8&dq=activity+theory+and+actor+network+theory&ots=cJN7MIKNjN&sig=rUiRTiKLw-JxfmMw_gn6fEQhu10. Accessed March 28, 2016.

Kukafka, R., Johnson, S. B., Linfante, A., & Allegrante, J. P. (2003). Grounding a new information technology implementation framework in behavioral science: A systematic analysis of the literature on IT use. *Journal of Biomedical Informatics, 36*(3), 218–227.

Kuutti, K. (1995). Activity theory as a potential framework for human-computer interaction research. In B. A. Nardi (Ed.), *Context and consciousness: Activity theory and human-computer interaction*. Cambridge: Massachusetts Institute of Technology.

Latour, B. (2005). *Reassembling the social: An introduction to actor-network-theory*. Oxford: Oxford University Press.
Lau, F. (2007). A proposed benefits evaluation framework for health information systems in Canada. *Healthcare Quaterly, 10*(1), 112–116.
Lau, F., Kuziemsky, C., Price, M., & Gardner, J. (2010). A review on systematic reviews of health information system studies. *Journal of the American Medical Informatics Association, 17*(6), 637–645. https://doi.org/10.1136/jamia.2010.004838
Law, J. (1999). After ANT: Complexity, naming and topology. In J. Law & J. Hassard (Eds.), *Actor network theory and after* (pp. 1–14). Oxford: Blackwell.
Law, J., & Hassard, J. (1999). *Actor network theory and after*. Oxford: Wiley-Blackwell.
Law, John (2004). After method: mess in social science research. London New York: Routledge. ISBN 9780415341752.
Leontiev, A. N. (2009). *Problems of the development of mind*. Kettering: Marxists Internet Archive.
McLean, C., & Hassard, J. (2004). Symmetrical absence/symmetrical absurdity: Critical notes on the production of actor network accounts. *Journal of Management Studies, 41*(3), 493–519. https://doi.org/10.1111/j.1467-6486.2004.00442.x
Meijden, M. J. V. D., Tange, H. J., Troost, J., & Hasman, A. (2003). Determinants of success of inpatient clinical information systems: A literature review. *Journal of the American Medical Informatics Association, 10*(3), 235–243.
Miettinen, R. (1999). The riddle of things: Activity theory and actor network theory as approaches to studying innovations. *Mind, Culture, and Activity, 6*(3), 170–195.
Muhammad, I., Teoh, S. Y., & Wickramasinghe, N. (2012). Why using actor network theory (ANT) can help to understand the personally controlled electronic health record (PCEHR) in Australia. *International Journal of Actor-Network Theory and Technological Innovation (IJANTTI), 4*(2), 44–60.
Mutch, A. (2002). Actors and networks or agents and structures: Towards a realist view of information systems. *Organization, 9*(3), 477–496. https://doi.org/10.1177/135050840293013
Nardi, B. A. (1996). *Context and consciousness: Activity theory and human-computer interaction*. Cambridge: MIT Press.
Ponemon Institute. (2014). The Imprivata report on the economic impact of inefficient communications in healthcare, independent research report conducted by Ponemon Institute LLC.
Protti, D. & Smit, C., (2006). The Netherlands: Another European country where GPs have been using EMRs for over twenty years. *Healthcare Information Management & Communications, 30*(3). Available at: http://www.healthcareimc.com/bcovers/PDFS/TheNetherlands.pdf
Sadeghi, P., Andreev, P., Benyoucef, M., et al. (2014). Activity theory driven system analysis of complex healthcare processes. In *Proceedings of Twenty Second European Conference on Information Systems ECIS'2014 Tel Aviv*.
Sharma, R., Southon, G., & Yetton, P. (1999). Successful IS innovation: The contingent contributions of innovation characteristics and implementation process. *Journal of Information Technology, 14*(1), 53–68. https://doi.org/10.1080/026839699344746
Singleton, V., & Michael, M. (1993). Actor-networks and ambivalence: General practitioners in the UK cervical screening programme. *Social Studies of Science, 23*(2), 227–264.
Smith, A. (2012). Cell Internet Use 2012. Pew Research Internet Project. Retrieved January 20, 2015, from http://www.pewinternet.org/2012/06/26/cell-internet-use-2012/
Stevenson, J., Nilsson, G., Petersson, G., & Johanssson, P. (2010). Nurses' experience of using electronic patient records in everyday practice in acute/inpatient ward settings: A literature review. *Health Informatics Journal, 16*(1), 63–72.
Tatnall, A., & Gilding, A. (2005). Actor-network theory in information systems research.
Varshney, U. (2014). Mobile health: Four emerging themes of research. *Decision Support Systems, 66*, 20–35.
Viitanen, J., Hypponen, H., Laaveri, T., Vanska, J., Reponen, J., & Winblad, I. (2011). National questionnaire study on clinical ICT systems proofs: Physicians suffer from poor usability. *International Journal of Medical Informatics, 80*(10), 708–725.

Vimarlund, V., & Timpka, T. (2002). Design participation as insurance: Risk management and end-user participation in the development of information system in healthcare organizations. *Methods of Information in Medicine, 41*(1), 76–80.
Vogel, D., Viehland, D., Wickramasinghe, N., & Mula, J. M. (2013). Mobile health. *Electronic Markets, 23*(1), 3–4.
Vygotsky, L. S. (1978). *Mind in society: Development of higher psychological process*. Cambridge: Harvard University Press.
Walsham, G. (1997). Actor-network theory and IS research: Current status and future prospects. *Information Systems and Qualitative Research, 466*, 80.
Williams-Jones, B., & Graham, J. E. (2003). Actor-network theory: A tool to support ethical analysis of commercial genetic testing. *New Genetics and Society, 22*(3), 271–296.
Wu, R. C., Lo, V., Morra, D., Wong, B. M., Sargeant, R., Locke, K., et al. (2013). The intended and unintended consequences of communication systems on general internal medicine inpatient care delivery: A prospective observational case study of five teaching hospitals. *Journal of the American Medical Informatics Association: JAMIA, 20*(4), 766–777. https://doi.org/10.1136/amiajnl-2012-001160
Yin, R. 2010 Case Study Research Sage, Thousand Oaks.
Yusof, M. M., Papazafeiropoulou, A., Paul, R. J., & Stergioulas, L. K. (2008). Investigating evaluation frameworks for health information systems. *International Journal of Medical Informatics, 77*(6), 377–385. https://doi.org/10.1016/j.ijmedinf.200

Chapter 13
Using Structuration Theory to Assist in Understanding the Implementation and Adoption of Health Information Systems

Imran Muhammad and Nilmini Wickramasinghe

13.1 Background

Increasingly health information systems (HIS) are introduced into health care as a facilitating tool to support patient care delivery and to improve care quality, safety and efficiency. The introduction of HIS comes with many challenges. These are due to the complexity of healthcare operations such as multidisciplinary characteristics, high stakes of life and death, the tensions between orderly routines and the need for flexibility, the tension between rationale and intuitive clinical judgement and various organisational and regulatory settings (Fichman et al. 2011; Thompson et. al 2008; Shaban 2005). In such a complex context, a good understanding of the facilitating role, i.e. whether and how HIS can support the clinician user in care delivery and also patient in managing and monitoring his/her health, is important. This can enable successful HIS design and implementation as well as superior care delivery.

Health care is an information-rich industry. The motivating notion in support of the introduction of IT (information technology) in healthcare service delivery is to improve the access and delivery of healthcare-related information across healthcare systems locally as well as globally for key stakeholders (e.g. service providers, consumers, government agencies and healthcare managers) reliably and securely so that improved health outcomes and quality of care can be increased significantly (Mort et al. 2009). Use of HIS can also help with cost savings, improving patient involvement and producing useable secondary data for further research and training (Car et al. 2008). However, the transformation from cabinets and paper files to computers and HIS software is not a candid proposition and is sometimes faced with

I. Muhammad · N. Wickramasinghe (✉)
Deakin University, Burwood, VIC, Australia

Epworth HealthCare, Richmond, VIC, Australia

N. Wickramasinghe, J. L. Schaffer (eds.), *Theories to Inform Superior Health Informatics Research and Practice*, Healthcare Delivery in the Information Age,
https://doi.org/10.1007/978-3-319-72287-0_13

many known and unknown hurdles, such as technological, organisational, financial and people issues, as a result of the complex and multifaceted environment of healthcare service delivery where different and important healthcare stakeholders (e.g. service providers, consumers, government agencies and healthcare managers) and technology interact with each other in very complex ways (Ammenwerth et al. 2006; André et al. 2008; Catwell and Sheikh 2009; Cresswell et al. 2010; DesRoches et al. 2008; Lorenzi et al. 2009).

Given the inherent complexities of healthcare operations, it is argued in this chapter that human and non-human actor interactions are challenging and need to be evaluated with theoretically informed techniques (Wickramasinghe and Schaffer 2010); one approach identified in the literature used to facilitate correct and accurate capturing of the complexities and levels of interactions in healthcare operations is to use a structuration theory (ST) (Muhammad et al. 2012; Cresswell et al. 2010). To determine the functionality of a system, it is important to understand the fit between technical subsystems and social subsystems in an organisation (Mitchell and Nault 2008). The emphasis is then not only on studying the impact of the technology on organisations and their work processes but also on the impact of social and people issues pertaining to technology and work processes (Cresswell et al. 2010). For this reason, it is also important to understand the interrelationship and interactions of the technical and social systems between each other (Coiera 2004).

The lens of structuration theory (ST) can be applied to analyse the data collected during the research. This can assist the researcher to understand the user requirements and their perceptions and expectations from the HIT implementation and to understand their needs and intentions to adopt the new e-health system.

This chapter shows the benefits of applying a structuration theory (ST) lens of analysis to the collective data set to further understand the richness and potential challenges, complications and general complexities of any/all people/technology interactions as the HIS implementation and adoption move forward. We believe that this can be achieved by the incorporation of an ST analysis as is illustrated in this chapter, and by doing an ST analysis a successful and more realistic mapping of the rich and complex environment which ultimately will ensure the appropriate design, development, implementation and adoption of the HIS solution will be enabled. This process serves to illustrate the power of such an ST analysis for a healthcare delivery context.

13.2 Theoretical Foundations

Healthcare systems are complex systems especially when they integrate with information technology. The challenge of this study is further complicated by the interaction of different human and non-human actors that mainly lead to failed technology-based healthcare interventions and implementations. As a result, failure rates are unsurprisingly high, costly and have far-reaching impacts (Cresswell et al. 2011). Thus, it becomes necessary and important to evaluate these interventions with theoretically informed techniques to enable a deeper understanding which in turn can facilitate a successful implementation and adoption of health information technology (Cresswell et al. 2011).

We believe that a sociotechnical systems perspective can provide the foundations for a better understanding of these systems so that there is a better evaluation and provision of specific solutions to address gaps in their current development, implementation and adoption. Furthermore, it can also enhance our understanding by providing a mechanism to study the relationships between technology, organisation, people, social and finance factors that influence the success of e-health implementation and adoption. We believe that a viable healthcare system can only be achieved if these considerations are jointly optimised.

Our goal was to investigate this in the specific context of the HIS, in Australia. The initial analysis and the conceptual framework presented for the HIS development in Australia to date show that the processes underlying the HIS development, implementation and adoption are inherently sociotechnical in nature. A sociotechnical approach of study therefore will allow for more flexibility in system design and adoption.

13.3 Structuration Theory (ST)

Structuration theory was developed by British sociologist Anthony Giddens (Giddens 2013). The purpose of this theory was to investigate the phenomenon of integrating two divergent standards of social thinking, namely, structuralism and functionalism, emphasising notions of social structure and interpretivism and bestowing prominence to human agency and meaning. It is important here to note that the experience of social actor and the existence of any form of social totality are not any concern of Giddens' investigation (Giddens 2013). Instead, in structuration theory, his main emphasis is on understanding how social practices are ordered across time and space. In structuration theory, Giddens (2013) tries to re-form structure and human agency as the duality of structure and action. In other words, social structure is drawn upon by agents in their day-to-day actions and is therefore produced and reproduced by this action. At the same time, action is both inhibited and empowered by structure (ibid). Accordingly, action is only possible then because of structure, and structure itself can only be instituted through action. It is important here to understand the Giddens (2013) meanings of agency and its operational processes in a structure.

In social science research, there exists a standing debate over the primacy of structure or agency in shaping human behaviour. According to Barker (2011) structure is the recurrent patterned arrangements which influence or limit the choices and opportunities available, whereas agency deals with the capacity of individuals to act independently and to make their own free choices. In structuration theory, micro- or macro-level analysis is done in isolation, and their individuality is not satisfactory (Barker 2011).

The goal of structuration theory is to interpret the relationship between human actions and social structures. The notion of structure is thought of as an immaterial notion. According to Walsham (1997), there are two basic elements of ST:

1. The way of capturing the two different levels of actions and structures with the help of duality of structure
2. The identification of vehicles or modalities that can help to link those two levels

This duality of structure is important in explaining how structures behave. Structures try to restrain the actions, and at the same time these structures are the product of human actions. Moreover humans produce or re-form structures by their actions through a linking expedient known as modalities (Hanseth et al. 2004).

In Hanseth and Monteiro, (1998) three modalities are identified—interpretative scheme, facility and norms. The interpretative scheme defines the phenomenon of agents understanding and then the procedures to institutionalise this developed understanding. It facilitates the shared stock of knowledge that humans extract while interpreting situations that lead to shared meanings and open communication channels. Facility refers to the mobilisation of dominant resources; in other words, it encompasses the media through which power is implemented.

For example, any IT-based system tries to build a system of domination (Hanseth and Monteiro 1998). The last modality, known as norms, controls actions through mobilisation of endorsements and defines the validity of relations (Hanseth and Monteiro 1998).

13.4 The Structuration Theory Approach to Evaluate HIS

To fully comprehend the successful development, implementation and use of HIS, it is important to investigate beyond the linear models of technology adoption, diffusion and transfer. Simple binary models are not enough because of the complex and dynamic nature of healthcare settings. The complex nature of interaction between the technology and social often renders the two inseparable (Williams-Jones and Graham 2003).

ST is considered an appropriate choice to analyse HIS because it can be used to identify and acknowledge the impacts of human and non-human, social or policy issues within the healthcare setting (Hanseth and Monteiro 1998). Further, ST is robust enough to accurately capture the complexities, nuances and richness of healthcare operations. In so doing, ST can also be used to investigate and theorise questions about how to identify the broader social structures of an organisation and consider the macro-environmental factors (McLean and Hassard 2004) for the analysis of the HIS.

The ability of agency and end-users to contest the problematisation of the technology can be affected by power structures already present in the network of human and non-human entities. These considerations are naturally relevant to the context of the HIS implementation and adoption in complex healthcare settings.

Any translation may succeed or fail, but only when failures of technology and networks occur one will be able to reveal the underlying reasons and embedded norms and values (Greenhalgh and Stones 2010; Law and Hassard 1999; Williams-Jones and Graham 2003). In an ST context, translation that has not properly incorporated the differences in social (nurse's perceptions, requirements and needs) and technology/system offerings has led to these issues arising. However, without ST it is also easy to dismiss the user perspective as "they just do not get it", which happens frequently in the implementation of information systems into healthcare contexts (Greenhalgh and Stones 2010).

Structuration theory is considered an appropriate choice for HIS implementation and adoption because it can identify and then acknowledge all human and non-human actors within the healthcare setting and any impact of their interaction on social or policy issues that might occur (Latour et al. 1996).

ST can also assist in understanding the active role of objects in shaping social realities by challenging the assumption of the separation between non-human and human worlds (Greenhalgh and Stones 2010; Law and Hassard 2004; Rydin 2010; Tobler 2008; Walsham 1997). This would assist researchers in studying the complexities of the relationships between human and non-human actors, the sustainability of power relationships between human actors and what kind of influence artefacts can have on human actors' relationships in transforming health care (Cresswell et al. 2010).

13.5 Development, Adoption, Implementation and Diffusion of the HIS Technology

A large number of health information systems have been implemented around the globe with mixed results, despite the claims that electronic health records (EHRs) can play a significant role in efficiency and effectiveness of healthcare service delivery. The literature provides evidence of failed clinical systems and lack of adoption by users (Basch 2005; DesRoches et al. 2008; Protti et al. 2009). Challenges and barriers to implementation and adoption of electronic health record have been extensively debated. We have divided these barriers into different categories ranging from environmental, social, technical and organisational (André et al. 2008). These factors can play a very crucial role in the decision-making process of technology adoption (Huang and Palvia 2001). In a healthcare service context where organisations are now required to work as a networked framework, health information technology implementation and adoption would be a more complex and challenging endeavour because of the different business processes, the available infrastructure, compatibility issues, decision centres, authorisation mechanisms and hierarchies, enterprise systems and data semantics (Avgerou 2008; Liu et al. 2011; Trudel 2010) and the nature of healthcare system as a complex adaptive system as stated by Leykum et al. (2009).

The most commonly discussed topics in Australian healthcare IT transformation include legal issues, individual privacy, health information security and ethics. Information is considered as the private property of the person about whom this information describes, so information privacy is defined as the ability of an individual to control the access to their own personal information (Culnan and Armstrong 1997; Staples 2007). Information privacy, security and confidentiality are very strongly observed in healthcare settings and, thus, are closely related to the use of e-health systems. Even though confidentiality, privacy and security are closely related, they are very much different concepts from each other. The right of a person or entity to be left alone and undisturbed is perceived as his/her right of privacy (Staples 2007). The right of someone in protecting his/her information from intentional or unintentional disclosure is confidentiality (Staples 2007). Security does not necessarily lead to privacy because trust must be considered in privacy protection. Hovenga et al. (2010, p. 77) described the relationship between security and privacy as:

> The concepts of security and privacy in health information systems are distinct but inextricably linked, like Siamese twins. The distinction can be expressed as follows: security is the protection of computers from people, and privacy is the protection of people from computers. The maintenance of privacy and security are two of the goals of a health informatics system.

The breach of privacy is a common concern among consumers and privacy advocates despite the HIS draft's (Personally Controlled Electronic health Record Act 2012) emphasis on the security and privacy of electronic health record of individuals as well as any information that is protected by law. Despite the placement of these requirements, the standards applied and the language used are vague, which can aggravate more confusion and raise concerns among both healthcare providers and consumers (Hoffinan and Podguski 2008).

The invasion of patient privacy can have a negative impact on the quality of patient health care (Parente and McCullough 2009). Hence, any technology use without proper security and privacy measures can pose a serious threat to patient-doctor relationships and it can lead to mistrust (ibid). Consequently, the patient may withhold important information from a healthcare service provider that can negatively impact healthcare service quality (ibid). Further standardisation is important for the setting of security and access rules for the system (Hoffinan and Podguski 2008). This has been identified as a policy issue, and a need for direct involvement of patients in consultation regarding development and implementation of the HIS system, these patients not being involved in interest groups and citizen privacy and information security groups, has been emphasised as policy issues mainly concerning EHR and e-health have been proved challenging and contentious (Showell 2011).

Financial issues such as initial implementation and adoption cost and total cost of ownership have been identified as a significant hurdle in adoption and implementation of health information technology, especially electronic health records (Aaronson et al. 2001; Aarts et al. 2004; Aarts and Koppel 2009; Abbott 2005; André et al. 2008; Ash et al. 2006; Ashish 2009; Bahensky et al. 2008; Bates 2005; Bernstein et al. 2007; Boonstra and Broekhuis 2010; Culnan and Armstrong 1997; Goldstein and Blumenthal 2008; HFMA 2006; Kaplan and Harris-Salamone 2009; Kennedy 2011; Liu et al. 2011; Thweatt and Kleiner 2007; Trudel 2010; Weimar 2009). These issues range from start-up costs to software upgrades and staff training. This is acknowledged that for sole practitioners, the capital cost of healthcare ICT is very high and not considered as a good investment for returns (Ashish 2009). The lack of incentives, budget overruns and high time costs are other financial concerns (Boonstra and Broekhuis 2010; Cohn et al. 2009; DePhillips 2007; Liu et al. 2011; Trudel 2010).

The common perception is that primarily economic benefits in using e-health technologies would benefit consumers and that they can use online services for simple health information and will undertake fewer GP visits and fewer consultations and tests and that governments would benefit from this where healthcare systems are more dependent on public funding. This scenario does not benefit healthcare service providers because they will lose business or will not be compensated for online consultations (Bates 2005; Cohn et al. 2009; Hikmet et al. 2008). The business model used in compensating healthcare service providers is a retrospective form of payment, e.g. a fee for service, the prospective form of payment, and this form of payment is not necessarily encouraging factors for e-health adoption for service providers (Cohn et al. 2009; Hennington and Janz 2007).

IT implementations can cause serious disruptions in services deliveries and in result productivity; healthcare services are one of the very critical areas of services that cannot afford disruptions (Bates 2005; Kralewski et al. 2010; Scott et al. 2005). Suspending operations whilst the healthcare system is being implemented and the staff is being trained is not possible in the healthcare industry; this can result in increased workload for staff as they may have to spend after hours' time for learning and training (Bates 2005; Kralewski et al. 2010; Scott et al. 2005). Private healthcare practices cannot afford suspension of their services for an extended period of time because of the permanent nature of patient visits and consultations; by doing so they would be running a risk of losing patients.

Many organisational barriers to implementation and adoption of e-health technologies in organisations have been reported in the literature, for example, poor governance, organisational culture and proper management of the change process that could harm the flow of transformation (Bernstein et al. 2007; Greenhalgh and Stones 2010; Hoffinan 2009; Kennedy 2011). These issues can aggravate the resistance to the change process and complicate the dissemination of the e-health technology. Due to the complexity of healthcare delivery systems, assimilation of information technology in health care needs a deeper understanding of organisational and environmental aspects of technology adoption and use (Catwell and Sheikh 2009; Yusof et al. 2008). Technological issues can also exacerbate the resistance to the adoption of health information technology. The lack of infrastructure and standards and protocols results in a fragmentation of healthcare information systems, and this contributes to creating a very complex situation for coordination

(Davidson and Heslinga 2007; HFMA 2006; Hoffinan and Podguski 2008; Kennedy 2011; Kralewski et al. 2010; Trudel 2010; Vitacca et al. 2009). The lack of interpretability between different healthcare delivery and management systems can hinder the expansion of the use of this technology and its sustainability (André et al. 2008; Gaylin et al. 2005; Kennedy 2011; Liu et al. 2011). Pre-implementation and post-implementation vendor support is another key concern for organisations (Kralewski et al. 2010; Cohn et al. 2009; Kennedy 2011; Liu et al. 2011; Trudel 2010; Tang et al. 2006). The lack of technical resources and experience with information technology implementation within healthcare settings are other problems faced by many (Torda et al. 2010; Trudel 2010; Liu et al. 2011; Kennedy 2011; André et al. 2008; Bath 2008; DePhillips 2007; Davidson and Heslinga 2007; McReavy et al. 2009). The accuracy of data obtained through a health information system and its ability in sorting, querying and validating data in some cases is very poor and is considered as a barrier for HIT adoption (Kimaro and Nhampossa 2004; Rosebaugh 2004; Rosenbloom et al. 2006).

People issues, ranging from user acceptance (Agarwal and Prasad 1997; Frame et al. 2008), perceived ease of use (Al-Azmi et al. 2009), lack of knowledge about the system (André et al. 2008; Bath 2008; Elrod and Androwich 2009; Kaplan and Harris-Salamone 2009; Liu et al. 2011), lack of training, lack of stakeholder consultation (Showell 2011), lack of willingness to assimilate the technology into daily routines and processes (Cash 2008; Davidson and Heslinga 2007; Kaplan and Harris-Salamone 2009; Ross et al. 2010), conflict between system and user-embedded values (Cash 2008; Kaplan and Harris-Salamone 2009), complex and complicated user interfaces (Yusof et al. 2007), conflict between physician activities and training schedules (André et al. 2008; Yusof et al. 2007; Kaplan and Harris-Salamone 2009) and complications in patient-provider communications, are some of the major concerns. It is paramount that the systems are user centric and have a good fit with user values as well as existing healthcare systems. Table 13.1 below further explains the nature of these issues and factors as they relate to the adoption and implementation of e-health technologies in complex healthcare settings.

Healthcare systems are complex systems especially when they integrate with information technology. This environment is further complicated by the interaction of different human and non-human actors that often lead to failed technology-based healthcare interventions and implementations, and hence, failure rates are unsurprisingly high, costly and have far-reaching impacts (Cresswell et al. 2011). Thus, it becomes necessary and important to evaluate these interventions with theoretically informed techniques to enable a deeper understanding which in turn can facilitate a successful implementation and adoption of health information technology (Cresswell et al. 2011).

Given the complex nature of healthcare system and the HIS adoption complexities described in previous sections, conceptualising and framing the critical factors for evaluating the system is important. Hence the next section of this chapter will explain the conceptual model derived from this literature review.

We contend that sociotechnical systems perspective can provide the foundations for a fuller understanding so that there is a better evaluation and provision of

Table 13.1 Key factors and issues regarding the adoption and implementation of e-health technologies

Factors and issues	Nature of factors and issues
Fit between task and technology	Sociotechnical
Technical support	Sociotechnical
Different HIT systems and their communication standards	Purely technical
Fragmentation	Purely technical
Fit between HIT and user skill	Sociotechnical
Protocols and standards	Purely technical
Provided security	Sociotechnical
Access rules	Sociotechnical
Technology infrastructure	Purely technical
Complex user interface	Purely technical
Difficult terminologies	Purely technical
User beliefs	Purely social
User attitude	Purely social
Alignment of technology with the values of the user	Sociotechnical
User training	Sociotechnical
Staffing and skills	Sociotechnical
Resistance to change	Purely social
Lack of user involvement in all the stages of system life cycle	Sociotechnical
Legislative and legal issues	Purely social
Stakeholder support	Purely social
Trust	Purely social
Ethics and privacy	Purely social
Complex nature of healthcare settings	Purely social
Lack of sustainable models for e-health solutions	Sociotechnical
Contextual and environmental factors	Purely social
Clarification of roles and responsibilities	Purely social
BPR	Sociotechnical
Health organisation and technology fit	Sociotechnical
Poor governance of health institutions and technology	Sociotechnical
Leadership	Sociotechnical
High time cost	Sociotechnical
Budget overruns	Sociotechnical
Technology cost	Sociotechnical
Business case	Purely social
Lack of incentives for service providers	Purely social

specific solutions to address gaps in their current development, implementation and adoption. Furthermore, it can also enhance our understanding by providing a mechanism to study the relationships between technology organisation, people, social and financial factors that influence the success of e-health implementation and adoption. We believe that a viable healthcare system can only be achieved if these considerations are jointly optimised.

13.6 Conceptual Framework

The initial conceptual framework for this chapter by identifying the human and non-human factors for successful HIS implementation and adoption was developed and presented. Five key considerations and factors were identified for the successful implementation and adoption of e-health solutions in general, namely, financial, organisational, social, people and technological factors at micro, meso, and macro level. These have facilitated the development of the proposed conceptual framework as presented in Fig. 13.1.

The Table 13.2 below maps the key identified factors specifically to the healthcare environment in Australia.

Considering the HIS shares many similar factors to other e-health solutions, it is logical to use these factors as the basis of our model. This conceptual model serves to capture the important aspects of the barriers and facilitators for the prediction of the successful adoption and implementation of the HIS. The proposed model identifies a network of different actors interconnected to each other. It further illustrates that a central issue with the evaluation of IT-based health care is influenced by the complexity of the evaluation objects and includes both social and technical considerations (Ammenwerth et al. 2006). For instance, the nature of the integration of healthcare information systems with the culture and business processes of healthcare organisations puts more emphasis on the evaluation methods and goes beyond the technology aspects of hardware and software, furthermore, external and internal environmental factors, and an understanding of the diverse nature of system effects in the healthcare settings is required (Ammenwerth et al. 2006). This emphasis is on creating a better fit between human, contextual and technological factors for the successful implementation and adoption of health information systems (Dansky et al. 1999; Kukafka et al. 2003; Yusof et al. 2008).

To study this complex network of interactions of humans with technology in organisations and certain individual levels, a sociotechnical system (STS) perspective is indeed prudent (Cresswell et al. 2011).

We note that in the conceptual model (Fig. 13.1), it is possible to view these factors at different levels, in particular micro-level issues (i.e. issues related to the individual user level), meso-level issues (i.e. issues related to the organisational level) and macro level issues (i.e. issues related to the government level) dealing with policy regarding funding and privacy aspects. However, it is important to remember that the actual factors are relevant at all levels (micro, meso and macro levels) and together form a heterogeneous network as per actor-network theory (Latour 2005), and thus it is important at least initially to view them at the same level much like the way actants are all treated equally in ANT (Latour 2005).

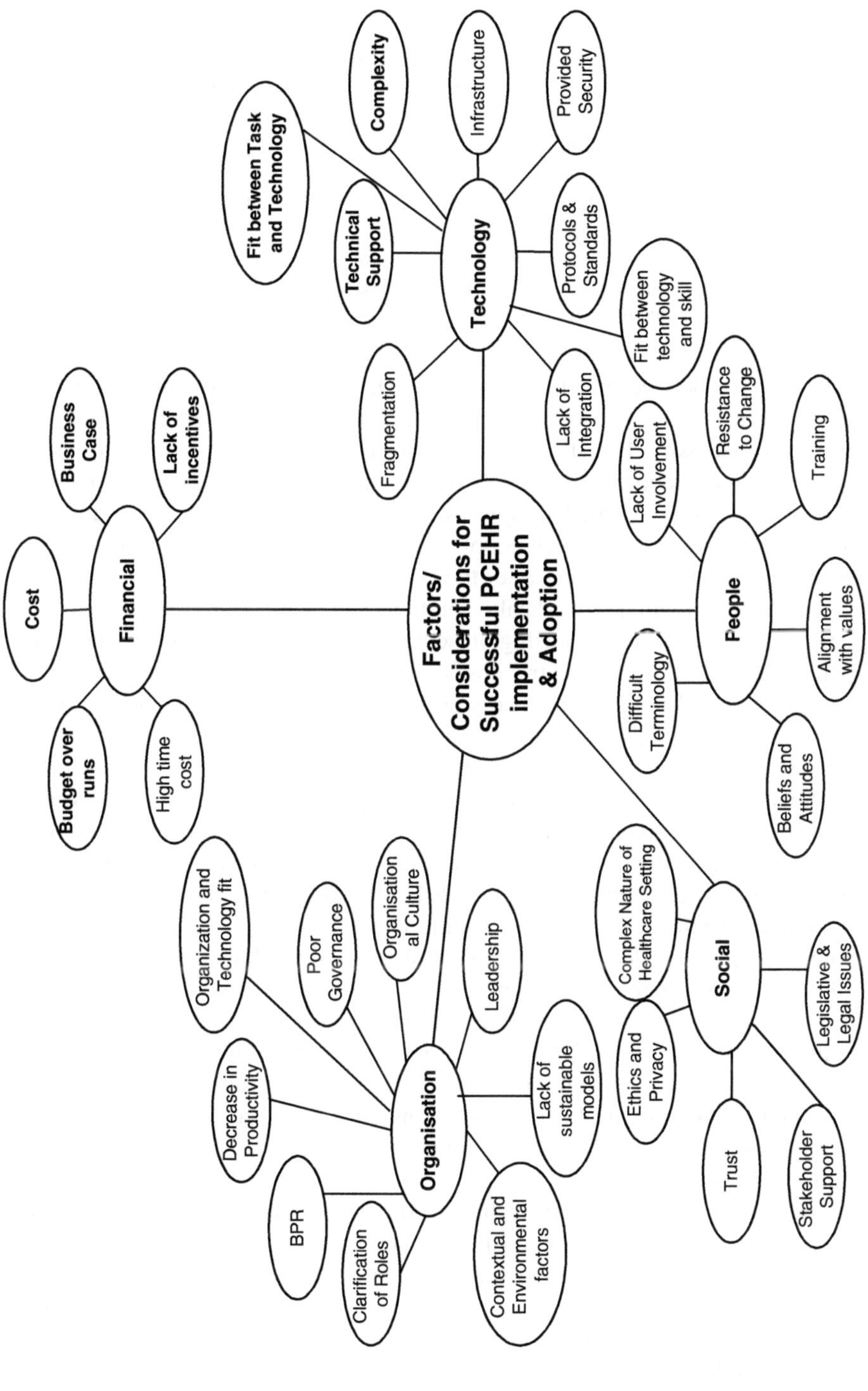

Fig. 13.1 Conceptual framework

Table 13.2 Mapping of key factors to the Australian healthcare environment

Key factors	Mapping with health care
Technology	HIS, fragmented healthcare systems such as radiology and labs
People	Healthcare consultants, GPs, specialists, allied healthcare service providers, clinic and hospital administrators, and healthcare insurance individuals
Social	Health-related legislation and laws, user trust, ethics and privacy rules, stakeholder support
Organisation	Hospitals, doctor clinics, allied health organisations, healthcare ministries, state and federal health organisations
Financial	Payers, funding organisations, private insurance, public insurance, healthcare direct and indirect cost, healthcare budgets, e-health costs. Doctor and other health service provider incentives

Therefore, we believe that to study this complex network of interactions of humans with technology in organisations and certain individual levels, a holistic approach is a necessity. Holistic means that analysis should be done as a whole including all the interdependent parts of the system and avoid any separate or individual analysis (Latour 2005). This approach serves to capture all issues relating to financial, organisational and social, people and technological factors during design, implementation and adoption phases of the HIS.

Our initial investigation into e-health solutions and their adoptions has served to indicate a great need to start focusing on social and organisational issues and shift away from the current techno centric obsession of how the technical system can be made to work right. The literature clearly outlines that the failure is not just because of a poor understanding of technological issues but also, and more importantly, about a lack of understanding and interest in organisational, cultural and social issues (Sharma et al. 1999). Ignoring the existing organisational workflows and social interactions in redesigning the organisational processes may hinder the implementation and adoption process, which could have adverse effects on healthcare service outcomes (Muhammad et al. 2012). Therefore the information system alone might not be the decisive factor, but the social factors are likely to have much more importance in the decision-making process. A sociotechnical design provides a well-thought-out approach to acknowledge the complexities of the healthcare environment and explain the interaction between a social system and a technology (Altman 1997; Atkinson et al. 2001; Coiera 2011). We believe, it is only by adopting a sociotechnical approach that it will be possible to not only fully capture the complexities and richness of healthcare operations but also be able to analyse them effectively and appropriately and thereby assess critical issues for successful e-health solutions to ensue.

The mainstream e-health and health information system implementation and adoption researchers tend to adopt a strong positivistic stance; they have used variance theories and factor-based approaches to create new knowledge about the phenomenon under investigation.

The basic assumption of these approaches is that cause-and-effect relationships are indistinct and prevalent when studying e-health implementations. Alternatively, there are researchers whose argument is that the study of health information systems and e-health implementation is a relatively new phenomenon and needs theoretically rich and informed research approaches to investigate the problem in hand.

For this chapter, the researchers have used sociotechnical theory supported by an interpretivist framework to better understand the complexity of implementation and adoption of HIS. This choice is consistent with many other researchers' view that structuration theory (ST) can help to understand the sociotechnical nature of information system in healthcare settings (Walsham 1997; Tobler 2008; Greenhalgh and Stones 2010; Cresswell et al. 2010; Timpka et al. 2007; Wickramasinghe and Bali 2009). In contrast of using popular adoption and diffusion theories to understand the implementation, adoption and use of the HIS—such as, the theory of reasoned action (TRA), the theory of diffusion and the technology acceptance model (TAM)—this chapter's choice was to use sociotechnical theory-based analysis lens because the HIS implementation and adoption in healthcare services sector need to understand the interaction between human and non-human actors. This chapter acquaints with the HIS and e-health researchers specifically to structuration theory (ST) as suitable theoretical framework for understanding the relationships between technologies, a non-human actor, and human actors such as key stakeholders in the HIS implementation and adoption and interpreting the processes and structures of organisations such as NEHTA and department of health and ageing.

A foremost issue in this study was to improve the understanding of the complexities of the HIS implementation and adoption. The use of structuration theory can explain the interactions and roles of some key actors.

Structuration theory was considered an appropriate choice for this chapter because it has helped the researcher to identify and then acknowledge all human and non-human actors within the healthcare setting and then study the impact of their interaction on social or policy issues that had impact on the HIS implementation and adoption (Latour 2003).

In summary, the way for academics to analyse future e-health implementation and adoptions is by understanding the interconnected perspectives of meaning, context, process, structure and technology.

13.7 Conclusion

The need for IT-based interventions in the healthcare services delivery to improve information and communication and thereby provide superior value-based care is well recognised globally. Different e-health solutions are being implemented with mixed success to address this challenge (Protti and Smit 2006; Basch 2005; DesRoches et al. 2008; Greenhalgh and Stones 2010). It is, therefore, important to evaluate these technologies with theoretically informed approaches to enjoy more successful outcomes.

We believe it is important to develop a deeper understanding of the constraint to the development, adoption, implementation and diffusion of these various HIS solutions. Specifically, we suggest that a sociotechnical, e.g. ST-based, approach can inform and facilitate such evaluations.

A sociotechnical approach of study will allow more flexibility in system design and adoption. We have argued that this approach will be of benefit to both practitioners for better design and implementation and researchers for better evaluation. One of the main challenges of technology-based organisational change research is to find the answer of an ontological question of balance between agency and structures (McPhee and Poole 2001; Tobler 2008).

This chapter has served to outline the key concepts of ST that are relevant in the context of the HIS adoption and implementation and discussed the appropriateness of an ST-based theoretical lens for the evaluation of HIS in very complex environment of healthcare service delivery.

References

Aaronson, J. W., Murphy-Cullen, C. L., Chop, W. M., & Frey, R. D. (2001). Electronic medical records: The family practice resident perspective. *Family Medicine, 33*(2), 128–132.

Aarts, J., Doorewaard, H., & Berg, M. (2004). Understanding implementation: The case of a computerized physician order entry system in a large Dutch University Medical Center. *Journal of the American Medical Informatics Association, 11*, 207–216.

Aarts, J., & Koppel, R. (2009). Implementation of computerized physician order entry in seven countries. *Health Affairs (Project Hope), 28*(2), 404–414.

Abbott, T. (2005). The adoption of eHealth in Australia. In The Health Informatics Conference Melbourne 2005. Melbourne.

Agarwal, R., & Prasad, J. (1997). The role of innovation characteristics and perceived voluntariness in the acceptance of information technologies. *Decision Sciences, 28*(3), 557–582.

Altman, R. B. (1997). Informatics in the care of patients: Ten notable challenges. *The Western Journal of Medicine, 166*(2), 118–122.

Al-Azmi, S., Al-Enezi, N., & Chowdhury, R. (2009). Users' attitudes to an electronic medical record system and its correlates: A multivariate analysis. *Health Information Management Journal, 38*(2), 33–40.

Ammenwerth, E., Iller, C., & Mahler, C. (2006). IT-adoption and the interaction of task, technology and individuals: A fit framework and a case study. *BMC Medical Informatics and Decision Making, 6*, 3.

André, B., Ringdal, G. I., Loge, J. H., Rannestad, T., Laerum, H., & Kaasa, S. (2008). Experiences with the implementation of computerized tools in health care units: A review article. *International Journal of Human–Computer Interaction, 24*(8), 753–775.

Ash, J. S., Sittig, D. F., Campbell, E., Guappone, K., & Dykstra, R. (2006). An unintended consequence of CPOE implementation: Shifts in power, control, and autonomy. In AMIA Annual Symposium Proceedings (Vol. 2006, p. 11).

Ashish, K. (2009). Use of electronic health records in U. S Hospitals Medical Benefits. https://doi.org/101056NEJMsa0900592, 25(10 SRC–GoogleScholar), 4–9.

Atkinson, C., Eldabi, T., Paul, R., & Pouloudi, A. (2001). Investigating integrated socio-technical approaches to health informatics (p. 10–pp SRC–GoogleScholar)

Avgerou, C. (2008). Information systems in developing countries: A critical research review. *Journal of Information Technology, 23*, 133–146.

Bahensky, J. A., Jaana, M., & Ward, M. M. (2008). Health care information technology in rural America: Electronic medical record adoption status in meeting the national agenda. *The*

Journal of Rural Health: Official Journal of the American Rural Health Association and the National Rural Health Care Association, 24(2), 101–105.
Barker, C. (2011). Cultural Studies: Theory and Practice (Fourth Edition edition). London: SAGE Publications Ltd.
Basch, P. (2005). Electronic health records and the national health information network: Affordable, adoptable, and ready for prime time? *Annals of Internal Medicine, 143*(3), 227–228.
Bates, D. W. (2005). Physicians and ambulatory electronic health records. *Health Affairs, 24*, 1180–1189.
Bath, P. (2008). Health informatics: Current issues and challenges. *Journal of Information Science, 34*(4), 501.
Bernstein, M. L., McCreless, T., & Côté, M. J. (2007). Five constants of information technology adoption in healthcare. *Hospital Topics, 85*(1), 17–25.
Boonstra, A., & Broekhuis, M. (2010). Barriers to the acceptance of electronic medical records by physicians from systematic review to taxonomy and interventions. *BMC Health Services Research, 10*(1), 231.
Car, J., Anandan, C., Black, A., Cresswell, K., Pagliari, C., McKinstry, B., et al. (2008). The impact of eHealth on the quality & safety of healthcare: A systematic overview and synthesis of the literature, report, NHS Connecting for Health Evaluation Programme.
Cash, J. (2008). Technology can make or break the hospital-physician relationship. *Healthcare Financial Management: Journal of the Healthcare Financial Management Association, 62*(12), 104–109.
Catwell, L., & Sheikh, A. (2009). Evaluating eHealth interventions: The need for continuous systemic evaluation. *PLoS Medicine, 6*(8), e1000126. https://doi.org/10.1371/journal.pmed.1000126
Cohn, K., Berman, J., Chaiken, B., Green, D., Green, M., Morrison, D., et al. (2009). Engaging physicians to adopt healthcare information technology. *Journal of Healthcare Management/ American College of Healthcare Executives, 54*(5), 291.
Coiera, E. (2004). Four rules for the reinvention of health care. *British Medical Journal, 328*(7449), 1197–1199.
Coiera, E. (2011). Do we need a national electronic summary care record? *The Medical Journal of Australia, 194*(2), 90–92.
Cresswell, K., Worth, A., & Sheikh, A. (2011). Implementing and adopting electronic health record systems: How actor-network theory can support evaluation. *Clinical Governance: An International Journal, 16*(4), 320–336.
Cresswell, K. M., Worth, A., & Sheikh, A. (2010). Actor-network theory and its role in understanding the implementation of information technology developments in healthcare. *BMC Medical Informatics and Decision Making, 10*, 67.
Culnan, M., & Armstrong, P. K. (1997). Information privacy concerns, procedural fairness and impersonal trust: An empirical investigation. Available at: http://citeseer.ist.psu.edu/viewdoc/summary?doi=10.1.1.40.5243
Dansky, K. H., Gamm, L. D., Vasey, J. J., & Barsukiewicz, C. K. (1999). Electronic medical records: are physicians ready? *J Healthc Manag, 44*(6), 440–454.
Davidson, E., & Heslinga, D. (2007). Bridging the IT – Adoption Gap for Small Physician Practices: An Action Research Study on Electronic Health Records. *Information Systems Management, 24*(1), 15.
DePhillips, H. A. (2007). Initiatives and barriers to adopting health information technology: A US perspective. *Disease Management and Health Outcomes, 15*(1), 1–6. Available at: http://ideas.repec.org/a/wkh/dmhout/v15y2007i1p1-6.html. Accessed September 27, 2011.
DesRoches, C. M., Campbell, E. G., Rao, S. R., Donelan, K., Ferris, T. G., Jha, A., et al. (2008). Electronic health records in ambulatory care – A national survey of physicians. *New England Journal of Medicine, 359*(1), 50–60. https://doi.org/10.1056/NEJMsa0802005
Elrod, J., & Androwich, I. M. (2009). Applying human factors analysis to the design of the electronic health record. *Studies in Health Technology and Informatics, 146*, 132–136.

Fichman, R. G., Kohli, R., & Krishnan, R. (2011). Editorial overview—the role of information systems in healthcare: Current research and future trends. *Information Systems Research, 22*(3), 419–428. https://doi.org/10.1287/isre.1110.0382

Frame, J., Watson, J., & Thomson, K. (2008). Deploying a culture change programme management approach in support of information and communication technology developments in Greater Glasgow NHS Board. *Health Informatics Journal, 14*(2), 125–139.

Gaylin, D., Goldman, S., Ketchel, A., Moiduddin, A., & Chicago, I. (2005). Community Health Center Information Systems Assessment: Issues and Opportunities Final Report (p. 125). NORC at the University of Chicago. Retrieved from http://aspe.hhs.gov/sp/chc

Giddens, A. (2013). The Constitution of Society: Outline of the Theory of Structuration. John Wiley & Sons.

Goldstein, M. M., & Blumenthal, D. (2008). Building an information technology infrastructure. *The Journal of Law, Medicine & Ethics: A Journal of the American Society of Law, Medicine & Ethics, 36*(4), 709–715, 609.

Greenhalgh, T., & Stones, R. (2010). Theorising big IT programmes in healthcare: Strong structuration theory meets actor-network theory. *Social Science & Medicine (1982), 70*(9), 1285–1294.

Hanseth, O., & Monteiro, E. (1998). Understanding information infrastructure. Unpublished Book, http://Heim.Ifi.Uio.No/~Oleha/Publications/Bok. Html. Retrieved from http://heim.ifi.uio.no/oleha/Publications/bok.pdf

Hanseth, O., Aanestad, M., & Berg, M. (2004). Guest editors' introduction: Actor-network theory and information systems. What's so special? *Information Technology & People, 17*(2), 116–123.

Hennington, A. H., & Janz, B., (2007). Information systems and healthcare XVI: Physician adoption of electronic medical records: Applying the UTAUT model in a healthcare context. *Communications of the Association for Information Systems, 19*(1), 5.

HFMA. (2006). Overcoming barriers to electronic health record adoption: Results of survey and roundtable discussions conducted by the Healthcare Financial Management Association. Available at: http://mhcc.maryland.gov/electronichealth/mhitr/EHR%20Links/overcoming_barriers_to_ehr_adoption.pdf. Accessed October 4, 2011.

Hikmet, N., Bhattacherjee, A., Menachemi, N., Kayhan, V. O., & Brooks, R. G. (2008). The role of organizational factors in the adoption of healthcare information technology in Florida hospitals. *Health Care Management Science, 11*(1), 1–9.

Hoffinan, L. (2009). Implementing electronic medical records. *Communications of the ACM, 52*(11), 18–20. https://doi.org/10.1145/1592761.1592770

Hoffinan, S., & Podguski, A. (2008). Finding a cure: The case for regulation and oversight of electronic health record systems. Harv. *JL & Tech., 22*, 103.

Hovenga, E. J. S., Kidd, M. R., Garde, S., & Cossio, C. H. L. (2010). *Health Informatics: An Overview* (1 edition). Amsterdam; Washington, DC: IOS Press.

Huang, Z., & Palvia, P. (2001). ERP implementation issues in advanced and developing countries. *Business Process Management Journal, 7*(3), 276–284. https://doi.org/10.1108/14637150110392773.

Kaplan, B., & Harris-Salamone, K. D. (2009). Health IT success and failure: Recommendations from literature and an AMIA workshop. *Journal of the American Medical Informatics Association, 16*(3), 291–299.

Kennedy, B. L. (2011). *Exploring the sustainment of health information technology: Successful practices for addressing human factors*. Northcentral University.

Kimaro, H., & Nhampossa, J. (2004). The challenges of sustainability of health information systems in developing countries: Comparative case studies of Mozambique and Tanzania *1*(1), 1–10.

Kralewski, J., Dowd, B. E., Zink, T., & Gans, D. N. (2010). Preparing your practice for the adoption and implementation of electronic health records. *Physician Executive, 36*(2), 30–33.

Kukafka, R., Johnson, S. B., Linfante, A., & Allegrante, J. P. (2003). Grounding a new information technology implementation framework in behavioral science: A systematic analysis of the literature on IT use. *Journal of Biomedical Informatics, 36*(3), 218–227.

Latour, B. (2003). *Reassembling the Social: An Introduction to Actor-Network-Theory*. Oxford: University Press.

Latour, B. (2005). *Reassembling the social: An introduction to actor-network theory*. Oxford: Oxford University Press.

Latour, B., Harbers, H., & Koenis, S. (1996). *On actor-network theory: A few clarifications*. London: Academic Press.

Law, J., & Hassard, J. (1999). *Actor network theory and after*. Wiley-Blackwell.

Law, J., & Hassard, J. (2004). *Actor-network theory and after*. Wiley-Blackwell.

Leykum, L. K., Pugh, J. A., Lanham, H. J., Harmon, J., & McDaniel, R. R. (2009). Implementation research design: integrating participatory action research into randomized controlled trials. *Implementation Science: IS, 4*, 69–69. https://doi.org/10.1186/1748-5908-4-69

Liu, L. S., Shih, P. C., & Hayes, G. R. (2011). Barriers to the adoption and use of personal health record systems. In *Proceedings of the 2011 iConference*, pp. 363–370.

Lorenzi, N., Kouroubali, A., Detmer, D. E., & Bloomrosen, M. (2009). How to successfully select and implement electronic health records (EHR) in small ambulatory practice settings. *BMC Medical Informatics and Decision Making, 9*, 15.

McLean, C., & Hassard, J. (2004). Symmetrical absence/symmetrical absurdity: Critical notes on the production of actor-network accounts. *Journal of Management Studies, 41*(3), 493–519. https://doi.org/10.1111/j.1467-6486.2004.00442.x

McPhee, R. D., & Poole, M. S. (2001). Organizational structures and configurations. In The new handbook of organizational communication: Advances in theory, research and methods (pp. 503–543).

McReavy, D., Toth, L., Tremonti, C., & Yoder, C. (2009). The CFO's role in implementing EHR systems: The experiences of a Florida health system point to 10 actions that can help CFOs manage the revenue risks and opportunities of implementing an electronic health record. Retrieved December 16, 2011, from http://findarticles.com/p/articles/mi_m3257/is_6_63/ai_n35529545/

Mitchell, V., & Nault, B. (2008). The emergence of functional knowledge in sociotechnical systems. https://pdfs.semanticscholar.org/5c3a/a7d7d20309ce9dc9572aa41915436ad31219.pdf

Mort, M., Finch, T., & May, C. (2009). Making and unmaking telepatients: Identity and governance in new health technologies. *Science, Technology & Human Values, 34*(1), 9–33.

Muhammad, I., Teoh, S. Y., & Wickramasinghe, N. (2012). Why Using Actor-Network Theory (ANT) Can Help to Understand the Personally Controlled Electronic Health Record (PCEHR) in Australia. *International Journal of Actor-Network Theory and Technological Innovation (IJANTTI), 4*(2), 44–60.

Parente, S., & McCullough (2009). Health information technology and patient safety: evidence from panel data. *Health Affairs, 28*(2). https://doi.org/10.1377/hlthaff.28.2.357, Accessed on Apr 10 2018.

Personally Controlled Electronic Health Record Act (2012).

Protti, D., & Smit, C. (2006). The Netherlands: Another European country where GPs have been using EMRs for over twenty years. *Healthcare Information Management & Communications, 30*(3). Available at: http://www.healthcareimc.com/bcovers/PDFS/TheNetherlands.pdf

Protti, D., Johansen, I., & Perez-Torres, F. (2009). Comparing the application of Health Information Technology in primary care in Denmark and Andalucía, Spain. *International Journal of Medical Informatics, 78*(4), 270–283. https://doi.org/10.1016/j.ijmedinf.2008.08.002

Rosebaugh, D. (2004). Getting ready for the software in your future. *Home Health Care Management Practice, 16*(3), 228–234. https://doi.org/1011771084822303259877

Rosenbloom, S. T., Qi, X., Riddle, W. R., Russell, W. E., DonLevy, S. C., Giuse, D., et al. (2006). Implementing pediatric growth charts into an electronic health record system. *Journal of the American Medical Informatics Association, 13*, 302–308.

Ross, S. E., Schilling, L. M., Fernald, D. H., Davidson, A. J., & West, D. R. (2010). Health information exchange in small-to-medium sized family medicine practices: Motivators, barriers, and potential facilitators of adoption. *International Journal of Medical Informatics, 79*(2), 123–129. https://doi.org/10.1016/j.ijmedinf.2009.12.001

Rydin, Y. (2010). Actor-network theory and planning theory: A response to Boelens. *Planning Theory, 9*, 265–268.

Scott, J. T., Rundall, T. G., Vogt, T. M., & Hsu, J. (2005). Kaiser Permanente's experience of implementing an electronic medical record: a qualitative study. BMJ (Clinical Research Ed.), 331(7528), 1313–1316.

Shaban, R. (2005). Theories of clinical judgment and decision-making: A review of the theoretical literature. *Australasian Journal of Paramedicine, 3*(1). Retrieved from https://ajp.paramedics.org/index.php/ajp/article/view/308

Sharma, R., Southon, G., & Yetton, P. (1999). Successful IS innovation: the contingent contributions of innovation characteristics and implementation process. *Journal of Information Technology, 14*(1), 53–68. https://doi.org/10.1080/026839699344746

Showell, C. M. (2011). Citizens, patients and policy: A challenge for Australia's national electronic health record. *Health Information Management Journal OnLine, 40*(2), 39–43.

Staples, W. G. (2007). Encyclopedia of Privacy: A-M. Greenwood Publishing Group.

Tang, P. C., Ash, J. S., Bates, D. W., Overhage, J. M., & Sands, D. Z. (2006). Personal health records: Definitions, benefits, and strategies for overcoming barriers to adoption. *Journal of the American Medical Informatics Association: JAMIA, 13*(2), 121–126. https://doi.org/10.1197/jamia.M2025

Thompson, R., Compeau, D., Higgins, C., & Lupton, N. (2008). Intentions to use information technologies: An integrative model.

Thweatt, E. G., & Kleiner, B. H. (2007). New developments in health care organisational management. *Journal of Health Management, 9*(3), 433–441.

Timpka, T., Bång, M., Delbanco, T., & Walker, J. (2007). Information infrastructure for interorganizational mental health services: An actor network theory analysis of psychiatric rehabilitation. *Journal of Biomedical Informatics, 40*(4), 429–437.

Tobler, N. (2008). *Technology, organizational change, and the nonhuman agent: Exploratory analysis of electronic health record implementation in a small practice ambulatory care*. Utah: The University of Utah.

Torda, P., Han, E. S., & Scholle, S. H. (2010). Easing the adoption and use of electronic health records in small practices. *Health Affairs (Project Hope), 29*(4), 668–675.

Trudel, M. C. (2010). *Challenges to personal information sharing in interorganizational settings: Learning from the Quebec Health Smart Card project*. London: The University of Western Ontario.

Vitacca, M., Mazzù, M., & Scalvini, S. (2009). Socio-technical and organizational challenges to wider e-Health implementation. *Chronic Respiratory Disease, 6*(2), 91–97.

Walsham, G. (1997). Actor-network theory and IS research: Current status and future prospects. In *Information Systems and Qualitative Research: Proceedings of the IFIP TC8 WG 8.2 International Conference on Information Systems and Qualitative Research, 31st May–3rd June 1997, Philadelphia, Pennsylvania, USA* (pp. 466–481).

Weimar, C. (2009). Electronic health care advances, physician frustration grows. *Physician Executive, 35*(2), 8–15.

Wickramasinghe, N., & Bali, R. K. (2009). The S'ANT imperative for realizing the vision of healthcare network centric operations. *International Journal of ActorNetwork Theory and Technological Innovation IJANTTI, 1*(1), 45–58.

Wickramasinghe, N., & Schaffer, J. (2010). *Realizing value driven e-Health solutions*. Washington DC: IBM Centre for the Business of government.

Williams-Jones, B., & Graham, J. E. (2003). Actor-network theory: a tool to support ethical analysis of commercial genetic testing. *New Genetics and Society, 22*(3), 271–296.

Yusof, M., Stergioulas, L., & Zugic, J. (2007). Health information systems adoption: Findings from a systematic review. *Studies in Health Technology and Informatics, 129*(Pt 1), 262.

Yusof, M. M., Papazafeiropoulou, A., Paul, R. J., & Stergioulas, L. K. (2008). Investigating evaluation frameworks for health information systems. *International Journal of Medical Informatics, 77*(6), 377–385. https://doi.org/10.1016/j.ijmedinf.2007.08.004

Chapter 14
Actor-Network Theory to Assist in Understanding the Implementation and Adoption of Health Information Systems

Imran Muhammad and Nilmini Wickramasinghe

14.1 Background

Globally, governments are increasingly investing in healthcare information technology (HIT), with an emphasis on electronic health records. This is in response to the immense and diverse pressures of changing patient demographics, healthcare services provision, financial implications, workforce shortages, advancements in medical technologies and their impact on healthcare demand and delivery as well as a move towards a system where interaction between healthcare providers and consumers can achieve maximum output with limited human and financial resources (Wickramasinghe and Schaffer 2010).

Healthcare services are very well established as an information-rich industry (ibid). The motivating notion in support of the introduction of IT (information technology) in healthcare service delivery is that if we can improve the ways of accessing and sharing information across healthcare systems by moving away from pen, paper and human memory towards a new environment, where key stakeholders (e.g. service providers, consumers, government agencies and healthcare managers) can reliably and securely share information electronically, health outcomes and quality of care can be improved significantly (Mort et al. 2009).

Use of HIT can also help with cost savings, improve patient involvement and produce useable secondary data for further research and training (Car et al. 2008). However, the transformation from cabinets and paper files to computers and HIS software is not a candid proposition and is sometimes faced with many known and unknown hurdles, such as technological, organisational, financial and people issues, as a result of the complex and multifaceted environment of healthcare service

I. Muhammad · N. Wickramasinghe (✉)
Deakin University, Burwood, VIC, Australia

Epworth HealthCare, Richmond, VIC, Australia

N. Wickramasinghe, J. L. Schaffer (eds.), *Theories to Inform Superior Health Informatics Research and Practice*, Healthcare Delivery in the Information Age,
https://doi.org/10.1007/978-3-319-72287-0_14

delivery where different human and non-human actors interact with each other in very complex ways (Ammenwerth et al. 2006; André et al. 2008; Catwell and Sheikh 2009; Cresswell et al. 2010; DesRoches et al. 2008; Lorenzi et al. 2009).

Given the inherent complexities of healthcare operations, it is argued in this chapter that human and non-human actor interactions are challenging and need to be evaluated with theoretically informed techniques (Wickramasinghe and Schaffer 2010). One approach identified in the literature used to facilitate correct and accurate capturing of the complexities and levels of interactions in healthcare operations is to use an ANT (Muhammad et al. 2012; Cresswell et al. 2010; Wickramasinghe et al. 2009).

To determine the functionality of a system, it is important to understand the fit between technical subsystems and social subsystems in an organisation (Mitchell and Nault 2008). The emphasis is then not only on studying the impact of the technology on organisations and their work processes but also on the impact of social and people issues pertaining to technology and work processes (Cresswell et al. 2010). For this reason, it is also important to understand the interrelationship and interactions of the technical and social systems between each other (Coiera 2004). The lens of actor-network theory (ANT) is useful in such contexts as it can be applied to analyse the data collected during the research. This can assist the researcher to understand the user requirements, their perceptions and expectations from the HIT implementation and to understand their needs and intentions to adopt the new e-health system.

This chapter shows the benefits of applying an actor-network theory (ANT) lens of analysis to the collective data set to further understand the richness of the actor-network theory (ANT) and potential challenges, complications and general complexities of any/all people/technology interactions as the HIS implementation and adoptions move forward to a large-scale implementation. We believe that this can be achieved by the incorporation of an ANT analysis as is illustrated in this chapter, and by doing an ANT analysis a successful and more realistic mapping of the rich and complex environment which ultimately will ensure the appropriate design, development, implementation and adoption of the HIS solution will be enabled. This process serves to illustrate the power of such an ANT analysis for a healthcare delivery context.

Healthcare systems are complex systems especially when they integrate with information technology. This environment is further complicated by the interaction of different human and non-human actors that often leads to failed technology-based healthcare interventions and implementations which are also costly and have far-reaching impacts (Cresswell et al. 2011). Thus, it becomes necessary and important to evaluate these interventions with theoretically informed techniques to enable a deeper understanding which in turn can facilitate a successful implementation and adoption of the intended health information technology (Cresswell et al. 2011).

We contend that a sociotechnical systems perspective can provide the foundations for a fuller understanding so that there is a better evaluation and provision of specific solutions to address gaps in their current development, implementation and adoption. Furthermore, it can also enhance our understanding by providing a mechanism to study the relationships between technology organisation, people and social and financial factors that influence the success of e-health implementation and adoption. We believe that a viable healthcare system can only be achieved if these considerations are jointly optimised.

14.2 Actor-Network Theory (ANT)

Actor-network theory (ANT) is a sociological theory developed by French sociologist Bruno Latour and Michel Callon and British sociologist John Law (Latour 2005; Law and Hassard 1999; Muhammad et al. 2013). Its fundamental stand is that technologies and people are linked in an often-complex network. ANT tries to bridge the gap between a sociotechnical divide by denying the existence of purely social or technical relations. In doing so, it takes a very radical stance and goes as far as challenging many of the conventional epistemological ideas and rejecting any distinction between subject or object, nature or culture and technology and society.

ANT assumes that each entity (such as technologies, organisations and humans) is an actor. Therefore, the actors have the potential to transform and mediate social relationships (Cresswell et al. 2010). ANT further emphasises that entities regardless of their nature, whether human, technologies or process, are not fixed. Thus, they do not have any significance on their own, but rather their significance depends on the nature of their relations with other entities in the network and their role which may change as their relations change (Law 2006). This means that neither actors nor their relations are static and permanent; they change over time and across social and political contexts (Singleton and Michael 1993).

Actors are essentially considered heterogeneous in nature, representing negotiations at different levels (e.g. political, social, technical and/or economic levels). Further, the degrees of commitment, skills, constraints and prejudice among actors also can vary. Often, these represent a mixture of one or two of social, technical or personal levels (Latour 2005). At the technical level, the role of technology may be involved to facilitate users by giving them accurate and up-to-date information when it is needed. The accuracy (effectiveness and efficiency) of the technology would be best determined or disputed by the users (nurses, clinicians, pharmacists and patients). To better understand relationships and how they create meaning and describe the role of different actors (e.g. the patient, GPs, nurses, different diagnostic tests, different medical technologies, different communication channels, standards, protocols and decision-makers and policymakers), ANT suggests we should think in terms of networks of relations or actor networks (Williams-Jones and Graham 2003).

14.3 Key Concepts of ANT

To apply ANT appropriately, it is first necessary to become familiar with the following key constructs and map them with the implementation and adoption of HIS.

Actor/Actant Actors are the web of participants in the network including all human and non-human entities. Because of the strong biased interpretation of the word actor towards human, the word actant is commonly used to refer both human and non-human actors (Wickramasinghe et al. 2012). Examples include humans, organisations, technology, technical artefacts and graphical representations.

Heterogeneous Network A network of aligned interests formed by the actors/actants. This is a network of materially different actors that is achieved by a great deal of work that both shapes those various social and nonsocial elements and disciplines them so that they work together, instead of making off on their own (Wickramasinghe et al. 2012).

Tokens/Quasi Objects Created through the successful interaction of actors/actants in a network and are passed between actors within the network. As the token is increasingly transmitted or passed through the network, it becomes increasingly punctualised and increasingly reified especially when the token is decreasingly transmitted or when an actor fails to transmit the token (Wickramasinghe et al. 2012).

Punctualisation Central to ANT. Within the domain of ANT, every actor/actant in the web of relations is connected to others and will be considered as a single object or concept in the same way as the concept of abstraction is treated in object-oriented programming. These sub-actors are sometimes hidden from normal view and can only be viewed in the case of a network breakdown. This concept is often referred as a depunctualisation. Because ANT requires all actors or sections of a network to perform required tasks and therefore maintain the web of relations, this becomes more focused when a breakdown in the network occurs. In case any actor ceases to operate or maintain its link, the entire actor network would break down resulting in punctualisation. Punctualisation is thus a process and cannot be achieved indefinitely rather it is a relational effect and is recursive in nature (Law and Hassard 1999).

Obligatory Passage Point (OPP) Broadly refers to a situation that must occur for all the actors to satisfy the interests that have been attributed to them by the focal actor. The focal actor defines the OPP through which the other actors must pass through and by which the focal actor becomes indispensable (Callon 1986).

Irreversibility The degree of irreversibility depends on the extent to which it is subsequently impossible to go back to a point where that translation was only one among others (Callon 1986) and the extent to which it shapes and determines subsequent translations (Latour 2005).

Given the very complex nature of healthcare operations (Lubitz and Wickramasinghe 2006), irreversibility is generally not likely to occur. However, it is vital that chains of events are continuously analysed in order that future events can be addressed as effectively and efficiently as possible.

To realise the importance of the application of ANT into the study of evaluation of the implementation and adoption of HIS, it is important to understand the key concepts of ANT and map them to the critical issues endured in HIS implementation and adoptions. An initial assessment of these key concepts and their mapping is provided in Table 14.1.

Irreversibility In the context of a very complex nature of healthcare operations, irreversibility is very less likely to occur and would be more dependent on social networks and the nature of interaction between human and non-human actors in the network. Here it is important to remember though the chain of events needs to be monitored carefully so the future events can be addressed in best possible manners.

14.4 Actor Networks

Actor networks are highly dynamic and inherently unstable in their nature. Understanding the alignment between people, technology, their roles, routines, values, training and incentives and the role of technology and how it can facilitate or negatively impact the work processes and tasks in an organisation can serve to stabilise these networks (Greenhalgh and Stones 2010; Wickramasinghe et al. 2011). Actor networks need to be continually maintained through the engagement (e.g. a process known as enrolment in ANT) of the different actors/actants involved in the process.

At times, actor networks may fail and hence may need to be replaced by other networks or by integrating new enrolments. The enrolment of new actors/actants leads to the reconfiguration of the networks as interests are translated to suit the needs of the wider body of actors. These actors then take part in a negotiation process to define the new identity of the actor networks. In this process, importance is placed on the actions of actors and networks and the interactions between different actors (e.g. social institutions, individuals, government, technology, communication channels, rules and regulations, protocols and work environment) (Wickramasinghe et al. 2011; Muhammad et al. 2013).

The origin of power and structure are the main sources and drivers of the existence of such actor networks. Thus, if there needs to be an understanding of the essential dynamics within such an actor network, it is important to understand and consider all the components that collaborate, co-operate and compete to lead to propagation and perseverance of ANT and how to unpack and then understand the underlying process and important components of actors and their networks that are

Table 14.1 Mapping of the HIS Implementation and Adoption with ANT

Key concepts of ANT	Mapping of the HIS implementation and adoption with ANT
Actor/actant	In the HIS context, actors/actants are different stakeholders in healthcare delivery settings such as technology (Web 2.0, databases, graphical user interfaces, IHI and different computer hardware and software) and people (service providers, healthcare funders, healthcare service recipients, healthcare organisations, suppliers and private health insurers as well as clinical administrative technologies, work process and health records) in the form of paper or electronic
Heterogeneous network	The HIS technology here is clearly a network of different applications in this context But it is important to understand that heterogeneous network in ANT requires to conceptualise the network as aligned interest including people, organisations, standards and protocols and their interaction with technology. The key here is a better alignment and representation of interests so the healthcare delivery can be improved
Tokens/quasi objects	In the HIS context, this translates to successful cost-effective and efficient healthcare delivery, such as for GPs treating patient by having a capability of sharing health information with other service providers and for patients who are on long-term medicine having capability to print prescription from home issued by their doctor through the HIS portal. It is important to understand here that to maintain the integrity of the network all the time is very important because if wrong information is passed through the network, the errors would be devastating because they can propagate quickly and will multiply
Punctualisation	For example, a computer on which one is working would be treated as a single block or unit. Only when it breaks down and needs help with spare parts can reveal the hidden chain of network consisting of different actors made up of people, computer parts and organisations. Similarly, in the HIS context, uploading health record of a patient is a consequence of the interaction and coordination of many subtasks. This only can be revealed if breakdown at this point occurs and depunctualisation of the network happens and all subtask would be carefully examined
Obligatory passage point (OPP)	In the HIS context, one can illustrate this by taking the example of access rights. The interface of the system is developed in a way that no service can access any record without using their IHI, which in this case constitute an obligatory passage point through which they must pass for their everyday activities

hidden and cannot readily be seen or understood (Harding 2004; Singleton and Michael 1993).

ANT assists in mapping the actors involved in the development, use and implementation of the HIS at micro, meso and macro levels, as well as the actor network of their engagement and some of the actors' connections. This task is complicated because the actors participate in many networks which may or may not overlap with the introduction of a technology solution nationwide.

Actor networks can be thought of as being fractal and expanding all the time with each actor becoming a node for another network (Law 1999). This complexity

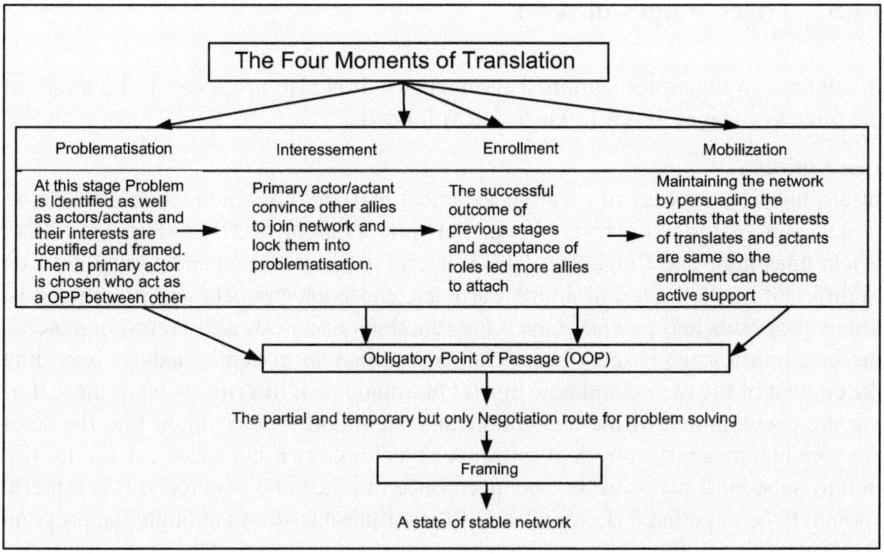

Fig. 14.1 Moments of translation in ANT (adapted from Muhammad et al. (2012))

makes it very difficult to separate the foreground from the background, and such a network is thus challenging to analyse. To overcome this complexity, it is useful to simplify the actor network, and this can be done using the concept of punctualisation or creation of black boxes (Law 2006).

For the purpose of analysis and despite a risk for oversimplification, networks that are stable and strong can be treated as an obligatory passage point (OPP) for some larger networks. The supporting network can then be black boxed. For example, within Fig. 14.1, each box of different levels are complex black boxes, each with its own internal network that can be further expanded or opened to create its own network. The actors of each black box not only interact with each other but also with various actors from additional external networks. Such networks are complex and dynamic in nature. For example, a change (government funding scheme, hospital policy, introduction of a new technology) will impact different actors and their interactions from multiple aspects, and the networks will reorganise and realign as acceptance and/or resistance is manifested.

ANT also advocates a focus on the multiple factors influencing the alignment of linkages between actors and their networks (Mol 2002), but does not emphasise the specific shape or structure of the actor network. For example, in the case of a healthcare decision support system, the technology could be different for different purposes. It may serve the purpose of its targeted audience and be accepted promptly or not serve the purpose and be resisted strongly by other actors. Hence, it is important to understand how actors can be brought together in a network and help them to keep participating in the network. The concept of translation can assist with this task (Law and Hassard 1999).

14.5 Three Stages of ANT

In addition to the aforementioned commentary, it is also necessary to be aware of the three key stages of ANT, which are as follows:

Inscription

Inscription is a process of creating technical text and communication artefacts to protect an actor's interests in a network (Latour 2005; Monteiro 2000; Wickramasinghe and Bali 2009). This is a term used for all text and communication in different media including journal articles, conference papers and presentations, grants proposals and patents. Given the functions of an e-health record in general, the inscription stage is most beneficial to facilitate an in-depth analysis regarding the content of the record and how this is communicated. Inscription takes place during the development of the technological system and its placement into the actor network that means the physical existence of technology is not necessary for inscription to happen. It needs to be convinced once in place and convinced it is forceful enough to be negotiated (Latour 2005). If inscription is strong enough, the program prescribed by it will be followed by other actors (Latour 2005). The stage of inscription starts as soon as system is conceptualised and documented. Inscription can help to understand the underlying assertions of actors; it asserts that technological artefacts always are embedded in developer's beliefs, social norms, user's beliefs and patron of use and assumptions about the system.

Translation

Translation is used to explain the process of creation of actor networks and the formation of ordering effects (Callon and Law 1988; Law 1991). As Latour (2005, p. 64) explains:

> ANT is the name of a movement, a displacement, a transformation, a translation, and enrolment. It is an association between entities which are in no way recognisable as being social in the ordinary manner, except in the brief moment when they are reshuffled together.

At this stage, all actors decide to be part of a specific network if it is worth building (Wickramasinghe and Bali 2009). A good example of this function is the formation of the National E-Health Transition Authority (NEHTA) in the Australian case study and the identification of GPs (general practitioners) as primary actors in the case of the HIS adoption and implementation. Translation is a vital element of ANT. This term is used to explain the process of creating actor networks and the formation of ordering effects (Callon 1986; Law and Callon 1992). The translation stage provides insights into how the HIS system can be integrated into the very complex work environment of healthcare services and delivery.

Translation encourages actors to be involved in the formation of the network and helps the primary actor to overcome resistance. Each actor in the network is an independent entity and regardless of its formation (e.g. a person, group, institute, company, process, hardware or software) will have its own set of diverse interests (Law and Callon 1992). Therefore, the network can only be stable if the interests of different actors can easily and continually be translated (Callon 1986).

The process of translation can also be called a process of negotiation. After the creation of a network, in the presence of many actors, a strong or primary actor would translate the interests of other actors into his/her own by negotiating with the other actors. At this stage, all actors decide to be (or not to be) part of the new network, which is usually dependent on the perceived benefit to themselves (Wickramasinghe and Bali 2009). Among human actors, the translation process is analogous to the negotiation of common interests, whereas the translation among human and non-human actors is typically negotiated through the design of scripts (Callon 1986).

The process of translation of actor/actant interests is achieved through a series of four moments of translation as shown in Fig. 14.1 (Callon 1986):

1. Problematisation
2. Interessement
3. Enrolment
4. Mobilisation

The concept of translation and its four moments is important. This aspect helps the reader to understand how different groups of actors/actants can be brought together to support a common goal and achieve successful enrolment to stabilise the network.

Any resistance to sociotechnical change can be met by reorganising the relations in actor networks and translating their interests into common goals. Counterclaims and disagreements that arise from different actors in a network can harm the stability of the network. In the vision for the HIS, concerns regarding aggravated healthcare costs, disparate patient information system and healthcare quality, safety and efficiency shaped the problematisation stage. The HIS is the primary actor as well as the OPP between other actors. Competing roles between the incoming primary actor (HIS) and the outgoing actor (paper-based documentation) require that links between the latter (paper) and other actors (e.g. nurses, medical staff, allied health professionals and patients) are weakened. In addition, the ties (interests) between the incoming actor (HIS) and the other actors need strengthening, through interessement, to be successful. If this process succeeds, then it can facilitate the enrolment stage in which actors accept and align their positions in new networks where the actor paper-based documentation leaves and the HIS enters. Mobilisation happens when the new networks become active and stable with the new actor.

The foundation of networks is built upon the rules of interactions between actors. Therefore, continuous translation of interests at different levels is a primary source of social order. It is therefore also important to understand the role of controlling elements and their influences and contribution (Law 2006).

Framing

Framing is an operation that can help to define actors and distinguish different actors and goods from each other (Callon 1999). This last and final stage in the ANT process can help a network to stabilise. At this stage, key issues and debates would already have been negotiated within the network, and technologies can become more stabilised over time (Wickramasinghe and Bali 2009).

14.6 The Actor-Network Theory Approach to Evaluate HIS

To fully comprehend the successful development, implementation and use of a new technology known as the HIS in health care, it is important to investigate beyond the linear models of technology adoption, diffusion and transfer. Simple binary models are not enough because of the complex and dynamic nature of healthcare settings. The complex nature of interaction between the technology and social often renders the two inseparable (Williams-Jones and Graham 2003).

ANT is considered an appropriate choice to analyse the HIS evaluation study because it can be used to identify and acknowledge the impacts of human and non-human, social or policy issues within the healthcare setting (Latour 2005). ANT is robust enough to accurately capture the complexities, nuances and richness of healthcare operations. In doing so, ANT can also be used to investigate and theorise questions about why and how networks come into existence, what sort of associations and impacts they can have on each other, how positions move and change in a network, how actors enrol and leave the network and most importantly how networks can achieve stability (Callon 1999; Doolin and Lowe 2002; McLean and Hassard 2004). An assumption of ANT theory is that if any new actor is enrolled or an old actor leaves a network it affects the whole network (Cresswell et al. 2010; Doolin and Lowe 2002).

The ability of actors and end users to contest the problematisation of the technology can be affected by power structures already present in the network. These considerations are naturally relevant to the context of the HIS implementation and adoption in complex healthcare settings.

Any translation may succeed or fail, but only when failures of technology and networks occur then one will be able to reveal the underlying reasons and embedded norms and values (Greenhalgh and Stones 2010; Law and Hassard 1999; Williams-Jones and Graham 2003). In an ANT context, translation that has not properly incorporated the differences in social (nurse's perceptions, requirements and needs) and technology/system offerings has led to these issues arising. However, without ANT it is also easy to dismiss the user perspective as "they just do not get it", which happens frequently in the implementation of information systems into healthcare contexts (Greenhalgh and Stones 2010).

Actor-network theory is considered an appropriate choice for HIS implementation and adoption because it can identify and then acknowledge all human and non-human actors within the healthcare setting and any impact of their interaction on social or policy issues that might occur (Latour et al. 1996).

In doing so, ANT can also help to investigate the question of why and how networks come into existence, what sort of associations and impact they can have on each other, how they move and change their position in a network, how they enrol and leave the network and most importantly how these networks can achieve stability (Doolin and Lowe 2002; Callon 1986; McLean and Hassard 2004) that would lead to successful implementation and adoption of proposed system. ANT's assumption that if any new actor is enrolled in the network or old actor leaves the network, it would affect the whole network (Cresswell et al. 2010; Doolin and Lowe 2002) will help us to understand the impact of the HIS on underlying structures of healthcare settings.

ANT can also assist in understanding the active role of objects in shaping social realities by challenging the assumption of the separation between non-human and human worlds (Greenhalgh and Stones 2010; McLean and Hassard 2004; Rydin 2010; Tobler 2008; Walsham 1997). This would assist researchers in studying the complexities of the relationships between human and non-human actors, the sustainability of power relationships between human actors and what kind of influence artefacts can have on human actors' relationships in transforming health care (Cresswell et al. 2010).

The rational to choose ANT to evaluate the HIS system is the strength of ANT's ability to identify and explore the real complexities involved in healthcare service delivery. Other approaches used to study information systems adoption, such as diffusion of innovation (DOI) theory, emphasise the properties of the technology or individual and organisation itself in isolation without considering the rules of their interaction. This approach can oversimplify the very complex nature of healthcare service delivery setting (Wickramasinghe and Bali 2009), whereas ANT's approach of investigation can cover these complexities by thoroughly studying the network of actors and their associations. Thus, ANT can provide a unique way to view HIS implementation and adoption studies.

14.7 Critique and Limitations of ANT

Although ANT has been applied to the implementation and adoption of many IT-based healthcare innovation studies (Berg et al. 2003; Cresswell et al. 2010, 2011; Hall et al. 2010), it is important to note that ANT has also been criticised for its limitations (Williams 2007; Cresswell et al. 2010, 2011; Greenhalgh and Stones 2010; Walsham 1997). Some of the key limitations of ANT identified in the literature include a lack of ability to consider the broader social structures (Walsham 1997) and a lack of ability to consider the macro-environmental factors (McLean and Hassard 2004). However, the advocates of ANT have argued that the macro level structures of the system or society are made up of the same artefacts so they can be analysed in the same way as micro level structures. Further the advocates of ANT have argued that ANT is flexible enough to allow different levels of analysis. Latour (2005) argues that differences between network and actor are two faces of the same phenomenon. Mixing structuration theory with ANT can help in overcoming this problem as it can link multiple levels of analysis from individual to organisation level settings (Walsham 1997).

Another criticism of ANT is its inability to explain the formation of relationships between actors and over changes of events in networks (Cresswell et al. 2011; Greenhalgh and Stones 2010; Kaghan and Bowker 2001). ANT's assumption of symmetry between the social and technological actors has also been criticised (Mutch 2002). There is an argument that all actors are not same as some can have more influence than others and human feelings and emotions can play strong role in different circumstances (Mutch 2002; Walsham 1997).

Another criticism of ANT relates to its methodological standing. It has been argued that ANT is a method of describing rather than explaining (Bloomfield 1991); however, Latour (2005) counters this criticism by explaining that ANT does not try to explain the actor's reasons for joining the network but searches for procedural activities that happen in negotiations between different actors. Thus, ANT never intended to explain the behaviour, but ANT is a way to understand why and how the actors behave (Law and Hassard 1999).

Lastly, the position of the researcher in the research is another criticism of ANT. The researcher's role in labelling actors, defining the passage point and scoping the actor network can be influential and can have an impact on the results. Thus the researcher should be critical in their labelling of actors and analysis in general and thereby be guided by the actors themselves.

To overcome these limitations, many researchers have suggested that ANT can be combined with other theoretical lenses such as structuration theory (ST) and strong structuration theory (SST) (Cresswell et al. 2011; Greenhalgh and Stones 2010; Trudel 2010; Walsham 1997).

14.8 Conclusion

The need for IT-based interventions in the healthcare service delivery to improve information and communication and thereby provide superior value-based care is well recognised globally. Different e-health solutions are being implemented with mixed success to address this challenge (Protti and Smit 2006; Basch 2005; DesRoches et al. 2008; Greenhalgh and Stones 2010). It is, therefore, important to evaluate these technologies with theoretically informed approaches to enjoy more successful outcomes.

We believe it is important to develop a deeper understanding constraint to the development, adoption, implementation and diffusion of these various HIS solutions. Specifically, we suggest that a sociotechnical, e.g. ANT-based, approach can inform and facilitate such evaluations.

A sociotechnical approach of study will allow more flexibility in system design and adoption. We have argued that this approach will be of benefit to both practitioners for better design and implementation and researchers for better evaluation. One of the main challenges of technology-based organisational change research is to find the answer of an ontological question of balance between agency and structures (McPhee and Poole 2001; Tobler 2008). This chapter has served to outline the key concepts of ANT that are relevant in the context of the HIS adoption and implementation and discussed the appropriateness of an ANT-based theoretical lens for the evaluation of HIS in very complex environment of healthcare service delivery. We have also noted that ANT has been criticised by several scholars because of its appropriateness as an ontology and/or epistemology (Latour 2005). Therefore, we recommend that to reduce the negative impact of these limitations, the use of structuration theory can be incorporated.

References

Ammenwerth, E., Iller, C., & Mahler, C. (2006). IT-adoption and the interaction of task, technology and individuals: A fit framework and a case study. *BMC Medical Informatics and Decision Making, 6*, 3.

André, B., Ringdal, G. I., Loge, J. H., Rannestad, T., Laerum, H., & Kaasa, S. (2008). Experiences with the implementation of computerized tools in health care units: A review article. *International Journal of Human–Computer Interaction, 24*(8), 753–775.

Basch, P. (2005). Electronic health records and the national health information network: Affordable, adoptable, and ready for prime time? *Annals of Internal Medicine, 143*(3), 227–228.

Berg, M., Aarts, J., & van der Lei, J. (2003). ICT in health care: Sociotechnical approaches. *Methods of Information in Medicine, 42*(4), 297–301. https://doi.org/10.1267/METH03040297.

Bloomfield, B. (1991). The role of information systems in the health service: Action at a distance and the fetish of calculation. *Social Studies of Science, 21*. SRC-GoogleScholar, 701–734.

Callon, M. (1986). Some elements of a sociology of translation: Domestication of the scallops and the fishermen of St. Brieuc Bay. In J Law (Ed.), Power, action and belief: A new sociology of knowledge (pp. 196–233). London: Routledge and Kegan Paul

Callon, M. (1999). Actor-network theory–the market test. *Actor Network Theory and After, 47*, 181–195.

Callon, M., & Law, J. (1988). Engineering and sociology in a military aircraft project: A network analysis of technological change. *Social Problems, 35*(3), 284–297.

Car, J., Anandan, C., Black, A., Cresswell, K., Pagliari, C., McKinstry, B., et al. (2008). *The impact of eHealth on the quality & safety of healthcare: A systematic overview and synthesis of the literature*, report, NHS Connecting for Health Evaluation Programme. London: Imperial College London.

Catwell, L., & Sheikh, A. (2009). Evaluating eHealth interventions: The need for continuous systemic evaluation. *PLoS Medicine, 6*(8), e1000126. https://doi.org/10.1371/journal.pmed.1000126

Coiera, E. (2004). Four rules for the reinvention of health care. *BMJ: British Medical Journal, 328*(7449), 1197–1199.

Cresswell, K., Worth, A., & Sheikh, A. (2011). Implementing and adopting electronic health record systems: How actor-network theory can support evaluation. *Clinical Governance: An International Journal, 16*(4), 320–336.

Cresswell, K. M., Worth, A., & Sheikh, A. (2010). Actor-network theory and its role in understanding the implementation of information technology developments in healthcare. *BMC Medical Informatics and Decision Making, 10*, 67.

DesRoches, C. M., Campbell, E. G., Rao, S. R., Donelan, K., Ferris, T. G., Jha, A., et al. (2008). Electronic health records in ambulatory care – A national survey of physicians. *New England Journal of Medicine, 359*(1), 50–60. https://doi.org/10.1056/NEJMsa0802005

Doolin, B., & Lowe, A. (2002). To reveal is to critique: Actor-network theory and critical information systems research. *Journal of Information Technology, 17*, 69–78.

Greenhalgh, T., & Stones, R. (2010). Theorising big IT programmes in healthcare: Strong structuration theory meets actor-network theory. *Social science & medicine (1982), 70*(9), 1285–1294.
Hall, L. M., Ferguson-Paré, M., Peter, E., White, D., Besner, J., Chisholm, A., et al. (2010). Going blank: Factors contributing to interruptions to nurses' work and related outcomes. *Journal of Nursing Management, 18*(8), 1040–1047.
Harding, S. G. (2004). *The feminist standpoint theory reader: Intellectual and political controversies*. New York: Routledge.
Kaghan, W., & Bowker, G. (2001). Out of machine age?: Complexity, sociotechnical systems and actor network theory. *Journal of Engineering and Technology Management, 18*, 253–269.
Latour, B. (2005). *Reassembling the social: An introduction to actor-network theory*. Oxford: Oxford University Press.
Latour, B., Harbers, H., & Koenis, S. (1996). *On actor-network theory: A few clarifications*. Cambridge: Academic Press.
Law, J. (1991). *A Sociology of monsters: Essays on power, technology, and domination*. London: Routledge.
Law, J. (1999). In J. Law & J. Hassard (Eds.), *After ANT: Complexity, naming and topology* (pp. 1–14). Oxford: Blackwell.
Law, J. (2006). *Networks, relations, cyborgs: on the social study of technology*. Retrieved from http://oro.open.ac.uk/21394/
Law, J., & Callon, M. (1992). The life and death of an aircraft: A network analysis of technical change. In *Shaping technology/building society: Studies in sociotechnical change* (p. 360). Cambridge, MA: The MIT Press.
Law, J., & Hassard, J. (1999). *Actor network theory and after*. Oxford: Wiley-Blackwell.
Lorenzi, N., Kouroubali, A., Detmer, D. E., & Bloomrosen, M. (2009). How to successfully select and implement electronic health records (EHR) in small ambulatory practice settings. *BMC Medical Informatics and Decision Making, 9*, 15.
Lubitz, D., & Wickramasinghe, N. (2006). Healthcare and technology: The doctrine of network-centric healthcare. *International Journal of Electronic Healthcare, 2*, 322–344.
McLean, C., & Hassard, J. (2004). Symmetrical absence/symmetrical absurdity: Critical notes on the production of actor-network accounts. *Journal of Management Studies, 41*(3), 493–519. https://doi.org/10.1111/j.1467-6486.2004.00442.x
McPhee, R. D., & Poole, M. S. (2001). Organizational structures and configurations. In *The new handbook of organizational communication: Advances in theory, research and methods* (pp. 503–543). Thousand Oaks: Sage.
Mitchell, V., & Nault, B. (2008). *The emergence of functional knowledge in sociotechnical systems*. Cambridge: Academic Press.
Mol, A. (2002). *The body multiple: Ontology in medical practice*. Durham/London: Duke University Press.
Monteiro, E. (2000). Actor-network theory and information infrastructure. *From Control to Drift*, 71–83.
Mort, M., Finch, T., & May, C. (2009). Making and unmaking telepatients: Identity and governance in new health technologies. *Science, Technology & Human Values, 34*(1), 9–33.
Muhammad, I., Teoh, S. Y., & Wickramasinghe, N. (2012). Why using Actor Network Theory (ANT) can help to understand the Personally Controlled Electronic Health Record (PCEHR) in Australia. *International Journal of Actor-Network Theory and Technological Innovation (IJANTTI), 4*(2), 44–60.
Muhammad, I., Teoh, S. Y., & Wickramasinghe, N. (2013). The need for a socio-technical analysis in e-health: The case of the PCEHR. *International Journal of E-Health and Medical Communications (IJEHMC), 4*(2), 65–79.
Mutch, A. (2002). Actors and networks or agents and structures: Towards a realist view of information systems. *Organization, 9*(3), 477.

Protti, D., & Smit, C. (2006). The Netherlands: Another European country where GPs have been using EMRs for over twenty years. *Healthcare Information Management & Communications, 30*(3). Available at: http://www.healthcareimc.com/bcovers/PDFS/TheNetherlands.pdf

Rydin, Y. (2010). Actor-network theory and planning theory: A response to Boelens. *Planning Theory, 9*, 265–268.

Singleton, V., & Michael, M. (1993). Actor-networks and ambivalence: General practitioners in the UK cervical screening programme. *Social Studies of Science, 23*(2), 227–264.

Tobler, N. (2008). *Technology, organizational change, and the nonhuman agent: Exploratory analysis of electronic health record implementation in a small practice ambulatory care*. Utah: The University of Utah.

Trudel, M. C. (2010). *Challenges to personal information sharing in interorganizational settings: Learning from the Quebec Health Smart Card project*. London: The University of Western Ontario.

Walsham, G. (1997). Actor-network theory and IS research: Current status and future prospects. In *Information Systems and Qualitative Research: Proceedings of the IFIP TC8 WG 8.2 International Conference on Information Systems and Qualitative Research* (pp. 466–481), 31st May–3rd June 1997, Philadelphia, Pennsylvania, USA.

Wickramasinghe, N., & Bali, R. K. (2009). The S'ANT imperative for realizing the vision of healthcare network centric operations. *International Journal of ActorNetwork Theory and Technological Innovation IJANTTI, 1*(1), 45–58.

Wickramasinghe, N., Bali, R. K., & Lehaney, B. (2009). *Knowledge management primer*. New York: Taylor & Francis.

Wickramasinghe, N., & Schaffer, J. (2010). *Realizing value driven e-health solutions*. Washington DC: IBM Centre for the Business of Government.

Wickramasinghe, N., Tatnall, A., & Goldberg, S. (2011). The advantages of mobile solutions for chronic disease management. In *PACIS 2011 Proceedings*. Available at: http://aisel.aisnet.org/pacis2011/214

Wickramasinghe, N., Tatnall, A., & Goldberg, S. (2012). Understanding the advantages of mobile solutions for chronic disease management: The role of ant as a rich theoretical lens. *International Journal of Actor-Network Theory and Technological Innovation, 4*(1), 1–12. https://doi.org/10.4018/jantti.2012010101.

Williams, R. (2007). Managing complex adaptive networks. In *Proceedings of the 4th International Conference on Intellectual Capital, Knowledge Management & Organizational Learning* (pp. 441–452).

Williams-Jones, B., & Graham, J. E. (2003). Actor-network theory: A tool to support ethical analysis of commercial genetic testing. *New Genetics and Society, 22*(3), 271–296.

Chapter 15
Activity Theory: A Comparison of HCI Theories for the Analysis of Healthcare Technology

Fabian Wiser, Carolin Durst, and Nilmini Wickramasinghe

15.1 Introduction

Information technology gains more and more significance in businesses all over the world. IT serves as an enabler for companies, and new opportunities and trends arise frequently: cloud computing, internet of things, or big data, for example. More than two trillion U.S. dollars have been spent in IT in 2016 (Statista 2016) and the branch will, as assumed, grow annually by 3.3% until 2020 (IDC 2016). By far the most rapidly growing IT sector is health care, with a compound annual growth rate of 5.7%, almost double the average percentage of all IT industries (IDC 2016). With this growth emerge more and more technical innovations.

Electronic health records, for example, revolutionize the handling of patient data, medical prescriptions, immunization dates, as well as allergies and progress notes. The electronic health record enables health institutions to transmit digital patient information between each other. Communication channels among clinics have become more efficient, which decreases work and costs for them. Also, a new technology called computerized physician order entry system has improved many processes within the healthcare sector. It features the automatization of medication ordering and guarantees more reliable orders.

However, there exist challenges: IT systems in health care are considered to be complex and critical due to the fact that they deal with human lives. An example of

F. Wiser (✉)
TU Braunschweig, Braunschweig, Germany

C. Durst
University Erlangen-Nuremberg, Nuremberg, Germany

N. Wickramasinghe
Deakin University, Burwood, VIC, Australia

Epworth HealthCare, Richmond, VIC, Australia

N. Wickramasinghe, J. L. Schaffer (eds.), *Theories to Inform Superior Health Informatics Research and Practice*, Healthcare Delivery in the Information Age,
https://doi.org/10.1007/978-3-319-72287-0_15

the dangers of using IT in health care is the case of the medical electron accelerator Therac-25, which caused several human deaths by massive radiation overdoses (Leveson and Turner 1993). For this reason, it is important to design, develop, and operate systems, bearing in mind the system's risks. Healthcare systems should not have any flaws which affect the patient's experience or the workflows in health institutions negatively.

In order to prevent such errors and risks, it is suggested to describe IT systems in health care with the social context they are embedded in. This approach has been confirmed as useful in former research (Riechert et al. 2016; Wiser et al. 2017).

Therefore, we want to investigate the use of a rich theoretical lens which is not yet applied extensively in the research of healthcare information technology, namely Activity Theory (AT). This paper presents the foundations of AT, as well as highlights its advantages for human–computer interaction analysis by comparing it with four other theories.

15.2 Methodology

The current investigation involves the comparison of five different human–computer interaction theories by means of the best suitability in the context of health care. These theories were selected due to their popularity and include: Activity Theory, Actor-Network Theory, Distributed Cognition, Structuration Theory, and Situated Action. The theories are compared in terms of a qualitative single case study literature review. Theories will be described in detail and finally compared in eight disciplines. The result of the case study should highlight the importance of AT in the analysis healthcare IT systems and undergird the reasons why AT is to be preferred over other HCI theories in health care.

15.3 Activity Theory

AT is a descriptive tool which tries to illustrate human practices and the social context in which they are embedded (Allert and Richter 2007). The history of AT can be divided into three generations.

15.3.1 Evolution of Activity Theory

First, the Russian psychologist Lev Vygotsky (1978) introduced the mediated act. For Vygotsky (1978) the interactions between human agents and objects are always connected by a mediating object. This mediator can be a tool, sign or cultural mean. For instance, a radiologist (subject) examines a patient (object) by the help of an MRI (mediating object).

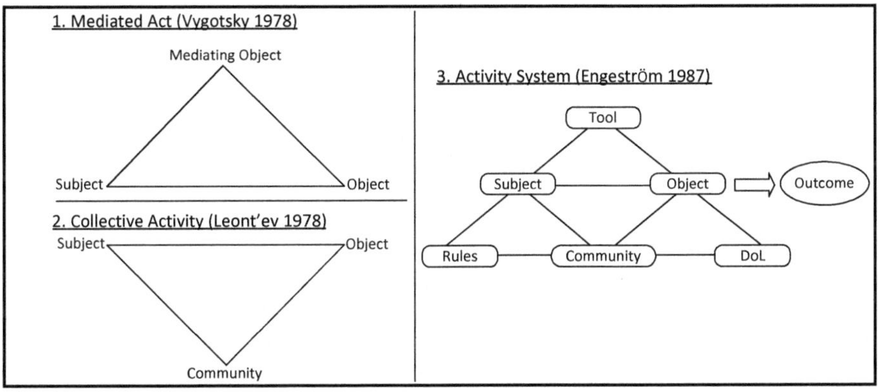

Fig. 15.1 Evolution of activity theory

Second, the Soviet developmental psychologist Leontiev (1978) extended Vygotsky's (1978) theory by the collective notion of activity (Bertelsen and Bødker 2003). He identified that, in order to describe an activity, it is necessary to take account of the community and the social context in which the activity is embedded (Leont'ev 1978). Regarding the example described above, the radiologist (subject) examines a patient (object). Throughout the process he is supported by nurses or other assistant doctors (community).

Further, Leontiev (1978) outlined the hierarchy of activity. According to him, an activity is driven by a motive and consists of several actions (Leont'ev 1978). These actions are following specific goals and again can be divided into operations (Leont'ev 1978). An operation is the smallest entity of the hierarchical structure and depends on its environmental conditions (Leont'ev 1978).

Lastly, Yrjö Engeström (1987) progressed the theories of Vygotsky and Leontiev into an applicable model of systemic structure of human collective activity (see Fig. 15.1) (Korpela 2000). Engeström's activity system is still today the most common variant for collective activities and, therefore, lays with Leontiev's hierarchical activity structure the foundation for today's research on AT (Kaptelinin and Nardi 2012).

Engeström's activity system incorporates subject, object, and community, as well as the mediating objects: tools, rules, and division of labor. All these elements then are transformed into an outcome. Table 15.1 describes briefly each component of the activity system.

Continuing the example, the radiologist (subject) would examine the patient (object) with the help of MRI (tool), in a hospital setting (community), in which several nurses, doctors and chief physicians work (division of labor). During examination the doctor must stick to general medical ethics and follow the principles of the hospital (rules). When the examination is done, a diagnosis protocol is written and the patient gets educated about their results (outcome).

Table 15.1 Activity theory—Description of elements (Kuutti 1996)

AT element	Description
Subject	The subject acts according to its own motives and goals. It is transforming the object into a specific outcome
Object	An object can be physical, less tangible (e.g. a plan) or not tangible at all (e.g. ideas). The object can alter and evolve during the activity is performed
Community	The community is the group or team in which the subject is performing the activity. It also includes persons who take an interest in the activity (stakeholders)
Tools	Tools mediate the relationship between subjects and objects. They can be of both physical (e.g. computers) and non-material nature (e.g. software, language)
Rules	Rules are explicit as well as tacit laws, norms, conventions and expectations. They determine the interaction between subject and its community
Division of labor	The definition of labor defines implicitly and explicitly the roles and hierarchy of the community with regards to the object
Outcome	The outcome is the modified and altered object after the execution of the activity

15.3.2 Contradictions in Activity Theory

Due to the fact that activities continuously evolve and alter, they are fundamentally marked by contradictions (Bertelsen and Bødker 2003). Contradictions are "historically accumulating structural tensions within and between activity systems"(Engeström 2001, p. 137). Engeström (1987) notes that they are a crucial factor for innovation and human learning. Moreover, he explains that there are four key kinds of contradictions in AT (Yrjö Engeström 1987):

First-level contradictions are contradictions which appear inside of a component (e.g. the existence of a conflict between rules).

Second-level contradictions occur between two components, such as subjects not complying with given rules.

Third-level contradictions describe potential problems caused by the relation between an existing activity system and its more evolved object or outcome (Kaptelinin and Nardi 2012). There can be resistance to alter and update an existing system.

Fourth-level contradictions refer to tensions in the network of neighboring activity systems. Whenever components or results are part of more than two activities a conflict can occur.

15.3.3 Principles of Activity Theory

The core principles describing rules and details of AT were elaborated by Leontiev (1978) and categorized in the work of Kaptelinin and Nardi (2006). The five principles are outlined in the subsequent paragraphs.

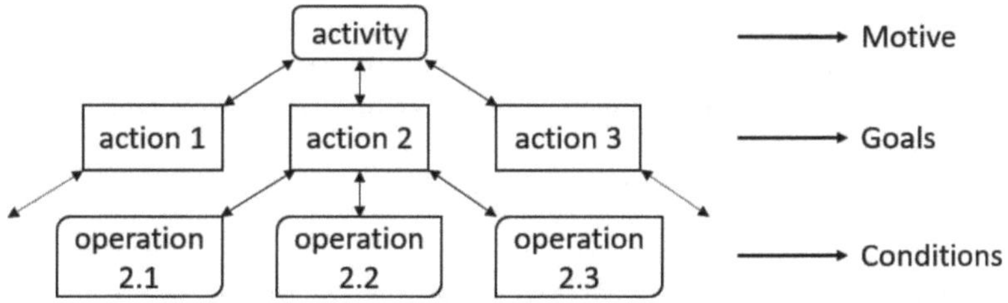

Fig. 15.2 Hierarchical structure of activity theory (adapted from Leont'ev 1978)

Object-orientedness describes the subject-object relationship in AT. It explains how all human activities are aimed towards their objects. These objects encourage and steer activities, which makes it necessary to analyze them in detail. Moreover, object-orientedness portrays the motivation of subjects to interact with particular objects to achieve an outcome. Here one can find a significant difference between the interaction with objects by humans and animals. In the animal world only physical things can be objects as they have no consciousness for immaterial things, such as language or information. Humans, though, can interact both with material and immaterial objects to accomplish a desired outcome.

Hierarchical structure: Hierarchy was already described in the prior section on the evolution of AT (see Fig. 15.2). In AT, the activity is divided into three layers: the activity layer, the action layer, and the operational layer. The activity layer illustrates how an activity is directed towards a motive. To satisfy the motive, several goal-related actions have to be conducted. A difference between humans and animals can be determined also in this principle. Unlike humans, most animals cannot differentiate between motives and goals, as they always act to their instincts and do not know that there are multiple solutions to solve a single problem. Actions consist out of operations which are dependent on the environmental conditions. Operations are either unconscious, e.g. using one's tongue while speaking, or automated procedures. Whenever an automated process fails, it becomes transformed into a manual and conscious action.

Kaptelinin and Nardi (2006) stress that *mediation* is the core dimension in which humans and animals differ. The success of the human species is owed by the usage of tools, whereas animals usually rely on claws, muscles, and other physical characteristics. AT argues that there is always a mediator with which humans interact to fulfill a motive and that this circumstance determines how humans behave. Car drivers, e.g., know the maps of their cities better than pedestrians, because the car allows them to see more from its infrastructure (Kaptelinin and Nardi 2012).

Internalization and externalization explain the distribution and re-distribution of tacit knowledge throughout the human world. In simple words, it emphasizes learning and teaching. By internalization, the actor deepens and incorporates external knowledge. Kaptelinin and Nardi (2012) provide the example of a young child who uses their fingers to count, but over time learns to count without any external means. On the other side, externalization delineates how tacit knowledge becomes explicit. This can be achieved by documentation, speaking, or just the modification of objects.

The final principle is *development*. It explains how activity systems alter over time and highlight the analyzation of the evolutionary process, which it gives insights on the modification of objects and shows how a society adapts to its environment and changes over time.

15.4 Other Human–Computer Interaction Theories

"If we focus only on practical usefulness and exclude explanation and interpretation, we do serious harm to our very nature as researcher" (Kuutti 2010, p. 717). With this statement, Kuutti (2010) highlights the key role of theory in activity assessment of human–computer interaction (HCI) systems.

Albeit there are many theories which try to describe complex actions and matters in information technology, it is a challenge to select the most suitable theory for one's own research purposes.

In the following sections, we want to introduce four other theories which are relevant for HCI and finally compare them with AT to highlight its suitability in the context of health care.

15.4.1 Actor-Network Theory

Actor-network theory (ANT) was developed by Bruno LaTour (1987) in the 1980s to understand innovation and knowledge creation in science. The theory aims to describe and uncover complexities in sociotechnical settings and emphasizes on the participation of non-human actors in social processes (Cressman 2009).

ANT consists of the following entities:

Actors, also called actants, can be either human or non-human and constitute everything which "accomplishes or undergoes an act" (Dankert 2011, p. 1). In AT they would represent subjects, objects and tools.

Networks connect actants with each other. They can be seen as the counterpart of the activity systems in AT. The network of ANT is not related to society or community. Networks appear, change, evolve and vanish during time (Principle of translation). A network only exists as long as its actants are interacting with each other.

The most central aspect of ANT is the principle of generalized symmetry (Reijo Miettinen 1999). This principle prescribes that networks consist out of actants, which can either be a human or a technological entity. Moreover, every actant, human or non-human, is assigned equal amounts of agency.

Another essential aspect of ANT is bilaterality of actants because every unit consists of social as well as technological portions. E.g. a website is technically based on programming code and servers, as well as socially based on the development team of the website.

Literature raises doubts on the usefulness of ANT in HCI. Firstly, problems arise out of the symmetrical language ANT uses. It contradicts the principle of Machiavellianism, dominating in western society, which argues that an actor always has to be human (Reijo Miettinen 1999). Secondly, the principle of symmetry does not show any hierarchical relationships, which makes application in corporations difficult. Therefore, Miettinen (2009) criticises that the semiotic vocabulary of ANT is not the right concept for describing HCI. Thirdly, Engeström has criticized ANT for reducing all actors into "black boxes without identifiable internal systemic properties and contradictions." (Engeström 2005).

15.4.2 Structuration Theory

Structuration theory (ST), developed by Giddens (1984), explains the interplay between society and the individual. Giddens outlines in his theory that social structures both have an impact on human activities and result from them. In one simple sentence: "Structure is both the medium and outcome of action"(Gehman 2008, p. 1). ST is premised on the three principles of *structures*, *systems*, and *duality of structure*.

Structures "are the resources and rules organized as properties of social systems" (Nyandiere et al. 2012, p. 388), whereby rules can be seen as universalizable procedures applied during social interaction, and resources are described as either authoritative, responsible for the distribution of power in a system, or of material nature (Gehman 2008). Moreover, agents play an elementary role for structure, as they consciously observe their environment and evaluate the actions of themselves and others (Gehman 2008).

According to Giddens (1984, p. 377), *systems* are "the patterning of social relations across time-space, understood as reproduced practices." That being said, systems constitute the routines for a context (Nyandiere et al. 2012).

The *duality of structure* explains that structure is both a mediator for actors and a result of social interaction. This means that actors have to align to certain structures while interacting with one another. As a cause of this interaction, new rules and resources can emerge which alter the system structure (Gehman 2008).

All in all, the focus of structuration theory is to explain how system structures change during time rather than how systems work in particular (Craib 1992).

The theory is criticized for its high level of abstraction (Nyandiere et al. 2012) and moreover does not provide descriptive tools to illustrate processes and uncover system problems. This circumstance makes it difficult to analyze specific HCI systems in detail and leads to the conclusion that structuration theory tends to be a useful tool to describe the evolution of a corporate culture rather than to illustrate specific activities (Jones and Karsten 2008).

15.4.3 Distributed Cognition

Hutchins (1986) developed the theory of distributed cognition (DCog) during the 1980s. His theory is grounded in cognitive sciences and cognitive anthropology. Hutchins (1986) contends that knowledge is not only existent in the individual but also within an individual's social and physical environment, respectively sociotechnical context. DCog encompasses the coordination between internal, which displays the individual's mind, and external structures, which is the individual's surrounding.

The "distributed" in DCog refers to dividing or splitting apart cognition among time, space, society, and artifacts, while "cognition" means the perception and interpretation of information by reading, watching, listening, learning, reasoning, etc. (Hutchins 1986).

DCog involves systems, environments, humans, and physical artifacts, and illustrates the interaction between these elements. E.g. a collaborative patient care system (system and physical resource) is implemented in a hospital (environment). Doctors, nurses, and patients (individuals) interact with the system. The theory is applied in the research areas of HCI, computer supported collaborative work, and computer supported collaborative learning. In literature DCog is applied in examples and case studies for ship navigation, aircraft cockpits, and the coordination of programmers (Hutchins 1986; Flor and Hutchins 1991).

DCog has profound similarities with AT because they share a common intellectual heritage (Halverson 2002). However, they diverge in the following points (Halverson 2002):

- Contrary to DCog, AT provides terms for its theoretical elements. Therefore, AT supports description and communication.
- In both theories, a system or activity has a certain outcome. In DCog this outcome is obtained by the work of several individuals, while in AT the focus is clearly on one protagonist who transfers an object into a result.
- The theoretical language between both theories is different: In AT exists the "social, cultural, historical and artifactual world" (Halverson 2002, p. 247). DCog is less complex and focuses on sociotechnical systems to describe humans and non-humans on an equal footing.
- The static activity systems highlight processes for both analysts and readers and, thus, feature descriptive and rhetorical power. In DCog the representation of processes lies in the hands of the researchers and provides no standardization, which would encourage comparability.
- The Venn-Diagram in Fig. 15.3 clarifies the differences and commonalities between AT and DCog.

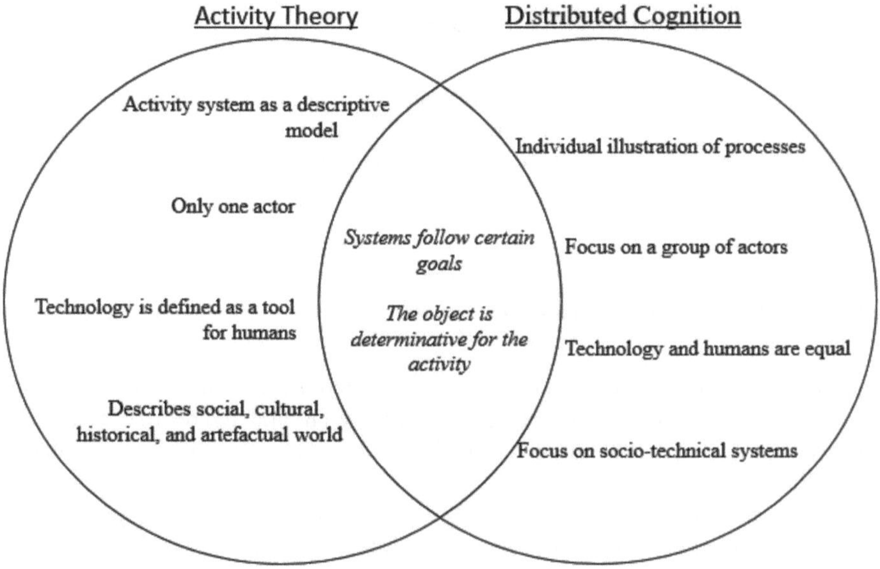

Fig. 15.3 Comparison of activity theory and distribute cognition

15.4.4 Situated Action

Situated action (SAct) was first introduced in 1987 in the book "Plans and Situated Action: the problem of human-machine communication" by Suchman (1986). SAct is principally based on anthropology and social sciences and has the intention to not only produce a formal model for knowledge and action, but to explore their relation in particular contexts in which they unanimously appear (Suchman 1986).

SAct underlines the wisdom of people and "how they use common-sense practices/procedures to produce, analyze and make sense of one another's actions and their local or situated circumstances" (Doerry 1995, p. 1). SAct portrays how individuals act in their situation and environment.

Suchman argues that, although people make plans for solving problems or interacting with their environment, in the end the situation can be different than expected and may alter the plan and therefore the behavior of the individual (Suchman 1986). She gives the example of going canoeing over falls to clarify this point (Suchman 1986): a canoeist can map their actions of paddling according to what they see. But when the paddler begins their adventure, they always have to adapt their plan according to the water streams or obstacles they have not spotted before.

The prior example illustrates that the "structuring of activities is not something which precedes it but can only grow directly out of the immediacy of the situation" (Nardi 1993, p. 36). Thus, only a temporal activity can be examined, but not an enduring pattern of interaction across situations (Nardi 1993). This makes the theory suitable for investigations regarding usability, as the handling of technology by diverse individual practitioners can be analyzed. However, an analysis of an overall process with all its interactors and social facets, like in AT, cannot be provided.

15.5 Comparison of HCI Theories

Now that four other theories to AT have been introduces, they will be evaluated in the next two sub-sections. First, the theories will be ranked according to their weight in research. Second, they will be examined and compared from eight different aspects.

15.5.1 Relevance of Theories

Looking for the occurrence of the previous presented theories in research literature gives insights on their relevance and popularity, even though the result of searching for certain strings in digital libraries provides rather a tendency than a clear evidence (Kaptelinin and Nardi 2012).

In this case, all four theories and AT were searched both on their names and, moreover, in relation to HCI. The results (see Table 15.2) show that AT is less popular than ST but with regards to HCI it is by far the most applied theory in research. ANT and SAct are the least popular theories. DCog is not as regularly applied as AT, but still has its reason for existence as several case studies have shown (Hutchins 1986; Flor and Hutchins 1991).

15.5.2 Final Comparison of HCI Theories

Due to the fact that this paper analyzes HCI theories in health care, we take the following eight aspects for a final comparison into account:

- *Social context:* Are human interactions and the social setting of a process or rather activity adequately represented?
- *Technical specifications:* Can the interaction with technology be depicted precisely?
- *Graphical tool*: Does the theory provide a model to illustrate and analyze HCI systems?

Table 15.2 Occurrence of theories in ACM Library—from 2.5 million references in computing (14.06.2016)

Search string	Number of hits	Search string	Number of hits
"Activity theory"	562	"Activity theory" && HCI	135
"Actor-network theory"	225	"Actor-network theory" && HCI	20
"Structuration theory"	1440	"Structuration theory" && HCI	21
"Distributed cognition"	397	"Distributed cognition" && HCI	78
"Situated action"	136	"Situated action" && HCI	29

- *Equality of technology and humans*: Are equal amounts of agency assigned to humans and non-humans?
- *Enhancements*: Is the theory evolving and slightly altering through time?
- *Popularity*: How relevant are the theories in today's research? (see Table 15.2)
- *General suitability:* Is it reasonable to apply the theory in a common organizational context?
- *Healthcare suitability:* Is it reasonable to apply the theory in a healthcare context?

The results of the comparison show that AT differentiates between clinicians and patients, defines information technology as a mediator and describes processes embedded in a medical context precisely by the application of activity systems (see Table 15.3). This makes it suitable for usage in health care, as the theory is more operational than ANT or other theories and capture the dynamics of IT in medical institutions accurately.

15.6 Discussion

Prior work has documented that Activity Theory is an effective tool for the analysis of sociotechnical systems in health care (Riechert et al. 2016; Wiser et al. 2017). However, these studies did not compare Activity Theory with other relevant HCI theories to stress the advantage of AT over them. For this reason, we conducted a qualitative case study in terms of a literature review. The results of this work have shown the following:

The application of Situated Action in health care is limited, but a reasonable case for an analysis with this theory could be for investigation of user-friendliness of newly introduced technology in clinics.

By the means of Structuration Theory the evolution of medical environments over a longer timespan can be investigated. However, technology is of secondary importance and therefore the theory is not appropriate for finding flaws in healthcare technology.

In Distributed Cognition and Actor-Network Theory technology and humans are on an equal footing regarding their power and rights within an activity. The disadvantages they have against Activity Theory in a health care is that the patient cannot be positioned as the central aspect of an activity. Moreover, in those theories the group is in focus. Thus, the theories cannot specifically illustrate how each individual behaves.

Activity Theory, in contrary, records a multifaceted network with all of the activity's social and technological units in order to illustrate the object oriented action triggered by the clinical person towards the patient using tools, like electronic patient health records. Finally, Activity Theory and its four levels of contradictions allows a precise documentation of flaws and categorizes them which can, when resolved, reduce risks for the patient's health and safety.

Table 15.3 Now that four other theories

Theory/ Aspect	Activity theory	Actor-network theory	Structuration theory	Distributed cognition	Situated action
Social context	Social setting is represented in subjects, objects, community, rules, and division of labour	Social actants, which partially have technical characteristics	Focus is on social structures and their evolution through time	A group of individuals is in foreground	The activities of individuals are paramount
Techical specifications	Technology is represented in the group of tools and is mediating social interaction	Technical actants, which partially have social characteristics	The term "system" includes social aspects. Technology is of secondary importance	Systems, technological environment and physical artifacts play a major role	Technologies are neglected: they only provide the situation for the individual
Equality of technology and humans	No, strict separation of human and technological entities	Yes, both humans and non-humans are seen as actants with equal rights	To some degree: humans and non-humans both alter system structures	Yes, humans and technology is on an equal footing	No, technologies provide the playground for social interaction
Graphical tool	Yes, the activity system illustrates the interplay of social and technical components	No	No	No	No
Enhancements	Yes	Limited	Limited	Yes	Limited
Popularity	High	Medium	Medium	High	Low
Suitability for information systems in organizations	Differentiation between IT and humans	Humans and IT contribute equally to the network	Documents the structural changes within the organizations caused by the implementation of IT	Possible analysis of employees, customers, IT, and business environment	Documents how humans adapt to IT in their organization
	Illustration of activities with the organizational and IT context they are embedded in	Illustration of activities with the organizational and IT context they are embedded in			
Suitability for information systems in health care	Differentiation between clinical staff and patients	Clinicians and patients contribute equally to the network	Without adaption, ST can only explain culture in HealthCare towards technology (see Groves et al. 2011)	Enables to understand roles of technology, patients, clincians, and environment (Hazlehurst et al. 2007)	Can only focus on the individual clinician or patient, but not on both at the same time
	Illustration of activities with the medical context they are embedded in	Illustration of activities with the medical context they are embedded in			Healthcare technology is seen as a circumstance humans have to adapt to

15.7 Conclusion

Concluding, Activity Theory is considered to be a useful theory for facilitating a better understanding of technologies in a healthcare context. Its contradiction layers help to unveil key issues which, when resolved, can lead to smoother system implementation and more streamlined processes.

Although Activity Theory is an appropriate method to analyze STS in health care, adding functionalities from the other HCI theories could lead to advanced insights: for example, aggregating situated action elements to AT for an emphasized analysis of people's reaction on IT or adding structuration theory for a sophisticated examination of the hierarchical changes caused by IT. However, changes in theory should be carried out with care so that principles of Activity Theory are not infringed upon (Kaptelinin and Nardi 2012).

References

Allert, H., & Richter, C. (2007). Activity systems and context working as core concepts in modeling socio-technical systems. *Proceedings of the 2007 workshop on Representation models and techniques for improving e-learning*, pp. 28–39.

Bertelsen, O. W., & Bødker, S. (2003). Activity theory. In J. M. Carroll (Ed.), *HCI models, theories, and frameworks* (pp. 291–324). San Francisco: Elsevier. https://doi.org/10.1016/B978-155860808-5/50011-3.

Craib, I. (1992). *Anthony giddens*. London, New York: Routledge.

Cressman, D. (2009). *A brief overview of actor-network theory: Punctualization, heterogeneous engineering & translation*. Paper for Simon Frasier University ACT Lab/Centre for Policy Research on Science & Technology (CPROST), 1–17. https://doi.org/10.3126/bodhi.v5i1.8053

Dankert, R. (2011). *Using Actor-Network Theory (ANT) doing research*. Retrieved June 12, 2016, from http://ritskedankert.nl/using-actor-network-theory-ant-doing-research/

Doerry, E. (1995). *Evaluating distributed environments based on communicative efficacy [inproceedings]*. Retrieved from http://www.sigchi.org/chi95/Electronic/documnts/doctoral/ed_bdy.htm

Engeström, Y. (1987). *Learning by expanding an activity-theoretical approach to developmental research* (1st ed.). Helsinki: Orienta-Konsultit Oy.

Engeström, Y. (2001). Expansive learning at work: Toward an activity theoretical reconceptualization. *Journal of Education and Work, 14*(1), 133–156. https://doi.org/10.1080/13639080020028747.

Engeström, Y. (2005). *Developmental work research: Expanding activity theory in practice*. Berlin: Lehmanns Media.

Flor, N. V., & Hutchins, E. L. (1991). A case study of team programming during perfective software maintenance. In *Empirical studies of programmers: Fourth workshop in proceedings* (p. 36).

Gehman, J. (2008). *Structuration theory summary*. Retrieved April 01, 2016, from http://www.joelgehman.com/resources/Giddens1984StructurationTheorySummary.pdf. Accessed on April 1, 2016.

Giddens, A. (1984). *The constitution of society: Outline of the theory of structuration*. Cambridge, Cambridgeshire: Polity Press.

Groves, P. S., Meisenbach, R. J., & Scott-Cawiezell, J. (2011). Keeping patients safe in healthcare organizations: a structuration theory of safety culture. *Journal of Advanced Nursing, 67*(8), 1846–1855.

Halverson, C. A. (2002). Activity theory and distributed cognition: Or what does CSCW need to DO with theories? *Computer Supported Cooperative Work (CSCW), 11*, 243–267. https://doi.org/10.1023/A:1015298005381.

Hazlehurst, B., McMullen, C. K., & Gorman, P. N. (2007). Distributed cognition in the heart room: how situation awareness arises from coordinated communications during cardiac surgery. *Journal of biomedical informatics, 40*(5), 539–551.

Hutchins, W. J. (1986). *Machine translation: Past, present, future*. Chichester: Ellis Horwood.

IDC. (2016). *Worldwide IT spending forecast to reach $2.7 trillion in 2020 led by financial services, manufacturing, and healthcare, according to IDC*. Retrieved October 1, 2016, from https://www.idc.com/getdoc.jsp?containerId=prUS41699316

Jones, M. R., & Karsten, H. (2008). Giddens's structuration theory and information systems research. *MIS Quarterly, 32*(1), 127–157. Retrieved from http://dl.acm.org/citation.cfm?id=2017378.2017385.

Kaptelinin, V., & Nardi, B. (2006). *Acting with technology: Activity theory and interaction design*. Cambridge: MIT Press.

Kaptelinin, V., & Nardi, B. (2012). *Activity theory in HCI: Fundaments and reflections*. San Rafael, CA: Morgan & Claypool.

Korpela, M. (2000). Activity analysis as a method for information systems development: General introduction and experiments from Nigeria and Finland. *Scandinavian Journal of Information Systems, 12*(1). pp. 191–210.

Kuutti, K. (1996). Activity theory as a potential framework for human-computer interaction research. In B. Nardi (Ed.), *Context and consciousness: Activity theory and human-computer interaction* (pp. 17–44). Cambridge and London: MIT Press.

Kuutti, K. (2010). Where are the Ionians of user experience research? In *Proceedings of the 6th Nordic conference on human-computer interaction: extending boundaries* (pp. 715–718). New York, NY: ACM. https://doi.org/10.1145/1868914.1869012

Latour, B. (1987). *Science in action : How to follow scientists and engineers through society*. Cambridge, MA: Harvard University Press.

Leont'ev, A. N. (1978). *Activity, consciousness, and personality*. Englewood Cliffs, NJ: Prentice Hall.

Leveson, N. G., & Turner, C. S. (1993). An investigation of the Therac-25 accidents. *Computer, 26*(7), 18–41. https://doi.org/10.1109/MC.1993.274940.

Miettinen, R. (1999). The riddle of things: Activity theory and actor network theory as approaches to studying innovations. *Mind, Culture, and Activity, 6*(3), 170–195. https://doi.org/10.1080/10749039909524725.

Miettinen, R. (2009). *Dialogue and creativity: Activity theory in the study of science, technology and innovations*. Berlin: Lehmanns. Retrieved from https://books.google.com.au/books?id=lETzCQAAQBAJ.

Nardi, B. A. (1993). Studying context: A comparison of activity theory, situated action models, and distributed cognition. In *Proceedings East–West conference on human–computer interaction* (pp. 352–359). Moscow: ICSTI.

Nyandiere, C. M., Kamuzora, F., & Lukandu, I. A. (2012). Application of structuration theory and activity theory in enterprise resources planning systems implementation for universities. *Computer Technology and Application, 3*, 385–394.

Riechert, J., Durst, C., & Wickramasinghe, N. (2016). The application of activity theory to explain collaborative technology use in healthcare: The case of a chemotherapy ordering system. *Proceedings of the 49th Hawaii International Conference on System Sciences (HICSS)*, pp. 989–997.

Statista. (2016). *Worldwide information technology (IT) spending forecast from 2014 to 2019 (in billion U.S. dollars)*. Retrieved October 1, 2016, from https://www.statista.com/statistics/480063/worldwide-it-spending-forecast/

Suchman, L. (1986). *Plans and situated actions*. New York: Cambridge University.

Vygotsky, L. S. (1978). In M. Cole, V. John-Steiner, S. Scribner, & E. Souberman (Eds.), *Mind in society: Development of higher psychological processes*. Cambridge: Harvard University Press.

Wiser, F., Durst, C., & Wickramasinghe, N. (2017). Analyzing collaborative patient care solutions using activity theory. *Proceedings of the 50th Hawaii International Conference on System Sciences (HICSS)*, pp. 901–909.

Chapter 16
Fit-Viability Model Examination of e-Health Solutions

Nilmini Wickramasinghe, Jonathan L. Schaffer, Juergen Seitz, Imran Muhammad, and Doug Vogel

16.1 Introduction

The successful adoption and implementation of health information systems (HIS) has been the subject of extensive research. However, the effect of cross-cultural issues including macro level or external factors such as political, social, economic, environmental infrastructure/technology, laws and regulations; messo-level or organisational factors such as leadership, management style, polices, structure; and micro-level or tactical factors such as information sharing, training and learning, technical staff or user behaviour have been less widely studied (OECD 2010a; b; Pearce and Haikerwal 2010; Porter and Guth 2012; Porter and Teisberg 2006; Wickramasinghe and Schaffer 2010). Yet, it is precisely these issues that separately, or in combination, derail numerous HIS implementations. To examine this dilemma, we proffer a fit viability model (FVM) to facilitate a better understanding of key issues. In so doing, we answer the research question: "How can a FVM assist in

N. Wickramasinghe (✉)
Faculty of Health, Deakin University, Melbourne, VIC, Australia

Health Informatics Management Unit, Epworth HealthCare, Richmond, VIC, Australia

J. L. Schaffer
Faculty of Health, Deakin University, Melbourne, VIC, Australia

Cleveland Clinic, Cleveland, OH, USA

J. Seitz
DHBW, Heidenheim, Germany

I. Muhammad
Faculty of Health, Deakin University, Melbourne, VIC, Australia

D. Vogel
Harbin Institute of Technology, Harbin, China

N. Wickramasinghe, J. L. Schaffer (eds.), *Theories to Inform Superior Health Informatics Research and Practice*, Healthcare Delivery in the Information Age,
https://doi.org/10.1007/978-3-319-72287-0_16

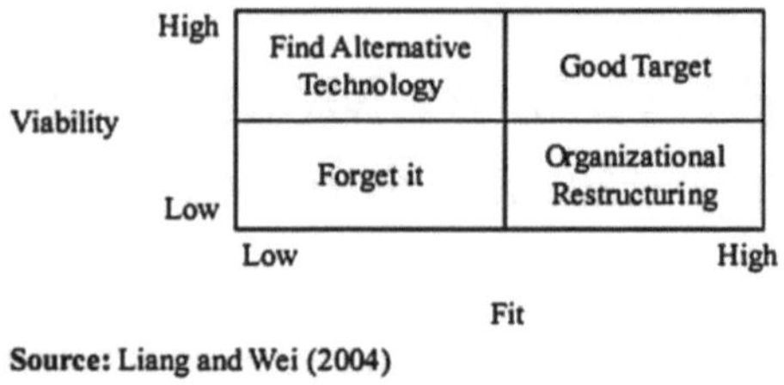

Fig. 16.1 FIT-Viability framework (Liang and Wei 2004)

unpacking cross-cultural issues in the adoption and implementation of HIS?" An exploratory multiple case study methodology is adopted.

16.2 Development of an Appropriate Conceptual Framework: The Fit-Viability Model

Tjan (2001) proposed fit viability dimensions for evaluating Internet initiative projects. Liang and Wei (2004), using these two dimensions and adding Task Technology Fit (TTF) theory, proposed a fit-viability model to study m-commerce applications. In their framework, viability measures the readiness of the organization for the technology adoption and implementation, and fit measures capabilities of the systems to optimally perform the required tasks. These two dimensions make a simple matrix with fit on horizontal and viability on vertical axes, as shown in Fig. 16.1.

By using the four corners of the matrix, organizations can make an informed decision for technology adoption and implementation and adjust accordingly. For example, developing countries could have better political stability, economic growth, better environment, and more stable telecommunication and information technology infrastructure, which in turn means that the system could rate high on viability but the task does not fit the nature of the designed system and hence would lead to unsuccessful results. For example, a multinational corporation (MNC) having operations in two different geographical locations such as USA and China could have high viability and high fit in the USA for a specific system, but high viability and low fit in China due to different data structures, reporting procedures and business processes. This means that the system has to be customized according to the local organizational and cultural requirements or the business has to go through organizational restructuring or Business Process Re-engineering (BPR), which could lead to complications, delays and budget overruns. Only those systems with both high task-technology fit and high viability are good and thus deemed likely to succeed.

16.3 Task-Technology Fit

The theoretical basis of the fit construct is derived from the Task-Technology Fit model which according to Goodhue (1995, 1998) argues that a fit between task characteristics and system features needs to be high for better performance and success. Further, this will have an effect on the decision making process of an organization. Research (Soh et al. 2000; Goodhue 1998) has indicated that if a system is more aligned with the requirements of the users there are greater chances of system success which leads to better performance. Hence, if the features offered by the system fit with the task requirements, users will be more inclined to adopt the system.

16.3.1 *Viability*

Viability refers to the degree of impact of national and organizational factors on a system adoption and implementation decision. At the national level, these factors include political and social, economic, environmental as well as infrastructure/technology factors. At the organizational level, literature has proposed many factors with strategic and tactical aspects (Umble et al. 2003; Poon and Wagner 2001). These factors include leadership, management style, polices, information sharing, training and learning, technical staff, and user behaviour. Taking the example of China, Huang and Palvia (2001) suggest that economic and technological factors are crucial in cross-cultural ERP system implementations, and ignoring these factors could lead to unsuccessful projects; Molla and Bhalla (2006) argue that stable economic growth and strong IT infrastructure could create better business environments and innovation adoption, positively affecting viability of the system.

16.3.2 *Proposed Framework*

The research framework shown in Fig. 16.2 illustrates the key constructs and factors affecting system implementations. Fit will be measured by matching the requirements of the organization with the functionalities offered by the system e.g. data format, operating procedures, and output format. Viability will be measured by assessing the impact of national and organizational factors on the adoption decision of the organization. This paper proffers that this is a robust and rich framework to evaluate large scale e-health systems. To do this we adopt a multiple case study approach as described in the Methodology section.

16.3.3 *Methodology*

Based on the criteria given by Yin (2014); the appropriate choice of methodology to test the use and usability of the proposed framework (Fig. 16.2) is qualitative multiple case study research because this is an exploratory study of a new or emerging phenomenon; namely health informatics solutions at national or

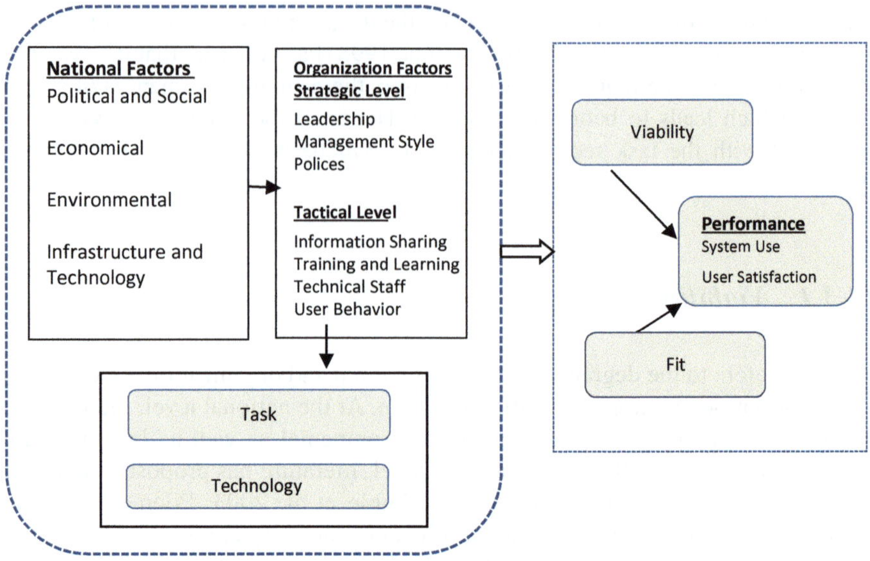

Fig. 16.2 Research framework

regional levels. Further, we wish to explore how solutions in different countries can be implemented successfully and what are the factors that impact on the implementation and adoption of these IS based interventions in healthcare contexts. Qualitative research is holistic, humanistic, and interactive to provide more focus support on the study of a complex phenomenon of human and system interaction and relationship; as in our research (Creswell 2009; Yin 2014), qualitative research can provide deeper understanding of the phenomenon as compared to quantitative study because of the exploratory nature of the study and focus which would not be on quantitative measures (Trochim and Donnelly 2008). The chosen case studies are from Australia, China, Germany, South Africa and the United States.

16.3.3.1 Case Vignettes

Multiple case studies of various solutions and technologies are now presented in turn. Data was collected using several techniques including unstructured interview, surveys and analysis of archival material. As far as possible the multiple stakeholder views in health care (i.e., provider, regulator, payer, hospital and patient perspectives) were captured. Data analysis included standard qualitative techniques such as thematic analysis where a priori themes were derived from the components in the conceptual model. The case studies all exemplify various aspects of the proffered conceptual model in this way serving to validate the model and demonstrate its usefulness in unpacking critical aspects with HIS implementation.

16.3.4 The German e-Healthcard

The basis for the German e-healthcard is the law requiring the upgrading of the public healthcare system (Gesetz zur Modernisierung der gesetzlichen Krankenversicherung), which passed the parliament November 14th, 2003 and is coded in § 291a of the 5th book of Code of Social Law (Sozialgesetzbuch). There were two different kind of functions defined: mandatory and optional functions. Mandatory functions are, for example, administrative data and electronic prescriptions. Optional functions include medical functions such as the emergency data record and the electronic patient record. Originally the e-healthcard should have been implemented by January 1st, 2006. In 2011 the e-prescription function was stopped. Now, since January 2014 the old card is replaced by the new chip style e-healthcard. (Federal Ministry of Health 2008; Gematik 2014).

As the project to implement the e-healthcard started in 2003 this means that the basic architecture is not state of the art anymore; eg regarding the specification that a maximum number of prescriptions of eight could be stored on the card. (Gematik 2008) For people with chronic diseases, this number is inadequate. Nowadays, the question is 'Is it necessary to store prescriptions on the card?' In 2003 the maximum bandwidth in Germany was 1.536 Mbit/s downstream and 0.384 Mbit/s upstream; in 2014 the maximum bandwidth is 50 Mbit/s upstream and 10 Mbit/s downstream (Telekom Deutschland GmbH 2014). In the age of cloud computing, the data volume of a single prescription is very small and the bandwidth is not a limiting issue. Data storage on the e-healthcard is no longer necessary or even desired. The more important aspect is data security. The existing encryption algorithms can provide adequate data protection. The key length of the asymmetric RSA algorithm is not limited to a certain length. Of course, nowadays with a shorter key, encrypted data can be decrypted in the future much faster. The length of the key can be defined depending on the life expectancy of the data and the criticality of the value of the data.

There are approximately 700 million prescriptions in Germany each year (Schweim 2007). The Ministry of Health estimated that nearly one billion Euro can be saved if these prescriptions are transferred to e-prescriptions. (Handelsblatt 2004) The whole process can be implemented as a process without any media disruptions. Ven if less than 100% of the prescriptions can be transferred to e-prescriptions, significant monetary savings can be experienced. Of course, it is neither efficient, nor effective to have two processes simultaneously: a paper-based process and an electronic process. As the acceptance is low and there will never be support of all stakeholders, the only opportunity to benefit from the electronic process without media disruptions is to offer the choice in which way a prescription is issued. In the process of a prescription we have at least three parties: the patient, the prescribing clinician and the pharmacy. Compared to money transfer using online banking, this process is more complex. The online banking process has at least two partners: the customer and the bank. Although this process is simpler, Germany has roughly 45 per cent of the population between 16 and 74 years of age who use online banking and approximately 40 million out of 93 million current accounts are online accounts (Leichsenring 2012). Positive experiences allow patients, prescribing clinicians and pharmacists to change their mind. There are techno phobic patients, clinicians and pharmacists, also in combination, which means a very much slower change of the process. But compared to no existing change in the process, this is more effective. Eight years have passed without an existing electronic process, without the opportunity to provide a tech savvy population to benefit from the transformed process. A tech savvy patient and a tech savvy clinician are essential for ultimate success.

Step by step the number of patients, the number of clinicians and the number of pharmacies will increase because they will benefit from the electronic processes. For example, besides young clinicians and new highly specialized ambulatory healthcare centers, hospitals also perceive the pressure of competition. They need an efficient and effective organization and can benefit from information technology adoption (Fähling et al. 2009a; b; Köbler et al. 2010). The data are available online and there are no media disruptions which have to be overcome. In contrast, well established clinicians with a stellar reputation, who don't store their data electronically even nowadays because they have their patients, don't have the pressure to change their processes and systems. They often have long waiting lists and their perception is that any change in the process and their behaviour means an investment which is, from their point of view, not worth making. (Dünnebeil et al. 2012).

It is often criticized that the informational self-determination is not provided (e. g. Gardt 2012; Chaos Computer Club e. V. 2014; Bündnis 'Stoppt die e-Card!' 2014). The idea of the system is that patients control which clinician or medical doctor has access to stored data like diagnostic findings (§ 295a 5th book of Code of Social Law). A medical doctor typically has access to these data only in the presence of a patient. The e-healthcard in combination with the PIN of the patient is needed to authorize access. There is, of course, no guarantee that the process works securely all the time and that there isn't any misuse of data. But the misuse of data results from the mistakes of people and criminal activities. Some of the published mistakes of people occurred in the early stage of implementation, where we still are, when the processes were not fully implemented in organizations (e. g. Gruhn 2014; Gruhn and Reisener 2014). Mistakes in the process shouldn't be reasons held against the e-healthcard itself. The card always worked properly. On the other side, the process without the e-healthcard also has its risks: correspondence between medical doctors takes place via email without any encryption, patient documents can be found everywhere in a doctor's office or a hospital without any protection, the access control to archives with patients documents is insufficient, and IT service staff have nearly full access to patients data and they are also able to manipulate data (Weichert 2006). For decades, medical doctors and hospitals have transferred data to clearing centers and insurance companies without any significant data protection.

Finally, it seems that there isn't a big difference between the old insurance card and the new e-healthcard. Both cards are used to identify and authorize people. But even if there aren't data stored anymore on the e-healthcard (except emergency data), the improvement of data security is significant because patients have the opportunity to control data flows between doctors as well as the data flow.

Further, the data stored in the telematics infrastructure are encrypted. The legal requirements for data privacy and data security are significant. In a case of emergency, people will probably not care about data privacy and data security if their lives depend on the availability of data.

16.3.5 *China*[1]

China has persistent and pervasive healthcare problems due to a paucity of resources and population pressure, not the least of which is a dramatic increase in the number of elderly with chronic diseases (Yun et al. 2012). The problems cannot be solved with new entrants into the medical profession mainly due to a relative lack of young people as a function of the one-child policy that has been in place for decades. Hospital visits can require 3 h of waiting in a queue for a 3 min appointment followed by another 3 h for payment consummation. However, not all is bleak since innovative solutions are emerging at community levels to deal with medical issues in a creative fashion. A salient example is the case of the Lujiazui Smart Community project in greater Shanghai.

The Lujiazui community has gone through a dramatic transformation (Lujiazui 2017). Located across from the Bund in Shanghai, the region was historically farm land that was prone to floods. More recently, the region has been transformed into a business district with over 160,000 people. However, the previous community was not displaced and still exists, primarily as a comparatively poor collection of relative illiterate elderly people with increasing prevalence of chronic diseases e.g., hypertension and type-2 diabetes. A large portion of this population is housebound. Interestingly, though, another part of the Lujiazui community population is characterized by professionals of various ages associated with the newly created business district. These professional have a variety of needs, including vaccinations for their children as well as normal population medical requirements (Yun et al. 2012).

A distinct portion of the professional portion of the population can be categorized as "young-elderly" (Lujiazui 2017). By nature, these are people between the ages of 60 and 75 who are entering a phase of life in which they are not working full time but still are energetic and wish to donate some time to society. As such, they can stay mentally active and ease the transition from a busy work-life to retirement. These young elderly come from a variety of backgrounds but, for the most part, are not medically trained (although there are some retired doctors and nurses).

To meet the diverse needs of the Lujiazui community, a non-profit organization has been created with a relatively small grant from the government (Yun et al. 2012). The organization is led by an energetic (and charismatic) former surgeon who points out that he can now affect the lives of hundreds of thousands of people rather than just thousands (as a surgeon). He regularly goes out in the community and is widely respected by the population in general.

[1] For this section – internal documents in Chinese which were translated to English were also used to provide the background.

The system supporting the community is not overly sophisticated and, for the most part, has been assembled by integrating various pieces of open-source software with heavy use of the Internet. Services delivered include online booking for clinic visits and help in locating drugs as well as home monitoring support, health data collection, coordinating follow-up by doctors and emergency help if necessary including finding an appropriate hospital. Additional services are information oriented e.g., advice on self-examination and healthcare alternatives.

A collection of small neighbourhood clinics deliver the services for those patients who are mobile. Unlike the hospitals, the visits are better scheduled in advance and organized around use of a community "smart-card" to handle administrative details. The clinics can deal with a wide range of "normal" medical issues but, of course, are not in a position to handle medical emergencies requiring hospital level attention. As such, they are only the first line of defence but can take a lot of pressure off of hospitals and, needless to say, are quite accessible e.g., within walking distance of patients requiring service.

A key element of service delivery is the use of 165 young-elderly volunteers who go out into the homes of those patients who are not mobile and require personal attention e.g., in measuring blood pressure and monitoring glucose levels. Training is provided in the organization's "university". The young-elderly volunteers are responsible for a given set of patients and have established trust along with the ability to recognize change over time (for better or worse) and recommend a visit to a medical professional if appropriate (or not). Volunteers are rewarded through recognition as well as discounts from local businesses appreciative of their community service.

Where possible, results are transmitted directly using wireless technologies e.g., smart-phone use by the patient or young-elderly care giver. Accumulated results are displayed visually on a patient-by-patient basis and reviewed by medical personnel to identify treatment effects and trends. If necessary, the patient can be transferred into a clinic (or hospital) if situations warrant but, for the most part, the patients remain at home confident that they are being properly cared for. Increasingly available sensor-based devices are anticipated to further automate data collection and transmission.

Over the past 8 months, the organization has dealt with over 10,000 patients and has been widely recognized as successful. It indeed has many visitors from other communities seeking to establish something similar in their own communities and has become self-supporting through minimal direct patient payment as well as insurance reimbursement. The success factors are many but can be categorized into macro, messo and micro issues in the general context of task-technology fit.

16.3.6 Macro

At a macro level, a variety of extenuating circumstances provided the opportunity for the Lujiazui community initiative. The general healthcare environment is fraught with problems and universally recognized as not being able to meet population needs, both in the present and, especially, in the future. As such, the government is willing to provide seed funding for alternatives, albeit envisioning that solutions will become self-sustaining as non-profits. The legal environment in China is relatively unrefined for these health related issues which further encourages new initiatives. Internet-based technology is widely available and highly accepted by the population in general e.g., a very high percentage of all ages have smart-phones. China has provided global leadership in IP6 implementation and looks forward to high levels of sensor-based and mobile applications. Components are not only manufactured in China but also made available for evaluation in a fashion uncommon to the rest of the world. Vendors are eager to supply prototypes for promotion and gathering of usage data.

16.3.7 Messo

At a messo level, a number of organizational factors have been especially influential in its success. As previously noted, the organization's gregarious leader is a unique individual with medical training as a surgeon but, more importantly, a commitment to community service and willingness to engage that is seldom witnessed. The management style is very participative, collaborative and transparent such that the (relatively few) employees enjoy access and have a consensual view of organizational objectives. The organization further relies on a strong group of dedicated volunteers (including young-elderly as previously noted). Policies are relatively few and the structure is fluid as a function of the circumstances. The organic nature of meeting community needs through beneficial services is well received and helps focus organizational effort.

16.3.8 Micro

At a micro level, information sharing is paramount and learning through the organization's "university" is highly encouraged. There is a relative minimal technical staff with a high level of involvement and presence in interactions as well as a focus on component integration, rather than traditional systems development, resulting in reasonably rapid response to change and a high level of system success in supporting relevant stakeholders. User behaviour is accordingly positive with respect to willingness to use existing system functions in addition to recommending change as warranted. Patients are grateful to have the services as a vital healthcare component and complement to hospital visits, which can be minimized.

16.3.9 Task-Technology Fit

From a task-technology fit perspective, the cumulative macro, messo and micro factors as previously noted work well in combination to get the system used and useful as intended, extending implementation beyond technical issues alone.

Careful monitoring (along with lots of stakeholder feedback) and evaluation with subsequent revision in mind assures that the system will continue to support the organization in a fruitful fashion and maximizes the probability of success. A key element of system evolution and development process success is working "with" stakeholders, not just "for" them in designing in an organic fashion focused on progressive removal of uncertainties. The system components are loosely (rather than tightly) coupled which enables flexibility and ease of change over time to meet evolving community needs and technological advances.

16.4 Australia: The Personally Controlled Electronic Health Record (PCEHR) or MyHealth Record

The terminology adopted in Australia for electronic record keeping and its e-health solution is known as the Personally Controlled Electronic Health Record (PCEHR) [later re-named MyHealth Record] which sits between individually-controlled health records and healthcare provider health records (DoHA and NEHTA 2011; Fig. 16.3). Thus, the PCEHR has a shared use and mixed governance model (DoHA and NEHTA 2011; Fig. 16.1).

Specifically, the PCEHR is a person-centric secure repository of electronic health and medical records of an individual's medical history that acts as a hub for linking hospital, medical and pharmaceutical systems using a unique patient identifier (NHHRC 2009, p. 134). One of its key features is that it captures information from different systems and presents this information in a single view to consumers and authorised service providers for better decision making about health and service delivery (DoHA and NEHTA 2011). This is a hybrid health information system that integrates web based personal health records with a clinical electronic health record system and allows shared access to both consumers and healthcare providers based on a shared responsibilities and mixed governance model. (Leslie 2011).

The PCEHR is designed to be a person-centric system where technology is implemented in a complex clinical and organisational environment and users consist of different sets of stakeholders including healthcare service providers, healthcare managers, government bodies, healthcare pressure groups and (most importantly) patients (DoHA and NEHTA 2011). Further, the PCEHR is a patient centric system and a model for increasing engagement by patients in their health-

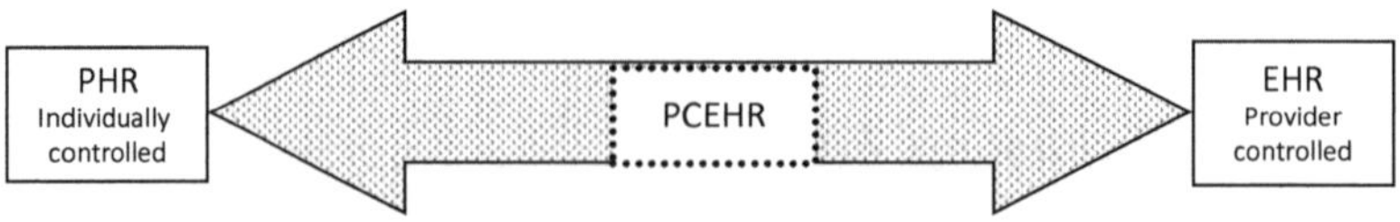

Fig. 16.3 The position of the PCEHR in the e-health solution spectrum

care and empowering them in this undertaking (DoHA and NEHTA 2011). The PCEHR utilises advances in technology most notably that of Web 2.0 which makes it possible to engage users by providing them interactive user interfaces (DoHA and NEHTA 2011). However, since going live in July 2012, it still continues to suffer from low adoption.

16.4.1 Macro

At a macro level the PCEHR was designed to fit the relatively unique and multifaceted Australian healthcare system which has federal and state jurisdictions. This structure serves to create quite a complex set of nested information flows as depicted in Fig. 16.4. Given the low adoption, it may have been more prudent to first streamline the macro processes and information flows and then deign a suitable technology solution to facilitate and support these.

16.4.2 Messo

The majority of healthcare providers are sceptical and concerned about aspects of the PCEHR. As was identified in several interviews, some legitimate concerns exist regarding who is liable for wrong data, the extra administrative tasks are not compensated and, until the PCEHR becomes the only system, all providers would need to maintain the previous legacy system(s) as well as the PCEHR solution. Thus, rational reasons around costs, increase in workflow and liability risks were among the most significant reasons for the lack of support for the PCEHR from healthcare providers.

16.4.3 Micro

Probably the most important aspect at the micro level is patient understanding. To date most Australian do not understand the PCEHR, how it impacts healthcare delivery and how it can help them manage their healthcare data. Further, and especially for those citizens who are not particularly IT savvy, there exists a significant learning curve to be overcome before one can easily enter data and/or monitor one's health records. In addition, if all of one's doctors have not opted into the system, then the previous system plus the PCEHR system must be maintained which adds a further burden to citizens at a time they are unwell and vulnerable. Further, patients were also concerned about the privacy and security of their medical data.

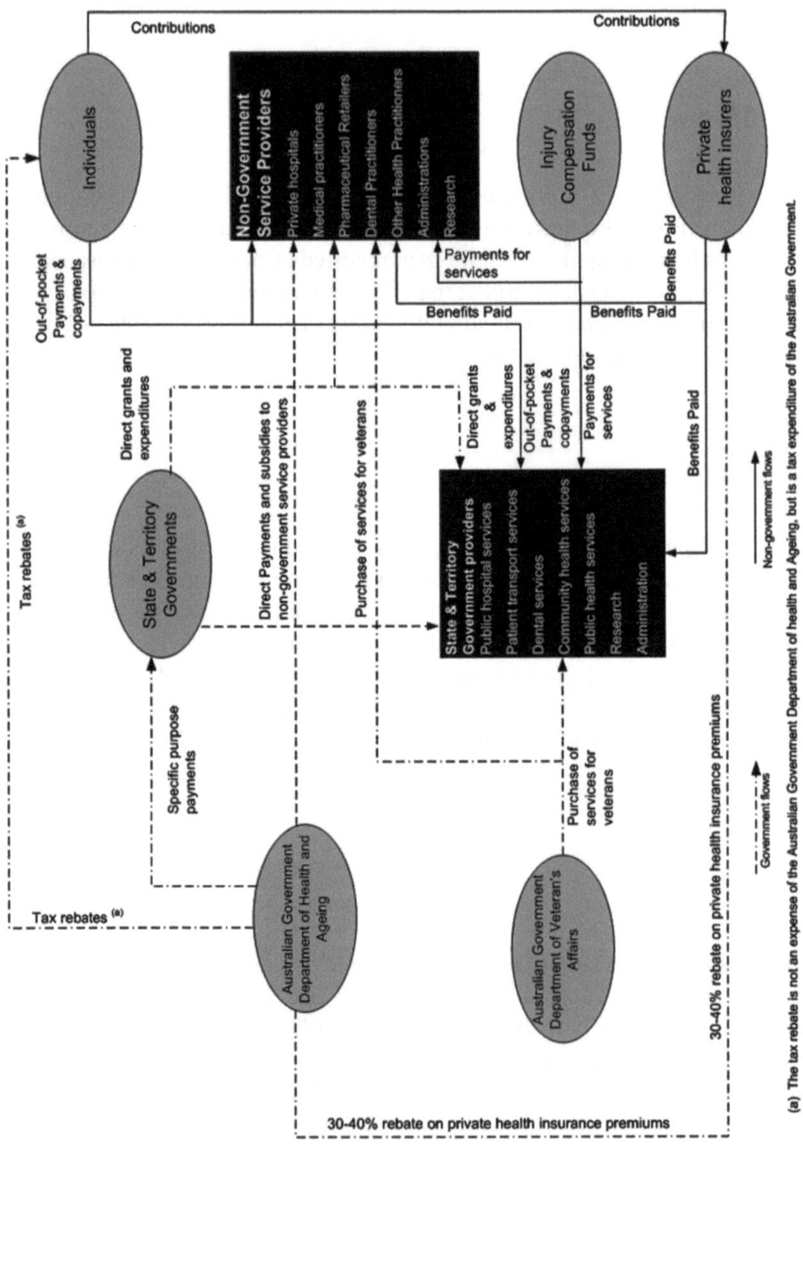

Fig. 16.4 The structure of Australian healthcare system and its flow of funds (AIHW 2010)

16.4.4 Task-Technology Fit

From a task technology fit perspective, it can be seen that while the PCEHR might have had laudable intentions and theoretically appears to be a sound solution to facilitate better healthcare delivery, in reality (at the macro, messo and micro levels) there are very real concerns pertaining to actualising this solution in practice. In fact, by applying the proffered task-technology fit framework to the case example of the PCEHR many of the critical issues that are proving to be significant barriers to the adoption of the PCEHR can be clearly identified.

16.4.5 South Africa

South Africa currently is faced with a burden of diseases and healthcare issues which deteriorate the quality of health care (Department of Health 2011) such as:

- HIV/AIDS and TB;
- Maternal, infant and child mortality;
- Non-communicable diseases; and
- Injury and violence.

In South Africa, the national health ministry is increasingly taking a stewardship role as part of a renewed focus on improving health information systems (Nel 2011). Further, the South African primary health care (PHC) system is undergoing a process of revitalisation in which the currently fragmented community-based 'outreach' functions are being prioritised for greater development, through integration with and management by the health department (Leon et al. 2012). However, the health sector's share of total government expenditure, allocations to the health sector in South Africa have been gradually declining from over 13% in 1997 to 11% in 2006 (Govender et al. 2008) making superior healthcare delivery challenging.

There are some instances of leadership in the health information field and the emergence of new technological platforms in South Africa of note such as a web-based routine district health information system (DHIS), an electronic record system for antiretroviral treatment and an eHealth strategy (Bowman 2014; Leon et al. 2012). However, there are several barriers related to broader health systems such as practices of healthcare workforce, the integration of new technology with existing information systems, sustainable funding and appropriate leadership to steer shifts to e-health technologies (Foster 2013; Horner et al. 2013; Leon et al. 2012) which serve to negate many of the positive benefits that might otherwise ensue. Furthermore, South Africa is faced with various challenges, including (Masilela et al. 2013):

- Widely differing levels of e-health maturity across and within provinces;
- Large number of disparate systems between which there is little or no interoperability and communication;

- Inequity of e-health services provided and expenditure on eHealth across Provincial and National Departments of Health;
- Expensive broadband connectivity; and
- Lack of capacity within the public health sector to drive the development and implementation of e-health.

The South Africa national eHealth strategy consists of the 10 strategic priorities for 2012 to 2017 (eHealth Strategy South Africa 2012), outlined below:

- Strategic Priority 1:

- Strategy and leadership international experience has shown that the successful implementation of eHealth is complex and that it requires a strong national e-health strategy.
- Strategic Priority 2:
- e-health stakeholder engagement needs effective collaboration in order to succeed.
- Strategic Priority 3:
- Standards and interoperability standards are the cornerstone of the e-health strategy implementation.
- Strategic Priority 4:
- e-health governance and regulation affects multiple stakeholder types and extends across multiple domains, including personal health, healthcare provision, ICT and management.
- Strategic Priority 5:
- Investment, affordability and sustainability before beginning any e-health project, financing must be procured and its sustainability protected over the duration of the project.
- Strategic Priority 6:
- Benefits realisation specific actions are required to ensure that e-health implementations deliver on their promise and that anticipated benefits are realised for all stakeholders.
- Strategic Priority 7:
- Capacity and workforce having adequate human resource capacity is essential to successful delivery on this e-health strategy.
- Strategic Priority 8:
- e-health Foundations incremental approach adopted by this strategy aims to deploy eHealth capability in a step-wise manner.
- Strategic Priority 9:
- Applications and tools to support healthcare delivery There is a wide range of digital applications and tools with the potential to support and improve healthcare delivery.
- Strategic Priority 10:
- Monitoring and evaluation of the e-health strategy It is essential to monitor and evaluate performance on the eHealth strategy on an ongoing basis.

A report provided in 2013 by Masilela et al., shows that, sadly, limited progress has been made towards addressing the following five strategic priority areas of the eHealth Strategy namely: Investment, Affordability and Sustainability; Benefits Realisation; Capacity and Workforce; eHealth Foundations; and Applications and Tools to support healthcare delivery (Masilela et al. 2013). In order to better address some of these strategic priority areas, Mxoli et al. (2014) believe that a Personal Health Record system (PHR) has the potential to improve the current state of health for South Africa through better decision-making, diagnosis and treatment, which will yield better health outcomes (Mxoli et al. 2014). This will need to be revisited in the future.

Given the current state of healthcare delivery and possible roles for technology solutions in this country, it is apparent that many of the challenges for South Africa with regards to embracing technology solutions to facilitate superior healthcare delivery reside at the macro and messo levels and until required policy, legislation structures and infrastructures are in place, it will not be possible to achieve significant and beneficial e-health solutions in this region.

16.5 US: Cleveland Clinic

In the US, healthcare delivery enabled through and supported by technology solutions varies across institutions and health systems. One leading example of realising benefits of e-health can be seen with the Cleveland Clinic, in Cleveland Ohio, USA. The Cleveland Clinic MyConsult application, an on-line second medical opinion system, serves to remove the geographic barriers to care by providing an online second medical opinion for those diagnoses with sufficient objective data for which a remote evaluation can be completed. The focus is to determine if the diagnosis is correct and if the patient is receiving optimal treatment. These patients can receive a second opinion without leaving their homes or travelling. Integration with the existing IT infrastructure includes network, interface engine, LDAP, DB, upload, EMR, security, financial, and materials management. Three structural layers are especially significant in this solution: first the external system to receive and organize these requests; second, the internal system to coordinate, consolidate, and organize per diagnosis; and third, the geographic issues from the international, national and regional unique markets. We suggest that this solution is possible because the necessary macro and messo requirements to enable this solution to be designed and implemented have been satisfied, and thus it is possible to focus on ensuring that micro level requirements are addressed and satisfied and, thus, the fit–viability model is satisfied. In particular, as there is a strong fit respectively between patient-user and clinical-user tasks and requirements, a high level of adoption and satisfaction is seen by both groups.

16.6 Discussion

As can be seen, the fit-viability model enables us to examine the role of various e-health solution is a systematic fashion. Further, it enables us to examine simultaneously the macro, messo and micro environments with their relative strengths and weaknesses to identify the potential success of any e-health solution. To illustrate the benefits of this approach and framework we have examined various solutions such as the PCEHR in Australia, the e-health solution in South Africa, the German e-health card, developments such as those by Google and Apple as well as e-health developments in China and the MyConsult solution at the Cleveland Clinic. We emphasise that these solutions are varied and the respective healthcare environments also differ, with some being predominantly private, others predominantly public and others (notable Germany and Australia) two tier in structure. In addition, we note that given the magnitude of the challenges in both US and South Africa we did not iterate all key issues under the micro, messo and macro levels but underscore the need for significant attention. Irrespective of the structure of the healthcare system, the fit-viability model is rich enough to enable us to map the respective system and thus compare and contrast both within and between e-health solutions. This makes it a powerful model indeed.

16.7 Conclusion

This chapter has set out to proffer a systematic approach to evaluate e-health solutions. We did this by first presenting the fit-viability model and then using this model to evaluate various e-health solutions throughout the world. This has served to provide a systematic analysis of these various e-health solutions at three levels; namely, the macro, messo and micro levels. In addition it is possible to identify the many strengths and weaknesses in the various e-health solutions and thereby begin to develop appropriate corrective measures to address current limitations as well as leverage strength of the respective solutions. We contend that this provides a very powerful analysis and will thus enabled better e-health solutions to exist. To date most e-health solutions have yet to realise their full potential and too many e-health solutions exceed their budgeted cost structure, have many problems, poor user satisfaction and/or uptake and increase, rather than decrease, healthcare costs. Hence, we are confident that use of the aforementioned model will serve to address this current dilemma with regarding to e-health solutions around the world.

References

AIHW. (2010). Retrieved December, 2014, from www.aihw.gov.au/publication-detail/?id=6442468376.

Bowman, R. J. (2014). Sage Health Solutions taps into a global sourcing network: Started by two sisters in South Africa, a small provider of medical supplies accepts an invitation from its biggest customer to join an electronic sourcing platform--then sees the technology as an opportunity to enable growth in a global scale. *Supplychainbrain, 18*(3), S42–S43.

Bündnis ,Stoppt die e-Card!. (2014). *Aktion, Stoppt die e-Card!* Retrieved August 8, 2014, from http://www.stoppt-die-e-card.de/.

Chaos Computer Club e. V. (2014). *Elektronische Gesundheitskarte*. Retrieved August 8, 2014, from http://www.ccc.de/de/elektronische-gesundheitskarte.

Creswell, J. W. (2009). *Research design: Qualitative, quantitative, and mixed methods approaches* (3rd ed.). Thousand Oaks, CA: Sage.

Department of Health. (2011). Retrieved December, 2011, from http://www.doh.gov.za/.

DoHA and NEHTA. (2011). *Concept of operations: Relating to the introduction of a Personally Controlled Electronic Health Record System (Article)* (p. 159). Retrieved from http://www.egov.vic.gov.au/focus-on-countries/australia/trends-and-issuesaustralia/e-health-australia/electronic-health-records-australia/concept-of-operationsrelating-to-the-introduction-of-a-personally-controlled-electronic-health-recordsystem.html.

Dünnebeil, S., Sunyaev, A., Blohm, I., Leimeister, J. M., & Krcmar, H. (2012). Determinants of physicians' technology acceptance for e-health in ambulatory care. *International Journal of Medical Informatics, 2012*(81), 1–15.

eHealth Strategy South Africa. (2012). Retrieved May, 2016, https://www.health-e.org.za/wp-content/uploads/2014/08/South-Africa-eHealth-Strategy-2012-2017.pdf.

Fähling, J., Köbler, F., Leimeister, J. M., & Krcmar, H. (2009a). *Wahrnehmung des Wertbeitrags von Informationstechnologie in deutschen Krankenhäusern – Eine empirische Studie*. Paper presented at the 9. Internationale Tagung Wirtschaftsinformatik, Wien, Austria.

Fähling, J., Köbler, F., Leimeister, J. M., & Krcmar, H. (2009b). Wahrnehmung des Wertbeitrags von Informationstechnologie in deutschen Krankenhäusern. *Krankenhaus-IT-Journal*, (1), 34–36.

Federal Ministry of Health. (2008). The electronic health card. https://www.commoncriteriaportal.org/files/ppfiles/pp0020_v2_ma1b.pdf.

Foster, R. (2013). Assessing the development process of the eHealth strategy for South Africa against the recommendations of the WHO/ITU National eHealth Strategy Toolkit. *Journal of the International Society for Telemedicine and eHealth, 1*(2), 62–72.

Gardt, M. (2012). Was hinter der E-Gesundheitskarte steckt. In *Die Welt*, 04.06.2012.

Gematik. (2008). *Speicherstrukturen der eGK für Gesundheitsanwendungen*. Retrieved August 8, 2014, from http://www.gematik.de/cms/de/spezifikation/release_0_5_3/release_0_5_3_egk/release_0_5_3_speicherstrukturen.jsp

Gematik. (2014). *Anwendungen der eGK*. Retrieved August 8, 2014, from http://www.gematik.de/cms/de/egk_2/anwendungen/anwendungen_1.jsp

Goodhue, D. L. (1995). Understanding user evaluations of information systems. *Management Science, 41*(12), 1827–1844.

Goodhue, D. L. (1998). Development and measurement validity of a task-technology fit instrument for user evaluations of information systems. *Decision Sciences, 29*(1), 105–138.

Govender, V., McIntyre, D., & Loewenson, R. (2008). *Progress towards the Abuja target for government spending on health care in East and Southern Africa*. Equinet discussion paper 60, April 2008. Retrieved November 11, 2008, http://www.tarsc.org/publications/documents/DIS6ofinABUJA.pdf

Gruhn, A. (2014). So wird meine Krankenversicherung gekapert. In *RP Online*, 26.06.2014. Retrieved August 8, 2014, from http://www.rp-online.de/wirtschaft/unternehmen/so-wird-meine-krankenversicherung-gekapert-aid-1.4341498

Gruhn, A., Reisener, T. (2014). So unsicher sind Patientendaten. In *RP Online*, 26.06.2014. Retrieved August 8, 2014, from http://www.rp-online.de/wirtschaft/so-unsicher-sind-patientendaten-aid-1.4341292

Handelsblatt. (2004). Reisepass und Gesundheitskarte mit Bits und Bytes. In *Handelsblatt*, 22.03.2004.

Horner, V., Rautenbach, P., Mbananga, N., Mashamba, T., & Kwinda, H. (2013). An e-health decision support system for improving compliance of health workers to the maternity care protocols in South Africa. *Applied Clinical Informatics, 4*(1), 25–36.

Huang, Z., & Palvia, P. (2001). ERP implementation issues in advanced and developing countries. *Business Process Management Journal, 7*(3), 276–284. https://doi.org/10.1108/14637150110392773.

Köbler, F., Riedl, C., Vetter C., Leimeister J. M., & Krcmar, H. (2010). Social connectedness on Facebook–An explorative study on status message usage; Paper presented at the 16th Americas Conference on Information Systems; Lima, Peru. p. 247.

Leichsenring, H. (2012). *Online banking auf dem Vormarsch.* Retrieved August 8, 2014, from http://www.der-bank-blog.de/online-banking-auf-dem-vormarsch/online-banking/6683/

Leon, N., Schneider, H., & Daviaud, E. (2012). Applying a framework for assessing the health system challenges to scaling up mHealth in South Africa. *BMC Medical Informatics and Decision Making, 12*(1), 123.

Leslie, H. (2011). *Australia's PCEHR challenge.* Retrieved from http://omowizard.wordpress.com/2011/08/30/australias-pcehr-challenge/

Liang, T.-P., & Wei, C.-P. (2004). Introduction to the special issue: Mobile commerce applications. *International Journal of Electronic Commerce, 8*(3), 7–17.

Lujiazui. (2017). Retrieved May, 2017, from http://www.shanghaidaily.com/district/pudong/Lujiazui-with-a-vision-for-the-future-and-a-place-in-the-world/shdaily.shtml

Masilela, T. C., Foster, R., & Chetty, M. (2013). The eHealth strategy for South Africa 2012-2016: How far are we? *South African Health Review*, 15–24.

Molla, A., & Bhalla, A. (2006). Business transformation through ERP: A case study of an Asian company. *Journal of Information Technology Case and Application Research, 8*(1), 34–54. https://doi.org/10.1080/15228053.2006.10856081.

Mxoli, A., Mostert-Phipps, N., & Gerber, M. (2014). *Personal health records: Design considerations for the South African context.* http://hdl.handle.net/10204/7712

Nel, P. S. (2011). *Human resources management.* Oxford: Oxford University Press.

NHHRC. (2009). *A healthier future for all Australians: National Health and Hospitals Reform Commission - Final report June 2009.* Australian Government Department of Health and Ageing. Retrieved from http://www.health.gov.au/internet/main/publishing.nsf/Content/nhhrc-report

OECD. (2010a). *Growing health spending puts pressure on government budgets.* Retrieved January 31, 2011, from http://www.oecd.org/document/11/0,3343,en_2649_ 34631_45549771_1_1_1_37407,00.html

OECD. (2010b). *OECD health data 2010.* Retrieved January 31, 2011, from http://stats.oecd.org/Index.aspx?DatasetCode=HEALTH

Pearce, C., & Haikerwal, M. C. (2010). E-health in Australia: Time to plunge into the 21st century. *The Medical Journal of Australia, 193*(7), 397–398.

Poon, P., & Wagner, C. (2001). Critical success factors revisited: Success and failure cases of information systems for senior executives. *Decision Support Systems, 30*(4), 393–418. https://doi.org/10.1016/S0167-9236(00)00069-5.

Porter, M. E., & Guth, C. (2012). *Redefining German health care moving to a value-based system.* Berlin, Heidelberg: Springer.

Porter, M. E., & Teisberg, E. O. (2006). *Redefining health care: Creating value-based competition on results.* Boston, MA: Harvard Business School Press.

Schweim, H. G. (2007). Die unerträgliche Geschichte der Gesundheitskarte in Deutschland. *GMS Medizinische Informatik, Biometrie und Epidemiologie, 3*(1), 1–5.

Soh, C., Kien, S. S., & Tay-yap, J. (2000). Enterprise resource planning: Cultural fits and misfits: Is ERP a universal solution? *Communications of the ACM, 43*(4), 47–51. https://doi.org/10.1145/332051.332070.

Telekom Deutschland GmbH. (2014). http://www.telekom.de

Tjan, A. K. (2001). Finally, a way to put your internet portfolio in order. *Harvard Business Review, 79*(2), 76.

Trochim, W., & Donnelly, J. (2008). *The research methods knowledge base* (3rd ed.). Mason, OH: Atomic Dog.

Umble, E. J., Haft, R. R., & Umble, M. M. (2003). Enterprise resource planning: Implementation procedures and critical success factors. *European Journal of Operational Research, 146*(2), 241–257. https://doi.org/10.1016/S0377-2217(02)00547-7.

Weichert, T. (2006). Datenschutzmanagement und Technikeinsatz. In *W & S Krankenhaus*, (Vol. 5, pp. 44–45).

Wickramasinghe, N., & Schaffer, J. (2010). *Realizing value driven e-Health solutions Improving Healthcare Series*. Washington, DC: IBM Center for the Business of Government.

Yin, R. K. (2014). *Case study research: Design and methods* (5th ed.). London: Sage.

Yun, Y., Huang, W., Seitz, J., & Wickramasinghe, N. (2012). e-health in China: An evaluation. In N. Wickramasinghe, R. Bali, R. Suomi, & S. Kirn (Eds.), *Critical Issues for the Development of Sustainable e-health Soltuions*. New York: Springer.

Chapter 17
Using Foucault to Understand Self-Monitoring in Chronic Disease Management

Nilmini Wickramasinghe and Steve Goldberg

17.1 Introduction

Today we are witnessing a rise in mobile solutions geared to assist in the monitoring and management of various health and wellness contexts such as diabetes and obesity. What is still unanswered is why some of these solutions work and some fail. We contend that this is connected to the issue of self-monitoring and explore this drawing upon Foucault to explain results from a clinical trial looking at the use of mobile solutions to facilitate superior diabetes self-care.

17.2 Background

In Australia alone, an estimated 275 individuals develop diabetes daily (Diabetes Australia 2016) making Australia a significant contributor to this projected trend. Further, an estimated 700,000 Australians, representing approximately 3.6% of the population, were diagnosed with diabetes in 2004–2005, while between 1989–1990 and 2004–2005, the proportion of Australians diagnosed with this disease more than doubled from 1.3 to 3.3% (Diabetes Australia 2016). Additionally, between 2000–2001 and 2004–2005, Australian diabetes hospitalizations increased by 35% from 1932 to 2608 hospitalizations per 100,000 people (AIHW 2008). Hence, most

N. Wickramasinghe (✉)
Deakin University, Melbourne, VIC, Australia

Epworth HealthCare, Richmond, VIC, Australia

S. Goldberg
Inet International Inc., Thornhill, ON, Canada

N. Wickramasinghe, J. L. Schaffer (eds.), *Theories to Inform Superior Health Informatics Research and Practice*, Healthcare Delivery in the Information Age,
https://doi.org/10.1007/978-3-319-72287-0_17

agreed that diabetes is one of the fastest-growing chronic diseases in Australia (AIHW 2008; Catanzariti et al. 2007; Chittleborough et al. 2007).

In addition to the unpleasantness of this disease to its sufferers, it must also be kept in mind that diabetes and its complications incur significant costs for carers, governments, and the entire health system (Geisler and Wickramasinghe 2005; Colagiuri et al. 2002). In the USA, between 2010 and 2011, costs associated with diabetes were US$174 billion ($116 billion direct medical costs and at least $58 billion indirect costs) (Help4Diabetes 2012), while in 2004–2005 direct healthcare expenditure on diabetes in Australia was AU$907 million, which constituted approximately 2% of the allocatable recurrent health expenditure in that year (AIHW 2008; Wickramasinghe et al. 2013). Further costs include societal costs that represent productivity losses for both patients and their carers (Colagiuri et al. 2002).

Recognizing the growing problem of this chronic disease as well as noting that during this same time there has been an exponential rise in the penetration, use, and uptake of mobile phone solutions and applications, it seemed logical to investigate the possibility of developing a mobile pervasive technology solution to support and facilitate better monitoring and management of individuals with diabetes, i.e., "DiaMonD" a pervasive smart diabetes monitoring solution.

17.3 Diabetes Care and the Importance of Self-Management

Today, there is no cure for diabetes. Successful treatment protocols require effective and ongoing lifestyle management in conjunction with careful attention and monitoring by healthcare professionals and patients (International Diabetes Federation 2015). In order to be effective, it is essential that patients are both informed and active participants in their treatment regimen (AIHW 2008; Zhang et al. 2011), thereby making self-monitoring an essential part of recommended diabetes care (ICIC 2008; Colagiuri et al. 1998; Poulton 1999; Rasmussen et al. 2001; Wellard et al. 2008).

However, self-monitoring is time-consuming and requires substantial self-discipline (AIHW 2007). Contemporary support strategies include regular assessment, goal setting, action planning, problem-solving, and follow-up (Kleinwechter et al. 2011).

Nevertheless, since effective self-monitoring often requires patient interaction with their healthcare professionals (ICIC 2008), difficulties often arise when diabetes sufferers encounter problems ranging from making appointments to needing to travel to many locations (Colagiuri et al. 1998; Poulton 1999; Britt et al. 2009).

Solutions for supporting self-monitoring to date (Rasmussen et al. 2001; Wellard et al. 2008) have not always been effective, as they have been complex and awkward for patients to embrace easily (Reach et al. 2005). It has been noted that computer-assisted telemedicine can help diabetes sufferers improve both their self-monitoring (Balas et al. 2004) and their relationship with healthcare professionals (Van Eyk and Baum 2002; Zgibor and Songer 2001), and thus the use of a pervasive smart mobile solution appears to be beneficial.

17.3.1 Gestational Diabetes

Gestational diabetes (GDM) is a form of diabetes and presents in pregnancy, usually detected by routine screening in asymptomatic women (Wickramasinghe et al. 2013). Typically, incidence is 4.6% of pregnancies, i.e., greater than 12,400 women per year in Australia (Crowther et al. 2005). Some women, especially those in whom the diagnosis of GDM was made early in pregnancy, may have preexisting undiagnosed diabetes. In Australia and New Zealand, universal screening for GDM is recommended by the Australasian Diabetes in Pregnancy Society (ADIPS) (Hoffman et al. 1998); however, the uptake of the recommendation is rather variable (Rumbold and Crowther 2001). Most commonly the diagnosis of gestational diabetes is made following routine screening at 24–28 weeks' gestation, with smaller numbers of women diagnosed earlier or later in pregnancy. Maternal complications of GDM include polyhydramnios and premature labor, preeclampsia, and perineal trauma (Rudi and Celler 2006). Perinatal complications include macrosomia, shoulder dystocia, bone fractures, and nerve palsy (Balas et al. 2004). It recurs in subsequent pregnancy in 30–80% of women, the incidence varying with ethnicity, being lower in Caucasian women (Bodenheimer et al. 2002).

Treatment of women with GDM aims to control maternal and therefore fetal, hyperglycemia, and the associated tendency to fetal hyperinsulinemia, which is at the root of the fetal complications (Metzger et al. 2008). Critical to the treatment of women with GDM then is careful and systematic monitoring of maternal glycemia and appropriate adjustment of lifestyle, dietary, and pharmacological therapy (Metzger et al. 2008; Crowther et al. 2005).

17.4 Foucault and Self-Monitoring

Foucault (1980, 1998) suggests an appropriate frame in which to understand self-monitoring behavior as surveillance. He claims that self-monitoring activities primarily serve the controlling principles of society and only secondarily serve the self-monitoring individuals themselves. Techniques and technologies align individual goals with organizational/institutional or societal goals, as prescribed in management control literature (Foucault 1980, 1998; Kelley 1990; Townley 1993).

Within regimes of disciplinary control (e.g., total institutions, such as the prison), Foucault describes how "architectures" (like Bentham's Panopticon) can be designed to induce people, regardless of their personality traits, to monitor their own behavior in conformance to specific guidelines or norms. Central to this understanding is the idea that power/knowledge is a unit of operation that can be exercised to exert control over others through dividing practices, scientific classifications, and subjectification. "Power is not something that is acquired, seized, or shared, something one holds onto or allows to slip away…" (Townley 1993). Power is relational; "…it becomes apparent when it is exercised … [and] is not associated with a particular institution, but with practices, techniques, and procedures" (Foucault 1980). Similarly, knowledge does not exist in isolation as independent and detached; "[k]nowledge is the operation of discipline. It delineates an analytical space and ... provides the basis for action and intervention" (Townley 1993). "It is not possible for power to be exercised without knowledge, it is impossible for knowledge not to engender power" (Foucault 1980).

While Foucault's analyses draw examples from eighteenth and nineteenth century historical contexts to shape integrated concepts of power, knowledge, and control (Poster 1990), contemporary historians, sociologists, and philosophers have linked those concepts to current processes of organization (Poster 1990; Rabinow 1991; Bourdieu 1990). Rules and professional norms are seen as social constraints that define the appropriate form of behavior in a specific context. Studies have shown that an individual will follow these guidelines even if it is not in his or her self-interest to do so (Bourdieu 1990). Although plausible explanations of this behavior do not necessarily demand a Foucauldian perspective, these findings have been interpreted as evidence of "subjectification." The idea of subjectivity and the role of the individual are recurrent themes throughout Foucault's work. "From a Foucauldian perspective, the human subject is not 'given' but produced ...constituted through correlative elements of power and knowledge" (Foucault 1980).

More importantly for this discussion, in the face of these processes of control, the individual is continually seeking techniques and strategies to increase or regain power/knowledge (Foucault 1980; Rabinow 1991). In terms of individual activity, subjectification involves three related practices with which individuals seek to shape their social worlds: self- understanding, self-observation (also understood as a form of surveillance that often involves computerized monitoring), and self-description (including many forms of computerized recording, profiling, and tracking) (Rabinow 1991). By engaging in these activities, individuals are, ironically, complicit in their own control. Poster (Poster 1990; Rabinow 1991; Bourdieu 1990) has further described the ways in which databases, intranets, and other ICTs serve to augment this participatory surveillance and the associated discourses of power/knowledge. Taken altogether, these empirically based extensions of Foucault's theoretical work into contemporary settings have spawned assertions that ideas about an information society are better understood as concepts about "societies of control" (Rabinow 1991).

17.5 Methodology

To examine the connections between self-monitoring, Foucault's power/knowledge dynamic, and chronic disease management, we analyze qualitative data gathered from a clinical trial that examined the use of a pervasive mobile technology solution to effect superior diabetes self-monitoring and management.

The central research question is as follows: how can we understand the drivers and effects of self-monitoring practices in the context of diabetes management and

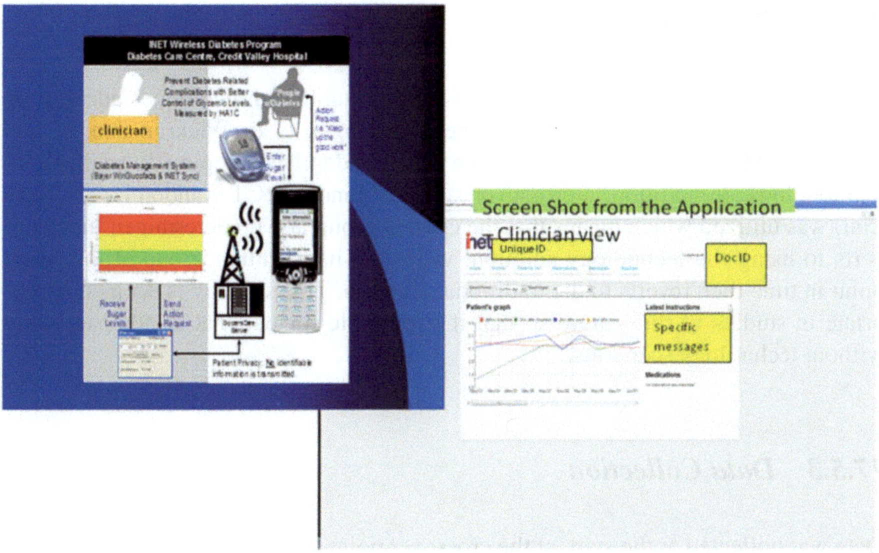

Fig. 17.1 The system in a nutshell

how can this in turn facilitate the use of mobile solutions to effect superior diabetes self-monitoring?

A single case study approach was adopted and the gathered qualitative data was evaluated using recognized qualitative techniques most notably thematic analysis. The data was gathered from a non-blinded clinical trial in Australia focusing on women suffering from GDM, carried out after all appropriate ethical clearances were received.

17.5.1 The Proffered Mobile Solution

The pervasive mobile solution used was grounded in a recognized chronic disease management as set out by Rachlis (2006). Integral to this model is the interaction between an informed patient and a proactive care team both of which is possible only with solutions that can facilitate better management and monitoring (Goldberg 2002a, b, c; Wickramasinghe and Goldberg 2003, 2004).

Succinctly, the final solution works as follows (Fig. 17.1a, b): the individual takes their blood glucose readings. These are then either directly transferred to the mobile device or manually entered and then sent to the designated member of the clinical care team who on reading the information can send a message back to the patient.

17.5.2 Research Design

The conducted clinical trials subscribed to the established techniques adopted by Wickramasinghe and Goldberg (Goldberg 2002a, b, c, d; Wickramasinghe and Goldberg 2003, 2004) to date, i.e., the AMR (adaptive mapping to realization) methodology. In addition, a crossover style unblended RCT (randomized control trial) was utilized which means that the control group at a predetermined time converts to using the technology solution, while the intervention group at this same point in time then reverts to the traditional solution. This strategy is deemed appropriate in studies of this nature so that it is possible for patients to compare with/without technology scenarios.[1]

17.5.3 Data Collection

Data was collected at the start, at the crossover point, and at the end of each respective patient's participation in the trial via an interview and the administration of open-ended questionnaires. In addition, clinician data was captured at the start and conclusion of the project via interview and the administration of open-ended questionnaires.

17.6 Summary of the Clinical Findings

The results to date of this research in progress include the establishment of an appropriate delivery framework and web-based conceptual model that are tailored to the private healthcare context in Australia. This is an essential first step in order to successfully apply the pervasive mobile solution. From this, it was possible to then program the solution to the required local processes and requirements. Once the solution was approved by the clinicians and ethics clearance received, it was then used in the technology arm of the trial.

Whether patients started with standard care and then migrated to the technology arm or vice versa, all patients interviewed have preferred the technology solution over the standard care approach. It is noted that the standard care approach essentially consisted of keeping logs of blood sugar readings and food intake and when required insulin usage. One patient noted (and all patients to date have expressed similar sentiments):

> …as a busy working person I have no time to note things down but with the mobile solution I can record things as I go so easily. I cannot believe this solution has not been used yet… (patient 3)

---

[1] www.implementationscience.com/content/4/1/69.

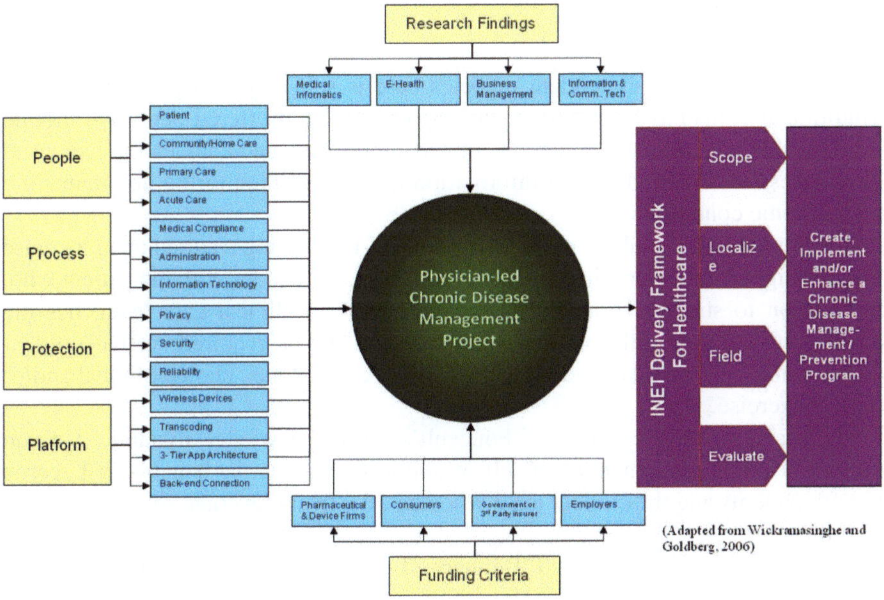

Fig. 17.2 Web-based model. Adapted from Wickramasinghe and Goldberg (2007)

In addition, on the clinical care team (obstetricians, diabetic educator, and endocrinologist) again without exception, all clinicians preferred the technology solution over the standard care approach. The questionnaires and debrief sessions also generated many useful and innovative suggestions for additional features such as an interactive food diary. In keeping with a user-centered design approach, these suggestions will now be incorporated into the technology solution for the next large-scale clinical trial. Moreover, the large-scale clinical trial will also enable us to test the generated hypotheses (Fig. 17.2).

As this was a pilot study, we cannot unequivocally state the benefits of such a pervasive technology solution in the enablement of heightened self-care by patients and providing clinicians to assist in the superior management, monitoring, self-care, and patient empowerment in the context of diabetes. We do however believe that fidelity and usability of the solution has been established and there is strong directional data to support the benefits of a pervasive technology solution in this context. We also note that key facilitators include clinician support and patient preference. The major limitation of this study is the small patient cohort or generally similar "typical" GDM patients; however, this was necessary to first establish proof of concept and comply with ethics requirements. Now that this has been established, we plan to expand the study to a larger patient population.

17.7 Discussion

Integral to effective and prudent diabetes care is self-monitoring by the patient. Traditionally, this has been done using logbooks. The proffered pervasive mobile solution serves to shift the dynamics of self-monitoring and enables the patient to have access to critical data and information to assist in monitoring and managing their chronic condition.

In our study, ICT-enabled monitoring and self-monitoring resulted in an increase in goal-aligned behavior. The impetus for this increase resides with the patient who, in addition to standard practice of meeting with the clinical care team, has the appropriate data and information when required and as required so that prudent decision-making can take place at the time it is required, i.e., choice of meal and/or type of exercise.

By analyzing this in terms of Foucault's power/knowledge dynamic, we can explain not only the dynamics of self- monitoring but also the benefits that accrue to both patients and the clinical team who can effectively leverage self- monitoring activities.

We find some evidence that ICT-enhanced self-monitoring is a widely practiced professional (and semiprofessional) activity in a survey study conducted by Kirsch et al. (2002), Kohli and Kettinger (2004), and Doolin (2004). Their research respectively addresses various aspects of control and management of information systems (IS) in both healthcare and non-healthcare contexts. We note, however, that our application of Foucault is one of the first in the context of patient-clinical care team dynamics where ICT has been used to enable and facilitate effective and efficient self-monitoring. The studies noted, however, do all identify that, "self-control will be exercised when behavior observability is low, or when outcome measurability is high" (Kirsch et al. 2002). This is definitely the case when monitoring and managing blood sugar readings in the context of diabetes as our trial data supports. We interpret this finding as further evidence of a power/knowledge dynamic in which the individual is continually seeking techniques and strategies to increase or regain power/knowledge (i.e., be in control of the disease) and of the effectiveness of ICT-enhanced self-monitoring to benefit not only the patient but also the clinical care team. Hence, our own findings, thus, strongly indicate that ICT-enhanced self-monitoring can establish a win-win scenario for patients and the clinical care team.

We believe our research has provided the uncovering of a new theoretical application. By combining the multidisciplinary work of Foucault in the context of chronic disease management in connection to ICT use provides a powerful lens in which to better understand how ICTs can be used more effectively and efficiently to effect superior chronic disease management. Moreover, it provides an opportunity to incorporate the methods and concepts discussed by Foucault, which some have noted surprising that it is lacking in the IS field (Rabinow 1991). Moreover, we note that given the current focus on the value agenda with diabetes being identified as a critical comorbidity, the role of self-monitoring in order to manage this chronic disease becomes vital. Our unpacking of self-monitoring using Foucault's power/

knowledge constructs helps to identify low-cost high-quality benefits of pervasive smart mobile solutions to address this current critical need which in turn serve to contribute to increasing and support value-driven healthcare delivery.

In addition, we believe the study starts to shed light on why some solutions are not as effective as others to impact behavior change in the context of noncommunicable chronic disease. Specifically, it would appear that solutions that do not aid the power/knowledge dimension, i.e., provide the patient with better and appropriate data, information, and/or knowledge, are likely not to be successful in facilitating self-monitoring and therefore also effecting the appropriate behavior modification.

17.8 Conclusions

The proceeding has served to describe a facet of the DiaMonD study which supports a pervasive smart mobile technology solution, which, while not exorbitantly expensive, has the potential to facilitate the superior monitoring and management of diabetes sufferers. The proposed solution enables patient empowerment by way of enhancing self-monitoring. Using Foucault's power/knowledge constructs, we have analyzed the dynamics of self-monitoring in this context to identify why it does indeed lend itself to superior outcomes as observed by the data from the clinical trial conducted. Clearly a small pilot trial cannot provide statistically significant results, but the goal of the study was to establish proof of concept and fidelity of the solution. Our directional data to date does, however, enable us to do this as well as answer the posed research question: can a pervasive mobile solution be used as an adjunct to support better blood sugar control of GDM patients? In particular, the benefits of such a technology are in the enablement of heightened self-care by patients by enabling superior and more effective and efficient self-monitoring to ensue and providing clinicians with germane data and relevant information to assist in their patients' control of blood sugars. Given the growing importance of self-management and self-monitoring to ensure better outcomes especially in regard to chronic disease, a deeper understanding of the underlying nuances regarding self-management becomes important. This chapter has assisted our understanding using the powerful lens of Foucault's power/knowledge dynamic. In closing we call for more confirmatory research to explore this further.

References

AIHW. (2007). *National indicators for monitoring diabetes: Report of the Diabetes Indicators Review Subcommittee of the National Diabetes Data Working Group in diabetes series 2007*. Canberra: The Australian Institute of Health and Welfare.

AIHW. (2008). *Australian facts 2008*. Canberra: Australian Institute of Health and Welfare.

Balas, E. A., Krishna, S., Kretschmer, R. A., Cheek, T. R., Lobach, D. F., & Boren, S. A. (2004). Computerized knowledge management in diabetes care. *Medical Care, 42*, 610–621.

Bodenheimer, T., Lorig, K., Holman, H., & Grumbach, K. (2002). Patient self-management of chronic disease in primary care. *JAMA, 288*(19), 2469–2475.

Bourdieu, P. (1990). *The logic of practice*. Stanford, CA: Stanford University Press.

Britt, H., Miller, G. C., Henderson, J., Bayram, C., Valenti, L., Harrison, C., et al. (2009). *General practice activity in Australia 2008-09*. Sydney: Australian Institute of Health and Welfare, and University of Sydney.

Catanzariti, L., Faulks, K., & Waters, A.-M. (2007). *National diabetes register: A statistical profile 1999-2005*. Canberra: Australian Institute of Health and Welfare.

Chittleborough, C. R., Grant, J. F., Phillips, P. J., & Taylor, A. W. (2007). The increasing prevalence of diabetes in South Australia: The relationship with population ageing and obesity. *Public Health, 121*(2), 92–99.

Colagiuri, S., Colagiuri, R., Grainger, D., Graham-Clarke, P., Davey, P., FitzGerald, P., et al. (2002). DiabCost Australia-assessing the burden of Type 2 diabetes in Australia. In *Diabetologia*. New York, NY: Springer.

Colagiuri, S., Colagiuri, R., & Ward, J. (1998). *National diabetes strategy and implementation plan* (pp. 1–281). Canberra: Diabetes.

Crowther, C. A., Hiller, J. E., Moss, J. R., McPhee, A. J., Jeffries, W. S., Robinson, J. S., et al. (2005). Effect of treatment of gestational diabetes mellitus on pregnancy outcomes. *New England Journal of Medicine, 352*(24), 2477–2486.

Diabetes Australia. (2016, April 11). *Diabetes in Australia*. Available from https://www.diabetesaustralia.com.au/diabetes-in-australia

Doolin, B. (2004). Power and resistance in the implementation of a medical management information system. *Information Systems Journal, 14*(4), 343–362.

Foucault, M. (1980). *Power/knowledge: Selected interviews and other writings, 1972-1977*. New York: Pantheon.

Foucault, M. (1998). *The will to knowledge: The history of sexuality* (Vol. I). London: Penguin.

Geisler, E., & Wickramasinghe, N. (2005). *The role and use of wireless technology in the management and monitoring of chronic diseases*. Paper presented at the IBM Center for The Business of Government, DC.

Goldberg, S. (2002a). *HTA presentation rendering component summary*. Internal INET documentation.

Goldberg, S. (2002b). *HTA presentational selection and aggregation component summary*. Internal documentation.

Goldberg, S. (2002c). *Wireless POC device component summary*. Internal INET documentation.

Goldberg, S. (2002d). Building the evidence for a standardized mobile internet (wireless) environment in Ontario, Canada. January Update, Internal INET Documentation, Ontario, Canada, INET.

Help4Diabetes. (2012). *Diabetes: A world wide epidemic*. [cited 2012 September 2012]. Available from http://www.hope4diabetes.info/general-information/diabetes-a-worldwide-epidemic.html

Hoffman, L., Nolan, C., Wilson, J. D., Oats, J. J., & Simmons, D. (1998). Gestational diabetes mellitus-management guidelines. The Australasian Diabetes in Pregnancy Society. *Medical Journal of Australia, 169*(2), 93–97.

ICIC. (2008). Improving chronic illness care: The chronic care model.

International Diabetes Federation. (2015). *IDF diabetes atlas* (7th ed.). Brussels: IDF.

Kelley, R. E. (1990). Managing the new workforce. *Machine Design, 62*(9), 109–113.

Kirsch, L. J., Sambamurthy, V., Ko, D.-G., & Purvis, R. L. (2002). Controlling information systems development projects: The view from the client. *Management Science, 48*(4), 484–498.

Kleinwechter, H., Schäfer-Graf, U., Bührer, C., Hoesli, I., Kainer, F., Kautzky-Willer, A., et al. (2011). *Gestationsdiabetes mellitus (GDM). Evidenzbasierte Leitlinie zu Diagnostik, Therapie u. Nachsorge der Deutschen Diabetes-Gesellschaft (DDG) und der Deutschen Gesellschaft für Gynäkologie und Geburtshilfe (DGGG)*. www.deutsche-diabetes-gesellschaft.de

Kohli, R., & Kettinger, W. J. (2004). Informating the clan: Controlling physicians' costs and outcomes. *MIS Quarterly, 28*, 363–394.

Metzger, B. E., Lowe, L. P., Dyer, A. R., Trimble, E. R., Chaovarindr, U., Coustan, D. R., et al. (2008). Hyperglycemia and adverse pregnancy outcomes. *The New England Journal of Medicine, 358*(19), 1991–2002.

Poster, M. (1990). *The mode of information: Poststructuralism and social context*. Chicago: University of Chicago Press.

Poulton, B. C. (1999). User involvement in identifying health needs and shaping and evaluating services: Is it being realised? *Journal of Advanced Nursing, 30*(6), 1289–1296.

Rabinow, P. (1991). *The Foucault reader*. London: Penguin.

Rachlis, M. (2006). Key to sustainable healthcare system (p. 2008), vol. 21. Retrieved June, 2006.

Rasmussen, B., Wellard, S., & Nankervis, A. (2001). Consumer issues in navigating health care services for type I diabetes. *Journal of Clinical Nursing, 10*(5), 628–634.

Reach, G., Zerrouki, A., Leclercq, D., & d'Ivernois, J. F. (2005). Adjusting insulin doses: From knowledge to decision. *Patient Education and Counseling, 56*(1), 98–103.

Rudi, R., & Celler, B. G. (2006). Design and implementation of expert-telemedicine system for diabetes management at home. In *Biomedical and Pharmaceutical Engineering, 2006. ICBPE 2006. International Conference on*. Singapore: IEEE.

Rumbold, A. R., & Crowther, C. A. (2001). Guideline use for gestational diabetes mellitus and current screening, diagnostic and management practices in Australian hospitals. *Australian and New Zealand Journal of Obstetrics and Gynaecology, 41*(1), 86–90.

Townley, B. (1993). Foucault, power/knowledge, and its relevance for human resource management. *Academy of Management Review, 18*(3), 518–545.

Van Eyk, H., & Baum, F. (2002). Learning about interagency collaboration: Trialling collaborative projects between hospitals and community health services. *Health & Social Care in the Community, 10*(4), 262–269.

Wellard, S. J., Rennie, S., & King, R. (2008). Perceptions of people with type 2 diabetes about self-management and the efficacy of community based services. *Contemporary Nurse, 29*(2), 218–226.

Wickramasinghe, N., & S. Goldberg. (2003). The wireless panacea for healthcare. In *Proceedings of 36th Hawaii international conference on system sciences*, Hawaii.

Wickramasinghe, N., & Goldberg, S. (2004). How M = EC^2 in healthcare. *International Journal of Mobile Communications, 2*(2), 140–156.

Wickramasinghe, N., & Goldberg, S. (2007). The Wi-INET model for achieving M-Health success. In D. Taniar (Ed.), *Encyclopedia of Mobile Computing and Commerce* (pp. 1004–1010). Hershey, PA: Information Science Reference. https://doi.org/10.4018/978-1-59904-002-8.ch168.

Wickramasinghe, N., Troshani, I., Rao, S., Hague, W., & Goldberg, S. (2013). A transaction cost assessment of a pervasive technology solution for gestational diabetes. In *Healthcare information technology innovation and sustainability: Frontiers and adoption* (p. 109). Hershey, PA: IGI Global.

Zgibor, J. C., & Songer, T. J. (2001). External barries to diabetes care: Addressing personal and health systems issues. *Diabetes Spectrum: A Publication of the American Diabetes Association, 14*(1), 23.

Zhang, F., et al. (2011). Increasing prevalence of gestational diabetes mellitus in Chinese women from 1999 to 2008. *Diabetic Medicine, 28*(6), 652–657.

Chapter 18
Healthcare Information Systems (HIS) Assimilation Theory

Hidayah Sulaiman and Nilmini Wickramasinghe

18.1 Introduction

Over the years, various innovations have been introduced into healthcare organisations in order to incorporate better use of technology, to aid decision-making and to facilitate the search for medical solutions. This allows integration between experts in the medical field either throughout the organisation or globally (Fadlalla and Wickramasinghe 2004).

Innovations such as electronic health record (EHR), hospital information system and telemedicine will generally bring about the usage of information systems as a means to provide better health services for the community and overcome challenges that have been perceived as cumbersome for people seeking medical treatment (Jha et al. 2008). Nevertheless, these innovations have not escaped from various challenges and issues both from internal and external factors (Wager et al. 2005).

The main aim is to eliminate manual processes that are now seen as a major hindrance to increasing organisational performance in terms of providing fast and efficient health services. The assimilation and use of information systems and information technology (IS/IT) have an important role in enhancing firm performance (Devaraj and Kohli 2003). Assimilation can be defined as the extent of which IS/IT are being used within the key processes and activities in an organisation. The stages of assimilation begin from the organisation's initial evaluation to its formal

H. Sulaiman (✉)
Information Systems Department, College of Computer Science and Information Technology (CSIT), Universiti Tenaga Nasional (UNITEN), Kajang, Selangor, Malaysia
e-mail: Hidayah@uniten.edu.my

N. Wickramasinghe (✉)
Epworth HealthCare, Richmond, VIC, Australia

Deakin University, Melbourne, VIC, Australia
e-mail: n.wickramasinghe@deakin.edu.au

N. Wickramasinghe, J. L. Schaffer (eds.), *Theories to Inform Superior Health Informatics Research and Practice*, Healthcare Delivery in the Information Age,
https://doi.org/10.1007/978-3-319-72287-0_18

adoption and end with a well-accepted deployment of the system to a point where it becomes part of the value chain activities in the organisation (Cooper and Zmud 1990; Fichman 2000; Setia et al. 2011). The final routinisation stage is where the system becomes part of the organisation's value chain activities (Zhu et al. 2006).

This chapter sets out to examine the implication of assimilation theory within the healthcare information systems' (HIS) use in public hospitals. HIS is a healthcare information system that integrates computer systems throughout the hospital in order to enhance the clinical and administrative function of a hospital (Kim et al. 2002). The HIS applications are also developed to communicate with the relevant medical departments at the health ministry especially in areas relating to human resources, finance and procurement. Through the development of a focused theory on innovation assimilation (Fichman 2000; Fichman and Kemerer 1999), technology-organisation-environment (Tornatzky and Fleischer 1990) and resource-based view of the firm (Bharadwaj 2000; Grant 1991, 1995; Huang et al. 2006; Khatri 2006; Ross et al. 1996), it was possible to provide a technology assimilation model for information technology (IT) managers, hospital chief information officers and IT executives involved in acquiring or deploying HIS. Combination of these theories was tailored specifically to the technology implemented in the healthcare setting, aimed at delivering better healthcare services.

The introduction of new technology begins with great enthusiasm and an extensive spread of initial excitement about the acquisition. However, the new technology fails to be deployed and sustained in many acquiring firms due to not meeting specific user requirements or too complicated to be used by the users (Fichman and Kemerer 1999). This then causes the existence of an assimilation gap for technology innovation as the initial acquisition of the technology does not always lead to sustained use of the technology (Fichman and Kemerer 1999; Mu et al. 2015).

Previous literature on technology innovation and diffusion was mostly based on the work of Rogers (1983) through the diffusion of innovation (DOI) theory (Agarwal et al. 1997; Ahmed et al. 2007; Burke et al. 2002; Gallivan 2001; Greenhalgh et al. 2004). The diffusion of innovation model by Rogers (1983) has been extended (Moore and Benbasat 1996) and has created an insightful role in producing concepts, terminologies and scope of the innovation field. Nevertheless the extended models are not always suitable for different innovations at different adoption context (Fichman 2000; Lee et al. 2013).

Rogers (2003) suggested that innovations in the non-profit sector often encounter huge diffusion difficulties especially with innovations that could provide benefit to the public. Hence a study that explores innovation issues is worth undertaking (Mcgrath and Zell 2001; Lee et al. 2013). A study that examines the organisation, people and technological level focusing on how technology can be sustained throughout the innovation assimilation stages is also deemed important. This study serves to fill a key void in the existing literature through the exploration of 'how' and 'why' people in the organisation reject or refuse to make use of a specific innovation after the acquisition process, which can ultimately cause discontinuance of the innovation (Greenhalgh et al. 2004). There is also a lack of theories being developed for a specific type of technology and for a particular adoption context such as the healthcare organisation due to the lack of generic theory in technology innovation (Fichman 2000; Yoo 2013). These factors together provide the motivation for this study in developing a technology innovation assimilation model for hospitals to successfully assimilate their healthcare information systems (HIS). Successfully assimilating HIS is also seen as having a possible impact on decreasing technology, organisation, environment and process issues pertaining to acquisition and deployment. As a result, successful assimilation of HIS would realise the objective of assisting work processes of the medical professionals to the benefit of the community at large.

18.2 Literature Review

The introduction of healthcare IS/IT technologies into the healthcare environment has led to increased efficiency in providing better services and improved processes for healthcare practitioners. Adoption of IS/IT in the healthcare industry is seen as a way of innovating with technology in order to bring about positive outcomes especially in assisting the work processes of the clinicians in the adopting organisation. Positive outcomes are not always the case in the healthcare environment (Allen 2000; Snyder-Halpern 2001; Cresswell and Sheikh 2013). Table 18.1 describes some research findings pertaining to IS/IT technology innovation that has been implemented in the healthcare industry and highlighting key issues, success stories and recommendations.

Table 18.1 provides a summary of healthcare IS/IT innovation adoption complexity which is similar to that of other industries. The healthcare IS/IT innovations are influenced by a wide variety of factors such as external environment, characteristics of the healthcare organisation, the technology readiness, knowledge readiness and process of implementing the technology (Snyder-Halpern 2001). Innovating with IS/IT does not always lead to success after immediate adoption (Swanson 2004; Wu and Chen 2014). Various publications in the literature highlight problems with healthcare IS/IT implementation and identify facilitators to assist firms in being successful with IS/IT implementation (Bradford and Florin 2003; Chatzoglou and Diamantidis 2009; Fehse et al. 2002; Fichman and Kemerer 1999; Øvretveit et al. 2007; Skok et al. 2001; Swanson 2004; Varonen et al. 2008; Walley and Davies 2002; Wickramasinghe 2000; Wickramasinghe and Goldberg 2008; Ahmadi et al. 2015b). Although IS/IT implementation success remains an essential focus area of IS/IT research, there is an increasing interest in addressing the issue of organisation assimilation of IS/IT innovation due to the importance of IS/IT efficiency in the adopting healthcare organisation (Fichman 2000; Gallivan 2001; Keim et al. 2005; Swanson 2004; Zhu et al. 2006; Ahmadi et al. 2015b). This study emphasises the focus on assimilation of HIS as an innovation to healthcare organisations through the influence of various established theories in information systems. The following sections will discuss the major theories that are significant to this context.

Table 18.1 Technology innovation evolution in health care

Technology innovation	Findings
Radio frequency identification (RFID)	The key factors in determining the successful adoption of RFID are the presence of a champion, technology push and need pull. Organisations also need not consider in adopting new technology unless reasons such as performance gap and market uncertainty were seen as crucial to the organisation (Lee and Shim 2007)
Electronic patient record (EPR)	Surgeons welcomed the EPR system as long as it provides direct clinical benefits to their work and eased their work practices (Jensen and Aanestad 2007)
Computerised physician order entry (CPOE)	Pathology laboratory had to go through various changes and adjustments in their work practices, responsibilities and procedures which cause frustration (Georgiou et al. 2007)
Electronic health record (EHR)	There is a need to have end-user participation in successfully implementing EHR. However, the EHR has to also provide relevance to the work practices of the end users in order to motivate users to participate. There should also be a careful balance in providing relevance and gaining participation from end users (Katsma et al. 2007)
Electronic medical record (EMR)	In assimilating EMR technology, these factors are associated with the physician's practices: Overcome learning barriers, related knowledge and diversity (Reardon and Davidson 2007)
Personal digital assistant (PDA)	PDAs have the potential to be accepted by nurses provided it contains more rich information about the patients, knowledge resources and functions for their daily work (Berglund et al. 2007)
Electronic signature	These are some of the significant factors which contribute to the adoption of electronic signature: Hospital size, adequate resources, vendor support and government policy (Chang et al. 2007)
Electronic medical record (EMR)	Challenges in implementing EMR include cost, difficulty in calculating return on investment, lack of education, physicians' and staff concerns, technology-related concerns, inadequate complementary changes to organisational processes, lack of IT support and lack of incentives. In order to overcome these challenges, the recommended measures include government level intervention and institutional level interventions (Radhakrishnan et al. 2008)
Electronic medical record (EMR)	The EMR failed to be introduced at hospitals in Japan due to the introduction costs to be very high. Besides that communication between EMR systems should also be standardised for future integration and interoperability (Yasunaga et al. 2008)
Mobile health applications	M-health is attracting a great deal of attention worldwide because it presents a unique way to provide information and resources to healthcare professionals and patients alike and may be a promising tool to support health care (Gagnon et al. 2016)
Big data analytics in health	Healthcare industry has not fully grasped the potential benefits to be gained from big data analytics. Big data analytics was suggested to be beneficial for healthcare information technology (IT) infrastructure, operational, organisational, managerial and strategic areas (Wang et al. 2016)
Internet of things (IoT) in health care	The use of IoT concept brought ease of use for the clinicians and patients since it could be applied to a variety of medical functionalities such as health monitoring and health management (Senthilkumar et al. 2016)

18.2.1 Diffusion of Innovation Theory

The diffusion of an innovation can be described as the process by which knowledge of an innovation spreads across a population and through the decisions made by a unit in the organisation whether or not the innovation is adopted or rejected (Carter et al. 2001; Rogers 2003). Rogers' (1983) work is considered ground-breaking with regard to technology innovation and diffusion; therefore most studies that focus on the diffusion of innovation with respect to technology begin with Rogers. Findings for Rogers' research indicate that adopters of most new innovations or ideas can be categorised as innovators, early adopters, early majority of adopters, late majority of adopters and laggards, based on the mathematically based Bell curve. Adoption over time will indicate an 'S-shaped curve' (an S curve) to show that the technology adopters may be slow at start, more rapid as adoption increases, and then ultimately arrive at a more stagnant rate. This is more widely known as the diffusion of innovation model (Rogers 2003). Table 18.2 provides a summary of the key findings from the diffusion of innovation literature.

Based on the cited literature in Table 18.4, there is a clear need for more research to be done on the IT innovation assimilation area grounded through the diffusion of innovation theory(s) in investigating the failure or rejection of innovation usage amongst a population in a particular context. The review of relevant theoretical research carried out in the area of IS/IT innovation assimilation based on the diffusion of innovation literature and specifically focused on the healthcare industry is discussed in the next section.

18.2.2 Theory of Innovation Assimilation

Innovation can be defined as an idea, practice, technology or entity that is considered to be new by an individual, a group or any other units of adoption (Rogers 2003). With innovation comes the processes initial discussion and idea for innovation generation, introduction of the idea for innovation, evaluation of the idea for innovation through the identification of needs and priorities of this new innovation. The process of innovation assimilation involves decisions made by members of the organisation relating to the possibility of the innovation being potentially useful in solving the organisational issues, followed by the adoption of the innovation and finally the institutionalisation of the innovation (Wu and Chen 2014; Greenhalgh et al. 2008; Li et al. 2005; Zhu et al. 2006).

The need for innovation assimilation can be seen in many of the HIS implementation literature (Heeks 2002; Jayasuriya and Anandaciva 1995; Littlejohns et al. 2003; Ahmadi et al. 2015a). In a study of the implementation of HIS in developing countries such as South Africa and the Philippines, the results of HIS evaluation reveal that three quarters of HIS applications were found to have failed with no evidence that the system has actually improved healthcare professional's productivity

Table 18.2 Findings in relation to diffusion of innovation literature

Category	Findings
Organisation	Organisations must understand and manage their implementation process especially management's recognition of critical issues to be raised and resolved throughout the implementation process. There is a need for strategy development and resource allocation by managers between design stage and implementation stage. Managerial influence is most likely higher at design stage rather than during the implementation. Managers have to understand the critical nature of timing if they are to shift and implement new technology using good IT innovation theories (Lyytinen and Rose 2003; Nambisan et al. 2017)
Technology innovation process or assimilation	Develop strategies for assimilating technologies into its operations through support, advocacy and total commitment. CIO's business and IT knowledge, relationship with top management and informal interaction with senior management team are found to be significant in influencing IT assimilation (Armstrong and Sambamurthy 1999) Introduction of the assimilation gap which provides a new way to assess the prospect of the innovation at the early stages of the entire diffusion cycle (Fichman and Kemerer 1999) There should be more research on technological innovation process (Allen 2000; West and Bogers 2014) Diffusion of innovation should be studied as a process consisting of multiple stages and measures (Carter et al. 2001; Wu and Chen 2014) Serious gap uncovered in finding out what processes are innovations in health care implemented and sustained in a particular context and how this process can be enhanced (Greenhalgh et al. 2004; Moullin et al. 2015). The concept of organisational assimilation of IT innovation is under explored in the literature (Swanson 2004; Mu et al. 2015)
Traditional diffusion of innovation (DOI) research	Adding 'result demonstrability', 'visibility', image and voluntariness to the initial five characteristics of innovation (Moore and Benbasat 1991) Due to the lack of general theory on innovation, the development of more middle range theory for specific technology and adoption context is recommended (Fichman 2000; Archibald and Clark 2014) The use of traditional diffusion models should be expanded to more complex, mandatory and deep usage (Chin and Marcolin 2001; Nan et al. 2014). Uses traditional DOI theory to frame and understand issues with ERP implementation (Bradford and Florin 2003; Rajagopal 2002; Akca and Ozer 2014). The traditional DOI model is able to accurately describe nurses' behaviour in adopting workplace innovation (Lee 2004; Archibald and Clark 2014)

(Littlejohns et al. 2003; Willcocks and Lester 1996). Some of the problems highlighted at the South African hospitals were related to infrastructure and implementation processes, such as delay in the network upgrades, delay in the development of the proposed modules, features that were too advanced for the healthcare personnel which required them to have intensive training, failure of maintenance support to provide quick and reliable services and frustration of personnel having to use selective passwords in accessing certain modules (Littlejohns et al. 2003). As a response to the resentment of the HIS usage, a new contract was given to a different company with the hope of improving the current problematic situation. This action failed to address the issues and, as a result, a new system was developed. The new system required all healthcare personnel to undertake training to be familiar with the new application (Littlejohns et al. 2003).

In the study of a healthcare facility in the Republic of the Philippines, the author concurs with Heeks (2002) who found that many of the developing countries are facing HIS sustainability issues caused by the failure to assimilate the design and actual implementation of systems in many hospitals (Heeks 2002). In the case of the hospital under study in the Philippines, the system acquired was based on a successful model in an American hospital, without considering the currently available IT resources in the Philippines' hospital. Cultural differences were not considered during the implementation of the HIS (Jayasuriya and Anandaciva 1995). The implementation process lacked a skilled project manager, lacked adequate technological infrastructure and proficient information management practices (Jayasuriya and Anandaciva 1995). Heeks's (2002) study showed that the hospital suffered from an assimilation gap during its implementation and operation (Heeks 2002; Jayasuriya and Anandaciva 1995). As a result of the assimilation gap, these systems did not meet the healthcare personnel's requirements and had to be abandoned within less than a year (Heeks 2002). Mismanagement of the implementation process of the HIS and the assimilation gap lead to the information system failing to realise its benefits at considerable monetary cost (Littlejohns et al. 2003). Therefore, a study on the processes of innovation assimilation is clearly important.

18.2.3 Technology-Organisation-Environment (TOE) Framework

In the discussion of assimilation gaps, facilitators that influence the innovation assimilation stages should be considered. Tornatzky and Fleischer (1990) introduced the technology-organisation-environment (TOE) framework in 1990. Their framework provides details that firms should consider when studying components that influence assimilation of technological innovation. These components are grouped in three aspects: technological context, organisational context and environmental context (Tornatzky and Fleischer 1990; Zhu et al. 2006; Wu and Chen 2014). The components are represented in Fig. 18.1.

The technology context comprises of the internal and external technologies pertaining to the firm involved and includes both equipment and processes (Tornatzky and Fleischer 1990). The organisational context involves the characteristics and resources of the firms such as firm size, managerial structure, human resources, amount of slack resources and linkages amongst employees. The environmental context includes the structure of the industry, the firm's competitors, the macroeconomic concept and the regulatory environment (Tornatzky and Fleischer 1990).

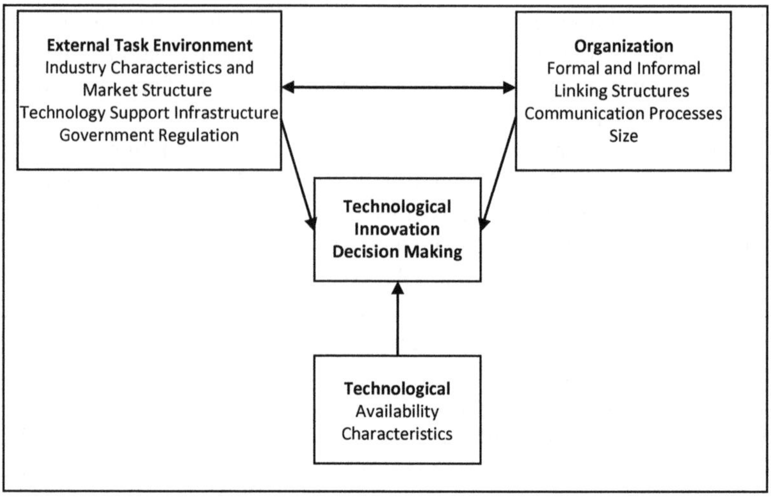

Fig. 18.1 The original TOE model (Tornatzky and Fleischer 1990)

These elements have been identified as being both the constraints and opportunities for technological innovation; thus these are also considered as components that influence the way a firm sees the need to and ways to adopt new technology.

This framework is also applied in the work of Zhu et al. (2006) studying factors that influence e-business assimilation stages in both developed and developing countries. However, the original diagram by Tornatzky and Fleischer (1990) has been modified to suit their study in an e-business context. The adapted model by Zhu et al. (2006) is depicted in Fig. 18.2. Results from the study of Zhu et al. (2006) indicate that factors such as technological readiness and regulatory environment are the most relevant factors in the innovation assimilation process—especially for developing countries. The organisational context which involves elements such as firm size and managerial obstacles has been verified through the IS literature which provides evidence of significant relationships of firm size and firm scope to IS/IT adoption and usage (Gurbaxani and Whang 1991; Zhu 2004).

Firm size is seen as an important organisational attribute for innovation diffusion (Rogers 2003; Nan et al. 2014). With regard to assimilation stages, Damanpour (1996) argued that the relationship between firm size and assimilation stages may differ due to differences in activities carried out in each of the assimilation stages. Zhu et al. (2006) noted that larger firms usually initiate and adopt innovations due to their resource advantages in terms of financial, managerial and technical resources.

The managerial obstacles' factor is referred to as the organisation's lack of managerial skills and efficiency in handling change management, thus causing ineffectiveness in managing technology adoption and adaptation (Zhu et al. 2006). This is in line with Mata et al. (1995) and Teo and Bhattacherjee's (2014) view that the ability to merge managerial and IS/IT skills is highly dependent on the firms' ability

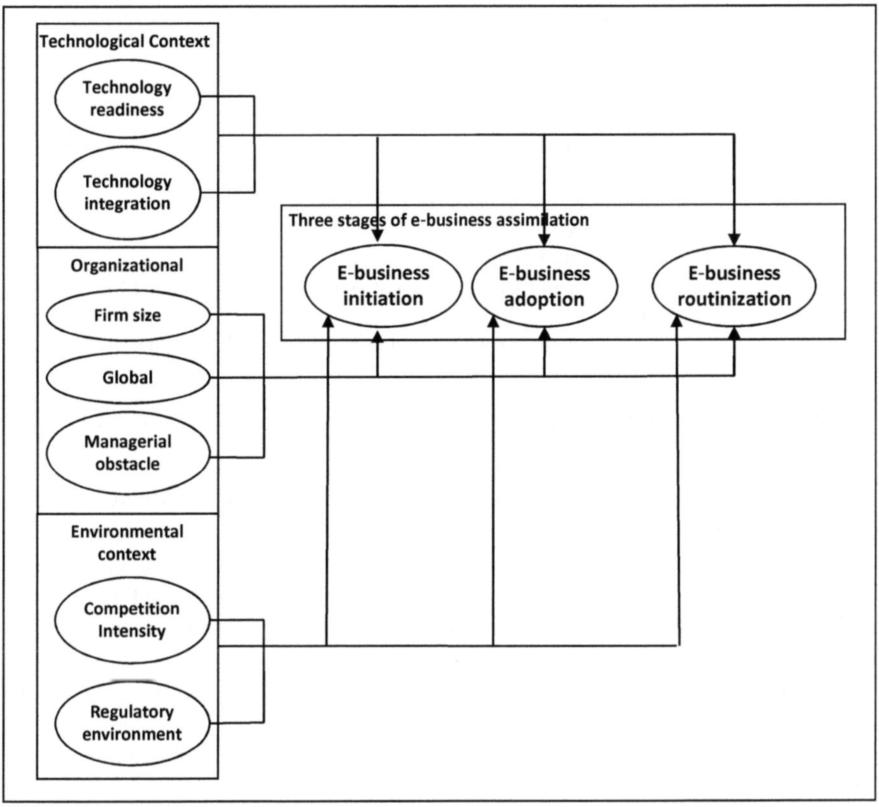

Fig. 18.2 E-business innovation assimilation model (Zhu et al. 2006)

to assimilate information technology. This then requires firms to possess relevant managerial skills and overcome barriers in adopting and assimilating new technology. Therefore, in line with the HIS assimilation study, this research will adapt some of the factors in the TOE framework, such as hospital size and managerial obstacles as facilitators to the success of HIS assimilation in a healthcare context.

18.2.4 IS/IT Resources in Resource-Based View

The IS/IT resources classification in the resource -based view literature begins with Grant's (1995) classification of key IS/IT-based resources and was categorised into:

1. IS/IT infrastructure: the tangible resource which includes IS/IT infrastructure components such as hardware and software.
2. IS/IT expertise: the human IS/IT resources which are divided into technical and managerial skills.

Table 18.3 IS/IT resource elements

Resource	Elements
IS/IT human resources	Strong competent technical skills Excellent understanding of the business Empowered IS/IT teams to work closely with clients in addressing business needs
Technology	Sharable technical platform and databases Well-defined technology architecture Data and platform standards
Relationship	Ownership and accountability of IS/IT projects from both IS/IT and client Top management leadership in establishing IS/IT priorities

3. IS/IT-enabled intangibles: the intangible IS/IT-enabled resources such as knowledge assets and customer service skills.

Ross et al. (1996) further extended the study by classifying that the relationship and use of resources such as IS/IT human resources, reusable technology infrastructure and strong IS/IT-business partner relationship together would result in faster strategic business needs in terms of cost-effectiveness as compared to the organisation's competitors. Description of these resources as defined by Ross et al. (1996) is listed in Table 18.3.

It is crucial for an IS/IT department to have strong IS/IT competencies and skills in order to be able to solve business problems and handle business opportunities through the use of information technology (Ross et al. 1996). This can be further enhanced by being able to understand organisational processes and work closely with clients in gathering the necessary problem-solving skills (Ross et al. 1996). With the IS/IT infrastructure, the importance of a sharable platform and technology is essential for integrating systems in the organisation in order to make IS/IT applications more cost-effective especially in the area of operations and support (Ross et al. 1996).

Merging the studies of both Grant (1995) and Ross et al. (1996), Bharadwaj (2000) extended these concepts of IS/IT resources through an empirical study of the relationship between the IS/IT resources to organisation's superior performance. Bharadwaj (2000) defines all three resources according to Grant's (1995) classification and refers to them as IT capabilities. The results indicate that firms should do much more than merely invest in IS/IT. Instead, firms should consider identifying ways in which to create a firm- wide IS/IT capability. The study by Bharadwaj (2000) also suggests that the identification of the most important IS/IT resources and skills is actually the search in understanding the nature of superior IS/IT performance (Bharadwaj 2000).

Huang et al. (2006) further explored the study by Bharadwaj (2000), through the similar usage of IS/IT resource-based view, and concentrated on the same three resources. Their study however is more focused on the use of the IS/IT resources in relation to IS/IT investment. An interesting outcome from Huang et al.'s (2006) study is the revelation that the IS/IT infrastructure and human IS/IT resources cannot directly influence firm's performance. However, the two resources provide an influence to intangible resources such as knowledge assets, improved customer service through IS/IT (as this makes the firm more responsive to customer's needs), management of organisational knowledge, better synergy between the vendor and customers, improved coordination and sharing of resources across organisational divisions (Bharadwaj 2000; Huang et al. 2006). Hence, these intangibles are grouped as IS/IT-enabled intangibles (Bharadwaj 2000) which will directly influence the firm's performance. Figure 18.3 denotes the original conceptual diagram used in Huang et al.'s (2006) research.

A study by Glaser (2002) on the strategic applications of IS/IT in healthcare organisation has brought about the identification of healthcare organisational IS/IT resources that were aimed towards 'furthering organisational strategies and advancing the organisation's abilities to achieve its goals'. The resources identified relevant to this study are listed in Table 18.4.

Based on the list defined by Glaser (2002), this research includes IT governance as part of the technology component in the conceptual framework. The technical architecture and IS/IT staff in Glaser's (2002) study are found to be similar to the definition of IS/IT infrastructure and human IS/IT resources from the previously mentioned literature on the use of IT resources in resource-based view.

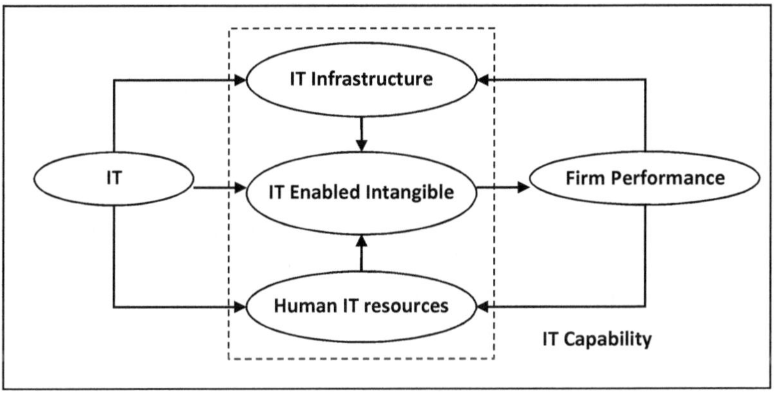

Fig. 18.3 Research framework in the study of Huang et al. (2006)

Table 18.4 Glaser's (2002) definition of the organisational IS/IT resources

Resource	Description
Technical architecture	Basic infrastructure comprising of networks, programming languages, operating systems, workstations and other basic technologies that form the foundation for the applications
IS/IT staff	Analyst, programmers and computer operators who manages IS/IT in the organisation
IT governance	Organisation mechanisms which include committees, policies, procedures and best practices by which IS/IT strategies are formed, priorities are set, standards are developed and projects are managed

To further strengthen the usage of the identified IT resources in this research, a conceptual study done by Khatri (2006) which identified important resources for a healthcare organisation through the literature on resource-based view is of relevance. It is interesting to note that the identified resources are similar to the resources identified by Grant (1995) and the resources tested by Bharadwaj (2000) and Huang et al. (2006). Khatri (2006) determined that it is worth examining the relationship between these resources and clinical outcomes through mediating variables such as organisational processes. Therefore, it is of significance to examine the influence of IS/IT infrastructure, human IS/IT resources and IS/IT intangibles to successfully assimilate HIS into a healthcare facility.

Assimilation in this research refers to the series of stages that the healthcare organisation has to undergo from the initial evaluation of the potential system to be acquired to the formal adoption and finally to the deployment of the system after which it becomes part of the organisation's value chain activities. This study theorises that new technology such as the HIS is introduced into a healthcare organisation with great enthusiasm and rapid acquisition but nevertheless fails to be thoroughly deployed and sustained in its use amongst healthcare professionals. The widespread acquisition of an innovation will not necessarily be followed by a widespread deployment and full utilisation by the acquiring organisation. An assimilation gap exists between the rate of acquisition and deployment, where certain barriers are claimed to have slowed the innovation diffusion process and caused a negative impact on deployment when compared to the acquisition (Fichman and Kemerer 1999).

Previous studies on technology assimilation have outlined a number of assimilation stages for success. These stages vary in their interpretations and can be presented in three stages or six stages depending on the technology innovation involved. Studies by Cooper and Zmud (1990) highlighted six stages from initiation and adoption as the 'early stages' and adaptation, acceptance, routinisation and infusion as the 'later stages'. Mata et al. (1995) identified three stages involving initiation, adoption and routinisation which cover most aspects of technology innovation assimilation stages. Applying the innovation assimilation concept to the healthcare setting, some researchers have classified the early assimilation stage as awareness and evaluation (Meyer and Goes 1988).

However, this study will adopt the view of Zhu et al. (2006) and Ammenwerth et al. (2005), in classifying both awareness and evaluation in the initiation stage in line with the conceptual framework of Thompson (1965) and many other empirical researchers (Agarwal et al. 1997; Chengalur-Smith and Duchessi 1999; Cooper and Zmud 1990; Gallivan 2001; Grover and Goslar 1993; Pierce and Delbecq 1977; Zhu et al. 2006; Zmud 1982) who consider 'initiation' to be the first stage in an assimilation stage (Fig. 18.4).

Following the initiation is the adoption stage, where adoption involves the successful usage of the technology acquired (Agarwal et al. 1997). A gap is identified between the stages of acquisition and adoption as there is usually the enthusiasm of acquiring new technology. Once it has been adopted however, the new technology failed to meet its purpose and was not able to sustain its use (Fichman and Kemerer

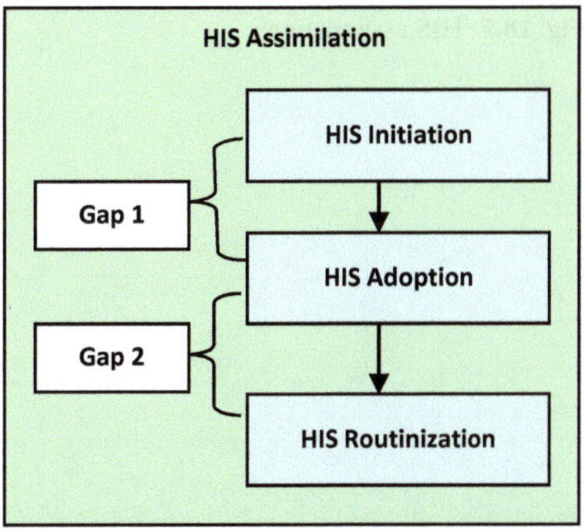

Fig. 18.4 HIS assimilation stages

1999). Therefore, adoption does not always indicate that the technology has been widely used in the organisation; adoption has to be followed by the utilisation and institutionalisation of the technology throughout the organisation (DeLone and McLean 1992; Devaraj and Kohli 2003; Sethi and King 1994; Zhu et al. 2006). Having found similarities in the assimilation concepts of this research to the study of Mata et al. (1995), the HIS assimilation stages described in this research go beyond the initiation and adoption stage to include routinisation. This stage refers to the 'later stage' of innovation diffusion to a point where the elaborated use of the HIS has become part of the value chain activities of the organisation and managerial systems (Pongpattrachai et al. 2009; Zmud and Apple 1992).

There exists another gap between adoption and routinisation which is highlighted after a new information technology has been adopted. The adoption-routinisation gap occurs when the organisation and its members lack sufficient knowledge to gain control and manage the system, thereby causing asynchrony with the fit between the technology implemented and the end user's work context (Fichman and Kemerer 1999; Zhu et al. 2006). As a result, the system is rarely used and may be totally abandoned. Considering the theoretical aspects and literature above, this study theorises three innovation assimilation stages, initiation, adoption and routinisation, and the assimilation gaps which will be explored in the healthcare setting.

18.2.5 The Technology-Organisation-Environment (TOE) Context

The theoretical model will include several concepts identified from the TOE framework, namely, those which have been identified to be relevant when studying developing countries. Amongst the selected concepts are regulatory environment, technology readiness elements, firm size and managerial obstacles (Fig. 18.5).

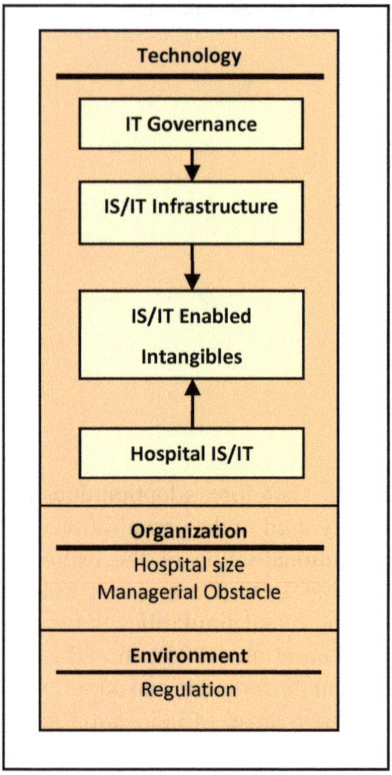

Fig. 18.5 HIS assimilation

18.2.5.1 Regulatory Environment

Regulatory environment is an important concept to consider, namely, in a country where the federal government has centralised control over the country's health policy through its constitutional powers. Hence the healthcare organisations must abide to any regulatory changes and implementation (Chee and Barraclough 2007). These impacts might involve elements such as support and funding provided for technology adoption (Chee and Barraclough 2007).

18.2.5.2 Technology Readiness

Technological readiness involves infrastructure, relevant systems, hardware and technical expertise which are considered important factors for successful IS/IT adoption (Armstrong and Sambamurthy 1999; Kwon and Zmud 1987). This concept is very similar to the concept of IS/IT resources in the resource-based view theory. Hence, this research will merge the TOE technology readiness concept with the IS/IT resources concepts from a combination of resource-based view literatures that relate to the influence of resources on organisation's processes (Bharadwaj 2000; Grant 1991, 1995; Huang et al. 2006; Khatri 2006; Ross et al. 1996).

Based on studies done by Grant (1995), Ross et al. (1996), Bharadwaj (2000) and Huang et al. (2006), the identification of resources for this research will include all of the three common resources—IS/IT infrastructure, human IS/IT resources and IS/IT-enabled intangibles. These resources are deemed significant in assessing the influence that the IS/IT resources could provide to the HIS innovation assimilation. Exploring how IS/IT infrastructure, human IS/IT resources and IS/IT intangibles are being utilised and how they can be leveraged in sustaining the use of HIS is deemed relevant.

Another concept that is specifically relevant to managing IS/IT is IT governance. Many organisations, including the healthcare industry, adopted IT governance to ensure that IS/IT is aligned with organisation goals and objectives (Cater-Steel and Tan 2005; Smaltz et al. 2007; Borousan et al. 2011). As an integral part of enterprise governance, IT governance consists of leadership, organisational structures and processes that ensure the organisation's IS/IT sustains and extends the organisation's strategy (Sallé 2004; Smaltz et al. 2007; Borousan et al. 2011). In order to sustain the use of technology, there is a necessity in establishing some order and control in the management of IS/IT resources (Zachman 1987; Ramadhani et al. 2013). Hence, in managing IS/IT resources, effective IT governance is required.

18.2.5.3 Firm Size and Managerial Obstacle

The firm size concept is incorporated in this study due to its importance for innovation diffusion (Rogers 2003) and to distinguish between activities that are carried out between large and small firms in each of the assimilation stages according to their resource advantage (Zhu et al. 2006).

The managerial obstacles under the organisational context are also considered an important concept as the success of innovation implementation will not only rely on the innovation itself and the behaviour of the adopters but also on the strength and support provided by the management (Attewell 1992; Greenhalgh et al. 2008; Yetton et al. 1999; Zmud 1984; Al Shaar et al. 2015). The managerial skills and efficiency of the management in handling change could determine the effectiveness of the innovation assimilation and thus also lead to sustained use.

18.2.6 Summary and Significance of Study Based on the Literature

The literature has indicated various issues pertaining to IS/IT assimilation and use in the healthcare industry. Issues with HIS assimilation are said to be potentially solved if there was a systematic approach to assimilation with the support of the facilitating components. The literature also identified gaps especially in the assimilation stages where clinical and non-clinical medical professionals tend to be enthusiastic about using the HIS at the beginning of its acquisition and the excitement tends to drop after its adoption.

Furthermore, mismatch of the HIS technology implemented with the work environment of the clinical and non-clinical medical professionals and the lack of knowledge in maintaining the HIS are also considered facilitators and contributors to the assimilation gap. The literature review has provided evidence that there is a need for a solid and robust assimilation model to ensure the success of HIS assimilation. This is crucial in assisting the clinical and non-clinical medical professionals to deliver better healthcare services to the community and realise the full benefits HIS has to offer.

18.3 Methodology

This study explores well formulated theories in a unique context that in turn leads to confirming, challenging and building upon these theories. Hence, a qualitative approach is deemed especially appropriate in studying a relatively new phenomenon that a specific population experiences, a new innovation in a particular context. A qualitative approach is suitable in exploring the identified research problems through the point of view of participants describing their issues and problems explicitly whilst using the HIS. This study also involves the study of social and cultural phenomena through interviews, documents and the researcher's impression as well as reaction to the identified context (Myers 2009).

A qualitative interview was conducted where participants were categorised into pilot study participants and main study participants. There were 2 participants for the pilot study and 31 participants for the main study conducted in a public hospital. The participant for the pilot study was a medical specialist from the identified public hospital and a subject matter expert on information systems in health care. The pilot study was conducted in order to gauge responses on the suitability of the interview questions and preliminary insights on the issue of HIS use in the selected case study.

The main study was conducted in the targeted public hospital as a single case with multiple embedded cases. Based on the criteria of the hospital being the first to implement a hospital-wide IS/IT and have undergone every stage of the HIS assimilation, the public hospital is seen as the most suitable choice to explore the identified problems. The participants for the main interview were recruited across multiple departments in the hospital ranging from senior clinicians who participated in the planning of the HIS to the junior medical team as well as the non-clinical personnel. In addition to the semi-structured interviews, this research also involved the use of multiple data collection methods such as data, methodological and interdisciplinary triangulation (Denzin and Lincoln 2005; Mantzana et al. 2007). Data was also collected through several other sources such as archival documents, minutes of meetings, consultancy reports and the organisation's website. It is also the aim of this research to enhance or build upon existing theories through the findings of the data collected. Therefore, this is in line with Eisenhardt's (1989) suggestion that the usage of multiple data collection methods supports triangulation and provides a concrete and solid foundation of theory building.

Interviews were transcribed and coded using the thematic coding technique. The use of thematic analysis was applied in the analysis of data in this research as it provides a structured way of understanding how to develop thematic codes and sense themes. The interviews were transcribed and themes were identified from the transcription. This research adopted the theory and prior research-driven approach in developing the themes and codes as this approach allows the use of existing themes and codes in order to replicate, extend or refute prior discoveries (Boyatzis 1998). Moreover, this approach was also chosen due to the flexibility to the researchers in developing their own codes and may want to rely on established theories to assist in the development of themes and codes.

18.4 The HIS Assimilation Model

Findings of this study identified four main contextual components consisting of people, process, technology and environment. Table 18.5 reveals elements that were identified as facilitators from the analysis of the data.

Findings indicate that out of seven initially identified elements, only four elements were consistent with the previous literature. These four elements are the clinical IS/IT experts, IT governance, healthcare IS/IT infrastructure and the regulatory

Table 18.5 Identified elements for assimilation model

Context	Element
People	Clinical IS/IT experts
	Medical staff
	Vendor
Process	IT governance
	Clinical governance
	Financial
	Procurement
Technology	Healthcare IS/IT infrastructure
	Software and hardware
	System design
	Performance
	Integration
Environment	Political
	Work culture
	Regulation
	Leadership

environment. The clinical IS/IT experts and healthcare IS/IT infrastructure elements provide support to the theoretical underpinning of the resource-based view of the firm, in which the human IS/IT resource and IT infrastructure are considered to be of importance in the adoption of information systems (Huang et al. 2006). The utilisation of these resources is also arguably able to leverage technology usage thus providing success to technology innovation (Bharadwaj 2000; Grant 1991, 1995; Huang et al. 2006; Khatri 2006; Ross et al. 1996). The IS/IT-enabled intangible element of customer service skills and knowledge, which was identified initially as a resource that could provide success to HIS assimilation, was scarcely discussed amongst interview participants. Further analysis indicated that these intangible elements were more of a barrier than a facilitator to the hospital. These barriers will be discussed further in subsequent sections.

The regulation element was an expected finding as the context of the case study was in a public hospital that adheres to all regulations posed by the government. The regulatory environment confirms the argument of Chee and Barraclough (2007) that healthcare organisations should abide by any regulatory changes and implementation as the government's regulatory influences would have an impact on the HIS assimilation in a hospital. The regulatory element also supports findings of Zhu et al. (2006) whereby regulation does actually provide an influence to the success of the technology assimilation.

The focus on HIS assimilation in the hospital supports the theory of diffusion modelling that, from a practical perspective, affects the larger portion of the hospital's population and further, from a technical perspective, appears to be successful based solely on the idea of having new innovation acquired in the organisation but nevertheless failed to be deployed (Fichman and Kemerer 1999).

Analysis of this study identified gaps between the assimilation stages, revealing global and local barriers that should be addressed in all and specific assimilation stages in order to provide successful HIS assimilation. Despite the elucidation of the global and local barriers, to obtain a more descriptive and consistent picture pertaining to successfully assimilation of the HIS, the people, process, technology and environment components were identified to provide key facilitators for success. Based on the barriers and facilitators identified, a better descriptive version of HIS assimilation model for hospitals is developed. This is illustrated in Fig. 18.6.

Findings of this study highlight that successful assimilation of the HIS in a public hospital is highly complex. The adoption and use of the HIS are relatively slow and require continuous improvement in sustaining its use. This view is supported in the literature by various scholars who support the contention that there are still issues with the healthcare sector that is slow in adopting HIS and sustaining the use of these systems (LeRouge and Wickramasinghe 2013; Spil and Stegwee 2001).

It is clear from the findings of this study that successful assimilation of an HIS involves more than proper planning and implementation at the initial stage. Successful assimilation also requires clinical governance in understanding the needs of healthcare IS/IT, the maintenance of the systems throughout adoption and the input of clinical IS/IT experts. Clinical management support in terms of technical knowledge and financial resources must be accompanied by strong leadership and

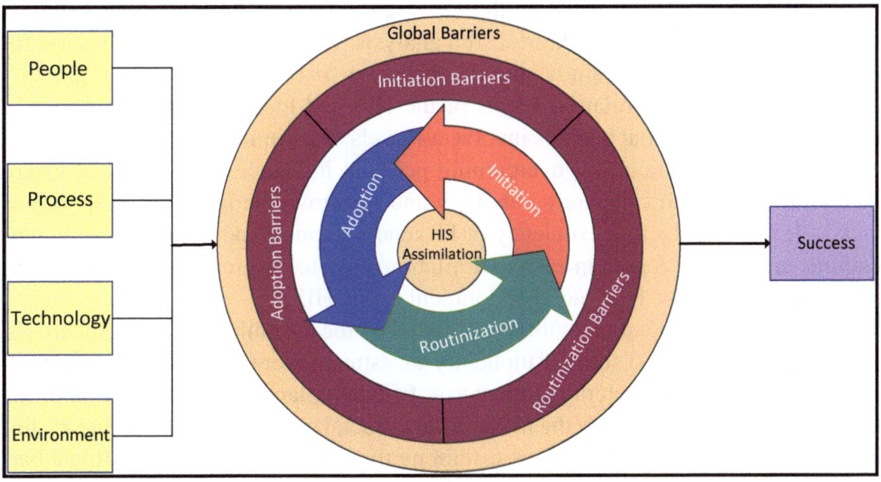

Fig. 18.6 The HIS assimilation framework

critical understanding of the demands of a computerised medical facility in order to promote the extensive use of HIS through to its routinisation stage. However, with the absence of good leadership and knowledge of the HIS demands, the system remains part of the organisation's value chain activities but has failed to meet its intended benefits. The absence of sufficient knowledge after a new IS/IT has been adopted in a healthcare facility is also supported by the findings of Fichman and Kemerer (1999) and further supported by Zhu et al. (2006) that the organisation and its members usually lack sufficient knowledge to gain control and manage the system after new IS/IT was adopted. This then causes an issue with the fit between the technology acquired and the end user's work context. As a result, systems may be abandoned or utilised less due to being irrelevant to the work environment.

HIS assimilation is important as healthcare organisations are facing crisis due to the global exponentially increasing healthcare costs, and government in most countries around the world believed that IS/IT is central in resolving this situation. Thus, it is apparent that a myriad of e-health and/or IS/IT innovation projects in health care are currently initiated and implemented in various countries. However, many of these initiatives and innovations are unsuccessful. Therefore, HIS assimilation offers a possible solution to ensure the likely success of HIS within the e-health projects.

Despite the numerous issues encountered by the medical staff of the public hospital, the HIS undeniably provided valuable assistance to the clinical work practices, especially in storing and retrieving information on patient's medical histories. The use of the HIS also promotes familiarisation of clinical computation amongst medical professionals. Efficient services providing almost immediate clinical test results have subsequently lead to easier and faster decision-making on the patient's medical treatment. The HIS has also been acknowledged as a medium of communication amongst medical staff in providing a diagnosis for cross department cases.

The HIS was initially found by this research to be poor in relation to sustained use. Through the findings of the research analysis, this was found to be the case for the public hospital understudy and is attributed to barriers that occur globally throughout all the assimilation stages of the HIS and locally at specific stages of HIS assimilation. Global barriers involve all levels of assimilation and include overcoming financial difficulties, overcoming political influences and a lack of up-to-date knowledge on healthcare technology and systems. The local barriers, such as lack of leadership, lack of efficiency of IT vendor support and proactive communications, must be addressed in each assimilation stage to ensure that preventive measures have been taken to avoid abandonment of the HIS.

Overcoming financial difficulties is crucial as the assimilation of healthcare IS/IT requires a prolonged state of monetary investment from the relevant stakeholders, especially during system maintenance. Efficient planning and allocation of the healthcare IS/IT budget from the investors are crucial in supporting the entire assimilation process which will result in sustaining the use of the HIS. The political barriers in many government organisations do cause complications in many parts of the organisation, particularly the work processes. Overcoming political barriers requires a change in work culture, good governance and a high degree of political and administrative commitment by the top government authorities. It is imperative to adopt a more transparent way of managing the current business practices relating to areas such as IT vendor selection and procurement processes. A strong senior management team that promotes accountability and transparency and upholds strong ethical values in realising organisational objectives in providing better health and quality of service to the people is essential.

An appointed champion amongst senior clinicians with strong healthcare IS/IT knowledge is mandatory to promote sustained use of the HIS, and a change in work culture is required to improve communication gaps between the medical and IS/IT field. It is crucial for both areas to understand the latest advancement in medical technology and to possess an understanding of clinical procedures in order to achieve the aims of having successful use of an end-to-end hospital IS/IT facility. Better communication amongst staff may also lead to an improved work culture and a more flexible and collaborative work environment.

In ensuring that the HIS is assimilated successfully in a healthcare facility, elements in the technology-organisation-environment framework (Tornatzky and Fleischer 1990) require further enhancement in tailoring the framework to the needs of a healthcare organisation. Hence, specifically for the healthcare context, the components of people, process, technology and environment can be postulated as being facilitators for technology innovation. As facilitators, they influence the way that the healthcare organisation realises the needs and searches for ways to adopt new technology. However, these facilitators are not without barriers that the organisation has to overcome, both globally and locally, in each stage of the innovation assimilation.

It is also due to these barriers that the gaps identified by Fichman and Kemerer (1999) and Zhu et al. (2006), pertaining to the level of enthusiasm amongst HIS users that is generally higher during initial stage of assimilation and lower during the later stages of assimilation, exist. In the context of a healthcare environment, being oblivious to these barriers during the initial stages causes the information systems deployment and adoption to result in disappointment or failure. Members of the healthcare organisation, not realising that other barriers exist in later stages of assimilation, are often deprived of or possess very limited skills and knowledge to use and maintain the HIS. Ultimately, this causes major misalignment between the new HIS being implemented and the medical professionals' work environment.

It should be noted that many of the findings, whilst they have not been explicitly discovered in the context of health care, have been discussed to a greater or lesser extent in other industries, such as banking, finance and telecommunication. Thus noting this occurrence in healthcare context indicates that in many ways health care is not so dissimilar to other industries.

18.5 Conclusion

The area of HIS assimilation requires further investigation especially in ensuring that IS/IT are being utilised despite the identified barriers. However, given the growing focus globally for an increasing need of IS/IT as a means to effecting and enabling superior HIS delivery, it becomes of vital importance to further explore the components of HIS assimilation. This is critical, and in order to understand the depth and breadth of this key process, it is essential that future studies build on the important findings of this study. The next step for assimilation research is to carry out more investigation to examine in greater detail the specific barriers and facilitators identified in this study in other healthcare contexts to provide more insights into HIS assimilation. Given the advancement in healthcare technologies with IoT health-enabled devices and big data analytics, it is of utmost importance for hospital administrators to ensure that the IS/IT systems are seamlessly assimilated throughout the healthcare facilities in order to be able to generate vast amount of data to be used for predictive analytics in making precise decisions.

Multiple case studies should be carried out in various hospitals achieving similar levels of HIS assimilation to further improve the generalisability of the findings. Given the growing significance that IS/IT will play in enabling superior healthcare delivery, the critical role for successful assimilation of HIS needs to be further addressed in this important area.

References

Agarwal, R., Tanniru, M., & Wilemon, D. (1997). Assimilating information technology innovations: Strategies and moderating influences. *IEEE Transactions on Engineering Management, 44*(4), 347–358.

Ahmadi, H., Nilashi, M., & Ibrahim, O. (2015a). Organizational decision to adopt hospital information system: An empirical investigation in the case of Malaysian public hospitals. *International Journal of Medical Informatics, 84*(3), 166–188.

Ahmadi, H., Nilashi, M., Ibrahim, O., Ramayah, T., Wong, M. W., Alizadeh, M., Jafarkarimi, H., & Almaee, A. (2015b). Exploring potential factors in total hospital information system adoption. *Journal of Soft Computing and Decision Support Systems, 2*(1), 52–59.
Ahmed, H., Daim, T., & Basoglu, N. (2007). Information technology diffusion in higher education. *Technology in Society, 29*(4), 469–482.
Akca, Y., & Ozer, G. (2014). Diffusion of innovation theory and an implementation on enterprise resource planning systems. *International Journal of Business and Management, 9*(4), 92.
Al Shaar, E. M., Khattab, S. A., Alkaied, R. N., & Manna, A. Q. (2015). The effect of top management support on innovation: The mediating role of synergy between organizational structure and information technology. *International Review of Management and Business Research, 4*(2), 499.
Allen, J. P. (2000). Information systems as technological innovation. *Information Technology and People, 13*(3), 210–221.
Ammenwerth, E., Gräber, S., Bürkle, T., & Iller, C. (2005). Evaluation of health information systems: Challenges and approaches. In T. A. M. Spil & R. W. Schuring (Eds.), *E-health systems diffusion and use: The innovation, the user and the use IT model* (pp. 212–236). Hershey, PA: Idea Group.
Archibald, M. M., & Clark, A. M. (2014). Twitter and nursing research: How diffusion of innovation theory can help uptake. *Journal of Advanced Nursing, 70*(3), e3–e5.
Armstrong, C. P., & Sambamurthy, V. (1999). Information technology assimilation in firms: The influence of senior leadership and IT infrastructures. *Information Systems Research, 10*(4), 304–327.
Attewell, P. (1992). Technology diffusion and organisational learning: The case of business computing. *Organisation Science, 3*(1), 1–19.
Berglund, M., Nilsson, C., Revay, P., Petersson, G., & Nilsson, G. (2007). Nurses' and nurse students' demands of functions and usability in a PDA. *International Journal of Medical Informatics, 76*(7), 530–537.
Bharadwaj, A. S. (2000). A resource-based perspective on information technology capability and firm performance: An empirical investigation. *MIS Quarterly, 24*(1), 169–196.
Borousan, E., Hojabri, R., Manafi, M., & Hooman, A. (2011). Balanced scorecard; a tool for measuring and modifying IT governance in healthcare organizations. *International Journal of Innovation, Management and Technology, 2*(2), 141.
Boyatzis, R. E. (1998). *Transforming qualitative information: Thematic analysis and code development*. Thousand Oaks, CA: Sage.
Bradford, M., & Florin, J. (2003). Examining the role of innovation diffusion factors on the implementation success of enterprise resource planning systems. *International Journal of Accounting Information Systems, 4*(3), 205–225.
Burke, D. E., Wang, B. B. L., Wan, T. T. H., & Diana, M. L. (2002). Exploring hospitals' adoption of information technology. *Journal of Medical Systems, 26*(4), 349–355.
Carter, F. J., Jambulingam, T., Gupta, V. K., & Melone, N. (2001). Technological innovations: A framework for communicating diffusion effects. *Information Management, 38*(5), 277–287.
Cater-Steel, A., & Tan, W. G. (2005). *Implementation of IT infrastructure library (ITIL) in Australia: Progress and success factors*. Paper presented to IT Governance International Conference, Auckland, New Zealand, 14–16 November 2005.
Chang, I. C., Hwang, H. G., Hung, M. C., Lin, M. H., & Yen, D. C. (2007). Factors affecting the adoption of perspective of hospital electronic signature: Executives' information department. *Decision Support Systems, 44*(1), 350–359.
Chatzoglou, P. D., & Diamantidis, A. D. (2009). IT/IS implementation risks and their impact on firm performance. *International Journal of Information Management, 29*(2), 119–128.
Chee, H., & Barraclough, S. (2007). *Health care in Malaysia: The dynamics of provision, financing and access*. Hoboken, NJ: Routledge.
Chengalur-Smith, I., & Duchessi, P. (1999). The initiation and adoption of client–server technology in organisations. *Information Management, 35*(2), 77–88.

Chin, W. W., & Marcolin, B. L. (2001). The future of diffusion research. *SIGMIS Database, 32*(3), 7–12.
Cooper, R. B., & Zmud, R. W. (1990). Information technology implementation research: A technological diffusion approach. *Management Science, 36*(2), 123–139.
Cresswell, K., & Sheikh, A. (2013). Organizational issues in the implementation and adoption of health information technology innovations: An interpretative review. *International Journal of Medical Informatics, 82*(5), e73–e86.
Damanpour, F. (1996). Organizational complexity and innovation: Developing and testing multiple contingency models. *Management Science, 42*(5), 693–716.
DeLone, W. H., & McLean, E. R. (1992). Information systems success: The quest for dependent variable. *Information Systems Research, 3*(1), 60–95.
Denzin, N. K., & Lincoln, Y. S. (Eds.). (2005). *The Sage handbook of qualitative research* (3rd ed.). Thousand Oaks, CA: Sage.
Devaraj, S., & Kohli, R. (2003). Performance impacts of information technology: Is actual usage the missing link? *Management Science, 49*(3), 273–289.
Eisenhardt, K. M. (1989). Building theories from case study research. *Academy of Management Review, 14*(4), 532–550.
Fadlalla, A., & Wickramasinghe, N. (2004). An integrative framework for HIPAA-compliant I*IQ healthcare information systems. *International Journal of Health Care Quality Assurance, 17*(2), 65–74.
Fehse, K. I. A., Krabbendam, K., & Boer, H. (2002). The role of politics in the implementation of information systems: A hospital case. *International Journal of Healthcare Technology and Management, 4*(3/4), 205–219.
Fichman, R. G. (2000). The diffusion and assimilation of information technology innovations. In R. Zmud (Ed.), *Framing the domains of IT management: Projecting the future through the past*. Cincinnati, OH: Pinnaflex.
Fichman, R., & Kemerer, C. (1999). The illusory diffusion of innovation: An examination of assimilation gaps. *Information Systems Research, 10*(3), 255–275.
Gagnon, M. P., Ngangue, P., Payne-Gagnon, J., & Desmartis, M. (2016). m-Health adoption by healthcare professionals: A systematic review. *Journal of the American Medical Informatics Association, 23*(1), 212–220.
Gallivan, M. J. (2001). Organisational adoption and assimilation of complex technological innovations: Development and application of a new framework. *SIGMIS Database, 32*(3), 51–85.
Georgiou, A., Westbrook, J., Braithwaite, J., Iedema, R., Ray, S., Forsyth, R., Dimos, A., & Germanos, T. (2007). When requests become orders - A formative investigation into the impact of a computerized physician order entry system on a pathology laboratory service. *International Journal of Medical Informatics, 76*(8), 583–591.
Glaser, J. P. (2002). *The strategic application of information technology in health care organisations*. San Francisco: Jossey-Bass.
Grant, R. M. (1991). The resource-based theory of competitive advantage - Implications for strategy formulation. *California Management Review, 33*(3), 114–135.
Grant, R. M. (1995). *Contemporary strategy analysis*. Oxford, UK: Balckwell.
Greenhalgh, T., Robert, G., Macfarlane, F., Bate, P., & Kyriakidou, O. (2004). Diffusion of innovations in service organisations: Systematic review and recommendations. *The Milbank Quarterly, 82*(4), 581–629.
Greenhalgh, T., Robert, G., & Bate, P. (2008). *Diffusion of innovations in service organisations: A systematic literature review*. Chichester: Wiley.
Grover, V., & Goslar, M. D. (1993). The initiation, adoption, and implementation of telecommunications technologies in U.S. organisations. *Journal of Management Information Systems, 10*(1), 141–163.
Gurbaxani, V., & Whang, S. (1991). The impact of information systems on organisations and markets. *Communications of the ACM, 34*(1), 59–73.
Heeks, R. (2002). Information systems and developing countries: Failure, success, and local improvisations. *The Information Society, 18*, 101–112.

Huang, S.-M., Ou, C.-S., Chen, C.-M., & Lin, B. (2006). An empirical study of relationship between IT investment and firm performance: A resource-based perspective. *European Journal of Operational Research, 173*(3), 984–999.

Jayasuriya, J., & Anandaciva, S. (1995). Compliance with an incident report scheme in anaesthesia. *Anaesthesia, 50*(10), 846–849.

Jensen, T. B., & Aanestad, M. (2007). Hospitality and hostility in hospitals: A case study of an EPR adoption among surgeons. *European Journal of Information Systems, 16*(6), 672–680.

Jha, A. K., Doolan, D., Grandt, D., Scott, T., & Bates, D. W. (2008). The use of health information technology in seven nations. *International Journal of Medical Informatics, 77*, 848.

Katsma, C. P., Spil, T. A. M., Ligt, E., & Wassenaar, A. (2007). Implementation and use of an electronic health record: Measuring relevance and participation in four hospitals. *International Journal of Healthcare Technology and Management, 8*(6), 625–643.

Keim, T., Malinowski, J., & Weitzal, T. (2005). *Bridging the Assimilation Gap: A User-Centered Approach to IT Adoption in Corporate HR Processes*. Paper presented to Americas conference on information systems (AMCIS), Omaha, NE, paper 220.

Khatri, N. (2006). Building IT capability in health-care organisations. *Health Services Management Research, 19*(2), 73.

Kim, C., Lee, J., & Kim, Y. (2002). Early stage evolution of a hospital information system in a middle income country: A case study of Korea. *International Journal of Healthcare Technology and Management, 4*(6), 514–524.

Kwon, T. H., & Zmud, R. W. (1987). Unifying the fragmented models of information systems implementation. In *Critical issues in information systems research* (pp. 227–251). Chichester: Wiley.

LeRouge, C., & Wickramasinghe, N. (2013). A review of user-centred design for diabetes-related consumer health informatics technologies. *Journal of diabetes science and technology, 7*(4), 1039–1056.

Lee, T.-T. (2004). Nurses' adoption of technology: Application of Rogers' innovation-diffusion model. *Applied Nursing Research, 17*(4), 231–238.

Lee, C.-P., & Shim, J. P. (2007). An exploratory study of radio frequency identification (RFID) adoption in the healthcare industry. *European Journal of Information Systems, 16*(6), 712–724.

Lee, S. G., Trimi, S., & Kim, C. (2013). Innovation and imitation effects' dynamics in technology adoption. *Industrial Management and Data Systems, 113*(6), 772–799.

Li, Y.-C., Chang, I.-C., Hung, W.-F., & Fu, H.-K. (2005). *The critical factors affecting hospital adoption of mobile nursing technologies in Taiwan*. Paper presented to proceedings of the 38th annual Hawaii international conference on system sciences (HICSS'05) - Track 6 - Volume 06.

Littlejohns, P., Wyatt, J. C., & Garvican, L. (2003). Evaluating computerised health information systems: Hard lessons still to be learnt. *BMJ, 326*(7394), 860–863.

Lyytinen, K., & Rose, G. M. (2003). The disruptive nature of information technology innovations: The case of internet computing in systems development organizations. *MIS Quarterly, 27*, 557–596.

Mata, F., Fuerst, W., & Barney, J. (1995). Information technology and sustained competitive advantage: A resource-based analysis. *MIS Quarterly*, (19: 4).

Mantzana, V., Themistocleous, M., Irani, Z., & Morabito, V. (2007). Identifying healthcare actors involved in the adoption of information systems. *European Journal of Information Systems, 16*, 91–102.

McGrath, C., & Zell, D. (2001). The future of innovation diffusion research and its implications for management: A conversation with Everett Rogers. *Journal of Management Inquiry, 10*(4), 386–391.

Meyer, A. D., & Goes, J. B. (1988). Organisational assimilation of innovations: A multilevel contextual analysis. *The Academy of Management Journal, 31*(4), 897–923.

Moore, G. C., & Benbasat, I. (1991). Development of an instrument to measure the perceptions of adopting an information technology innovation. *Information Systems Research, 2*(3), 192–222.

Moore, G. C., & Benbasat, I. (1996). Integrating diffusion of innovations and theory of reasoned action models to predict utilization of information technology by end-users. In *Diffusion and adoption of information technology* (pp. 132–146). New York: Springer.

Moullin, J. C., Sabater-Hernández, D., Fernandez-Llimos, F., & Benrimoj, S. I. (2015). A systematic review of implementation frameworks of innovations in healthcare and resulting generic implementation framework. *Health Research Policy and Systems, 13*(1), 16.

Mu, E., Kirsch, L. J., & Butler, B. S. (2015). The assimilation of enterprise information system: An interpretation systems perspective. *Information Management, 52*(3), 359–370.

Myers, M. (2009). *Qualitative research in business and management*. London: Sage.

Nambisan, S., Lyytinen, K., Majchrzak, A., & Song, M. (2017). Digital innovation management: Reinventing innovation management research in a digital world. *MIS Quarterly, 41*(1), 223.

Nan, N., Zmud, R., & Yetgin, E. (2014). A complex adaptive systems perspective of innovation diffusion: An integrated theory and validated virtual laboratory. *Computational and Mathematical Organization Theory, 20*(1), 52–88.

Øvretveit, J., Scott, T., Rundall, T. G., Shortell, S. M., & Brommels, M. (2007). Improving quality through effective implementation of information technology in healthcare. *International Journal for Quality in Health Care, 19*(5), 259–266.

Pierce, J. L., & Delbecq, A. L. (1977). Organisation structure, individual attitudes and innovation. *The Academy of Management Review, 2*(1), 27–37.

Pongpattrachai, D., Cragg, P., & Fisher, R. (2009). *Spreadsheet infusion in small audit firms in Thailand*. Paper presented to americas conference on information systems (AMCIS), San Francisco, CA.

Radhakrishnan, A., David, D., & Zaveri, J. (2008). *Challenges with adoption of electronic medical record systems*. Hershey, PA: IGI Global.

Rajagopal, P. (2002). An innovation--diffusion view of implementation of enterprise resource planning (ERP) systems and development of a research model. *Information Management, 40*(2), 87–114.

Ramadhani, D. P., Kurniati, A. P., & Maharani, W. (2013). IT governance analysis of XYZ hospital based on COBIT 4.1. In *The Proceedings of The 7th international conference on information and communication technology and systems (ICTS)*.

Reardon, J. L., & Davidson, E. (2007). An organisational learning perspective on the assimilation of electronic medical records among small physician practices. *European Journal of Information Systems, 16*(6), 681–694.

Rogers, E. (1983). *Diffusion of innovations* (3rd ed.). New York: Free Press.

Rogers, E. (2003). *Diffusion of innnovations* (5th ed.). New York: Free Press.

Ross, J. W., Beath, C. M., & Goodhue, D. L. (1996). Develop long-term competitiveness through IT assets. *Sloan Management Review, 38*(1), 31.

Sallé, M. (2004). *IT service management and IT governance: Review, comparative analysis and their impact on utility computing*. Palo Alto, CA: HP Laboratories.

Senthilkumar, R., Ponmagal, R. S., & Sujatha, K. (2016). Efficient health care monitoring and emergency management system using IoT. *International Journal of Control Theory and Applications, 9*(4), 137–145.

Sethi, V., & King, W. R. (1994). Development of measures to assess the extent to which an information technology application provides competitive advantage. *Management Science, 40*(12), 1601–1627.

Setia, P., Setia, M., Krishnan, R., & Sambamurthy, V. (2011). The effects of the assimilation and use of IT applications on financial performance in healthcare organisations. *Journal of the Association for Information Systems, 12*(3), 1.

Skok, W., Kophamel, A., & Richardson, I. (2001). Diagnosing information systems success: Importance- performance maps in the health club industry. *Information Management, 38*(7), 409–419.

Smaltz, D. H., Carpenter, R., & Saltz, J. (2007). Effective IT governance in healthcare organisations: A tale of two organisations. *International Journal of Healthcare Technology and Management, 8*(1/2), 20–41.

Snyder-Halpern, R. (2001). Indicators of organisational readiness for clinical information technology/systems innovation: A Delphi study. *International Journal of Medical Informatics, 63*(3), 179–204.

Spil & Stegwee (2001) Strategies for healthcare information systems IGI, Hershey.
Swanson, E. (2004). How is an IT innovation assimilated. In *IT innovation for adaptability and competitiveness* (pp. 267–287). New York: Springer.
Teo, T. S., & Bhattacherjee, A. (2014). Knowledge transfer and utilization in IT outsourcing partnerships: A preliminary model of antecedents and outcomes. *Information Management, 51*(2), 177–186.
Thompson, V. A. (1965). Bureaucracy and innovation. *Administrative Science Quarterly, 10*(1), 1–20.
Tornatzky, L. M., & Fleischer, M. (1990). *The process of technological innovation*. Lexington, MA: Lexington Books.
Varonen, H., Kortteisto, T., Kaila, M., & EBMeDS Study Group. (2008). What may help or hinder the implementation of computerized decision support systems (CDSSs): A focus group study with physicians. *Family Practice, 25*(3), 162–167.
Wager, K. A., Lee, F. W., & Glaser, J. P. (2005). *Managing health care information systems: A practical approach for health care executives*. San Francisco: Wiley.
Walley, P., & Davies, C. (2002). Implementing IT in NHS hospitals - Internal barriers to technological advancement. *International Journal of Healthcare Technology and Management, 4*(3/4), 259–272.
Wang, Y., Kung, L., & Byrd, T. A. (2016). Big data analytics: Understanding its capabilities and potential benefits for healthcare organizations. *Technological Forecasting and Social Change, 126*, 3.
West, J., & Bogers, M. (2014). Leveraging external sources of innovation: A review of research on open innovation. *Journal of Product Innovation Management, 31*(4), 814–831.
Wickramasinghe, N. (2000). IS/IT as a tool to achieve goal alignment. *International Journal of Healthcare Technology and Management, 2*(1), 163–180.
Wickramasinghe, N., & Goldberg, S. (2008). *Critical success factors for delivering M-health excellence*. Hershey, PA: IGI Global.
Willcocks, L., & Lester, S. (1996). Beyond the IT productivity paradox. *European Management Journal, 14*(3), 279–290.
Wu, L., & Chen, J. L. (2014). A stage-based diffusion of IT innovation and the BSC performance impact: A moderator of technology–organization–environment. *Technological Forecasting and Social Change, 88*, 76–90.
Yasunaga, H., Imamura, T., Yamaki, S., & Endo, H. (2008). Computerizing medical records in Japan. *International Journal of Medical Informatics, 77*(10), 708–713.
Yetton, P., Sharma, R., & Southon, G. (1999). Successful IS innovation: The contingent contributions of innovation characteristics and implementation process. *Journal of Information Technology, 14*(1), 53–68.
Yoo, Y. (2013). The tables have turned: How can the information systems field contribute to technology and innovation management research? *Journal of the Association for Information Systems, 14*(5), 227.
Zachman, J. (1987). Framework for information systems architecture. *IBM Systems Journal, 26*(3), 276.
Zhu, K. (2004). The complementarity of information technology infrastructure and E-commerce capability: A resource-based assessment of their business value. *Journal of Management Information Systems, 21*(1), 167–202.
Zhu, K., Kraemer, K. L., & Xu, S. (2006). The process of innovation assimilation by firms in different countries: A technology diffusion perspective on E-business. *Management Science, 52*(10), 1557–1576.
Zmud, R. W. (1982). Diffusion of modern software practices: Influence of centralization and formalization. *Management Science, 28*(12), 1421–1431.
Zmud, R. W. (1984). An examination of "Push-Pull" theory applied to process innovation in knowledge work. *Management Science, 30*(6), 727–738.
Zmud, R., & Apple, L. (1992). Measuring technology incorporation/Infusion. *Journal of Product Innovation Management* 9(2), 148–155.

Part III
Specific Solutions and the Principles of Knowledge Management

Chapter 19
Knowledge Management to Address Real Healthcare Needs: The Case of Allergy Care in Australia

Nilmini Wickramasinghe and Peter Haddad

19.1 Introduction

The Australasian Society of Clinical Immunology and Allergy (ASCIA) defines allergy as a medical condition that *occurs when a person's immune system reacts to substances in the environment that are harmless for most people. These substances are known as allergens and are found in house dust mites, pets, pollen, insects, molds, foods, and some medicines* (ASCIA 2013). Allergy including asthma incidents is steadily increasing and thus becoming a major health concern in many of these countries. This includes allergic rhinitis, drug allergy, food allergy, insect allergy, skin allergy, sinusitis, and general allergy (Pleis et al. 2009). These different types of allergy have different prevalence rates in different countries, but they all have an increased trend in common (AAAAI 2015). For example, 7.5% of the population in the USA were diagnosed with hay fever in 12 months in 2011–2012, and 8% of the population had a food allergy (Haahtela et al. 2013). This problem appears to be more acute in Australia, where allergy and immune diseases are among the fastest growing chronic conditions in the country (ASCIA 2013). According to the latest figures (ASCIA 2013, 2014), almost 20% of the Australian population has an allergic disease, and this prevalence is increasing. Hospital admissions for anaphylaxis (severe life threatening allergic reaction) have increased fourfold in the last 20 years. Not only has this increase occurred in adults, but it has also hit newborn infants, as food-induced anaphylaxis has doubled in the last 10 years, and 10% of infants now have an immediate food allergy (ASCIA 2013). Autoimmune diseases

N. Wickramasinghe (✉)
Epworth HealthCare, Richmond, VIC, Australia

Deakin University, Burwood, VIC, Australia

P. Haddad
Deakin University, Melbourne, VIC, Australia

N. Wickramasinghe, J. L. Schaffer (eds.), *Theories to Inform Superior Health Informatics Research and Practice*, Healthcare Delivery in the Information Age,
https://doi.org/10.1007/978-3-319-72287-0_19

have also caused serious health problems to Australians. Today, there exist over 100 different autoimmune diseases that affect 5% of Australians and lead to significant disability. These figures agree with another study that reports exponential increases in food allergy diagnosis in recent decades (Wang and Sampson 2011).

Data generated from a local HealthNuts study has also identified an increase of 20% sensitization, and a 10% challenge confirmed food allergy rate in 12-month-old Melbourne infants (Osborne et al. 2011). Further, there were 4.1 million Australians (19.6%) having at least one allergy, and the average Australian allergic person with 1.74 allergies, forecasting of 70% in the number of Australians with allergies affected from 4.1 million now to 7.7 million by 2050, and an increased proportion affected from 19.6 to 26.1% if the trends back then continued (Access Economics Pty Limited 2007).

As in other developed countries, these increased rates of allergy diagnosis in Australia are representing a real concern at the national level. Not only have these figures caused significant health problems for the Australian population, but they also have had notable economic impacts. 7.8 billion Australian dollar was the calculated cost of allergies in Australia in 2007. This is due to different interrelated factors like lower productivity ("presenteeism" $4.2 billion), direct medical costs ($1.2 billion), lower employment rates ($1.1 billion), absenteeism and lost household productivity ($0.2 billion), and premature death ($83 million) (Cook et al. 2007; Sampson 2002, 2009).

Two burdens appear to have played key roles in making the allergy management even more challenging in the Australian context. Firstly, there is a lack of public awareness about the impact and appropriate management of allergy and immune diseases (AAAAI 2015; ASCIA 2013). This is in part due to the fact that allergy is evolving and many do not look at allergy as a serious medical condition like cancer or diabetes (ASCIA 2013). Secondly, access to care is difficult, even in metropolitan areas, due to the high number of patients and low number of appropriately trained healthcare professionals, resulting in long waiting times to see a specialist, which also causes negative consequences on patients and their possible treatment care plans (AAAAI 2015).

These two challenges, and the nature of allergy conditions and required treatments, are causing allergy patients to be seen by different healthcare professionals for allergy screening and/or follow-up (Haddad et al. 2015). This starts with general practitioners, or family doctors, who would refer patients to a specialist if needed. Two problems face this model of provisioning allergy care in Australia. Firstly, it is not an unusual clinical practice for clinicians to provide patients with a copy of their skin prick testing (SPT) results each time the test is performed as well as keep a record of the test in either written or electronic form in their patient database. As allergy services are currently stretched, there are frequently prolonged waiting times for food allergy review, particularly in the public sector. It is not uncommon for patients to be seen by different allergy practitioners for follow-up testing in the longer term (Gordois et al. 2007). In the interim patients are frequently encouraged to attend their general practitioner for food allergy follow-up that may include intermittent evaluation of yearly or second yearly allergen-specific immunoglobulin E (sIgE) testing to the food allergen(s) in question. In the event that these levels are low or approaching negative re-referral for follow-up and consideration of formal inpatient challenge may be appropriate. In this situation it is not uncommon that previous test results are not readily available for comparison. There is some evidence to suggest that the rate of change in SPT size or sIgE levels over time may help in predicting the development of tolerance (Australian Doctor 2015; Haddad et al. 2015).

Secondly, there has been no specific or agreeable knowledge among healthcare professionals to manage these referrals. A recent study (Smith et al. 2016) reviewed 100 consecutive general practitioner (GP) referrals to a hospital allergy clinic were reviewed to determine whether patients could be seen in a community-based clinic led by a general practitioner with special interest (GPwSI) allergy. The results showed that at 25–50% of allergy referrals to the selected hospital-based service could be dealt with in a GPwSI clinic, thereby diversifying the patient pathway, allowing specialist services to focus on more complex cases, and reducing the waiting time for first appointments. These two and other problems have motivated the need to redesign the model of provisioning care allergy (Warner et al. 2006).

Based on these circumstances, health information exchange solutions have been touted to be helpful to address the issue of interorganizational health information exchange (HIE) (Walker et al. 2005). The literature is rich with studies that evaluate the impact of HIE in health care in general. Walker et al. (2005) created an HIE taxonomy and found that a fully standardized HIE that also takes interoperability into consideration may yield a net value of $77.8 billion per year upon the full implementation. Similarly, Bailey et al. (2013) found that HIE was associated with 64% lower odds of repeated diagnostic imaging in an emergency evaluation of back pain (p. 16), and another study found that HIE access was associated with an annual cost savings of $1.9 million, and hospital readmission reductions accounted for 97.6% of the total cost reduction for the population of the study (Frisse et al. 2012). Hence, this study is an attempt to leverage the possibilities of HIE to facilitate better flows of knowledge and information within and across allergy care providers and their patients.

19.2 Research Aim and Question

This study addresses a key practical need by designing a comprehensive solution that utilizes information and communication technology (ICT) to facilitate knowledge flow among allergy care providers and also between patients and their healthcare providers as explained below.

Hence, this study answers the following research question:

- *How can information and communication technology be designed to facilitate superior knowledge flow in the context of allergy care delivery?*

In answering this question, this study also identifies the challenges and opportunities of information and communication technology in managing allergy care delivery. Hence, the following sub-questions are also addressed:

- *What are the technical challenges faced in designing information systems to facilitate knowledge flow in the context of allergy care delivery?*
- *What are the enablers and barriers to design such information systems?*

To answer these questions, this study uses the approach of knowledge management as a theoretical underpinning.

19.3 The Approach of Knowledge Management

Given the increased rates of allergy diagnoses in developed countries, this study attempts to solve a current business challenge by increasing the efficiency and efficacy of the core business processes for allergy care providers. The theory of knowledge management (KM) is deemed appropriate to ground this study (Holsapple 2013; Power et al. 2015; Wang et al. 2014; Wickramasinghe et al. 2009).

Knowledge management is an emerging management approach that aims at responding to the increasing need to better management of the ever-increasing data stored in databases or even information that is being exchanged throughout different and complex networks (Geisler and Wickramasinghe 2009). The literature shows a number of definitions of knowledge management. For example, Lee (2001) looks at knowledge management as a discipline that promotes an integrated approach to identifying, managing, and sharing all of an enterprise's information needs. These information assets may include databases, documents, policies, and procedures as well as previously unarticulated expertise and experience resident in individual workers (Geisler and Wickramasinghe 2009). Another perspective is also centered on collecting data and transferring these data from raw materials into information elements, which in turn are assembled and organized into context-relevant structures that represent knowledge (Saint-Onge 1996). Another interesting aspect on defining knowledge management is centered on enabling individuals in an organization to collectively acquire, share, and leverage knowledge to achieve business objectives (Duffy 2001; Geisler and Wickramasinghe 2005).

The tools, techniques, and tactics of knowledge management approach are increasingly being used and recognized by organizations (Geisler and Wickramasinghe 2009; Wickramasinghe et al. 2009). The primary drivers for knowledge management in the last decades have been (1) the global trend to invest in information and communication technology since the late 1980s and (2) the dilemma of lack of tools that domesticate the expertise within the organizations when senior executives leave their organizations (Holsapple 2013; Wickramasinghe et al. 2009).

Knowledge management is not limited to the context within organizations, but it also covers the interorganizational activities pertaining to knowledge flow, transfer, and management (Agrawal 2001; Wang et al. 2014). In their review of the factors affecting knowledge flow and sharing between different unities (organizations or individuals), Battistella et al. (2015) found that trust, intensity of the connections, and, they added, the distances that exist between parties, in particular the organizational distance, the physical distance, the distance of the knowledge base, the cultural distance, and the normative, play key roles in determining the success of knowledge management practices both interpersonally and interorganizationally.

Even though knowledge management has been used to highlight the interorganizational knowledge flow, examining this concept in health care is still developing in the literature (Holsapple 2013; Power et al. 2015; Wang et al. 2014; Wickramasinghe et al. 2009). This research is a contribution to this effort.

19.3.1 Knowledge Management for Health Care

The allure of knowledge management to control and facilitate knowledge transfer and flow has been appealing for the healthcare context, and it is becoming an established discipline with many applications and techniques (El Morr and Subercaze 2010). It is especially useful given the nature of health care, as a data and an information-intensive industry (Wickramasinghe and Schaffer 2010).

Further, with the ever-increasing volume of data being produced daily in the electronic medical records (EMR) and clinical databases, knowledge management approaches provide a tool-rich platform to perform pattern-identification tasks, such as detecting associations between certain risk factors and outcomes, ascertaining trends in healthcare utilization, or discovering new models of disease in populations (Holmes et al. 2002).

Today the literature has a plethora of studies that utilize the principles of knowledge management in the context of health care, such as clinical decision making (Balas et al. 2004; Lobach et al. 2012), knowledge translation (Straus et al. 2013) and flow (Lin et al. 2012), and mobilization of knowledge (Davies et al. 2016).

In their comprehensive assessment of applying knowledge management in the healthcare industry, Wickramasinghe et al. noted that the gap between data collection and data comprehension and analysis is becoming more problematic, given the increased volume and complexity of clinical data, which, in on one or other, reflects the complexity of the health care itself (Wickramasinghe et al. 2009).

19.3.2 The Application of Knowledge Management on This Study

Utilizing the tools, tactics, and techniques that knowledge management offers is deemed appropriate for this research for the following reasons:

First, the designed database is expected to produce high volumes of data on different types of allergy in different age groups. Not only is the volume demanding, but also the complexity of the produced data is an issue. Those two factors combined make the use of knowledge management prudent to maximize the benefit of using the designed database.

Second, knowledge management will help bridge the gap between data collection as a routine procedure and data comprehension and analysis as an innovative and iterative process. This is highly important based on the explanation aforementioned.

Third, it will help clinicians to better understand their patients' data with less effort and time, which, in turn, increases the efficiency and efficacy of their daily operations.

Fourth, the aim of this study is to create a reliable and exchangeable knowledge among different allergy treatment providers, rather than merely creating the database. This is the core interest of knowledge management approach, by moving from raw knowledge (data), which is much context-dependent, to knowledge and then wisdom, which are much more context-independent (Wickramasinghe et al. 2009).

19.4 The Proposed System

The proposed solution is a web portal and a mobile app that utilize a comprehensive database at the back end as Fig. 19.1 illustrates.

The proposed system addresses the need for a timely access to the latest information of allergy patients irrespective of their care providers. This system will be designed to do the following:

1. Enabling allergy care providers and receivers to access accurate real time and digitized data on their patients' care plans, treatments, and progress

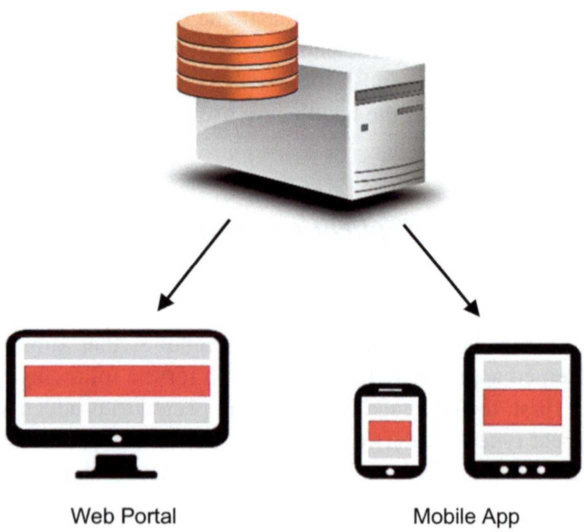

Fig. 19.1 The generic design of the proposed solution

2. Raising the awareness of allergy care by providing educational materials on allergy and its needed treatments
3. Enhancing the knowledge flow between patients and their care providers by including the system smart alerts and notifications on needed follow-ups

The system will enable two way communications between allergy patients and their care providers, so patients will be able to ask their health professionals questions on their care needs and allergy management plans.

Building the system has two phases: first building the prototype by using MySQL, PHP, and JavaScript. This includes building the backbone database and testing it against the design requirements. The design requirements are determined by discussions with allergy care providers at the selected case as the next section will show. The next step is to test the designed system and how it fits the design requirements and the purpose it addresses, i.e., facilitating superior knowledge flow in the context of allergy care delivery.

Patients' data will be secured using recommended protocols by industry partners. During the prototype phase, the researchers are using a dummy data set.

19.5 Methodology and Research Design

This study adopts single case study (Yin 2003) and design science research methodology (DSRM) (Peffers et al. 2007). Case study research has proven to be "*well-suited to capturing the knowledge of practitioners and developing theories from it*" (Benbasat et al. 1987, p. 370). Also, the main focus of this study is to design an IS/IT that facilitates knowledge transfer and sharing among different allergy care providers. Hence, the use of (DSRM is deemed appropriate for this study (Peffers et al. 2007). DSRM is a process model that helps carry out researchers on designing artifacts to serve in the area of IS. This methodology is widely used quantitatively to improve existing solutions or qualitatively to create new solutions to unsolved problems (Gregor and Hevner 2013). In this research, this methodology is used qualitatively given the nature of this study as it aims at creating a novel solution for an existing problem (von Alan et al. 2004), namely, the fragmented chain of knowledge sharing among allergy care providers. Hevner (2007) conceptualizes DSRM in three cycles, namely, relevance cycle, rigor cycle, and design cycle. According to this framing, design science research starts with the relevance cycle whose role is centered on providing the requirements for the research by identifying the opportunity/problem to be addressed. The rigor cycle is centered on providing past knowledge to the research project to insure its innovation (p. 90), and the design cycle concentrates on building the artifacts and processes and evaluating them (Hevner 2007). As this research is in its initial stages, the relevance and design cycles are relevant to this study at this stage. Upon the building of the solution, the rigor cycle will be addressed. Table 19.1 summarizes how the relevance and design cycles are mapped to this study.

Table 19.1 Mapping DSRM (Peffers et al. 2007) to the proposed system

DSRM activity	Activity description	Application on this study
Problem identification and motivation	Defining the specific research problem and justifying the value of a solution based on knowledge of the state of the problem	With the increasing rates of food allergy diagnosis (Osborne et al. 2011) and the stretches allergy care is experiencing (Bell and Busse 2013), the lack of a computerized information and communication system to support knowledge flow among allergy care providers is clear, and the need to address this gap is established
Definition of objectives of the solution	The objectives can be qualitative or quantitative, i.e., create or improve an artifact, respectively, based on knowledge of the state of the problem and current solutions, if any, and their efficacy	The objective is qualitative, as this research aims to create an artifact to address the fragmented nature of allergy care (Duncavage and Hagaman 2013). Not only does the designed solution attempts to address the technical, cultural, and principle challenges, but it also explores the role of information and communication technologies in managing knowledge flow among allergy care providers and patients and their communities
Design and development	Creating the artifact, including the desired functionality and its architecture based on knowledge of theory that can be used to bear in a solution	The artifact is to be designed to facilitate knowledge sharing and flow among different allergy care providers by having a central database that can be accessed by care providers and receivers to have instant access to the latest results and treatment plans. To do so, the design phase is conducted collaboratively between the researchers and the clinicians at the selected case
Demonstration	Demonstrate the use of the artifact to solve the problem	The artifact is to be tested and tried, and then in-depth analysis will be performed to measure the extent to which the proposed system helps solve the problem
Evaluation	Iterate back to better design the artifact if needed	As needed, iteration back will take place, based on in-depth analyses to identify rooms of improvement
Communication	Publish and let the value of the solution talk about itself	Conference publications and other presentation activities to develop the project further and share the findings with interested stakeholders

19.5.1 Settings and Participants

The design phase of this study was guided by discussions with clinicians in the selected case. The selected case is a pediatric allergy clinic in Melbourne, Australia. The output of these discussions was a set of design requirements and recommendations. Randomly selected de-identified existing patients' records from this clinic will be used to help establish the main structure of the proposed system. Upon completing the design phase, the prototype will be tested at the selected case.

19.5.2 Data Collection Plan and Techniques

Through the initial discussions with the clinicians at the selected case, we have established that the need for an information system that enables knowledge sharing and flow among different allergy care providers and their patients is greatly needed. Once the prototype is designed, a focus group will target up to five clinicians who work for the selected clinic. They are recruited based on their daily interaction with patients and their records. Those who participate in the focus group will be requested to complete a follow-up survey for data triangulation. Patients who visit the clinic during the 3-month trial period will be asked if they wish to participate in the study (again subscribing to all ethical requirements) and if so will then be randomly selected into the respective arms of the two-arm trial (as described above). All patients will receive equal care and attention irrespective of their participation or not in the study.

19.6 Results to Date and Discussion

Currently, the initial prototype has been designed including the structure of the backbone database, and the web portal, and testing them both by using a dummy data set. The initial results show that the database is capable to be the backbone supporting system. The next step is to use real de-identified data to test its scalability in real time. The majority of design requirements were met during the design, plus subscribing to the DSRM approach. This also will be confirmed during the second phase of the study.

This research has a number of implications for both theory and practice. From theoretical perspective, this research addresses an urgent need to address the inter-organizational knowledge flow and the potential role of information technology and communication in this regard, specifically in a healthcare context. It also aims at highlighting the technical challenges that may affect the use of such systems and limit their usability. In addition, a further theoretical aspect is the application of DSRM in a healthcare context.

From the perspective of practice, we highlight several key aspects as follows:

First, the proposed solution is an attempt to address the three problems facing the current model of allergy care, namely, the lack of awareness of allergy care requirements (by enabling educational contents for allergy patients); difficulty accessing specialized allergy care (by increasing the efficiency of care delivery through the use of information technology), as well as the nature of allergy care; and the need for higher coordination among different care providers.

Secondly, this solution has the potential to enhance the long-term follow-up of patients attending for comprehensive food allergy management at healthcare contexts.

Thirdly, this project has great potential to be patented and commercialized again bringing kudos and financial benefits to healthcare contexts.

Fourthly, the outputs of this study are far reaching to patients and their communities in developed countries, particularly in Australia, where allergy rates are among the highest in the world. It is expected that there will be instant and long-term clinical benefits by facilitating proactive and protective allergy care and management practices.

The next step of this research is to examine the usability and fidelity of the proposed system at the selected case. The outputs of this testing will be used to further enhance different design and functionality aspects of the proposed system.

19.7 Conclusion

The proceeding has served to outline a research in progress study that serves to address a healthcare need drawing upon the tools, techniques, and tactics of knowledge management. Specifically, a knowledge-based ICT solution is designed and developed using a DSRM to address current key issues in the delivery of care for patients suffering from allergies. The developed prototype will now be tested to establish usability, fidelity, and patient centeredness. In this way, the impact of the proffered system as a decision support tool powered by integrating key aspects of the tools, techniques, and technologies of knowledge management to enable superior value-based care delivery will be identified and realized.

Acknowledgment We would like to thank Dr Joan Smart and Ms Catherine Han Lin for the help provided in this study; their efforts and insights are highly appreciated.

References

AAAAI. (2015). *Allergy statistics*. Retrieved May 10, 2016, from http://www.aaaai.org/about-aaaai/newsroom/allergy-statistics

Access Economics Pty Limited. (2007). *The economic impact of allergic disease in Australia: Not to be sneezed at*. Balgowlah, NSW: Australasian Society of Clinical Immunology and Allergy (ASCIA).

Agrawal, A. K. (2001). University-to-industry knowledge transfer: Literature review and unanswered questions. *International Journal of Management Reviews, 3*(4), 285–302.

ASCIA. (2013). *Allergy and immune diseases in Australia (AIDA) report 2013*. Melbourne, Australia.

ASCIA. (2014). ASCIA 2014 abstract index. *Internal Medicine Journal, 44*, 35–37. https://doi.org/10.1111/imj.12548.

Australian Doctor. (2015). *GPs earmarked for greater role in allergy care*. Retrieved May 16, 2016, from http://www.australiandoctor.com.au/news/latest-news/gps-earmarked-for-greater-allergy-care-role

Bailey, J. E., Pope, R. A., Elliott, E. C., Wan, J. Y., Waters, T. M., & Frisse, M. E. (2013). Health information exchange reduces repeated diagnostic imaging for back pain. *Annals of Emergency Medicine, 62*(1), 16–24. https://doi.org/10.1016/j.annemergmed.2013.01.006.

Balas, E. A., Krishna, S., Kretschmer, R. A., Cheek, T. R., Lobach, D. F., & Boren, S. A. (2004). Computerized knowledge management in diabetes care. *Medical Care, 42*, 610–621.

Battistella, C., De Toni, A. F., & Pillon, R. (2015). Inter-organisational technology/knowledge transfer: A framework from critical literature review. *The Journal of Technology Transfer, 41*, 1195–1234.

Bell, M. C., & Busse, W. W. (2013). Severe asthma: An expanding and mounting clinical challenge. *The Journal of Allergy and Clinical Immunology: In Practice, 1*(2), 110–121.

Benbasat, I., Goldstein, D. K., & Mead, M. (1987). The case research strategy in studies of information systems. *MIS Quarterly, 11*(3), 369–386.

Cook, M., Douglass, J., Mallon, D., Mullins, R., Smith, J., & Wong, M. (2007). *The economic impact of allergic disease in Australia: Not to be sneezed at*. Balgowlah: Australasian Society of Clinical Immunology and Allergy.

Davies, H., Powell, A., & Nutley, S. (2016). Mobilizing knowledge in health care. In *The Oxford handbook of health care management*. Oxford: Oxford University Press.

Duffy, J. (2001). The tools and technologies needed for knowledge management. *Information Management, 35*(1), 64.

Duncavage, J., & Hagaman, D. D. (2013). Practical aspects of integrating allergy and pulmonology management into a rhinology practice: The Vanderbilt ASAP experience. *Current Opinion in Otolaryngology & Head and Neck Surgery, 21*(1), 74–78.

El Morr, C., & Subercaze, J. (2010). Knowledge management in healthcare. In *Handbook of research on developments in e-health and telemedicine: Technological and social perspetives* (pp. 490–510). Hershey, PA: IGI Global.

Frisse, M. E., Johnson, K. B., Nian, H., Davison, C. L., Gadd, C. S., Unertl, K. M., et al. (2012). The financial impact of health information exchange on emergency department care. *Journal of the American Medical Informatics Association, 19*(3), 328–333.

Geisler, E., & Wickramasinghe, N. (2005). The role and use of wireless technology in the management and monitoring of chronic diseases. D.C.

Geisler, E., & Wickramasinghe, N. (2009). *Principles of knowledge management: Theory, practices, and cases*. Armonk, NY: M.E. Sharpe.

Gordois, A., Armour, C., Brillant, M., Bosnic-Anticevich, S., Burton, D., Emmerton, L., et al. (2007). Cost-effectiveness analysis of a pharmacy asthma care program in Australia. *Disease Management and Health Outcomes, 15*(6), 387–396.

Gregor, S., & Hevner, A. R. (2013). Positioning and presenting design science research for maximum impact. *MIS Quarterly, 37*(2), 337–355.

Haahtela, T., Holgate, S., Pawankar, R., Akdis, C. A., Benjaponpitak, S., Caraballo, L., et al. (2013). The biodiversity hypothesis and allergic disease: World allergy organization position statement. *World Allergy Organization Journal, 6*(1), 3.

Haddad, P., Smart, J., Sango, X., Kanagalingam, S., Moghimi, H., Han-Lin, C., & Wickramasinghe, N. (2015). *Allergy database Epworth research week*. Melbourne: Epworth Research Institute.

Hevner, A. R. (2007). A three cycle view of design science research. *Scandinavian Journal of Information Systems, 19*(2), 4.

Holmes, J. P., Abbott, P., Cullen, R. N., Moody, L., Philips, K., & Zupan, B. (2002). Clinical data mining: Who does it, and what do they do? *Paper presented at the AMIA 2002 Symposium*.

Holsapple, C. (2013). *Handbook on knowledge management 1: Knowledge matters* (Vol. 1). Heidelberg: Springer.

Lee, J.-N. (2001). The impact of knowledge sharing, organizational capability and partnership quality on IS outsourcing success. *Information Management, 38*(5), 323–335.

Lin, C., Wu, J.-C., & Yen, D. C. (2012). Exploring barriers to knowledge flow at different knowledge management maturity stages. *Information Management, 49*(1), 10–23.

Lobach, D., Sanders, G. D., Bright, T. J., Wong, A., Dhurjati, R., Bristow, E., et al. (2012). Enabling health care decision making through clinical decision support and knowledge management. *Evidence Report/Technology Assessment, 203*, 1–784.
Osborne, N. J., Koplin, J. J., Martin, P. E., Gurrin, L. C., Lowe, A. J., Matheson, M. C., et al. (2011). Prevalence of challenge-proven IgE-mediated food allergy using population-based sampling and predetermined challenge criteria in infants. *The Journal of Allergy and Clinical Immunology, 127*(3), 668–676.e662. https://doi.org/10.1016/j.jaci.2011.01.039.
Peffers, K., Tuunanen, T., Rothenberger, M. A., & Chatterjee, S. (2007). A design science research methodology for information systems research. *Journal of Management Information Systems, 24*(3), 45–77.
Pleis, J. R., Lucas, J. W., & Ward, B. W. (2009). Summary health statistics for US adults: National Health Interview Survey, 2008. Vital and health statistics. Series 10, Data from the National Health Survey (242), pp. 1–157.
Power, D. J., Sharda, R., & Burstein, F. (2015). *Decision support systems*. Hoboken: Wiley.
Saint-Onge, H. (1996). Tacit knowledge the key to the strategic alignment of intellectual capital. *Planning Review, 24*(2), 10–16.
Sampson, A. P. (2009). FLAP inhibitors for the treatment of inflammatory diseases. *Current Opinion in Investigational Drugs, 10*(11), 1163–1172.
Sampson, H. A. (2002). Improving in-vitro tests for the diagnosis of food hypersensitivity. *Current Opinion in Allergy and Clinical Immunology, 2*(3), 257–261.
Smith, H. E., Wade, J., & Frew, A. J. (2016). What proportion of adult allergy referrals to secondary care could be dealt with in primary care by a GP with special interest? *Clinical and Translational Allergy, 6*(1), 1–6. https://doi.org/10.1186/s13601-016-0091-1.
Straus, S., Tetroe, J., & Graham, I. D. (2013). *Knowledge translation in health care: Moving from evidence to practice*. Chichester: Wiley.
von Alan, R. H., March, S. T., Park, J., & Ram, S. (2004). Design science in information systems research. *MIS Quarterly, 28*(1), 75–105.
Walker, J., Pan, E., Johnston, D., Adler-Milstein, J., Bates, D. W., & Middleton, B. (2005). The value of health care information exchange and interoperability. *Health Affairs, 24*, 10–18. https://doi.org/10.1377/hlthaff.W5.10.
Wang, J., & Sampson, H. A. (2011). Food allergy. (science in medicine) (disease/disorder overview). *Journal of Clinical Investigation, 121*(3), 827.
Wang, S., Noe, R. A., & Wang, Z.-M. (2014). Motivating knowledge sharing in knowledge management systems a quasi–field experiment. *Journal of Management, 40*(4), 978–1009.
Warner, J. O., Kaliner, M. A., Crisci, C. D., Del Giacco, S., Frew, A. J., Liu, G. H., et al. (2006). Allergy practice worldwide: A report by the World Allergy Organization Specialty and Training Council. *International Archives of Allergy and Immunology, 139*(2), 166–174.
Wickramasinghe, N., Bali, R. K., Lehaney, B., Schaffer, J., & Gibbons, M. C. (2009). *Healthcare knowledge management primer*. Hoboken: Taylor and Francis.
Wickramasinghe, N., & Schaffer, J. L. (2010). *Realizing value driven e-health solutions, Improving healthcare series*. Washington, DC: IBM Center for the Business of Government.
Yin, R. K. (2003). *Case study research: Design and methods* (3rd ed.). Thousand Oaks, CA: Sage.

Chapter 20
Embracing the Principles of Knowledge Management to Structure a Superior IT Healthcare Paradigm

Nilmini Wickramasinghe, James Choi, and Jonathan L. Schaffer

20.1 Introduction

Health care is an information-rich, knowledge-intensive environment. In order to treat and diagnose even a simple condition, a physician must combine many varied data elements and information streams. Such multispectral data must be carefully integrated and synthesized to allow medically appropriate management of the disease. Given the need to combine data and information into a coherent whole and then disseminate these findings to decision-makers in a timely fashion, the benefits of ICT to support physician decision-making and other stakeholders throughout the healthcare system are clear (Wickramasinghe et al. 2005b). In fact, we see the proliferation of many technologies such as HER (health electronic records), PACS (picture archive computerized systems), CDSS (clinical decision support systems), etc.

However, and paradoxically, the more investment in ICT by healthcare organizations, the more global health care appears to be hampered by information chaos, which in turn leads to inferior decision-making, ineffective and inefficient operations, exponentially increasing costs, and even loss of life (Wickramasinghe et al. 2005b; Wickramasinghe 2008a). We believe the reason for this lies in the essentially platform-centric application of ICT within health care to date, which at the micro

N. Wickramasinghe (✉)
Health Informatics Management Unit, Epworth HealthCare, Richmond, VIC, Australia

Faculty of Health, Deakin University, Melbourne, VIC, Australia
e-mail: n.wickramasinghe@deakin.edu.au

J. Choi
Yale University, New Haven, CT, USA

J. L. Schaffer
Faculty of Health, Deakin University, Melbourne, VIC, Australia

Cleveland Clinic, Cleveland, OH, USA

N. Wickramasinghe, J. L. Schaffer (eds.), *Theories to Inform Superior Health Informatics Research and Practice*, Healthcare Delivery in the Information Age,
https://doi.org/10.1007/978-3-319-72287-0_20

level do indeed bring some benefits, but at the macro level only add to the problem by creating islands of automation and information silos that hinder rather than enable and facilitate the smooth and seamless flow of relevant information to any decision-maker when and where such information is required.

In order to understand the role for technology in healthcare delivery, it is first important to understand the unique aspects of the healthcare industry, the key challenges, and the components of the healthcare value proposition. Unlike most other industries, health care has the unique structure that the receiver of the services (i.e., the patient) is often not the predominant payer for those services (i.e., the insurance company or government). Moreover, any healthcare intervention is complex and typically involves directly or indirectly a multiplicity of players including providers, payers, patients, and regulators. This then leads to many economic dilemmas such as moral hazard, orthogonal considerations pertaining to cost versus quality, and information asymmetry which in turn have the potential to create obstacles in an attempt to deliver efficient and effective health care (Wickramasinghe and Silvers 2003; Wickramasinghe et al. 2006; von Lubitz and Wickramasinghe 2006a). In order to ameliorate these problems, relevant data, pertinent information, and germane knowledge play a vital role and can only be obtained via the prudent structure and design of technology (Wickramasinghe and Schaffer 2006; Wickramasinghe 2007a, 2008b). Of equal significance are the major challenges facing today's healthcare organizations, i.e., demographic challenges, technology challenges, and finance challenges (Wickramasinghe and Schaffer 2006; Wickramasinghe 2007a, 2008b; von Lubitz and Wickramasinghe 2006b).

Demographic challenges are reflected by longer life expectancy and an aging population; technology challenges include incorporating advances that keep people younger and healthier; and finance challenges are exacerbated by the escalating costs of treating everyone with the latest technologies. Healthcare organizations should respond to these challenges by focusing on three key solution strategies, which taken together form the healthcare value proposition (Wickramasinghe 2008b), namely:

1. Access—caring for anyone, anytime, anywhere, and when and where the patient requests
2. Quality—offering world-class care and establishing integrated information repositories
3. Value—providing effective and efficient healthcare delivery at minimal cost

These three components are interconnected such that they continually impact on the other and all are necessary to meet the key challenges facing healthcare organizations today. In such a context, it is only through the judicious application of technology solutions that superior healthcare delivery can be effected (Wickramasinghe et al. 2005b; Wickramasinghe 2008b).

Recognizing the need for technology solutions does not in and of itself translate into realizing the full potential afforded by the technology. To truly realize the full potential, it is imperative to understand the healthcare technology paradigm, develop a sustainability model for the effective use of technology in a specific context, and then successfully design and implement the patient-centric technology solution. Many of the problems with technology use are connected to the platform-centric nature of these systems and the fact that they cannot support seamless transfer of data and information. This challenge, on top of already inferior healthcare processes, leads to the realizing of inferior, not superior, healthcare delivery. Hence, it is of paramount importance to focus on designing effective and efficient healthcare processes enabled with technology to support the delivery of superior health care and thus better access, quality, and value.

To address this current and significant chasm facing healthcare delivery in the United States, the proposed paper will serve to integrate key management theories and outline the importance of embracing the tools, technologies, tactics, and techniques of knowledge management in order to design a ubiquitous healthcare grid. This new network-centric paradigm, which is grounded in a process-oriented view of KM (knowledge management) and the seminal work of von Lubitz and Wickramasinghe (2005a, 2006b), Boyd and COL USAF (1987), and Wickramasinghe et al. (2009a) is essential to provide a robust technology infrastructure capable of enabling seamless transfer of necessary healthcare information to whom it is needed when it is needed so that superior patient-centric healthcare delivery will ensue and the US healthcare system will once again regain its premier status.

20.2 Process-Oriented Knowledge Generation

Knowledge management is a relatively recent management technique designed to make sense of this information chaos by applying strategies, structures, and techniques to apparently unrelated and seemingly irrelevant data elements so that germane knowledge can be extracted (Wickramasinghe et al. 2005b; Wickramasinghe and Schaffer 2006; Wickramasinghe 2007a, 2008a, b; von Lubitz and Wickramasinghe 2005a). This knowledge can then serve, in support of decision-making, effective and efficient operations as well as enable an organization to reach a state of information superiority. Critical to knowledge management is the application of ICT [ibid]. However, it is the configuration of these technologies that is important to support the techniques of knowledge management.

Within knowledge management, the two predominant approaches to knowledge generation are people centric and technology centric (von Lubitz and Wickramasinghe 2005a; Wickramasinghe 2005; Bali et al. 2009). A people-oriented perspective draws from the work of Nonaka as well as Blacker and Spender (von Lubitz and Wickramasinghe 2005a; Wickramasinghe 2005; Bali et al. 2009; Nonaka and Nishiguchi 2001; Nonaka 1994; Newell et al. 2002). Essential to this perspective of knowledge creation is that knowledge is created by people and that new knowledge or the increasing of the extant knowledge base occurs as a result of human cognitive activities and the effecting of specific knowledge transformations [ibid], Fig. 20.1a.

The processes of creating and capturing knowledge, irrespective of the specific philosophical orientation (i.e., Lockean/Leibnitzian versus Hegelian/Kantian), are the central focus of both the psychosocial (people) and algorithmic (technology) theories of knowledge creation. However, to date, knowledge creation has tended to be approached from one or the other perspective, rather than a holistic, combined perspective (von Lubitz and Wickramasinghe 2005a; Wickramasinghe 2005; Bali et al. 2009). Figure 20.1a highlights the essential aspects of the three well-known psychosocial knowledge creation theories, namely, Nonaka's knowledge spiral and Spender's and Blackler's respective frameworks, into one integrative framework by showing that it is possible to change the form of knowledge, i.e., transform existing tacit knowledge into new explicit knowledge and existing explicit knowledge into new tacit knowledge or to transform the subjective form of knowledge into the

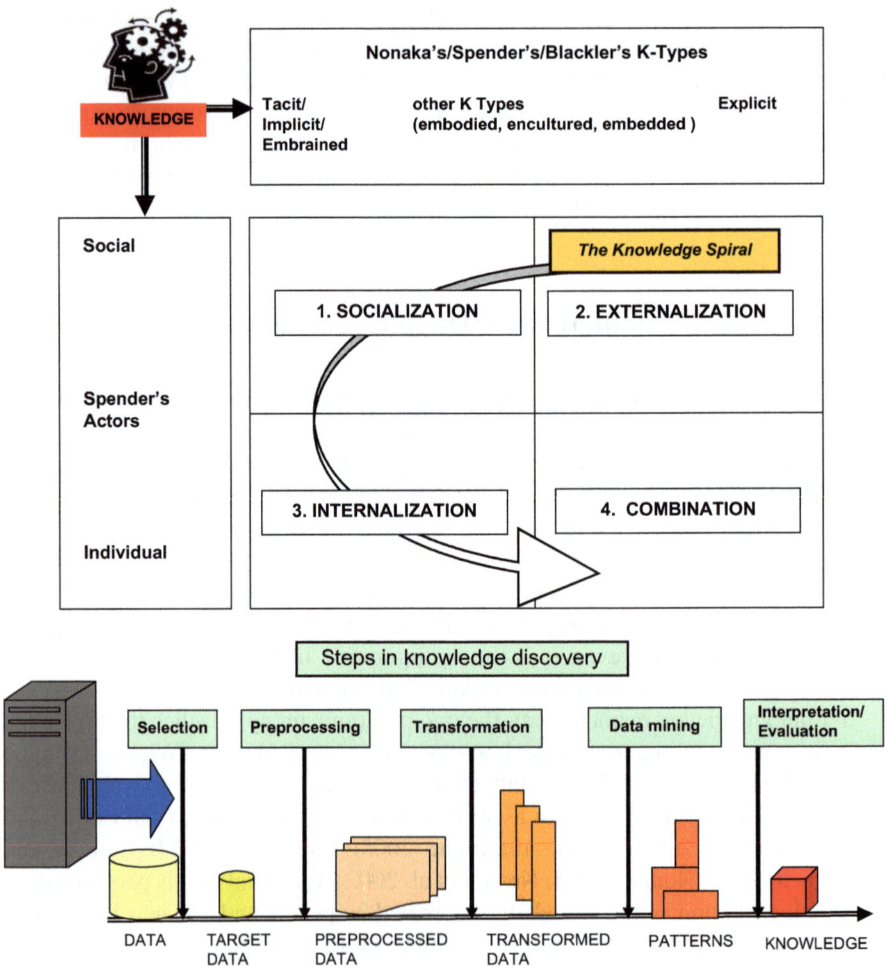

Fig. 20.1 (**a**) People perspective of knowledge generation. (**b**) Technical perspective of knowledge generation. (**c**) Process perspective of knowledge generation. Adapted from Bali et al. (2009)

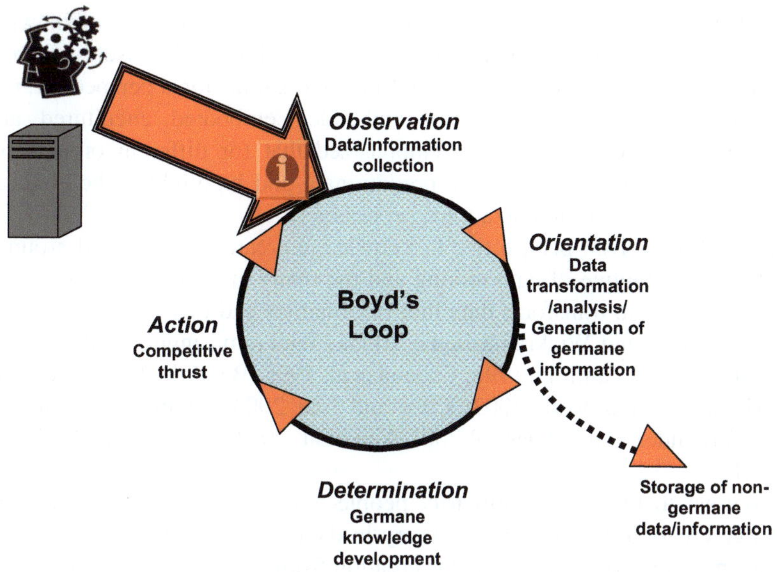

Fig. 20.1 (continued)

objective form of knowledge (von Lubitz and Wickramasinghe 2005a; Wickramasinghe 2005; Bali et al. 2009).

In effecting such transformations, the extant knowledge base as well as the amount and utilization of the knowledge within the organization increases. According to Nonaka (1994):

1. Tacit to tacit (socialization) knowledge transformation usually occurs through apprenticeship-type relations where the teacher or master passes on the skill to the apprentice.
2. Explicit to explicit (transformation) knowledge transformation usually occurs via formal learning of facts.
3. Tacit to explicit (externalization) knowledge transformation usually occurs when there is an articulation of nuances; for example, as in health care if a renowned surgeon is questioned as to why he does a particular procedure in a certain manner, by his articulation of the steps the tacit knowledge becomes explicit.
4. Explicit to tacit (internalization) knowledge transformation usually occurs as new explicit knowledge is internalized; it can then be used to broaden, reframe, and extend one's tacit knowledge.

The two other primarily people-driven theories that focus on knowledge creation as a central theme are Spender's and Blackler's respective frameworks (von Lubitz and Wickramasinghe 2005a; Wickramasinghe 2005; Bali et al. 2009; Newell et al. 2002). Spender draws a distinction between individual knowledge and social knowledge, each of which he claims can be implicit or explicit [ibid]. Spender's definition of implicit knowledge corresponds to Nonaka's tacit knowledge. However, unlike Spender,

Nonaka doesn't differentiate between individual and social dimensions of knowledge; rather he just focuses on the nature and types of the knowledge itself. In contrast, Blackler [ibid] views knowledge creation from an organizational perspective, noting that knowledge can exist as encoded, embedded, embodied, encultured, and/or "embrained." In addition, Blackler emphasized that for different organizational types, different types of knowledge predominate and highlighted the connection between knowledge and organizational processes [ibid].

A technology-driven perspective to knowledge creation is centered around the computerized technique of data mining and the many mathematical and statistical methods available to transform data into information and then meaningful knowledge (von Lubitz and Wickramasinghe 2005a; Wickramasinghe 2005; Bali et al. 2009; Adriaans and Zantinge 1996; Cabena et al. 1998; Bendoly 2003; Fayyad et al. 1996; Holsapple and Joshi 2002; Choi and Lee 2003; Chung and Gray 1999; Becerra-Fernandez and Sabherwal 2001; Yen et al. 2004; Award and Ghaziri 2004; Fig. 20.1b).

In contrast to the above, primarily people-oriented frameworks pertaining to knowledge creation, knowledge discovery in databases (KDD), and more specifically data mining approach knowledge creation from a primarily technology-driven perspective. In particular, the KDD process focuses on how data is transformed into knowledge by identifying valid, novel, potentially useful, and ultimately understandable patterns in data (von Lubitz and Wickramasinghe 2005a; Wickramasinghe 2005; Bali et al. 2009; Adriaans and Zantinge 1996; Cabena et al. 1998; Bendoly 2003; Fayyad et al. 1996; Holsapple and Joshi 2002; Choi and Lee 2003; Chung and Gray 1999; Becerra-Fernandez and Sabherwal 2001; Yen et al. 2004; Award and Ghaziri 2004). KDD is primarily used on data sets for creating knowledge through model building or by finding patterns and relationships in data using various techniques drawn from computer science, statistics, and mathematics. From an application perspective, data mining and KDD are often used interchangeably. Figure 20.1b presents a generic representation of a typical knowledge discovery process. Knowledge creation in a KDD project usually starts with data collection or data selection, covering almost all steps in the KDD process; the first three steps of the KDD process (i.e., selection, preprocessing, and transformation) are considered exploratory data mining, whereas the last two steps (i.e., data mining and interpretation/evaluation) in the KDD process are considered predictive data mining.

Unlike the aforementioned approaches, a process-centric approach to knowledge creation not only combines the essentials of both the people-centric and technology-centric perspectives but also emphasizes the dynamic and ongoing nature of the process. Process-centered knowledge generation is grounded in the pioneering work of Boyd and his OODA Loop, a conceptual framework that maps out the critical process required to support rapid decision-making and extraction of critical and germane knowledge (von Lubitz and Wickramasinghe 2005a; Boyd and COL USAF 1987; Wickramasinghe et al. 2009a; Wickramasinghe 2005; Bali et al. 2009). Colonel Boyd initially focused on the art of air warfare and the need to develop situational awareness, assess the options available, and make the critical decision to remaining airborne while the enemy became embedded in the terrain below. In fact, this seminal decision model had applicability to warfare, management, and many other operational situations.

The OODA loop is based on a cycle of four interrelated stages essential to support critical analysis and rapid decision-making that revolve in both time and space: observation followed by orientation, then by decision, and finally action (OODA). At the observation and orientation stages, implicit and explicit inputs are gathered or extracted from the environment (observation) and converted into coherent information (orientation). The latter determines the sequential determination (knowledge generation) and action (practical implementation of knowledge) steps [ibid], Fig. 20.1c. The outcome of the action stage then affects, in turn, the character of the starting point (observation) of the next revolution in the forward progression of the rolling loop.

Given that health care is such a knowledge-rich environment that requires rapid decision-making to take place that has far-reaching consequences, a process-centered approach to knowledge generation is most relevant and forms the conceptual framework for network-centric healthcare operations.

20.3 Network-Centric Healthcare Operations

Health care, like all activities conducted in complex operational space, affects and requires the functioning of three distinct entities, i.e., people, process, and technology. To capture this dynamic triad that continually impacts all healthcare operations, the doctrine of healthcare network-centric operations is built around three entities that form mutually interconnected and functionally related domains. Specifically, these domains include (von Lubitz and Wickramasinghe 2006a, b):

1. A physical domain that represents the current state of healthcare reality that encompasses the structure of the entire environment healthcare operations intend to influence directly or indirectly, e.g., elimination of disease, fiscal operations, political environment, patient and personnel education, etc. and also has data within it that are the easiest to collect and analyze, especially that they relate to the present rather than future state.
2. An information domain that contains all elements required for generation, storage, manipulation, dissemination/sharing of information, and its transformation and dissemination/sharing as knowledge in all its forms.
3. A cognitive domain that constitutes all human factors that affect operations.

It is within the cognitive domain that deep situational awareness is created, judgments made, and decisions and their alternatives are formulated.

In essence, these domains cumulatively serve to capture and then process all data and information from the environment, and given the dynamic nature of the environment, new information and data must always be uploaded. Thus, the process is continuous in time and space captured by the "rolling nature" of Boyd's OODA Loop, i.e., grounded in the process-oriented perspective of knowledge generation.

20.4 ICT Use in Healthcare Network-Centric Operations

The critical technologies for supporting healthcare network-centric operations are not new, rather they are reconfigurations of existing technologies including web and Internet technologies. The backbone of the network is provided by a healthcare information grid (von Lubitz and Wickramasinghe 2006a, b; Wickramasinghe et al. 2009a). Figure 20.2 depicts the essential grid architecture.

The three essential elements of the grid architecture are the smart portal which provides the entry point to the network, the analytic node, and the intelligent sensors (von Lubitz and Wickramasinghe 2006a, b). Taken together these elements make up the knowledge enabling technologies to support and effect critical data, information, and knowledge exchanges that in turn serve to ensure effective and efficient healthcare operations.

In network-centric healthcare operations, the entry point or smart portal must provide the decision-maker with pertinent information and germane knowledge constructed through the synthesis and integration of a multiplicity of data points, i.e., support and enable OODA thinking. Unlike current web pages in general and especially current medical web portals and online databases such as MEDLINE that provide the decision-maker with large amounts of information that he/she must then synthesize and determine relative and general relevance, i.e., they are passive in nature, the smart portal enables the possibility to access the critical information required to formulate the action (practical implementation) stage of Boyd's Loop.

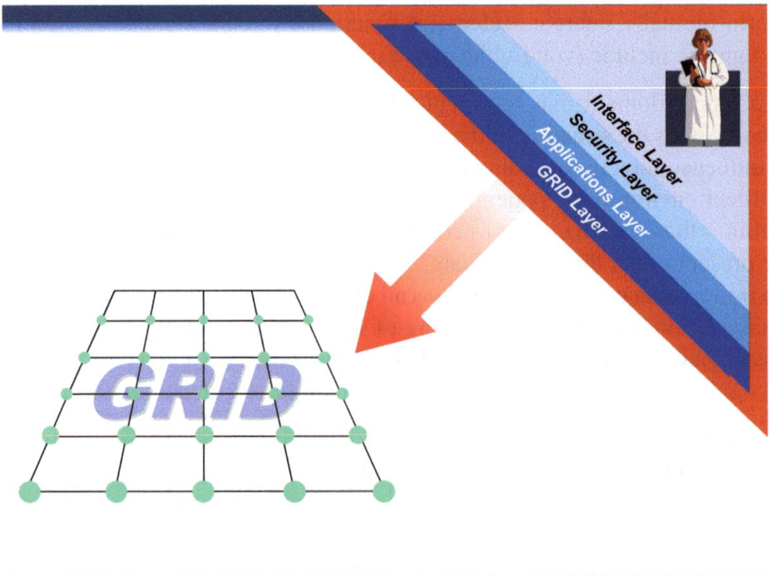

Fig. 20.2 Schematic for Network Centric HealthCare Operations. Adapted from Bali et al. (2009)

In addition, the smart portal includes the ability to navigate well through the grid system; i.e., the smart portal must have a well-structured grid map to identify what information is coming from where (or what information is being uploaded to where). In order to support the ability of the smart portal to bring all relevant information and knowledge located throughout the grid system to the decision-maker, there must be universal standards and protocols that ensure the free-flowing and seamless transfer of information and data throughout the healthcare information grid, the ultimate in shared services. Finally, given the total access to healthcare information grid provided by the smart portal to the decision-maker, it is vital that the highest level of security protocols are maintained at all times, thereby ensuring the integrity of healthcare information grid. Figure 20.3 captures all these key elements of the smart portal.

The analytic nodes of the healthcare information grid perform all the major intelligence and analysis functions and must incorporate the many tools and technologies of artificial intelligence and business analytics including OLAP (online analytical processing), genetic algorithms, neural networks, and intelligent agents in order to continually assimilate and analyze critical data and information throughout the grid system and/or within a particular domain. The primary role of these analytic nodes is to enable the systematic and objective process of integrating and sorting information or support the orientation stage of Boyd's Loop. Although we discuss the functional elements of the analytic node separately, it is important to stress that the analytic node is in fact part of the smart portal. In fact, the presence of the analytic node is one of the primary reasons that the smart portal is indeed "smart" or active rather than its more passive distant cousin the integrated e-portal that dominates many intranet and extranet sites of e-businesses today.

The final important technology element of the healthcare information grid is the intelligent sensor. These sensors are essentially expert systems or other intelligent detectors programmed to identify changes to healthcare information grid and data and/or information within a narrow and well-defined spectrum, such as an unusually high outbreak of anthrax in a localized geographic region, which would send a message of a possible bioterrorism attack warning to the analytic node or perhaps the possibility of spurious or corrupt data entering the healthcare information grid system. The sensors are not necessarily part of the smart portal and can be located throughout healthcare information grid independent of the analytic nodes and smart portals Figure 20.3 depicts the three essential technical components of healthcare information grid.

20.5 Knowledge Development, Support, and Dissemination

When the articular surfaces of a patient's knee degenerate, the patient's mobility becomes painful and limited. As with the tires on a car, the more mileage driven and the harder the driving and the rougher the road's surface, the tire tread becomes worn. Replacing the tires and replacing the knee's articular surfaces are comparable

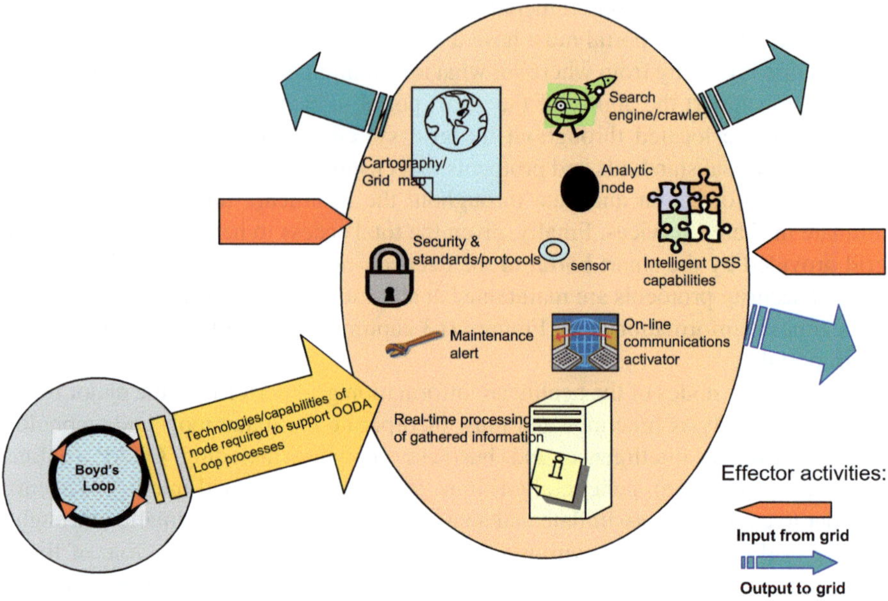

Fig. 20.3 Smart portal (adapted from Bali et al. 2009)

in general concept. Certain tires match with certain vehicles, certain types of roads, and certain driving demands. The same is true for patients to some extent. Knowing the patient's attributes is critical to achieving an optimal outcome after knee replacement. Patients with advanced degeneration of their hips and knees can have their function improved and the pain alleviated with arthroplasty of the knee in which the articular surfaces of the femur, tibia, and patella are replaced with implants.

The OODA loop applies to knee arthroplasty as it does to air warfare. The arthroplasty orthopedic surgeon must observe the patient during the history and exam phase; must orient by synthesizing all of the data obtained during those phases; must make decisions based on the data from those phases and the patient's medical, surgical, and medication history; and must act accordingly. That latter activity includes designing a perioperative course that will mitigate and manage the patient's comorbidities; prescribe a preoperative course of activities that will optimize the postoperative course; schedule the surgery with the recommended anesthetic technique, equipment, implants, and personnel; and start the postoperative phase planning including any hospital stay, postoperative monitoring, discharge planning including physical therapy and weight bearing, and assistive device demands.

Prior to the day of surgery when the operation begins in the operating room, there are a large number of interdependent specific processes that must be completed. Each process requires data input and produces a data output such as patient history, diagnostic tests, and consultations. Keeping the process moving for each patient and maintaining a full schedule for the surgeon and the hospital are challenges that require accurate and timely information for successful process completion and achieving the goals for each patient, surgeon, and the hospital simultaneously (Wickramasinghe et al. 2009b).

Scheduling and executing an operative procedure represents an ideal opportunity for the application of the OODA loop and knowledge management techniques. All of the requisite data elements are not always maximized or, in many cases, not collected in advance of the procedure. One of the authors (JLS) has developed a knowledge-based approach to evaluation and scheduling that collects the requisite data during the initial clinical evaluation; mitigates the clinical issues in advance of the procedure; determines, schedules, and broadcasts to the team the personnel, equipment, and plan for surgery; and also determines and schedules the postoperative plans including discharge disposition and rehabilitation plan before the procedure.

This system has proven effective by identifying crucial variances, minimizing those variances, and helping to address those variances when they do inevitably occur.

The interaction between these data elements is not always maximized in terms of operating room scheduling and completion of the procedure. Surgeons are experiencing little change in system capacity, but are being told to improve efficiency and output, improve procedure time, and eliminate redundancy. As each of the individual processes is often dependent on a previous event, the capture of event and process data in a data warehouse is necessary in order to evaluate past events based on actual events, i.e., the data, and then make systematic improvements. The diagnostic evaluation of this data set and the reengineering of each of the deficient processes will then lead to increased efficiency. Prescriptive reengineering is then possible using the OODA loop evaluations in combination with existing knowledge and data mining techniques to examine the clinical and business processes. The care continuum can be evaluated and scrutinized to improve the efficiency and quality of the process, and value would thus be maximized (Wickramasinghe et al. 2009b).

20.6 Discussion and Conclusion

At its most fundamental, and maybe also the most naïve, health care is about assuring and maintaining individual's adequate level of health necessary to function as a fully capable member of the society. In reality, health care, particularly in its global context, became a business growing at an unprecedented rate, where global disparities in healthcare delivery become increasingly more apparent, where technology emphasizes them rather than assists in their obliteration, and where the current expenditure of trillions of dollars yearly appears to have no impact at all. Part of the problem rests with the fact that the majority (if not all) solutions to the healthcare crisis are, essentially, platform-centric, i.e., concentrated on the highly specific needs of a specialty (e.g., molecular biology), an organization (e.g., hospital), or a politically defined region (e.g., US or EU). Hence, most of the technology-based solutions, while highly functional and of unquestionable benefit to their users, fail to act as collaborative tools assisting in the unification rather than subdivision of effort. Highly useful information generated within individual systems is, for all practical purposes, lost since it is inaccessible to others either because of its incompatibility with different operational platforms or simply because others are not even aware of its existence! The latter issue becomes particularly significant when relevant information exists within healthcare-unrelated domains.

We believe that adoption of the network-centric approach that is integrally connected to the process perspective of knowledge management may provide at least part of the solution, especially at the worldwide level of health care. The concept is not new. In 1994, Lindberg described a vision of global information infrastructure based on extensive implementation and exploitation of US leadership in high-performance computing, networking, and communications in developing a large-scale, technology-based approach to health care (Lindberg 1994). During the same decade, the US Department of Defense, followed by military establishments worldwide, adopted the notion of network-centric operations as the most viable solution to the ever-increasing complexity of military operations (Alberts et al. 2000). Similar concepts are brought to life in multilayered, dynamic business activities (Wickramasinghe 2003). Healthcare operations are equally complex, if not more so, than either business or military ones. Their information/knowledge needs are equally multispectral and intense. And while health care is, indeed, about providing an individual with easy access to healthcare provider and providing the provider with tools to provide adequate health care, it all takes place in a vastly more complicated environment of economies, policies, and politics and, far too frequently, conflicts. We believe, therefore, that in similarity to the two other fields of human activity to which health care is (maybe unfortunately) also related—business and war—health care needs to expand its incursion into the world of ICT to the concept of network centricity and pursue it with utmost vigor. As already demonstrated in practice [ibid], network-centric operations increase efficiency, reduce cost, and increase chance of success. All of these are of critical importance in the conduct of a single, most expensive, and yet significantly inefficient activity known to humankind—the conduct of global healthcare operations.

Acknowledgment Rajeev K Bali for his helpful insights on early drafts of this chapter.

References

Adriaans, P., & Zantinge, D. (1996). *Data mining*. Boston: Addison-Wesley.

Alberts, D. S., Garstka, J. J., & Stein, F. P. (2000). *Network centric warfare: Developing and leveraging information superiority* (pp. 1–284). Washington, DC: CCRP Publication Series (Dept. of Defense). Retrieved from http://www.dodccrp.org/publications/pdf/Alberts_NCW.pdf.

Award, E., & Ghaziri, H. (2004). *Knowledge management*. Upper Saddle River: Prentice Hall.

Bali, R., Wickramasinghe, N., & Lehany, B. (2009). *KM primer*. Hoboken, NJ: Routledge.

Becerra-Fernandez, I., & Sabherwal, R. (2001). Organizational knowledge management: A contingency perspective. *Journal of Management Information Systems, 18*(1), 23–55.

Bendoly, E. (2003). Theory and support for process frameworks of knowledge discovery and data mining from ERP systems. *Information Management, 40*, 639–647.

Boyd, J. R., & COL USAF. (1987). *Patterns of conflict, unpublished briefing*. Accessible as essence of winning and losing, from http://www.d-n-i.net

Cabena, P., Hadjinian, P., Staler, R., Verhees, J., & Zanasi, A. (1998). *Discovering data mining from concept to implementation*. Upper Saddle River: Prentice Hall.

Choi, B., & Lee, H. (2003). An empirical investigation of KM styles and their effect on corporate performance. *Information Management, 40*, 403–417.

Chung, M., & Gray, P. (1999). Special section: Data mining. *Journal of Management Information Systems, 16*(1), 11–16.

Fayyad, U., Piatetsky-Shapiro, G., & Smyth, P. (1996). From data mining to knowledge discovery: An overview. In U. Fayyad, G. Piatetsky-Shapiro, P. Smyth, & R. Uthurusamy (Eds.), *Advances in knowledge discovery and data mining*. Menlo Park, CA: AAAI Press/The MIT Press.

Holsapple, C., & Joshi, K. (2002). Knowledge manipulation activities: Results of a Delphi study. *Information Management, 39*, 477–490.

Lindberg, D. (1994). Global information infrastructure. *International Journal of Bio-Medical Computing, 34*(1-4), 13–19.

Newell, S., Robertson, M., Scarbrough, H., & Swan, J. (2002). *Managing knowledge work*. New York: Palgrave.

Nonaka, I. (1994). A dynamic theory of organizational knowledge creation. *Organization Science, 5*, 14–37.

Nonaka, I., & Nishiguchi, T. (2001). *Knowledge emergence*. Oxford: Oxford University Press.

von Lubitz, D., & Wickramasinghe, N. (2005a). Creating germane knowledge in dynamic environments. *International Journal of Innovation Learning, 3*(3), 326.

von Lubitz, D., & Wickramasinghe, N. (2006a). Key challenges and policy implications for governments and regulators in a networkcentric healthcare environment. *International Journal of Electronic Government, 3*(2), 204–224.

von Lubitz, D., & Wickramasinghe, N. (2006b). Healthcare and technology: The doctrine of networkcentric healthcare. *International Journal of Electronic Healthcare, 4*, 322–344.

Wickramasinghe, N. (2003). Do we practice what we preach: Are knowledge management systems in practice truly reflective of knowledge management systems in theory? *Business Process Management Journal, 9*(3), 295–316.

Wickramasinghe, N. (2005). Knowledge creation: A meta-framework. *International Journal of Innovation and Learning, 3*(5), 558.

Wickramasinghe, N. (2007a). A web-based knowledge management system for cardiovascular disease. *International Journal of Biomedical Engineering and Technology, 1*(2), 111–127.

Wickramasinghe, N. (2007b). Fostering knowledge assets in healthcare with the KMI model. *International Journal of Management and Enterprise Development, 4*(1), 52–65.

Wickramasinghe, N. (2008a). The health care intelligence continuum: Key model for enabling KM initiatives and realising the full potential of SMT in healthcare delivery. *International Journal of Biomedical Engineering and Technology, 1*(4), 415–427.

Wickramasinghe, N. (2008b). From data to decisions: A knowledge management approach for productivity increase in a radiology department. *International Journal of Biomedical Engineering and Technology, 1*(3), 259–272.

Wickramasinghe, N., Bali, R., Lehany, B., Gibbons, C., & Schaffer, J. (2009a). *HCKM primer*. Hoboken, NJ: Routledge.

Wickramasinghe, N., Bali, R. K., Gibbons, M. C., Choi, J. H. J., & Schaffer, J. L. (2009b). A systematic approach: Optimization of healthcare operations with knowledge management. *Journal of Healthcare Information Management, 23*, 44–50.

Wickramasinghe, N., Bloomendal, H., de Bruin, A., & Krabbendam, K. (2005a). Enabling innovative healthcare delivery through the use of the focused factory model: The case of the spine clinic of the future. *International Journal of Innovation and Learning, 2*(1), 90–110.

Wickramasinghe, N., Geisler, E., & Schaffer, J. (2005b). Realizing the value proposition for healthcare by incorporating km strategies and data mining techniques with the use of infor-

mation communication technologies. *International Journal of Healthcare Technology and Management, 7*(3/4), 303–318.
Wickramasinghe, N., Misra, S., Jenkins, A., & Vogel, D. (2006). The competitive forces facing e-health. *International Journal of Healthcare Information Systems and Informatics, 1*(4), 68–81.
Wickramasinghe, N., & Schaffer, J. (2006). Creating knowledge driven healthcare processes with the intelligence continuum. *International Journal of Electronic Healthcare, 2*(2), 164–174.
Wickramasinghe, N., & Silvers, J. B. (2003). IS/IT the prescription to enable medical group practices to manage managed care. *Health Care Management Science, 6*(2), 75–86.
Yen, D., Chou, D., & Cao, J. (2004). Innovation in information technology: Integration of web and database technologies. *International Journal of Innovation and Learning, 1*(2), 143–157.

Chapter 21
The Impact of Impaired Executive Functions of ADHD Adults on the Use of IS: Psychologists' Perceptions

Bader Binhadyan and Nilmini Wickramasinghe

21.1 Introduction

The use of IS in mental health often called e-mental health (eMH) has introduced tools that are able to enhanced treatment and enable early interventions for common mental health issues (Lal and Carol 2014; Musiat and Tarrier 2014). eMH has the ability to improve accessibility, reduce cost, provide treatment flexibility, and offer better consumer interactivity and engagement (Lal and Carol 2014). Furthermore, eMH can enhance other tools and services that overcome issues that already exist in the current mental health service care delivery. These include improving lack of access due to location, time, or financial difficulties (Booth et al. 2004; Whittaker et al. 2012), reducing stigma incurred by seeing a therapist (Christensen and Ian 2010; Burns et al. 2010), and improving the therapists' time and efficacy (Jorm et al. 2007, 2013).

eMH provides treatments, interventions, and support to people with different mental disorders through assistive technology such as short message service (SMS), email, website, chat/instant messaging (IM) tools, social media, video/audio over the Internet, as well as smartphones and tablets (Anthony et al. 2010; Christensen and Katherine 2013; e-Mental Health Alliance 2014; Whittaker et al. 2012). However, Lal and Carol (2014) also notes that eMH has a number of disadvantages that might affect the implementation of eMH programs, which lack quality control and accessibility and are limited to people who are familiar with using technology.

B. Binhadyan
Health Informatics Management Unit, Epworth HealthCare, Richmond, VIC, Australia

N. Wickramasinghe (✉)
Health Informatics Management Unit, Epworth HealthCare, Richmond, VIC, Australia

Faculty of Health, Deakin University, Melbourne, VIC, Australia
e-mail: n.wickramasinghe@deakin.edu.au

N. Wickramasinghe, J. L. Schaffer (eds.), *Theories to Inform Superior Health Informatics Research and Practice*, Healthcare Delivery in the Information Age,
https://doi.org/10.1007/978-3-319-72287-0_21

Table 21.1 Impaired executive functions associated with ADHD by (Brown 2006, 2008)

EF cluster	Functions
Activation	Task initiation, organization, prioritization, time estimation
Focus	Focusing, sustaining, or shifting attention to tasks
Effort	Regulating alertness, sustaining effort, and processing speed
Emotion	Managing frustration and regulating emotions
Memory	Storing and retrieving information and utilizing working memory
Action	Self-regulation and self-monitoring

Notwithstanding these disadvantages, there appears to be a great potential for eMH in the context of young adults with mental disorders (Burns et al. 2010; Webb et al. 2008) such as attention deficit hyperactivity disorder (ADHD).

ADHD is a neurodevelopmental disorder, which is characterized by inappropriate persistent symptoms of inattention, hyperactivity, and impulsivity (American Psychiatric Association 2013). Globally, prevalence of ADHD rates is estimated at 3.4% in adults (Fayyad et al. 2007). Inattention is related to issues with concentration; adults with ADHD often display a lower attention span than what it is expected for everyday routine and find it difficult to remain focused a given task (Barkley et al. 2008; Pope 2010). They also appear to make mistakes due to lack of attention to detail or inability to follow directions or remember what the requirements of the tasks were (Barkley et al. 2008) and have issues with initiating and completing a task (Du Paul et al. 2009).

Hyperactivity symptoms in adults are more refined than in childhood, which presents itself as restlessness, racing thoughts, unreasonable talking, or trying to do many things at once (Barkley et al. 2008; Murphy et al. 2002). Lamberg (2003) argues that individuals with ADHD frequently search for high stimulation and have intolerance of boredom. Impulsivity symptoms or having difficulties in self-control which results in acting impulsively without any regard for the consequences are also common symptoms (Okie 2006).

In addition, it has been found among adults with ADHD population that many have obtained less formal education and/or lower performance ranks while in high school (Mannuzza et al. 1998), have higher unemployment, show antisocial behavior, and experience alcohol and drug abuse (Pope 2010), and suffer impairment in executive function (EF). EF is correlated with the underlining issues of ADHD which are associated with differences in the neurobiological structure and function of adults with ADHD brain (Ramsay and Anthony 2007). Brown (2006, 2008) identified six clusters of EF that are associated with ADHD, i.e., activation, focus, effort, emotion, memory, and action. These clusters are outlined in Table 21.1.

The recognized treatment of ADHD is based on multimodal approach which consists of four components: medication, therapy, coaching, and education (NICE 2008). Stimulant medication is commonly used for ADHD (Wilens et al. 2008). Therapy—also known as psychotherapy—is the use of psychological approaches by mental health providers to treat mental health issues. It is focused on assisting a

Table 21.2 Assistive technology tools found in ADHD, the treatment components

Treatment	Tools	References
Coaching	Smartphones or SMS reminder	Prevatt et al. (2011)
	Alarm and computerized reminders (online calendars, email notification)	Young and Jessica (2006)
	Email coaching and time management	Swartz et al. (2005)
Therapy	Neurofeedback therapy	Arns et al. (2009), Arns et al. (2014), Lansbergen et al. (2011), Wang and Hsieh (2013)
	CBT/Internet-based CBT	Pettersson et al. (2014), Wilens et al. (1999), Young and Jessica (2012), Beck et al. (2010), Klingberg et al. (2005), Westerberg et al. (2007)
Education	Informative website for intervention Social media	Murphy (2005), Reijnders et al. (2015)

person to change and overcome issues in his/her life. ADHD coaching is used in executive coaching and life skill coaching which involves time management, organization, and problem solving to help the students to change their behavior and improve social and academic skills (Quinn 2001). In education, it helps adults with ADHD to understand how such a disorder can affect multiple areas of their lives which will result in reducing symptoms, improving functioning, and preventing negative consequences of ADHD (Wender et al. 2001).

However, previous studies have indicated that there are some issues with this current model of treatment. Side effect and limited effectiveness are some of the disadvantages of stimulant medications (Asherson, as cited in Salomone et al. 2016). The other components of the multimodal approach that focuses on the cognitive and behavioral issues can target the underlining issues with ADHD (Chacko et al. 2014), such as EF impairment.

There a number of assistive technology tools used in the treatment of ADHD. Some of the assistive technology tools that have been found in the literature and previous studies are listed in Table 21.2. EF might impact on the successful use of assistive technologies which has influenced this research.

The role of IS in mental health remains in its early stages; therefore, the aim of this research, which is a part of a bigger long-running project, is to explore factors impacting the use of IS in treatments of adults with ADHD. These factors are best examined using a qualitative approach to identify barriers and enablers that might influence the use of IS behavior by clinicians and adults with ADHD. The research gap exists in developing a theory that will employ assistive technology tools and framework to assist in providing better treatment options for individuals with ADHD in Australia. In order to provide a recommendation based on psychologists' perception of the existing issue and after undertaking literature review, the question of this research is "What are the factors impacting the use of IS in adult ADHD treatment?".

21.2 Methodology

The methodology employed to assist in answering the research question is grounded theory described by Strauss and Corbin (1990). This research serves to investigate barriers and enablers of the use of assistive technology tools in the treatment and management of adults with ADHD. Further this research serves to explore the area of IS in mental health, especially in the treatment of adults with ADHD. It is a new emerging area that is not well researched to date and hence fits perfectly with the theoretical nature of grounded theory.

Analysis within the research followed the systematic design in grounded theory. This focuses on the use of the data analysis steps of open, axial, and selective coding suggested. Strauss and Corbin (1990) define a grounded theory as one that is "inductively derived from the study of the phenomenon it represents. That is, it is discovered, developed and provisionally verified through systematic data collection and analysis of data pertaining to that phenomenon. Therefore, data collection, analysis and theory stand in reciprocal relationship with each other" (Strauss and Corbin 1990, p. 23).

Qualitative methods usually produce huge amounts of data which are not in a standard format and are not easily measured, analyzed, and reduced (Yin 2009). Grounded theory has structured analytical processes that allow the researcher to organize these data, finding relationships between them and then providing answers to the research questions. Grounded theory was adopted as lenses of analysis. In addition, Cummings and Elizabeth (2011) note that grounded theory has been seen a powerful tool when it comes to the development of health informatics' frameworks and/or applications. Furthermore, grounded theory, like other forms of qualitative research methods, has key concepts which differentiate this methodology from others. The research will follow the systematic design in grounded theory which focuses on the use of data analysis steps of open, axial, and selective coding.

21.2.1 Data Gathering and Coding

Grounded theory's analytical process consists of three subcoding processes: open coding, axial coding, and selective coding (Strauss and Corbin 1990). During these processes, the coded references were labeled or given a name that carefully describes the selected words, sentence, or paragraph. This serves to ease identification of relationships between concepts and categories. "The greatest tools researchers have to work with are their minds and intuition. The best approach to coding is to relax and let your mind and intuition work for you" (Corbin and Strauss 2008, p. 160).

For this research, 12 psychologists were recruited to participate. The targeted participants were divided in four equal groups. Each group was allocated to a case study and a protocol. The participants were selected based on four dimensions: educational level, years of experience, specialized in ADHD, and offering Internet technology as a treatment tool.

- She/he is specialized in treating adults with ADHD.
- She/he has a minimum of 10 years of experience.
- Offering at least one of IS tools to deliver his/her services, i.e., Skype, email, or SMS.

21.2.2 Open Coding

Open coding is the first process to increasing making sense of the gathered data and the first stage of the grounded theory analytical process. The research starts by carefully examining words and phrases of each of the sentences of a paragraph to identify categories from the data without any early perception of concepts. This means setting aside preconceived concepts about what the researcher expects to find and letting the data and interpretation of it guide analysis (Corbin and Strauss 2008).

During this process, the data was broken into discrete parts and closely examined for both differences and similarities which enable fine discrimination and differentiation among categories (Strauss and Corbin 1990); vents, happening, objects, and action/interaction which were found to be conceptually similar in nature or related in meaning were grouped under more abstract concepts termed "categories" (Strauss and Corbin 1998, p. 102).

Corbin and Strauss (2008) remark that "concepts can range from lower-level concepts to higher-level concepts. Higher-level concepts are called categories/themes and categories tell us what a group of lower-level concepts are pointing to or are indicating. All concepts, regardless of level, arise out of the data" (p. 160). "In later analytic steps, such as axial and selective coding, data are reassembled through statements about the nature of relationships among the various categories and their subcategories. These statements of relationship are commonly referred to as a 'hypothesis'" (Strauss and Corbin 1998, p. 103).

21.2.3 Axial Coding

The aim of axial coding process is to start shaping higher-level concepts (core categories/themes) from the open coding process, exploring the relationship between initial concepts. In addition, "The purpose of axial coding is to begin the process of reassembling data that were fractured during open coding. In axial coding, categories are related to their subcategories to form more precise and complete explanations about phenomena" (Strauss and Corbin 1998). Technically, axial coding is done by relating categories to subcategories along the lines of their properties and dimensions, and it looks at how categories crosscut and link.

21.2.4 Selective Coding

The aim of selective coding is to integrate and refine the themes/categories into a theory that justifies the phenomenon being investigated. "Concepts that reach the status of a category are abstractions. They represent the stories of many persons or groups reduced into … highly conceptual terms" (Corbin and Strauss 2008, p. 103).

The first step in integration is to decide upon a core category. The core category represents the main theme of the research and is the concept which all the other concepts will be related to (Corbin and Strauss 2008; Strauss and Corbin 1990). Furthermore, the other categories/themes are integrated around the central category to form a cohesive theory.

21.2.5 Memo

Writing memos is an essential part of doing grounded theory. Memos can include the products of analysis or directions for the analyst. Glaser (1978) referred to memos as "the theorizing write-up of ideas about codes and their relationships as they strike the analyst while coding" (p. 83). They are intended to be conceptual and analytical not descriptive, and they benefit the researcher to be aware of his own potential effects on the data (Strauss and Corbin 1990). Writing memos continuously during the analysis process allows the researcher to investigate, explicate, and theorize the emergent themes.

Memos start in parallel with open coding and are produced continuously in grounded theory from the start of the analysis process until reaching closure (Fernández 2004). Further, they contain the actual products of grounded theory analytical coding processes (open, axial, and selective), or theoretical notes, which may conclude the analysis or keep the analyst's thoughts and ideas about theoretical sampling and other issues (Strauss and Corbin 1998).

Memos are considered the vehicle for creativity for this research journey and can be viewed as the center of ideas and thoughts for the developments of the emergent theory. During different stages of the analysis process, memos develop and grow, and they remain significant documents for this research. This is because they store the development, ideas, thoughts, as well as feelings and hints of this research and researcher. Strauss and Corbin (1998) mention that the risk of failing to remodeling the details of the research without memos is high (Strauss and Corbin 1998). Table 21.3 outlines memo development and task at each coding process of the grounded theory analytical process (Strauss and Corbin 1998).

Table 21.3 Memo involvement and development during the analytical process

Coding	Memos
Open	In this process, memos contain thoughts, impressions, and directions to oneself Initial categories' notes Early concepts that pertain to categories and some dimensions and properties
Axial	The memos during this stage relate to categories and resume developing them based on their dimensions and properties
Selective	The memos throughout this process are theoretical and operational notes which relate to filling in themes and refining the theory

21.3 Findings

This section will present the findings of the data gathered from the 12 interviews with psychologists. The themes that emerged from the analysis of interviews and supporting statements made by participants are outlined. This will provide the basis from which the core themes were theorized. The interrelationships between the themes have been analyzed.

21.3.1 Patient Factors Influencing IS Usability

The essence of this theme is that participants perceive that factors, which are aspects related to common neurobehavioral aspects of ADHD, can impact on the use of IS by adults with ADHD. The analysis of data highlights relationships between adults with ADHD and their use of assistive technology. These factors are classified into two groups which include EF ability attributes. The analysis shows that EF ability factors with adults with ADHD are increased with the use of assistive technology tools, as discussed in Table 21.4. Participants believe that these preference factors have the ability to influence the use of IS in treatment delivery by adults with ADHD.

21.3.1.1 EF Ability Factors

The concept consists of participants' views of the use of IS relying on issues related to EF ability associated with ADHD. The perceived EF ability factors found in the data refer to the cognitive skills that adults with ADHD are required to perform: (1) start, plan, and organize, (2) sustain and shift attention, (3) maintain mood and emotions, (4) regulate and monitor behavior in regard to the task, (5) recall and remember task-related information, and (6) regulate and monitor performance for successful execution of a given task. All of these factors are perceived by participants to influence the use of assistive technology tools as listed in Table 21.4.

Table 21.4 EF abilities and use of assistive technologies

EF ability	Multimodal approach, assistive technologies
Planning and management	Online calendar or to-do lists, clock time, time management personal cloud storage service
Attention	Time alarms, multiple alarms
Emotional control	CBT, ACT
Self-reinforcement	Support and interaction with external factors
Working memory	Multiple alarms, cloud-based applications
Self-regulation	Support and interaction with external factors

Planning and Management

The core of this category contains participants' view of the use of assistive technology tools to assist adults with ADHD with planning and management issues of EF, including poor organizational skills and difficulty prioritizing and activating. Most of the participants perceived the role of assistive technology tools is to represent this EF ability by visualization of perception of time and information. The representation of time is by using clock time pacing and backward planning approach that includes measuring the completion of task by using the predictable way of clock time. For example, they request their clients to calculate travel time between places or make the start point of any task being earlier than the actual starting time. As an example, P1-C2 request their adults with ADHD to calculate travel time between places or make the start point of any task being earlier than the actual starting time.

> Maybe we have to help them put in, instead of aiming to get there at one thirty when they're supposed to be, maybe we say to them, "Aim to get there at one fifteen" because, inevitably–because they run late all the time or things like that.

Majority of participants believe that issues to this EF ability can be assisted by externalizing management skills by using tools to represent management and organization by visualizing the perception of time. These tools include to-do lists, cloud-based file management systems, and location reminders. Cloud storage services are helpful in improving the management and organization skills as reported by the participants. All of these were present in the data, and the following is an example of this.

> Then there's apps, like, to-do lists, which– and there's ones that have avatars … and you get points for kind of doing the things that you need to do.

However, the analysis shows that the issues correlated with this EF ability are perceived by participants to influence the use of assistive technologies by adults with ADHD. Some participants believe that because adults with ADHD are unable to organize tasks and have issues deciding which tasks or project are more important, adopting these assistive technology tools is not going to be useful. Majority of adults with ADHD have difficulties in converting or breaking down process into smaller approach tasks.

> Nine times out of ten–organization, time management, and breaking jobs down into steps... Once they learn to plan on a piece of paper–they learn to plan a time–I'll encourage them to find a calendar.

Attention

Adults with ADHD related issues with their EF ability to focus can be assisted by using assistive technology tools. This includes representation of time and making it physically, visually, and audibly tangible by using clock, alarm systems, or phone reminders. However, the use of tools is believed to be impacted by the level of EF ability to focus, sustain, and shift attention as discussed earlier in this research.

This representation is seen by participants to be useful in improving adults with ADHD issues with attention. Multiple alarm options can improve issues with shifting attentions between tasks as perceived by a participant. Most of the participants believe that providing tools that represent time visually or in audio which provides repeated distraction approach temporarily improves issues related to shifting and sustaining attention. As an example, participant P1-C1 claims that having two alarm systems can improve adults with ADHD's EF ability to switch and shift between tasks.

> Sometimes we put on timers for forty-five minutes, so then we have a forty-five-fifteen kind of work aspect, and then they use timers for forty-five minutes...., so there's this ability to shift between tasks.

However, these issues with difficulties with attention of EF-impaired ADHD are seen by participants to impact the use of assistive technology tools. This level of distractibility is perceived by participants to result in less productive use of these assistive technology tools which impact on adults with ADHD performance of completing tasks using these tools.

> But you have to be careful with these guys [Adults with ADHD] because they will actually find apps for themselves, try them, and then try and fiddle with them.... And it [task] never gets done because they're trying to make it work].

Emotional Control

The analysis shows that adults with ADHD often have issues with regulating emotions of EF which are seen by majority of participants to impact on how adults with ADHD interact with assistive technology tools. Issues with emotion indicate high level of frustration and difficulty in regulation of emotions and mood. The fear emotion or feeling overwhelmed is seen by participants to affect the use of assistive technology tools.

> The more intelligent these guys [Adults with ADHD] are, the more they will go and find all these little bits and pieces to try and make it work and get overwhelmed with all these bits and pieces.

Working Memory

Adults with ADHD have difficulties in recalling and holding information. Visualizing the information to represent working memory ability by using assistive technology. Technologies, such as phone, the Internet, and cloud-based applications, are used to enhance treatments of ADHD and believed by the participants to be beneficial. They can better help issues with working memory. Participants see using multiple alarms can help to improve the multitasking skills and shifting between tasks.

> I think technology is very, very good for Adults with ADHD because with working memory problems you increase the size of working memory by having IT.

Participants believe that assistive technology tools that present their content using only text are not suitable for these individuals. These executive functions can impact on the effectiveness of the use of these tools. As an example, participants who are text heavy will present issues that impact on these assessments' accessibility. As an example, a participant, P1-C3, claims that *MoodGYM*, which is an online CBT tool, is heavy texted which makes it not stabile for ADHD.

> Some of them like MoodGYM are so text heavy and for someone with ADHD it's like—it's great content there, but I don't know anyone with ADHD that's finished it. So that accessibility part again.

Self-Regulation and Motivation

Adults with ADHD often have issues with motivation, self-regulation, and self-monitoring that are related to EF impairment. Participants use assistive technology to represent information related to this ability in a form of feedback or rewards approach. The data analysis shows that creating rewards and positive feedback using assistive technology (e.g., mobile apps) can work as externalized source of motivation. Participants perceive that using IS tools, such as mobile apps, that provide motivational words or visualize the task performance progress. These types of tools encourage adults with ADHD to stay motivated.

> one of my clients showed it to me and it said, "Procrastinate later," and then the little—you know how it says accept or deny on the buttons usually? One says, "Okay, I'm motivated." The other button said, "Stop yelling at me." Okay, so some clients have been finding that that's been very, very useful for them.

Participants believe that feedback on task performance is seen as a useful tool to improve the lack of motivation issues in ADHD. Setting up a feedback approach that allows both clinicians and adults with ADHD to exchange information with regard to task progress can improve issues associated with impaired self-regulation in ADHD.

> they can say, "Yeah, you're on the right track," or, "You're completely missing the point." That can then motivate the behavior much more readily because they're getting the feedback that they need because they can't judge it themselves. Okay?

21.3.1.2 Clinicians Supervision and Mentoring

The data shows that clinicians' supervision and mentoring skills may influence adults with ADHD use of assistive technology. Clinicians' support and supervisions are seen by participants as important elements of clinicians that contribute to the use of these assessments. The analysis shows that majority of participants [who are also clinicians] provide training methods to improve technology skills for adults with ADHD. They also act as a support system that assist adults with ADHD to choose the suitable assistive technology tools to their requirements. This act is seen to improve the level of interaction with technology by encouraging adults with ADHD to choose and try specific assessments.

> Meeting regularly by phone or in person to check in on how the actions that they have undertaken to do have worked and whether they're staying on track.

This impact is believed by some participants to prevent undesirable outcomes that adults with ADHD might face. These outcomes include untrusty assessments or increasing the level of inattention. Most of P/participants see the absence of clinician supervision can impact the use of these assessments and increase the possibility of risk failure and negative outcome.

> don't encourage them to troll the internet, typing in "ADHD" and see what comes up because there's so much misinformation out there and the world is full of people who are self-diagnosed, which doesn't help much.

This level of support is found in the data to be impacted by age of clinicians and knowledge. As an example, a participant, P2-N4, claims that because of his/her age and lack of knowledge about the new available IS-based assessments, he/she will refer their adults with ADHD to his/her kids.

> I don't know much about that technology so I can't tell people about it. I think, you know, I'd have to refer them to my kids.

21.4 External Factors Influencing Use of Assistive Technology

The data shows that external factors refer to individual skills (beyond clinicians and adults with ADHD) that are found in direct environments (home or education or the Internet) of adults with ADHD. Individuals and their skill and environment are listed in Table 21.5. The impact of these factors enhances the adults with ADHD care process.

These include home, clinic, education, and virtual environments, and actors include clinicians, family members, educators, and online users. The analysis shows that the supervision and support and level of awareness of these actors influence the use of IS-based assessments. Participants perceived that although tertiary education provides assistive technology tools for university students with ADHD, education system and structure can influence a negative use of these assessments and negatively impact ADHD performance.

Table 21.5 External factors enhancing the role of IS

Individual	Skills	Environment
Family/friend	Technology literacy Communication	Home
Educator	Awareness Communication	Education
Online user	Communication Support	The Internet

21.4.1 Family Member Support

Family members as an external factor influence adults with ADHD and the use of IS. Family member support is perceived by participants to be a factor that impacts effectiveness of the usability of IS-based assessment. Parental support is a key success factor of treatment for children and adolescents with ADHD, and the absence of this support can present an issue for adults with ADHD.

> Like, if you're targeting university students, then it's going to need to be scaled to a point which is—some individuals, some eighteen year olds, this is their first opportunity to be looking after themselves. They really still are adolescents. It needs to be scaled down, because there's a big difference from an eighteen-year-old, who's for the first time driving to university because mum's always driven them to school.

Some participants believe the support that is provided by a family member can facilitate the adoption of technology in the treatment of adults with ADHD. As an example, a participant, P3-C and E4, claimed that having someone who has knowledge and understanding of the use of technology has facilitated the use of IS-based treatment assessment that she/he introduced to her/his adult with ADHD.

> A couple of people I'm thinking of–they've got partners who are very IT savvy and they've set up other systems in the home that kind of help them stay organized.

21.4.2 Educator Interaction and Awareness

The core of this concept is that educators in the environment of adults with ADHD influence the use of IS-based assessments. Educators in tertiary education are useful for ADHD students. Participants perceive that a good quality educator can improve issues with executive functions, which is found in the analysis to have a positive relationship with the use of assistive technology tools. Technology literacy and ADHD awareness are seen to influence the level of support and acceptance of ADHD students. Participants believe that these assessments improve the performance of these students and provide better human interaction between students and education providers. This interaction is able to improve the level of motivation and behavior of ADHD students.

> Really good tutors often are the savior for a lot of these university people because they'll help them break the tasks down, keep them on track, ask for a draft of, you know, the first part of an assignment.

However, the unstructured way of education which is believed to be a huge challenge for adults with ADHD. Some participants perceive that issues with education structure are positively related to decreased motivation level of adults with ADHD and reduced effectiveness of the use of IS-based assessments.

> So, you know, just the whole, kind of, lecture format doesn't work for them...Then they choose not to attend. "Oh, I can just listen to it online, or whatever." And so then they avoid going to the actual physical lecture and they miss out on really important information experience.

Majority of participants believe that online users in virtual environment of adults with ADHD can influence the use of IS treatment. Connected treatment in socio-technical systems approach can enhance and encourage adults with ADHD to use these assessments. This enhancement is seen by participants as diminishing the sense of isolation and increasing the level of motivation among these individuals. Other available assessments, such as online CBTs, which are not socially connected, can increase the sense of isolation.

> For an online CBT, I think you're going to have to go with something like that has been done for groups because you're targeting the mass... Part of the group, though, is the normalization of it, whereas if it's online, you're still an individual. You're still isolated. Nobody else has this stuff going on for them in their head.

21.5 Discussion

As mentioned, this research is part of a bigger project, and the outcome of this research contributed to the development of a theory of that project. Only two themes have been reported in this research which are attributes of adults with ADHD that impact the use of IS tools, such as assistive technology, and external factors that include this use. These attributes are listed in Table 21.6.

This research has shown that most participants' perception of the current available treatment assistive technology tools that are used by adults with ADHD are beneficial. These tools are used as assistive methods to support the deficit in the EF associated with ADHD. The best use of assistive technology tools can improve issues in impaired EF affected by ADHD. The perceived outcome of using these tools in the treatment of adults with ADHD is outlined in Table 21.7. Furthermore,

Table 21.6 ADHD and IS attributes

Aspect	Attributes
Adult with ADHD	The ability of EF (planning and management, attention, emotional control, self-reinforcement, working memory, and self-regulation)
Technology	Usability, availability, and accessibility

Table 21.7 Factors of the use of IS and EF ability

EF ability	Process	Assistive technology tools	Perceived outcome
Planning and management	Visualization of perception of time and information	Online calendar or to-do lists, clock time, time management personal cloud storage service	Improved organization and time management skills
Attention	Externalizing time visually and audibly	Time alarms, multiple alarms	Improved issues with attention and shifting attention
Emotional control	Relies on the other improved EFs	CBT ACT	Improved issues with high level of frustration
Working memory	Visualizing the information	Multiple alarms, cloud-based applications	Working memory capacity aid
Self-regulation	Visualizing the information	Support and interaction with external factors	Improved motivation

the best use of IS relies on the alignment between the attributes which is more important than the actors' attributes individually. For example, adults with ADHD attributes (adults with ADHD's EF abilities, technology literacy, and skills), and the best alignment is when a technology tool is closely related to the specific impaired EF of a particular individual. The alignment between attributes of adults with ADHD age and gender and of technology usability impact on the use of IS.

The successful use of assistive technology tools relies on the ability of action, attention, and self-regulation of EF associated with adults with ADHD. Some participants argue that the successful use of IS-based technology treatment assessment tools depends on adults with ADHD high level of organization skills and self-regulation aspects and the low level of distractibility of technology tools. Adults with ADHD often have issues with organization skills and have low level of self-regulation.

Any poor alignment between them can negatively impact on the best alignment between ADHD and IS attributes refer to Table 21.7. For instance, the participants perceived that if an adult with ADHD has a deficit in EF ability of planning and management which preventing his/her to priorities or/and break down task into smaller processes, the alignment between ADHD and IS attributes will not meet for their purposes, technology attributes of usability in particular.

The data shows that the enhancement action that most participants employ to improve this poor alignment is by providing cognitive skill coaching and training needed to improve this impaired EF before introducing IS-based technology treatment assessment. This enhancement action is often delivered based on face-to-face or paper-based delivery approach. Most of participants argue that enhancing these issues associated with impairment of EF actors by using paper-based tools is related to the successful use of IS-based assessment.

Consistent with the literature, Roper (2007) conducted a study on online learning and individuals skills, yet the mental health of these students was not indicated in the study. This study showed that the successful use of online learning in general is based on the students' ability to organize themselves. However university students with ADHD have lower motivation in using learning technologies compared to students without disabilities (Parker and Banerjee 2007).

The study also provides an example of the use of grounded theory in an eMH context.

21.6 Conclusion

In conclusion, most of the current IS tools that target adults with ADHD are perceived by participants to be useful. These tools are used as assistive tools by externalizing the EF. These tools are generic tools, such as online calendar, online management and planning tools, alarm, smartphone, GPS, and so on. The participants believe that the functionality of such tools is able to improve issues in the certain areas affected by ADHD. Multiple alarms, for instance, can be able to improve multitasking issues and attention. Calendar and online diary can be used to improve planning difficulties associated with ADHD.

Health EF abilities will increase the chances of successful use of IS in the treatment of adults with ADHD. This means clinicians are recommended to improve the cognitive skills of a patient before or during the introduction of assistive technology tools as perceived by most participants.

References

American Psychiatric Association. (2013). *Diagnostic and statistical manual of mental disorders (DSM-5®)*. Arlington, VA: American Psychiatric.

Anthony, K. N., Merz, D. A., & Goss, S. (2010). *The use of technology in mental health: Applications, ethics and practice*. Springfield, Ill: Charles C Thomas.

Arns, M. D., Sabine, Strehl, U., Breteler, M., & Coenen, A. (2009). Efficacy of neurofeedback treatment in ADHD: The effects on in attention, impulsivity and hyperactivity: A meta-analysis. *Clinical EEG and Neuroscience, 40*(3), 180–189.

Arns, M. H., Hartmut, & Strehl, U. (2014). Evaluation of neurofeedback in ADHD: The long and winding road. *Biological Psychology, 95*, 108–115.

Barkley, R. A., Murphy, K. R., & Fischer, M. (2008). *ADHD in adults:What the science says.* New York: Guilford.

Beck, S. H., Christine, A., Puffenberger, S. S., Benninger, K. L., & Benninger, W. B. (2010). A controlled trial of working memory training for children and adolescents with ADHD. *Journal of Clinical Child & Adolescent Psychology, 39*(6), 825–836.

Booth, M. L., Bernard, D., Quine, S., Kang, M. S., Usherwood, T., Alperstein, G., et al. (2004). Access to health care among Australian adolescents young people's perspectives and their sociodemographic distribution. *Journal of Adolescent Health, 34*(1), 97–103.

Brown, T. E. (2006). Executive functions and attention deficit hyperactivity disorder: Implications of two conflicting views. *International Journal of Disability, Development and Education, 53*(1), 35–46.

Brown, T. E. (2008). ADD/ADHD and impaired executive function in clinical practice. *Current Psychiatry Reports, 10*(5), 407–411.

Burns, J. M., Davenport, T. A., Durkin, L. A., Luscombe, G. M., & Hickie, I. B. (2010). The internet as a setting for mental health service utilisation by young people. *Medical Journal of Australia, 192*(11), S22.

Chacko, A., Kofler, M., & Jarrett, M. (2014). Improving outcomes for youth with ADHD: A conceptual framework for combined neurocognitive and skill-based treatment approaches. *Clinical Child and Family Psychology Review, 17*(4), 368–384.

Christensen, H. H., & Ian, B. (2010). E-mental health: A new era in delivery of mental health services. *Medical Journal of Australia, 192*(11), S2.

Christensen, H. P., & Katherine. (2013). Information technology as the key to accelerating advances in mental health care. *Australian and New Zealand Journal of Psychiatry, 47*(2), 114–116.

Corbin, J., & Strauss, A. (2008). *Basics of qualitative research: Techniques and procedures for developing grounded theory* (3rd ed.). Thousand Oaks, CA: Sage.

Cummings, E. B., & Elizabeth M. (2011). Grounded theory evolution and its application in health informatics. In *Proceedings of the ITCH.*

Du Paul, G. J., Weyandt, L. L., O'Dell, S. M., & Varejao, M. (2009). College students with ADHD. *Journal of Attention Disorders, 13*(3), 234–250.

e-Mental Health Alliance. (2014). *e-Mental Health Services in Australia 2014: Current and future*. Retrieved from online, https://emhalliance.fedehealth.org.au/wp-content/uploads/sites/42/2014/10/e-Mental-Health-in-Australia-2014.pdf

Fayyad, J., De Graaf, R., Kessler, R., Alonso, J., Angermeyer, M., Demyttenaere, K., et al. (2007). Cross–national prevalence and correlates of adult attention–deficit hyperactivity disorder. *The British Journal of Psychiatry, 190*(5), 402–409. https://doi.org/10.1192/bjp.bp.106.034389.

Fernández, W. (2004). The grounded theory method and case study data in IS research: Issues and design. In *Proceedings of the information systems foundations workshop: constructing and criticising.*

Glaser, B. G. (1978). *Theoretical sensitivity: Advances in the methodology of grounded theory* (Vol. 2). Mill Valley, CA: Sociology Press.

Jorm, A. F., Morgan, A. J., & Malhi, G. S. (2013). The future of e-mental health. *Australian and New Zealand Journal of Psychiatry, 47*(2), 104–106.

Jorm, A. F., Wright, A., & Morgan, A. J. (2007). Where to seek help for a mental disorder? *The Medical Journal of Australia, 187*(10), 556–560.

Klingberg, T., Fernell, E., Olesen, P. J., Johnson, M., Gustafsson, P., Dahlström, K., et al. (2005). Computerized training of working memory in children with ADHD-A randomized, controlled trial. *Journal of the American Academy of Child & Adolescent Psychiatry, 44*(2), 177–186.

Lal, S. A., & Carol, E. (2014). e-Mental health: A rapid review of the literature. *Psychiatric Services, 65*(1), 24–32.

Lamberg, L. (2003). ADHD often undiagnosed in adults: Appropriate treatment may benefit work, family, social life. *JAMA, 290*(12), 1565–1567.

Lansbergen, M. M., van Dongen-Boomsma, M., Buitelaar, J. K., & Slaats-Willemse, D. (2011). ADHD and EEG-neurofeedback: A double-blind randomized placebo-controlled feasibility study. *Journal of Neural Transmission, 118*(2), 275–284.

Mannuzza, S., Klein, R. G., Bessler, A., Malloy, P., & La Padula, M. (1998). Adult psychiatrics tatus of hyperactive boys grown up. *The American Journal of Psychiatry, 155*(4), 493–498.

Murphy, K. (2005). Psychosocial treatments for ADHD in teens and adults: A practice-friendly review. *Journal of Clinical Psychology, 61*(5), 607–619.

Murphy, K. R., Barkley, R. A., & Bush, T. (2002). Young adults with attention deficit hyperactivity disorder: Subtype differences incomorbidity, educational, and clinical history. *The Journal of Nervous and Mental Disease, 190*(3), 147–157.

Musiat, P., & Tarrier, N. (2014). Collateral outcomes in e-mental health: A systematic review of the evidence for added benefits of computerized cognitive behavior therapy interventions for mental health. *Psychological Medicine, 44*(15), 3137–3150. https://doi.org/10.1017/S0033291714000245.

NICE. (2008). *Attention deficit hyperactivity disorder: Diagnosis and management.* Retrieved from, https://www.nice.org.uk/guidance/cg72

Okie, S. (2006). ADHD in adults. *New England Journal of Medicine, 354*(25), 2637.
Parker, D. R., & Banerjee, M. (2007). Leveling the digital playing field assessing the learning technology needs of college-bound students with LD and/or ADHD. *Assessment for Effective Intervention, 33*(1), 5–14.
Pettersson, R., Söderström, S., Edlund-Söderström, K., & Nilsson, K. W. (2014). Internet-based cognitive behavioral therapy for adults with ADHD in outpatient psychiatric care. *Journal of Attention Disorders, 21*(6), 508–521.
Pope, D. (2010). The impact of in attention, hyperactivity and impulsivity on academic achievement in UK university students. *Journal of Further and Higher Education, 34*(3), 335–345.
Prevatt, F. L., Georgios, K., Bowles, V., & Garrett, L. (2011). The use of between session assignments in ADHD coaching with college students. *Journal of Attention Disorders, 15*(1), 18–27.
Quinn, P. (2001). *ADD and the college student: A guide for high school and college students with attention deficit disorder*. Washington DC: Magination Press.
Ramsay, J. R., & Anthony, L. (2007). *Cognitive-behavioral therapy for adult ADHD: An integrative psychosocial and medical approach* (1st ed.). Hoboken: Routledge.
Reijnders, J., van Heugten, C., & van Boxtel, M. (2015). Keep your brain fit! a psychoeducational training program for healthy cognitive aging: A feasibility study. *Educational Gerontology, 41*(8), 613–620. https://doi.org/10.1080/03601277.2015.1024554.
Roper, A. R. (2007). How students develop online learning skills. *Educause Quarterly, 30*(1), 62.
Salomone, S., Fleming, G. R., Bramham, J., O'Connell, R. G., & Robertson, I. H. (2016). Neuropsychological deficits in adult ADHD evidence for differential attentional impairments, deficient executive functions, and high self-reported functional impairments. *Journal of Attention Disorders*. https://doi.org/10.1093/ije/dyt261.
Strauss, A., & Corbin, J. (1990). *Basics of qualitative research: Grounded theory procedures and techniques*. Newbury Park, CA: Sage.
Strauss, A., & Corbin, J. (1998). *Basics of qualitative research: Techniques and procedures for developing grounded theory* (2nd ed.). Newbury Park, CA: Sage.
Swartz, S. L., Prevatt, F., & Proctor, B. E. (2005). A coaching intervention for college students with attention deficit/hyperactivity disorder. *Psychology in the Schools, 42*(6), 647–656.
Wang, J. R., & Hsieh, S. (2013). Neurofeedback training improves attention and working memory performance. *Clinical Neurophysiology, 124*(12), 2406–2420.
Webb, M., Burns, J., & Collin, P. (2008). Providing online support for young people with mental health difficulties: Challenges and opportunities explored. *Early Intervention in Psychiatry, 2*(2), 108–113.
Wender, P. W., Lorraine, E., & Wasserstein, J. (2001). Adults with ADHD. *Annals of the New York Academy of Sciences, 931*(1), 1–16.
Westerberg, H., Jacobaeus, H., Hirvikoski, T., Clevberger, P., Ostensson, M. L., Bartfai, A., & Klingberg, T. (2007). Computerized working memory training after stroke-A pilot study. *Brain Injury, 21*(1), 21–29.
Whittaker, R., Merry, S., Stasiak, K., McDowell, H., Doherty, I., Shepherd, M., et al. (2012). MEMO—A mobile phone depression prevention intervention for adolescents: Development process and postprogram findings on acceptability from a randomized controlled trial. *Journal of Medical Internet Research, 14*(1), e13. https://doi.org/10.2196/jmir.1857.
Wilens, T. E., Adler, L. A., Adams, J., Sgambati, S., Rotrosen, J., Sawtelle, R., et al. (2008). Misuse and diversion of stimulants prescribed for ADHD: A systematic review of the literature. *Journal of the American Academy of Child & Adolescent Psychiatry, 47*(1), 21–31.
Wilens, T. M., Stephen, P., Biederman, J., Abrantes, A., Hahesy, A., & Spencer, T. J. (1999). Cognitive therapy in the treatment of adults with ADHD: A systematic chart review of 26 cases. *Journal of Cognitive Psychotherapy, 13*(3), 215–226.
Yin, R. K. (2009). *Case study research: Design and methods* (Vol. 5). Thousand Oaks: Sage.
Young, S. B., & Jessica, B. (2006). *ADHD in adults: A psychological guide to practice*. Chichester: Wiley.
Young, S. B., & Jessica, B. (2012). *Cognitive-behavioural therapy for ADHD in adolescents and adults: A psychological guide to practice*. Chichester: Wiley. Wiley.com.

Chapter 22
The Development of Intelligent Patient-Centric Systems for Health Care

Arturo Caronongan III, Hannah Gorgui-Naguib, and Raouf N. G. Naguib

22.1 Introduction

Artificial intelligence (AI) is defined as 'a field of science and engineering concerned with the computational understanding of what is commonly called intelligent behaviour and with the creation of artefacts that exhibit such behaviour' (Shapiro 1992). Through a vast amount of data sets as input, systems are able to perform a series of algorithms to produce computational models and provide a decision as an output. Many technology vendors have made investments towards AI to provide solutions and services with the use of their technology, such as Microsoft, Google, Apple, IBM, and Amazon to name a few (Chouffani 2016). One of the domains that AI has been extensively studied in is the field of health care, specifically developing an AI-driven healthcare system.

One of the major goals of the modern healthcare system is to offer quality healthcare services to individuals in need (Kamruzzaman et al. 2006). In order for that goal to be achieved, it is important to undergo a successful early diagnosis of a disease so that the most appropriate treatment can be administered, leading to a better patient outcome (Ifeachor et al. 1998; Teodorescu et al. 1998). As such, there is a need for AI computational models/algorithms that can aid in diagnosing, with reliable accuracy, a patient's condition given a series of data.

A. Caronongan III
De La Salle University, Manila, Philippines
e-mail: arturo.caronongan@delasalle.ph

H. Gorgui-Naguib
King's College London, London, UK

R. N. G. Naguib (✉)
Liverpool Hope University, Liverpool, UK

BIOCORE Research & Consultancy Ltd, Liverpool, UK

N. Wickramasinghe, J. L. Schaffer (eds.), *Theories to Inform Superior Health Informatics Research and Practice*, Healthcare Delivery in the Information Age,
https://doi.org/10.1007/978-3-319-72287-0_22

22.2 Artificial Neural Networks

Artificial neural networks (ANNs) have drawn tremendous interest due to their demonstrated successful applications in many pattern recognition and modelling arenas (Rumelhart et al. 1988), particularly in processing data for biomedicine (Nazeran and Behbehani 2001). Neural networks have also been demonstrated to be very useful in many biomedical areas, such as assisting in diagnosing diseases, studying pathological conditions, and monitoring treatment outcomes (Kamruzzaman et al. 2006).

ANNs are computational paradigms that operate with the resemblance of a biological nervous system (Sordo 2002). They are also referred to as connectionist systems, parallel distributed systems, or adaptive systems, because they are composed of a series of interconnected processing elements that operate in parallel. First represented as a binary threshold function (McCulloch and Pitts 1943), the ANN was eventually developed into a perceptron as a practical model (Rosenblatt 1958). The perceptron is most popularly represented as a multilayer feedforward system, where networks are made up of several layers of neurons. Such model (Fig. 22.1) is often made up of the input layer, the middle or hidden layer(s), and the output layer, each of which is fully connected to each other with numerical weights associated (Ramesh et al. 2004). One important feature of the ANN is its ability to *learn* through a training environment relying on backpropagation, where the neural network performs repeated adjustments of its weights to simulate learning (Werbos 1974).

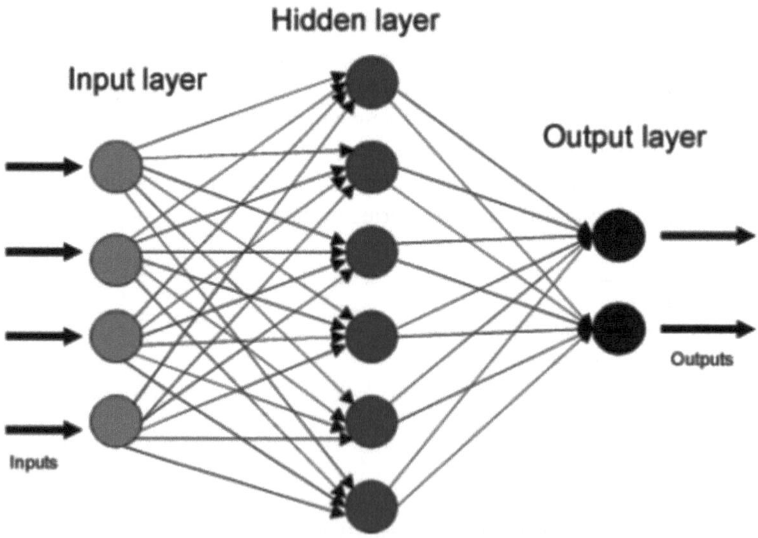

Fig. 22.1 The artificial neural network (Ramesh et al. 2004)

22.2.1 Artificial Neural Networks for Diagnosis

An instance where ANNs have been applied within the medical domain is for clinical diagnosis (Baxt 1995), along with image analysis in radiology, data interpretation in intensive care settings, and waveform analyses, particularly in oncology (Naguib and Sherbet 2001; Ramesh et al. 2004). One example of such system is PAPNET, an automated neural network-based computer programme for assisted screening of Pap (cervical) smears (Boon et al. 1993). A Pap smear test examines cells taken from the uterine cervix for signs of any malignancy where a properly taken and analysed Pap smear can detect very early slightly abnormal squamous cells. Detected early, cervical cancer has an almost 100% chance of cure through the removal of such possible precancerous cells performed as an outpatient procedure (Sordo 2002). In addition, a Bayesian posterior probability (BPP) distribution function in a neural network input selection was designed to assist gynaecologists in the preoperative discrimination between benign and malignant ovarian tumours (Verrelst et al. 1998). The network used data from 191 consecutive patients for training with the results from the neural network being validated by experienced gynaecologists. Another example is a neural network called ProstAsure index which can classify prostate tumours as benign or malignant with a diagnostic accuracy of 90%, a sensitivity of 81%, and a specificity of 92% (Stamey et al. 1996). Further studies in the applications of ANNs to prostate cancer involved the development of techniques for the analysis of conventional and experimental prognostic markers (Naguib and Hamdy 1998; Naguib et al. 1998).

There are several systems available for the diagnosis and selection of therapeutic strategies in breast cancer. A neural network judged the possible recurrence rate of tumours correctly in 960 of 1008 cases by using data from lymphatic node-positive patients, based on tumour size, number of palpable lymphatic nodules, tumour hormone receptor status, etc. It was reported that similar results were obtained by neural network evaluation of the parameters of the BI-RADS standardised code system (Baker et al. 1995). To predict metastases in breast cancer patients, an entropy maximisation network (EMN) was applied (Choong 1994). EMN was used to construct discrete models that predicted the occurrence of axillary lymph node metastases in breast cancer patients, based on characteristics of the primary tumour, using a series of clinical and physiological features. Similarly, the prediction accuracy of artificial neural networks and other statistical models for predicting breast cancer survival was compared (Burke et al. 1995). In that study, ANNs using the backpropagation algorithm, compared with the TNM staging system (tumour size, number of nodes with metastatic disease, and distant metastases), proved to be more accurate in predicting the 5-year survival of 25 cases.

In addition to breast cancer, a multilayer perceptron proved to be a reliable decision support tool for the prognosis and the extent of hepatectomy of patients with hepatocellular carcinoma (Hamamoto et al. 1995).

Using the backpropagation learning algorithm and a radial basis function (RBF) network, a diagnostic aid system for the serum electrophoresis procedure was developed. The serum electrophoresis is a standard laboratory medical test for diagnosing pathological conditions, such as liver cirrhosis or nephrotic syndrome (Sordo 2002). Results confirmed the feasibility of the network as an architecture for medical diagnosis with respect to the provided input (Costa et al. 1998). Similarly, diagnosing bowel disease was aided with the assistance of an adaptive resonance theory mapping neural network using 23 features extracted from 280 inflammatory bowel disease instances and was used to classify as either Crohn's disease or ulcerative colitis (Cross and Harrison 1998).

22.2.2 Assistive EEG Analysis

Neural networks have also been used in electroencephalography (EEG) analysis, particularly in diagnosing neurological diseases (de Haan et al. 2009). One such disease, epilepsy, is characterised by sudden recurrent and transient disturbances of mental function and/or movement of the body that result from excessive discharging of groups of brain cells. The detection of an abnormal EEG plays an important role in the diagnosis of epilepsy (Kamath et al. 2006): spikes or spike discharges are transient waveforms present in the human EEG and have a high correlation with seizure occurrence. There is a general agreement that automated spike detection is a well-recognised task for an ANN in a neurodiagnostic laboratory; therefore, identification and scoring of spikes in the EEG signal are necessary tasks to determine the diagnosis of epilepsy. Using a three-layer feedforward backpropagation (BP) network trained with raw EEG data yielded respectable results in detecting spikes during or before an onset of an epileptic seizure (Özdamar and Kalayci 1998). Raw EEG signals recorded from the scalp and intracranial electrodes of two epileptic patients were also considered, where the EEG recorded acted as an input to discrete time recurrent multilayer perceptrons which concluded that intracranial recordings provided better results in identifying spikes (Petrosian et al. 2000). A further study indicated that using an enhanced cosine radial basis function neural network was able to perform EEG classification with an extensive parametric and sensitivity analysis to validate the robustness of the classifier in diagnosing epilepsy (Ghosh-Dastidar et al. 2008).

Another neurological disease that has been analysed using EEG scans is Alzheimer's disease (AD). The disease onset usually takes place post 60 years old, and the risk of AD goes up with age, such that approximately 5% of men and women between ages 65 and 74 have AD and nearly half of those who are aged 85 and older may have the disease (Kamath et al. 2006). However, AD is not a normal part of ageing, and an analysis of EEG scans of patients with AD revealed abnormal frequency signatures (Moretti et al. 2004). Continuous EEGs (as well as their wavelet-filtered sub-bands) from parieto-occipital channels of ten early AD patients and ten healthy controls were used as input into recurrent neural networks (RNNs) for training and testing purposes (Petrosian et al. 2001). The study indicated that features derived from wavelet analysis, combined with the RNN approach, may be useful in analysing long-term continuous EEGs for early identification of AD. In addition, neural network analysis combined with graph theory for the analysis of topological changes in large-scale functional brain networks found that the brain network organisation in patients with AD deviated from the optimal network structure towards a more random type (de Haan et al. 2009).

Developing assistive technology for patients through EEG analysis can be achieved through a brain-computer interface (BCI) that operates on the principle that non-invasively recorded cortical EEG signals contain information about an impending task intended by the user. That task can be identified by an ANN (Kamath et al. 2006), where it is imperative that the intention of the user is translated into a signal interpretable towards a control movement (Blanchard and Blankertz 2004) using either a regression or classifier algorithm (McFarland and Wolpaw 2005; Penny et al. 2000). One application of a BCI involves being a patient-centric medium for controlling a motorised device (such as a wheelchair or a home appliance) or performs computer-related tasks (e.g. moving a mouse or typing on the keyboard) despite being hindered by a physical disability such as paralysis. The design of an assistive BCI system ranges from components such as EEG amplifiers, a feature extractor, a pattern recognition system for the analysis of signals, and a mechanical interface to achieve the motor component of the task. Software for feature extraction and recognition must be optimised for rapid response, and the mechanical device coupled to a BCI should be easy to operate. Due to this, it is imperative that the algorithms used for classifying patterns through EEG signals in the BCI are as efficient and effective as possible. A variety of classifier algorithms that have been used in BCI have been described by Lotte et al. (2007) and can be seen in Table 22.1. Depending on the features selected, it is important to be aware as to which algorithm is considered as the most appropriate, depending on the specifications of the system's design, particularly the features selected and its intended users.

22.2.3 Imaging Towards a Patient-Centric Medium

As indicated in the previous studies, EEG analysis is useful in diagnosing diseases in neurology, but the main underlying foundation is being able to detect patterns in the EEG of patients through imaging. Imaging is an important area for the application of ANNs (Egmont-Petersen et al. 2002), particularly in medicine, as pattern recognition is widely used to identify and extract important features from medical images (Shuttleworth et al. 2008; Jiang et al. 2010; Hilado et al. 2014). Medical images, such as radiographies, computed tomography (CT), and magnetic resonance imaging (MRI), are some of the most used imaging input media towards healthcare-centric computational models using neural networks.

Using certain imaging principles such as filtering, segmentation, and edge detection techniques, cellular neural networks were able to improve the resolution in brain tomographies, which in turn enabled the improved detection of microcalcifications

Table 22.1 A summary of the qualities of classification algorithms used by brain-computer interface (BCI) (Lotte et al. 2007)

	Linear	Non linear	Generative	Discriminant	Dynamic	Static	Regularized	Stable	Unstable	High dimension robust
FLDA	X			X		X		X		
RFLDA	X			X		X	X	X		
Linear-SVM	X			X		X	X	X		X
RBF-SVM		X		X		X	X	X		X
MLP		X		X		X			X	
BLR NN		X		X		X			X	
ALN NN		X		X		X			X	
TDNN		X		X	X				X	
FIRNN		X		X	X				X	
GDNN		X		X	X				X	
Gaussian NN		X		X		X			X	
LVQ NN		X		X		X			X	
Perceptron	X			X		X		X		
RBF-NN		X		X		X			X	
PeGNC		X		X		X	X		X	
Fuzzy ARTMAP NN		X		X			X		X	
HMM		X	X		X				X	
IOHMM		X		X	X				X	
Bayes quadratic		X	X			X			X	
Bayes graphical network		X	X			X			X	
k-NN		X		X		X			X	
Mahalanobis distance		X		X		X			X	

in mammograms by refining the global frequency correction (Aizenberg et al. 2001). Another study had ANNs trained to recognise regions of interest (ROIs) corresponding to specific organs within electrical impedance tomography (EIT) images of the thorax, where the network allowed automatic selection of optimal pixels based on the number of images, in which each pixel is classified as belonging to a particular organ (Miller 1993). ANNs have also been applied to microscope images to classify blood cells. Combined with the use of a neural network classifier, ROIs were extracted using global threshold methods, morphological filters, and connected-component labelling for the classification of red blood cells as normal or abnormal. This achieved an overall average accuracy of 83% (Tomari et al. 2014). Using a multispectral imaging approach, ANNs were used for automated melanoma detection (Tomatis et al. 2003). That study involved analysing lesions by a telespectrophotometric system prior to surgery. Through a reduction in dimension by factor analysis techniques, the ANN was able to achieve results of 78% sensitivity and 76% specificity for the validation set.

Using a variety of image processing algorithms, a cardiovascular image analysis software package, named Segment, was used in MRI, CT, single-photon emission computer tomography (SPECT), and positron emission tomography (PET) for the analysis of automated segmentation of the left ventricle, myocardial viability analysis, and quantification of MRI flow (Heiberg et al. 2010). The image processing algorithms used ranged from ROI analysis, automated segmentation, flow quantification, linear analysis, and image fusion. The user interface of Segment is displayed in Fig. 22.2, while Fig. 22.3 shows an overview of the Segment system.

22.2.4 Towards Assistive Drug Administration and Patient Care

In developing patient-centric systems, it is important that we take into consideration studies that involved the development or analysis of drugs administered to patients. It is also important to evaluate and determine the parameters needed for utmost patient care by selecting the most effective treatment options given the patient's circumstances (Sordo 2002).

Digoxin (DGX) is a drug widely used for treating various cardiovascular diseases, such as congestive cardiac failure and symptomatic alterations of the heart rate such as auricular fibrillation and paroxysmal supraventricular tachycardia, by improving the effective behaviour of the heart and by relaxing the heartbeat. However, the main drawback of using this drug is the possibility of intoxication in the patient. A study used ANNs to determine a patient's risk of digoxin intoxication (Camps-Valls and Martin-Guerrero 2006). The study had patients classified as patients with high risk of intoxication (DGX levels >2 ng/mL) and patients with low risk of intoxication (DGX levels <2 ng/mL). Two hundred and fifty-seven patients were included and monitored in the study. Data collected included anthropometrical

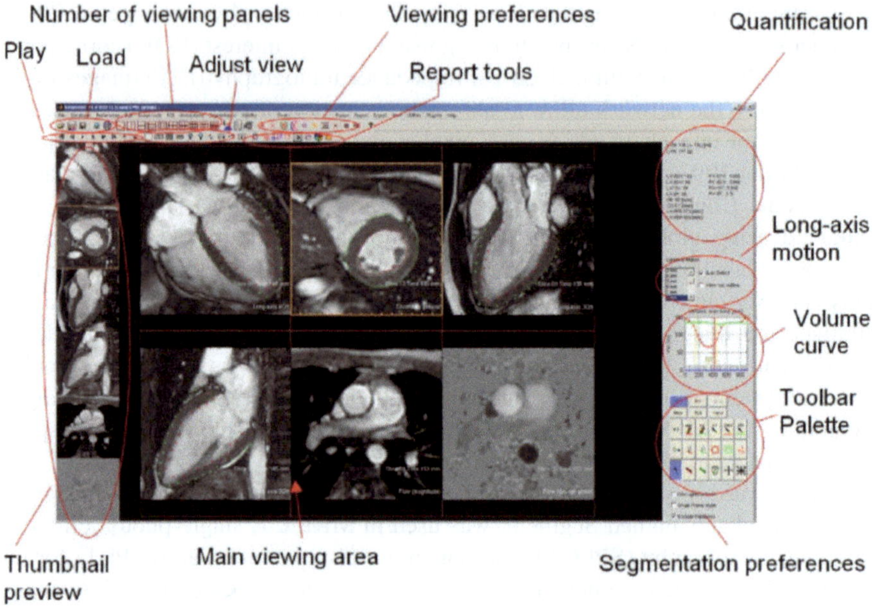

Fig. 22.2 User interface of Segment: A cardiovascular image analysis software package (Heiberg et al. 2010)

data of the patient (age, sex, height, and total body weight), renal function parameters (creatinine level and creatinine clearance), indicators of existing interaction with other drugs (treatment with amiodarone), daily dosage, and the administration rate (times per week). The study used a multilayer perceptron trained by the eigensystem realisation algorithm (ERA) (Gorse et al. 1997) which improved results of the classical backpropagation learning algorithm, compared to other neural approaches, such as radial basis function neural networks (RBFNNs) and one-class one-network (OCON) neural networks (Camps-Valls et al. 2003).

In anaesthesia, designers have employed ANNs in order to measure and provide more quantitative information to surgical teams in relation to the depth of the drugs administered (Robert et al. 2002a, b). The variety of features used to quantify the state of consciousness and effectiveness included traditional EEG measures (power in delta, theta, alpha, and beta bands), features derived from bispectra, mutual information (MI), and nonlinear dynamic (chaos) models of the EEG signal (Ortolani et al. 2002; Zhang and Roy 2001; Zhang et al. 2001). In addition, another study presented an approach based on MI to predict response during isoflurane anaesthesia (Huang et al. 2003). The MI of EEG recorded from four cortical electrodes was computed from 98 consenting patients prior to incision during isoflurane anaesthesia of different levels. The system was able to correctly classify purposeful response with an average accuracy of 91.84% of the cases.

ANNs were also used to monitor kidney patients who undergo cyclosporine A (CyA) treatment (Camps-Valls et al. 2003). CyA is still the drug of choice for

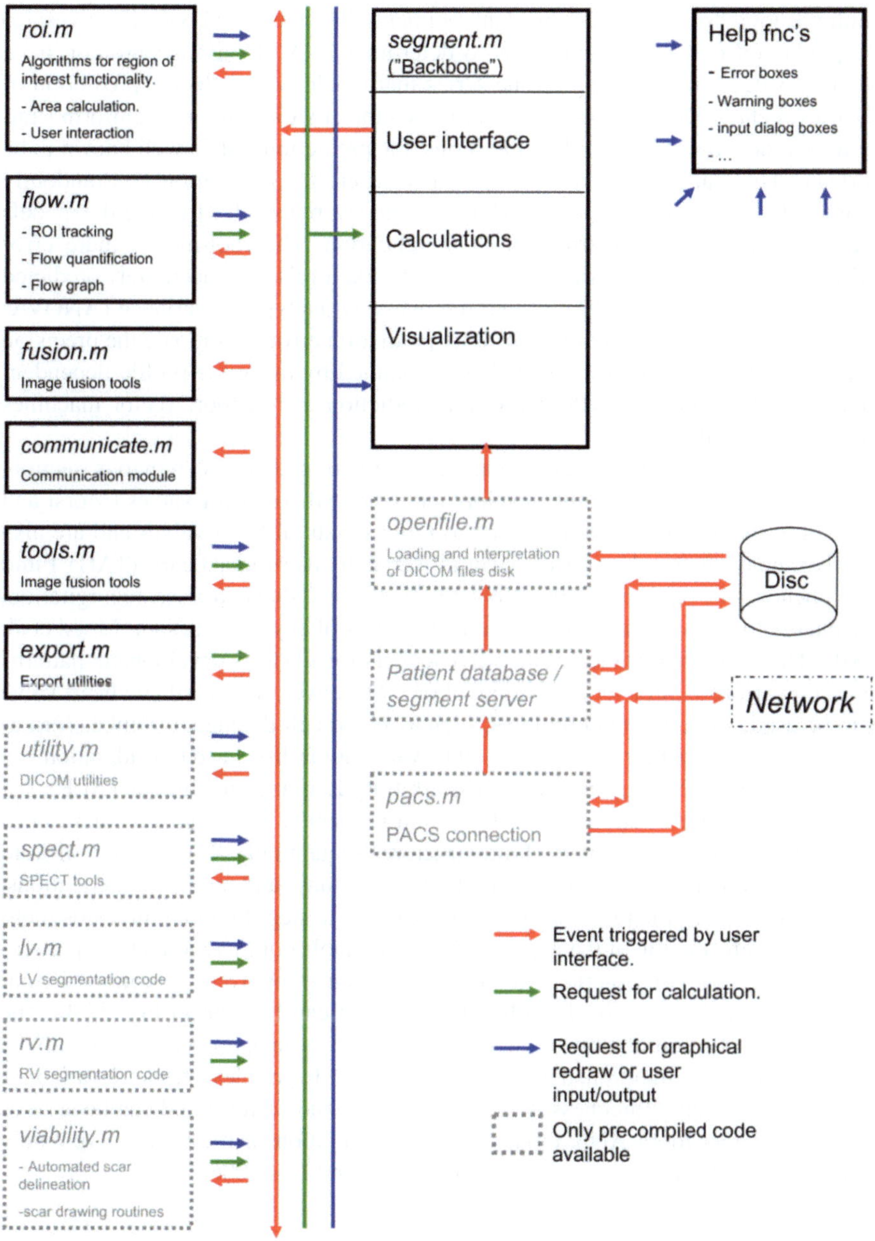

Fig. 22.3 Overview of the Segment software package and the transaction analysis between interfaces (Heiberg et al. 2010)

immunosuppression in renal transplant recipients. The study had two objectives: (a) the prediction of CyA trough levels to determine CyA blood concentration from previous values by following a time series methodology and (b) the prediction of CyA level class. Due to high inter- and intra-subject variability, non-uniform sampling, and nonstationarity of the time series, the prediction task is well known to be intricate. The study consisted of 57 patients, where the population was randomly assigned to two groups: 39 patients (665 patterns) were used for training the models and 18 patients (427 patterns) for their validation. The root-mean-square error (RMSE) was used as a measure of precision. Blood levels were accurately predicted with an error margin of 20% through the one-way analysis of variance (ANOVA) method by using the mean of the absolute prediction error to compare the precision of the models, with the best results being obtained by using the profile-dependent support vector regression (PD-SVR) for prediction and support vector machines (SVM) for classification.

In addition to cardiovascular imaging as mentioned in the previous section, ANNs can also be used for the development of prosthetic heart valves (Morsi and Das 2006), which are commonly used to replace natural heart valves and are also widely used in ventricular assist devices (VAD) in total artificial hearts (TAH). Fluid flow phenomena, particularly in vitro velocity profiles, shear stresses, regurgitation, and energy losses, contribute to the clinical success of any valve design (Morsi et al. 2001). Thus, the optimisation of the valve leaflet or wall stress development patterns relies on various parameters (Lin et al. 2004). Moreover, if a prosthetic heart valve is to be used, valve-related problems, such as blood cell damage, thrombus formation, calcification, and infection, as well as valve durability, need consideration.

Several numerical techniques, such as arbitrary Lagrangian-Eulerian (ALE), fictitious domain/mortar element (FD/ME), and immersed boundary (IB), have been examined to solve the problem (fluid-structure) sequentially. The solution of fluid forces is obtained using the conservation of law of mass and momentum equations, and then the structural solution follows for each time step. In all the methods mentioned, the deformation of the mesh poses a formidable computational task, particularly in the case of complex geometric problems involved in cardiovascular application (an example of the solution procedure can be seen in Fig. 22.4). The development of a neural network model can be used as an approach to deal with the optimisation issues mentioned using a dataset of fluid variables, structure variables, tube diameter, leaflet thickness, Reynolds number, and so forth and can be used as input parameters to an ANN model, with an estimation of the heart valve leaflet deflection with time as an output variable (Morsi and Das 2006).

22.3 Hidden Markov Models in Patient-Centric Analysis

Aside from ANNs in general, hidden Markov models (HMMs) can also be used in analysing circumstances beneficial towards a patient-centric system. An HMM is a statistical model in which the system being modelled is assumed to be a Markov

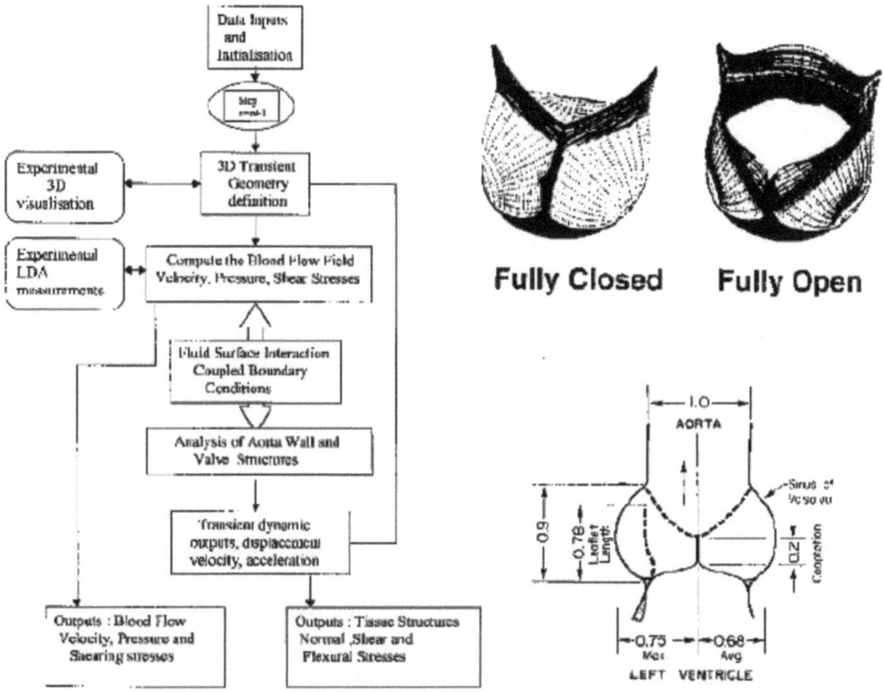

Fig. 22.4 Tri-leaflet heart configurations for closed and open valves (Morsi and Das 2006; Morsi 2014)

process with hidden states (Cooper and Lipsitch 2004). The outputs of the hidden states are observable and are represented as probabilistic functions of the state. A general approach to estimating parameters of continuous-time Markov chains from discretely sampled data was used in analysing hospital-acquired infections (Ross and Taimre 2007). Hospital-acquired infections caused by transmissible nosocomial pathogens have been widely studied due to the detrimental effects of the infections, resulting in possible loss of life, as well as in high demands on healthcare resources. Reports state that 1 in 10 patients admitted to a hospital will acquire a nosocomial infection, resulting in approximately 5000 deaths and costs amounting to one billion pounds per annum (Inweregbu et al. 2005), with reports of nosocomial infections being continually on the rise. Focus has thus turned on developing strategies for limiting the occurrence of such infections through improved hygiene practices among healthcare workers, selective antibiotic use, and isolation (human-human distancing) strategies. In their study using HMMs, Cooper and Lipsitch (2004) developed a methodology which was combined with a new stochastic model for the transmission of hospital-acquired infections—one which accounts for dynamic bed occupancy—providing a method for estimating the parameters of such systems. In the study, particular attention was given to modelling dynamic bed occupancy as

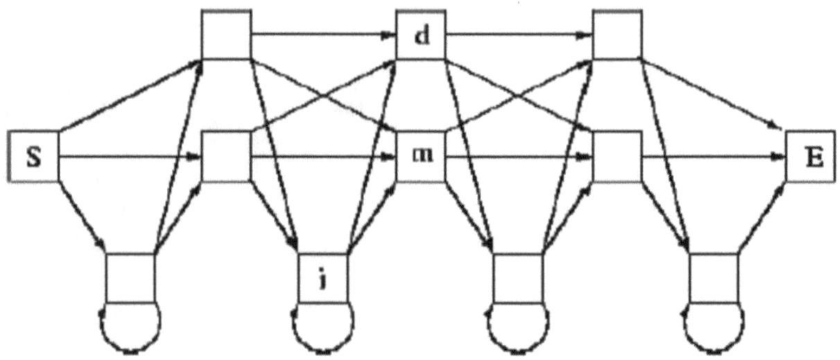

Fig. 22.5 Standard HMM architecture developed by Ohlsson et al. (2001). *(S and E denote start and end state, respectively, while the delete, main, and insert states are marked as d, m, and i)*

a necessary parameter in predicting patients who may begin exhibiting symptoms of hospital-acquired infections.

HMMs have also been used for predicting body trajectories for cancer progression, where conditional probabilities of clinical data were modelled using HMM techniques (Ohlsson et al. 2001). In that study, each potential body site was encoded by an N-letter code, and a disease trajectory was described in terms of a string of letters. Patient database records were then represented by start- and endpoints through the architecture illustrated in Fig. 22.5. The approach was explored using pathological data for non-Hodgkin lymphoma, augmented with an artificial database generated according to observed distributions in the clinical data. For the HMMs, a Bayesian approach was taken using the hybrid Monte Carlo method, producing an ensemble of models rather than a single one. In addition, Simöes (2010) made use of an emission probability value for detecting possible aberrations that could occur during cancer progression. In this study, an additional value was placed between the transition of states to represent the possibility of mutations occurring from one phase to another and which are undetected in laboratory procedures. A representation of the study is shown in Fig. 22.6.

As mentioned previously, administering drugs to patients is one of the important procedures in patient care; however, it is important to take note of possible adverse drug reaction as it is one of the leading causes of injury or death among patients undergoing medical treatments. This is due to adverse reactions not being thoroughly identified prior to a drug being made available on the market. Sampathkumar et al. (2014) developed an HMM-based system for mining online healthcare fora and extracting reports of adverse drug side effects (some of which are given in Table 22.2) from messages to use them as early indicators to assist in post-marketing drug surveillance. The system's architecture is presented in Fig. 22.7. The study also made use of an annotated dataset which was used in the training and validation of the HMM-based text mining system illustrated in Fig. 22.8. The results from a tenfold cross-validation of the manually annotated dataset yielded on average an F-score of 0.76 from the HMM classifier, compared to 0.575 from the baseline classifier.

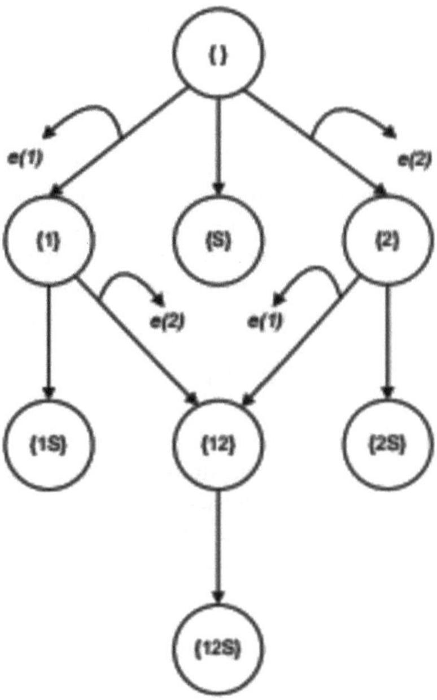

Fig. 22.6 HMM architecture developed by Simöes (2010). *(s values mark a stop state and the e represents emission values between states)*

Furthermore, the study also managed to discover some novel adverse side effects, using the aforementioned computational models, which could potentially be classified as adverse drug reactions.

22.4 Conclusions: Challenges in Developing Intelligent Patient-Centric Systems

The future potential success of AI in the development of patient-centric intelligent systems is directly related to the careful consideration and design of the theories and architectures involved in any such system. As described, developing applications towards patient-centric procedures is a well-appraised challenge in the domain of AI. As ANNs and HMMs are non-application-specific computational models, various theoretical and application research studies have been attained, all with varying degrees of success. Nevertheless, the challenge lies in which part of the classification process the ANN or HMM is to be applied. It is clear that their nonlinear representation abilities can address highly complex problems, and it is this attribute which should be further exploited through their usage to address a single element in the overall automated classification process.

In terms of designing intelligent systems, in particular, that cater towards the healthcare industry, there continues to be a need for novel approaches that apply the complexities of hospital operations and offer much needed productivity gains in resource usage and providing services to patients. Despite improvements in technology

Table 22.2 Mined side effects of drugs from different sources using HMM (Sampathkumar et al. 2014)

Drug name	Prescribed for	Common ADRs in drug package inserts	Common ADRs mined from medications.com	Novel side-effects mined from medications.com
Lisinopril	High blood pressure (hypertension), congestive heart failure, improve survival after a heart attack	Headache, dizziness, cough, fatigue, rash, diarrhea, nausea, cramps	Cough (12.57%), dizziness (2.77%), headache (1.81%), fatigue (1.49%), cramps (1.38%), diarrhea (0.96%), nausea (0.75%), rash (0.43%)	Hearing loss (0.53%), hair loss (0.53%), shingles (0.43%), fits (0.32%)
Prednisone	Allergic disorders, skin conditions, ulcerative colitis, arthritis, lupus, breathing disorders	Anxiety, dizziness, depression, insomnia, headache, nausea, moon face, elevation in blood pressure, behavioral and mood changes, weight gain	Anxiety (5.57%), insomnia (3.15%), depression (2.97%), dizziness (2.41%), mood swings (2.41%), weight gain (1.86%), nausea (1.3%), moon face (1.11%)	Hives (1.3%), acid reflux (0.37%), avascular necrosis (0.37%), dry mouth (0.37%)
Singulair	Asthma, allergic rhinitis	Upper respiratory infection, fever, headache, pharyngitis, cough, abdominal pain, diarrhea, influenza, rhinorrhea, sinusitis	Headache (2.02%), infection (1.12%), cough (1.12%), fever (0.90%), diarrhea (0.45%), sinusitis (0.45%), inflammation (0.45%)	Seizure (6.28%), depression (3.59%), nightmares (3.36%), aggression (2.91%), mood swings (2.02%), suicide (1.35%), suicidal thoughts (0.9%)
Topamax	Seizures, migraine headaches	Anorexia, paresthesia (tingling), fatigue, nervousness, weight decrease, somnolence, dizziness, infection, flushing, psychomotor slowing, difficulty with memory	Tingling (5.64%), weight toss (4.14%), memory loss (3.76%), numbness (2.26%), dizziness (2.26%), tired (1.88%), sleepy (1.13%)	Hair loss (3.01%), depression (2.26%), stress (1.88%), aches (1.88%), anxiety (1.13%), diarrhea (1.13%), dry mouth (1.13%), itching (1.13%)

and the translation of numerous studies from labs to daily use in hospitals and medical practices, the health research community still faces one of the greatest challenges in relation to effective AI adoption. Issues, such as those presented by big data, necessitate the development of novel computational techniques to handle the large volumes of data available, along with their variability and velocity, with efficiency and in the

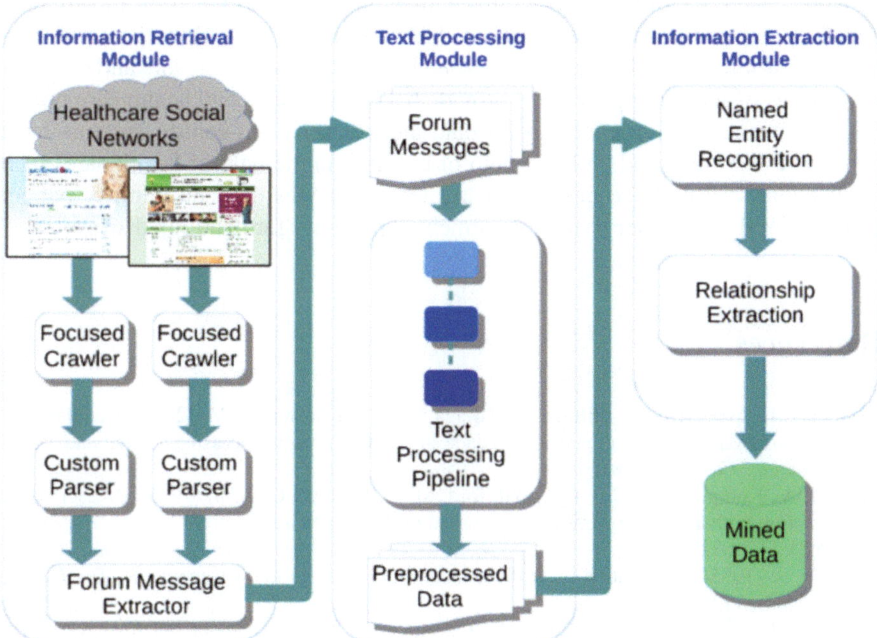

Fig. 22.7 System architecture of the mining system for adverse drug reactions (Sampathkumar et al. 2014)

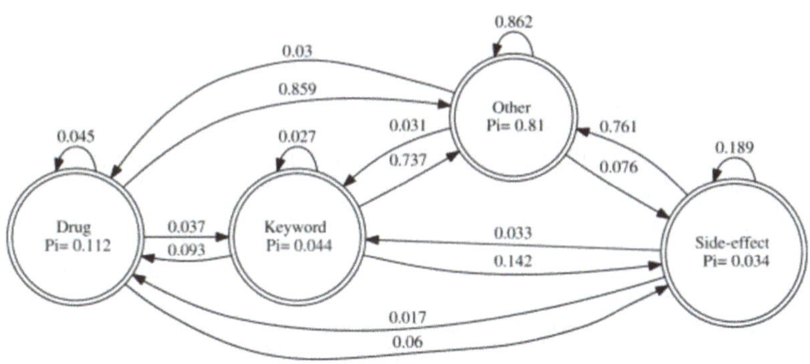

Fig. 22.8 Resulting HMM obtained from the training set (Sampathkumar et al. 2014)

least amount of processing time. There are cases when instantaneous and accurate results may be important in the immediate diagnosis and treatment of patients. Another issue exists where the use of technology should not go against the design of effective human-computer interfaces. Humans should be able to better interact with the data, and communication could be integrated with the flow of information, despite the presence of complex computational models integrated within such systems (Khanna et al. 2013).

Nonetheless, the presence of AI in healthcare applications has been shown to be beneficial in providing more sophisticated techniques in aiding physicians with performing various clinical tasks and allowing hospitals to accommodate and discover new means of servicing patients to provide better treatments and health care procedures. From assistive technology to data analytics, patient-centric systems have continued to evolve, and with the help of research in the field of health care, such applications will produce more sophisticated techniques that can improve patient care and produce a wider array of treatment approaches for handling disease.

References

Aizenberg, I., Aizenberg, N., Hiltner, J., Moraga, C., & Zu Bexten, E. M. (2001). Cellular neural networks and computational intelligence in medical image processing. *Image and Vision Computing, 19*(4), 177–183.

Baker, J. A., Kornguth, P. J., Lo, J. Y., Williford, M. E., & Floyd, C. E., Jr. (1995). Breast cancer: Prediction with artificial neural network based on BI-RADS standardized lexicon. *Radiology, 196*(3), 817–822.

Baxt, W. G. (1995). Application of artificial neural networks to clinical medicine. *The Lancet, 346*(8983), 1135–1138.

Blanchard, G., & Blankertz, B. (2004). BCI competition 2003 – Data set IIa: Spatial patterns of self-controlled brain rhythm modulations. *IEEE Transactions on Biomedical Engineering, 51*(6), 1062–1066.

Boon, M. E., Kok, L. P., & Under, J. (1993). Neural network processing can provide means to catch errors that slip through human screening of pap smears. *Diagnostic Cytopathology, 9*(4), 411–416.

Burke, H. B., Rosen, D. B., & Goodman, P. H. (1995). Comparing the prediction accuracy of artificial neural networks and other statistical models for breast cancer survival. In G. Tesauro & D. S. Touretzky (Eds.), *Advances in neural information processing systems 7* (Vol. 7, pp. 1063–1067). Cambridge: MIT Press.

Camps-Valls, G., Porta-Oltra, B., Soria-Olivas, E., Martín-Guerrero, J. D., Serrano-López, A. J., Pérez- Ruixo, J. J., et al. (2003). Prediction of cyclosporine dosage in patients after kidney transplantation using neural networks. *IEEE Transactions on Biomedical Engineering, 50*(4), 442–448.

Camps-Valls, G., & Martin-Guerrero, J. D. (2006). Neural and kernel methods for therapeutic drug monitoring. In *Neural networks in healthcare: Potential and challenges* (pp. 238–261). Hershey, PA: IGI Global.

Choong, P. L. (1994). Breast cancer prognosis using the EMN architecture. *Proceeding of the IEEE World Congress on Computational Intelligence, 6*, 3516–3520.

Chouffani, R. (2016). Four uses for artificial intelligence in healthcare. SearchHealthIT, Newton, MA. Retrieved March 02, 2017, from http://searchhealthit.techtarget.com/tip/Four-uses-for-artificial-intelligence-in-healthcare

Cooper, B., & Lipsitch, M. (2004). The analysis of hospital infection data using hidden Markov models. *Biostatistics, 5*(2), 223–237.

Costa, A., Cabestany, J., Moreno, J., & Calvet, M. (1998). Neuroserum: An artificial neural NetBased diagnostic aid tool for serum electrophoresis. In *Third international conference on neural networks and expert systems in medicine and healthcare* (pp. 34–43).

Cross, S. S., & Harrison, R. F. (1998). Making the distinction between Crohn's disease and ulcerative colitis by histopathological examination: A comparison of human performance, Logistic Regression and Adaptive Resonance Theory Mapping Neural Networks (ARTMAP). In *Third international conference on neural networks and expert systems in medicine and healthcare* (pp. 116–124).

de Haan, W., Pijnenburg, Y. A., Strijers, R. L., van der Made, Y., van der Flier, W. M., Scheltens, P., et al. (2009). Functional neural network analysis in frontotemporal dementia and Alzheimer's disease using EEG and graph theory. *BMC Neuroscience, 10*(1), 101.

Egmont-Petersen, M., de Ridder, D., & Handels, H. (2002). Image processing with neural networks – A review. *Pattern Recognition, 35*(10), 2279–2301.

Ghosh-Dastidar, S., Adeli, H., & Dadmehr, N. (2008). Principal component analysis-enhanced cosine radial basis function neural network for robust epilepsy and seizure detection. *IEEE Transactions on Biomedical Engineering, 55*(2), 512–518.

Gorse, D., Shepherd, A. J., & Taylor, J. G. (1997). The new ERA in supervised learning. *Neural Networks, 10*(2), 343–352.

Hamamoto, I., Okada, S., Hashimoto, T., Wakabayashi, H., Maeba, T., & Maeta, H. (1995). Prediction of the early prognosis of the hepatectomized patient with hepatocellular carcinoma with a neural network. *Computers in Biology and Medicine, 25*(1), 49–59.

Heiberg, E., Sjögren, J., Ugander, M., Carlsson, M., Engblom, H., & Arheden, H. (2010). Design and validation of segment-freely available software for cardiovascular image analysis. *BMC Medical Imaging, 10*, 1.

Hilado, S. M. D., Gan Lim, L. A., Naguib, R. N. G., Dadios, E. P., & Avila, J. M. C. (2014). Implementation of wavelets and artificial neural networks in colonic histopathological classification. *Journal of Advanced Computational Intelligence and Intelligent Informatics, 18*(5), 792–797.

Huang, L., Yu, P., Ju, F., & Cheng, J. (2003). Prediction of response to incision using the mutual information of electroencephalograms during anaesthesia. *Medical Engineering & Physics, 25*(4), 321–327.

Ifeachor, E. C., Sperduti, A., & Starita, A. (1998). *Neural networks and expert systems in medicine and health care*. Singapore: World Scientific Publishing.

Inweregbu, K., Dave, J., & Pittard, A. (2005). Nosocomial infections. *Continuing Education in Anaesthesia Critical Care & Pain, 5*(1), 14–17.

Jiang, J., Trundle, P., & Ren, J. (2010). Medical image analysis with artificial neural networks. *Computerized Medical Imaging and Graphics, 34*(8), 617–631.

Kamath, M. V., Upton, A. R., Wu, J., Bajaj, H. S., Poehlman, S., & Spaziani, R. (2006). Artificial neural networks in EEG analysis. In R. Begg, J. Kamruzzaman, & R. Sarker (Eds.), *Neural networks in healthcare: Potential and challenges* (pp. 177–194). Calgary, AB: Idea Group.

Kamruzzaman, J., Begg, R., & Sarker, R. (2006). Overview of artificial neural networks and their applications in healthcare. In R. Begg, J. Kamruzzaman, & R. Sarker (Eds.), *Neural networks in healthcare: Potential and challenges* (pp. 1–19). Calgary, AB: Idea Group.

Khanna, S., Sattar, A., & Hansen, D. (2013). Artificial intelligence in health – The three big challenges. *The Australasian Medical Journal, 6*(5), 315–317.

Lin, Q., Morsi, Y. S., Smith, B., & Yang, W. (2004). Numerical simulation and structure verification of jellyfish heart valve. *International Journal of Computer Applications in Technology, 21*(1–2), 2–7.

Lotte, F., Congedo, M., Lécuyer, A., Lamarche, F., & Arnaldi, B. (2007). A review of classification algorithms for EEG-based brain-computer interfaces. *Journal of Neural Engineering, 4*(2), R1.

McCulloch, J., & Pitts, W. A. (1943). Logical calculus of the ideas imminent in nervous activity. Reprinted in *Embodiements of Mind* (1965).

McFarland, D. J., & Wolpaw, J. R. (2005). Sensorimotor rhythm-based brain-computer interface (BCI): Feature selection by regression improves performance. *IEEE Transactions on Neural Systems and Rehabilitation Engineering, 13*(3), 372–379.

Miller, A. S. (1993). *The application of neural networks to imaging and signal processing in astronomy and medicine*. Doctoral Dissertation. Southampton, UK: University of Southampton.

Moretti, D. V., Babiloni, C., Binetti, G., Cassetta, E., Dal Forno, G., Ferreric, F., et al. (2004). Individual analysis of EEG frequency and band power in mild Alzheimer's disease. *Clinical Neurophysiology, 115*(2), 299–308.

Morsi, Y. S. (2014). Bioengineering strategies for polymeric scaffold for tissue engineering an aortic heart valve: An update. *The International Journal of Artificial Organs, 37*(9), 651–667.

Morsi, Y., Ahmad, A., & Hassan, A. (2001). Numerical simulation of the turbulent flow field distal to an aortic heart valve. *Frontiers of Medical and Biomedical Engineering, 11*(1), 1–11.

Morsi, Y. S., & Das, S. (2006). Computational fluid dynamics and neural network for modeling and simulations of medical devices. In *Neural networks in healthcare: Potential and challenges* (pp. 262–283). Hershey, PA: IGI Global.

Naguib, R. N. G., & Hamdy, F. C. (1998). A general regression neural network analysis of prognostic markers in prostate cancer. *Neurocomputing, 19*(1–3), 145–150.

Naguib, R. N. G., Neal, D. E., & Hamdy, F. C. (1998). Neural network analysis of combined conventional and experimental prognostic markers in prostate cancer: A pilot study. *British Journal of Cancer, 78*(2), 246–250.

Naguib, R. N. G., & Sherbet, G. V. (2001). *Artificial neural networks in cancer diagnosis, prognosis and patient management*. Boca Raton, FL: CRC Press.

Nazeran, H., & Behbehani, K. (2001). Neural networks in processing and analysis of biomedical signals. *Nonlinear Biomedical Signal Processing Fuzzy Logic Neural Networks and New Algorithms, 1*, 69–97.

Ohlsson, M., Peterson, C., & Dictor, M. (2001). Using hidden Markov models to characterize disease trajectories. In *Proceeding of the neural networks and expert systems in medicine and healthcare conference* (pp. 324–326).

Ortolani, O., Conti, A., Di Filippo, A., Adembri, C., Moraldi, E., Evangelisti, A., et al. (2002). EEG signal processing in anaesthesia. Use of a neural network technique for monitoring depth of anaesthesia. *British Journal of Anaesthesia, 88*(5), 644–648.

Özdamar, Ö., & Kalayci, T. (1998). Detection of spikes with artificial neural networks using raw EEG. *Computers and Biomedical Research, 31*(2), 122–142.

Penny, W. D., Roberts, S. J., Curran, E. A., & Stokes, M. J. (2000). EEG-based communication: A pattern recognition approach. *IEEE Transactions on Rehabilitation Engineering, 8*(2), 214–215.

Petrosian, A., Prokhorov, D., Homan, R., Dasheiff, R., & Wunsch, D. (2000). Recurrent neural network based prediction of epileptic seizures in intra- and extracranial EEG. *Neurocomputing, 30*(1), 201–218.

Petrosian, A. A., Prokhorov, D. V., Lajara-Nanson, W., & Schiffer, R. B. (2001). Recurrent neural network-based approach for early recognition of Alzheimer's disease in EEG. *Clinical Neurophysiology, 112*(8), 1378–1387.

Ramesh, A. N., Kambhampati, C., Monson, J. R. T., & Drew, P. J. (2004). Artificial intelligence in medicine. *Annals of the Royal College of Surgeons of England, 86*(5), 334–338.

Robert, C., Gaudy, J. F., & Limoge, A. (2002a). Electroencephalogram processing using neural networks. *Clinical Neurophysiology, 113*(5), 694–701.

Robert, C., Karasinski, P., Arreto, C. D., & Gaudy, J. F. (2002b). Monitoring anesthesia using neural networks: A survey. *Journal of Clinical Monitoring and Computing, 17*(3), 259–267.

Rosenblatt, F. (1958). The perceptron: A probabilistic model for information storage and organization in the brain. *Psychological Review, 65*(6), 386–408.

Ross, J. V., & Taimre, T. (2007). *On the analysis of hospital infection data using Markov models*. April 30, 2017, from http://citeseerx.ist.psu.edu/viewdoc/summary?doi=10.1.1.296.8724

Rumelhart, D. E., McClelland, J. L., & PDP Research Group. (1988). *Parallel distributed processing* (Vol. 1). IEEE.

Sampathkumar, H., Chen, X. W., & Luo, B. (2014). Mining adverse drug reactions from online healthcare forums using hidden Markov model. *BMC Medical Informatics and Decision Making, 14*(1), 91.

Shapiro, S. C. (1992). Encyclopedia of artificial intelligence (2nd ed., pp. 54–57). New York: Wiley.

Shuttleworth, J. K., Todman, A. G., Naguib, R. N. G., Newman, R. M., & Bennett, M. K. (2008). Texture analysis and classification techniques for cancer diagnosis. In O. C. L. Haas & K. J. Burnham (Eds.), *Intelligent and adaptive systems in medicine*, *Series in medical physics and biomedical engineering* (pp. 331–368). New York and London: Taylor and Francis.

Simöes, M. (2010). *A hidden Markov model for cancer progression*. Master's thesis, KTH School of Computer Science and Communication, Stockholm.

Sordo, M. (2002). Introduction to neural networks in healthcare. *OpenClinical Document: Knowledge Management for Medical Care*.

Stamey, T. A., Barnhill, S. D., Zhang, Z., Madyastha, K. R., Prestigiacomo, A. F., Jones, K., et al. (1996). Effectiveness of ProstAsure™ in detecting prostate cancer (PCa) and benign prostatic hyperplasia (BPH) in men age 50 and older. *Journal of Urology, 155*, 436A.

Teodorescu, H.-N. L., Kandel, A., & Jain, L. C. (1998). *Fuzzy and neuro-fuzzy systems in medicine* (Vol. 2). Boca Raton, FL: CRC Press.

Tomari, R., Zakaria, W. N. W., Jamil, M. M. A., Nor, F. M., & Fuad, N. F. N. (2014). Computer aided system for red blood cell classification in blood smear image. *Procedia Computer Science, 42*, 206–213.

Tomatis, S., Bono, A., Bartoli, C., Carrara, M., Lualdi, M., Tragni, G., et al. (2003). Automated melanoma detection: Multispectral imaging and neural network approach for classification. *Medical Physics, 30*(2), 212–221.

Verrelst, H., Vandewalle, J., De Moor, B., & Timmerman, D. (1998). Bayesian input selection for neural network classifiers. In *Proceeding of the third international conference on neural networks and expert systems in medicine and healthcare (NNESMED'98)* (pp. 125–132).

Werbos, P.J. (1974). *Beyond regression: New tools for prediction and analysis in the behavioral sciences*. PhD thesis, Harvard University, Cambridge, MA.

Zhang, X. S., & Roy, R. J. (2001). Derived fuzzy knowledge model for estimating the depth of anesthesia. *IEEE Transactions on Biomedical Engineering, 48*(3), 312–323.

Zhang, X. S., Roy, R. J., Schwender, D., & Daunderer, M. (2001). Discrimination of Anesthetic states using mid-latency auditory evoked potentials and artificial neural networks. *Annals of Biomedical Engineering, 29*(5), 446–453.

Chapter 23
Applying the Practice Theoretical Perspective to Healthcare Knowledge Management

Obinna Anya, Hissam Tawfik, and Raouf N. G. Naguib

23.1 Introduction

In health care, knowledge management is primarily focused on providing clinical practitioners with appropriate knowledge resources, including techniques, strategies, tools and processes, for making the best patient care decisions at the point of need. A popular means for incorporating knowledge resources into the healthcare decision-making process is through evidence-based practice (EBP). EBP is the conscientious use of current best evidence in making decisions about patient care (Sackett et al. 2000). In practice, it offers a set of methods established upon explicit scientific criteria that allow the clinical practitioner to assess available research, clinical guidelines and other information resources prior to applying them to clinical decision-making.

As greater issues of social and organizational contexts in health care began to emerge—including considerations of a patient's unique health state and diagnosis, their individual risks, benefits of potential interventions, hospital norms and practices and patient's preferences and values—the practical applicability of EBP has been challenged. Despite its popularity and a "gold standard" status, Gabbay and le May (2011), in an ethnographic study of the use of clinical evidence by primary

O. Anya
IBM Research-Almaden, San Jose, CA, USA
e-mail: o.anya@ieee.org

H. Tawfik
Leeds Beckett University, Leeds, UK
e-mail: h.tawfik@leedsbeckett.ac.uk

R. N. G. Naguib (✉)
Liverpool Hope University, Liverpool, UK

BIOCORE Research & Consultancy Ltd, Liverpool, UK
e-mail: r.naguib@ieee.org

N. Wickramasinghe, J. L. Schaffer (eds.), *Theories to Inform Superior Health Informatics Research and Practice*, Healthcare Delivery in the Information Age,
https://doi.org/10.1007/978-3-319-72287-0_23

care physicians in the United Kingdom and the United States, observed that EBP is faltering because it focuses hugely on an idealized model of how clinicians ought to use the best evidence and pays little attention to the actual practices of clinical decision-making. The authors conclude that in addition to using the best evidence, clinicians in day-to-day decision-making often deploy a set of internalized, tacit-based and collectively reinforced guidelines that serve as the clinicians' "knowledge-in-practice-in-context". The approach emphasizes the role of collaboration, context and practice, rather than idealized rules, in guiding actions during clinical decision-making. For example, in co-located healthcare settings, the use of evidence often transpires in the midst of problem-based conversational encounters between clinicians about a clinical case at hand, joint critical appraisal of research evidence, a guideline or patient's medical record, referrals to a secondary care specialist or team-based formulation of a care plan or workflow (Abidi 2006). Decision support in such contexts typically occurs interactively and extemporaneously (Mejia et al. 2010; Whittaker et al. 1994) and is largely driven by a common ground offered by the clinicians' shared context of work and "knowledge-in-practice-in-context" (Kuziemsky and Varpio 2010; Gabbay and le May 2011).

In addition, a critical review of existing literature shows that a competent and accountable use of a system in a hospital is inseparable from a body of local work practices that go beyond clinical workflow representations, and through which an awareness of real-world clinical contexts, implicit local work structures, constraints and specific patient-centred needs could be constructed to facilitate effective cross-boundary healthcare knowledge management and decision support (Chaiklin 2011; Gabbay and le May 2011; Schatzki 2012; Button and Harper 1996; Brézillon 2011; Allert and Richter 2008; Tawfik et al. 2012). However, existing healthcare knowledge management systems lack sufficient capability to support problem-solving and facilitate clinical decision support based on practice-centred knowledge about a work situation. This provokes a number of challenges for cross-boundary knowledge management and decision support. How do we enable cross-boundary clinical decision support in a manner that allows for the construction of awareness of a clinical work process and available knowledge resources at the work practice level? Would such approach sufficiently take account of the situated and socially mediated nature of located work practices, clinical encounters, organizational circumstances and patients' specific needs? How do we enable accurate perceptions of work situations across boundaries of workplaces and organizations? How do we enable a suggestion or "second opinion" emanating from a user in a remote organization to be easily applied to support problem-solving and decision-making in another work context in spite of the lack of shared context of work for supporting cohesive interaction and knowledge sharing between the work settings?

In this chapter, we describe a research effort targeted at developing an e-health system for clinical decision support and knowledge sharing across organizational and geographical boundaries, using the practice theoretical approach. The chapter concludes with a roadmap for the critical goal of designing healthcare knowledge management systems and user interfaces that meet the information, collaboration and workflow needs of healthcare professionals at the point of care.

23.2 Practices, Context and Healthcare Knowledge Management

Drawing upon respective work in knowledge management, human-computer interaction and the social sciences, this section provides a brief introduction to the concept of practice. The goal is to ground the application of the practice theoretical perspective in the underlying assumptions of the practice theories. In addition, the section aims to relate the discussion to relevant concepts and techniques in healthcare knowledge management and context-aware computing.

At the core, our approach to the practical theoretical perspective discussed in the chapter is the relationship between knowledge artefacts, context and situation and how that relationship enables an awareness of a community's work practice, i.e. their evolving approach to activity. Context is dynamically constituted through activity involving people and artefacts in a specific setting; it is not just "out there" but is consciously and purposefully generated through people's interaction with artefacts and the environment as represented in their practices (Dourish 2004). This interaction is both shaped by situation and the result of specific historical, cultural and ontological processes within which work is transformed. Practice theories are valuable in explicating human activities and practices in real-world situations, bringing to light "the conflux of multifaceted, shifting, intertwining processes that comprise human thought and behaviour", which are necessary for the development of effective healthcare knowledge management systems (Nardi 1996).

23.2.1 *Healthcare Knowledge Management*

Conceptually, healthcare knowledge management (KM) is characterized as "the systematic creation, modelling, sharing, operationalization and translation of healthcare knowledge to improve the quality of patient care" (Abidi 2008). It is aimed at promoting and providing optimal, effective and pragmatic healthcare knowledge and resources to clinical professionals (as well as patients and individuals) for the purpose of effecting high-quality, well-informed and cost-effective patient care decisions at the point of need. In practice, it is concerned with techniques, tools and processes for capturing, representing, organizing, synthesizing and operationalizing the different modalities of healthcare knowledge (including experienced-based know-hows) in order to realize comprehensive, validated and accessible healthcare knowledge resources for delivering quality and timely patient care decisions.

At a high level, knowledge management involves four major steps of capturing/creating/generating knowledge, representing/storing knowledge, accessing/using and disseminating/transferring knowledge (Davenport and Prusak 1998; Wickramasinghe and Davison 2004). The process of knowledge capture or creation generally has tremendous implications for the entire knowledge management process, which requires an understanding of the knowledge construct, as well as of its context. However, knowledge is not a simple construct, particularly in health care, where its creation, use and sharing are heavily reliant practices that support common perceptions of the construct being used or shared (Wickramasinghe 2009). This is primarily as a result of the subjective nature of knowledge, which makes it dynamically malleable to the social, organizational and cultural practices of a community of practice. These attributes make it possible to transform knowledge from one form to another, e.g. from explicit knowledge to tacit knowledge and vice versa, following Nonaka's famous knowledge spiral model, and to apply various forms and modalities of knowledge in a single clinical case or decision-making situation, for example, the use of various forms of knowledge and clinical workflows within the "clinical mindline" construct developed by Gabbay and le May (2011). However, it poses a number of challenges to knowledge sharing across communities and organizational boundaries in health care. As noted by Abidi (2008), a healthcare knowledge management system ought to address the following activities and challenges:

- The need to capture, represent, model, organize and synthesize the various forms and different modalities of healthcare knowledge in order to realize comprehensive, valid and accessible knowledge resources for patient care decision-making
- The challenge of accessing, sharing and disseminating current and case-specific knowledge to healthcare stakeholders and patients in usable formats
- The need to operationalize and utilize healthcare knowledge, within clinical workflows and acceptable organizational contexts, to provide pragmatic patient care services, such as decision support and care planning at the point of need

Over the years, healthcare knowledge management, as a set of practices for effecting collaborative and quality patient care, has focused on three overarching themes, namely, streamlining the nature of knowing in the healthcare sector, identifying the types of knowledge management tools and initiatives that are suitable for the healthcare sector and minimizing the barriers, while strengthening the enablers, to the take up of knowledge management practices (Nicolini 2008).

23.2.2 The Concept of Practice

Work practice can be defined as "the ways of doing work, grounded in tradition and shared by a group of workers" (Bødker 1991). It is a "customary way of doing things" (Allert and Richter 2008), and, according to Reckwitz (2002), it incorporates an appreciation of a people's cultural and historical phenomena as well as the specific contexts of their actions. The importance of practice lies in its ability to locate the precise situation of work; the design of computer support for work, by default, implies the design for the work situations of the users.

Practice refers to human everyday practical activity through which we share cooperatively produced understandings and knowledge about the world and our activities (Bødker 1991). However, practice has been generally overlooked theoretically and is often taken as a "thin" term with little meaning, a term denoting a loose family of not necessarily coherent ideas and always treated as a background concept (Kirsh 2001; Hopwood 2010; Chaiklin 2011). Some thinkers conceive of practice, minimally, as arrays of activity, while others yet theorize practice as the skills, tacit knowledge and presuppositions that underpin activities.

The practice theoretical perspective is underlined by the following key assumptions, which are critical to effectively applying the practice theory for collaborative knowledge management support (Allert and Richter 2008):

- Practices are socially mediated in that they are shaped by, and evolve within, social communities and can even become part of the communities' identity (Büscher et al. 2001; Wenger 1998).
- Practices entail both a momentum of stability as well as change. While practices manifest and reproduce historically developed patterns of activity, they are also open to change in that the concrete activities have to be continuously adapted to new situations and changing conditions (Chaiklin 2011).
- Even though practices are often characterized by the use of particular artefacts (e.g. giving a PowerPoint presentation), practices are not determined by these artefacts in a strict sense. This difference is due to the fact that an artefact becomes a tool only when interpreted as such within a social and historical context.
- Practices do not exist in isolation but are part of a larger network of practices that is dependent on a broad-based notion of context. Practices are interrelated as both individual and collective actors, as well as artefacts are usually enrolled and used in several practices simultaneously.
- Practice is the research object to which studies of cultural-historical theory is directed (Chaiklin 2011). As a result, any scientific understanding of work practice must include some analysis of the socio-historical context in which the practice becomes enacted, since practice acts as a scaffold to augment and direct human actions (though in a non-deterministic way) within a work context.
- Practice represents a meaning-processing system, which processes information by constructing meaning, uniting action and meaning. It is essentially concerned with the ways in which actions can be rendered as meaningful, i.e. how a particular action, for example, becomes meaningful or is interpreted by certain people by virtue of where it was performed, when it was performed and with whom or what (Dourish 2004; Wenger 1998).

The concept of work practice offers an approach for organizing tools, actors and resources in a work environment, as well as for portraying how and why certain tools, actors and resources are used in certain knowledge use and sharing activities in relation to prevailing local contexts.

23.2.3 The Role of Context

One of the most significant elements that has emerged from work practice studies over the last two decades is the notion of the situatedness of work (Szymanski and Whalen 2011). This perspective argues that work, as well as knowledge use and sharing, contrary to the commonly held views of plans and rationalistic thinking, unfolds in response to the contingencies of a situation. Context allows us to address the situatedness and knowledge use and sharing and to recognize in the application of the practice theoretical perspective that knowledge sharing in health care is heavily reliant on practices that support common perceptions of shared knowledge artefacts. Practice is intrinsically linked with contexts so much so that each produces and locates the other in a complex interplay of socially produced knowledge, practices and relations (Saltmarsh 2009).

Similar to many applications for personalized support and intelligent services, healthcare knowledge management systems are highly dependent on their execution context (Bricon-Soufa and Newman 2007). A common definition of context considers it as "any information that can be used to characterize the situation of an entity", where an entity refers to a person, place or object that is considered relevant in an interaction sequence (Dey 2001). Context is critical in the design of care support systems for the elderly because of its ability to enable us to construct and maintain awareness of a person's activities, status or context in different settings; yet, it has remained a poor source of information in computing environments (Dey 2001). As a result, the term has been considered differently by different authors—as the surroundings of the interaction between the user and the application (Coutaz et al. 2005), what is needed to characterize and encode the situation of an entity, information about the activity or task the user is currently performing or what is needed to understand what people do and how and why they achieve and maintain a mutual understanding of the context for their actions (Dourish 2004).

23.3 Applying the Practice Theoretical Perspective

In this section, we describe how a practice-centred approach to healthcare knowledge management could contribute to the challenge of building computer applications that allow individuals to more effectively construct and convey information about their contexts of work, including actual work practices, local circumstances and varying work situations in a manner that facilitates cross-boundary knowledge sharing and decision support beyond what is currently offered by existing workflow-based approaches. A practice theoretical perspective allows us to uncover the specific details of knowledge use and sharing at the work practice level, i.e. the level at which work unfolds in the actual sense. Under the EBP approach, evidence is often generated out of controlled experiments, and, as a result, their use often guides knowledge reuse at an abstract level and hardly incorporates details of actionable tasks and processes necessary for accomplishing work in a real-world context (Anya and Tawfik 2016; Anya et al. 2010).

23.3.1 Capturing Practice-Related Knowledge

The first step in applying the practice theoretical perspective is to capture practice-related knowledge. Practice-related knowledge belongs to the form of knowledge known as tacit or "know-how", rather than explicit or factual knowledge (Wickramasinghe and Davison 2004). It is also hugely a subjective form of knowledge.

To address these challenges, we carried out a user-centred study of clinical work practices in order to understand the "what", "how" and "why" behind their knowledge use and sharing practices for patient care support. The goal is to provide a user-centred basis for our approach to applying the practice theoretical perspective to healthcare knowledge management and to identify design requirements to inform the development of technological support and e-health decision support. Specifically, we believe that by collecting an account of the various ways by which clinicians often contextualize procedures, improvise practices in order to accommodate for peculiar workplace circumstances and specific patient-centred needs and seek to construct meaning out of their local interactions with technologies, one can provide some useful insights into the design of knowledge management systems for e-health decision support at a work practice level. The details of the study appear in Tawfik et al. (2012). The findings indicate that differences in clinical practices and approaches to knowledge use and sharing among clinicians are associated with differences in local work contexts across work settings but are moderated by their adherence to best practice guidelines and the need for patient-centred care. The study further reveals that an awareness, especially of the ontological, stereotypical and situated practices, plays a crucial role in adapting knowledge for patient care decision support (Table 23.1).

23.3.2 Modelling Practice-Related Knowledge

In this section, we describe our approach to modelling practice-related knowledge use and sharing, which is concerned with using the knowledge acquired from a work process ("know-how") to enable context-aware patient care decision support. Our approach combines adaptations of the activity system and the situation awareness theory in a model that considers non-workflow-based aspects of work, e.g. the situated factors of a work environment in order to accommodate accounts of the situated perspective of healthcare knowledge use and sharing.

A work practice model brings out details of the rich contextual framework in which work unfolds and suggests lines of enquiry that would potentially lead to

Table 23.1 Process-data vs. practice-based data in healthcare KM (Adapted from Leidner et al. 2006)

Element	Process-based knowledge	Practice-based knowledge
Role	Handle task execution	Mainly act to influence task execution based on prevailing circumstances of work
Nature of knowledge	Formal work specifications, domain rules and conceptual knowledge	Informal specifications, common sense knowledge, world views, local norms, organizational values and beliefs, power structures, rituals, stories and myths
	Rigid and generic, i.e. independent of work settings	Flexible and easily adapts to changes in local work settings, e.g. availability of tools and services
Type of knowledge	Explicit knowledge—codified in rules, tools and processes	Mostly tacit knowledge—unarticulated knowledge not easily captured or codified
Context/model type	Mostly ontological context and domain model and stereotyped context	Mostly situated context and situation model and often stereotyped context
Means of transmission	Formal controls, procedures and standard operating procedures with heavy emphasis on information technologies to support knowledge creation, codification, transfer and decision support	Informal social groups that engage in storytelling and improvisation
Affecting factors	Factors within internal work processes, e.g. task methods	External factors, such as economic status, government policies and regional agenda
Means of enabling awareness	Through formal processes	Through the extent of influence on work processes in order to enable or constrain them
Means of mediation	Rules, tools, roles, subjects and objects	Tools, roles, subjects and objects, community, history and social and cultural practices
Paradigm	Rationalistic thinking, task structures, workflow-based technologies	Activity, cultural-historical and social theories
Practice system category	Ontological, stereotyped	Situated, stereotyped
Benefits	Provides structure to harness generated ideas and knowledge	Provides an environment to generate and share high-value tacit knowledge for decision support
	Achieves scale in knowledge reuse	Provides spark for fresh ideas and responsiveness to changing environment
Disadvantages	Fails to tap into tacit knowledge. May limit innovation and forces participants into fixed patterns of thinking	Can result in inefficiency. Abundance of ideas with no structure to implement them

(continued)

Table 23.1 (continued)

Element	Process-based knowledge	Practice-based knowledge
Role of information technology	Heavy investment in IT to connect people with reusable codified knowledge	Moderate investment in IT to facilitate conversations and transfer of tacit knowledge and "influencers" for more adaptive cross-boundary decision support

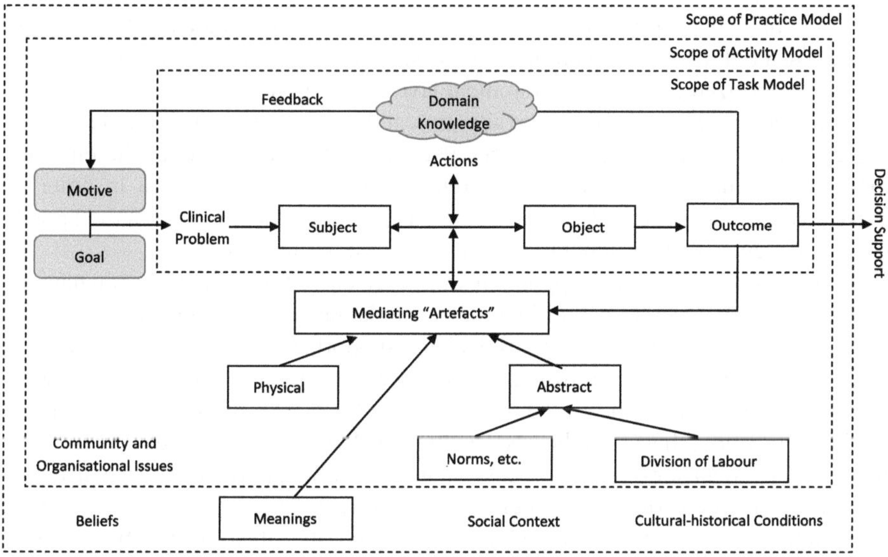

Fig. 23.1 Scope of a practice-based knowledge management model highlighting the role and relationships among various elements of work practice in enabling an understanding of knowledge use at the work practice level (Adapted from Wilson 2006)

enhanced adaptive cross-boundary support to work, which a less detailed analysis would not suggest. To further highlight this, we extended a process model of activity proposed by Wilson (2006) and show how a work practice model offers a much wider scope than an activity or a task model for understanding the context and setting in which we perform our activities. Figure 23.1 shows how work is realized within this system from the perspective of a work process, driven by motive and goal and directed (by work practice elements and activity factors) towards a desired outcome (Wilson 2006).

In order to appropriately model these situation-dependent factors, we employ the use of a situation awareness model. We describe this situation awareness model and show how we have integrated it into the work practice model. At the core of the situation awareness model is a situation model—a "setting" consisting of entities and interactions among entities, which one becomes aware of via the situation awareness model. The notion of a situation model enables us to understand "the complete state of the universe [of work] at an instant of time" in relation to what influences a clinician's actions and task requirements. We will show in the next section how we have further incorporated context modelling into a practice model in order to portray the subsets of this universe that are considered "contextually relevant" to decision-making at any instant (Dourish 2004).

Next, we apply the situation awareness model proposed by Endsley (1995). The primary basis of the situation awareness model, as we apply it to this work, is to gain an understanding of the state of a clinical work situation with a view to knowing how information, events and one's own actions (or those of others) will impact the goals and objectives of providing the best possible care to the patient. Based on his well-known definition of situation awareness, Endsley's situation awareness model can be categorized into three hierarchical levels: perception of elements in current situation, comprehension of current situation and projection of future status. At the perception level, the model recognizes necessary information about the environment. The comprehension level interprets the perceived information in order to make sense of the current of the environment. The projection level uses the knowledge of the current environment to predict its possible future states.

Endsley's model has been applied in areas such as air traffic control, ship navigation and military operations but includes a fundamental assumption that makes it unsuitable to cross-boundary clinical decision support. The researcher assumes that the agent seeking to gain an awareness of a situation and to influence his/her decision by the elements in the situation is a direct observer of the situation. In cross-boundary e-health, this is not the case; a clinician A wanting to provide a suggestion to support the decision-making process of another clinician, B, who is in a different workplace or even geographical region, is not a direct observer of the situation B is in. As a result, we have refined the basic structure of the situation awareness model by inserting two new levels—conceptualization and stereotyping between perception and comprehension—and moving projection to the decision support phase. Figure 23.2 depicts the resultant model for enabling healthcare knowledge management from a practice theoretical perspective and consists of four phases: *perception of work situation*, *conceptualization of work domain*, *stereotyping of work locality and comprehension of work status and problem requirements*.

The model allows information interchange and decision support across clinical work settings and disparate practice systems. In principle, it aims to generate contextually enriched knowledge in order to adaptively support decision in a specific work context by explicating the forms of work practices in a specific work setting and consequently tailoring an information item (which we refer to as a suggestion), which originates from a different work setting, to fit into the practices and problem-solving patterns in the user's work context in a way that accommodates for both institution-specific and situation-dependent variations in care.

Typically, when people provide suggestions towards assisting other people, e.g. in online forums, they usually provide the information item in a general context or, at least, in terms of their own individual contexts and experiences. As has been argued in this work, people in different work settings, e.g. clinicians—owing to differences in work culture, available resources and expertise, patients' needs and institutional agenda—have evolved work practices that conform to their work

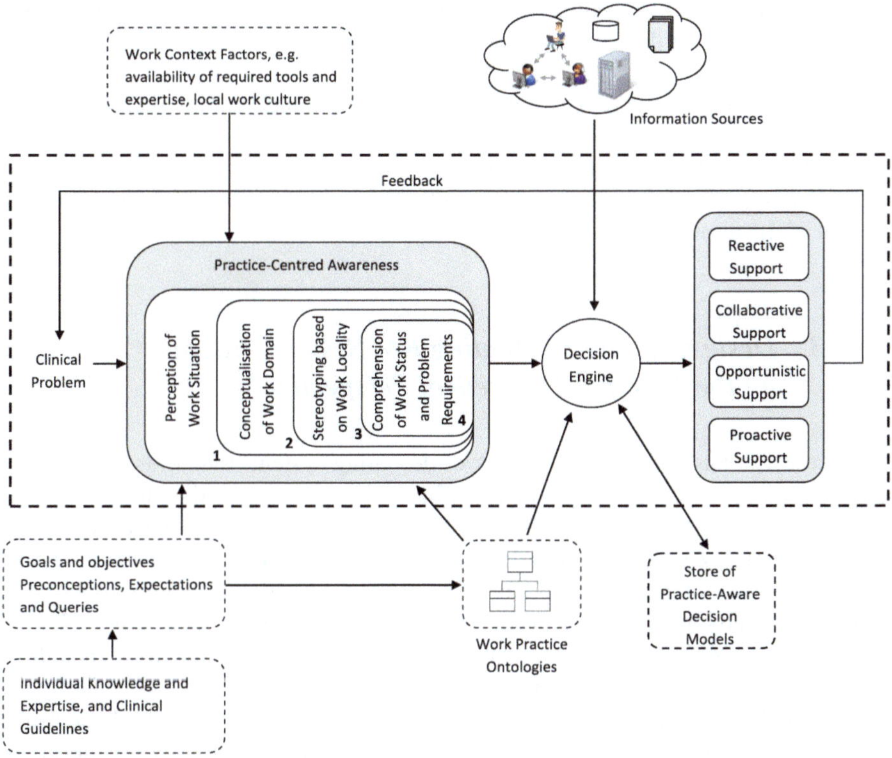

Fig. 23.2 A practice-centred knowledge management model (Adapted from Endsley 1995)

contexts and seek to address their individual issues. We posit that in order to be effective, a suggestion needs to adapt to the various ways by which a user works. As a result, our context-morphing approach aims to restructure (i.e. customize) the information content of a suggestion in order to add value to the ways by which clinicians often contextualize problem-solving procedures in order to accommodate for specific local contexts and individual patient-centred needs (Harrison et al. 2010; Gabbay and le May 2011). To achieve this, our approach focuses on the following actions:

- Improvise: What resources, tools, expertise and standardized services does the user lack? How do they make up for them by virtue of their work practices? How can the suggestion provided help users in accomplishing this in relation to their overall work goal and expected solution?
- Influence: What internal (person-related and organization-dependent) and external (e.g. regional policies) factors have shaped the user's decision-making? How do the factors affect the decision quality? How can the suggestion provided help ensure quality?

- Augment: How can the suggestion enrich the user's work practices and existing information towards achieving the overall work goal and expected solution and vice versa?
- Explain: How can the suggestion help offer an explanation or justification for the user's work practices (Kofod-Petersen and Aamodt 2009)?
- Apply: Here the suggestion is directly applied to user work context without any action on it. This occurs where the work context of the suggestion provider and that of the user are similar.

23.3.3 Designing and Evaluating KM Systems Based on the Practice Theoretical Perspective

Most research has approached the task of designing systems that relate to the context of computation by focusing on the technical issues associated with context, e.g. the syntactic connections between different concepts or the use of sensor technologies to enable systems to respond to changes in the computational environment (Dourish 2004; Kaenampornpan and O'Neill 2005). However, much effort is still required to study and analyse context from a knowledge-level perspective (Newell 1981). By seeking to construct a computational model of context of work, including organizations of people, tools and resources for work, as well as the underlying motives and circumstances of problem-solving, our approach aims to build decision support systems that are aware of their "context" through an ontology of "the structure of a total world" (Newell 1981). From a knowledge-level perspective, a thrust of this research is to understand the "work practices" of clinicians across various regional and organizational work settings in order to enable context-aware decision support in a manner that takes account of the "bounded rationality" across work setting (Simon 1991).

23.4 Discussion and Concluding Remarks

Although this chapter explored the application of the practice theoretical perspective to healthcare knowledge management, the specific approach described is based on the activity theory and the theory of situation awareness. Whereas activity theory belongs to the family of practice theories (Foot 2014), allowing us a lens for uncovering the real actions of practitioners as they engage in clinical decision; the theory of situation awareness provides a framework for the perception of environmental elements and events with respect to the time and place of decision-making. Their combined used enables the exploration of how practice can be used, managed and transformed to suit various clinical problem situations and patients' needs. The approach blurs the distinction between action and context to explore the notion that practice supports common perception of shared knowledge items within and across communities of practice. A key thesis of the chapter is that the dynamics of knowledge management in patient care decision-making is complex and particularly challenging when knowledge is shared across community and organizational boundaries in collaborative health care. The process is reliant on contextual features that support common perceptions of shared information and usually occurs within a complex structure of clinical work practices that is shaped by a wide range of factors, including organizational culture, local contexts, socially constructed traditions of actions, experiences and patients' circumstances, which vary across organizational and community settings.

We argue that an integrated approach to understanding knowledge management in health care is needed and could lead to the design of improved system to support better knowledge use and sharing at the point of care and point of need. A large part of the paradox of healthcare knowledge management is that though information technology has enabled a knowledge-rich healthcare system with accessible databases and repositories, healthcare knowledge remains largely underutilized, and often wrongly utilized, in patient care decision-making. Addressing the problems facing the healthcare sector from a knowledge management perspective calls for an integrated approach with the capability to manage the tension between evidence-based practice and practice-based evidence, which in many ways has a lot in common with the tension between process data or between explicit knowledge and tacit knowledge. A practice theoretical perspective would enable healthcare organizations to uncover and understand the communication and coordination practices that make for more effective and efficient patient care decision-making. By making their knowledge explicit and adhering to evidence-based standards, healthcare organizations will be more suitably equipped to develop standardized practice management techniques.

Besides knowledge management, the potential role of the practice theoretical perspective in healthcare knowledge management resonates strongly with one of the major concerns of the computer-supported cooperative work community with health care, namely, investigating how healthcare decision-making is collaboratively and practically achieved in various work contexts and designing systems to support that process (Fitzpatrick and Ellingsen 2013). Against this background, a practice theoretical perspective to healthcare knowledge has a lot to offer to computer-supported cooperative work research, including providing a framework to foster the articulation and sharing of clinical, operational knowledge and experiences in collaborative health care.

While a practice theoretical perspective is highly valuable in understanding and utilizing non-explicit and less evidence-based types of knowledge and making such knowledge assets more explicit, implementing healthcare knowledge management systems based on the practice theoretical perspective is hugely challenging. As noted by the areas of focus in this chapter, the challenges stem from the difficulty in capturing practice-related knowledge, modelling practice-related knowledge and designing and evaluating systems that are built and based on that approach. Recent trends in health care, including the proliferation of online healthcare knowledge resources easily available to patients, as well as new innovations in telemedicine, pose enormous challenges to healthcare knowledge management. We believe that addressing some of them effectively and efficiently would impact on elements of the practice theoretical perspective.

References

Abidi, S. S. R. (2006). Healthcare knowledge sharing: Purpose, practices and prospects. In R. Bali & A. Dwivedi (Eds.), *Healthcare knowledge management: Issues, advances and successes* (pp. 65–86). New York: Springer.

Abidi, S. S. R. (2008). Healthcare knowledge management: The art of the possible. In D. Riaño (Ed.), *Knowledge management for health care procedures, Lecture notes in computer science* (Vol. 4924). Berlin: Springer.

Allert, H., & Richter, C. (2008, April 1–2). Practices, systems, and context working as core concepts in modeling socio-technical systems. In M. Möller, T. Roth-Berghofer, & W. Neuser (Eds.), *Proceedings of the fifth international workshop on philosophy and informatics, WSPI 2008*, Kaiserslautern.

Anya, O., & Tawfik, H. (2016). Designing for practice-based context-awareness in ubiquitous e-health environments. *Computers & Electrical Engineering, 61*, 312–326. Retrieved August 24, 2016, from https://doi.org/10.1016/j.compeleceng.2016.08.012

Anya, O., Tawfik, H., Amin, S., Nagar, A., & Shaalan, K. (2010). Context-aware knowledge modelling for decision support in e-health. In *International joint conference on neural networks (IJCNN)* (pp. 1–7).

Bødker, S. (1991). Activity theory as a challenge to systems design. In H.-E. Nissen, H. K. Klein, & R. Hirschheim (Eds.), *Information systems research: Contemporary approaches and emergent traditions*. Amsterdam: North Holland.

Brézillon, P. (2011). Context-based management of practices. In *International workshop on modeling and reasoning in context, Karlsruhe, Germany*. Berlin, Germany: Springer.

Bricon-Soufa, N., & Newman, C. R. (2007). Context awareness in health care: A review. *International Journal of Medical Informatics, 76*, 2–12.

Büscher, M., Gill, S., Mogensen, P., & Shapiro, D. (2001). Landscapes of practice: Bricolage as a method for situated design. *CSCW, 10*, 1–28.

Button, G., & Harper, R. (1996). The relevance of 'work-practice' for design. *CSCW, 4*(4), 263–280.

Chaiklin, S. (2011). The role of practice in cultural-historical science. In M. Kontopodis, C. Wulf, & B. Fichtner (Eds.), *Children, development and education: Cultural, historical, anthropological perspectives* (pp. 227–246). Dordrecht: Springer.

Coutaz, J., Crowley, J. L., Dobson, S., & Garlan, D. (2005). Context is key. *Communications of the ACM, 48*, 49–53.

Davenport, T., & Prusak, L. (1998). *Working knowledge: How organizations manage what they know*. Boston: Harvard Business School Press.

Dey, A. K. (2001). Understanding and using context. *Personal and Ubiquitous Computing, 5*, 4–7.

Dourish, P. (2004). What we talk about when we talk about context. *Personal and Ubiquitous Computing, 8*(1), 19–30.

Endsley, M. R. (1995). Toward a theory of situation awareness in dynamic systems. *Human Factors, 37*(1), 32–64.

Fitzpatrick, G., & Ellingsen, G. (2013). A review of 25 years of CSCW research in healthcare: Contributions, challenges and future agendas. *Journal of CSCW, 22*, 609–665.

Foot, K. A. (2014). Cultural-historical activity theory: Exploring a theory to inform practice and research. *Journal of Human Behavior in Social Environment, 24*(3), 329–347.

Gabbay, J., & le May, A. (2011). *Practice-based evidence for healthcare: Clinical mindlines*. London: Routledge.
Harrison, M. B., Légaré, F., Graham, I. D., & Fervers, B. (2010). Adapting clinical practice guidelines to local context and assessing barriers to their use. *Canadian Medical Association Journal, 182*(2), E78–E84.
Hopwood, N. (2010). *Dwelling in complexity: Relational-ecological understandings of context, space, place, and the body in professional practice*. Presented at the AARE international research in education conference, Melbourne.
Kaenampornpan, M., & O'Neill, E. (2005). Integrating history and activity theory in context aware system design. In *International workshop on exploiting context histories in smart environments, pervasive '05*, Munich, Germany.
Kirsh, D. (2001). The context of work. *Human Computer Interaction, 16*(2–4), 305–322.
Kofod-Petersen, A., & Aamodt, A. (2009). Case-based reasoning for situation-aware ambient intelligence: A hospital ward evaluation study. In *International conference on case-based reasoning ICCBR'09* (pp. 450–464). Berlin, Germany: Springer.
Kuziemsky, C.E., & Varpio, L. (2010). Describing the clinical communication space through a model of common ground–you don't know what you don't know. *AMIA Annual Symposium* (pp. 407–411).
Leidner, D., Alavi, M., & Kayworth, T. (2006). The role of culture in knowledge management: A case study of two global firms. *International Journal of e-Collaboration, 2*(1), 17–40.
Mejia, D. A., Favela, J., & Morán, A. L. (2010). Understanding and supporting lightweight communication in hospital work. *IEEE Transactions on Information Technology in Biomedicine, 14*(1), 140–146.
Nardi, B. (1996). *Context and consciousness: Activity theory and human-computer interaction*. Cambridge, MA: MIT Press.
Newell, A. (1981). The knowledge level. *AI Magazine, 33*, 1–20.
Nicolini, D. (2008). Managing knowledge in the healthcare sector: A review. *International Journal of Management Review, 10*(3), 245–263.
Reckwitz, A. (2002). Towards a theory of social practices: A development in culturalist theorizing. *European Journal of Social Theory, 5*(2), 243–263.
Sackett, D. L., Straus, S. E., Richardson, W. S., Rosenberg, W., & Haynes, R. B. (2000). *Evidence-based medicine: How to practice and teach EBM* (2nd ed.). New York: Churchill Livingstone.
Saltmarsh, S. (2009). Researching context as a 'practiced place'. In B. Green (Ed.), *Understanding and researching professional practice* (pp. 153–163). Rotterdam: Sense Publishers.
Schatzki, T. R. (2012). A primer on practices: Theory and research. In *Practice-based education, Practice, education, work and society series* (Vol. 6, pp. 13–26).
Simon, H. (1991). Bounded rationality and organizational learning. *Organization Science, 2*(1), 125–134.
Szymanski, M. H., & Whalen, J. (Eds.). (2011). *Making work visible: Ethnographically grounded case studies of work practice*. Cambridge, UK: Cambridge University Press.
Tawfik, H., Anya, O., & Nagar, A. K. (2012). Understanding clinical work practices for cross-boundary decision support in e-health. *IEEE Transactions on Information Technology in Biomedicine, 16*(4), 530–541.
Wenger, E. (1998). *Communities of practice: Learning, meaning and identity*. Cambridge, UK: Cambridge University Press.
Whittaker, S., Frohlich, D., & Daly-Jones, O. (1994). Informal workplace communication: What is it like and how might we support it? In *Proceedings of the SIGCHI conference on human factors in computing systems: Celebrating Interdependence (CHI 1994)* (pp. 131–137), Boston, MA.
Wickramasinghe, N. (2009). Healthcare knowledge management: Incorporating the tools, technologies, strategies, and process of knowledge management to effect superior healthcare delivery. In R. Bali, & A. Dwivedi (ed.) *Healthcare knowledge management: issues, advances, and successes*, (pp. 87–103). Berlin: Springer.

Wickramasinghe, N., & Davison, G. (2004). Making explicit the implicit knowledge assets in healthcare: The case of multidisciplinary teams in care and cure environments. *Health Care Management Science, 7*(3), 185–195.

Wilson, T. D. (2006). A re-examination of information seeking behaviour in the context of activity theory. *Information Research, 11*(4), 11–14.

Chapter 24
Contemporary Developments in e-Health

Indrit Troshani and Nilmini Wickramasinghe

24.1 Introduction

Digitally enabled technologies including ICTs can support the achievement of health goals. ICT have the potential to transform the manner in which health services are delivered (WHO 2011). e-Health is defined as the use of ICT to improve health and healthcare outcomes (Lintonen et al. 2007; Mackert et al. 2009). e-Health is an emerging field which comprises the intersection of numerous disciplines, including medicine, biomedical engineering, computer and information science, statistics, health promotion and marketing, and management science (Anderson 1997; Chiasson and Davidson 2004; Wickramasinghe et al. 2007). ICT are touted to offer a huge potential to raise the quality, increase the efficiency, and decrease the costs of primary, secondary, and tertiary health care (Heinzelmann et al. 2005). Additionally, these technologies can empower patients to better understand their medical conditions and take responsibility by making informed decisions about such conditions (Raisinghani and Young 2008). More specifically, the espoused benefits of e-health include preventing and controlling of diseases by way of facilitating health information acquisition (Baker et al. 2003), customizing and personalizing information dissemination (Tate et al. 2006), detecting and treating diseases (Thomas et al. 2002), and encouraging the adoption of healthy lifestyles including weight control, physical activity, and quitting smoking (Tate et al. 2003).

For example, chronic diseases, such as diabetes in addition to having a huge impact on the diabetes sufferers themselves as previously illustrated, can also be

I. Troshani (✉)
Adelaide Business School, The University of Adelaide, Adelaide, SA, Australia
e-mail: indrit.troshani@adelaide.edu.au

N. Wickramasinghe
Deakin University, Burwood, VIC, Australia
e-mail: n.wickramasinghe@deakin.edu.au

N. Wickramasinghe, J. L. Schaffer (eds.), *Theories to Inform Superior Health Informatics Research and Practice*, Healthcare Delivery in the Information Age,
https://doi.org/10.1007/978-3-319-72287-0_24

very costly to treat (AIHW 2007, 2008). Yet, pervasive diabetes monitoring solutions can offer enormous benefits which include efficient and accurate monitoring and control of glucose levels and minimizing unnecessary hospitalizations or even just doctor visits (Wickramasinghe et al. 2009). These solutions have also been shown to improve patients' quality of life by preventing and controlling disease progress and instilling preventative behaviors among diabetes sufferers (Bali et al. 2013; Koch 2006; Wickramasinghe et al. 2010).

In this context, Chiasson and Davidson (2004) argue that although there is an increasing number of contributions to e-health research, knowledge in this area remains limited and underdeveloped. Additionally, as Koch (2006) and WHO (2011) argue, most modern developed healthcare systems are experiencing many challenges such as:

- Increasing demand for healthcare services due to increasing aging populations and changed lifestyles resulting often in chronic diseases
- Increasing demand for healthcare accessibility (e.g., home care)
- Increasing need for efficiency, personalization, and quality equity in health care
- Increasing and chronic staff shortages
- Limited budgets

There is widespread agreement in the literature that e-health can help in addressing these challenges. Thus, knowledge and understanding of current e-health trends can be useful in assisting researchers address these challenges since it can help understand why pervasive e-health solutions emerge and how they are shaped. Additionally, it can assist e-health scholars channel their research efforts. Thus, the aim of this chapter is to identify existing trends in e-health research. Having extensively reviewed extant research, we first discuss health education, electronic health records (EHR), standardization, and m-health. The chapter is subsequently concluded with a discussion of research directions.

24.2 Electronic Health Records (EHRs)

Electronic health records (EHRs) represent medical information concerning patients which is meant to support healthcare-related activities and evidence-based medical decision that support both directly or indirectly. This information is collected longitudinally during patient visits at any healthcare delivery setting (Raghupathi and Kesh 2009). In addition to patient demographics, EHRs also include past medical history such as medications, problems, immunizations, radiology and laboratory results, and progress notes (Raghupathi and Kesh 2009). It is anticipated that in the future EHRs will offer rich medically relevant information in addition to text. EHRs will include still images, echocardiograms, endoscopies, and even video recordings of patient interviews or visits which will enable convenient access to expertise that is located remotely and even facilitate training of medical practitioners (Heinzelmann et al. 2005).

EHRs can offer many benefits including complete, accurate, error-free universally accessible lifetime patient health information (Raghupathi and Kesh 2009). They also offer significant productivity improvements in the healthcare industry (von Lubitz and Wickramasinghe 2006). In a healthcare setting where healthcare costs are steadily increasing, while pressures are growing to satisfy unmet needs and increasing competition, the promises of EHRs to offer quality and productivity constitute the main driving forces for developing them.

There are a number of risks that need to be mitigated as EHR development progresses and design issues addressed. Although EHRs offer many benefits, healthcare professionals may find that with EHRs they may be exchanging a set of issues with one another. For example, issues experienced with traditional manual paper-based patient record systems such as lost patient charts, poor handwriting, and missing information may be exchanged with issues with data capture problems, computer crashes, programming errors, and susceptibility for viruses and other malware which are likely to affect EHRs and potentially render them useless (Glaser and Aske 2010; Goldschmidt 2005).

Another major issue with EHRs concerns the privacy and security of confidential personal medical and health information (Rao Hill and Troshani 2010; Troshani and Rao Hill 2009). For example, unethical use of such information for personal gain by disgruntled or unethical employees or even legislated use of private information without an individual's prior consent constitute serious risks that need to be mitigated as EHRs are developed (Goldschmidt 2005). Thus, the question that needs further research is if the espoused benefits of EHRs will indeed outweigh their risks and development costs (Rash 2005).

Extant research shows that EHR design and development have been constrained by major challenges (Raghupathi and Kesh 2009). First, the literature suggests that existing EHRs seem to be driven by specific vendors or technologies and ignore the diverse and complex nature of modern healthcare settings and processes (Blobel 2006). For example, driven by specific vendors, existing EHRs do not appear to comply with portability standards (Hippisley-Cox et al. 2003; Troshani and Lymer, 2010). Additionally, almost all exiting EHRs are based on relatively simple relational database applications which consist of patient data entry forms and report generation capabilities, but which lack the capacity to be interoperable in large-scale distributed environments and to inexpensively scale up to fully functional applications (Hippisley-Cox et al. 2003; Raghupathi and Kesh 2009). One possible way to address these issues is to take a holistic network-centric view to EHR design (von Lubitz and Wickramasinghe 2006; Troshani et al. 2015).

24.3 Using Blockchain Technology for EHR Management

While the risks discussed in the previous section can be critical and can affect EHR management, new technology has emerged that can help mitigate them. For example, blockchain technology can be used to manage EHR. A blockchain is a distributed database system that keeps track of a records (Molteni 2017; Tapscott and Tapscott 2016). As records are added to the blockchain, they are ordered in blocks, and each block contains timestamp links to the related blocks.

Blockchain records are secure and easily verifiable. As events or transactions that are captured as records occur, decentralized verification of their authenticity is carried out by majority consensus in networks (Ekblaw et al. 2016).

That is, a record capturing an event becomes part of the blockchain if and only if significant effort is made by players in the network validating its genuineness and authenticity. Additionally, because network consensus is always required, alteration of records becomes very difficult and expensive. That is, blockchain technology ensures that the effort required to alter a record (e.g., for the purpose of committing fraud, etc.) always exceeds the benefits or gains that result from attempts to alter the record. This reduces incentives of individuals or groups to change blockchain records which indicates that what is in the blockchain is accurate and authentic (Molteni 2017).

Because the blockchain is managed autonomously in peer-to-peer network, information in it is not stored in a single location and is always available to use and verify and not susceptible to loss (e.g., because part of the network fails). Additionally, because verification and recording of information is carried out by the network, the need for intermediating role of trusted authority or central server is significantly reduced or, depending on application, even eliminated (Ekblaw et al. 2016).

While in its purest form information in the blockchain is available to anyone, it is possible to create a blockchain where permissions concerning the right of individuals to add, record in, and read information on a block chain can be easily controlled. Private blockchains, as opposed to public blockchains, can be suitable tools for EHR management (Buterin 2015).

24.4 Health Education

Recent research has stressed the need for improving health literacy and education, particularly, because it can have a huge impact on individual quality of life, public health, and even more broadly, on national economies (Ball and Lillis 2001; Gazmararian et al. 2005; Mackert et al. 2009). Many organizations around the world are using pervasive e-health technologies to address health literacy and education problems. The main reason for this is attributed to the fact the e-health technologies offer adaptability, cost-effectiveness, and accessibility (Eysenbach 2007). In addition to this, findings reported in Ball and Lillis (2001) concerning a study conducted by Deloitte and Touche and VHA Inc. reveal that two thirds of the US patients do not receive any literature in relation to their medication conditions. At least in part, this is getting patients to take matters into their own hands and look for medical information online (Ball and Lillis 2001; Wickramasinghe et al. 2009).

One of the technologies that is receiving much attention is Web 2.0. It offers online activities that encourage interactivity and collaboration through interpersonal networking and personalization while also fostering a sense of community among users (Abram 2005). There are many Web 2.0 applications that offer a huge potential for health literacy and healthcare education (Boulos and Wheeler 2007) including wikis, blogs, podcasting, RSS feeds, social networking applications, and instant messaging (IM). We explain these in turn and illustrate them with examples about how they are being used in relation to health literature and education (Sharif et al. 2014, 2015).

A *wiki* is a collaborative application that allows users to provide content while also enabling that content to be edited by anybody (Boulos et al. 2006). In healthcare settings, wikis can be used for knowledge sharing (e.g., http://www.wikisurgery.com). Additionally, wikis offer strong localization capabilities enabling non-English posts as well. For example, DiabetesPost at http://www.diabetespost.com/ enables posts to be made in Arabic.

Blogs enable users to provide online journals or web diaries that can be easily published and updated chronologically on issues of interest or on common themes including health literacy and education (Boulos et al. 2006). Some of the most notable health education blogs include http://drugscope.blogspot.com and http://biographyofbreastcancer.blogspot.com. As blog users are not necessarily professionals, there is a substantial risk for misinformation, although, according to Boulos et al. (2006), inherent "collaborative intelligence" acts as a built-in quality control and assurance mechanism for blogs (Sharif et al. 2014, 2015).

Podcasts are location- and time-independent digital files that can be downloaded automatically by free software on portable devices, such as Apple iPods/iPads or MP3/MP4 players and played by users at their leisure (Boulos and Wheeler 2007). Notable examples of health education podcasts include http://healthliteracyoutloud.com.

RSS (Really Simple Syndication) feeds are protocols that are used to indicate updates or additions to content to websites or blogs as per user-defined queries or requirements (Boulos and Wheeler 2007). Typically, RSS works when users subscribe to RSS feeds using RSS aggregators that are typically supported in modern browsers. Aggregators crawl selected websites regularly and display feeds to users enabling them to conveniently and quickly overview updates on specific topics at any point in time at the selected websites (Boulos and Wheeler 2007).

Social networking applications enable forming of groups of individuals that share common interests or circumstances. For example, http://www.depressionnet.com.au is an Australian online community that provides comprehensive information for people living with depression. A similar social networking application is the CURE DiABETES group at http://groups.myspace.com/cureDiABETES which is run by patients and supporters in order to help and support diabetes sufferers (Sharif et al. 2016).

Instant messaging (IM) constitutes real-time online interaction between two or more users who can share text, audio, video, and other types of files. A nurse-led web chat application enabling the public to interact with qualified nurses was well received by patients (Eminovic et al. 2004).

As patients wish to interact and exchange increasingly more information with healthcare providers, opportunities exist for using Web 2.0 tools and applications to enable or facilitate these interactions for literacy development and education purposes. By emphasizing education, these tools empower patients to take responsibility for their conditions, thereby making them active and responsible participants in their treatment regimen (Boulos et al. 2006; Boulos and Wheeler 2007; Mackert et al. 2009; Nicholas et al. 2001).

24.5 Standardization

Standardization entails developing standards in the development and provision of pervasive e-health applications and limiting the use of other options (Choudrie et al. 2003; Damsgaard and Lyytinen 2001; King et al. 1994; Troshani and Lymer 2010). Standards constitute conventions that are needed for the structure and behavior of computing functions, formats, and processes (Engel et al. 2006). Standards play a critical role in the transmissions of electronic information, and as such, standard development, that is, standardization, is essential for the development and widespread diffusion of pervasive e-health applications. Lack of standardization can create interoperability issues adversely impacting information exchange between and among various e-health applications, that is, e-health applications can become "information islands" and thus present difficulties to integrate with larger healthcare systems (Tang et al. 2006).

For example, standards developed for electronic payments in the finance and banking sectors worldwide have been highly successful and have become widely diffused due to the national and international standardization approaches adopted and coordination among key stakeholders (WHO 2011). Similarly, governments and industry associations are collaborating by way of the Global Harmonization Task Force in order to develop standards for medical technologies (WHO 2011).

Standardization facilitates both integration and interoperability, thereby enabling industry growth and development, while lack thereof can make the development of pervasive e-health applications and their integration prohibitively costly (Engel et al. 2006; Koch 2006; Lee et al. 2009). Standardization can include many aspects of e-health, ranging from terminology, text/image communications, health hardware devices, and even security and privacy (Lee et al. 2009). For example, South Korean e-health initiatives are considering the US Health Insurance Portability and Accountability Act (HIPAA) as a security standard for medical data and the International Classification of Diseases (ICD) for terminology standardization (Lee et al. 2009).

24.6 m-Health

Mobile health or simply m-health is defined as a component of e-health, whereby medical practice is supported by mobile devices including mobile phones and personal digital assistants (PDAs) or any other wireless devices (WHO 2011). According to the International Telecommunications Union (ITU), there are over 5 billion wireless subscribers in the world, over 70% of which reside in low- to middle-income countries (ITU 2010). The widespread accessibility and availability of mobile phones makes these devices very powerful media for reaching individuals generally (e.g., with general health promotion messages) and patients suffering from various medical conditions, in particular, by way of mobile health applications.

Evidence collected in a recent World Health Organization (WHO) study shows that there are numerous activities of m-health services that are currently being offered in member countries including health call centers, emergency toll-free telephone services, managing emergencies and disasters, mobile telemedicine, appointment reminders, community mobilization and health promotion, treatment compliance, mobile patient records, information access, patient monitoring, health surveys and data collection, surveillance, health awareness raising, and decision support systems (ITU 2010). While 83% of WHO member states offer at least one of these m-health services, many offer 4–6 with the most popular m-health services being health call centers (59%), emergency toll-free telephone services (55%), managing emergencies and disasters (54%), and mobile telemedicine (49%) (WHO 2011). As might be expected, the WHO study also shows that counties in the high-income group have implemented a greater range of m-health initiatives than those in the lower-income groups, while m-health call centers and healthcare help lines appear to be popular across all income groups (WHO 2011). Additionally, all income categories identified competing m- and e-health priorities was one of the greatest barriers to m-health adoption (WHO 2011).

A recent study carried out by PriceWaterhouseCoopers's Health Research Institute (HRI) presents the case for the market for m-health applications and services. For example, in a recent survey they conducted, they found that 40% of respondents are willing to pay for remote health monitoring devices and monthly service fees to send data automatically to their doctors, while, based on these respondents, HRI estimate that the annual market for mobile health monitoring devices ranges between $7.7 and 43 billion (PWC 2010).

The PWC study also identifies three main business models that can be viable in the m-health market (PWC 2010). First, the *operational/clinical business model* enables all healthcare stakeholders including providers, payers, medical device, and drug companies to use m-health applications to run their operations more efficiently. Second, the *consumer products and services model* provides unique value-added m-health applications to individuals. Third, the *infrastructure business model* offers connecting and secure infrastructures that enable m-health information and services (PWC 2010). Further research is required to evaluate the viability and effectiveness of these models in practice.

24.7 Conclusion and Future Research

The healthcare industry is under increasing pressure worldwide from many challenges including quality improvements, chronic staff shortages, and limited resources including financial and human resources. The use of ICT to enable health care and improve health outcomes, e-health, is touted to transform the healthcare industry and help address these challenges. Although, the number of contributions in e-health research is steadily growing, knowledge in this area remains still at an embryonic stage (Chiasson and Davidson 2004). Having extensively reviewed extant research, we have discussed current e-health trends including health education, electronic health records (HER), standardization, and m-health. We believe that this discussion can assist e-health scholars hone in their efforts and extend existing limited research in these areas.

For successful implementations to become a reality in the identified areas, adoption of corresponding e-health applications by both patients and healthcare providers is necessary (Raisinghani and Young 2008). In order for adoption to occur, coordinated campaigns are needed to establish public awareness and understanding concerning the value of e-health applications. These campaigns can encourage open learning and information sharing. Additionally, given the complexity of e-health applications and diversity of stakeholders that they may ultimately affect, partnerships should be fostered between the different stakeholders including vendors, patients, providers, insurers, and drug and medical device companies as well as between public and private sectors (Raisinghani and Young 2008).

New research directions can extend the areas identified in the previous sections in many ways. First, controlled studies can focus on longitudinal analyses and investigations targeting the adoption of e-health applications and services in the identified areas (Cline and Haynes 2001; Wickramasinghe et al. 2016). Second, cost/benefits evaluations can be carried out to assess whether the costs involved in developing e-health applications can be offset by espoused benefits that these applications promise to offer (Halkias et al. 2008). Third, further research needs to investigate the demographics of the patients seeking to use e-health applications, how they use them, the information they seek and its quality, and how their behaviors can be affected (Wyatt 1997). This can also help identify underserved communities, thereby, address equity concerns. Finally, further research can also examine the manner in which public policy can assist the development of e-health applications (e.g., subsidies, training) (Cline and Haynes 2001; Troshani et al. 2012).

References

Abram, S. (2005). Web 2.0-huh? Library 2.0, librarian 2.0. *Information Outlook, 9*(1), 44–45.

AIHW. (2007). *National indicators for monitoring diabetes: Report of the diabetes indicators review subcommittee of the national diabetes data working group*. AIHW cat. no. CVD 38. Canberra, Australia: AIHW.

AIHW. (2008). *Diabetes: Australian facts 2008*. Canberra, ACT: Australian Institute of Health and Welfare.

Anderson, J. G. (1997). Clearing the way for physicians' use of clinical information systems. *Communications of the ACM, 40*(8), 83–90.

Baker, L., Wagner, T. H., Singer, S., & Bundorf, M. K. (2003). Use of the internet and e-mail for health care information: Results from a national survey. *Journal of American Medical Association (JAMA), 289*(18), 2400–2406.

Bali, R., Troshani, I., Goldberg, S., & Wickramasinghe, N. (Eds.). (2013). *Pervasive health knowledge management*. New York: Springer.

Ball, M. J., & Lillis, J. (2001). E-health: Transforming the physician/patient relationship. *International Journal of Medical Informatics, 61*(1), 1–10.

Blobel, B. G. M. E. (2006). Advanced EHR architectures-promises or reality. *Methods of Information in Medicine, 45*(1), 95–101.

Boulos, M. N. K., Maramba, I., & Wheeler, S. (2006). Wikis, blogs and podcasts. A new generation of web-based tools for virtual collaborative clinical practice and education. *British Medical Journal, 6*, 41. http://www.biomedcentral.com/1472-6920/6/41.

Boulos, M. N. K., & Wheeler, S. (2007). The emerging web 2.0 social software: An enabling suite of sociable technologies in health and health care education. *Health Information and Libraries Journal, 24*(1), 2–23.

Buterin, V. (2015). *On public and private blockchains*. Ethereum Blog: Ethereum Foundation. Retrieved March 03, 2017, from https://blog.ethereum.org/2015/08/07/on-public-and-private-blockchains/

Chiasson, M., & Davidson, E. (2004). Pushing the contextual envelope: Developing and diffusing IS theory for health information systems research. *Information and Organization, 14*(3), 155–188.

Choudrie, J., Papazafeiropoulou, A., & Lee, H. (2003). A web of stakeholders and strategies: A case of broadband diffusion in South Korea. *Journal of Information Technology, 18*, 281–290.

Cline, R. J. W., & Haynes, K. M. (2001). Consumer health information seeking on the internet: The state of the art. *Health Education Research, 16*(6), 671–692.

Damsgaard, J., & Lyytinen, K. (2001). The role of intermediating institutions in the diffusion of electronic data interchange (EDI): How industry associations intervened in Denmark, Finland, and Hong Kong. *The Information Society, 17*(3), 195–210.

Ekblaw, A., Azaria, A., Halamka, J. D., & Lippman, A. (2016). *A case study for blockchain in healthcare: "MedRec" prototype for electronic health records and medical research data*. White Paper. Boston: MIT Media Lab and Beth Israel Deaconess Medical Center. Retrieved March 03, 2017, from https://www.healthit.gov/sites/default/files/5-56-onc_blockchainchallenge_mitwhitepaper.pdf

Eminovic, N., Wyatt, J. C., Tarpey, A. M., Murray, G., & Ingrams, G. J. (2004). First evaluation of the NHS direct online clinical enquiry service: A nurse-led web chat triage service for the public. *Journal of Medical Internet Research, 6*, e17. http://www.jmir.org//2/e17/.

Engel, K., Blobel, B., & Pharow, P. (2006). Standards for enabling health informatics interoperability. In A. Hasman, R. Haux, J. Van Der Lei, E. De Clercq, & F. H. R. France (Eds.), *Ubiquity: Technologies for better health in aging societies, Studies in health technology and informatics* (Vol. 124, pp. 145–150). Amsterdam: IOS Press.

Eysenbach, G. (2007). Credibility of health information and digital media: New perspectives and implications for youth. In B. E. Metzger & A. J. Flanagin (Eds.), *Digital media, youth, and credibility*. Cambridge, MA: MIT Press.

Gazmararian, J., Curran, J., Parker, R., Bernhardt, J., & DeBuono, B. (2005). Public health literacy in America: An ethical imperative. *American Journal of Preventative Medicine, 28*(3), 317–322.

Glaser, J., & Aske, J. (2010). Healthcare IT trends raise bar for information security. *Healthcare Financial Management, 64*(7), 40–44.

Goldschmidt, P. G. (2005). HIT and MIS: Implications of health information technology and medical information systems. *Communications of the ACM, 48*(10), 69–74.

Halkias, D., Harkiolakis, N., & Thurman, P. (2008). Internet use for health-related purposes among Greek consumers. *Telemedicine and e-Health, 14*(3), 255–260.

Heinzelmann, P. J., Lugn, N. E., & Kvedar, J. C. (2005). Telemedicine in the future. *Journal of Telemedicine and Telecare, 11*, 384–390.

Hippisley-Cox, J., Pringle, M., Cates, R., Wyna, A., Hammersley, V., Coupland, C., et al. (2003). The electronic patient record in primary care–regression or progression? A cross sectional study. *British Medical Journal, 326*, 1439–1443.

ITU. (2010). *The world in 2010: ICT facts and figures*. Geneva: International Telecommunications Union (ITU). http://www.itu.int/ITU-D/material/FactsFigures2010.pdf.

King, J. L., Gurbaxani, V., Kraemer, K. L., McFarlan, K. L., Raman, K. S., & Yap, C. S. (1994). Institutional factors in information technology innovation. *Information Systems Research, 5*(2), 139–169.

Koch, S. (2006). Home telehealth-current state and future trends. *International Journal of Medical Informatics, 75*, 565–576.

Lee, M., Min, S. D., Shin, H. S., Lee, B. W., & Kim, J. K. (2009). The e-health landscape: Current status and future prospects in Korea. *Telemedicine and e-Health, 15*(4), 362–369.

Lintonen, T. P., Konu, A. I., & Seedhouse, D. (2007). Information technology in health promotion. *Health Education Research, 23*(3), 560–566.

Mackert, M., Love, B., & Whitten, P. (2009). Patient education on mobile devices: An e-health intervention for low health literate audiences. *Journal of Information Science, 35*(1), 82–93.

Molteni, M. (2017). *Moving patient data is messy, but blockchain is here to help*. San Francisco: Wired.com. Retrieved March 03, 2017, from https://www.wired.com/2017/02/moving-patient-data-messy-blockchain-help/

Nicholas, D., Huntington, P., Williams, P., & Blackburn, P. (2001). Digital health informatin provision and health outcomes. *Journal of Information Science, 27*(4), 265–276.

PWC. (2010). *Healthcare unwired: New business models delivering care anywhere*. Los Angeles: Health Research Institute and PriceWaterhouseCoopers.

Raghupathi, W., & Kesh, S. (2009). Designing electronic health records versus total digital health systems: A systemic analysis. *Systems Research and Behavioural Science, 26*(1), 63–79.

Raisinghani, M. S., & Young, E. (2008). Personal health records: Key adoption issues and implications for management. *International Journal of Electronic Healthcare, 4*(1), 67–77.

Rao Hill, S., & Troshani, I. (2010). Factors influencing the adoption of personalisation mobile services: Empirical evidence from young Australians. *International Journal of Mobile Communications, 8*(2), 150–168.

Rash, M. C. (2005). Privacy concerns hinder electronic medical records. *The Business Journal of the Greater Triad Area, 4*, 4–6.

Sharif, M., Troshani, I., & Davidson, R. (2014). Adoption of social media services: The case of local government organizations in Australia. In T. E. Sun & J. Yearwood (Eds.), *Handbook of research on demand-driven web services: Theory, technologies and applications* (pp. 287–303). Hershey: IGI Global.

Sharif, M., Troshani, I., & Davidson, R. (2015). Public sector adoption of social media. *Journal of Computer Information Systems, 55*(4), 53–61.

Sharif, M., Troshani, I., & Davidson, R. (2016). Determinants of social media impact in local government. *Journal of Organizational and End User Computing, 28*(3), 82–103.

Tang, P. C., Ash, J. S., Bates, D. W., Overhage, J. M., & Sands, D. Z. (2006). Personal health records: Definitions, benefits, and strategies for overcoming barriers to adoption. *The Journal of the American Medical Informatics Association, 13*(2), 121–126.

Tapscott, D., & Tapscott, A. (2016). *Blockchain revolution: How the technology behind bitcoin is changing money, business, and the world*. New York: Penguin Random House LLC.

Tate, D. F., Jackvony, E. H., & Wing, R. R. (2003). Effects of internet behavioral counseling on weight loss in adults at risk for type 2 diabetes. *Journal of American Medical Association (JAMA), 289*(14), 1563–1571.

Tate, D. F., Jackvony, E. H., & Wing, R. R. (2006). A self-regulation program for maintenance of weight loss. *New England Journal of Medicine, 355*(15), 1563–1571.

Thomas, B., Stamler, L. L., Lafreniere, K. D., Out, J., & Delahunt, T. D. (2002). Using the internet to identify women's sources of breast health education and screening. *Women & Health, 36*(1), 33–48.

Troshani, I., & Lymer, A. (2010). Translation in XBRL standardization. *Information Technology and People, 23*(2), 136–164.

Troshani, I., Goldberg, S., & Wickramasinghe, N. (2012). A regulatory framework for pervasive e-health: A case study. *Health Policy and Technology, 1*(4), 199–206.

Troshani, I., Parker, L., & Lymer, A. (2015). Institutionalising XBRL for financial reporting: Resorting to regulation. *Accounting and Business Research, 45*(2), 196–228.

Troshani, I., & Rao Hill, S. (2009). Linking stakeholder salience with mobile services diffusion. *International Journal of Mobile Communications, 7*(3), 269–289.

von Lubitz, D., & Wickramasinghe, N. (2006). Healthcare and technology: The doctrine of networkcentric healthcare. *International Journal of Electronic Healthcare, 2*(4), 322–344.

WHO. (2011). *mHealth: New Horizons for health through mobile technologies*. Geneva: World Health Organization (WHO).

Wickramasinghe, N., Bali, R. K., & Tatnall, A. (2007). Using actor network theory to understand network centric healthcare operations. *International Journal of Electronic Healthcare, 3*(3), 317–328.

Wickramasinghe, N., Troshani, I., & Goldberg, S. (2009). Supporting diabetes self-management with pervasive wireless technology solutions. *International Journal of Healthcare Delivery Reform Initiatives, 1*(4), 17–31.

Wickramasinghe, N., Troshani, I., & Goldberg, S. (2010). An investigation into the use of pervasive wireless technologies to support diabetes healthcare. In A. Coronato & G. De Pietro (Eds.), *Pervasive and smart technologies for healthcare, Ubiquitous methodologies and tools* (Vol. 114–129). New York: IGI Global.

Wickramasinghe, N., Troshani, I., & Tan, J. (Eds.). (2016). *Contemporary consumer health informatics*. Cham: Springer.

Wyatt, J. C. (1997). Commentary: Measuring quality and impact of the World Wide Web. *British Journal of Medicine, 314*, 1879–1881.

Chapter 25
A Systematic Framework to Assess EMRs and EHRs

Rima Gibbings and Nilmini Wickramasinghe

25.1 Background

Electronic medical records (EMRs) are health information systems that gather, store, process, and retrieve patient information from multiple sources. EMRs were created to enhance legibility, organization, and access in an industry that historically was responsible for handling massive amounts of data, created by record keeping, compliance and regulatory notes, and patient care (Raghupathi 2010). The US healthcare system is infamous for its high cost and modest population health outcomes compared to other developed countries. Increased US healthcare cost is due to the liberal use of medical tests and imaging technologies accompanied by fewer frequent primary care interactions. These results are further exacerbated by the limited attention given to US social services which directly influence population health outcomes negatively. According to the Organization for Economic Cooperation and Development (OECD), in 2013 US healthcare spending was 17.1% of the GDP, while France healthcare expenditure consumed only 11.6% of the GDP, and in UK the share was even lower, at 8.8% (Fund 2013). Although public healthcare programs in the USA only covered 34% of the population (in 2013), per capita spending was recorded at $4197 which is one of the highest among all developed countries. Healthcare system in the UK on the other hand covers the entire population with a per capita spending of $2802 annually. One of the main reasons for US high healthcare spending is the higher consumption of diagnostic technology. In 2013, US clinicians prescribed 240 CT exams per 1000 people, while the number of prescribed tests for the same number of the population was only at 193 in France. Compared to

R. Gibbings
UIC University of Illinois at Chicago, Chicago, IL, USA

N. Wickramasinghe (✉)
Deakin University, Kew East, VIC, Australia

N. Wickramasinghe, J. L. Schaffer (eds.), *Theories to Inform Superior Health Informatics Research and Practice*, Healthcare Delivery in the Information Age,
https://doi.org/10.1007/978-3-319-72287-0_25

the OECD median of 136, both countries were considered as above average. The USA is expected to consume more resources in health care and ultimately result in higher cost. However, the health outcomes of Americans do not reflect such expenditure trends. Life expectancy in the USA was recorded at 78.8 years in 2013, which is lower than the median of the OECD recorded at 81.2 years. Also infant mortality in the USA in the same year was reported at a higher rate of 6.1 deaths per 1000 live births which was higher than the median of the OECD rate of 3.5 deaths. Poor health indicators for Americans in addition to faded presence of social programs are associated with higher rates of obesity which leads to chronic conditions such as hypertension and cardiovascular diseases. However, there are factors that even for healthy Americans who are nonsmokers and who maintain a healthy lifestyle, risks of morbidity and mortality are higher than their OECD counterparts which could be justified by limited support for social determinants of health in the USA.

The effect of EMR on overall patient healthcare outcomes is categorized within three different classes: (1) Enhancing the quality of care, (2) Reducing healthcare cost, and (3) Resolving medical errors (Linder et al. 2007). With the immense impact of modern technology in the field of medicine and health, all facets of healthcare delivery (diagnosis, treatment, patient-physician interaction, and clinical communication) are rapidly transforming and causing the formation of newly designed standards of care. From wristbands that indicate the level of patient activity to sensors monitoring the cardiac patient's heart rate periodically, clinicians are presented with a large breadth and volume of data/information that needs organization and application. Furthermore, highly complex transplant surgeries and the utilization of robotic technology in many of healthcare treatment plans are continuously increasing patient (and their caregivers) expectations. Finally, new forms of communication and the free availability of medical knowledge are enhancing the patient-physician and clinician-clinician communication standards and resulting in new models that promote transparency and group evaluation. Higher level of care standards is accompanied with the need for reliable communication. Most healthcare encounters are sufficiently adequate to improve patient care outcomes; however timely communication and patient care coordination are major challenges in the treatment process. Failure in the efficient delivery of care promotes redundancy in lab tests and wasteful drug consumption, which in turn drives the cost of health care to uncontrollable levels.

Clinical communication relying on handwritten notes unquestionably increases the potential for error and medical flaws. EMR systems are designed to reduce and eventually eliminate human-based errors, however.

25.2 EMR History

Prior to the nineteenth century, medical diagnosis was mostly based on the subjective evaluation of patient-presented symptoms instead of a comprehensive physical evaluation. This trend dramatically changed when the quantitative measurements in clinical practice were introduced by French Clinical School and German laboratory medicine's systematic recording methods of clinical interactions, which in turn enhanced the volume and need for organization of clinical data, which ultimately was enhanced into paper files in nineteenth century medical centers of Paris and Berlin (Gillum 2013).

In the nineteenth century, the New York Hospital was preserving copies of physician notes related to patient disease history, its cause, and treatments provided in the library for future references. By the end of same century, medical record's role evolved to serve as legal documentation in insurance and malpractice disputes. This development urged hospital officials to exert detailed supervision on the process of gathering and preserving patient medical records (Siegler 2010). Harvard Medical School modeled the case history method utilized in Harvard Law School to organize patient medical records that included family history, patient habits, previous illnesses, present illness, physical examination, admission urine and blood analyses, routine daily medical notes, and discharge notes. Another model promoting medical data organization was developed in the beginning of the twentieth century by Henry S. Plummer who was dissatisfied by the long delays associated with obtaining medical notes from physicians regarding each given patient. This dissatisfaction motivated Dr. Plummer to enhance both education and patient care by creating efficient medical records through his dossier model that is still being utilized at Mayo Clinic. The model simply followed basic privacy and accessibility-enhancing techniques through assigning numbered envelopes to each patient and placing all patient-related information into the given envelope that is safely reserved in a centralized location within the clinic (Camp et al. 2008).

The earliest concept of computerized record keeping including patient medical record information was materialized as early as the 1960s by Larry Weed. The idea promoted a problem-oriented medical record that will encompass more than just patient diagnosis and will potentially enable third party clinical staff to independently review patient cases and treatment. In 1969 Larry Weed introduced the problem-oriented medical record (POMR) concept to enhance the record keeping knowledge to the cause of medical conditions instead of a narrow focus on the treatment process. These systems were also known as clinical information systems. Accompanied with the POMR trend was the development of Health Evaluation through Logical Processing (HELP) system which promoted the use of patient medical data/information to assist clinicians with decision support systems.

In the 1980s many hospitals and care organizations experienced the benefits of EMRs and EHRs and thus formed technical teams to pursue a customized standardization of the new method (Atherton 2011).

In 1991, the Institute of Medicine published a comprehensive report encouraging clinical practices to adopt the clinical data management tool introduced under EMR and EHR models, which mainly focused on the safe conversion of paper-based medical records into EHRs. Furthermore in 2000, the IOM published another report that aimed at addressing medical errors under the title "To Err is Human" that emphasized the role of EHRs in the safe storage and retrieval of patient records (Atherton 2011). In 2004 in his State of the Union address, President Bush mentioned the importance of medical records management in reducing cost, enhancing efficiency, and avoiding medical errors (Post 2004). In 2009, President Obama merged the EHR requirement into the American Recovery and Reinvestment Act (ARRA) to be ultimately included in the Health Information Technology for Economic and Clinical Health Act (HITECH) which promoted the technology by rewarding practices (who can prove meaningful use of EHRs) with financial reimbursements.

25.2.1 Problems in EMR/EHR

EMRs and EHRs are considered computerized medical information systems that are responsible for collecting, gathering, and displaying patient information and patient-clinician documented interaction/encounter details. As evident by the name of the newly introduced systems, EMRs and EHRs were designed and implemented to introduce the appropriate contribution of informatics in the healthcare industry. However many obstacles have proven to hinder the progress and adoption of the medical record systems:

- Health care is one of the most heavily regulated and complex industries in the USA that consumes more than 17% of the annual national GDP. The introduction of Medicare and Medicaid in the 1960s, although a commendable effort by US government to provide medical coverage to the elderly and disabled in the country, sharply increased the demand on an industry that unfortunately was left with a stagnant if not decreasing levels of supply/resources. The Patient Protection and Affordable Care Act, also known as Obamacare, unfortunately added to this imbalance by expanding coverage to include most of the uninsured population while only modestly succeeding in the implementation of cost reduction policies. On the other hand, cost inflation in health care was impacted by legislator interference almost in all aspects of health care. Different administrations on both sides of the isle have continuously introduced new regulations to either nationalize or monopolize healthcare resources since 1910. Restricting the medical licensure, enforcing the federal certificate-of-need for construction of medical facilities, and monopolizing prescription drugs by enhancing and extending patent duration contributed in the shrinking of the resource pool of the medical industry, nationalizing health care for a large portion of the population in the USA (elderly and disabled) through Medicare and Medicaid, and monopolization of payers by exempting the large health insurance companies from most federal regulation like the antitrust laws.
- EMR and EHR workflow adoption challenges create resistance among clinicians and especially physicians who mostly control care cost. Physicians are expecting for EMR systems to increase the accurate flow of information in the diagnosis and treatment processes which will ultimately enhance their service delivery performance. However many physicians have a customized routine for providing care, and furthermore they trickle down a certain structure of delegated

responsibilities to their staff. EMRs are created mostly by software companies who consider certain requirements mandated by the "Meaningful Use" act, but they fail to incorporate configuration and customization to the degree that allows clinics and hospitals to continue their tasks with minimal interruption.

- Introducing EMR/EHR systems has a negative impact on clinical communication. Physicians are required to enter patient-related data and details regarding patient interaction in the short patient visit time that is on average less than 15 min. This reduction in the quality of physician-patient communication influences patient education and the human factor that is vital for building a reliable relationship with patients. Robust physician-patient communication will result in improved decision-making and healthcare outcomes.
- Training during and before the implementation of EMR/EHR could be time-consuming and costly in the adoption process. To replace the existing paper-based or less efficient computerized medical information system with a new EMR/EHR system, organizational leadership encounters resistance from physicians and other clinical staff. It is vital for the training phase to identify the computer skills of staff members to target sufficient training on an individual basis. Also it is important to provide system implementation pilot periods that will facilitate a smooth transition. Factors such as responsive customer service team, feedback solicitation from users, and video/audio training tools embedded or accompanied with the system could improve the adoption process.
- Interoperability issues between different EMR/EHR systems could pose major challenges in the implementation process. Communication between EMR systems is not fully standardized yet, and the Department of Health and Human Services plans to have full interoperability between all disparate EMR systems by 2024. However different care organizations set up similar EMR systems differently, and in many cases physician practices utilize EMR systems based on their parent organization preference which could create more interoperability issues between their office and other clinical organizations that are regularly communicating with them.
- Adoption of EMR system adds new tasks to an already busy clinical staff. Entering data and retrieving information from different pages of a given EMR system take precious time away from clinical staff that are already overwhelmed with a high volume of patients and heavy schedules. Physicians are required to divide their time between clinical care, answering patient phone calls, and reviewing prescription and lab order requests. The newly introduced tasks by the EMR system add to this workload with a promise of long-term efficiency results.

25.3 Most Popular EMR/EHR Systems

After the enforcement of several phases of the "Meaningful Use" act, many providers have been under extreme pressure to comply with the implementation of electronic medical records and complying with the requirements of supervisory

EHR Vendor Market Share by Practice Size

Rank	Vendor Name	Number of Physicians in Practice					
		1 to 3	4 to 10	11 to 25	26 to 40	41+	Overall
1	Epic	9.8%	21.4%	33.9%	40.1%	43.5%	12.4%
2	eClinicalWorks LLC	10.7%	8.9%	5.1%	2.8%	1.0%	10.3%
3	Allscripts	7.6%	10.8%	10.7%	9.9%	7.0%	8.2%
4	**Practice Fusion**	**7.9%**	**1.2%**	**0.2%**	**0.0%**	**0.0%**	**6.5%**
5	NextGen Healthcare	4.8%	7.7%	7.9%	3.9%	3.5%	5.4%
6	Cerner Corporation	3.5%	5.7%	8.7%	10.5%	9.0%	4.1%
7	athenahealth, Inc	4.0%	2.8%	1.2%	0.6%	0.5%	3.7%
8	GE Healthcare	2.9%	5.6%	6.4%	8.0%	4.5%	3.5%
9	Greenway Health	3.3%	4.6%	2.6%	0.6%	1.0%	3.5%
10	McKesson	3.3%	2.4%	2.0%	4.7%	1.5%	3.1%
11	AmazingCharts.com, Inc	2.6%	0.4%	0.0%	0.0%	0.0%	2.1%
12	MEDITECH	1.7%	2.3%	3.8%	2.2%	1.0%	1.9%
13	13 e-MDs, Inc.	1.9%	1.1%	0.4%	0.3%	0.0%	1.7%
14	Care360, Quest Diagnostics	1.8%	0.3%	0.1%	0.0%	0.0%	1.5%
15	Office Ally	1.3%	0.2%	0.0%	0.0%	0.0%	1.1%
16	MEDENT-Community Computer Service Inc.	1.0%	1.4%	0.6%	0.0%	0.0%	1.1%
17	NexTech Systems Inc.	1.1%	0.5%	0.0%	0.0%	0.0%	0.9%
18	Aprima Medical Software, Inc	1.0%	0.6%	0.2%	0.3%	0.0%	0.9%
19	ADP	1.0%	0.3%	0.0%	0.0%	0.0%	0.9%
20	TRAKnet Solutions	1.0%	0.3%	0.0%	0.0%	0.0%	0.9%
21	All Other Vendors (466)	27.8%	21.5%	16.2%	16.3%	27.5%	26.5%
	TOTAL	100%	100%	100%	100%	100%	100%

Fig. 25.1 Vendor share by practice size (Shay 2016)

healthcare information system bodies. According to Practice Fusion blog, there are over 1000 vendors that develop EMR/EHR systems in the current market. The top selection points of the current EMR/EHR systems are their compliance with meaningful use regulations, leaving a large area of medical practice requirements unfulfilled and creating a significant proportion of the clinical staff unsatisfied. The top five EHR vendors are Epic, eClinicalWorks LLC, Allscripts, Practice Fusion, and NextGen Healthcare (Shay 2016) (Fig. 25.1).

25.3.1 Epic

Founded in 1979 by its current CEO, Judy Faulkner, Epic is one of the most popular (if not the most popular) patient record health information system in the market. Some of its clients are Oakland, Calif.- based Kaiser Permanente, Cleveland Clinic, Johns Hopkins Medicine in Baltimore, UCLA Health in Los Angeles, Arlington-based Texas Health Resources, Massachusetts General Hospital in Boston, Mount Sinai Health System in New York City, and Duke University Health System in Raleigh, NC. It is estimated that about 51% of Americans have an Epic record. Epic has a good reputation among its users and has achieved the No. 1 Overall Software Suite for 2013 by KLAS Research. Unlike its competitors Epic has not joined the CommonWell Health Alliance that is active in increasing interoperability between EHR platforms; instead Epic has partnered with health industry leaders like Kaiser Permanente, Walgreens, and Surescripts to form Carequality. Carequality is an effort to increase data exchange between hospitals, physicians, payers, retail clinics, and other healthcare stakeholders. Epic is also considered as one of the more expensive EMR products in the market which require a significant investment on the healthcare organization part. It has been estimated that Epic system implementation in Duke University Health System had a price tag of $700 million, and for Kaiser Permanente the cost reached the $4 billion mark (Gregg 2014).

25.3.2 eClinicalWorks EHR Suite

Founded in 1999, eClinicalWorks has attempted at replacing paper-based communication between physician practice and healthcare entities that are involved with patient care such as pharmacies, test labs, and hospitals. With its cloud-based EHR system, eClinicalWorks covers about 800,000 medical staff/users. Some of the benefits offered by the EHR system are their free conversion (from any other EHR system to eClinicalWorks), free on-site training, and free startup implementation. However as a web-based product, eClinicalWorks does not provide the opportunity for organizations to host their own data and EHR system. Pricing of eClinicalWorks starts at $375/monthly per each provider for practices that include from 1 to 9 providers. In 2014, according to KLAS rating report, the average EHR system scored a 6.3, when eClinicalWorks rated a 7 for meeting ACO requirements (ctsguides 2016). One of the main advantages of the eClinicalWorks EHR is that it serves small, medium, and large healthcare organizations.

25.3.3 Allscripts

Allscripts is a Chicago-based company that was founded in the 1980s. With 180,000 physicians and 45,000 practices utilizing their product, it is considered as one of the more popular EHR systems currently available in the market. Allscripts provides a wide range of templates to a variety of specialties which motivates healthcare organizations active in different aspects of care to consider their product. Another main advantage of the system is its interoperability aspect. Allscripts is capable of communicating with over 50,000 pharmacies for e-prescribing and more laboratories (according to the company claims) than any other EHR systems available in the market. According to their website, Allscripts has won the No. 1 top Ambulatory EHR Vendor in user satisfaction pool from Black Book Rankings and the 2014 No. 1 Best Global Acute EMR and KLAS Category Leader. Allscripts also uses different speech recognition tools to extract patient and physician input with minimum effort; furthermore the system also parses the data entered to identify structured data that are relevant in billing and practice processes (Capterra 2015).

25.3.4 Practice Fusion

Founded in 2005 Practice Fusion is a cloud-based and web-based medical health record platform provider for healthcare organizations. Practice Fusion has a client base of 30,000 physician practices and a large integrated system that can connect to a variety of labs, imaging centers, billing solutions, and third-party applications. The EHR system does not restrict its clients to number of users or number of patient records. User feedback indicates a deficiency in the customized templates that are beneficial to specialties. A major advantage of the system is its free support in addition to assigned and dedicated support personal to given users. Practice Fusion is keen in providing dedicated training videos to different layers of clinical staff (physicians, nurses, physician assistants, and administrative staff), and it provides a tool to enable practices in their Meaningful Use evaluation process. Offering a unique pricing model, Practice Fusion is a free EHR service that follows the Google model, by providing free services to its users and utilizing them as the marketing base for its advertisements (AKA revenue source).

25.3.5 NextGen Healthcare

NextGen Healthcare was established 25 years ago to assist providers with solutions that enhance health information system technology and to facilitate a smooth transition to value-based purchasing. A main indicator of the company success is their significant cliental presence of 33% in Accountable Care Organizations (ACOs), and another 40% of the primary care physicians who purchase the NextGen products are accredited by Patient-Centered Medical Homes (PCMHs). Such contribution is mainly attributed to the use of health quality measures in the product which is helpful in value-based purchasing. With such high user numbers of 150 million patients, receiving care from NextGen Healthcare offered interoperable solutions that integrate a wide variety of care facilities, and 40 million patients regularly use their patient portal to communicate with physicians; the system claims both user-friendliness and easy adoption of clinical processes (NexGen Healthcare 2016). The system is considered expensive and does not offer many customization options; instead it requires its future clients to be already upgraded to ICD-10 which could be considered as a limitation (Parker n.d.).

25.4 EMR/EHR Rubric Systems

With the universal demand for healthcare applications, many challenges emerge that need to be addressed. Complex medical systems that include diagnostic and treatment procedures along with bulky administrative transactions often dictate specific system customization. In addition, many health facilities render a unique combination of health services under given diagnostic codes with specific clinical staff preferences that create an exclusive need for system management. To address such challenges and enhance the performance of clinical facilities, system engineers and application developers are designing sophisticated applications that are tailored to their clients' needs and obligations. In the process of such development, it is imperative to consider the healthcare privacy laws such as HIPAA and recognize elevated patient expectations due to medical modernization. To satisfy all the requirements with few comprehensive systems, essential rubric items need to be considered and measured in all developed applications:

- *Seamless integration of developed applications with healthcare procedures:* Identifying perfect systems require a smooth conversion from existing EMRs or paper-based systems to newly adopted systems. Achieving such conversion demands a clear understanding of the necessary requirements of a given facility combined with the skill set of the clinical and administrative staff. Gathering existing procedural flow and business model-related data must incorporate organizational reporting methods, structures, and preferences. Adopting software systems without taking such details into consideration will cause staff resistance and costly procedural redundancy. Clinical and administrative staff usually continue conducting their daily tasks with familiar and more preferable methods and resist adding additional workload to their daily obligations. Organizations that do not consider such disadvantages usually experience failed software adoption processes and are in risk of spending additional funds and effort for a minimal return.
- *Designing and developing configurable healthcare systems:* Hectic clinical operations usually demand certain prioritization in the organizational workflow, and clinicians are led by medical emergencies and patient needs to organize their daily routines. However, certain healthcare applications (EMRs and EHRs) limit their users into a controlled set of options that determine and operate in opposition to existing routines. These constraints will ultimately lead to either abandoning time-consuming operations that are not configurable to a given organizational clinical preferences or circumnavigating such processes and repurposing tasks to fit them in their daily workload. In both of these conditions, risks of redundancy, staff resistance, and prolonged implementation periods will deplete organizational resources and negatively impact performance measures.
- *Including patient care coordination in EMR/EHR systems:* Newly adopted systems are more successful when they include and track patient participation in the process of care (treatment and follow-up). Many healthcare applications are limiting their patient coordination by incorporating electronic communication with patients or their caregiver. Although patient communication in the process of treatment is critical, it is not sufficient based on the new demands imposed by care coordination provisions and tightly coupled reimbursement regulations with healthcare outcome measures. To satisfy care coordination, EMRs/EHRs need to introduce a classification of services provided and determine the level of coordination necessary within

each class. Measuring patient-clinician coordination will establish reasonable clinical outcome expectations and assist clinical staff in determining the next appropriate steps and increase overall satisfaction. Such measures should be implemented via the inclusion of clinical data and expert input.

- *Enhancing user-friendliness in healthcare applications:* Intuitive user interface (UI) features such as touch screen monitors, mobile applications, self-describing UI labels, and audio/video training systems that are accompanied with superb costumer service commitment are all essential user interaction components that are pursued in most healthcare applications. EMR/EHR systems that are not responsive to the technological advances usually fail to recognize the exact needs of their users and subsequently become detached from their client base. Technological advances play a major role in enhancing the performance of healthcare clinicians. Duplicating monotonous tasks that are both time-consuming and costly to the clinician workload by user-friendly devices that both measure and record patient status will increase the overall outcome and enhance efficiency dramatically. Clinicians are overwhelmed with hectic schedules, and they normally perform identical set of tasks such as measuring patient vital signs per each given visitation; utilizing precise handheld devices will enhance their performance and provide busy clinicians with much needed free time to interact with their patients and boost their clinical training. Also administrative staff will be able to interact at a faster and more reliable manner with their designated web pages which ultimately enhances clinical efficiency and increases strategic visibility into the organizational tasks.
- *System interoperability and data sharing:* Communication within different layers of healthcare facilities and functioning units regularly poses genuine challenges. EMR/EHR systems that plan interoperability and communication features within their applications are recognizing such a sincere demand and being responsive to their user's needs. Accountable Care Organizations, Physician groups, emergency care centers, and state governing organizations are in constant and urgent need for continuous and reliable communication. To satisfy their need, it is essential for EMR/EHR systems to provide accurate and comprehensive mapping tools that allow clinicians and administrative staff to interpret and convert large amount of clinical data into transferrable files (in accordance to established standards) that are communicable in a short amount of time. On another hand scanning tools that incorporate intelligent text recognition features could remarkably enhance system usability and clinical efficiency.
- *Healthcare application rollout strategies:* Newly implementation software applications require many preparation steps in order to ensure a successful adoption process. Organized rollout implementation phases are usually improved by more experienced systems. Evaluating targeted user computer skills and their availability is the first and possibly most important rollout consideration in the case of any newly adopted system. EMR/EHR systems that have a proven record of success and verified user satisfaction should be considered as superior systems to their counterparts. Supportive customer service is another important concept in the process of software rollout. Users measure system success by level of their

success and speed of their interaction with given application features. If the process of the initial human interaction is hindered by numerous unresponsive questions and scenarios, users lose interest and desire in training and becoming better familiarized with the new application.

References

Atherton, J. (2011). Development of the electronic health record. *AMA Journal of Ethics, 13*(3), 186–189.

Camp, C., Smoot, R. L., Kolettis, T. N., Groenewald, C. B., Greenlee, S. M., & Farley, D. R. (2008). Patient records at mayo clinic: Lessons learned from the first 100 patients in Dr Henry S. Plummer's Dossier Model. *Mayo Clinic Proceedings, 83*(12), 1396–1399.

Capterra. (2015). *Capterra Medical Software Blog*. Retrieved from http://blog.capterra.com/ehr-software-comparison-brief-overview-of-the-top-10-ehrs/

ctsguides. (2016). *eClinicalWorks*. Retrieved from http://www.ctsguides.com/medical/eclinicalworks/

Fund, T. C. (2013). *U.S. health care from a global perspective spending, use of services, prices, and health in 13 countries*. Retrieved from http://www.commonwealthfund.org/publications/issue-briefs/2015/oct/us-health-care-from-a-global-perspective

Gillum, R. F. (2013). From papyrus to the electronic tablet: A brief history of the clinical medical record with lessons for the digital age. *The American Journal of Medicine, 126*(10), 853–857.

Gregg, H. (2014). *10 things to know about epic*. Chicago, IL: Becker's Hospital Review. Retrieved from http://www.beckershospitalreview.com/lists/10-things-to-know-about-epic.html.

Linder, J., Ma, J., Bates, D., Middleton, B., & Stafford, R. (2007). Electronic health record use and the quality of ambulatory care in the United States. *Archives of Internal Medicine, 167*(13), 1400–1405. Retrieved from http://www.ncbi.nlm.nih.gov/pubmed/17620534.

NexGen Healthcare. (2016). *Corporate Fact Sheet*. Retrieved from https://www.nextgen.com/About-NextGen/Newsroom/Corporate-Fact-Sheet

Parker, S. (n.d.). *EHR Vendor*. Retrieved from http://www.curemd.com/EHR-vendor-pricing-comparison.pdf

Post, W. (2004). Text of President Bush's 2004 State of the Union Address. http://www.washingtonpost.com/wp-srv/politics/transcripts/bushtext_012004.html

Raghupathi, W. (2010). Data mining in health care. In S. Kudyba (Ed.), *Healthcare informatics: Improving efficiency and productivity* (pp. 211–223). Oxfordshire, UK: Taylor & Francis.

Shay, R. (2016, January 1). *Practice Fusion Blog*. Retrieved from http://www.practicefusion.com/blog/ehr-adoption-rates/

Siegler, E. L. (2010). The evolving medical record. *Annals of Internal Medicine, 153*(10), 671–677.

References

Chapter 26
Integrating Hospital Records and Home Monitoring by mHealth Apps

Sara Marceglia, Giuseppe Pozzi, and Elena Rossi

26.1 Introduction

Over the last decades, the amount of patients affected by chronic diseases and the duration of their treatments dramatically increased, with related costs reaching outstanding levels.

In some chronic diseases, the acute phase may require hospitalization, while the long-term treatment, following the acute phase, can be managed outside the hospital (Rossi et al. 2015). Thus, home monitoring has been regarded to as the key to increase the quality of life of chronic patients and to reduce the economic and social costs for such patients.

At home, the role of the caregiver is to be extended from the classical "formal" caregiver (specialized physicians and nurses, as in a traditional hospital environment) to the "informal" caregiver represented by the relatives of the patient and sometimes the patient him/herself. This requires that every caregiver, experienced or newcomer, must be suitably trained to face the situation. Such a training requires a strict interaction with the monitoring instrumentation. Hence, in order to provide patients with suitable care when at home, the education of home caregivers and the deployment of home monitoring devices and tools are needed.

The widespread diffusion of smartphones, following those of tablets and of PCs, sets up a suitable technological skill level which is an optimal starting point.

S. Marceglia (✉)
Dipartimento di Ingegneria e Architettura, Università degli Studi di Trieste, Trieste, Italy
e-mail: smarceglia@units.it

G. Pozzi · E. Rossi
Dipartimento di Elettronica, Informazione e Bioingegneria, Politecnico di Milano, Milan, Italy
e-mail: giuseppe.pozzi@polimi.it; elena.rossi@polimi.it

N. Wickramasinghe, J. L. Schaffer (eds.), *Theories to Inform Superior Health Informatics Research and Practice*, Healthcare Delivery in the Information Age,
https://doi.org/10.1007/978-3-319-72287-0_26

Connecting monitoring instrumentation to smartphones is thus a natural approach to such needs, achieving high-quality home monitoring.

However, while stand-alone mobile applications (mApps) even on smartphones do not feature extremely complex requirements in terms of connection to external devices (and/or to external information systems), mApps devoted to monitoring patients or treatments face a more critical environment: privacy, security, safety, robustness, and accuracy are only some of the issues that characterize the medical domain when compared to all the other domains that can benefit from technology. The added value of health mApps (mobile health apps, mhApps) resides in the possibility to share the information acquired on the patient to the care team, in order to design and implement appropriate interventions. However, the care team refers to electronic health record (EHR) and hospital information systems (HIS) as their main working tools. To ensure proper communication to and from the care team, data acquired from monitoring instrumentation through mhApps must hence be transferred to EHR and/or HIS, in a secure and reliable connection. Privacy is extremely important and data collected at home by mhApps must not be intercepted by a man-in-the-middle, and must fit into the EHR/HIS so that the physicians can be informed as soon as these data are available.

The bi-directional exchange of data between mhApps and EHR/HIS can be seen as part of a broader philosophy known as "health information exchange" (HIE). HIE improves the speed, quality, safety, and cost of patient care by allowing all the healthcare providers (doctors, nurses, pharmacists, etc.) and patients to access and share patient's vital medical information in an appropriate and secure environment (http://www.healthit.gov/providers-professionals/health-information-exchange/what-hie). This approach opens the future possibility of enabling individuals to contribute to their health records, directly involving them in their own care.

However, extending the information—collected via mhApps and included in the EHR/HIS—to the patient/caregiver, as well as granting them the access to healthcare data and documents, still does not have a strong theoretic background at the time of writing.

26.2 Background

The scenario of HIE involves different actors. Among them, the most involved in the generation and use of healthcare data and document can be divided in four categories:

- Healthcare professionals belonging to the same institution
- Healthcare professionals belonging to different institutions
- Patients
- Researchers

In a simplified framework, each of them can either "view information" or "insert information" or "update information" or "download information" to/from each of their main health data/information recording tools: the EHR, as main tool for patient's data collection for healthcare professionals; the personal health record (PHR), as main tool for personal health-related data collection for patients; and the clinical report form (CRF), as main tool for research data collection for researchers. However, at present, the widespread adoption of smartphones, tablets, and other mobile technology introduced personal mhApps among the available tools for patients. Table 26.1 summarizes the current rights of each category to each tool. The first column of Table 26.1 is a subset of the five standard SQL commands for authorizations to data manipulation: insert, delete, update, query, and reference. In the current context, the reference command does not apply (it is used when building up a database table where one attribute of the current table refers to attributes of other tables), and the delete command generally does not apply to any EHR (where data can never be deleted). The "retrieve" action basically consists of a query command over data from one single patient; the "insert/update" action consists of insert or modify commands over data from one single patient; and the "query" action consists of a query command over data from a set of patients, where data are extracted for population-oriented research.

The current norms, standards, and recommendations available at the European, the USA, and, in general, international levels regarding health information exchange in the light of the available EHR functional models—as defined by the HL7 RIM (HL7 2008), the ISO/HL7 10,871 norm (International Standard Organization 2010), and the OpenEHR initiative—provide the regulatory framework for the information exchange in four categories: the EHR-EHR data exchange within the same institution; the EHR-EHR data cross-institutional exchange; the EHR-PHR exchange; and the EHR-clinical report form (CRF) exchange. In general, whereas the EHR/EHR category is well covered by available standards and recommendations, all the other categories are still underrepresented. More specifically, the ISO 13606 family (International Standard Organization 2010) provides the general framework for EHR-EHR communication, including the reference model (part 1), the specification of semantic archetypes for semantic interoperability, data consistency and data quality (parts 2 and 3), the management of security issues (part 4), and the interface specifications (part 5). HL7 version 3 (HL7 2008) and HIE integration profiles provide the specifications for the implementation of the communication architecture in the EHR-EHR category (Marceglia et al. 2015a, Marceglia et al. 2015b). Healthcare data and information are exchanged either using standard messages (HL7-based) or using structured documents (HL7 Clinical Document Architecture, release 2, CDA-2). For example, some CDA-2 implementation guides ground the exchange of structured documents between PHRs (PHR-PHR exchange) and between CRFs (CRF-CRF exchange). A part from the HIE XPHR profile that provides specifications for including information coming from the EHR into the PHR, none of the available standard covers the exchange of information from the patient tools to the EHR. Also mhApps are not yet considered in the recommendation framework.

Table 26.1 Rights (privileges), category of user, and type of tool when accessing clinical data stored by a EHR/HIS

Actions	Actors	Electronic health record (EHR)	Personal health record (PHR)	Clinical research form (CRF)	mhApp
Retrieve	Healthcare professional (same institution)	Already in place	If patient provides access, but untrusted data	If involved in the clinical trial	Patient's monitoring medication tracking communication
	Healthcare professional (other institutions)	Envisaged, with some experiences ongoing: Cross- border/ EPSOS (Europe) meaningful use (the USA)	If patient provides access, but untrusted data	If involved in the clinical trial	
	Patient	Envisaged, with some experiences ongoing: PA-EHR (patient-accessible EHR)	By definition	No	Responsible for its use
	Researcher	Envisaged	Possible but not envisaged	If set up for multicenter clinical trial	No
Insert/ update	Healthcare professional (same institution)	Already in place	Available in some cases of PHRs with direct download from EHR	If involved in the clinical trial	Upload prescriptions therapy suggestions
	Healthcare professional (other institutions)	Possible by adding new documents to the EHR	Available in some cases of PHRs with direct download from EHR	If involved in the clinical trial	
	Patient	Problem of faithful information	By definition	No	Responsible for its use
	Researcher	Possible but not envisaged	Possible but not envisaged	If set up for multicenter clinical trial	No
Query	Healthcare professional (same institution)	Already in place	If patient provides access, but untrusted data	If involved in the clinical trial	Retrieve consensus documents
	Healthcare professional (other institutions)	Envisaged, with some experiences ongoing: Cross-border (Europe) meaningful use (the USA)			
	Patient	Envisaged, with some experiences ongoing: blue button	By definition	No	Responsible for its use
	Researcher	Envisaged to facilitate research (ongoing)	Possible but not envisaged	If set up for multicenter clinical trial	Can use personalized apps for data collection in clinical trials

26.3 Theoric Conceptual Model for the Integration

An integrated care system is composed by an EHR or HIS, or even both of them, where data can be manipulated (i.e., inserted, deleted, or updated), and a set of different applications, possibly running on different computer systems, involving different agents and caregivers, receiving information by different sources and instrumentation, and managing all of these aspects in an harmonious/orchestrated manner. The conceptual framework for the bi-directional integration between the EHR side and the personal application side is based on the following functional requirements:

- Accurate information representation: the requirement refers to the way that information is properly represented both internally to the system (e.g., data structures, tables, dictionary of terms, glossary, etc.), and externally (e.g., how information is reported to the users, according to their authorizations and their roles: analytically, or referring to a single patient, or synthetically, referring to groups of patients or the entire observed population). Internal representation of information is to be shared by all the applications, including mobile ones, if they have to access to data stored by the EHR/HIS.
- Data protection: the requirement refers to access control over data. Generally, information about a patient is considered private and sensitive, and data stored within the EHR/HIS are available to authorized personnel, only. If the patient is monitored/treated at home, some data must be available outside the strict boundaries of the EHR/HIS, and made available to the mhApp. In a complementary way, data acquired by the mhApp must be received by the EHR/HIS and internally stored. As a consequence, particular attention is to be paid to protect these information at any time, i.e., when stored inside the EHR/HIS, when stored by the mhApp, and when transmitted to/from the EHR/HIS.
- Patient education and training: the requirement refers to the minimal skills required to the patient and to the home caregiver. The user of the smartphone must be capable of running the mhApp, of properly managing it, and of being aware of the nature of personal health data.
- Information tracking: the requirement refers to keeping track of every information, including where, when, and in which circumstances it has been acquired. Since data can be acquired externally from the hospital, i.e., at home, such detail may significantly influence data and their consideration by the physician when reviewing the condition of the patient.

Basing on these requirements, we can theorize the architectural framework composed by the following modules (i.e., software components) and depicted in Fig. 26.1:

- Concept translator: this module aims at interfacing different sets of terms and glossaries, as well as database table and attribute names, which can be used by the EHR/HIS and the mhApp. This should ensure semantic integration, even though the level of health literacy of patients/caregivers is not as high as that of healthcare professionals.

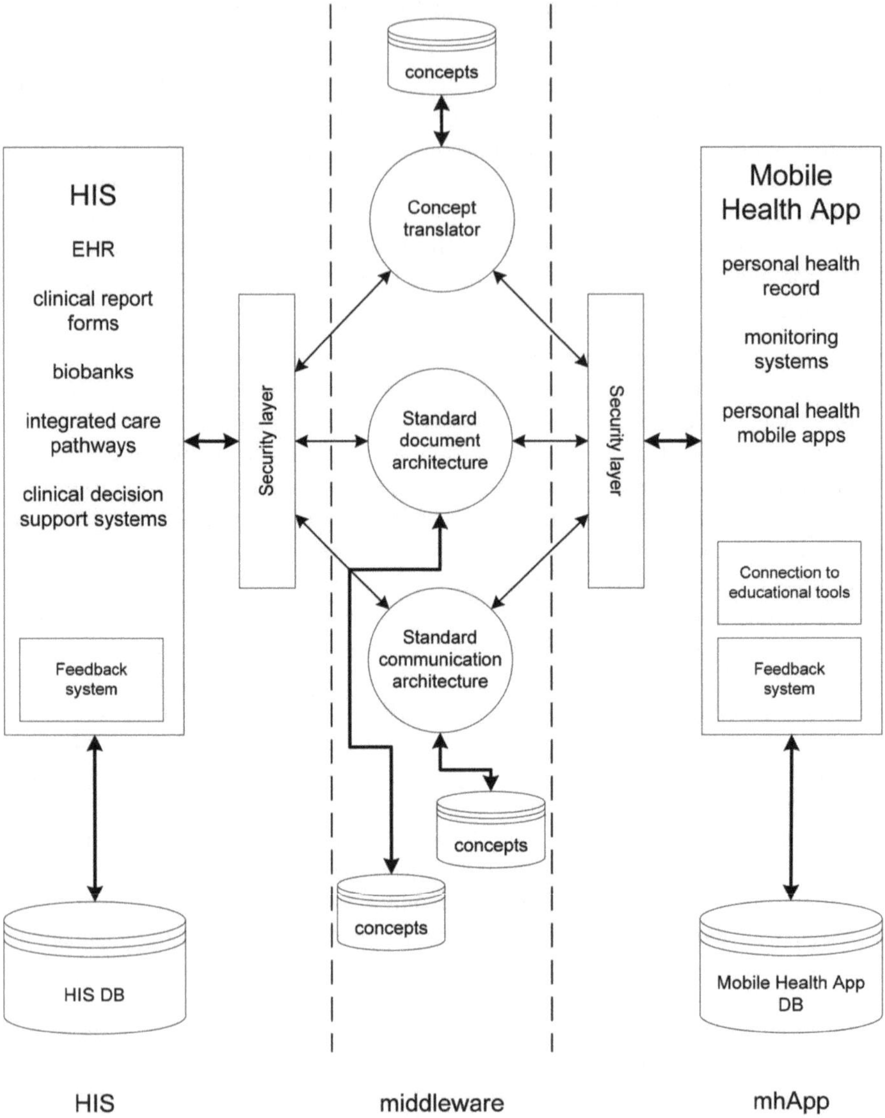

Fig. 26.1 An overall architecture for an integrated care system, where the intermediate layer (middleware) enables data communication between mobile health applications (mhApp) and the hospital information systems (HIS) through the adoption of standard documents—(Adapted from Marceglia et al. 2015a)

- Security tools/data protection policies: these modules have to properly manage the protection of data when stored within the databases (EHR/HIS and on the mobile side) and when transferred to/from the mhApp.
- Standard document and communication architectures: the system has to implement available (or newly proposed) standards, which include EHR-PHR data exchange, X-PHR Integrating the Healthcare (HIE) profile, HL7 Clinical Document Architecture release 2 (CDA-2) "Personal Health Monitoring Record", to enable the bi-directional data exchange among the two main components.
- Connection to educational tools: these modules aim at training the caregivers and, possibly, the patient on how to use the mhApp. A good training is fundamental for a correct use of the mhApp.
- Feedback system: these modules aim at validating if the data entered by the caregiver at home or the patient are correct. Would any inconsistency or incompleteness of data be discovered, a feedback is to be immediately sent out.

26.4 Exemplary Implementation of the Theoric Model

As case study for the theoric model, we can consider the telemonitoring of patients at risk of congestive heart failure (Marceglia et al. 2015a). The telemonitoring process can be summarized as follows:

- The process starts with the patient admission for an acute episode. After proper management of the acute episode, the clinician prescribes patient's monitoring at home and patient's home therapy using the institutional EHR system.
- The prescription, including both the monitoring and the medication instructions, is sent to a patient's mHealth app dedicated to telemonitoring.
- After receiving the prescription, the app creates the monitoring and medication calendar accordingly. At the scheduled time, the app prompts an alert to the patient to do an action (start the monitoring session or take the medication).
- The action produces a result (the medication administration log or the result of the monitoring) that generates a report.
- The report is sent back directly to the institutional EHR for the clinician who will review it to decide whether or not to call the patient for a visit.

Figure 26.2 represents a possible system implementation, in which the connection between the EHR side and the mHealth app side is implemented by the exchange of encrypted XML-based CDA-2 structured documents. The document sent from the EHR to the mHealth App can be broadly defined as a "prescription," representing an indication of action that comes from the clinician, and it is direct to the patient (e.g., monitoring action, rehabilitation exercise, medication regimen, nutritional advice, etc.). The content of the prescription depends on the specific patient's condition. The prescription is generated as a structured clinical document in the EHR (Fig. 26.2a) using the standard terminology implemented in the EHR, and it is uploaded in the EHR system clinical data repository. The structured CDA document

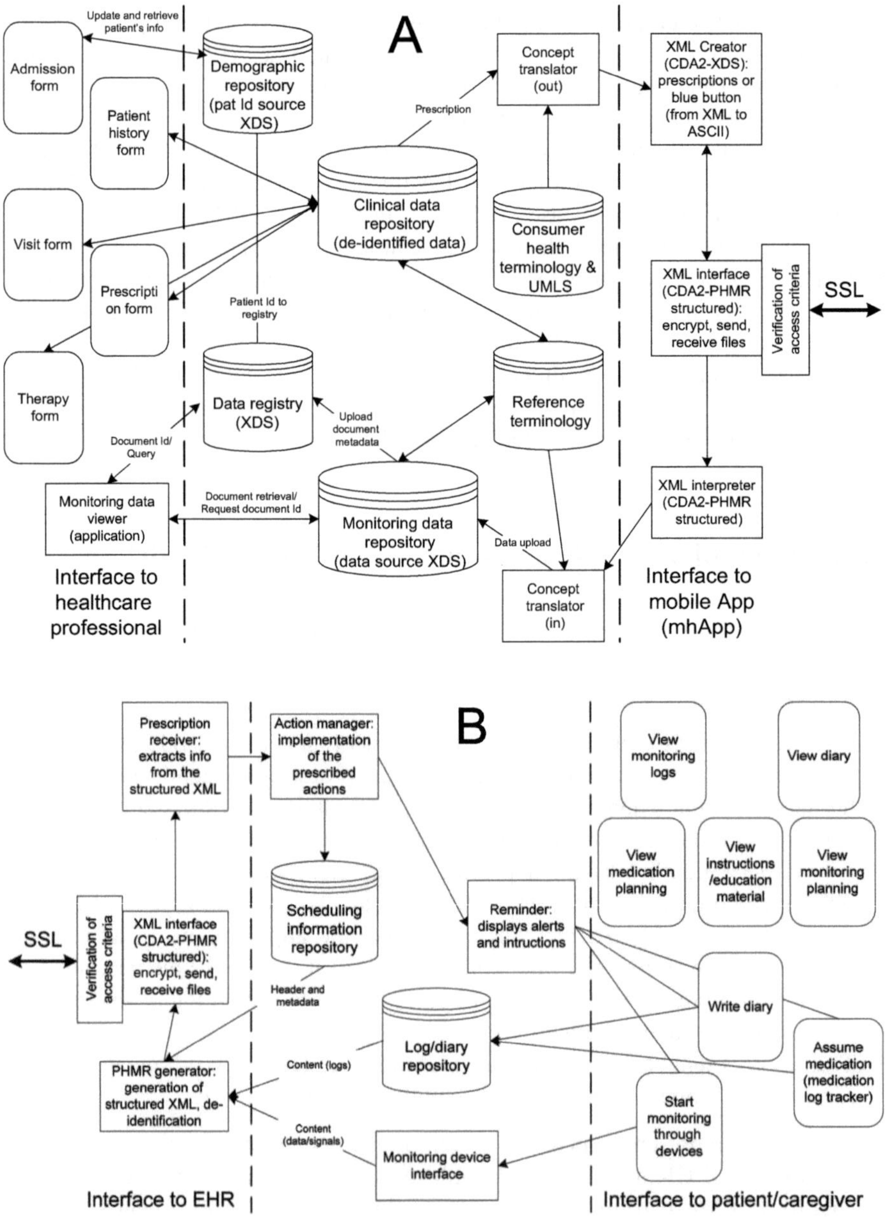

Fig. 26.2 Possible implementation architecture of the information exchange between the personal mHealth app and the EHR system: (**a**) EHR system side (top); (**b**) mHealth app side (bottom)

to be sent to the patient is then created starting from the original prescription that is "translated" for patients understanding using UMLS mapping to the consumer health vocabulary (CHV). The document must contain only the patient identification number and not the patient's demographic information that are stored in the demographic data repository on the EHR side. After encryption, the document is sent through a secure connection (SSL) and received by the mHealth app (Fig. 26.2b) that sets the appropriate actions (e.g., medication/monitoring remainders, rehabilitation exercises to be presented to the patient, etc.). The patient, using the app, generates monitoring information that can be either logging data (e.g., medication compliance tracking) or data/signals coming from monitoring devices. Whatever the information type, the mHealth app generates, encrypts, and sends to the EHR a structured CDA-2 "monitoring report," with appropriate header, metadata, and content, but without any patient identification information. Also, the app should not store in the device memory the information generated and sent. Once the "monitoring report" is received by the EHR (Fig. 26.2a), it should not be stored within the clinical data repository, but it should be sent to a dedicated repository (Monitoring Data Repository in Fig. 26.2a) that can be managed according to the Cross-Enterprise Document Sharing (XDS) HIE profile for information retrieval.

26.5 Model Discussion

A proper discussion of the described model has to consider both the major advantages and the critical issues which still remain unresolved and need further investigation.

26.5.1 Major Advantages

Adopting an integrated care system, as described above, may introduce some advantages, in terms of increased quality of care along with reduced economic and social costs. Major advantages deal with:

- Continuity of treatment/care and of monitoring: the patient can continue the treatment and/or the care at home, for the chronical evolution of the pathology after the acute step in a hospital. Being at home and continuously monitored by mhApps and by suitable instrumentation and tools will guarantee the patient a uniform level of care together with a better quality of life: any abnormal event, change in the patient's status, or even emergency will automatically be detected immediately and suitably dealt with.
- Avoid duplication and redundancy, as well as potential errors and misunderstanding: mhApps which run strictly connected to the EHR/HIS do not require to have local copy of acquired data, which may go lost in case of off-line asynchronous

transferal to the main database. Data are not replicated, are not saved into temporary tables, and are not redundant. The overall quality of data, both for patient-oriented and for population-oriented analyses, is thus guaranteed and preserved.

- Better communication between patients and healthcare professionals (medical and nurses): a proper communication channel and data exchange between the patient and the caregivers at home rely on a good, bi-directional communication channel between homecare tools and the EHR/HIS. By using mhApps such a better communication is easily achieved.
- Meaningful use: the bi-directional exchange of data and documents between patients and healthcare professionals is part of the stage 3 of the meaningful use program (http://www.cdc.gov/ehrmeaningfuluse/timeline.html) that envisages the adoption of interoperable EHR systems with wider access to health information for patients.
- Patient involvement and engagement: involving the patient as an active agent in the care process is extremely important, both in terms of quality of collected data and in terms of his/her psychological role. Moreover, some data which describe the condition of the patient cannot be described in a better way if not directly by the patient him-/herself: no one else can better describe that.

26.5.2 Critical Issues

Adopting an integrated care system, as described above, may introduce some critical issues which are to be continuously monitored. Major critical issues deal with:

- Security and control: as healthcare data are considered extremely sensitive and private (i.e., of the patient him-/herself), security controls must be performed to ensure data integrity. Since the mobile environment is usually considered as "unsafe" and prone to attacks, the bi-directional data exchange between mhApps and EHR systems deserves particular attention. Moreover, mhApps can insert, delete, and update stored information, thus possibly introducing new risks.
- Authorized access to data: home caregivers and patients must own suitable authorizations to access information, according to well-defined access policies. In fact, some data can be read but can't be updated or deleted: on the other side, some data can be inserted by mhApps, on condition that the user is properly identified. This requires a strong mechanism of validating and authorizing access to stored data.
- Information accuracy for patient-generated data: poor health literacy may lead to low data quality which, in turn, may lead to incorrect decisions, treatments, and care, with unwanted consequences. Thus, the accuracy of acquired data—especially for those acquired outside the hospital—is a critical issue to be considered, as in any health-related domain.

- Continuous monitoring of critical parameters and automatic detection of critical situations: home-generated data, as well as hospital-generated ones, may hide or highlight critical situations, abnormalities, and sudden worsening of patient's condition. As a consequence, alarms, which can be activated within the hospital over hospital-generated data, must be properly activated also over home-generated data. The detection mechanism is thus to be made available over data managed by mhApps, too.

26.6 Future Trends

As the present scenario remains scattered, the future trend claims for an increased interoperability among different applications. This can be achieved by the definition of appropriate standards for the implementation of the bi-directional exchange of data and documents between institutional systems and mhApps for the patient and of appropriate business models ensuring that the added value of such information exchange is sustainable by the healthcare systems (Rossi 2016).

Portability and platform independence of both the professional and the patient side are another future development for integrated eHealth, in the light of a broader health information exchange.

In the vision of a future national and transnational interoperability between mhApps and EHR systems of different enterprises, the definition of minimum datasets of header information for message exchange and their format should also be evaluated.

Finally, technological interoperability won't be enough to implement integrated care: the semantic integration between electronic medical records and electronic social records (i.e., those tracking patient's information for social care) should be boosted in order to entirely follow patient's care pathways.

26.7 Conclusions

The technological integration of the healthcare professional and the patient environments will lead to a fully integrated care, thus ensuring better quality of care and of life, especially for chronic patients. Provided that the technological tools of these two environments are deeply different in terms of data security and privacy, as well as of data accuracy and quality due to the different level of education and engagement, such integration faces big challenges. Available technological and semantic standards do not cover the exchange of information between mhApps for patients and institutional health information systems/EHRs, patient-generated data need to be reliable and appropriately represented to be included in the EHR, ad hoc security and privacy strategies have to be developed to ensure healthcare data protection, and patients and caregivers need support to act into the care pathway. Once these issues will become part of the implementation process of both institutional systems and patients' mhApps, the integration will be achieved.

References

HL7. (2008, February). *Implementation guide for CDA release 2.0 personal healthcare monitoring report (PHMR). Health Level Seven International. Draft standard for trial use. Release 1.1*. Retrieved 2017, May 15, from http://www.hl7.org/implement/standards/product brief.cfm?product id=120

International Standard Organization. (2010, October). *ISO 13606-1:2008 health informatics—electronic health record communication*. Retrieved 2017, May 15, from https://www.iso.org/standard/40784.html

Marceglia, S., Fontelo, P. A., Rossi, E., & Ackerman, M. J. (2015a). A standards-based architecture proposal for integrating patient mhealth apps to electronic health record systems. *Applied Clinical Informatics, 6*(3), 488–505, eCollection 2015. doi: https://doi.org/10.4338/ACI-2014-12-RA-0115

Marceglia, S., Fontelo, P. A., & Ackerman, M. J. (2015b). Transforming consumer health informatics: Connecting CHI applications to the health-IT ecosystem. *JAMIA, 22*(e1), e210–e212. https://doi.org/10.1093/jamia/ocu030.

Rossi, E. (2016). *Integrating the home and the professional care environments through standards: A prototype for tDCS home monitoring*. Unpublished doctoral dissertation, Politecnico di Milano, Milano, Italy. Retrieved from http://hdl.handle.net/10589/114516

Rossi, E., Fontelo, P. A., Ackerman, M. J., Pozzi, G., & Marceglia, S. (2015). A prototype of mobile app/EHR communication through standards for home treatment of transcranial direct current stimulation. In P. Balakrishnan, J. Srivatsava, W. Fu, S. M. Harabagiu, & F. Wang (Eds.), *2015 International Conference on Healthcare Informatics, ICHI 2015, Dallas, TX, USA, October 21–23, 2015* (pp. 310–315). Washington, DC: IEEE Computer Society. Retrieved from http://doi.ieeecomputersociety.org/10.1109/ICHI.2015.44.

Chapter 27
An Investigation on Integrating Eastern and Western Medicine with Informatics

Catherine Han Lin, Angela Wei Hong Yang, David Phillips, and Nilmini Wickramasinghe

27.1 Introduction

Integrating western medicine (WM) with Chinese medicine (CM) has been a feature in China since WM was introduced to the country in the mid-nineteenth century of the Qing dynasty (Lin et al. 2015b). Today, it is common that patients are treated with both types of medicine (Chan et al. 2010). Although this integration has been very popular in China, it is relatively new to western countries. WM uses disease diagnosis with the foundation of pathological examination of individual organ functions or malfunctions (Chan et al. 2010). CM, on the other hand, is largely a philosophy, although it has been in practice for thousands of years, based on its incredible values in healing and well-being. The lack of scientific and medical evidence is one of the major reasons that CM has not been fully accepted and integrated into the western healthcare system (Lin et al. 2015b). The situation, however, has altered in recent times. Studies have shown that CM is used in treatment plans either as ingredients (Chan et al. 2010; Chau et al. 2009; Wang et al. 2011) or to improve physical and emotional well-being (Molassiotis et al. 2005). The World Health Organization's

C. H. Lin (✉)
Deakin University, Burwood, VIC, Australia
e-mail: lcatheri@deakin.edu.au

A. W. H. Yang
RMIT University, Melbourne, VIC, Australia
e-mail: angela.yang@rmit.edu.au

D. Phillips · N. Wickramasinghe
Deakin University, Burwood, VIC, Australia
e-mail: david.phillips@deakin.edu.au; n.wickramasinghe@deakin.edu.au

N. Wickramasinghe, J. L. Schaffer (eds.), *Theories to Inform Superior Health Informatics Research and Practice*, Healthcare Delivery in the Information Age,
https://doi.org/10.1007/978-3-319-72287-0_27

(WHO) traditional and complementary medicine (T&CM) strategy 2014–2023 urges its member countries to promote integrating "T&CM services and self-health care into national health systems" as stated by general director Margaret Chan (WHO 2013). WHO's goal and vision is to have a blended system which takes the best of both types of medicine and compensates for the potential weaknesses in each (Lin et al. 2015b; WHO 2013). Lin et al. studied the current and future movements of CM and WM integration and suggested that some developed countries (such as Australia, Canada, and England) are in a situation where WM predominates, with CM as a complementary and alternative medicine (CAM). National regulation, policies, and standards are established, and CM practices are partially integrated in these settings (Lin et al. 2015b). Furthermore, health insurance companies cover percentages of CM claims, and qualified CM practitioners must comply with the regulations.

In the process of this WM/CM integration, information systems and technology (IS/IT) can play a key contribution. Developments can already be found in various applications and systems. For example, these include expert systems (Lam et al. 2012), knowledge-based systems such as database/warehouse functions (Huang and Chen 2007) and diagnosis, and treatment assistant systems (He et al. 2006). These systems have shown that IS/IT is an essential tool in assisting CM to be accepted into mainstream medicine practices. Nonetheless, literature reviews show that the existing CM IS/IT developments have limitations, and there is a lack of suitable synthesis for this unique combination (Lin et al. 2015a; Yang et al. 2009).

This paper serves to extend Churchman's inquiring systems to depict CM as a combination of Hegelian and Kantian inquiring systems with the support of Singerian, Lockean, Leibnizian inquiring systems and knowledge management (KM) features and by doing so enable a deeper understanding of CM so then it might be possible to design a patient management system (PMS) to support CM practice in a given clinic.

27.2 Problems and Challenges of CM Developments

Medical developments in the twenty-first century have arisen from a multitude of factors, including a rapid increase in chronic diseases such as diabetes, a lack of resources in both drug manufacturing and medical funding, as well as educated patients who seek for better and holistic treatment of their illnesses and well-being (Lin et al. 2015b). Integrating WM with CM is a new approach that has shown some remarkable achievements in this aspect (Chan et al. 2010). Like any major change, challenges and problems are to be expected (Savery 2015). This section reviews some of the major concerns in this regard.

27.2.1 Different Regulations and Standards

Research shows that most developed countries classify CM as a type of CAM (WHO 2013). Regulations and experiences differ between countries; for example, Australia is at a stage where CM practitioners are expected to be qualified, and WM doctors who are trained and have knowledge in CM can be found in many medical clinics (Lin et al. 2015b). Specifically, with regard to Australia, (1) the CM profession is included in the National Registration and Accreditation Scheme (NRAS). A national registration of practitioners, acupuncturists, and dispensers of Chinese herbal medicine commenced on July 1, 2012 (AHPRA 2014; CMBA(c) 2012). (2) Policies, registration guidelines, codes, and standards are created and published to assist the CM medical profession. Accreditation standards and processes for consultation were developed by the Australian Health Practitioner Regulation Agency (AHPRA) and Chinese Medicine Board of Australia (CMBA) (AHPRA 2014). (3) CM undergraduate and postgraduate courses are offered in the Australian tertiary education system. (4) A CMBA website was created which enables online service delivery and communication. The Chinese Medicine Portal was created in 2009 and serves as an online CM knowledge pool where information and clinical data can be retrieved and accessed (Yang et al. 2009). (5) AHPRA will directly allocate cost funding to CMBA to assist various activities undertaken by the agreement and strategies (AHPRA 2014).

Regarding other western jurisdictions, in Switzerland, CM was covered by the nation's basic health insurance program in 1999 but was taken out in 2005 except CM acupuncture (Busato et al. 2006; Okma et al. 2010). In most of Europe, it is illegal to sell manufactured unlicensed herbal medicines without the appropriate license (Fan et al. 2012). In the UK, the 2009 "Statutory Regulation of Practitioners of Acupuncture, Herbal Medicine, Traditional Chinese Medicine and other Traditional Medicine Systems Practised in the UK" states that all CM practitioners must be qualified and regulated (Holmes 2011). In the USA, CM is recognised as dietary supplements and is regulated by the Dietary Supplement Health and Education Act (DSHEA) (Chau and Wu 2006). Hence, CM is loosely regulated and assessed compared to WM. Patients' safety is a major concern.

In summary, different levels of legal foundations to establish quality and safety standards for CM and its practice exist in some countries on a national basis. An internationally recognised standard should be enforced to avoid confusion, aid in coordination, and mitigate any health risks. Building on the existing contributions from Australia and other countries, future works may include increasing all aspects of WM and CM integration (Lin et al. 2015a). For example, (a) combining and integrating existing CM databases to international recognised format and standards, (b) making global standardised CM practice regulations and guidelines that can be accessed online, and (c) developing suitable IS/IT solutions for various CM practice, and gradually achieving WHO's goal of a blended system. The current research focuses on finding the suitable synthesis to justify the IS/IT development in supporting managing the patients' information at the clinic level.

27.2.2 CM IS/IT Developments and Challenges

The rich traditional knowledge of CM has helped the Chinese for thousands of years, integrating this medicine practice to the western world involves transferring this massive knowledge (Chan et al. 2015). So far, many databases, repositories, and information systems (IS) have been created (Chan et al. 2015). For example, the Traditional Chinese Medicine Information Database from the National University of Singapore contains information on 1,588 commonly used prescriptions, 1,313 herbs, and 5,669 herbal ingredients (Chan et al. 2010; TCM-ID 2015). The University of Michigan Comprehensive Herbal Medicine Information System for Cancer includes 527 anticancer herbal formulations (Chan et al. 2010; Fang et al. 2005). Some CM expert systems and applications are developed for certain diseases or particular treatment. For example, a Chinese acupuncture expert system can assist physicians on acupuncture prescription, needle insertion position, and acupuncture point usage (Lam et al. 2012). Recent research studies addressing major IS/IT activities in CM are summarised in Table 27.1 below.

Studies have shown that the existing IS/IT developments have several limitations, such as (1) selective information and lack of comprehensive data on the number of Chinese herbs with no or limited resources in Chinese acupuncture or vice versa (Yang et al. 2009); (2) most of the IS/IT system solutions are created in China or Asia, with limited scientific and evidence-based research in western countries (Lukman et al. 2007); (3) there is not a theory to support the IS/IT development in the integration of these medicines (Lin et al. 2015b). Further, a study of the current CM clinic management systems (consisting of Smart TCM Australia, TCM Herbalist Israel, TCM Organiser Canada, and Shen Professional Venezuela) also indicates some significant concerns including (a) incorrect use of the Chinese language as well as lack of translation into other languages apart from Chinese and English (Lin et al. 2015b); (b) lack of multi-user systems which can accommodate administrator, physician, and dispenser (Lin et al. 2015b); and (c) current systems that cannot be used on multiple platforms and devices (Lin et al. 2015b).

The most important limitation to the further application of CM is that the synthesis of IS/IT developments so far have been mainly studied and applied to WM (Lin et al. 2015b). This study suggests that blindly adopting these theories and technologies is not the best solution for CM. This view is supported in practice in other domains, for example, when we look at enterprise resource planning (ERP) systems, such as SAP and Oracle, as they have failed to conquer the Chinese market by simply applying the same tools and techniques without first understanding and mapping the underlying circumstances and requirements (Xue et al. 2005). To avoid similar failures, it is therefore necessary to systematically examine past experiences with WM IS/IT developments and develop a theoretical foundation that is suitable for CM practice. Hence, we analyse the different inquiring and knowledge management systems in this domain drawing upon the work of Churchman (1971).

Table 27.1 Summary of existing CM IS/IT developments (sourced from Lukman et al. 2007)

IS/IT	Group	Description	Examples
Databases	Database	Repository, database containing detailed information on CM formulas, syndromes, herb information including pharmaceutical name; botanical name; multilingual pronunciation; distribution of the herb; properties (characteristics); channels (meridians) entered; medical functions; actions and indications; chemical ingredients; recommended dosage; samples of formulae, toxicity, side effects, and cautions; basic molecular properties; optimised 3D structures; origins; and clinical effects	Chinese herb dictionary: Complementary and alternative healing university (Chu 2013)
	Dictionary		3D structure database of components from Chinese traditional medicinal herbs (Qiao et al. 2002)
	Knowledge base grid		Phytochemical databases of Chinese herbal constituents and bioactive plant compounds with known target specificities (Ehrman et al. 2007)
	Information system		
Data mining	CM data mining and biomedical mining systems	Data mining tools for CM herbs and formulations	MeDisco/3T—Text mining for clinical Chinese herbal medical knowledge discovery (Zhou et al. 2005)
		Information management system of CM syndrome	
		Study on combination of hierarchical cluster approach and Bayesian networks	Data mining system for multi-dimensional data analysis (Li et al. 2004)
		Research approach and method including harmony learning and model selection	Structural learning of graphical models and its applications (Deng et al. 2005)
CM diagnosis assistance	Diagnosis systems and approaches	Individual diagnosis and treatment assistance system including pulse-measuring points on wrists and their corresponding organs; electronic-brain medical erudite medical expert system; analysis packages of tongue and facial images, odour, speech, and pulse; and fuzzy expert systems assisting diagnosis for certain disease	Expert system for diagnosis in CM (Wang et al. 2004)
			Web-based CM diagnosis system (Huang and Chen 2007)
			Pulse analysis & diagnosis system (He et al. 2006)
			Fuzzy logic and its applications in medicine (Phuong and Kreinovich 2001)

27.2.3 Inquiring Systems

C. West Churchman defines the five inquiring systems as Leibnizian, Lockean, Hegelian, Kantian, and Singerian (Churchman 1971). Each of these represents a type of inquiring organisation from a system view of knowledge creation, examination, and management (Churchman 1971). This theory has been adopted, improved, and implemented in many IS/IT research paradigms and developments (Parrish Jr and Courtney 2012; Wickramasinghe 2005). Below is a summary of these systems.

The *Leibnizian* inquiring system uses formal logic and analysis to generate fact nets and manipulate explicit knowledge (Churchman 1971; Courtney et al. 2005; Hall and Croasdell 2005). Tacit knowledge gets little emphasis, and new knowledge is generated as an externalisation of editing and systemizing. Most suited IS/IT models to this type of systems are expert systems (Hall and Croasdell 2005; Mason and Mitroff 1973; Parrish Jr and Courtney 2012). The *Lockean* inquiring system contains communities sharing a common mind-set; knowledge is constructed through attention to symbolic references such as legends and/or well-respected authorities (Hall and Croasdell 2005; Mason and Mitroff 1973; Nonaka et al. 1998; Parrish Jr and Courtney 2012). IS/IT used in this type of system includes data warehouses (storing observations), data mining (analysing the observations), and groupware tools like emails (facilitating the communication and sharing) (Parrish Jr and Courtney 2012). The *Singerian* inquiring system generates cycles of processes which resolve problems and disagreements by introducing new variables and laws to provide guidance and overcome inconsistencies at each cycle, until the problem is fully investigated and understood from all sides (Hall and Croasdell 2005; Mason and Mitroff 1973; Parrish Jr and Courtney 2012). All forms of knowledge including tacit and explicit, deep and shallow, declarative and procedural, and exoteric and esoteric are considered, measured for improvements, and judged by both organisational and society ethical standards (Hall and Croasdell 2005; Mason and Mitroff 1973; Nonaka et al. 1998; Parrish Jr and Courtney 2012). The *Singerian* approach is best supported by networks based on groupware and web-based to allow virtual information gathering and learning because of its need to include a wide range of individual stakeholders (Hall and Croasdell 2005; Mason and Mitroff 1973; Parrish Jr and Courtney 2012). The *Hegelian* inquiring system builds new synthesis by reflecting and resolving diametrically opposed perspectives. It tries to understand all behaviours, forms, processes, methods, arguments, and technology (Hall and Croasdell 2005; Mason and Mitroff 1973; Parrish Jr and Courtney 2012). IS/IT solutions that support *Hegelian* inquiring systems include groupware, document management solutions, and repositories that hold the debate data for better understanding of each other's proposals (Hall and Croasdell 2005; Mason and Mitroff 1973; Parrish Jr and Courtney 2012). The *Kantian* inquiring system generates hypothesis based on multiple perspectives and inputs from various knowledge sources. It uses explicit and tacit knowledge to consider the many interpretations of the inputs; in this process, the inquirer can study and determine different ways, modelling, methods, and techniques to incorporate the new knowledge (Hall and Croasdell 2005; Mason and Mitroff 1973; Parrish Jr and Courtney 2012). Examples of IS/IT using Kantian systems are the World Wide Web (www), databases, model management systems, decision support systems (DSS), and effective information systems (Hall and Croasdell 2005; Mason and Mitroff 1973; Parrish Jr and Courtney 2012).

27.2.4 Inquiring System for WM

Healthcare information systems (HIS) have been largely developed to produce expert systems, theorem-proving systems, problem-solving and DSS, algorithm-generating systems, databases, and repositories in WM (Ferlie et al. 2012; Liao 2003). Hence, the existing HIS developments and solutions are mostly in the categories of Leibnizian and Lockean inquiring systems. For example, these include electronic knowledge repositories storing codified knowledge for future reuse and clinical DSS-linking characteristics of patients with chest pain to software algorithms recommending specific action (Ferlie et al. 2012). An early form of Kantian inquiring system can be found in some DSS which takes information from various data sources and uses this data to provide assistance with the structured portion of the semi-structured; however the human decision maker must rely on intuition and experience to assist them with the unstructured portions (Parrish Jr and Courtney 2012). Singerian inquiring system's emphasis on ethical behaviour can be seen in most HIS where medical ethics and professionalism are mandatory and expected to maintain strictly in practice. An example of this is a DSS which is developed and implemented with the guidance and principles of patient safety, quality performance, regulations, and policies (Parrish Jr and Courtney 2012).

27.3 Methodology

A mixed research method was chosen to address the research question because it allows exploring the issues faced by individuals (Venkatesh et al. 2013), in particular, the CM practitioners, and it enables identifying the facets and proposes productivity framework in order to better understand the proposed concept. Specifically, the research adopts case study methodology techniques in selecting the case clinics as well as conducting the interviews. Design science methodology was also employed in this research to carry out processes in producing the proposed PMS.

27.3.1 Case Study (CS)

CS methodology is a commonly used and well-recognised research strategy in healthcare services and IS research. It attempts to examine a contemporary phenomenon in its real-life context (Yin 1999, 2013). Through a typical CS, the research solution will be further supported by experiments which capture the circumstances and conditions of everyday and/or commonplace situations. In selecting the case clinics, this research uses a range of selection criteria including, for example, clinic size, number of patients and clinical staffs, and usage of both Chinese herbal medicine and acupuncture. The sample clinics must meet all the requirements and sign ethics agreements to participate in this research. Interviewing is one of the most familiar strategies for collecting qualitative data. It can provide important insights into the events or shortcuts to the prior history which helps to identify other relevant sources of evidence (Flick 2009; Yin 1999, 2013). This research will conduct semi-structured interviews with questions that are designed with experts' assistance and existing documents from the study field. It is anticipated that open and broad questions will be asked at the beginning of the interviewing process, where the interviewee groups can express their opinions and/or propose their own insights into certain occurrences and for further inquiries. Interviewee groups from the case clinic include the CM physician, acupuncturist, administrator, and dispenser. Each interview is scheduled for about 20 min and will be audio recorded, and notes will be taken by the interviewer.

27.3.2 Design Science (DS)

DS methodology has its roots in the field of engineering and science. It "seeks to create innovations that define the ideas, practices, technical capabilities, and products through which the analysis, design, implementation, management, and use of information systems can be effectively and efficiently accomplished" (von Alan et al. 2004). DS has been commonly used in IS/IT researches because it is aimed at developing executive information systems and supporting emerging knowledge processes with effective development methods and system solutions for particular user group requirements or models (Lewis 2015; Vaishnavi and Kuechler 2015; von Alan et al. 2004). Furthermore, Von Alan et al. provided a DS IS research framework and set of guidelines and practical rules for IS researchers to follow. Based on this framework, the research has four processes:

1. Problem verification—this means that the research problem is confirmed and documented as additional supporting evidence to the research literature. Interviews are carried out and guided by the interview questions. Data is collected, categorised, and stored in a database.
2. Solution design—the PMS is designed. A solution framework and structure is crafted for the research problem tailored to the current CM clinic practices. Therefore data analysis is performed in two major phases. First, the existing clinical (as-is) situation will be modelled, described, and analysed. Then, areas of improvements are identified according to the proposed PMS structure. The new (to-be) system is analysed, explained, and modelled.
3. Evaluation—this is conducted to ensure rigour; the modules of the proposed system are evaluated, refined, and tested with specification, expectation, and precise scope.
4. Summarise results—this is the final stage of the research. Findings, publications, and a thesis are the expected outcomes.

27.3.3 Data Collection and Analysis

A thematic analysis is used in this research as a facilitator to assist communication between the above-mentioned research methodologies, as it allows communication between different qualitative methods (Flick 2009). When reviewing the collected data, the researchers identify themes (such as CM herbs, acupuncture, treatment formulas, etc.), separate similarities and differences, and then refine and sort the data into different categories for further analysis. Periodical and ad hoc peers and participants' debriefing and checking are mandatory in this research as it helps to increase the rigour of the research. This is because it can (1) keep everyone informed and on track, (2) reduce communication errors and prevent/remove potential risks that may be caused by the lack of communication and misunderstanding, and (3) allow timely correction and recovery. Modelling and testing techniques are also used to capture the situation of the case clinics and the PMS solution.

27.4 Preliminary Results

Apart from the inquiring systems, KM systems are designed and developed to enhance knowledge-intense tasks, processes, and projects for the purpose of knowledge creation, storage, retrieval, transfer, refinement, reuse, revision, and feedback (Maier and Hädrich 2011). Hence KM architecture and characteristics are important elements which should be considered in CM developments.

27.4.1 CM IS/IT Development Design

Typical KM systems contain data and knowledge sources (including organisational internal and external information, data warehouses, document management, personal information management, content management, and groupware), infrastructure services (providing basic functionality for communication, data and electronic assets management, extraction, transformation, and loading), integration services (managing knowledge from a variety of sources), knowledge services (involving discovery functions such as searching, mining, navigation, and visualisation; publication functions like structuring, formats, and contextualisation; collaboration functions including skill/expert management, knowledge sharing, awareness, and experience management; learning functions that use tools and techniques for authoring, managing courses, tutoring, learning paths, and examinations), personalisation services, and access services (Maier and Hädrich 2011).

This research analyses the CM clinics' information and knowledge through a case study approach. It looks into the clinics' IT infrastructure services for messaging and file transferring. It also investigates how the clinic manages external information, such as films and laboratory test results in assisting diagnosis and treatments. The research also analyses 1) if any expert knowledge system is used in the clinic. 2) if the physicians use any decision support system (DSS) in assisting diagnosis and treatments. 3) how the clinic manages its reporting and standards required by the authorities, and, 4) how the clinic practitioners search, order, and manage their medical/herb information. The research also addresses how the clinics manage its practitioners' personal devices and applications as well as access level and security.

27.4.2 Preliminary/Expected Results

Guided by the aspects from the inquiring systems and KM, this research proposes that CM IS/IT developments should follow a synthesis that is a combination of Hegelian and Kantian inquiring systems with the support of Singerian, Lockean, and Leibnizian inquiring systems and KM features. This is discussed in detail in the next section. As an extension of the proposal, a PMS is built for the CM clinics. Fig. 27.1 maps the system architecture of the PMS.

The PMS follows the CM IS/IT structure allowing negotiation and consultation between different systems, applications, and world views. It also has the intention to integrate WM and CM accordingly via the connection to different databases and accessing different network system functions for inquiring and confirmation.

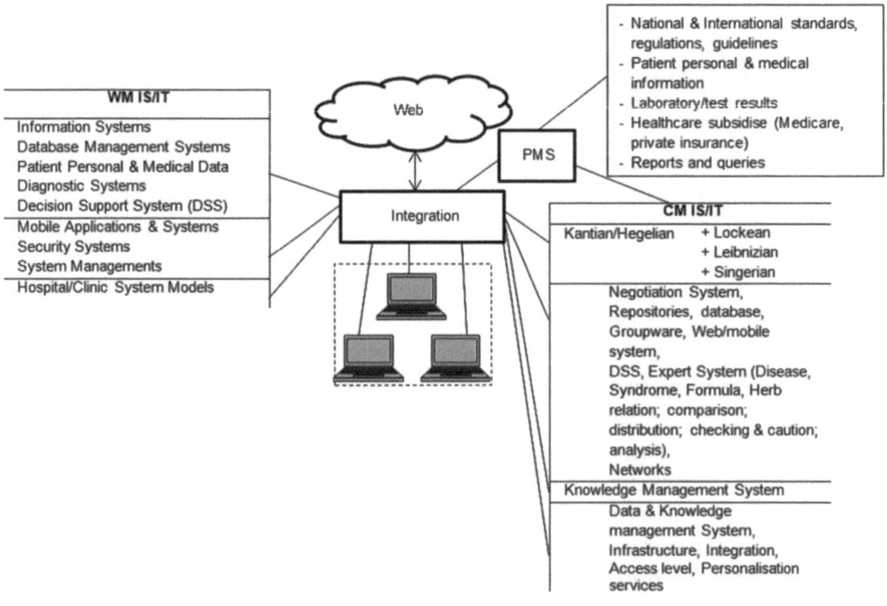

Fig. 27.1 PMS system design

For example, a patient's medical history (other than CM medical history), which is stored in another database, can be obtained. Likewise, a WM doctor can access the patient's CM medical history (stored in bilingual format) to gain better understanding of the patient's overall health problem at the point of care.

The PMS is designed to comply with the national and international CM practice regulations, guidelines, and standards. According to CMBA, it should contain information about:

- Patient personal and medical data including cultural background information.
- Up-to-date sickness/problem/medication lists and its diagnosis and treatment plans.
- Records of patients' progress, communications with other health service providers, and any discussion about possible side effects or alternative forms of treatments.
- Detailed records of prescriptions including name, strength, quantity, dose, instructions for use, number of repeats, and start and end dates.
- Vital signs and changes including allergies and warnings.
- Incorporate clinical laboratory test results.
- Provide a summary of care records for patients in case of referral or transition.
- All detailed procedures conducted (acupuncture points and stimulation methods).
- Generate reports, invoices, and rebates (CMBA(d) 2012).

All of the above must be protected with access passwords and kept for at least 7 years (CMBA(d) 2012). Therefore, a security archiving service may be necessary.

Information provided by the PMS can be used for (1) knowledge sharing (Leibnizian inquiring system) between WM, CM, community, and society, (2) further knowledge creation and transforming for both types of medicine practice, and (3) providing sources for studies on clinical trials and evidence-based research.

27.5 Discussion

CM is unique and follows a philosophy of systematic balance of Yin and Yang—opposite yet interdependent objects (Bing and Hongcai 2010; Chan et al. 2010). It emphasises inner, self-controlled system connectivity and balance between Yin and Yang energy, with any disorder being a result of failure and/or imbalance of the system (Huang and Chen 2007; Lu et al. 2004; Zhao et al. 1994). Hence, an important element in CM practice is resolving, strengthening, and rebalancing the system with duality wisdom (Wickramasinghe 2005). This is a typical Hegelian inquiring system which tries to resolve conflicts and proposes enlarged synthesis; as a result the problem is completely dissolved (Courtney et al. 2005; Hall and Croasdell 2005; Morr 2010). As indicated by Wickramasinghe that KM involves recognising the dualities in all knowledge creation and transformation (tacit/explicit, Lockean &

Leibnizian/Hegelian & Kantian, subjective/objective, people/technology), in doing so "a more complete and richer picture of knowledge is created and hence the impact to knowledge management" (Wickramasinghe 2005). Hegelian's ability to understand all types of inputs supports CM's comprehensive and systematic view of human diseases.

CM diagnosis methods are different to WM. In summary, it uses four diagnosis methods: inspection (understand and predict the pathological changes by observing abnormal changes in the patient's vitality, colour, appearance, secretions, and excretions), auscultation and olfaction (listening and smelling), inquiring (asking about the patient's condition), and palpation (placing the physician's first three fingers on the radial artery of a patient's wrist to detect different pulse qualities) (Huang and Chen 2007; Zhao et al. 1994). These four approaches are used in combination in every diagnosis and cannot be separated or omitted (Zhu and Wang 2011). A correct diagnosis can only be made based on a comprehensive and systematic analysis of a patient's condition at the point of care. A CM physician's tacit knowledge and thorough analysis of each patient's unique health condition is a key which differentiates between the two types of medicinal practices. This is a category of Kantian inquiring systems, as hypotheses are generated on the basis of the inputs received from various knowledge sources (Churchman 1971; Parrish Jr and Courtney 2012).

CM treatments can be any of the following: herbs (including leaves, seeds, roots, flowers, fruits, minerals, and animal products); acupuncture, moxibustion, tuina (Chinese remedial massage), cupping, qigong, and diet therapy (Zhu and Wang 2011). All treatments aim to increase human body's resistance to diseases and prevention by improving the interconnections among self-controlled systems (Lu et al. 2004). These multiple compounds, methods, and diversities indicate that CM is a Kantian system because it incorporates multiple perspectives and facts to determine different models and/or system design to discover and distribute information. It is aimed at achieving the best-fit between itself and the environment.

To define a suitable CM inquiring system, we also need to consider that Kantian and Hegelian systems rely on the Leibnizian inquiring system's fact net to generate knowledge (Churchman 1971; Parrish Jr and Courtney 2012), so the Leibnizian inquiring system is included as part of the knowledge base. Furthermore, Singerian inquiring systems' emphasis on ethical conduct is important. Patient safety, interests, and social justice must be considered and built-in as principles and guidelines in any CM IS/IT developments and solutions. Table 27.2 illustrates this research's perspective.

27.6 Research Contribution and Future Development

This research presents a synthesis which extends Churchman's inquiring systems theory into a new domain within health care and combining the inquiring system with a design science approach for actually designing and developing a proposed

Table 27.2 CM inquiring system (source from Lin et al. 2015b)

Inquiring systems	Hegelian	Kantian	Singerian	Leibnizian	Lockean
Western medicine		WM are more Lockean, Leibnizian, Singerian, and Kantian inquiring systems			
Chinese medicine		Diagnosis: Inspection, auscultation and olfaction, inquiring, palpation Treatments: Herbs, acupuncture, moxibustion, tuina, cupping, qigong, and diet therapy CM is more Hegelian, Kantian inquiring systems with supports from Singerian and Leibnizian			

solution. The proposed PMS provides an example and suggestion for CM clinics to migrate from a manual system to a IS/IT solution. This in-progress research intends to also demonstrate integration between WM and CM, through a designed system architecture. The research project can be used as assistance for both the CMBA and the individual CM practitioners in maintaining regulations and standards. It is a reference and resource for both types of medicine's research and education. This theoretical extension and the proposed system can be further developed and customised to other areas in the same domain.

References

AHPRA, C. (2014). *Chinese medicine regulation at work in Australia, 2013/14*. Retrieved from https://www.ahpra.gov.au/Publications/Corporate-publications/Annual-reports.aspx

Bing, Z., & Hongcai, W. (2010). *Basic theories of traditional Chinese medicine*. London: Singing Dragon.

Busato, A., Eichenberger, R., & Kunzi, B. (2006). Extent and structure of health insurance expenditures for complementary and alternative medicine in Swiss primary care. *BMC Health Services Research, 6*, 132. https://doi.org/10.1186/1472-6963-6-132.

Chan, E., Tan, M., Xin, J., Sudarsanam, S., & Johnson, D. E. (2010). Interactions between traditional Chinese medicines and Western therapeutics. *Current Opinion in Drug Discovery & Development, 13*(1), 50–65.

Chan, K., Hu, X.-Y., Razmovski-Naumovski, V., & Robinson, N. (2015). Challenges and opportunities of integrating traditional Chinese medicine into mainstream medicine: A review of the current situation. *European Journal of Integrative Medicine, 7*(1), 67–75.

Chau, A. C., Cheung, R. T., Jiang, X., Au-Yeung, P. K., & Li, L. S. (2009). Increased brain activation in motor cortex after acupuncture treatment for motor recovery in chronic stroke patients. *The Open Rehabilitation Journal, 2*, 89–94.

Chau, C. F., & Wu, S. H. (2006). The development of regulations of Chinese herbal medicines for both medicinal and food uses. *Trends in Food Science & Technology, 17*(6), 313–323.

Chu, J. H. K. (2013). *Chinese herbal medicine dictionary*. Retrieved from http://alternativehealing.org/chinese_herbs_dictionary.htm

Churchman, C. W. (1971). *The design of inquiring systems basic concepts of systems and organization*. New York: Basic Books.

CMBA(c). (2012). *<CMBA-Continuing-Professional-Development.pdf>*.

CMBA(d). (2012). *CMBA-guidelines-for-patient-records*. Chinese Medicine Board of Australia. Retrieved from http://www.chinesemedicineboard.gov.au/Codes-Guidelines.aspx.

Courtney, J. F., Haynes, J. D., & Paradice, D. B. (2005). *Inquiring organizations: Moving from knowledge management to wisdom*. Hershey, PA: IGI Global.

Deng, K., Liu, D., Gao, S., & Geng, Z. (2005). Structural learning of graphical models and its applications to traditional Chinese medicine. In *Fuzzy systems and knowledge discovery* (pp. 362–367). Berlin: Springer.

Ehrman, T. M., Barlow, D. J., & Hylands, P. J. (2007). Phytochemical databases of Chinese herbal constituents and bioactive plant compounds with known target specificities. *Journal of Chemical Information and Modeling, 47*(2), 254–263.

Fan, T.-P., Deal, G., Koo, H.-L., Rees, D., Sun, H., Chen, S., et al. (2012). Future development of global regulations of Chinese herbal products. *Journal of Ethnopharmacology, 140*(3), 568–586.

Fang, X., Shao, L., Zhang, H., & Wang, S. (2005). CHMIS-C: A comprehensive herbal medicine information system for cancer. *Journal of Medicinal Chemistry, 48*(5), 1481–1488.

Ferlie, E., Crilly, T., Jashapara, A., & Peckham, A. (2012). Knowledge mobilisation in healthcare: A critical review of health sector and generic management literature. *Social Science & Medicine, 74*(8), 1297–1304.

Flick, U. (2009). *An introduction to qualitative research*. Thousand Oaks, CA: Sage.

Hall, D. J., & Croasdell, D. (2005). *Inquiring organizations: An organizational form perspective*. Calgary, AB: Idea Group.

He, X., Huang, W., Lu, M., Xue, W., & Lu, Y. (2006). *Research and application of data mining in individual diagnosis and treatment based on Chinese traditional medicine*. Paper presented at the GrC.

Holmes, D. (2011). UK moves to ensure "access to unlicensed herbal medicines". *The Lancet, 377*(9776), 1479–1480.

Huang, M.-J., & Chen, M.-Y. (2007). Integrated design of the intelligent web-based Chinese medical diagnostic system (CMDS)–systematic development for digestive health. *Expert Systems with Applications, 32*(2), 658–673.

Lam, C. F., Leung, K. S., Heng, P. A., Lim, C. E., & Wong, F. W. (2012). Chinese acupuncture expert system (CAES)-a useful tool to practice and learn medical acupuncture. *Journal of Medical Systems, 36*(3), 1883–1890. https://doi.org/10.1007/s10916-010-9647-0.

Lewis, S. (2015). Qualitative inquiry and research design: Choosing among five approaches. *Health Promotion Practice, 16*(4), 473–475.

Li, C., Tang, C., Peng, J., Hu, J., Zeng, L., Yin, X., et al. (2004). TCMiner: A high performance data mining system for multi-dimensional data analysis of traditional Chinese medicine prescriptions. In *Conceptual modeling for advanced application domains* (pp. 246–257). Basel: Springer.

Liao, S.-H. (2003). Knowledge management technologies and applications—Literature review from 1995 to 2002. *Expert Systems with Applications, 25*(2), 155–164.

Lin, C. H., Wei, A., Yang, H., Pittayachawan, S., Vogel, D., & Wickramasinghe, N. (2015a). *Inquiring knowledge management systems–A Chinese medicine perspective*. Paper presented at the System Sciences (HICSS), 2015 48th Hawaii International Conference on.

Lin, C. H., Yang, A. W. H., Pittayachawan, S., & Wickramasinghe, N. (2015b). *An analysis on the utilisation of health information technology to support clinical operation of Chinese medicine*. Hershey, PA: IGI Global.

Lu, A.-P., Jia, H.-W., Xiao, C., & Lu, Q.-P. (2004). Theory of traditional Chinese medicine and therapeutic method of diseases. *World Journal of Gastroenterology, 10*(13), 1854–1856.

Lukman, S., He, Y., & Hui, S. C. (2007). Computational methods for traditional Chinese medicine: A survey. *Computer Methods and Programs in Biomedicine, 88*(3), 283–294. https://doi.org/10.1016/j.cmpb.2007.09.008.

Maier, R., & Hädrich, T. (2011). Knowledge management systems. In D. Schwartz & D. Te'eni (Eds.), *Encyclopedia of knowledge management* (2nd ed., pp. 779–790). Hershey, PA: Information Science Reference.

Mason, R. O., & Mitroff, I. I. (1973). A program for research on management information systems. *Management Science, 19*(5), 475–487.
Molassiotis, A., Fernadez-Ortega, P., Pud, D., Ozden, G., Scott, J. A., Panteli, V., et al. (2005). Use of complementary and alternative medicine in cancer patients: A European survey. *Annals of Oncology, 16*(4), 655–663.
Morr, C. E. (2010). Health care virtual communities: Challenges and opportunities. In M. M. Cruz-Cunha, A. J. Tavares, & R. J. Simoes (Eds.), *Handbook of research on developments in e-health and telemedicine: Technological and social perspectives* (pp. 278–298). Hershey, PA: Medical Information Science Reference.
Nonaka, I., Reinmoeller, P., & Senoo, D. (1998). The 'ART' of knowledge: Systems to capitalize on market knowledge. *European Management Journal, 16*(6), 673–684.
Okma, K. G., Cheng, T.-M., Chinitz, D., Crivelli, L., Lim, M.-K., Maarse, H., & Labra, M. E. (2010). Six countries, six health reform models? Health care reform in Chile, Israel, Singapore, Switzerland, Taiwan and The Netherlands. *Journal of Comparative Policy Analysis, 12*(1–2), 75–113.
Parrish, J. L., Jr., & Courtney, J. F. (2012). Inquiring systems: Theoretical foundations for current and future information systems. In *Information systems theory* (pp. 387–396). Berlin: Springer.
Phuong, N. H., & Kreinovich, V. (2001). Fuzzy logic and its applications in medicine. *International Journal of Medical Informatics, 62*(2), 165–173.
Qiao, X., Hou, T., Zhang, W., Guo, S., & Xu, X. (2002). A 3D structure database of components from Chinese traditional medicinal herbs. *Journal of Chemical Information and Computer Sciences, 42*(3), 481–489.
Savery, J. R. (2015). Overview of problem-based learning: Definitions and distinctions. In *Essential readings in problem-based learning: Exploring and extending the legacy of Howard S. Barrows* (pp. 5–15). West Lafayette, IN: Purdue University Press.
TCM-ID. (2015). *Traditional Chinese medicine information database*. Singapore: Department of Computational Science, National University of Singapore. http://tcm.cz3.nus.edu.sg/group/tcm-id/tcmid_ns.asp.
Vaishnavi, V. K., & Kuechler, W. (2015). *Design science research methods and patterns: Innovating information and communication technology*. Boca Raton, FL: CRC Press.
Venkatesh, V., Brown, S. A., & Bala, H. (2013). Bridging the qualitative-quantitative divide: Guidelines for conducting mixed methods research in information systems. *MIS Quarterly, 37*(1), 21–54.
von Alan, R. H., March, S. T., Park, J., & Ram, S. (2004). Design science in information systems research. *MIS Quarterly, 28*(1), 75–105.
Wang, X., Qu, H., Liu, P., & Cheng, Y. (2004). A self-learning expert system for diagnosis in traditional Chinese medicine. *Expert Systems with Applications, 26*(4), 557–566. https://doi.org/10.1016/j.eswa.2003.10.004.
Wang, X., Sun, H., Zhang, A., Sun, W., Wang, P., & Wang, Z. (2011). Potential role of metabolomics approaches in the area of traditional Chinese medicine: As pillars of the bridge between Chinese and Western medicine. *Journal of Pharmaceutical and Biomedical Analysis, 55*(5), 859–868.
WHO. (2013). *WHO traditional medicine strategy: 2014–2023*. Geneva: World Health Organization.
Wickramasinghe, N. (2005). The phenomenon of duality: A key to facilitate the transition from knowledge management to wisdom for inquiring organizations. In J. Courtney, J. Haynes, & D. Paradice (Eds.), *Inquiring organizations: Moving from knowledge management to wisdom* (pp. 272–315). Hershey, PA: IGI Global.
Xue, Y., Liang, H., Boulton, W. R., & Snyder, C. A. (2005). ERP implementation failures in China: Case studies with implications for ERP vendors. *International Journal of Production Economics, 97*(3), 279–295.

Yang, A. W., Allan, G., Li, C. G., & Xue, C. C. (2009). Effective application of knowledge management in evidence-based Chinese medicine: A case study. *Evidence-based Complementary and Alternative Medicine, 6*(3), 393–398. https://doi.org/10.1093/ecam/nem124.

Yin, R. K. (1999). Enhancing the quality of case studies in health services research. *Health Services Research, 34*(5 Pt 2), 1209.

Yin, R. K. (2013). *Case study research: Design and methods*. Thousand Oaks, CA: Sage publications.

Zhao, Y., Tsutsui, T., Endo, A., Minato, K., & Takahashi, T. (1994). Design and development of an expert system to assist diagnosis and treatment of chronic hepatitis using traditional Chinese medicine. *Informatics for Health and Social Care, 19*(1), 37–45.

Zhou, X., Liu, B., & Wu, Z. (2005). Text mining for clinical Chinese herbal medical knowledge discovery. In *Discovery science* (pp. 396–398). Berlin: Springer.

Zhu, B., & Wang, H. (2011). *Basic theories of traditional Chinese medicine*. London: Singing Dragon.

Epilogue

As the twenty-first century unfolds, the role for health informatics will continue to grow in importance. Our dependence on technology to facilitate superior healthcare delivery will be unparalleled. However, the key question remains and perhaps becomes more significant with time: "How can we design and develop successful solutions and monitor their effectiveness to provide for further improvements?"

The answer is not simple, but we believe it lies partly in identifying an appropriate theoretical lens from which to analyze the web of healthcare stakeholders, the complexities and nuances, as well as the dynamic and chaotic operations that often occur. To assist in this regard, we hope the preceding pages have served to highlight critical aspects of key theories for various aspects of technology-enabled healthcare delivery and provided some answers and helpful hints and most importantly stimulated further thought.

We apologize in advance for providing only a taste of the issues at hand. We hope that we have left our readers with an appetite for more and a desire to actively participate in this dynamic and evolving field.

N. Wickramasinghe, J. L. Schaffer (eds.), *Theories to Inform Superior Health Informatics Research and Practice*, Healthcare Delivery in the Information Age,
https://doi.org/10.1007/978-3-319-72287-0

Index

A
Acceptance, 294
Activity theory (AT)
  actions and operations, 192
  contradictions, 238
  description, 192
  evolution
    collective notion of activity, 237
    Engeström's activity system, 237, 238
    examination, 237
    hierarchy of activity, 237
    human collective activity, 237
    mediated act, 236
  fundamental building block, 192
  human activity, 192
  in IS, 193, 194
  principles
    development, 240
    hierarchical structure, 239
    internalization and externalization, 239
    mediation, 239
    object-orientedness, 239
  rules and division, labour, 192
Actor-network theory (ANT)
  accuracy, 221
  actors, 189, 190, 221, 240
  aims, 240
  aspects, 240
  competing roles, 227
  concepts
    actor/actant, 222
    heterogeneous network, 222
    irreversibility, 222, 223
    and mapping, 223
    obligatory passage point (OPP), 222
    punctualisation, 222
    tokens/quasi objects, 222
  criticism, 191
  critique and limitations, 229, 230
  description, 189
  entity, 189
  foundation of networks, 227
  framing, 227
  fundamental stand, 221
  HIS evaluation
    ability of actors and end -users, 228
    binary models, 228
    complexities, nuances
      and richness, 228
    diffusion of innovation
      (DOI) theory, 229
    implementation and adoption, 228, 229
    translation, 228
  hospital messaging, 190
  inscription, 226
  lens, 220
  limitations, 191
  moments of translation, 225
  networks, actor
    complexity, 224
    enrolment, new actors/actants, 223
    healthcare decision support system, 225
    oversimplification risk, 225
    power and structure, origin of, 223
    role of technology, 223
  resistance, to sociotechnical change, 190
  sociotechnical approach, 230
  sociotechnical change, resistance to, 227
  social/technical relations, 189
  sociotechnical approaches, 186

N. Wickramasinghe, J. L. Schaffer (eds.), *Theories to Inform Superior Health Informatics Research and Practice*, Healthcare Delivery in the Information Age,
https://doi.org/10.1007/978-3-319-72287-0

Actor-network theory (ANT) (*cont.*)
  translation, 226, 227
  usefulness of, 241
Adaptive mapping to realization (AMR) methodology, 81
Adoption
  acquisition stage, 294
  and adaptation, 290
  HIS, 220, 222, 223, 228, 229
  information systems, 300
  IS/IT in healthcare industry, 285
  organisational issues, 287
  and routinisation, 295
  'S-shaped curve', 287
"AlgorithmHolder", 180
Allergen-specific immunoglobulin E (sIgE) testing, 312–313
Allergy
  aspects, practices, 319, 320
  asthma incidents, 311
  autoimmune diseases, 311
  definition, 311
  diagnosis, 311
  DSRM
    cycles, 317
    data collection plan and techniques, 319
    mapping, 318
    process, 317
    selected case, 318
  ICT, 313
  interorganizational knowledge flow, 319
  knowledge management (*see* Knowledge management)
  management, 312
  proposed solution, 316, 317
  rates, allergy diagnosis, 312
  real de-identified data, 319
  types, 311
Ambient assisted living (AAL), 9
American Recovery and Reinvestment Act (ARRA), 406
Analysis of variance (ANOVA) method, 364
Arbitrary Lagrangian-Eulerian (ALE), 364
Area under the curve (AUC), 67
Artificial intelligence (AI)
  AI-driven healthcare system, 355
  ANNs (*see* Artificial neural networks (ANNs))
  computational models/algorithms, 355
  definition, 355
  drug administration and patient care
    in anaesthesia, 362
    ANOVA method, 364
    CyA, 362, 364
    data collection, 361
    DGX, 361
    ERA, 362
    numerical techniques, 364
    prosthetic heart valves, 364
    RBFNNs and OCON, 362
    Reynolds number, 364
  in healthcare applications, 370
  patient-centric intelligent systems, 367
  technologies, 355
Artificial neural networks (ANNs), 66–67
  applications, 357
  backpropagation learning algorithm and RBF network, 357
  as connectionist systems, 356
  EIT, 361
  EMN, 357
  feature, 356
  for biomedicine, 356
  for clinical diagnosis, 357
  imaging, 359
  model, 356
  multispectral imaging approach, 361
  PAPNET, 357
  as parallel distributed systems/adaptive systems, 356
  perceptron, 356
  regions of interest (ROIs), 361
  Segment, 361–363
  tumours, recurrence rate, 357
Assimilation, *see* Healthcare information systems (HIS) assimilation theory
Attention deficit hyperactivity disorder (ADHD)
  hyperactivity symptoms, 338
  inattention issues, 338
  neurodevelopmental disorder, 338
  See also Executive function (EF)
Australasian Diabetes in Pregnancy Society (ADIPS), 78
Australia
  adaptions and experiences, 121
  opt-in to an opt-out model, 121
Australian healthcare system
  adoption strategy, 117
  challenges, 118, 119
  financial support, 117
  infrastructure, 118
  legislative framework, 117
  My Health Record platform, 118
  PCEHR system, 117
  technologies, health care, 118
  user access and accessibility, 118
Axial coding process, 341

B
Bayesian posterior probability (BPP) distribution function, 357
Behavioral interventions, 164, 165, 180
Big data, 368
Blockchain technology, 393, 394
Boyd OODA loop
  arthroplasty orthopedic surgeon, 332
  germane knowledge, 328
  and knowledge management techniques, 333
  process-oriented perspective, knowledge generation, 329
  stages, 329
Brain-computer interface (BCI), 359, 360
Business process modeling notation (BPMN), 7
Business value of IT, 37, 38, 40
  conceptual model
    clinical practices (people), 155
    delivery operations (processes), 154, 155
    healthcare ecosystem (society), 152, 153
    system structure (organisation), 153, 154
  portfolio
    defined, 148
    Enterprise of Healthcare Delivery, 151, 152
    firm-wide infrastructure, 149
    heterogeneous perspective, 150
    information technology architecture, 149
    informational, 150
    infrastructure, 150
    management objectives, 148–150
    and strategy, 149, 150
    transactional, 150

C
Calorie Cruncher, 12–13
Causal analysis, 64
Chief Finance Officer (CFO), 44
Chinese acupuncture expert system, 430
Chinese medicine (CM)
  case study (CS) methodology, 433, 434
  developments, IS/IT
    activities, described, 431
    Chinese acupuncture expert system, 430
    described, 430
    ERP systems, 430
    expert systems and applications, 430
    limitation, 430
    Traditional Chinese Medicine Information Database, 430
  diagnosis methods, 438
  inquiring systems, 438, 439 (*see also* Inquiring systems)
  integration, with WM, 428
  KM systems, 435
  philosophy, 427
  regulations and standards, 429
  scientific and medical evidence, 427
  self-controlled system, 437
  T&CM strategy, 428
  treatments, 438
Chronic disease, 127, 391
  management, 77–79, 129, 130
  See also Diabetes
Churchman's inquiring systems, 428, 431, 432, 438
Cleveland Clinic MyConsult application, 265
Clinic management systems, 430
Clinical data repository (CDR), 144, 155
Clinical decision support systems (CDSS), 144, 155, 323
Clinical information systems (CIS)
  CPOE, 25
  descriptions, 21
  descriptive analysis, 24
  EMRs, 25
  healthcare industry, 19
  in-house and external training, 25
  investigation areas, 24
  IS/IT, 19
  limitations, 25
  online survey, 20
  overall user satisfaction, 19
  respondents, 20
  systems compatibility with clinicians' tasks, 26
  training and technical support channels, 26
  training and technical support satisfaction, 23–24
  user satisfaction, 20–23
Clinical protocols, 7
Clinical report form (CRF), 417
Cluster analysis, 96, 97, 99, 101–105
Communication Platform, 190
Communications technologies, 109, 111, 112
Complementary and alternative medicine (CAM), 428, 429
Computerised practitioner order entry (CPOE), 144
Context
  definition, 380
  and practice, 380
  user and the application, 380
Corporate Governance of IT, 38
Critical success factors (CSF), 39
Cyclosporine A (CyA), 362, 364

D

Data collection strategy, 82
Data mining, 56, 57
Data quality
  data inaccuracy, 33
  health outcome, 32
Database, 312, 314–319
Decision support systems (DSS), 432, 433, 436
Decision trees (DT), 65
Design artifacts
  instantiations, 4
  methods, 4
  models, 4
Design cycle, 14
Design science research (DSR) methodology
  artifacts, 3
  blood glucose monitoring, 10–12
  Calorie Cruncher, 12–13
  healthcare applications, IT solutions, 4
  healthcare field challenges, 4, 5 (*see also* Healthcare projects)
  human organizations, 3
  innovative artifacts, 3
  public health and clinical arenas, 4
  technology and science knowledge base enhancement, 3
  three-cycle DSR method, 14, 15
Design science research methodology (DSRM), 317–320
Design science theory, 96, 97, 106
Diabetes
  anticipated benefits and potential outcomes, 135
  control and management, 128
  costs for carers, 272
  GDM (*see* Gestational diabetes mellitus (GDM))
  HbA1c blood test, 128
  information management processes, 130
  insulin, use of, 134
  management
    as 'batch' data transfer, 130
    blood sugar levels, 129
    glucose monitoring technology, 129
    mobile phone technology, 129
    readings, for type 1/2 diabetic, 129
    self-management protocols, 129
  noncommunicable diseases, 128
  prevalence, 128
  qualitative techniques, 134
  quasi-experimental approach, 134
  questionnaires and de-brief sessions, 135
  "technology solution" or "standard care", 134
  uncontrolled, 128
Diabetes care
  age-adjusted comparative prevalence, 76
  Australian diabetes hospitalization rate, 75
  complications, 76
  components, 85, 88–89
  dimensions, 87–88
  mobile internet subscriptions, 75
  societal costs, 76
Diabetes monitoring device (DiaMonD), 81
Diabetes monitoring solutions, 392
Diagnosis-related groups (DRG), 111
DiaMonD study, 272, 279
Diffusion of innovation (DOI) theory
  description, 287
  literature findings, 287, 288
  Rogers' research, 287
  'S-shaped curve', 287
Digital health ecosystems, 7
Digoxin (DGX), 361
Distributed cognition (DCog)
  collaborative patient care system, 242
  similarities, with AT, 242
  theory, 242

E

E-business innovation assimilation model, 291
Educator interaction and awareness, 348–349
e-Health
  adoption and implementation, 208, 209
  in Australia (*see* Australian healthcare system)
  benefits, 391
  challenges, modern developed systems, 392
  country's e-health potential, 112
  defined, 111
  economic benefits, 207
  electronic medical records, adoption of, 112, 113
  ethical concerns, 112
  evidence-based methods and approaches, 112
  functions and capabilities, 112
  in Germany (*see* German healthcare system)
  global digital health market, 109, 110
  implementation and adoption, 207, 398
  on macro-environmental factors, 121
  and mobile health (*see* m-Health)

research directions, 398
scope of and macro-economic factors, 113, 114
stakeholders, 113
standardization, 396
technologies, 391
Eigensystem realisation algorithm (ERA), 362
Electrical impedance tomography (EIT), 361
Electroencephalography (EEG)
AD analysis, 358, 359
BCI, 359, 360
neural networks, 358
RNN approach, 358
Electronic health card (EHC)
acceptance, 116
challenges, 116
data security, 114
goal, 113
required and optional information, 115
strategical conception and implementation, 115
Electronic health records (EHR)
accurate information representation, 419
benefits, 393
blockchain technology, 393, 394
clinical data management tool, 405
communication channels, 235
computerized medical information systems, 406
concept translator, 419
connection to educational tools, 421
data protection, 419
design and development, 393
and EMR systems (*see* EMR/EHR systems)
feedback system, 421
and health education, 394–396
hospitals and care organizations, 405
images, 392
information tracking, 419
integrated care system, 419
medical history, 392
obstacles, 406
patient education and training, 419
privacy and security, 393
revolution, 235
security tools/data protection policies, 421
standard document and communication architectures, 421
Electronic medical administration records (eMAR), 155
Electronic medical records (EMRs), 8, 155
case history method, 405
classes, on overall patient healthcare outcomes, 404
clinical communication, 404
computerized record, 405
history, medical diagnosis, 404
hospitals and care organizations, 405
life expectancy, in USA, 404
medical data organization, 405
patient disease, 405
POMR concept, 405
programs, health care, 403
US healthcare system, 403
e-mental health (eMH)
defined, 337
tools and services, 337
treatments, interventions and support, 337
EMR/EHR systems
Allscripts, 409
on clinical communication, 407
complex medical systems
applications with healthcare procedures, 411
challenges, 411
configurable healthcare systems, 411
diagnostic and treatment procedures, 410
interoperability and data sharing, 412
organized rollout implementation, 412
patient care coordination, 411
user-friendliness, 412
computerized medical information systems, 406
eClinicalWorks, 409
entering data and retrieving information, 407
Epic, 408, 409
health care, 406
interoperability issues, 407
NextGen Healthcare, 410
obstacles, 406
Practice Fusion, 410
training, 407
workflow adoption challenges, 406
Enterprise resource planning (ERP), 430
Evidence-based practice (EBP), 375, 376, 380
Executive function (EF)
ADHD issues, 338
assistive technologies, 344
assistive technology tools, 339
axial coding process, 341
clinicians' support and supervisions, 347
data gathering and coding, 340–341
emotional control, 345–346

Executive function (EF) (*cont.*)
grounded theory, 340
impaired, 338
IS in mental health, role of, 339
open coding process, 341
perceived ability factors, 343
planning and management, 344–345
psychotherapy, 338
selective coding process, 342
self-regulation and motivation, 346–347
side effect and limited effectiveness, 339
stimulant medication, 338
working memory, 346
writing memos, 342, 343

F
Fictitious domain/mortar element (FD/ME), 364
Fit-viability model, 252, 266
viability, 253
Fogg's Behavior Model (FBM)
classification, 182
data layer, 174
indicator terms, 171
influencing factors, 167
personal factors, 165
and TTM, 165
Framing, ANT, 227

G
General practitioner with special interest (GPwSI) allergy, 313
German healthcare system
challenges, 116
data security, 114
EHC, 113–115
EU initiatives and funding schemes, 114
governmental and policy support, 113
technology and infrastructure, 115, 116
telemedicine, 113
user access and accessibility, 116
German healthcare telematics architecture, 7
Gestational diabetes mellitus (GDM)
ADIPS, 78
before and after breakfast, 133
fetal hyperinsulinemia, 78
longitudinal multi-country study, 77
mobile solution, 135
prevalence, 76, 129
research results, 81, 82
self-management, 77
standard care, 135
tight control and management, 129
type 1 and type 2, 78
Global healthcare operations, 323
Grounded theory
analytical process, 340, 341
defined, 340
eMH, 351
memos, 342
structured analytical processes, 340

H
Haemoglobin A1c (or HbA1c), 128, 131
Hawaii International Conference on Systems Sciences (HICSS), 38
Health and fitness service
at App Store, 163
goal, 164
proportion of users, 163
Health ecosystem, 152
Health education
blogs, 395
challenges, modern developed systems, 392
instant messaging (IM), 395
podcasts, 395
RSS feeds, 395
social networking applications, 395
wiki, 395
Health electronic records (HER), 323
Health Evaluation through Logical Processing (HELP) system, 405
Health informatics, 96
Health information exchange (HIE), 313
categories, 416
defined, 416
EHR functional models, 417
framework, 416
healthcare data and information, 417
SQL commands, 417
Health information systems (HIS)
agency and end-users, 204
ANT analysis (*see* Actor network theory (ANT))
breach of privacy, 206
complexity, 201
conceptual framework, 210–213
conceptualising and framing, factors, 208
development, implementation and use, 204
facilitating role, 201
fit-viability model, 252, 266
functionality, 220

implementation and adoption, 205, 220
invasion of patient privacy, 206
IT, 201
pre-and post-implementation vendor support, 208
security and privacy, 206
ST (*see* Structuration theory (ST))
task technology fit see (*see* Task technology fit)
translation, 205
use, 201
user acceptance, 208
Health Information Technology for Economic and Clinical Health Act (HITECH), 406
Health care
business value, IT (*see* Business value, IT)
communication and delivery, 185
communication inefficiencies, 186
IS (*see* Information systems (IS))
knowledge management, 315
patient-centric systems (*see* Patient-centric systems) (*see* Risk prediction models)
social and organizational contexts, 375
value-based care delivery systems, 147
'value', in healthcare, 147, 148
Healthcare doctrines
domains, 329
Healthcare informatics
case study (CS) methodology, 433, 434
design science (DS) methodology, 434
thematic analysis, 435
Healthcare information systems (HIS), 433
Healthcare information systems (HIS) assimilation theory
acquisition and deployment, 285
applications, 284
assimilation, defined, 283
communication amongst staff, 302 (*see also* Diffusion of innovation theory)
e-health projects, 301
elements, 299, 300
facilitators, 302
global barriers, 302
innovations, 283
medical solutions search, 283
non-profit sector innovations, 284
public hospitals, 284
senior management team, 302
specific user requirements, 284
successful assimilation, 300
technology innovation and diffusion, 284
technology innovation evolution, 285, 286 (*see also* Theory of innovation assimilation)
TOE (*see* Technology-organisation-environment (TOE) framework)
Healthcare information technology (HIT)
on electronic health records, 219
use of, 219
Healthcare management
description, 323
global healthcare operations, 323
ICT, 323
information asymmetry, 324
solution strategies, 324
technology paradigm, 324
technology, role of, 323, 324
Healthcare operations
See also Network-centric healthcare
Healthcare projects
business intelligence and data analytics, 8
clinical protocols, 7
delivery services, 9
eHealth systems, 10
EMRs, 8
governance of, medical and healthcare resources, 8
medical devices, 7
medical systems, 5–7
pharmaceutical systems, 10
public health and preventive care, 9
research areas, DSR papers, 5, 6
TCM, 10
Healthcare services
as information-rich industry (ibid), 219
Healthcare systems
AR-DRG system, 111
challenge, 202
demographic similarities, 111
in developed countries, 110
DRG system, 111
primary insurance, 110
sociotechnical systems, 203
universal two-tiered system, 110
Healthcare technology paradigm, 324
Hegelian inquiring system, 437
Hermeneutics
description, 30
getaway for patient, healthcare services, 29, 30
healthcare professionals, 30
information engineering development, 32
information technology innovation continuum, 29

Hermeneutics (*cont.*)
IS research, 31
IT healthcare solution, 29
IT-/IS-related studies, 31 (*see also* Mobile Health (mHealth))
object/phenomenon, 31
patients and medical professionals, 32
secondary artefacts, 31
study interpretation, Bible, 31
Hidden Markov models (HMMs)
administering drugs, 366
architecture, 367
Bayesian approach, 366
description, 364
hospital-acquired infections, 365
mining system, 366, 368, 369
nosocomial infections, 365
patient database records, 366
Home monitoring
caregivers and deployment, 415
economic and social costs, 415
Hospital communication
conceptual framework, 194–196
health information technology, 188
initial analysis and conceptual framework, 189
mHealth interventions, 187
pagers and phone conversations, 185
sociotechnical systems perspective, 188
Hospital Secure Messaging, 190
Human activity, 192–194
Human-computer interaction (HCI) theories
ANT, 240, 241
AT (*see* Activity theory (AT))
comparison, theories, 244–246
distributed cognition (DCog), 242
situated action (SAct), 243
ST, 241
Hyperactivity symptoms, 338

I

Impact analysis, 64
Implementation, HIS, 220, 222, 223, 228
See also Actor network theory (ANT)
Independent variables, 60–62
InfoLinks, 176, 177
InfoProviders, 176, 177
Information and communication technology (ICT), 313, 314, 318–320, 391, 398
Information asymmetry, 324
Information communication technologies (ICT), 79, 127, 128, 186, 187, 196, 325
healthcare network-centric operations, 330–332
KM (*see* Knowledge management (KM))
physician decision-making support, 323
Information management
aims, 130
blood glucose readings, 131
blood monitoring processes, 131
continued information sharing, 133
daily glucose readings, 131
feedback, to patient, 133
patient glucose readings, 131
project team, 130
real-time information exchange, 133
system-based development, 130
Information systems (IS)
and ADHD attributes, 349
AT, 193, 194
case study (CS) methodology, 433, 434
CM developments (*see* Chinese medicine (CM))
design science (DS) methodology, 434
developments, CM, 430, 431 (*see* Executive function (EF))
and EF ability, 350
external factors, 348
family members, 348
health care
care delivery, 142
e-health, 143
investments, 143
IS/IT applications, 143–145
IT spending, by industry in 2014-2015, 142, 143
on macro level, initiatives, 143
patient outcomes, 142
spending, on software, 143
structures, e-health initiatives, 143
use of, 142
participants, 347
Information systems/information technology (IS/IT), 19
Information technology (IT)
challenges, 235
CM developments (*see* Chinese medicine (CM))
design science (DS) methodology, 434
developments, CM, 430, 431
health care
capital, types of, 146
categories, 146
clinical IS/IT neglected, 147
components, 146
contradictory results, 147

delivery, 145
'health information technology capacity' and quality of care, 146
limitations, 145
medical information technology capital, 146
sociotechnical perspective, 147
structural equation modelling, 146
system specificity, 146
limitations, 141
opportunities and trends, 235
Innovation
in health care, 4
low user acceptance and high failure rates, 4
ongoing EMRs research, 8
Rigor Cycle, 14
Inquiring systems
Hegelian, 432
Kantian, 432
Leibnizian, 432
Lockean, 432
Singerian, 432
for WM, 433
Inscription, ANT, 226
Integrated care system
advantages, 423, 424
authorized access to data, 424
continuous monitoring, 425
information accuracy for patient-generated data, 424
security and control, 424
Integrating health records
caregiver, role of, 415
chronic diseases, 415
education, 415
mobile applications (mApp), 416
Intellectual properties (IP) assets, 38
Interoperability, 20, 23, 24, 26
IS/IT governance
accountability and responsibility, 38
board-related issues, 39
business processes, 39
business value, 37
CFO, 44
clinical and business domains, 45
collection and analysis, 42–43
Corporate Governance of IT, 38
criteria, 44
CSF, 39
domains, 39
factors affect, 51
healthcare contexts, 37
HICSS, 38
in healthcare model, 51
industries, 40
IT projects, failure of, 45
IT Steering Committee, 44
IT-enabled solutions, 37
people factors, 46–47
PMO, 43
PRINCE2, 43
process factors, 44, 47
research methodology, 41
research objectives and questions, 40–41
research strategy, 41–42
robust IT governance, requirements, 49
technology factors, 47–48
value and business value, 40

K

Knowledge discovery in databases (KDD), 328
Knowledge management (KM)
activities and challenges, 378
architecture and characteristics, 435
Boyd OODA Loop, 328, 329
characterization, 377
collaborative and quality patient care, 378
context, 377, 380
cross-boundary clinical decision support, 376
data and knowledge sources, 435
data base, designed, 315
data collection, 316
decision-making, health care, 387
definitions, 314
description, 325
EBP, 375
echnology-driven perspective, 328
efficiency and efficacy, of clinicians daily operations, 316
for health care, 315
goal, 377
"gold standard" status, 375
Hegelian and Kantian inquiring systems, 436
human-computer interaction, 377
ICT applications, 325
infrastructure services, 435
integrated approach, 387
integration services, 435
interorganizational activities, 314
interorganizational knowledge flow, 315
KDD process, 328

Knowledge management (KM) (*cont.*)
knowledge capture/creation, process of, 377
knowledge services, 435
"knowledge-in-practice-in-context", 376
people centric and technology centric approaches, 325
personalisation, 435
PMS, 436
practice, concept of, 378, 379
practice theoretical perspective (*see* Practice theory)
primary drivers, 314
psychosocial and algorithmic theories, 326
research proposes, 436
Spender's and Blackler's respective frameworks, 327, 328
steps, 377
support and dissemination, 331–333
tools, techniques and tactics, 314
transformations, 327

L
Laboratory information systems (LIS), 144
LACE index, 67
Law enforcement, 58
Logistic regression (LR), 64
Low-cost intervention for disease control (LIFE) project, 8

M
Machine learning algorithms, 32–34
Medical devices, 7
Medical systems
bounded care-giving environments, 5
design components, 7
projects and artifacts, 7
Medicine, 356, 359
Medicine 2.0 application, 95
Mobile app, 316
Mobile applications (mApps)
EHR and HIS, 416
external information systems, 416
HIE, 416
privacy, 416
Mobile health (m-Health)
accessibility and availability, 397
applications, 187
business models, 397
data accuracy and information technology, 33, 34
data inaccuracy, 32
defined, 397
income categories, 397
integral, 187
interventions, 187
mobile devices, 397
platforms, 187
services, 397
trials, 187
Mobile phone technology, 129
Mobile solutions, 130, 131, 135, 271, 272, 275, 276, 278, 279

N
Network-centric health care
artificial intelligence and business analytics, 331
Boyd's Loop stage, 331
Boyd's OODA Loop, 329
domains, 329
grid architecture, 330
information and germane knowledge, 330
medical web portals and online databases, 330
sensors, 331
smart portal elements, 331, 332
Neurodevelopmental disorder, 338
Nursing documentation (ND), 144

O
One-class one-network (OCON) neural networks, 362
Ontology, diabetes care, 83–87
Open coding process, 341
Open-ended questionnaires, 276
Order entry (OE), 144

P
Pagers, 185, 186
Patient management system (PMS), 428, 433–437, 439
Patient Protection and Affordable Care Act, 406
Patient-centric systems
AI, 355
ANNs (*see* Artificial neural networks (ANNs))
designing intelligent systems, 367
developing applications, 367
HMMs, 364–369
modern healthcare system, 355
Penalized regression analyses (PRA), 64

People factors, 46–47
Personal health record (PHR), 417
Personally Controlled E-Health Records (PCEHR), 117, 118
  described, 260
  features, 260
  macro level, 261
  messo level, 261
  micro level, 261
  person-centric system, 260
  task technology fit perspective, 263
  Web 2.0, 261
Pervasive mobile solution, 78–79, 275, 276, 278
Pervasive mobile technology, 274
Pervasive technology, 79, 83, 89
Pharmaceutical systems, 10
Pharmacy management system (PMS), 145
Physician documentation (PD), 145
Picture archive computerized systems (PACS), 323
Positron emission tomography (PET), 361
Power/knowledge, 273, 274, 278–279
Practice theory
  capturing practice-related knowledge, 381
  challenges, 381
  in clinical practices, 381
  for collaborative knowledge management support, 379
  context, role of, 380
  goal, 381
  KM systems, 382–383, 386
  knowledge use and sharing, 380
  modelling practice-related knowledge, 381, 383–385
Practice-related knowledge, 381
Predictive analytics
  empirical model building, 56
  finance, 57–58
  healthcare/healthcare analytics, 58
  hospital readmissions, 55
  insurance, 57
  law enforcement, 58
  patient-specific information, 56
  preventive measures, 55
  readmissions cost, 55 (*see also* Risk prediction models)
  sales and marketing, 57
  scheduled and unscheduled readmissions, 56
Problem Classification Scheme, 33
Problem identification and motivation, 105
Process factors, 47
Project management office (PMO), 43
ProstAsure index, 357

Q
Quadri-link cluster analysis, 104
Quadri-link model, 99, 100

R
Radial basis function neural networks (RBFNNs), 362
Radial-basis function (RBF) network, 357
Radiology information system (RIS), 145
Random forests (RF), 66
Randomized control trial (RCT), 81
Readmission period, 60
Readmissions
  cost of, 55
  hospital, 55
  period, 60
  prediction model, 59
  scheduled and unscheduled, 56
Receiver operating characteristic (ROC) curve, 67
Recurrent neural networks (RNNs), 358
Regression analysis, 60, 62–64
Regulatory environment, 296
Relevance cycle, 14
Rigor cycle, 14
Risk prediction models
  ANN, 66–67
  applied methods, 63
  C-statistics, 67, 68
  DT, 65
  independent variables, 60–62, 68
  issues, 60
  LACE algorithm, 67
  LACE index, 67
  object of investigation, 60
  performance comparison, 68, 69
  readmission period, 60
  regression analysis, 62–64
  retrospective studies, 59
  RF, 66
  sample size, 59
  split ratio, 59
  SVMs, 64–65
  systematic analyses, 59
RiskViewBuilder, 180
RiskViewDirector, 180

S

Secure connection (SSL), 423
Secure messaging, 190
Segment, 361–363
Selective coding process, 342
Self-monitoring
 clinical trials, 276
 diabetes care
  computer-assisted telemedicine, 272
  contemporary support, 272
  GDM, 273
 in management-control literature, 273
 pervasive mobile technology solution, 274
 as surveillance, 273
Serum electrophoresis, 358
Service archetype
 concrete functional, 169
 concrete requirements, 169
 defined, 167
 features for, 171, 179
 functional requirements, 169
 objective, 169
 requirement derivation, 169, 170
 target groups, 180
 types, 170
ServiceCards, 172–174, 180, 182
Single-photon emission computer tomography (SPECT), 361
Situated action (SAct), 243
Skin prick testing (SPT), 312, 313
Smart phone health applications, 130, 135
Smartphone
 usage, 163
Social media, 95–97, 105, 106
Social Question Answering (SQA) service
 algorithms, 101
 cluster analysis groups, 97
 cluster similar answers, questions and users, 101
 design and development, 106
 design science, 96
 Drugs.com question and answer site, 102
 evaluation, 106
 features, 98–100
 health informatics, 96
 healthcare SQA services, 95
 individual behaviors, 95
 keyword-based clustering, 97
 objective, solution, 105
 problem identification and motivation, 105
 quadri-link cluster analysis, 96, 101
 quadri-link model, 99, 100
 samples, 103
 sets of entities, 98
 social media, 96
 valuable knowledge repository, 95
Sociodemographic target group, 165, 167
Sociotechnical systems, 240, 242, 245
Split ratio, 59
"Standard care" protocols, 134
Standardization, 396
Structuration theory (ST)
 abstraction, 241
 in Australian healthcare IT transformation, 206
 duality of structure, 241
 facility, 204
 financial issues, 206
 functionality, system, 202
 goal of, 204
 human and non-human relationships, 205
 implementation and adoption, EHRs, 205
 IT implementations, 207
 lens of, 202
 modalities, 204
 re-form structure and human agency, 203
 in social science research, 203
 standards, social thinking, 203
 in structuration theory, 203
 structures, 241
 systems, 241
 user requirements, 202
Subjectification, 273, 274
Support vector machines (SVMs), 64–65
SWOT analysis, German and Australian e-health system
 advantages and disadvantages, 119–121
 applications, 119
 implementation, 119
 opportunities, 122–123
 threats for, 123

T

Tailored interventions
 classification, of requirements, 168, 169
 concrete requirements, 168
 implementation
  data layer, 175, 176
  logic layer, 177–179
  presentation layer, 178–180
 implemented service, 175
 for mobile devices
  abstraction, 173
  design patterns, 173
  feed, with ServiceCards, 172

first external actor, 172
platform system architecture, 174
precontemplation and contemplation stage, 174
second external actor, 172
structure, software, 171
use case diagram, 171
non-functional requirements, 168
precontemplation stage, 174
prototype, 175
prototypical implementation, 171
software requirements, 168
solutions and impact, for consumers, 180–182
type, of requirements, 168
Task technology fit (TTF), 252, 263
Australia (*see* Personally Controlled Electronic Health Record (PCEHR))
China
careful monitoring, 260
clinics, 258
Lujiazui community, 257
macro level, 258
messo level, 259
micro level, 259
organization, 257
resources and population pressure, 257
services, 258
system evolution and development process success, 260
training, 258
wireless technologies, 258
German e-healthcard, 255, 256
methodology, 253, 254
research framework, 253
South Africa
challenges, 263
diseases and healthcare issues, 263
district health information system (DHIS), 263
eHealth Strategy, 265
national health ministry, 263
primary healthcare (PHC) system, 263
strategic priorities, for 2012 to 2017, 264
technology solutions, 265
US, 265
Technological readiness, 296, 297
Technology factors, 47–48
Technology-organisation-environment (TOE) framework
adoption stage initiation, 294
adoption-routinisation gap, 295
assimilation, 294
clinical and non-clinical medical professionals, 298
clinical outcomes, 294
components, 289, 290
cost-effective, 292
E-business innovation assimilation model, 290, 291
environmental context, 289
firm size, 290
firm size concept, 297
firms, 292
HIS assimilation stages, 295
IS/IT resources classification, 291, 292
managerial obstacles, 297
managerial obstacles' factor, 290
methodology, 298–299
organisational IS/IT resources, 293
regulatory environment, 296
research framework, 293
technological readiness, 296, 297
"Technology solution" protocols, 134
Telemedicine, 113, 114, 127
Telemonitoring process, 421, 423
Theory of innovation assimilation
cultural differences, 289
defined, 287
healthcare personnel, 288
HIS implementation literature, 287
information system failure, 289
organisational issues, 287
Theory of knowledge management (KM), 314
Therac-25, 236
Three-cycle DSR method, 14, 15
Time series analyses, 64
Traditional Chinese medicine (TCM)\, 10
Training and technical support satisfaction, 23–24
Translation, ANT, 226, 227
Transtheoretical model (TTM)
on staging algorithm, 165
processes of change, 167
service archetype, 167
sociodemographic target groups, 165
stages, 165

U

User satisfaction
comparison, 23
overall satisfaction, selected cases, 22
respondents, 22
User-centered design (UCD) approach, 79

V
Value
  and business value, 37, 40
  description, 38
  IS/IT health care, 40
  IT investments, 38
Visiting medical officers (VMOs), 46

W
Web 2.0, 395, 396
Web portal, 316, 319
Web-based conceptual model, 276, 277
Web-based model, 79, 80, 131, 132
Western medicine (WM)
  developments, 428
  inquiring system, 433
  integration, with CM, 428
  IS/IT developments, 430
  patient's CM medical
    history, 437
  patient's medical history, 437
  PMS, 437
Work practice
  definition, 378
  for collaborative knowledge
    management support, 379
  for organizing tools, actors and
    resources, 379
  theoretical perspective, 379
Working memory, 346
Writing memos, 342, 343

MIX
Papier aus verantwortungsvollen Quellen
Paper from responsible sources
FSC® C105338
www.fsc.org

If you have any concerns about our products,
you can contact us on
ProductSafety@springernature.com

In case Publisher is established outside the EU,
the EU authorized representative is:
Springer Nature Customer Service Center GmbH
Europaplatz 3, 69115 Heidelberg, Germany

Printed by Libri Plureos GmbH
in Hamburg, Germany